The **Rough Guide** to

Kerala

written and researched by

David Abram

with additional research by

José Navarro

ROUGH
GUIDES

NEW YORK · LONDON · DELHI

www.roughguides.com

Contents

The Kuttanad backwaters colour section following p.112

Playing gods colour section following p.256

◄◄ Elephants line up at an *utsavam* ◄ The Malabar Coast

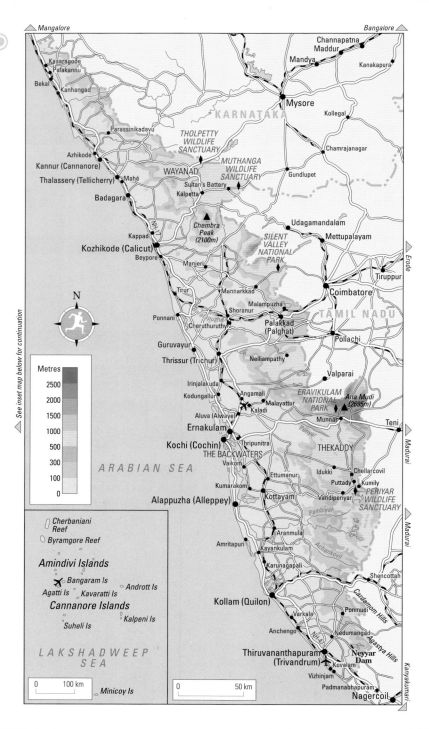

Introduction to
Kerala

Green and gold are the defining colours of Kerala: green for the tropical lushness that bursts from every patch of ground in the state; gold for the prosperity that has for many thousands of years been a consequence of this abundance. You see the two in combination everywhere, in the borders of the white cotton mundu worn by Keralan men, in the ceremonial umbrellas hoisted over temple deities as they're processed on elephant back during festivals, and in the make-up of the kathakali hero, framed by his trademark jewel-encrusted headdress.

 Gold and green will also dominate your first impressions of Kerala if, like most travellers, you arrive by plane from the Arabian Sea. Landing at Thiruvananthapuram (Trivandrum) or Kochi (Cochin), a flash of vivid golden sand brings the ocean to an abrupt end, giving way to a carpet of brilliant vegetation: bands of shaggy coconut palms interwoven by tangled rivers, canals, lagoons and water-logged rice paddy that stretch to a horizon bounded by forested mountains.

The lower slopes of the Western Ghats, less than 100km inland, are the source of the aromatic **spices** that drew traders from across the world to the shore known for centuries as the Malabar Coast. Ships from ancient Sumeria and Rome, China, the Arabian peninsula, Persia, East Africa, Portugal, Holland and Great Britain sailed to India's southwestern seaboard to fill their holds with pepper, cinnamon, cardamom and ginger. They brought with them a cornucopia of new ideas, technologies, foodstuffs and religions, which the Keralans embraced and made their own.

Scan the skyline of any town in the state today and you'll see, rising from the red-tiled rooftops alongside mosque minarets and the brass finials of Hindu temples, whitewashed church gables whose congregations claim descent from converts evangelized by Saint Thomas in the first century AD. In Fort Cochin, the region's pre-eminent colonial trading post, cantilevered fishing nets introduced by Chinese immigrants hang like giant predators along a waterfront dotted with Portuguese *palacios*, Dutch merchants' mansions, British warehouses and Jewish synagogues.

Adaptability and openness to the outside world continue to be central to the Keralan character. When recession started to bite in the 1970s, many **Malayalis** (a name derived from the official state

Fact file

• Edged by 580km (360 miles) of coastline, Kerala is 130km (76 miles) wide at its broadest point and covers a total surface area of 38,863 square kilometres; it takes around 12hr to ride from one end to the other by train.

• In March 2001 (the date of the last census) the population of Kerala stood at 31.8 million, of whom 56 percent were Hindu, 25 percent Muslim and 19 percent Christian.

• Both the literacy rate (91 percent) and life expectancy (73 years) are the highest in India. GDP hovers around Rs12,000 (£147/$294) per head.

• Malayalam is the official language of the state and the mother tongue of nearly all Keralans (also known as "Malayalis"). English is most people's second language, and is widely spoken in large towns, resorts and in businesses across the state.

▲ Tea plantation, near Munnar

language, Malayalam) left to work in the Persian Gulf. Now remittance cheques sent home by them account for twenty percent of GDP.

Behind the state's economic success story lies its long-standing policy of **universal education**. Thanks to enthusiastic patronage from the region's ruling maharajas and, after Independence, successive communist governments, Kerala enjoys the highest literacy rates of any Indian region and has led the field when it comes to gender equality and family planning.

In Fort Cochin, cantilevered Chinese fishing nets hang like giant predators along a waterfront dotted with Portuguese *palacios*, Dutch merchants' mansions, British warehouses and Jewish synagogues

Yet while innovation has always been central to Kerala's prosperity, Malayalis remain staunchly **conservative**. Traditional dress is the norm, even in the cities, while the old hierarchy of caste, in spite of decades of social reform, continues to dominate political life. From the visitor's point of view, this can have its downsides – not least the fact that most temples remain off-limits to non-Hindus. But it also accounts for the survival of Kerala's extraordinary **traditional arts scene**. A wealth of Malayali music, dance and ritual drama forms continue to be widely performed and enjoyed across the state, in precisely the same contexts as they have for centuries. In the case of *kudiyattam*, the most archaic of all, the masked plays audiences watch today have remained completely unchanged since the time of the Roman empire. One of the world's most elaborate systems of holistic medicine, **ayurveda**, has also been kept alive for thousands of years in Kerala, where it now enjoys a new lease of life as a spa therapy.

Moreover, thanks to Kerala's go-ahead tourism industry, you can enjoy these unique cultural phenomena from the comfort of some truly wonderful **accommodation**. Whether an ancestral *tharavadu* mansion made of teak or a converted *kettu vallam* rice barge in the backwaters, a British tea planter's bungalow high in the Cardamom Hills or a royal hunting

▲ Vizhinjam, near Kovalam

lodge lost in the jungle, heritage hotels and homestays run by local families offer plenty of excuses to get off the beaten track and will deepen your experience of a region that, for all its paradoxes and contradictions, never fails to astonish.

Where to go

Beaches loom large on most tourist itineraries of Kerala, and given the state's 580-kilometre, sand-splashed shoreline, you'd expect to be spoilt for choice. In reality, however, only a handful of resorts offer the combination of safe swimming, convenient accommodation and tolerant local attitudes to swimwear necessary for a stress-free beach holiday. The granddaddy of them all, and the corner of the Keralan coast where most charter holiday-makers end up, is **Kovalam**, half-an-hour south of the state capital and international airport at Thiruvananthapuram. Huddled behind a trio of beautiful palm-backed bays, Kovalam started out as a backpackers' hangout, and still offers a wide choice of places to stay and eat. But after a decade of haphazard development, it possesses much less character than locations further south, dotted along the endless sandy beaches stretching from the nearby fishing anchorage of **Vizhinjam** to **Poovar**. Stacked up the steep terraces behind a line of secluded coves and local fishing beaches, gated hotels have mushroomed in the coconut groves here, offering upscale retreats and rejuvenation packages.

If you're spending any time in or around Kovalam, you're bound at some stage to be tempted inland for a day's sightseeing in **Thiruvananthapuram (Trivandrum)** – an easy-going, leafy city boasting a spectacular Dravidian-style temple, a huge royal palace, a Raj-era museum, an art gallery and a thriving performing arts scene, as well as lots of good places to eat and shop.

An hour's drive north of Thiruvananthapuram, **Varkala** is Kerala's other main seaside resort. Spread beneath a backdrop of dramatic red cliffs, its golden beach has for many centuries served as an important Hindu pilgrimage site, although these days the locals who come here to cast the ashes of deceased relatives into the surf are far outnumbered by Westerners enjoying the sublime views, succulent seafood and sunset yoga sessions.

The laterite cliffs taper into long white sandbars and lagoons as you press north from Varkala into the **Kuttanad backwaters**. A busy highway and rail line scythe through the middle of this uniquely beautiful region, which forms a maze of looping rivers and canals extending from the former spice port of **Kollam (Quilon)** in the south to the outskirts of Kochi in the north. But the only way to really do it justice is by boat, whether a local ferry or a *kettu vallam* rice barge. Most of these graceful vessels work out of **Alappuzha (Alleppey)**, which is perfectly placed for forays out onto the ethereal waters of **Vembanad Lake** and holds an outstanding range of typically Keralan homestays, heritage hotels and lakeside resorts.

One of the most scenic ferry routes from Alappuzha, taking in an extraordinary vista of glassy lagoons and palm-encrusted islands, heads east to **Kottayam**, a predominantly Syrian-Christian market town in the heart of the Keralan lowlands. Further east, beyond the rubber plantation belt,

▲ A boat in the backwaters

lie the **Western Ghats**, South India's highest range. Surrounded by miles of grassy peaks and rainforest, **Periyar** is one of the country's top wildlife sanctuaries, visited in great numbers for its wild elephants which, if you're lucky, you can watch at close quarters on a bamboo raft safari across the reserve's central lake.

From Periyar, a dreamy road journey across mountainsides wrapped in tea estates, coffee plantations and cardamom forest takes you up to **Munnar**, the centre of Kerala's tea industry. The town serves as a springboard for some superb trekking opportunities, while its refreshingly cool climate offers a welcome respite from the humidity of the coastal plains.

Back at sea level, **Kochi (Cochin)**, the state's largest city, has dominated life in **central Kerala** since the Portuguese first sited a fort overlooking its harbour mouth. These days, Keralans come to the modern district of **Ernakulam**, on the mainland, to shop for expensive wedding saris and gold jewellery. Tourists, on the other hand, gravitate to the former colonial enclave of **Fort Cochin**, a ferry ride across the water, whose time-worn streets hold the finest crop of early European architecture in Asia, including the church where Vasco da Gama was buried.

Older, more indigenous traditions tend to form the focus of journeys north of Kochi, into the state's cultural heartland around the town of **Thrissur**. Aside from being the venue for Kerala's largest temple festival, **Puram**, Thrissur and its surrounding villages are also the spiritual home of the region's own female classical dance form, **mohiniyattam**, the martial-art-influenced **kathakali** dance-drama, and its ancient Sanskrit predecessor, **kutiyattam**, which have for centuries brought gods and demons from the *Mahabharata* and *Ramayana* to Keralan villages.

▼ Christmas in Kochi

Insulated from the tourist enclaves of the south by an eight- to twelve-hour train ride, **northern Kerala** and its capital **Kozhikode (Calicut)** see comparatively few visitors. But the region holds enormous potential for independent travel, with its own distinctive, Muslim-influenced atmosphere and some superb heritage homestays and ayurvedic spas.

For most visitors, however, the main incentives to venture up north are the extraordinary Hindu spirit-possession rituals known as **theyyattam**, held in villages throughout the winter around the coastal town of **Kannur (Cannanore)**. While you're in the region, other destinations worth extending your trip to reach include the wonderfully unspoilt **Valiyaparamba backwaters**, and the exquisite **Wayanad** hill tract, which holds some of southern India's finest rainforest and mountain scenery, and some superbly situated eco-resorts.

When to go

The **best time to visit** Kerala is between late-December and February, when the skies are clear and humidity at its least debilitating. From March onwards, the heat and stickiness become increasingly uncomfortable in the pre-monsoon build up. After a month of intense sunshine alleviated by short showers, the rains erupt in earnest in the first week of June, with a massive storm that sweeps off the Arabian Sea. This is considered the auspicious time to begin a course in ayurvedic treatment, but a beach holiday is out as the sand often disappears under the high tides and crashing waves. The second annual monsoon – known as the "retreating" monsoon because its prevailing winds are in the northeast – lasts from October to December. Although lighter than its predecessor, it leaves the skies frequently overcast and is accompanied by high humidity levels.

Average temperatures and rainfall

	Jan	Feb	March	April	May	June	July	Aug	Sept	Oct	Nov	Dec
Kochi (Cochin)												
Av daily max (°C)	31	31	31	31	31	29	28	28	28	29	30	30
Rainfall (mm)	23	20	51	126	297	723	592	353	195	340	178	41
Thiruvananthapuram (Trivandrum)												
Av daily max (°C)	30	31	32	31	31	29	28	28	28	29	29	30
Rainfall (mm)	20	20	43	122	249	331	215	164	123	271	207	73

things not to miss

It's not possible to see everything that Kerala has to offer in one trip – and we don't suggest you try. What follows, in no particular order, is a selective taste of the region's highlights: idyllic beaches, outstanding monuments, spectacular festivals and great places to stay. They're arranged in five colour-coded categories, which you can browse through to find the very best things to see and experience. All highlights have a page reference to take you straight into the guide, where you can find out more.

01 **Kalarippayattu** Page **100** • Kerala's acrobatic martial art has ancient roots, but enjoys a passionate following in special gyms across the state.

02 **Ayurveda** Page **110** • Pamper yourself with a full-body massage or follow a more elaborate course of holistic herbal treatment in any one of dozens of spas.

03 **Lighthouse Beach, Kovalam** Page **112** • Kovalam is the state's liveliest resort, ranged over three palm-fringed bays.

05 **Nishagandi Festival** Page **98** • The cream of South Indian music and dance, including uniquely Keralan forms such as *mohiniyattam*, performed at an open-air auditorium in Thiruvananthapuram.

04 **Padmanabhapuram Palace** Page **119** • The high-watermark of traditional Keralan architecture.

06 **Kathakali** Page **187** & *Playing gods* colour section • The extraordinary make-up and costumes of Kerala's trademark ritual theatre generate an unforgettable atmosphere.

07 **Keralan murals** Page 156 •
Kerala's finest medieval murals line
the gateway of the Mahadeva temple in
Ettumanur.

09 **Sadya** Page 41 • The ultimate
Keralan banana-leaf feast, served
during the annual harvest festival of Onam,
and in simpler versions at everyday "meals"
joints.

08 **Puram, Thrissur** Page 202
• The biggest and most thrilling of
all Kerala's temple *utsavams*, centered on a
huge elephant procession; smaller events are
staged across the state between November
and February.

10 **Kerala Kalamandalam,
Cheruthuruthy** Page 209 •
Visit the state's foremost performing arts
academy to see how *kathakali*, *mohiniyattam*
and other traditional forms are taught.

11 **Snake boat races** Pages **146** & **156** • With prows shaped like rearing cobras, traditional Keralan longboats are raced at various locations during the early monsoon.

12 **Munnar** Page **211** • The high peaks, forests and wildlife sanctuaries around the tea-growing town of Munnar are riddled with superb trails – home of the elusive Nilgiri tahr.

13 **Theyyattam** Page **245** & *Playing gods* **colour section** • Gods possess the bodies of dancers dressed in outlandish, elaborate masks and costumes during rituals held in small village temples around Kannur (Cannanore).

14 **Lakshadweep Islands** Page **194** • Exquisitely translucent seas and coral reefs enfold this remote archipelago, 400km west of the Keralan mainland.

15 Heritage homestays, Alappuzha Page **141** • Packed around the canals of the archetypal backwater town are a dozen or more homestays in characterful nineteenth-century houses.

16 Backwater cruises, Kuttanad Page **144** & *The Kuttanad backwaters* **colour section** • Explore the famous Kuttanad backwater region in a converted rice barge or (more eco-friendly) punted canoe.

17 Fort Cochin Page **182** • The cosmopolitan history of Kerala's colonial trade is evocatively preserved in the backstreets of Fort Cochin, along with the famous Chinese fishing nets.

18 Periyar Page **159** • View wild elephants and other large mammals, including occasional tigers, on a bamboo raft or jungle trek, guided by local tribal people.

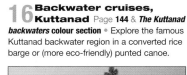

19 Papanasam beach, Varkala Page **126** • Varkala's amazing red cliffs provide the perfect backdrop for bodysurfing and sunset yoga sessions.

Basics

Basics

Getting there

Most visitors to Kerala fly into either Kochi (Cochin) or Thiruvananthapuram (Trivandrum), though the northern city of Kozhikode (Calicut) also has an international airport. From the UK, getting there by air will mean at least one change of plane – normally in the Gulf. Travellers from North America can expect an additional stopover in London – though there are direct flights from the US and Canada to the Gulf, and to Mumbai in India. Flying from Australia or New Zealand requires a minimum of one change, usually in Southeast Asia or Hong Kong, and often another in Chennai or Mumbai.

Airfares always depend on the **season**, with the highest being from roughly November to March, when the weather in Kerala is best; fares drop during the shoulder seasons – April to May and August to early October – and you'll get the best prices at the height of the monsoons, in June and July. Fares peak in November, around Diwali (the "Festival of Lights") as Indian emigrants travelling home for holidays with their families create a surge in demand, and over Christmas and New Year.

A long list of **operators** run **package holidays** to Kerala, based around beach stays in Kovalam or Varkala, which include the cost of the flight and hotel. Some also offer special-interest tours, ranging from textiles to religion, food and wildlife. In addition, many companies will arrange tailor-made tours, and can help you plan your own itinerary. For a list of operators running tours to Kerala, see p.23.

Finally, if India is only one stop on a longer journey, you might want to consider buying a **Round-the-World** (RTW) ticket: Mumbai features on many "off-the-shelf" itineraries. Figure on £950–1500/$1850–2900 for a RTW ticket including India, open for one year.

Flights from the UK and Ireland

There are no direct flights from the **UK** to Kerala. The most convenient route is to fly scheduled **via Colombo** with SriLankan Airlines (from around £460), or through one of the **Gulf States** with a carrier such as Qatar Airways, Emirates, Etihad or Gulf Air.

Either way, you're looking at a total flying time of between eleven and twelve hours, plus the stopover.

Routing passengers through their hub city, Doha, Qatar Airways offer the most consistently competitive fares, with tickets starting at around £400 or less. They have daily onward departures to all three airports in Kerala. Transit times with Qatar are short (typically between one and two hours); this is handy if your outbound flight leaves on time, but a major drawback if it doesn't, as missed connections can mean a frustrating extra day killing time in Doha. Indian carriers offering flights to Kerala from the UK via the Gulf include Air India, Indian Airlines and Jet.

Economy-class **fares** from London to Thiruvananthapuram/Kochi range from as little as £400 with Qatar Airlines, to nearly double that with Emirates.

An alternative route, which can save you money but invariably increases travelling time, is to fly **via Mumbai** and pick up a domestic connection there. Carriers with direct daily flights to Mumbai from London include British Airways (who offer good-value deals from around £400), the pricier Air India and Jet Airways. For the onward leg to Kerala, you can either opt for one of the scheduled domestic companies – Indian Airlines, Jet or Sahara – or their low-cost competitors: Air Deccan, Paramount, Kingfisher, GoAir and Air India Express. Of the bunch, Jet is the most dependable and flexible, but also the most expensive, with fares to Kochi/Thiruvananthapuram starting at £60 one way. You can book their tickets through agents in the UK and Ireland, or via the Jet Airways website (see p.23). Indian Airlines' fares are comparable with those of Jet, but the nation's domestic carrier is notoriously unreliable, with frequent delays and poor service; their online booking is also more hit and miss.

Starting from as low as Rs1000 (£12.50) plus taxes, the lowest fares of all for the journey between Mumbai and Kerala are with Web-based carriers Deccan Air and Paramount. The one catch here is that booking can be difficult for anyone who doesn't have a credit or debit card registered in India.

E-tickets issued by domestic carriers should, in theory, be honoured without any problems, but it's always worth getting this down in writing from the airline and/or your agent before leaving home. Otherwise you might find yourself being asked to pay all over again when you transfer in Mumbai; Indian Airlines are particularly prone to this.

There are no direct flights to anywhere in South India from **Ireland**. Your best bet is to link up with a scheduled or charter departure from London.

Flying by charter from the UK

Weekly **charter flights** leave on Sundays during the winter from London Gatwick to Thiruvananthapuram in southern Kerala. Indian regulations strictly prohibit the sale of charter **flight-only tickets** to Kerala from outside India. However, tour operators who pre-purchase blocks of seats on the charters and want to sell off unused ones at discounted rates get around the regulations by pretending that these seats are bundled with budget (or "bunkhouse") accommodation, issuing "dummy vouchers" with the ticket. There's nothing to stop you from purchasing one of these and ditching the voucher once you've arrived. It can still work out much cheaper than a scheduled flight via Mumbai, especially if you manage to pick up a last-minute bargain (two-week deals regularly drop to £299). However, certain **restrictions** apply (see below). One of these is a **limit of 28 days** to the maximum period for which any charter ticket is valid.

Flights from the US and Canada

Whether you fly to Kerala from the **US** and **Canada** via Europe (from the East Coast) or over the Pacific (from the West Coast), it's a long haul, involving one or more intermediate stops. Air India and Jet Airways both fly to Mumbai direct from New York, but you'll arrive fresher and less jet-lagged if you stop over for a few days somewhere en route. Agents will often break the journey into two sections anyway, which allows a wider choice of carriers for the transatlantic (or transpacific) leg.

From the **East Coast**, you'll stop over somewhere in Europe (most often London), the Gulf, or both. Figure on at least eighteen hours' total travel time. Prices are most competitive out of New York, where the cheapest low-season consolidated fares to Thiruvananthapuram/Kochi hover around US$1300 (rising to US$1750 in high season). From Washington or Miami, figure on US$1400 in low season, US$2000 in high

Charter flights: rules and restrictions

The Indian Civil Air Authority imposes **three major restrictions** on travel by charter flight to Kerala.

1. Charter tickets are valid for a maximum period of 28 days. If you wish to stay in India for longer, you'll have to fly scheduled to India and then catch a domestic flight via Mumbai or another Indian hub.

2. It is illegal to fly into India on a charter flight and out on a scheduled one, and vice versa. Indian travel agents do not always tell you this when you book, however, and are not liable should you be refused permission to board your flight.

3. Holders of Indian passports are not allowed to purchase charter tickets.

Fly less – stay longer! Travel and climate change

Climate change is the single biggest issue facing our planet. It is caused by a build-up in the atmosphere of carbon dioxide and other greenhouse gases, which are emitted by many sources – including planes. Already, flights account for around 3–4% of human-induced global warming: that figure may sound small, but it is rising year on year and threatens to counteract the progress made by reducing greenhouse emissions in other areas.

Rough Guides regard travel, overall, as a global benefit, and feel strongly that the advantages to developing economies are important, as are the opportunities for greater contact and awareness among peoples. But we all have a responsibility to limit our personal "carbon footprint". That means giving thought to how often we fly and what we can do to redress the harm that our trips create.

Flying and climate change

Pretty much every form of motorized travel generates CO_2, but planes are particularly bad offenders, releasing large volumes of greenhouse gases at altitudes where their impact is far more harmful. Flying also allows us to travel much further than we would contemplate doing by road or rail, so the emissions attributable to each passenger are greater. For example, one person taking a return flight between Europe and California produces the equivalent impact of 2.5 tonnes of CO_2 – similar to the yearly output of the average UK car.

Less harmful planes may evolve but it will be decades before they replace the current fleet – which could be too late for avoiding climate chaos. In the meantime, there are limited options for concerned travellers: to reduce the amount we travel by air (take fewer trips, stay longer!), to avoid night flights (when plane contrails trap heat from Earth but can't reflect sunlight back to space), and to make the trips we do take "climate neutral" via a carbon offset scheme.

Carbon offset schemes

Offset schemes run by **climatecare.org**, **carbonneutral.com** and others allow you to "neutralize" the greenhouse gases that you are responsible for releasing. Their websites have simple calculators that let you work out the impact of any flight. Once that's done, you can pay to fund projects that will reduce future carbon emissions by an equivalent amount (such the distribution of low-energy lightbulbs and cooking stoves in developing countries). Please take the time to visit our website and make your trip climate neutral.

www.roughguides.com/climatechange

season; from Chicago, US$1800/2200; and from Dallas/Fort Worth, US$2000/3000.

From the **West Coast**, it works out slightly quicker to fly west rather than east – a minimum of 22 hours' total travel time – and there may not be much difference in price.

From **Canada**, typical discounted low and high-season fares to Kochi from Montreal, Toronto and Vancouver are Can$2250/2850.

Flights from Australia, New Zealand and South Africa

Only Qantas flies direct from **Australia** to India, with flights from both Sydney and Melbourne to Mumbai; expect to pay around Aus$1900. Most travellers, however, make at least one change of plane in a South or Southeast Asian hub city: flights with carriers such as SriLankan Airlines, Singapore Airlines and Malaysia Airlines are considerably cheaper at around Aus$1600. That said, there is a huge choice of airlines flying to the region, and in order to get the best price most agents will combine two or more carriers. Because of higher demand, the best-value tickets are generally from Australia's east coast.

From **New Zealand**, the cheapest fares to South India are in the NZ$2000–2250 range if you depart from Auckland; add on approximately NZ$150 for flights from Wellington or Christchurch. There are no direct flights, and most travellers change in one of the major Australian cities or in Hong Kong.

From South Africa you can either fly direct to Mumbai from Johannesburg with South African Airlines from around ZAR4000 (flying time 8hr 30min), and pick up an onward domestic flight to Kerala from there, or go indirect via the Gulf, which will be cheaper, but involve one more change.

RTW fares from all three countries can take in India; tickets stopping in Mumbai are available with Thai Airways, Air New Zealand, Qantas and Malaysia Airlines, starting from around Aus$3500, NZ$4550 or ZAR12,500.

Airlines, agents and operators

Online booking

ⓦ www.expedia.co.uk (in UK),
ⓦ www.expedia.com (in US),
ⓦ www.expedia.ca (in Canada)
ⓦ www.lastminute.com (in UK)
ⓦ www.makemytrip.com (in US)
ⓦ www.opodo.co.uk (in UK)
ⓦ www.orbitz.com (in US)
ⓦ www.travelocity.co.uk (in UK and Ireland)
ⓦ www.travelocity.com (in US)
ⓦ www.travelocity.ca (in Canada)
ⓦ www.zuji.com.au (in Australia)
ⓦ www.zuji.co.nz (in NZ)

Airlines

Aeroflot US ☏ 1-888-686-4949, Canada ☏ 1-416-642-1653, ⓦ www.aeroflot.com.
Air Canada Canada ☏ 1-888-247-2262, ⓦ www.aircanada.com.
Air France UK ☏ 0870 142 4343, Republic of Ireland ☏ 01/605 0383, US ☏ 1-800-237-2747, Canada ☏ 1-800-667-2747, ⓦ www.airfrance.com.
Air India UK ☏ 020 8560 9996 or 8745 1000, US ☏ 1-800-223-7776, Canada ☏ 1-416-865-1033, Australia ☏ 02/9283 4020, New Zealand ☏ 09/631 5651, ⓦ www.airindia.com.
Air India Express India 022/22796330, ⓦ www.airindia.com.
Air New Zealand Australia ☏ 13 24 76, New Zealand ☏ 0800/737000, ⓦ www.airnewzealand.com.
Alitalia UK ☏ 0870 544 8259, Republic of Ireland ☏ 01/677 5171, US ☏ 1-800-223-5730, Canada ☏ 1-800-361-8336, ⓦ www.alitalia.com.

All Nippon Airways US ☏ 1-800-235-9262, ⓦ www.anaskyweb.com.
Asiana Airlines US ☏ 1-800-227-4262, ⓦ www.flyasiana.com.
British Airways UK ☏ 0870 850 9850, Republic of Ireland ☏ 1890/626 747, US and Canada ☏ 1-800-247-9297, Australia ☏ 1300/767177, New Zealand ☏ 09/966 9777, South Africa ☏ 011/441 8600, ⓦ www.ba.com.
Cathay Pacific US ☏ 1-800-233-2742, Australia ☏ 13 17 47, New Zealand ☏ 09/379 0861, South Africa ☏ 011/700 8930, ⓦ www.cathaypacific.com.
Delta Air Lines US and Canada ☏ 1-800-221-1212, ⓦ www.delta.com.
Emirates UK ☏ 0870 243 2222, US ☏ 1-800-777-3999, Australia ☏ 03/9940 7807, New Zealand ☏ 09/308 3352, South Africa ☏ 0861/363 738, ⓦ www.emirates.com.
Etihad UK ☏ 020 8735 6700, US ☏ 0212-984-1878, Australia ☏ 02/9293 2855, South Africa ☏ 011/343 9140, ⓦ www.etihadairways.com.
Gulf Air UK ☏ 0870 777 1717, Republic of Ireland ☏ 0818/272 818, US ☏ 1-888-359-4853, South Africa ☏ 011/268 8909, ⓦ www.gulfairco.com.
Jet Airways UK ☏ 020 8970 1525, US ☏ 1-800-225-522, ⓦ www.jetairways.com.
KLM Royal Dutch Airlines UK ☏ 0870 507 4074, Australia ☏ 1300/303747, New Zealand ☏ 09/309 1782, South Africa ☏ 011/881 9600, ⓦ www.klm.com.
Kuwait Airways US ☏ 1-201-582-9200, ⓦ www.kuwait-airways.com.
Lufthansa UK ☏ 0870 837 7747, Republic of Ireland ☏ 01/844 5544, US ☏ 1-800-645-3880, Canada ☏ 1-800-563-5954, Australia ☏ 1300/655727, New Zealand ☏ 09/303 1529, South Africa ☏ 011/325 1925, ⓦ www.lufthansa.com.
Malaysia Airlines US ☏ 1-800-552-9264, Australia ☏ 13 26 27, New Zealand ☏ 0800/777747, ⓦ www.malaysia-airlines.com.
Northwest/KLM Royal Dutch Airlines US and Canada ☏ 1-800-225-2525, ⓦ www.nwa.com.
Oman Air UK ☏ 0870 770 7319, Republic of Ireland ☏ 01/844 7376, ⓦ www.omanair.aero.wy.
Pakistan International Airlines UK ☏ 0800 587 1023, US ☏ 1-800-578-6786 or 1-212-760-8484, ⓦ www.piac.com.pk.
Qantas UK ☏ 0845 774 7767, Republic of Ireland ☏ 01/407 3278, US ☏ 1-800-227-4500, Australia ☏ 13 13 13, New Zealand ☏ 09/357 8900, South Africa ☏ 011/441 8491, ⓦ www.qantas.com.
Qatar Airways UK ☏ 0870 770 4215, US ☏ 1-877-777-2827, Canada ☏ 1-888-366-5666, Australia ☏ 03/8676 6400, South Africa ☏ 021/936 3080, ⓦ www.qatarairways.com.

Royal Brunei Airlines UK ☎020 7584 6660, ⊛www.bruneiair.com.

Royal Jordanian UK ☎020 7878 6300, US ☎1-800-223-0470, Canada ☎1-800-363-0711, ⊛www.rja.com.jo.

Royal Nepal Airlines US ☎1-800-266-3725, ⊛www.royalnepal.com.

Sahara Airlines UK ☎0870 127 1000, US ☎1-212-685-5456, Canada ☎1-416-966-4825, ⊛www.airsahara.net.

Saudi Arabian Airlines UK ☎020 7798 9898, US ☎1-800-472-8342, ⊛www.saudiairlines.com.

Singapore Airlines US ☎1-800-742-3333, Canada ☎1-800-663-3046, Australia ☎13 10 11 or 02/9350 0262, New Zealand ☎0800/808909, ⊛www.singaporeair.com.

Silk Air Singapore ☎1800-224 4243, ⊛www.silkair.com.

South African Airways South Africa ☎0861/359 722, ⊛www.flysaa.com.

SriLankan Airlines UK ☎020 8538 2001, US ☎1-877-915-2652, Canada ☎1-416-277-9000, Australia ☎02/9244 2234, New Zealand ☎09/308 3353, ⊛www.srilankan.aero

Swiss UK ☎0845 601 0956, US ☎1-877-359-7947, Australia ☎1300/724666, New Zealand ☎09/977 2238, ⊛www.swiss.com.

Thai Airways UK ☎0870 606 0911, US ☎1-212-949-8424, Canada ☎1-416-971-5181, Australia

☎1300/651960, New Zealand ☎09/377 3886, ⊛www.thaiair.com.

United Airlines UK ☎0845 844 4777, US ☎1-800-241-6522, ⊛www.united.com.

Virgin Atlantic Airways UK ☎0870 380 2007, US ☎1-800-821-5438, ⊛www.virgin-atlantic.com.

Domestic airlines

Air Deccan ⊛www.airdeccan.net.

Air India ⊛www.airindia.com.

Air India Express ⊛www.airindiaexpress.in

GoAir ⊛www.goair.in.

Indian Airlines ⊛www.indian-airlines.nic.in.

IndiGo Airlines ⊛www.goindigo.in.

Jet Airways ⊛www.jetairways.com.

Kingfisher Airlines ⊛www.flykingfisher.com.

Paramount Airways ⊛www.paramountairways.com.

Air Sahara ⊛www.airsahara.net.

Spicejet ⊛www.spicejet.com.

Tour operators

Abercrombie and Kent UK ☎0845 070 0600, ⊛www.abercrombiekent.co.uk, Australia ☎1300/851800, New Zealand ☎0800/441638, ⊛www.abercrombiekent.com.au. Upmarket two-week bespoke and set itineraries covering the main highlights, with stays in luxury hotels.

Adventure Center US ☏ 1-800-228-8747, ⓦ www.adventurecenter.com. "Spice tour" of Kerala, featuring a backwater trip.

Adventure Company UK ☏ 01420 541007, ⓦ www.adventurecompany.co.uk. Five well-thought-out itineraries, featuring Kerala on longer tours of South India.

Andrew Brock/Coromandel UK ☏ 01572 821330, ⓦ www.coromandelabt.com. Several options, including "Dawdling through Kerala" in an Ambassador, with trips on the backwaters and into the hills.

Audley Travel UK ☏ 01869 276222, ⓦ www.audleytravel.com. Privately guided, tailor-made itineraries covering all the usual sights, plus a handful of off-track destinations.

Bales UK ☏ 0845 057 1819, ⓦ www .balesworldwide.com. Escorted tours, varying in length from six to twenty-five days and featuring the main cities, hill stations, spice plantations and the backwaters.

Butterfield & Robinson US ☏ 1-800-6781/1477 or 1-866-551-9090, ⓦ www.butterfield.com. Bespoke tours, with an emphasis on walking and cycling. Also runs a six-day spice plantation tour in Kerala.

Classic Oriental Tours Australia ☏ 1300/747400, ⓦ www.classicoriental.com.au. Wide choice of tours encompassing three-day city breaks, a seven-day Kerala tour and a 22-day itinerary which includes Periyar Wildlife Park.

Cox & Kings UK ☏ 020/7873 5000, ⓦ www .coxandkings.com. Wide range of five- to nine-day tours.

Essential India UK ☏ 01225 868544, ⓦ www .essential-india.co.uk. A range of tours, from nine days to sixteen, covering Kerala.

Exodus UK ☏ 0870 240 5550, ⓦ www .exodustravels.co.uk. Experienced specialists in small-group itineraries, treks and overland tours.

First Choice UK ☏ 0870 850 3999 (or ☏ 0870 757 2757 for flights only), ⓦ www.firstchoice.co.uk. Standard resort packages to Goa, at various prices, and with a range of extension tours of the backwaters.

Hayes & Jarvis UK ☏ 0870 366 1636, ⓦ www.hayesandjarvis.co.uk. Luxury two-week sun breaks in resort hotels south of Kovalam.

High Places UK ☏ 0845 257 7500, ⓦ www .highplaces.co.uk. Biking, hiking and backwater boat rides around the state's tourist hotspots.

Imaginative Traveller UK ☏ 0800 316 2717, ⓦ www.imaginative-traveller.com. A choice of South Indian tours, combining Kerala's highlights with those of neighbouring states.

Insider Tours UK ☏ 01233 2811771, ⓦ www .insider-tours.com. The most original, "hands-on"

and ethical itineraries on the market, taking you to off-track corners of the state, including backwaters, hills, wildlife reserves and beaches.

Jewel in the Crown UK ☏ 01293 533338, ⓦ www.jewelholidays.com. Established Kerala specialist, offering a wide range of beach-based holidays.

JMC UK ☏ 0870 750 5711, ⓦ www.jmc.com. Owned by Thomas Cook, this big firm offers a broad range of package holidays at competitive prices.

Kerala Connections UK ☏ 01892 722440, ⓦ www.keralaconnect.co.uk. Established Kerala specialist whose tailor-made trips cater for a range of budgets, reflecting their expert knowledge of the state's lesser-known nooks and crannies. They also offer extensions to Lakshadweep and the Maldives.

Myths and Mountains US ☏ 1-800-675-6984 or 1-775-832-5454, ⓦ www.mythsandmountains .com. Special-interest trips, tailor-made or group, with an emphasis on culture, crafts, religion and traditional medicine. The "Real South India" tour includes heritage properties, ayurvedic massage and medicine and a stay on a houseboat, while the "Yoga, meditation and ayurveda" trip (of the same length) visits various ashrams and ends with three days in an ayurvedic resort.

On the Go Tours UK ☏ 020 7371 1113, ⓦ www.onthegotours.com. Tailor-made tours or a set itinerary around central Kerala's must-sees.

Peregrine Adventures Australia ☏ 1300/854444, ⓦ www.peregrine.net.au. Offers a fourteen-day tour of South India which includes Kochi, Periyar Wildlife Park and the backwaters.

Pettitts India UK ☏ 01892 515966, ⓦ www .pettitts.co.uk. Their "Rural Images of Kerala" tour ventures further off the beaten track than most, with the emphasis on culture, and nights in some choice homestays and heritage hotels.

SD Enterprises UK ☏ 020 8903 3411, ⓦ www .indiarail.co.uk. Run by Indian railway experts, SD Enterprises puts together complex itineraries for independent travellers wanting to explore India by train, as well as budget packages to Kerala.

Somak Holidays UK ☏ 020 8423 3000, ⓦ www.somak.co.uk. Top-end package tour covering the backwaters, beaches and hill resorts.

Soul of India UK ☏ 020 8901 7320, ⓦ www .soulofindia.com. Escorted and tailor-made spiritual journeys/pilgrimages, including a "Hindu and Christian South India" trip and an ayurveda tour that includes a seven-day rejuvenation programme at the *Taj Garden Retreat* in Kumarakom.

Trans Indus Travel UK ☏ 020 8566 2729, ⓦ www.transindus.co.uk. Wide range of South India tours, including a nine-day tour around Kerala and the Malabar coast.

Voyages Jules Verne UK ☎ 0845 166 7003, ⓦ www.vjv.co.uk. Thirteen classic India-wide heritage tours, but only one in the South. The "Splendours of the South" is a fourteen-day trip which covers wildlife, temples and the backwaters.

Western & Oriental Travel UK ☎ 0870 499 1111, ⓦ www.westernoriental.com. Award-winning upmarket agency with a wide range of itineraries. These include a "Mind, Body, Spirit" trip with a focus on yoga and ayurveda.

Wilderness Travel US ☎ 1-800-368-2794, ⓦ www.wildernesstravel.com. Their seventeen-day "Treasures of South India" tour takes in the highlights of Tamil Nadu alongside those of central Kerala and its backwaters.

Worldwide Quest Adventures US ☎ 1-800-387-1483, ⓦ www.worldwidequest.com. Their whistlestop "Sandalwood and Spices" tour calls at Periyar and Cochin en route between Tamil Nadu and Goa.

Recommended travel agents

ebookers UK ☎ 0800 082 3000, ⓦ www.ebookers.com; Republic of Ireland ☎ 01/488 3507, ⓦ www.ebookers.ie. Low fares on an extensive selection of scheduled flights and package deals.

Make My Trip US toll free ☎ 1-800-INDIA-10 or 1-877-845-3596; Australia ☎ 1300/664404; ⓦ www.makemytrip.com. Reliable online India specialist offering access to rock-bottom discounted international and domestic fares, with offices in the US and Australia.

North South Travel UK ☎ 01245 608291, ⓦ www.northsouthtravel.co.uk. Friendly, competitive travel agency offering discounted fares worldwide – profits are used to support projects in the developing world, especially the promotion of sustainable tourism.

STA Travel UK ☎ 0871 230 0040, ⓦ www.statravel.co.uk; US ☎ 1-800-781-4040, ⓦ www.statravel.com; Australia ☎ 13 47 82, ⓦ www.statravel.com.au; New Zealand ☎ 0800/474400, ⓦ www.statravel.co.nz; South Africa ☎ 0861/781781, ⓦ www.statravel.co.za. Worldwide specialists in independent travel; also student IDs, travel insurance, car rental, rail passes, and more. Good discounts for students and under-26s.

Trailfinders UK ☎ 0845 058 5858, Republic of Ireland ☎ 01/677 7888, Australia ☎ 1300/80212; ⓦ www.trailfinders.com. One of the best-informed and most efficient agents for independent travellers.

Getting around

With private car ownership still very much the preserve of India's moneyed classes, most Keralans get about on public transport, which means services are frequent and inexpensive (though perhaps not quite as comfortable as what you're used to back home). Wherever you're travelling, you won't have to wait long for a train, bus or ferry to appear – as often as not, already crammed to bursting point with passengers. For shorter journeys, auto-rickshaws and taxis are just as ubiquitous, while visitors with limited time may opt for a car and driver to whisk them around, or even catch a flight from one end of the state to the other.

By train

If you're spending your holiday exclusively in Kerala and not aiming to venture further afield in South India, chances are you probably won't travel very much by **train**. Given the hassles and delays that invariably attend most rail journeys in the state, it's nearly always quicker to go by bus or taxi – at least for short hops between towns and cities. That said, time your journey well and start close to your train's original point of departure (before it's had time to get seriously delayed), and rail travel can be an enormously enjoyable way to experience Kerala. People from all walks of life use the railways, from crisp-shirted businessmen cocooned from the heat in **air-conditioned** (abbreviated in this book and throughout

Kerala itself as a/c) compartments, to the hoi polloi, crushed into "unreserved" carriages, with their never-ending procession of hawkers, beggars, buskers, hustlers and chai-coffee sellers.

The **main line** runs the length of the state, connecting the major towns and cities of the coastal strip before heading north towards Goa and Mumbai. In addition, a couple of **branch lines** peel eastwards across the mountains into neighbouring Tamil Nadu, and there's a quiet back line cutting through Alappuzha and the Kuttanad region.

Types of train

While planning your journey, the first thing you need to do is settle on a specific train. Not all services travel at the same speed or offer the same degrees of comfort. Running twice weekly from Thiruvananthapuram up to Goa, via Kochi and Kozhikode, the fastest is the special a/c *Rajdhani* – one of Indian Railways' flagship trains. **Daily intercity services**, called "**express**" or "**mail**", cover the same route but stop a lot more frequently, and vary greatly in the amount of time they take to travel between stations. They are, however, still much faster than local "**passenger**" trains, which seem to spend a lot less time moving than they do marooned in the middle of nowhere at invisible signals.

Each service has a name and number. Timetables can be consulted at any station, or online at ⓦwww.indianrail.gov.in.

Classes of train travel

Indian Railways distinguishes between no fewer than seven **classes of travel**, though they will not all be available on every train. Moreover, unless you're planning to cover a long journey (such as the nine-hour haul from Thiruvananthapuram to Kozhikode), it's unlikely you'll need to fathom the intricacies of overnight travel, for which berths have to be reserved well in advance.

Travelling in the day, the important distinction is between regular "**unreserved**" or **third** class – how most of the locals will be travelling – and pricier a/c **second** or **first** – where most tourists end up, and which you pay between three and five times more for. Which of these will suit you is a matter of personal taste, but be warned that although "unreserved" class may be more picturesque, it'll certainly be a lot more uncomfortable, hot and dirty, with hard wooden seats and nasty smells emanating from the toilets.

Air-conditioned travel, unavailable on slower "passenger trains", falls into five categories, but the one you're most likely to come across is second-class two-tier. The name refers to the number of upholstered sleeper bunks that swing down from the walls of the compartments. In the daytime, these are fixed to the walls; the seats below can then accommodate six people, with another two on the opposite side of the corridor. Daytime passengers not staying on the train through the night, when the berths are lowered and seating space is limited, may purchase two-tier a/c tickets an hour or so before departure if there's room. Easily distinguished by their sealed-in windows, a/c carriages are usually coupled to the front of the train, and are always staffed by uniformed ticket inspectors and pantry-car attendants.

"Ladies-only" compartments exist on many trains; they can be full of noisy kids, but offer single women some respite from the incessant staring of open general carriages. Some stations also have ladies-only waiting rooms.

Timetables

Timetables for all mail, express and superfast trains are available online at ⓦwww.indianrail.gov.in, though the website is poorly designed and takes some getting used to. You can also check fares and availability online. Alternatively, pick up a copy of the biennial **Trains at a Glance**, available from information counters and newsstands at all main stations, and from IR agents abroad (see p.28). The same outlets

---

At the end of each chapter in this book, you'll find a **Travel details** section summarizing major transport connections in the relevant state. In addition, **Moving on** boxes at the end of each major city give details of onward transport from that city.

also stock the handy **Jaico Timetable booklet**, published by the state tourism department every month. For only Rs12, you can pocket a concise, well-set-out, up-to-date summary of all train services between major towns and cities – it also has info on bus, ferry and flight timings.

Rail **fares** are calculated according to the exact distance travelled. *Trains at a Glance* prints a chart of fares by kilometres, and also gives the distance in kilometres of stations along each route in the timetables, making it possible to calculate what the basic fare will be for any given journey – all much easier online, once you've worked out the peculiarities of the site.

Advance booking and sleeper trains

For shorter journeys of up to a few hours on passenger, mail or express trains, you won't need to book a seat during the day – just turn up at the station thirty to sixty minutes before departure and join the scrum around the ticket hatch on the station concourse. Where available, you can specify what class you'd like to travel in; if you don't state a preference, you'll be issued with the cheapest standard fare in "unreserved" (sometimes also referred to as "general") class. Note that it's possible to upgrade later by swapping carriages and paying the TC (Ticket Controller) the difference – technically, this isn't allowed, but rail staff tend to be sympathetic towards foreigners who unwittingly find themselves in unreserved carriages.

Longer journeys can last all night, in which case you'll need to reserve a berth. This is where the various classes really start to show. In **"unreserved"**, you'll be lucky to find so much as a square foot of floor space. Unless desperate, even travellers on the tightest of budgets should reserve a bunk in **sleeper class** (also called "second-class non-a/c" or "second-class reserved"), which costs Rs301 per 1000km and entitles you to a swing-down, slatted bunk in a three-tier compartment. Next up the scale is **second-class a/c**, which costs Rs845/1221 per 1000km, depending on whether it's two- or three-tier (ie with four or six bunks per compartment); this is by far the most common form of a/c sleeper travel, available on almost every express and mail train, and

comes complete with fresh cotton sheets, pillows and optional meals freshly cooked in an attached "pantry car". Finally, **first-class a/c**, the poshest of all, is reserved for only the swankiest of trains (such as the bi-weekly *Rajdhani* to Goa), costing upwards of Rs2159 per 1000km (including meals) – more than flying in many instances.

Buying tickets

Tickets can be booked in person at the station itself. In the big cities, huge computerized reservation halls process streams of passengers from 8am until 8pm, Monday to Saturday, and until 2pm on Sundays. Queues and waiting times tend to be long.

First off, fill in the requisite paper form with your personal details and the number, name and date of the train you wish to catch (available online, from *Trains at a Glance*, or, if you're lucky, from the desk clerk when you reach the head of the queue). Once you've paid for your ticket, check to make sure the dates and other details are correct, and that it is "confirmed" not "wait listed", in which case an ominous "W" will appear next to your berth number. This means your place hasn't been "confirmed", and that whatever number is listed next to the "W" on your ticket will be your position in a waiting list for allocation of unclaimed berths.

Women should note that most station booking halls have "ladies' queues"; travelling in a mixed group or couple, a woman will find it easier to get all the tickets if she queues up on her own.

As demand for all berths is high year-round, reservations should be made as far in advance as possible – ideally at least a couple of weeks before your intended departure date, or a minimum of 36 hours. To avoid having to trek out to the station again, travellers following tight itineraries tend to buy departure tickets from particular towns the moment they arrive. At most large stations, it's also possible to reserve tickets for journeys starting elsewhere in the state.

If there are no places available on the train you want, ask if any seats or berths have been set aside as a **"tourist quota"** This special allocation, reserved for foreign passport holders, is available in advance, but usually only from major or originating stations.

Alternatively, **online ticket reservation** is also now available (from anywhere in the world) via the **Indian Railway Catering and Tourism Corporation** (ⓦwww.irctc.co.in). Major foreign credit cards are accepted. The service charge is only Rs40 for second class and Rs60 for first. You just need to set up an account and password the first time you log on, after which you can access your personal travel record, check your reservations and, if need be, cancel any of them. Again, only a small fee is deducted before the refund is directly credited back to your card.

Many **travel agents** will also secure rail tickets for a fairly reasonable fee of Rs25–50. Failure to buy a ticket at the point of departure will result in a stiff **penalty** if the ticket controller finds you.

Indian Railways sales agents abroad

Australia Adventure World ☎02/9956 7766, ⓦwww.adventureworld.com.au.
UK SD Enterprises ☎020 8903 3411, ⓦwww.indiarail.co.uk.

Cloakrooms

Most stations in Kerala have **cloakrooms** (sometimes called "parcel offices") for passengers to leave their baggage. These can be very handy if you want to go sight-seeing in a town and move on the same day. In theory, you need a current train ticket or Indrail pass to deposit luggage, but they don't always ask; they may, however, refuse to take your bag if you can't lock it. Losing your reclaim ticket also causes problems. Make sure, when checking baggage in, that

the cloakroom will be open when you need to pick it up. The standard charge is currently Rs10 for the first 24 hours, Rs12 for the next 24 hours and Rs15 per day thereafter.

By air

Kerala has three civil **airports**: Thiruvanan-thapuram (ⓦwww.trivandrum-airport.com); Kochi (ⓦwww.cochin-airport.com); and Kozhikode (ⓦwww.kozhikode-airport.com). The vast majority of passengers using them tend to be en route to or from the Gulf States, but there are also plenty of flights between the three cities. It takes only forty minutes to fly from the capital to Kochi and fifty minutes to reach Kozhikode – the trip between Kochi and Kozhikode takes thirty minutes.

Air India Express (☎0484/238 1885, ⓦwww.airindiaexpress.in) operates the largest number of flights within the state, with the national domestic carrier, Indian Airlines – or just plain "Indian" as it recently rebranded itself (toll free ☎1800/180 1407, ⓦwww .indian-airlines.nic.in) – a close second. The smaller but dependable Air Sahara (toll free ☎1800/223020, ⓦwww.airsahara.net) also operates the routes, as does the no-frills airline, Air Deccan (☎3900 8888 or ☎m98403 77008, ⓦwww.airdeccan.net).

Fares fluctuate according to the time of year and availability, but can easily be checked online.

Booking tickets

Tickets are most easily booked at the airlines' offices, addresses for which are listed in the relevant city accounts

Tatkal tickets

Though regarded as something of a rip-off in India, Indian Railways' late-availability reservation system, or **Tatkal**, can be a great help for foreign tourists. A quota of ten percent of places is reserved on most trains under this scheme, which are bookable at any computerized office. Tickets are released five days before the train departs, with an extra charge of Rs150 in sleeper class, and Rs300 in first or a/c sleepers (Rs75/200 during low season, July 15 to Sept 15). The real catch, however, is that you also have to pay for the entire length of the journey from originating to terminating station, however much or little of the ride you do (hence the rip-off), so Tatkal is obviously not worth it if you want to get on, say, the Thiruvananthapuram–Goa Rajdhani Express between Kollam and Kochi. If the amount of the route you are planning to cover makes the cost worthwhile, though, you're pretty well guaranteed to find a place, especially if you get in early.

throughout this guide. **Booking online** can be less straightforward, as airlines tend to refuse payments by credit or debit cards not registered in India. Moreover, check-in clerks in some airports may not be geared up to accept **e-tickets**, insisting that passengers re-book and pay in cash for a conventional paper ticket. This problem should have been resolved in March 2007, when the industry supposedly dispensed with paper tickets altogether, but it's worth checking the situation before departure, especially if you're transferring from an international to a domestic carrier on arrival in India (and particularly if you're travelling on Indian Airlines).

By bus

Although generally less comfortable than travelling by train, **buses** fill in the gaps in the rail network, and can be quicker. They go almost everywhere, and more frequently than trains (though mostly in daylight hours).

Services vary somewhat in price and standard. Painted in distinctive red and cream, those run by the government bus company, **KSRTC** (the Kerala State Road Transport Company), tend to be the most ramshackle of all. Invariably jam-packed, they cover both short and very long distances; in the latter case, express services are run which have limited stops. In more widely travelled areas there are usually additional **private** buses offering more leg-room and generally travelling faster – not necessarily a plus point when you consider the dilapidated state of the vehicles.

Some clue as to comfort can be gained from the description given to the bus. "Ordinary" buses usually have minimally padded fixed upright seats. "Deluxe", "Luxury" and even "Super-deluxe" are fairly interchangeable terms and when applied to government buses may hardly differ from "ordinary". Usually they refer to private services, though, and should then guarantee a softer, sometimes reclining, individual seat. You can check this out when booking, and it's also worth asking if your bus has a video or music system – if so, the deafening noise will prevent any chance of sleep. Always try to avoid the back seats – they accentuate bumpy roads, launching you into the air several times a minute. Try to sit in the middle of the bus for safety.

Luggage travels in the hatch on private buses, sometimes at a small extra charge. You can usually squeeze it into an unobtrusive corner inside state-run vehicles, although you may occasionally be requested to store it on the roof (passengers travelling on the roof is a rare event these days); check that it's well secured and not liable to get squashed. Baksheesh (see p.68) is in order for whoever puts it up there for you.

Booking tickets

Buying a bus ticket is usually less of an ordeal than buying a train ticket, although at large city bus stations there may be twenty or so counters, each assigned to a different route. When you buy your ticket you'll be given the registration number of the bus and, sometimes, a seat number. As at railway stations, there is usually a separate, quicker, ladies' queue, although it may not be signed in English.

You can always get on ordinary state buses without a ticket, while at bus stands outside major cities it's usually possible to pay on board, though you have to be sharp to secure a seat. Prior booking is usually available and is recommended for express state buses and private services; it's worth checking the precise departure point with the agent. You can usually pay on board private buses, too, although that reduces your chances of a seat.

By boat

Ferries are a prominent feature of life in the **backwater regions** of Kerala, where they form essential links between disparate villages and market towns. Cheap, regular and reliable, they're also a great way for tourists to experience this unique part of the country.

The other place you're likely to use a ferry is in **Kochi**. Municipal ferries chug throughout the day and evening across the city's busy harbour, connecting the main jetty in Ernakulam with various islands and promontories, including Fort Cochin.

Full details of routes and fares appear along with useful travel hints in the relevant sections of the Guide. For an overview of backwater travel by **tourist boats** – including *kettu vallam* rice barges around Alappuzha and the Kuttanad region – see our dedicated box on p.144 and the "Backwaters" colour section.

By car

It's much more usual for tourists in Kerala to be driven than it is for them to drive; car rental firms operate on the basis of supplying **chauffeur-driven vehicles**.

Chauffeur-driven car hire

Arranged through tourist offices or local car rental firms, a chauffeur-driven car will start from about Rs1000–1200 per day, usually including 200km, with additional kilometres charged at the rate of Rs 6–7/km per day. On longer trips, the driver sleeps in the car, for which his firm may charge an additional Rs150–200. You should generally tip the driver Rs100–150. For more advice on hiring a car with a driver, see below.

Most tourists succumb to the romance of that quintessentially Indian automobile, the **Hindustan Ambassador** Mark IV, based on the design of the old British Oxford Morris. Sadly, however, the car's appalling suspension and back-breaking seats make it among the most uncomfortable rides in the world. Older models, in particular, can make for some gruelling journeys, with dashboards that become burning-hot and suffocating fumes plaguing the front seats. All in all, you'll be much better off in a modern two- or four-door hatchback – ask your rental company for the options.

Self-driving car rental

The big international chains, Avis (ⓦwww .avis.com) and Hertz (ⓦwww.hertz.com), usually have their offices in the upmarket hotels of major cities and are the best bet for **self-drive car** rental; contact numbers for them are listed throughout the Guide. In India the charge is much the same as it would be to be driven by a chauffeur, with a Rs1000 deposit against damage, though if you pre-book in your home country it can cost a lot more.

Driving in Kerala is not for beginners. If you do drive yourself, expect the unexpected, and count on other drivers taking whatever liberties they can get away with. Traffic circulates on the left, but don't expect road regulations to be obeyed. In the city, it's heavy and particularly undisciplined: vehicles cut in and out without warning, and you have to cope with pedestrians, cyclists

Renting a car: some tips

Renting a car and driver in Kerala can result in all manner of problems, most of them based on misunderstandings that could have been avoided at the planning stage. The following pointers should help you negotiate a smoother trip.

- Always compare prices between companies (bearing in mind that Rs1000–1200 for 200km and Rs6–7/km thereafter is standard).
- You should fix your itinerary, the approximate mileage, travelling time, pick-up and drop-off locations – and, crucially, who is paying for fuel, road taxes and tolls, and the driver's overnight allowance – with the rental company in advance.
- Pin the details of any agreement down in a written contract.
- Should a deposit be required (one may be asked for, but you're entitled to refuse), it's a good idea to wait until the time of departure to pay it – otherwise a different car may turn up from the one you agreed to. The remaining balance should be settled on the last day of the trip. Whatever happens, never pay the full amount in advance and always insist on a receipt for any money you hand over.
- Never leave your passport or a credit card slip as security.
- Ideally, meet the driver (especially if it is for a long journey) ahead of departure, in order to ensure that his English is up to the task.
- Before leaving, check the vehicle (brakes, lights, indicators, steering).

and cows wandering nonchalantly down the middle of the road as if you don't exist. In the country the roads are narrow, in terrible repair and hogged by overloaded Tata trucks that move aside for nobody. To overtake, sound your horn – the driver in front will signal if it is safe to do so; if not, he will wave his hand, palm downwards, up and down. The vast number of potholes doesn't make for a smooth ride either, and during the monsoon, roads can become flooded and dangerous; rivers burst their banks and bridges get washed away. Ask local people before you set off, and proceed with caution, sticking to main highways as much as possible. It is very dangerous to drive at night – not everyone uses lights, and bullock carts don't have any.

You should have an **international licence** to drive in Kerala. **Insurance** is compulsory, but not expensive. Car seat-belts are not compulsory but very strongly recommended. **Accident** rates are high, and you should be on your guard at all times. If you do have an accident, it might be an idea to leave the scene quickly and go straight to the police to report it; mobs can assemble fast, especially if pedestrians or cows are involved.

Fuel is reasonably cheap, at around Rs44 per litre, but the state of the roads will take its toll, and mechanics are not always very reliable, so a knowledge of **vehicle maintenance** is a help, as is a check-over every so often to see what all those bone-shaking journeys are doing to your car. Luckily, if you get a flat tyre, puncture-wallahs can be found almost everywhere.

By motorbike

It is hard to overstate the sense of freedom that breezing around the backroads of Kerala can bring. On a **rented bike** you can reach the state's remote beaches and cover long distances with relative ease, and air temperatures are warm enough to mean you don't have to keep wrapping and unwrapping layers each time you stop and start.

The downside, of course, is that two-wheelers can be perilous. Kerala's roads rank among the most dangerous on the planet, and at least a half of all recorded traffic accidents in the state are motorcycle riders or their pillion passengers. Before driving away, therefore, ensure the lights and brakes are in good shape, and be especially vigilant at night: many roads are poor and unlit, and stray cows and carts can appear from nowhere. Another hazard to look out for are the **speedbreakers** that slow progress on all Keralan roads. These speed-bumps, often of massive proportions, are rarely marked, and regularly cause accidents when riders hit them at speed.

Motorcycles are available for rent in the coastal resorts of Kovalam and Varkala. Officially, you need an **international driver's licence** (IDP, type #1949, available through post offices, the AA or RAC in the UK) to rent and ride anything, but in practice a standard licence will suffice if you're stopped and asked to produce your papers by the local police.

Helmets are also compulsory: you're unlikely to be stopped for not wearing one on country backroads, or riding around the resorts, but out on the main highways the police will often wave you over and spot-fine you if you're bare-headed. In any case, it makes sense to wear one given how dangerous the Keralan roads can be. The owner of your rented motorbike should be able to provide an Indian-made helmet, but it may not fit and isn't likely to be of the best quality; you might want to consider investing in a new one (they're available in Thiruvananthapuram's Chalai Bazaar area) or, better still, bringing one from home which you know hasn't been cracked.

Rates for motorbikes vary according to season, duration of rental and vehicle; most owners also insist on a deposit and/or passport as security. The cheapest bike, a scooter-style Honda Activa 100cc, which has automatic gears, costs around Rs250 per day. These are reliable and fine for buzzing to the beach and back, but to travel further you need a bit more power. Other options include the perennially stylish Enfield Bullet 350cc, although these are heavy, unwieldy and – at upwards of Rs350 per day – the most expensive bike to rent. For all-round performance and manoeuvrability, you can't beat the fast and light Yamaha RD, Honda Splendor and Baja Pulsars. Essentially Japanese-designed bikes built

When renting a motorcycle, always try for one that's less than a year old – Kerala's roads play havoc with suspension and brakes, and maintenance standards might not always be what you're used to at home. Take the bike out for a quick spin before you start to negotiate the price: test the brakes and lights and check the tyre treads. Its owner should also provide a helmet and insurance papers.

It's also a good idea to know in advance where the best **accident and emergency units** are located.

under licence (and with inferior materials) in India, they're economical on fuel and generally well suited to the windy Keralan roads. They go for Rs250–300, depending on what kind of shape the vehicle is in and how long you rent it for.

Two-stroke **fuel** is sold at service stations (known locally as "petrol pumps") in the main towns and along the national highway. In out-of-the-way places, it's also sold in mineral water bottles at general stores or through backstreet suppliers. But you should avoid these whenever possible as some bulk out their petrol with low-grade kerosene or industrial solvent, which makes engines misfire and smoke badly.

As a rule of thumb, a newish 100cc scooter or geared bike should manage at least 35–40km per litre. Be warned, however, that **fuel gauges** rarely work, and those that do shouldn't be trusted. When riding in remote areas of the state where fuel stops may be few and far between, take a spare litre with you.

Most villages also have a **motorcycle-repair** specialist (or a "puncture–wallah"), although in theory the person you rented your machine from should foot the bill for routine maintenance (including punctures, blown bulbs and any mechanical failures). Damage to the bike incurred during a road traffic accident, of course, has to be paid for by you. It is important you agree on such details with the owner before driving away; you should also exchange mobile (cell) phone numbers.

Cycling

Indian-made, gearless **Hero bicycles** – ideal for a gentle jaunt along the shady backlanes of the coast but hard work over longer distances – may be rented in most towns and resorts. The going rate varies between Rs50 and Rs100 per day, and you could be asked to leave a **deposit**, or even your passport, as security – though you should think twice about doing this, perhaps suggesting a photocopy instead.

If you plan to spend a couple of months or more in Kerala, **buying** your own cycle is worth considering. Standard Heroes cost Rs2000–Rs2500, depending on the model and what frills you choose to add. There are bicycle shops in all major towns and cities, although you may have to order and wait a week or two.

Up in Periyar, you can also rent modern, European-made **mountain bikes** for longer cycle rides through the Cardamom Hills – for more details, see p.162.

Bringing a bike from abroad requires no *carnet* or special paperwork, and most airlines allow you to take cycles at no extra cost – though they may insist on them being flat-packed in cardboard covers (available through good cycle shops). Spare parts and accessories may be of different sizes and standards in Kerala, though, and you may have to improvise. Bring basic spares and tools and a pump. Panniers are the obvious thing for carrying your gear, but fiendishly inconvenient when not attached to your bike, and you might consider sacrificing ideal load-bearing and streamlining technology for a backpack you can lash down on the rear carrier.

City transport

City transport takes various forms, with **buses** the most obvious. These are usually single-decker, and can get unbelievably crowded.

If you're visiting a variety of places around town, consider hiring a **taxi**, **rickshaw** or **auto-rickshaw** for the day. Find a driver who speaks English reasonably well, and agree a price beforehand. A taxi for a day will cost around Rs800–1000, an auto-rickshaw Rs400–500.

Taxis

Taxis are usually rather battered Ambassadors or old Fiat Padminis, but these older models are gradually being usurped by more modern vehicles. With any luck, the driver will agree to use the **meter**; in theory you're within your rights to call the police if he doesn't, but the usual compromise is to agree a fare for the journey before you get in. Naturally, it helps to have an idea in advance of what the fare should be, though any figures quoted in this or any other book should be treated as being the broadest of guidelines only. From places such as main stations, you may be able to find other passengers to share a taxi to the town centre; many stations, and certainly most airports, operate **prepaid taxi schemes** with set fares that you pay before departure; more expensive prepaid limousines are also available.

Auto-rickshaws

The **auto-rickshaw**, that most Indian of vehicles, is the front half of a motor-scooter with a double seat mounted on the back. Cheaper than taxis, better at nipping in and out of traffic, and theoretically metered (again, in most places they probably won't use them and you should agree a fare before setting off), auto-rickshaws are a little unstable and their drivers often rather reckless, but that's all part of the fun. In Kerala, rickshaw-wallahs – recognizable by their official khaki shirts – are strictly unionized, which means they tend not to overcharge tourists who don't know what the correct fares should be – although don't bank on this.

Accommodation

In Kerala, perhaps more than anywhere else in India, getting your choice of accommodation right will make or break your holiday. While rarely less than acceptable, standards and styles in all categories differ enormously. The reason for this is the varying speeds with which local hotel and guesthouse owners have adapted to recent changes in the tourism market. Whereas a decade ago, a basic room with running water was all that most visitors expected, now places to stay stand at the centre of the Kerala experience. Traditional architecture, verandas with lovely views and the chance to see period properties from the comfort of an antique bed are the reason many people come – and few leave disappointed.

Whatever your budget, you can expect to stay in some truly memorable places, ranging from old wooden *tharavadu* homesteads surrounded by rice fields to ivy-fronted British bungalows on tea estates high in the hills, village huts in the backwaters, and beachside resorts offering sea views from their overflow pools.

Prices, particularly in tourist centres, are high by Indian standards, but compared with Western countries, room tariffs offer amazing value for money.

Hotels and guesthouses

There is a huge variety of hotels, guesthouses and lodges throughout Kerala, ranging from tiny flea-bitten holes costing under Rs150 to super-luxurious giants that will set you back hundreds of dollars for a night.

Checkout time varies – in some places, such as hill stations or beach resorts, 9–10am is the norm, while in upper-bracket places it is more likely to be noon. Across most of the region, however, at least in the

Accommodation price codes

All **accommodation prices** in this book have been categorized according to the price **codes** below, which correspond to the cost of a double room in shoulder season (Nov to mid-Dec & mid-Jan to Feb).

Rooms covered under codes ❶ and ❷ are usually very basic but often include en-suite (attached) bathrooms and sometimes even a TV; some will have shared bathrooms (non-attached). You can expect hotel rooms in codes ❸ and ❹ to be attached, most likely with a TV, and have a better standard of decor and furnishing and maybe a balcony; some of the cheaper a/c rooms fall into this category or, if non-a/c, will have mosquito nets provided. Hotels in codes ❺ and ❻ are guaranteed to be smart, spacious, more tastefully furnished and more often than not a/c; breakfast may be included too. Hotels in codes ❼ and ❽ become positively luxurious, almost invariably with a/c, and boast far better facilities (such as swimming pools) and service; most top-end Indian business hotels belong here. Code ❾ is the preserve of the five-stars run by companies such as the Taj Group, as well as upscale heritage homestays or boutique hotels pitched at well-heeled foreign tourists; these provide quality to match anywhere in the world.

In non-touristy parts of the region, and in most major towns and cities, accommodation prices will be the same throughout the year. But in the resorts along the coast, and in wildlife sanctuaries and hill stations, rates fluctuate wildly with demand, inflating two- or three-fold during peak season (mid-Dec to mid-Jan).

Price code **spans** in the Guide usually indicate the cost of the cheapest non-a/c and cheapest a/c rooms, where applicable. All **taxes** are included in the rates we quote.

❶ up to Rs200	❹ Rs500–1000	❼ Rs2000–3000
❷ Rs200–300	❺ Rs1000–1500	❽ Rs3000–5000
❸ Rs300–500	❻ Rs1500–2000	❾ Rs5000 and upwards

budget to lower mid-range bands, places operate a 24-hour system, under which you are simply obliged to leave by the same time as you arrived.

Unfortunately not all hotels have **single rooms**, so it generally works out more expensive to travel alone, although you may be able to negotiate a slight discount for single occupancy of a double. It's not unusual to find rooms with three or four beds, however – great value for **families** and small groups.

In cheap hotels and hostels, you needn't expect any additions to your basic bill, but as you go up the scale you'll find **taxes** and **service charges** creeping in, sometimes adding as much as a third on top of the original tariff. Taxes vary but service is generally ten to fifteen percent. These hidden charges are usually added to your bill.

Officially, all establishments are obliged to provide a printed tariff list and most in fact do. However, like most other things in India,

the price of a room may well be open to **negotiation**. If you think the rate is too high, or if all the hotels in town are empty, try haggling: you'll nearly always be offered a reduction.

Inexpensive hotels

While accommodation prices in Kerala are generally on the up, there's still an abundance of **cheap hotels and lodges**, catering for backpacking tourists and less well-off Indians. Most charge Rs150–250 for a double room, and outside the big cities some have rates below Rs100.

Budget accommodation tends to be cheaper the further you get off the beaten track; it's most expensive in the resorts of Kovalam and Varkala, where prices are at least double those for equivalent accommodation in most other areas.

Cold showers or "bucket baths" are the order of the day – not really a problem in Kerala as the heat means that, except in the hills, you're unlikely to want hot water. Moreover, even cold water never comes out of the tap very cold, and by mid-afternoon can be positively warm if it's been sitting in a tank on the roof.

Even so, it's always wise to check out the state of the bathrooms and toilets before taking a room; most will be spotless, but you can never be sure. And not all will have Western, "sit-down" loos.

Mid-range hotels

You don't need to pay through the nose for creature comforts in Kerala. A large, clean double, with a freshly made bed, your own spotless bathroom with sit-down toilet, cable TV and hot and cold running water can still cost under Rs400 (£5/$10). Extras that bump up the price include taxes, mosquito nets, a balcony and, above all, **air-conditioning**. Many medium-priced hotels also have attached **restaurants**, and even room service.

The walls and floors of new hotels tend to be lined with marble (or some imitation), which can make them feel totally characterless. They are, however, much cleaner than older hotels, where dirt and grime clings to cracks and crevices, and damp quickly devours paint. Some mid-range hotels also feel compelled to furnish their rooms with wall-to-wall carpeting, which often smells due to humidity and damp.

Upmarket hotels

Kerala has devised its own spin on the conventional five-star campus, relocating **antique wood houses** (*tharavadu*) from villages to luxury resort enclaves on the coast and backwaters. Well-to-do families with beautiful old country mansions have also started to open their doors to guests, charging five-star tariffs for the privilege. And in the Western Ghats of inland Kerala, you'll find so-called **eco-resorts**, often consisting of tree houses or thatched, village-style mud huts equipped with low-impact comforts.

Modern deluxe establishments – slicker, brighter and far more businesslike – tend to belong to chains, including the Indian-owned Taj Group, which owns some of the state's finest hostelries. It's becoming more common for luxury chains to quote tariffs in US dollars (or euros in the case of places south of Kovalam), starting at $100 and rising to a hefty $500 – sometimes even more for suites. In converted palaces and heritage hotels, however, you'll still get excellent value for money, with rates only just beginning to approach those of their counterparts back home.

Note that only the standard "rack rates" will be offered to you if you walk into a top hotel direct, though special reductions are available online. You may also find **discounts** through travel agencies (listed in the Guide) offering up to sixty percent off certain luxury hotels, depending on the season.

Homestays

"Homestay" accommodation, where you pay to stay in family houses, is a rapidly growing trend in Kerala. It comes in various forms, from no-frills annexes tacked on to the back of an existing block to beautifully designed guest wings in period buildings, with antique furniture and private gardens. Home-cooked food is generally available, and you'll find most host families bring a strong sense of vocation to their business, interacting with guests at meal times and showing them around the local area – all of which can make for a very memorable and rewarding experience.

Rates vary according to the quality of accommodation and food, but tend to be slightly higher than comparable hotel accommodation. Reviews of homestays appear throughout the Guide; bookings are best made direct by telephone, or online via the homestay's website. Unlike more formal or luxury hotels, advance payments by credit card are not usually required to secure the reservation: a follow-up confirmation call a day or two before arrival will suffice.

Hostels

YMCAs and **YWCAs** in Kerala are confined to big cities and offer exceptional value – which is why they're invariably fully booked. We list several in the Guide, and if you're hoping to stay in one, make a booking by telephone several weeks in advance.

Staying in religious communities

Religious institutions offer accommodation for pilgrims and visitors, and may put up tourists; a donation is often expected, and certainly appreciated, but some of the bigger ones charge a fixed nominal fee. **Ashrams** are another source of rooms, especially if you are taking a course at the institution in question; again, some have fixed charges, others simply ask for donations.

Food and drink

One of the major highlights of any trip to Kerala is the food. For anyone used to the heavy, over-spiced curries typically dished up in "Indian" restaurants abroad, the subtlety of South Indian cuisine will come as a revelation. Keralans, in particular, bring the same ingenuity and wealth of deep-rooted traditions to food preparation that they've brought to bear on their sacred arts and festivals – with results that are no less sophisticated or surprising.

The fertile climate, soils, seas and inland waterways of the state have provided Keralan cooks with an uncommon variety of ingredients, augmented over the centuries by many others imported by traders and colonizers – not least the chilli, which came to Kerala with the Portuguese. They have always been quick to adapt to new culinary trends, and the recent boom in tourism means a host of familiar dishes are also on offer in the resorts, often given a local twist.

By Western standards, eating out in Kerala is extremely cheap. Even in a smart five-star restaurant, you'll rarely notch up a bill of over Rs1000 (£12.50/$25.00), while in a workaday local diner, a filling, delicious, freshly cooked feast comprising a dozen or more different dishes can be had for a mere Rs30 (£0.40/$0.80) or less.

Veg vs non-veg

Many Hindu castes in Kerala abstain from eating meat and seafood, while some orthodox Namboodiri Brahmins will not even eat onions or garlic, or any food cooked by anyone outside their household.

Eating places always state whether they are vegetarian or non-vegetarian – "**veg**" or "**non-veg**". Sometimes you will come across restaurants advertising both veg and non-veg, indicating they have two separate kitchens and, often, two distinct parts to the restaurant so as not to contaminate or offend their vegetarian clientele. You'll also see "**pure veg**" advertised, which means that no eggs or alcohol are served.

Veganism as such is not common, however, so if you're vegan you'll need to be fairly vigilant and enquiring. Dairy products, for example, are present in most Keralan sweets, and in many restaurants and homes ghee (unclarified butter) is used for frying.

As a rule, **meat-eaters** should exercise caution in Kerala: even when meat is available, especially in the larger towns, its quality is not assured and you won't get much in a dish anyway – especially in railway canteens where it's mainly there for flavouring. Note that what is called "mutton" is in fact goat. Hindus, of course, do not eat beef, and Muslims shun pork, but Christians throughout the state place both at the heart of their own brand of regional cooking.

Fish is popular throughout Kerala, particularly in the coastal towns and beach resorts, and fish dishes, whether as steaks or in curries, are often beautifully cooked and very good value.

Where and when to eat

Finding somewhere decent to eat in Kerala is rarely a problem. In towns and cities, hygienic South Indian-style cafés and restaurants compete for custom on seemingly every street corner, open from dawn until late at night. In the resorts, prices in places oriented towards foreigners tend to be much higher, and the quality of cooking much patchier, but you'll be spoilt for choice, with everything from fresh local seafood to pizzas and pasta, German-Bakery cakes and healthy green salads.

As for authentic Keralan food (covered under a separate heading on p.39), it's impossible to beat proper home cooking, which you'll be able to enjoy in homestays and small guesthouses all over the state. That said, the delicious, fresh and cheap fare served in **thattukada** hot meals stalls (see p.40) comes pretty close.

Breakfast

Keralans are early risers, especially women in the villages, who invariably start the day in the pre-dawn darkness with a quick glass of chai before getting stuck into a couple of hours' grinding rice, coconut and spices for the day's meals. **Breakfast** proper gets under way when the kids are up, and consists of **pootu** – cylinders of roughly pounded rice and coconut steamed together in hollowed-out bamboos (or, more often these days, in aluminium tubes) – or **appam** – soft, slightly cupped rice pancakes that are deliciously spongy in the centre. **Iddiappams**, a kind of vermicelli, are another breakfast staple, made by squeezing runny rice dough through a special press and then steaming it. These are accompanied by the sweetest Keralan bananas, and maybe a cup of warm milk, or else with saucers of spicy **egg masala**, a rich, tasty gravy based on onions which is poured over the *pootu*, *appam* or *iddiappam* and eaten with the fingers.

Washed down with cups of strong, milky chai or local filter coffee, versions of the standard Keralan breakfast are served in tea shacks (*chayakada*) and corner cafés all over the state – mostly to men, who use the opportunity to read the local paper and debate the latest political scandals.

> In the South – perhaps even more so than elsewhere – **eating with your fingers** is *de rigueur*, and cutlery may not always be available. Wherever you eat, remember to use only your right hand (see p.66), and wash your hands before you start. Use the tips of your fingers to avoid getting food on the palm of your hand.

In larger towns and cities, however, a more generic, **South Indian-style breakfast** prevails, based on dishes originally devised in the Karnatakan pilgrimage town of Udipi. These include scrumptious deep-fried savoury doughnuts made of chickpea flour called **vada**, and circular steamed rice cakes, or **iddlis**, which are broken up and soaked in **sambar** (a chilli-hot, sour, watery broth) or mushed together with **chatni** (a tangy paste, often made with ground coconut and finely chopped fresh green chillis).

You'll find *iddli-vada-sambar* breakfasts being dished up from dawn onwards, and around the clock in railway and bus stations. By 11am, however, most places will have switched to their lunchtime "meals" menu (see below).

Opening times are more erratic in the resorts of Kovalam and Varkala, where cafés serve a hotchpotch of travellers' standards such as banana pancakes, muesli, toast, omelettes, porridge (not always oatmeal), lassis and fruit shakes. Proper espresso is also widely available, along with freshly baked wholemeal bread, croissants (or a heavy, stodgy version of them) and copious fresh fruit salads with honey, grated coconut and yoghurt (curd).

If you're staying in a smart hotel, **buffet breakfasts** are the norm, consisting of limp versions of Western food and even limper South Indian dishes that won't be a patch on what you can order for Rs10 in the nearest village.

Lunch: "Meals Ready"

"Meals" restaurants or **canteens** are among the best places to try genuine South Indian cuisine. Found all over Kerala, usually clustered around major bus stations and bazaars with a sign saying "Meals

Ready" out front, they are a fast, cheap (around Rs25–35), informal and hygienic way to fill your stomach – and the food is usually terrific.

It's served either on a fresh plantain leaf or, more commonly these days, on large, round stainless steel trays (called by their North Indian name, thalis), with six to eight different preparations spooned by a succession of waiters into little bowls, along with blobs of pickle (*achar*) and sprinkles of salt.

The conventional Keralan way to approach the meal is to break the **papadam**, the crisp-fried wafer that normally appears first – into the heap of **rice** that comes shortly after. On to this mound you pour whichever of the fiery red *sambar* or lentil-based **dhals** take your fancy. Mix them into a manageable sludge (with the fingers of your right hand only, of course) and shovel into your mouth, without getting any on your face or shirt-front – not as easy as it may sound.

After the *ozhikan* (literally "to pour over") dishes, comes the *rasam*, a watery, hot soup soured with *kodampuli* (a kind of tamarind) or *kokum*, which is intended to aid digestion. Then you move on to the thicker vegetable dishes, known as "gravies", at least one of which in Kerala will be an **avial** – steamed root vegetables coated in roughly ground coconut and yoghurt. Waiters continually patrol the dining hall, refilling any bowls that get emptied and loading more rice onto your banana leaf or tray (Keralans get through an unbelievable quantity of rice in the course of an average lunch and will find your apparent lack of appetite amusing).

Servings of vegetables, dhal, *rasam* and rice are "unlimited" (they'll keep coming until you can't manage any more), but you may have to pay a tiny bit extra if you want a second helping of yoghurt, served in its pure form as "curd", which rounds every Keralan meal off: mix it into the last of your rice (Keralans will always accept a final spoonful for the purpose) – it'll help balance the heat of the spices. "Deluxe" meals will also include a small helping of sweet rice and mung bean pudding called **payasam**, deliciously spiced with cardamom and, in swankier places, saffron.

This is the generally accepted running order of dishes in Kerala, but meals are done differently in other states and there are really no hard-and-fast rules. The only no-no that's guaranteed to attract the attention of the whole restaurant, and have your fellow diners chuckling into their lunches, is if you inadvertently mix up the *payasam* with the savoury curries.

However well you manage, some good-natured curiosity is bound to attend the spectacle of a foreigner eating with his or her hands – though not as much as you'll attract by asking for a knife or fork. When you're done, head for the little tap in the corner to wash off the remnants.

As well as its main canteen or dining hall, most meals joints have a fancier a/c section (often upstairs and next door) where better-off middle-class diners, and women, can eat in greater comfort. The food's identical, but you'll pay Rs10–20 more for it.

Some places also have separate veg and non-veg sections (see p.36). In Kerala, non-veg "meals" are the same as "veg" ones, except they come with an additional chunk of fried fish or "mutton" curry.

Snacks: udipi cooking

Most, but not all, "meals" restaurants in Kerala serve menus of lighter, more generic South Indian snacks – though not usually at the same time. The so-called **udipi** menu – referring to a cuisine that was originally developed by Brahmin priests of the famous Krishna temple at Udipi, coastal Karnataka, but which has since spread all over the country – starts early for breakfast (see p.37) but is generally suspended 11am–3pm for lunch meals.

In the afternoon, *iddli-vada-sambar-chatni* (see p.37) returns to the menu, along with the quintessential and most scrumptious of all *udipi* snacks, the **masala dosa**. Made from a batter of partly fermented rice and lentil flour, *dosas* are fried like French crepes on hot griddle irons until they're crunchy on the outside. Into the centre of the pancake is then spooned a blob of spicy potato masala, often packed with chunks of green vegetables, coconut, freshly chopped coriander and curry leaves. It's served while still hot with an accompaniment of *sambar* and *chatni*.

Many delicious versions of the basic *dosa* appear on *udipi* menus: a **rawa dosa** has semolina added to its batter, which is mixed with chopped onions and poured in sweeping, cross-hatched patterns on to the griddle to create an extra crunchy mesh. Order a "roast" or "**paper dosa**" and you could end up with a wafer thin tube a couple of feet long.

Uttappams are another delicious *udipi* speciality – again, made from semi-fermented rice flour, but poured more thickly on the griddle, and served with a layer of green chillis, coriander, *sambar* and *chatni*. The tasty "cheese *uttappam*" offers a contemporary spin on the dish, featuring chopped tomatoes and finely grated cheese – South India's answer to the pizza.

Hotel restaurants

Nearly every hotel or lodge in Kerala, no matter how small, has a restaurant attached to it. The smarter ones tend to be where the local middle-classes dine out, served by teams of brisk waiters wearing black ties and waistcoats. At lunchtime, fancy versions of the standard thali meal, featuring North Indian dishes and extra sweets and nibbles, are offered (typically for around Rs100–120) alongside the standard **multi-cuisine menu**. This is generally divided into four sections: North Indian, South Indian, Continental and Chinese.

Dishes generally can cost anywhere between Rs75 and Rs250, depending on how flash the hotel is, and vary greatly in quality. Stick to the Indian options and you won't go far wrong. "Chinese" can mean a whole range of culinary possibilities, few of them resembling anything authentically Chinese, but spicy and full of flavour nonetheless. Except in the top hotels, which employ internationally trained chefs, Continental (Western-style) dishes are the ones to avoid.

Tourist restaurants

In the southern Keralan resorts of Kovalam and Varkala, the majority of café-restaurants lining the beach front and clifftops bear little resemblance to the places where locals eat. Staffed by emigrant workers from Nepal or northern India, most are seasonal bamboo and palm-thatch shacks that open for breakfast and stay open through the day and evening, serving a huge, catch-all menu of dishes tailored for the spice-sensitive Western palate.

After sunset, **seafood** takes centre stage, with the day's catch displayed on ice slabs out front to attract custom. Seer fish, marlin, kingfish, barracuda, shark and swordfish are the star attractions, along with calamari (squid), fresh tiger or king prawns, crab and lobster (the latter imported and often previously frozen). You select your fish (or crustacean), and decide how you want it cooked (pan-fried with butter and garlic is best, but they'll also bake it dry in a tandoori oven with *tikka* spices on request); then settle down with a beer for a long wait.

Always ask the price before you order (anywhere between Rs100 and Rs200 is the norm). It's also worth checking the size of the portion you'll get for that price in advance.

Keralan food

Kerala can boast one of the richest and most varied cuisines in India – so much so, in fact, that it's misleading to talk of a single style of cooking. Over the centuries, each of the region's many castes, sub-castes, religious minorities, traders and colonial overlords adapted the wealth of produce available locally – whether bitter gourds, mangos, jackfruit, tapioca or plantain – and created their own distinctive culinary traditions. All of them, however, retain certain common traits, notably the prominence of locally grown spices (such as cumin, pepper, turmeric, cinnamon, cloves and curry leaves) in elaborate combinations with fresh coconut and chillis.

Refined in the kitchens of Keralan palaces and temples, the cooking of Namboodiri Brahmins, the highest Hindu caste, is one of the oldest styles. Strictly vegetarian, it's based on the ayurvedic principle that flavours should promote a harmonious balance (*rasa*) of mind and body. Whereas Namboodiris prefer non-stimulant *satvic* foods (such as unpolished grains and pulses, nuts, fruit and fresh vegetables), lower castes make greater use of the innumerable spices that flourish in Kerala's moist, tropical climate, using them to enhance the strong tastes of meat and fish.

Freed of the dietary taboos imposed on higher-caste Hindus and Muslims, Syrian-Christians are resolutely "non-veg", relishing beef, pork and duck, as well as all manner of exotic river fish and seafood. In the far north, Moppila Muslims fused the recipes of their Arab forefathers with the indigenous cuisine of the Malabar Coast to devise the delicious biriyanis and *pathiri* rice-flour breads still enjoyed in the homes and neighbourhood restaurants of Kozhikode. By contrast, the dishes once prepared by Cochin's Jewish, Anglo-Indian and Indo-Portuguese households have all but disappeared, and is preserved only in a handful of speciality restaurants for the enjoyment of tourists.

Rice

Rice, in various, often unrecognizable forms, is the basic staple of every Keralan meal, eaten three or more times each day. For lunch, local people get through gigantic heaps of the stuff, usually the kind known in Malayalam as *puzhukkalari*. This local rice, a slightly reddish-streaked variety with plump, separate grains, has a much-enriched vitamin and mineral content – the result of it having been soaked and parboiled while still "raw", before being only partly milled. It's far more sustaining and tasty than the totally white, fluffy, fully milled *pachari* which the rest of India eats. In "meals" restaurants, you're always presented with a choice between the two.

As well as being prepared for lunch, rice may be coarsely pounded, blended into a batter and steamed in moulds as *pootu*, or finely ground and squeezed into a paste through small holes to create Keralan-style vermicelli, or *iddiappam*. *Appam*, steamed pancakes much loved by Syrian-Christians in particular, are also made from rice flour – after it's been made into batter and fermented overnight to give a subtle, yeasty flavour. *Appam* really come into their own in combination with rich, full-flavoured Christian *ishtews* (stews), such as those made from lamb for the traditional Easter meal.

Up in the northern Malabar region around Kozhikode (Calicut), local Moppila Muslims have their own type of flatbread made from rice flour, called *pathiri*. They're eaten in various forms: steam-cooked, flavoured with fish, shallow fried, dipped in egg or layered with coconut.

Finally, rice also forms the basis of the definitive Keralan dessert, *payasam* (see Desserts, p.46).

Vegetables and pulses

In Kerala, being a strict **vegetarian**, or even a vegan, is nothing like the privation it is often construed as in the West. On the contrary, vegetarian Malayali cooking is considered by many as the *haute cuisine* of South India – a testament to both the extraordinary wealth of fresh produce

Home cooking

Although typical Keralan breakfasts are widely available and local dishes feature in the South Indian thalis served at "meals" restaurants across the state, the best, most authentic food of all is that prepared in homes. Most Keralan women, even those with servants to help in the kitchen, are expert cooks, trained by generations of mothers, grandmothers, aunts and elder sisters. One of the great attractions of **homestay accommodation** (see p.35) is that it allows you to sample their hidden skills, and even learn them yourself on cookery courses.

Another, more accessible source of great Keralan food is the local **thattukada**, or hot meals stall. In towns and cities all over the state, these pop up from around 7pm on street corners, beachfronts and intersections to provide wholesome, freshly cooked local meals at low prices – mostly for men working away from home. From steaming vats and sizzling griddles, platefuls of delicious green-bean curry, dhal and egg masala are spooned piping hot onto fresh *appam*, *iddiappam* and *parottas*, which you eat on tin plates while seated on rough wooden benches. And the cost of this great food is negligible: you'd have to have the appetite of a sumo wrestler to spend more than Rs30 at a *thattukada*.

Sadyas

Thiruvonam, the final day of the spring harvest festival, **Onam**, is when Keralans welcome the mythical King Mahabali into their homes, holding a sumptuous family banquet, for which everyone dresses up in their finest new Onam clothes, or *onakkodi*.

Served on glossy green plantain leaves, the meal – known as a *sadya*, or *onasadya* – is the culmination of ten days' festivities and takes a suitably elaborate form. As many as a couple of dozen different preparations may be included in the feast, all of them scrupulously vegetarian and cooked according to traditional recipes. An extraordinary array of tastes are encompassed – sour, tangy, hot, bitter and sweet – but each should, in principle, be balanced by another, promoting equilibrium and a sense of wellbeing in mind and body afterwards – as per the precepts of ayurveda.

The order and style of serving are conducted with a similarly rigid attention to detail. Starting on the tapered side of the leaf (always placed pointing to the left), the *upperi* come first (both plain, and plastered in sticky *jaggery* as *sharkaravaratti*). Next to them are spooned blobs of *nakkam* – an array of mango and lime pickles, and pungent ginger-based condiments called *inji thayyir* – followed by the *ozhikan*, runny dhals and *sambars* in little terracotta pots which will later be poured over the rice. Thicker vegetable *kootu* – including at least one kind of mild *avial* and watery pumpkin or cucumber *olan* (see "Vegetables", p.44) – go immediately to their right, but above the dividing spine of the leaf. When the *kootu* are in place, the guests are seated, the rice is served and the eating can begin – with the pouring of the *ozhikan* over the rice.

The final course, *maduram* (literally "sweet"), will consist of at least two, and possibly three or four, different *payasam* (see "Desserts", p.46). When that's finished, the diners fold their plantain leaves away from them and heave themselves over to the wash basin for a rinse off.

Sadyas are an ancient Keralan tradition that's re-invented itself with the changing patterns of modern life, not least because it tends to unite family members living in different districts or countries. Traditionally, the job of preparing them kept the women folk in most Hindu households busy for days, but it's more common now for professional caterers to do most of the hard work.

available in local markets and the ingenious techniques Keralans have devised over the centuries to enhance their flavour.

Dishes tend to have two parts to their name: the main ingredient followed by the way it's prepared. There are literally hundreds of possibilities for both, but you'll find the same terms cropping up time and again on menus.

Nearly all of them will contain coconut in some form. For cooking, the flesh of the nut is scraped from the shell and mashed or ground (traditionally with a heavy stone mortar and pestle, but more often with an electric blender in modern kitchens). It adds richness, texture and substance – as well as protein – to dishes, and has a soothing effect on the piquancy produced by the pepper, fresh ginger and chopped green chillis that,

along with curry (*karhi*) leaves and at least five spices, are added for flavour.

One of the most popular stock recipes for vegetables in Kerala is *avial*, in which lightly boiled or steamed hard vegetables, particularly okra ("ladies' fingers") are dressed with a sauce made from roughly grated coconut and yoghurt. Notable for not containing any oil, it is said to have been invented by a sixteenth-century king after his kitchen ran out of cooking oil on the twenty-ninth day of a thirty-day feast.

Thoran is another light, oil-free concoction you'll see everywhere, in many different forms. After being poached in a wok, the main vegetable ingredients are overlaid with a paste made from fresh coconut and shallots. Spinach *thoran* is a Malayali favourite, often served with prawns sautéed

Keralan spices

Aromatic spices have been used to **flavour** food, as **medicines**, and in religious **rituals** for many thousands of years in Kerala. Traders from Sumeria first sailed across the Arabian Sea in the third millennium BC in search of cinnamon and cardamom – centuries before the Romans mastered the monsoon winds and used them to reach the Malabar's pepper, the "black gold", prized in Europe as a taste enhancer and preservative. Pepper also enticed the Portuguese to South India at the end of the fifteenth century, and provoked a series of vicious wars whose repercussions can still be discerned in the region. Indeed, few aspects of life in Kerala have not been shaped by spices in some way. Eaten by every Keralan every day, they're still a major source of export dollars and a defining feature of the landscape of the interior hills, where they're grown on sprawling plantations.

Pepper

The flowering **pepper** vine is indigenous to Kerala, where – as *kurumulakku* – it has been cultivated for as long as there has been agriculture, both as a food additive and cure-all. Dark red when fully matured, its berry becomes the familiar, wrinkly brown peppercorn after being dried. The root of the English word for the plant derives from the ancient Sanskrit *pippali*, whence the Latin *piper* – the root of the term "to pep up" (as in "pep pills"). India is the world's third largest producer, exporting between 50,000 and 70,000 tonnes annually. The International Pepper Exchange is situated in the historic district of Mattancherry, Kochi.

Curry leaf

Although little used in the West, the small, waxy green leaves of the humble curry plant, which is grown in most Keralan backyards and kitchen gardens, find their way into nearly every Malayali dish. It tends to be added fresh, at a late stage of cooking, in a *tarka* – a hot oil of sizzling mustard seeds and shallots – the resulting flavour blends wonderfully well with coconut milk. Its Tamil name, *kaddi patta*, would have been familiar to the first European traders in South India and is almost certainly the source of the English term "curry", although it's rarely used in the ready-ground "curry powders" sold abroad. In ayurvedic medicine, the plant is held to strengthen the functions of the stomach and is often prescribed as a mild laxative; its anti-diabetic properties have also been substantiated by Western scientific research.

Cinnamon

Cinnamon, a native to South India, comes from the reddish-brown bark of a tree whose English name derives from the Indonesian for "sweet wood". Long before the Portuguese intensified its production on the Malabar, it had a voracious market in the lowlands of central Europe – modern day Hungary and Poland. These days, most of what passes for cinnamon in Western supermarkets is in fact cassia, an inferior relative, which scientists have recently found contains a toxic compound causing liver and kidney damage. By contrast, the real thing is still extensively cultivated in Kerala – where it's known as *patta* – and is prized for its anti-oxidant properties. Originally planted by British East India Company entrepreneurs in the eighteenth century, the largest plantation in the state is situated just outside the northern town of Thalassery (Tellicherry).

Cardamom

Kerala is the world's largest producer of **cardamom** – *elakka* in Malayalam – a relative of the ginger plant which grows wild in the shady monsoon forests of the Western Ghat mountains, where it has for centuries also been cultivated as a secondary crop to coffee. Kumily, near the famous Periyar Wildlife Sanctuary, hosts the busiest cardamom auction house in the world. The wonderful fragrance is especially loved by Malayalis when used in the sweet rice-based dessert *payasam* (*kheer* in northern India). The earliest mention of the plant's medicinal properties appears in the Sanskrit treatise on medicine, the Charaka Samitha, dating from the second century BC.

Cloves

Cloves (*kariampu* in Malayalam) are the dried flower buds of a tree native to the Spice Islands of Indonesia. Its English name is thought to come from the French for "nail" (*clou*). Although used much more in North Indian cooking than in the kitchens of the South, it is a key ingredient in Keralan biriyani, a speciality of the Muslim Moppila community of the northern Malabar region. Cloves, and the essential oil pressed from them, are also much used in ayurveda; Western science has recently been researching their potential as a treatment for multiple sclerosis.

Chillis

A type of capsicum native to South America, the **chilli pepper** – called *unakka mulaku chuvanna* in Malayalam – was first introduced to India by the Portuguese, probably through the now defunct Malabari port of Muziris, since when it has become one of the main ingredients in Indian cookery. The unripe, green form of the fruit is particularly popular in Kerala, where it's added in thin slices to most vegetable dishes. Dried red chillis, when fried in oil with mustard seeds at the start of cooking, lend a deliciously smoky, dark, hot flavour which South Indians love. You might see fresh chillis, both red and green, strung with lime above doorways, or waved over the heads of loved ones with curry leaves and a little ash from the hearth to ward off evil spirits.

Cumin

Cumin, a member of the parsley family known as *jeerakam* in Malayalam, was probably brought to the region by Arab traders from its native North Africa. Few Keralan dishes don't contain at least a sprinkling of its seeds, either whole (fried in oil) or ground. The English name for the spice has ancient roots: etymologists trace it back to the Sumerian *gamun*, a word discovered on clay tablets written in the third millennium BC.

Coriander

Coriander (*malli* in Malayalam) crops up alongside cumin in most Keralan recipes, typically in ground form. Its leaf (*malli illa*) is chopped fresh with lime juice and mixed with onions and cayenne pepper to create a pungent, crunchy salad, often served as a side dish in Malayali rice meals. It grows everywhere in the state and you'll see huge bushels of it on sale in local markets.

Turmeric

A rhizome closely related to ginger, **turmeric** – *manjal* in Malayalam – is another native of the region, although these days most of what's sold in the state is imported from Maharashtra. Frequently mentioned in ancient Tamil literature, it is still used extensively both in cooking (primarily for its brilliant yellow colour) and medicine. Susruta's *Ayurvedic Compendium*, dating from 250 BC, recommends turmeric to relieve the effects of food poisoning. In recent decades, Western scientists have also been experimenting with it as a treatment for depression and Alzheimer's. In the West, you'll find turmeric masquerading as the food additive E100 – a yellow dye – and as a sun screen.

Ginger

Some debate surrounds the origins of **ginger**, but it is almost certainly native to southern India, where references to "singabera" regularly appear in ancient Sanskrit texts. Vast quantities were imported from the Malabar Coast by the Romans, who prized it for its medicinal properties rather than taste. Later, along with black pepper, the rhizome, which Malayalis call *inji*, formed the backbone of the Arab-controlled trade between the Malabar and East Africa. By the sixteenth century in England, a mere pound of it cost the same as a sheep.

Herbalists the world over still prescribe ginger for rheumatoid arthritis, migraine and sore throats, to improve circulation and reduce fat deposits in the arteries. Ayurvedic practitioners in Kerala also regard it as a powerful cure for cholera, anorexia and diseases affecting the liver – uses increasingly supported by scientific research.

In Malayali and most other Indian cooking, ginger is often paired with garlic to make a punchy, flavoursome paste – especially popular among Muslim and Christian Keralans as a meat tenderizer.

Raw cane sugar

The English word **"sugar"** is believed to come from the ancient Sanskrit *sarkkara*, which suggests Subcontinental origins for a plant known in Europe since the time of the Greek historian Herodotus, who wrote of it in the fifth century BC. Proof that sugar had long been cultivated in South India comes in the Atharva Veda (c. 1500–800 BC) where the sweet cane is called *ikshu*, described as an offering in Brahmanical sacrifices. Production of solid sugar by boiling the cane juice to make lumpy, brown *jaggery* (known in Malayalam as *sarkkarra* and in the rest of India as *guda*, or *gur*) was also first discovered in India, during the first millennium BC.

In the fourteenth century, when the Moroccan Ibn Battuta praised the sugar canes of Kerala as the best in the world, the only sweetener widely available outside Asia was honey. Later, the British East India Company imported thicker kinds of sugar cane to the region from their Caribbean plantations, since when it's been a major cash crop.

Both the roots and stems are widely used in ayurvedic medicine to treat infections, anaemia, jaundice and low blood pressure. But a more common incarnation is as a pick-me-up, sold in juice form from *jaggery* stalls on street corners throughout the state. Solid raw sugar cane also finds many uses in cooking, not least to sweeten *payasam*.

Kodampuli

Kodampuli is a kind of black tamarind, which looks and smells not unlike some kind of exotic animal dung, but which Malayalis adore for the distinctively sour flavour it imparts, especially to fish curries. South Indians all have their own versions (in Goa and the Konkan coast, dried *kokum* fruit and green mango seeds are used for the same purpose, while the Tamils prefer tamarind paste); Malayalis prize *kodampuli* over all others. Expat workers returning to their jobs in the Gulf will frequently take packets of the stuff back in their suitcases.

in garlic and ginger. A dish very similar to it, and which is often served on Hindu feast days such as Onam, is **pachadi**, where the vegetables are finished with curry leaves and mustard seeds spluttered in hot oil. Bottle gourd (*kambalanga*) or cucumber (*vellarika*) and boiled lentils (*gram* or *urud dhal*) tend to be the main components of **olan**, a particularly wholesome stew that's closely associated with the Nair community. It too gets a final coating (*tarka*) of hot oil

flavoured with whole mustard seeds and curry leaves.

Other distinctively Keralan vegetable dishes include **kadala**, a mixture of chickpeas and onions, and **kootu**, in which Bengali *gram* (maize flour) lentils (*kadalapparippu* in Malayalam) are cooked with plantain (*pachhakai*), elephant yam (*chena*) and snake gourd (*padavalanga*).

Another vegetable you may not recognize, either on market stalls or your plate, is tapioca, known in Malayalam as *kapad*. Produced from the root of the cassava plant, this rather bland, starchy staple is rich in carbohydrate, vitamins and minerals, and sometimes takes the place of rice to accompany fish. Although served in many village homes, it rarely appears on restaurant menus.

Meat

Meat may be considered highly polluting among upper-caste Hindus, but it's central to the diets of Kerala's Christian and Muslim minorities. Syrian-Christians, in particular, have a reputation for being die-hard carnivores, enjoying both beef (strictly avoided by all caste Hindus, and pork (prohibited in Islam), as well as all kinds of poultry (hence the huge flocks of ducks you'll see waddling around the backwaters and paddy fields of central Kerala).

Eaten on festive occasions such as Easter and Christmas, **lamb ishtew** is the quintessential Syrian-Christian dish. To the uneducated eye it looks not unlike its Irish namesake, but the sauce is enriched with coconut and the aromas of cardamom, cinnamon, ginger and pepper, with heaps of green chillis for heat. It's nearly always mopped up with steaming hot *appam*, as indeed is its drier cousin, **erachi olathu**, for which pieces of lamb are simmered in ground fennel seeds and other spices before the moisture is reduced, leaving a tasty, slightly crunchy coating on the meat. Duck curry (**tahorava kootu**) and country chicken curry (**kozhi kootu**) are two other Christian standards, though they're prepared differently by different sects, and from region to region: in Thrissur, for example, chicken curry is likely to be a dark brown colour because of its base of fried, grated coconut, whereas in Kochi it'll come Goan-style as a fiery, red and sour **vindaloo**, reflecting the city's former Portuguese influence.

Among the Moppila Muslims of the north, mutton (goat rather than sheep) is more often the meat of choice – consumed as kebabs or as mince, or packed into *pathiri* flatbreads. For wedding feasts, caterers still serve the classic Moppila delicacy, **aadu nirachathu** – lamb with a rich stuffing of chicken and egg.

Fish

In spite of diminishing stocks, fish remains the principal source of protein for Kerala's poorer and low-caste communities – Hindu, Christian and Muslim alike – especially along the coast. **Mackerel** and **sardines** are eaten almost daily as part of the lunchtime rice plate, deep-fried in crunchy coats of millet or in dry *thorans* called *karimeen pollichathu*. When soured with *kodampuli* (a kind of tamarind), and simmered in a hot red curry sauce using an earthen pot (*chatti*), they're transformed into *meen vattichathu*.

Choice cuts from the catches landed by the deep-sea trawlers each day nearly all end up on the tables of Kerala's foreign tourists in resorts such as Varkala and Kovalam. Marlin, barracuda, kingfish, pomfret, shark, tuna and – tastiest of all – seer fish are available from November until March.

In Keralan homes, and traditional Malayali restaurants around the state, you're more likely to be served river fish caught in the lagoons and backwaters. Distinguished by its gold and green stripes, the flat *karimeen*, or "pearlspot", is the best-loved of all, occupying a comparable place in Keralan culture to fish and chips in Britain or salted cod in Portugal. It's caught at night using lights: the fish are attracted to the surface and snatched by hand from the water. It's most often eaten after being marinated in spices and steam-baked in a banana leaf as *karimeen pollichathu*.

The other typical Malayali fish dish you'll see on menus everywhere is *moillee* (sometimes spelled "moily"), a simple but delicious curry in which slices of fish (kingfish is best) are simmered in a typically Keralan mixture of coconut juice, green chillis, ginger and curry leaves. It's quick to cook and perfect with local red *puzhukkalari* rice.

Chips: upperi

One of the most pervasive aromas of any Keralan market is the smell of frying plantain chips – *upperi* in Malayalam. They're made in a similar way to potato fries, only in vats of bubbling coconut oil, using thin slices of unripe, raw plantain, a kind of tough, savoury banana. In recent years, sweeter, ripe plantain has started to come into fashion, and you'll also occasionally see lumps of

Ten great places to eat authentic Keralan food

Ariya Niwas Aristo Junction, **Thiruvananthapuram**. The definitive Keralan banana-leaf thali. See p.104.

New Mubarak off Press Rd, **Thiruvananthapuram**. Famous little backstreet Malabari-Muslim restaurant where seafood and tapioca (*kapad*) are the house specialities. See p.105.

Fry's Village Restaurant Chittoor Rd, next to old Mymoor Cinema, **Ernakulam**. Mountainous Moppila-style biriyanis and proper steamed rice cakes, as eaten in thousands of Keralan villages. A city institution. See p.190

The History Brunton Boatyard, Bellar Rd, next to **Fort Cochin**'s Government Jetty. The cosmopolitan gastronomic heritage of Cochin on a single menu. See p.190.

The Old Courtyard 1/371–2 Princess St, **Fort Cochin**. Fine dining in the most picturesque colonial courtyard of the old quarter. See p.191.

Fort House Fort House Hotel, 2/6A Calvathy Rd, **Fort Cochin**. Served on a jetty jutting into the harbour, specialities here include a definitive *karimeen pollichathu*. See p.190.

Zains Convent Cross Rd, **Kozhikode**. The Holy Grail of Moppila cooking, where you can eat sublime *pathiris*, dipped in egg or layered with coconut. See p.234.

Paragon off the Kannur Rd, **Kozhikode**. You won't tuck into a better fish *moillee* anywhere than at the *Paragon*, the place to enjoy local Malabari cuisine at down-to-earth prices. See p.234.

Ayesha Manzil Court Road, **Kannur Cannanore**. Delightful homestay whose owner runs popular courses in north-Keralan-style Malabari cooking. See p.244.

Karimpunkala 6km south of **Kottayam** on the MC Rd, at Nattakom-Palam. Legendary in Kottayam for its sumptuous, village-style seafood *sadyas* and fresh toddy. See p.153.

Haritha Farms ("The Pimenta") Kadalikad, off the Muvattupuzha–Thodupuzha Rd, 38km southwest of **Thattekkad**. Wonderful Syrian-Christian dishes are part of the appeal of this organic farmstay, and you can learn how to cook them here, too. See p.196.

---

tapioca (*kapad*) and slender strips of jackfruit being deep-fried in the same way.

Upperi are an essential constituent of any Onam *sadya* feast (see p.41), where they're often served smothered in a paste made from *jaggery* (raw sugar cane) – a delicacy known as *sharkaravaratti* that used to be reserved for the highest castes only, but is nowadays enjoyed across the social spectrum, notably at wedding feasts.

Sweets and desserts

In common with their compatriots elsewhere in India, Malayalis have a fiendishly sweet tooth, especially when it comes to that most Keralan of delicacies, *halwa*. A speciality of the Kozhikode (Calicut) region of northern Kerala, *halwa* is a sticky brown sweet made from a base of rice flour (rather than wheat, favoured in similar preparations in other parts of India) and molasses or raw sugar cane (rather than refined white sugar). This mixture is then diluted with lots of coconut milk and slow-simmered and stirred for hours until it starts to thicken, when ghee (purified butter)

or coconut oil and *gram* (maize flour) are poured in.

Over the years, the Arab-influenced confectioners of the Malabar region added various kinds of nuts and dried fruit (such as dates, pineapples and figs) and many garish colourings to the basic *halwa* recipe. Stroll along the high altar of Keralan *halwa*, Mithai Theruvu (aka SM – "Sweet Market" – St) in central Kozhikode, and you'll be dazzled by brightly lit blocks in a vast range of colours.

A less dentally corrosive Keralan dessert, which you'll be served to round off any substantial Malayali meal, is **payasam**, a southern version of the North Indian *kheer* closely resembling rice pudding, only much lighter, and delicately spiced with cardamom. Unlike its northern cousin, *payasam* is prepared with coconut instead of cow's milk. For centuries, Brahmin priests at the Guruvayur temple have made huge vats of it each day to give as offerings to the Krishna deity, dispensing it afterwards to worshippers as *prasad*, or sacred "blessed" (see p.275).

Payasam also features prominently in Onam *sadyas* (see p.41), where it comes in two forms: white *paal payasam*, made with rice and sugar, and dark brown *parippu payasam*, enriched with mung beans and molasses. You also sometimes come across a version made with bananas and pineapple (*pazham payasam*) and another, *ada pradhaman*, derived from cooked rice flakes, which has a different texture.

Fruit

What **fruit** is available varies with region and season, but there's always a fine choice. Remember that it should always be peeled first. Roadside vendors often sell cut and peeled fruit that is sprinkled with salt and spices, but don't buy it if it looks like it's been hanging around for a while.

Mangos are usually on offer by late March, but not all are sweet enough to eat fresh – some are used for pickles or curries. Keralans are picky about their mangos, the ripeness of which they gauge by feel and smell before buying. Among the varieties appearing at different times in the season – from spring to summer – look out for Alphonso, which is grown in Goa, and Langra, which is grown all over the South, including Kerala. Oranges and tangerines are generally easy to come by, as are sweet melons and thirst-quenching watermelons, but Kerala is famous above all

for its numerous kinds of **bananas**, which are available all year round. Try the delicious red bananas of Kovalam, or the Nanjangod variety, which are considered by many in the city as the best, and most extravagant (at Rs5 or so per fruit). While travelling on buses, bananas provide a good fallback in places where safe, nourishing and hygienic food might not otherwise be readily available and they're especially good for upset or sensitive stomachs. Note that certain types, however, such as the Nendrakai variety are used only for cooking.

Other **tropical fruits** available year-round include coconuts, papayas (pawpaws) and pineapples; lychees and pomegranates are more seasonal. Among less familiar fruit, the *chikoo* which looks like a kiwi and tastes a bit like a pear, is well worth trying, as is the water-melon-sized jackfruit (*chakkai* in Malayalam), whose spiny green exterior encloses sweet, slightly rubbery yellow segments each containing a seed. The custard apple, its knobbly green case housing a scented white pulp with large black seeds, is another inter-esting seasonal fruit, with a sweet, creamy texture that does indeed resemble custard.

Drinks

Kerala is home to some of the world's premium **coffee**-growing areas and in many places coffee rivals tea in popularity. Filter

---

Paan

It's not quite as popular in the South as it is in northern India, but you'll still see Keralans spitting red stuff onto the streets of major cities. This is not blood, but juice produced by chewing **paan** (also known as *paan* masala), a digestive and mild stimulant.

A *paan* consists of chopped or shredded nut (always referred to as betel nut, though in fact it comes from the areca palm), wrapped in a leaf (which *does* come from the betel tree). It may be prepared with ingredients such as *katha* (a red paste, *chuna* (slaked white lime, to activate the betel), *mitha masala* (a mix of fennel seeds, sweet spices and other flavourings) and *zarda* (chewing tobacco, not to be swallowed on any account, especially if made with *chuna*). The triangular package thus formed is wedged inside your cheek and chewed slowly; in the case of *chuna* and *zarda paans*, you spit out the juice as you go. *Paan* is an acquired taste; novices should start off – and stick – with the sweet and harmless *mitha* variety, which is the most benign form and easier to ingest.

Paan is sold by paan-wallahs, often from tiny stalls squeezed between shops. *Paan*-wallahs develop big reputations and some of the more extravagant concoctions come wrapped in edible silver and, in some rare cases, even gold foil; these are often produced at weddings.

coffee is drunk weak (by Western standards), milky and sweet. There's a whole ritual attached, with the hot coffee poured in flamboyant sweeping motions between tall glasses to cool it down. One of the best places to get a decent cup is the *India Coffee House* cooperative chain, which has one or two branches in every Keralan town. Good vacuum-packed filter coffee, grown in Coorg (Kodagu) in Karnataka, is available but is yet to have an impact in cafés and restaurants.

India's undisputed national drink, however, is **tea** (or **chai**) – grown on the border of Kerala and Tamil Nadu. The tea gardens of the Nilgiris produce fine, full-flavoured teas and often carry a high price tag to match the altitude. Tea is sold by chai-wallahs on just about every street corner, and is traditionally prepared with lots of milk and sugar (though if you're quick off the mark you can usually get them to hold the sugar – ask for "sugar separate"). Ginger, pepper and/or cardamoms may also be added to make a *masala* chai. English tea it isn't, but many travellers find it an irresistible brew. In tourist spots and upmarket hotels, you can get a pot of European-style "tray" tea, which generally consists of a tea bag in lukewarm water – you'd do better to stick to the pukka Indian variety, unless you are in a traditional tea-growing area.

Soft drinks are widely available throughout India. Global brands like Coca Cola and Pepsi are sold alongside locally produced alternatives such as Campa Cola (innocuous), Thums Up (not unpalatable), Gold Spot (fizzy orange) and Limca (rumoured to have dubious connections to Italian companies and to contain additives banned there). All contain a lot of sugar but little else.

Bottled water is available everywhere. In some tourist places you can refill your own bottle with treated or boiled water, a popular initiative to help reduce street refuse. For more on bottled water, see the box on p.51.

Tender **coconut water** from green coconuts is delicious, very healthy (good if you have an upset stomach) and often the cheapest drink available. Green coconuts are common in coastal areas and are sold on the roadside by vendors who will hack off the top of the coconut for you with a

machete and give you a straw to suck up the coconut water (you then scoop out the flesh and eat it).

India's greatest cold drink, **lassi** – originally from the north but now available throughout India – is made with beaten curd and drunk either salted, sweetened with sugar or mixed with fruit. It varies widely from smooth and delicious to insipid and watery, and is sold at virtually every café, restaurant and canteen in the country.

Freshly made **fruit juices** are a real Keralan speciality. They are available everywhere from around Rs20, and are a wonderfully refreshing, healthy and heat-beating alternative to fizzy drinks. A couple of precautions apply though: firstly, make sure no ice is added (it won't have been made from purified water); and secondly, make sure the fruit is peeled to order and that your juice isn't made from something that's been hanging around for an hour or more, attracting flies.

Alcohol

Outside tourist resorts such as Varkala and Kovalam, where drinking is a major part of the beach café scene, **alcohol** is an exclusively male pastime, enjoyed in the seclusion of local toddy shops where men gather to get sozzled on cheap local hooch (bootleg liquor, often stiffened up with dangerous additives). This has taken a terrible toll on family life, especially among the working classes and peasantry; as a consequence, politicians searching for votes have from time to time played the **prohibition** card.

Kerala's licensing laws are particularly strict in the south. Prohibitive fees have to be paid by all except government agencies, such as the Kerala Tourist Development Corporation, who thus have a virtual monopoly on beer parlours throughout the state. However, alcohol is generally available in most mid- and upscale hotels, while big towns and cities all have "liquor" or "beverage" shops.

Beer and toddy

Beer is widely available, if rather expensive by local standards. Prices vary from Rs60–80 for a 650ml bottle. Kingfisher is the leading brand, and the one containing the least glycerine, added as a preservative. Whatever you order, it'll be much more palatable if it's served cold. Unfortunately, however, in all but the swankiest five-star restaurants it tends to be brought to your table in discreet teapots and drunk out of china cups to disguise the contents (few restaurants have liquor licences), or wrapped in brown paper and hidden under the table – all of which will warm the beer up and render its additives more noticeable.

Kerala's home-grown alternative to beer is **toddy**, or *kallu* in Malayalam. Made by fermenting coconut sap, it comes in three varieties: *madhurakkallu* ("sweet toddy"), tapped in the cool hours of early morning and very mild; *andikkallu*, a slightly stronger version tapped in the evening; and *muttankallu*, which is left to brew for at least 24 hours and thus has a higher alcohol content. None, however, have a kick comparable to that of commercial beer, unless – as is often the case – it's been spiked with something. The sedative diazepam (Valium) – nicknamed *aana mayakki* (literally "elephant sedative") in Malayalam – is these days the drug of choice deployed by unscrupulous toddy-wallahs and is responsible for an upsurge of addiction across the state.

If you learn to read only one word in Malayalam, it will probably be the one for toddy shops (*kally shaap*), which appears on little black and white signs wherever a shack is open for business. Because of the prevalence of adulteration, it's not a good idea to wander into any old one and order a glass; but your hotel and guesthouse owners will know where the reputable places are, and a trip to one of these can be a memorable experience, not least because along with the toddy, they tend to serve great local food such as fried sardines and *karimeen*.

Spirits and other liquor

Spirits usually take the form of "Indian Made Foreign Liquor" (IMFL), made to different recipes from their Western counterparts, although foreign spirits, such as various brands of Scotch whisky, Smirnoff vodka, Southern Comfort and Bacardi rum are increasingly gaining a foothold. Some types of Indian whisky aren't too bad, and are affordable in comparison. Indian gin and brandy can be pretty rough, though the rum is sweet and distinctive. Steer well clear of illegally distilled *arak*, which often contains methanol (wood alcohol) and other poisons. A look through the press, especially at festival times, will soon reveal numerous cases of blindness and death as a result of drinking bad hooch (or "spurious liquor" as it's called).

Wine

In addition to spirits, India produces several varieties of **wine**, grown in the temperate uplands of neighbouring Maharashtra and Karnataka. The industry is still in its infancy, but with the help of technologies and expertise imported from overseas, standards are steadily improving. By Indian standards, even the cheapest brands, such as Vin Ballet and Riviera, are pricey (around Rs200 in Kerala's government "beverage shops"), and can easily double your restaurant bills. Still more expensive, and correspondingly easier drinking, are Grover's dry white, and Chantilly. At the top end of the market, (Rs600–850 in a resort restaurant) are Grover's La Reserve, Sula Chenin Blanc and wines from India's foremost winery, Chateau Indage. The latter, while the best on offer, are comparable with cheap South American or Bulgarian wines you'd expect to pick up for less than £5 in the UK. For those who really want to push to boat out, high-end restaurants also serve a selection of New World wines, at prices marginally higher than you'd expect to pay back home.

As for **sparkling wines**, you've a choice between Marquise de Pompadour (a crisp, refreshing champagne made from a blend of Chardonnay, Pinot Noir and Ugni Blanc grapes), or Joie-Cuve Clos (a better-structured sparkling wine with a fruit-filled bouquet, not unlike Cava).

Health

The salubrious breezes of the Malabar make for a generally healthy climate, and if you are careful, you should be able to get through any holiday in the region with nothing worse than a mild dose of "Kerala belly". The important thing is to keep your resistance high by maintaining a balanced diet and getting plenty of sleep, and to be very aware of health risks such as poor hygiene, untreated water, mosquito bites and undressed open cuts.

Medical resources for travellers

For up-to-the-minute information, make an appointment at a **travel clinic**. These clinics also sell travel accessories, including mosquito nets and first-aid kits. There is plenty of India-specific **information online**, covering which vaccinations are required, and giving details on specific diseases and conditions, drugs and herbal remedies: check out the websites ⓦwww.fitfortravel.scot.nhs.uk, ⓦwww.travelvax.net and ⓦwww.tripprep.com. You could also consult the *Rough Guide to Travel Health* by Dr Nick Jones.

Travel clinics

In the UK and Ireland

Hospital for Tropical Diseases Travel Clinic UK ☏020 7387 4411, ⓦwww.thehtd.org.

MASTA (Medical Advisory Service for Travellers Abroad) UK ☏0870 606 2782, ⓦwww.masta-travel-health.com. Forty clinics across the UK.
Nomad Pharmacy UK ⓦwww.nomadtravel.co.uk. Clinics in London, Southampton and Bristol.
Tropical Medical Bureau Republic of Ireland ☏1850/487674, ⓦwww.tmb.ie.

In the US and Canada

CDC 1-877-394-8747, ⓦwww.cdc.gov. Official US government travel health site.
Canadian Society for International Health ⓦwww.csih.org. Extensive list of travel health centres in Canada.
International Society for Travel Medicine ⓦwww.istm.org. A full list of clinics worldwide specializing in travel health.

In Australia, New Zealand and South Africa

Travellers' Medical & Vaccination Centre ⓦwww.tmvc.com.au. Website lists travellers'

A traveller's first-aid kit

Below are items you might want to take, especially if you're planning to go trekking – all are available in India itself, for a fraction of the price you might pay at home:
- Antiseptic cream
- Insect repellent and cream such as Anthisan for soothing bites
- Plasters/Band-Aids
- A course of Flagyl antibiotics
- Water sterilization tablets or water purifier
- Lint and sealed bandages
- Knee supports
- Imodium (Lomotil) for emergency diarrhoea treatment
- A mild oral anesthetic such as Bonjela for soothing ulcers or mild toothache
- Paracetamol/aspirin
- Multivitamin and mineral tablets
- Rehydration sachets
- Hypodermic needles and sterilized skin wipes

What about the water?

One of the chief concerns of many prospective visitors to Kerala is whether the water is safe to drink. To put it simply, it's not, though it's usually your unfamiliarity with Indian micro-organisms which generally causes the problems rather than any great virulence in the water itself.

As a rule, it is not a good idea to drink **tap water**, although in big cities it is usually chlorinated. However, you'll find it almost impossible to avoid untreated tap water completely: it is used to make ice, which may appear in drinks without being asked for, to wash utensils and so on. In the resorts, an increasing number of restaurants these days use the **Aquaguard** purification system, which removes just about all impurities, rendering the water pretty safe – but only assume as much if you can see a unit on the wall.

Bottled water, available everywhere these days, may seem like the simplest and most cost-effective solution, but it has some major drawbacks. The first is that the water itself might not always be as safe as it seems. Independent tests carried out in 2003 on major Indian brands revealed levels of **pesticide** concentration up to 104 times higher than EU norms. Top sellers Kinley, Bisleri and Aquaplus were named as the worst offenders. The second downside of bottled water is the **plastic pollution** it causes. Visualize the size of the pile you'd leave behind you after getting through a couple of bottles per day, and imagine that multiplied by four million, and you have something along the lines of the amount of non-biodegradable landfill waste generated each year by tourists alone.

The best solution from the point of view of your health and the environment is to purify your own water. **Chemical sterilization** is the cheapest method: **iodine** isn't recommended for long trips owing to its long-term side effects, but **chlorine** is completely effective, fast and inexpensive, and you can remove the nasty taste it leaves with neutralizing tablets or lemon juice.

Alternatively, invest in some kind of **purifying filter** incorporating chemical sterilization to kill even the smallest viruses. An ever-increasing range of compact, lightweight products are available these days through outdoor shops and large pharmacies, but anyone who's pregnant or suffers from thyroid problems should check that iodine isn't used as the chemical sterilizer.

---

medical and vaccination centres throughout Australia, New Zealand and South Africa.
Netcare Travel Clinics ⓦ www.travelclinic.co.za. Travel clinics in South Africa.

Precautions

The lack of sanitation in India can be exaggerated; it's not worth getting too worked up about, or you'll never enjoy anything. A few **common-sense precautions**, however, are in order, bearing in mind that things such as bacteria multiply far more quickly in a tropical climate, and your body will have little immunity to Indian germs.

For details on the **water**, see the box above. When it comes to **food**, tourist restaurants and Western dishes are more likely to cause you problems than that at most local places, which tend to offer only a

limited menu, prepared fresh each day for a brisk trade. When eating in beach cafés and shacks, be particularly wary of prepared dishes that have to be reheated – they may have been on display in the heat and flies for some time. Anything that is boiled or fried (and thus sterilized) in your presence is usually all right, though meat can sometimes be dodgy: even if it's kept in the refrigerator it'll often be stored for too long (because in Kerala it's comparatively expensive) and power cuts are frequent outside the main cities. Raw unpeeled fruit and vegetables should always be viewed with suspicion, and you should avoid salads unless you know they have been soaked in purified water.

Be vigilant about **personal hygiene**. Wash your hands often, especially before eating. Keep all cuts clean – treat them with iodine or antiseptic – and cover them up to prevent infection. Be fussier than usual about sharing things like drinks and cigarettes, and never share a razor or toothbrush. It is also inadvisable to go around barefoot – and best to wear flip-flop sandals, including in the shower.

Advice on avoiding **mosquitoes** is offered under the section on malaria opposite. If you do get bites or itches try not to scratch them: it's hard, but infection and tropical ulcers can result if you do. Tiger balm, calamine lotion, antihistamine cream and even dried soap may relieve the itching.

Finally, especially if you are going on a long trip, have a **dental check-up** before you leave home. If you do go down with tooth trouble, however, don't despair. Kerala has plenty of international-standard dentists, many of them set up expressly for foreign custom. One that can be recommended in Kochi is the Emmanuel Dental Centre, Noble Square, Kadavanthara (℡0484/220 7544, Ⓦwww.cosmeticdentalcentre.com).

Vaccinations

No **inoculations** are legally required for entry into India, but meningitis, typhoid and hepatitis A jabs are recommended, and it's worth ensuring that you are up to date with tetanus, polio and other boosters. All vaccinations can be obtained in Thiruvananthapuram and Kochi; just make sure the needle is new or provide your own.

The frequency with which **hepatitis A** strikes travellers makes a strong case for immunization. Transmitted through contaminated food and water, or through saliva, it can lay a victim low for several months with exhaustion, fever and diarrhoea – and may cause liver damage. The Havrix vaccine has been shown to be extremely effective; though expensive, it lasts for up to ten years. Symptoms by which you can recognize hepatitis include a yellowing of the whites of the eyes, nausea, general flu-like malaise, orange urine (though dehydration could also cause that) and light-coloured stools. If you think you have it, avoid alcohol, try to avoid passing it on and get lots of rest. More serious is **hepatitis B**, passed on like AIDS through blood or sexual contact. There is a vaccine, but it is only recommended for those planning to work in a medical environment, or in rural areas and not for tourists.

Typhoid, also spread through contaminated food or water, is endemic in Kerala, but rare outside the monsoon. It produces a persistent high fever with malaise, headaches and abdominal pains, followed by diarrhoea. Vaccination can be by injection (two shots are required, or one for a booster), giving three years' cover, or orally – tablets, which are more expensive but easier on the arm.

Most medical authorities now recommend vaccination against **meningitis** too. Spread by airborne bacteria (through coughs and sneezes, for example), it attacks the lining of the brain and can be fatal. Symptoms include fever, a severe headache, stiffness in the neck and a rash on the stomach and back. If you think you may have meningitis, seek immediate medical attention.

You should have a **tetanus** booster every ten years whether you travel or not. Tetanus (or lockjaw) is picked up through contaminated open wounds and causes severe muscular spasms; if you cut yourself on something dirty and are not covered, get a booster as soon as you can.

Assuming that you were vaccinated against **polio** in childhood, only one (oral) booster is needed during your adult life. Immunizations against mumps, measles, TB and rubella are a good idea for anyone who wasn't vaccinated as a child and hasn't had the diseases.

Rabies is a problem in Kerala, as in the rest of the country. The best advice is to give dogs and monkeys a wide berth, and not to play with animals at all, no matter how cute they might look. A bite, a scratch or even a lick from an infected animal could spread the disease; wash any such wound immediately but gently with soap or detergent, and apply alcohol or iodine if possible. Find out what you can about the animal and swap addresses with the owner (if there is one) just in case. If the animal might be infected, or the wound begins to tingle and fester, act immediately to get treatment – rabies is invariably fatal once symptoms appear. There is a vaccine, recommended if you plan to work in rural areas, but it is expensive and only effective for a maximum of three months.

Malaria and other mosquito-borne diseases

The Keralan government recently declared that malaria had been eradicated from the state, but the truth is it hasn't, and protection remains absolutely essential. The disease, caused by a parasite carried in the saliva of female Anopheles mosquitoes, is endemic everywhere in South India and is nowadays regarded as the big killer in the Subcontinent. It has a variable incubation period of a few days to several weeks, so you can become ill long after being bitten. Programmes to eradicate the disease by spraying mosquito-infested areas and distributing free preventative tablets have proved disastrous; within a short space of time, the Anopheles mosquitoes develop immunities to the insecticides, while the malaria parasite itself constantly mutates into drug-resistant strains, rendering the old cures ineffective.

Prophylaxis

It is vital to take **preventative tablets** according to a strict routine, and to cover the period before and after your trip. The most commonly used drug is **chloroquine** (trade names include Nivaquin, Avloclor and Resochin): you usually take two tablets weekly, but India has chloroquine-resistant strains, and you'll need to supplement it with daily **proguanil** (Paludrine) or weekly **Maloprim**.

Malarone is the newest addition to the armoury against the deadlier *Plasmodium falciparum* strain, and is increasingly prescribed for people travelling to areas like Kerala where chloroquine- and other drug-resistant forms of malaria are present. Studies have claimed it to be 98 percent effective and to have relatively few side-effects. The main drawback is that it's expensive and is only licensed for use for 28 days (although in practice it's probably safe for longer). Malarone is taken once daily with food or milk, starting two days before entering a malaria risk area and continuing daily until seven days after leaving the area. Children can also take it. **Mefloquine** (Lariam) is now seldom recommended by doctors owing to its potentially disastrous side effects.

Side effects of other anti-malarial drugs may include itching, rashes, hair loss and sight problems. Chloroquine and quinine are safe during pregnancy, but most other anti-malarials should be avoided. As the malaria parasite can incubate in your system without showing symptoms for more than a month, it is essential that you continue to take preventative tablets for at least four weeks after you return home: the most common way of catching malaria is when travellers forget to do this.

Symptoms

The first **signs of malaria** are remarkably similar to a severe flu – shivering, burning fever and headaches – and come in waves, usually beginning in the early evening. They may take months to appear but if you suspect anything, go to a hospital or clinic immediately for a blood test. Malaria is not infectious, but some strains are dangerous and can prove fatal when not treated promptly, such as the virulent choloquine-resistant strain, **cerebral malaria**.

Preventing mosquito bites

The best way of avoiding malaria, of course, is to **avoid mosquito bites**. Sleep under a **mosquito net** if possible – one which can hang from a single point is best (you can usually find a way to tie a string across your room to hang it from). Burn mosquito **coils**, which are readily available in South India, though you should avoid them if you suffer from asthma. Plug-in **vapour mats or oil evaporators** are increasingly popular. When out after dusk, smother yourself in mosquito **repellent**. An Indian brand, Odomos, is widely available, very effective and has a pleasant lemon scent, though most travellers tend to bring a DEET-based spray from home; people with sensitive skin are advised to use the new wrist and ankle bands instead, as they are equally as effective as spray. A more natural alternative for those with sensitive skin is **citronella** or Mosi-guard Natural, made in the UK from a blend of **eucalyptus oils**.

Although they are active from dusk till dawn, female Anopheles mosquitoes prefer to bite in the **evening**, so be especially careful at that time. Wear long sleeves, skirts or trousers, avoid dark colours, which attract mosquitoes, and ensure you have repellent on exposed skin.

Dengue fever, Japanese encephalitis and Chikungunya

Another illness spread by mosquito bites is **dengue fever**, whose symptoms are similar to those of malaria, with the additional symptom of aching bones. There is no vaccine available and the only treatment is complete rest, with drugs to assuage the fever. Occurrences are pretty rare but tend to come in mini-epidemics. **Japanese encephalitis**, yet another mosquito-borne viral infection causing fever, muscle pains and headaches, has been on the increase in recent years in rural rice-growing areas during and just after monsoon, though there have been no reports of travellers catching the disease and you shouldn't need the vaccine. The same is true of the African disease **Chikungunya**, a relatively rare form of viral fever that has afflicted most parts of South India over the past few years, notably Alappuzha (Alleppey) in southern Kerala, where it caused at least 125 deaths in 2006. The name is derived from the Makonde word meaning "to bend" referring to the doubled-up posture that's a common symptom of Chikungunya.

Intestinal troubles

Diarrhoea is the most common bane of travellers. When mild and not accompanied by other major symptoms, it may just be your stomach reacting to unfamiliar food. Accompanied by cramps and vomiting, it could well be food poisoning. In either case, it will probably pass of its own accord in 24–48 hours without treatment. In the meantime, it's essential to replace the fluids and salts you're losing, so take lots of water with oral **rehydration salts** (commonly referred to as ORS, or called Electrolyte in India). If you can't get ORS, use half a teaspoon of salt and eight of sugar in a litre of water. Travel clinics and pharmacies sell double-ended moulded plastic spoons with the exact ratio of sugar to salt. If you are too ill to drink, seek medical help immediately.

While you are suffering, it's a good idea to avoid greasy food, heavy spices, caffeine and most fruit and dairy products. Some say bananas and pawpaws are good, as are *kitchri* (a simple dhal and rice preparation), rice soup and coconut water. Curd or a soup made from Marmite or Vegemite (if you happen to have some with you) are forms of protein that can be easily absorbed by your body when you have the runs. Drugs like Lomotil or Imodium simply plug you up – undermining the body's efforts to rid itself of infection – though they can be useful if you have to travel. If symptoms persist for more than a few days, a course of antibiotics may be necessary; this should be seen as a last resort, and only used following medical advice.

It's a good idea to look at what comes out when you go to the toilet. If your diarrhoea contains blood or mucus, the cause may be dysentery or giardia. With a fever, it could well be caused by **bacillic dysentery**, and may clear up without treatment. If you're sure you need it, a course of antibiotics such as tetracycline should sort you out, but they also destroy gut flora in your intestines, which help protect you (curd can replenish them to some extent). If you start a course, be sure to finish it, even after the symptoms have gone.

Similar symptoms, without fever, indicate **amoebic dysentery**, which is much more serious, and can damage your gut if untreated. The usual cure is a course of Metronidazole (Flagyl) or Fasigyn, both antibiotics which may themselves make you feel ill, and must not be taken with alcohol; avoid caffeine, too. Symptoms of **giardia** are similar – including frothy stools, nausea and constant fatigue – for which the treatment again is Metronidazole. If you suspect that you have any of these, seek medical help, and only start on the Metronidazole if there is blood in your diarrhoea and it is impossible to see a doctor.

Finally, bear in mind that oral drugs, such as malaria pills and the contraceptive pill, are likely to be largely ineffective if taken while suffering from diarrhoea.

Bites and creepy-crawlies

Biting insects and similar animals other than mosquitoes may also aggravate you.

The obvious ones are **bed bugs** – look for signs of squashed ones around cheap hotel beds. An infested mattress can be left in the hot sun all day to get rid of them, but they often live in the frame or even in walls or floors. Other notorious culprits are **sandflies**, whose bites can become unbearably itchy. Head and body **lice** can also be a nuisance, but medicated soap and shampoo (foreign brands are normally more effective) usually see them off. Avoid scratching bites, which can lead to infection, sometimes in dangerous forms such as **septicemia** or **tropical ulcers**. Bites from ticks and lice can spread **typhus**, characterized by fever, muscle aches, headaches and, later, red eyes and a measles-like rash. If you think you have it, seek treatment.

Worms may enter your body through skin (especially the soles of your feet) or food. An itchy anus is a common symptom, and you may even see them in your stools. They are easy to treat: if you suspect you have them, get some worming tablets such as Mebendazole (Vermox) from any pharmacy.

Snakes are unlikely to bite unless accidentally disturbed, and most are harmless in any case. The best way to avoid them is to walk heavily, and never poke around holes or crevices in the ground. It's also a good idea to wear sturdy shoes rather than flip-flops at night. It's rare to get bitten but if you do, try to identify the snake and seek immediate medical help: anti-venoms are available in most hospitals, A few **spiders** have poisonous bites too, as do scorpions and some centipedes, but they hardly ever prove fatal. **Leeches** may attach themselves to you in jungle areas. Remove them with salt, a lighter, or a lit cigarette; never just pull them off.

Heat trouble

The sun and the heat can cause a few unexpected problems. Many people get a bout of **prickly heat** rash before they've acclimatized – an infection of the sweat ducts caused by excessive perspiration that doesn't dry off. A cool shower, zinc oxide powder (sold in India) or talcum powder, and loose cotton clothes should help. **Dehydration** is another possible problem, so make sure you're drinking enough liquid, and drink rehydration salts when hot and/or tired. The main danger sign is irregular urination (only once a day, for instance). Dark urine probably means you should drink more.

Don't underestimate the power of the Keralan **sun**. A high-factor sunblock is vital on exposed skin, especially when you first arrive, and on areas newly exposed by haircuts or changes of clothes. A light hat is also a very good idea, especially if you're doing a lot of walking around.

Finally, be aware that overheating can cause **heatstroke**, which is potentially fatal. Signs are a very high body temperature without a feeling of fever, headaches and disorientation. Lowering body temperature (a tepid shower for example) and resting in an air-conditioned room is the first step in treatment.

HIV and AIDS

The increasing presence of **AIDS** has only recently been acknowledged by the Keralan government as a major problem. Should you need an injection or a transfusion while in the region, make sure that new, sterile equipment is used; any blood you receive should be from voluntary rather than commercial donor banks. Try to bring needles from home in your first-aid kit. If you have a shave from a barber, make sure he uses a clean blade, and don't submit to processes such as ear-piercing, acupuncture or tattooing unless you can be sure that the equipment is sterile.

Getting medical help

Pharmacies can usually advise on minor medical problems, and most **doctors** in Kerala speak English. Many hotels also have a doctor on call. Basic medicaments are made to Indian Pharmacopoea (IP) standards, and most medicines are available without prescription – although always check the sell-by date.

Hospitals vary in standard; those in the big cities are generally world-class, and university and medical-school hospitals are best of all. **Private clinics** and mission hospitals are often better than state-run ones, but may require patients (even emergency cases) to buy necessities such as medicines, plaster casts and vaccines and to pay for X-rays before procedures can be carried out. Costs are a fraction of private health care in the West, though be sure to keep all original documents and receipts to claim money back on insurance if need be. **Government hospitals** provide all surgical and aftercare services free of charge, and in most other state medical institutions, charges are usually so low that for minor treatment the expense may well be lower than the initial "excess" on your insurance. You will need a companion to stay, or you'll have to come to an arrangement with one of the hospital cleaners, to help you out in hospital – relatives are expected to wash, feed and generally take care of the patient.

Addresses of foreign consulates (who will advise in an emergency), and of clinics and hospitals can be found in the Listings sections for major towns in this book.

The media

Boasting literacy rates of around 88 percent for women and 91 percent for men, Kerala is by far the most media-oriented state in India, producing a string of regional dailies with readerships that outstrip most British tabloids. Furthermore, with the advent of satellite and cable, dozens of new TV channels have sprung up, both in English and Malayalam. Radio has a similarly wide range of stations, though it tends to be more localized and there is less programming in English.

Newspapers and magazines

Keralans have an insatiable appetite for news, views, information and gossip, and newsstands across the state groan under the weight of publications both in English and Malayalam. With a circulation close to 1.5 million and a readership of around nine million, the undisputed ruler of the region's **newspaper** roost is the mighty *Malayala Manorama*, the state's oldest daily. Like its main rival, *Mathrubhumi* (circulation one million), the *Manorama* comes in multiple editions from a string of different production centres covering all fourteen districts of the state. News coverage in all of them is irreverent and critical of the local and national government by Indian standards, with a fair measure of satirical sketches, cartoons and scandalmongering – in addition to all the usual movie and celeb tittle tattle. An English version of the paper appears online at Ⓦ www.manoramaonline.com and is an excellent source of in-depth news on Kerala.

The most prominent national dailies are *The Hindu*, *The Hindustan Times*, *The Statesman*, the *Times of India*, *The Economic Times* and *The Indian Express*, all of which have regional pages and inserts and are widely read across South India; the *Deccan Herald* is a southern paper, though widely read all over India.

All English-language Indian newspapers are pretty dry, though written in a somewhat breathless style that's littered with quaintly dated expressions. Criminals are "miscreants" who get "nabbed" after being "swooped on" by the police, or else "abscond" from the crime scene. Rioters are "stone pelters" who "go berserk" before being "*lathi* charged" (broken up by police with sturdy bamboo canes); rather demurely, victims of massacres "expire" rather than die.

All the major Indian newspapers have **websites** (see below), with the *Times of India*, *The Hindu* and *The Hindustan Times* providing the most up-to-date and detailed news services.

A number of *Time/Newsweek*-style **news magazines** have hit the market over the past decade, with a strong emphasis on politics. Published by *Malayala Manorama*, the one with the best coverage of Keralan news is *The Week*. Others worth a browse are the top-selling *India Today*, published independently, *Frontline*, published by *The Hindu* and *Outlook*, which is easily readable and covers the widest range of subjects. These often give a clearer picture of national politics than the dailies and also cover more international news. *Business India* is more financially oriented, and the *India Magazine* more cultural. Film fanzines and gossip mags are very popular; *Screen* and *Filmfare* are the best, though you'll have to be reasonably *au fait* with Indian movies to follow a lot of the coverage. Magazines and periodicals in English cover all sorts of popular and minority interests, and there are plenty of sports publications, especially on cricket.

Two- to three-day-old editions of **foreign publications** such as the *International Herald Tribune*, *Time*, *Newsweek*, *The Economist* and the international edition of the British *Guardian* are all available from major bookshops in the main cities, the most upmarket hotels, and some other outlets in a few tourist centres, but they're rather expensive (particularly considering you can now read most of them online for free). Expat-oriented bookstalls stock slightly out-of-date and expensive copies of magazines like *Vogue* and *NME*.

Indian news online

Ⓦ **www.guardian.co.uk/india** High-quality news features are the meat of this "Special Report" section of the *Guardian*'s award-winning website, which also has links to its archived India articles and an excellent dossier on Kashmir. Access is free.

Ⓦ **www.manoramaonline.com** You can access an English version of Kerala's top-selling Malayali paper for all the state's current news, and there's an archive search facility for back-browsing.

Ⓦ **www.samachar.com** One of the best news gateway sites, featuring the headlines of and links to leading Indian newspapers.

Ⓦ **www.tehelka.com** Alternative news magazine, based in Delhi, famous for exposing corruption scandals in the national government, but it also has coverage of Keralan events.

Ⓦ **timesofindia.indiatimes.com**; Ⓦ **www .hinduonline.com**; Ⓦ **www.hindustantimes .com**; Ⓦ **www.deccanherald.com** The websites of some of India's leading daily papers, with detailed national coverage. The *Deccan Herald* site has a fast-loading text-only format.

Radio

BBC World Service radio can be picked up on short wave, although reception quality is highly variable. The wavelength also changes at different times of day. In the early morning, try 5970Khz; during much of the day 15310Khz or 17790Khz; and in the evening, 9740Khz or 11955Khz. A full list of the World Service's many frequencies appears on the BBC website (Ⓦ www.bbc .co.uk/worldservice). **Government** radio also has some broadcasts in English.

Television

With its diet of largely sober, edifying programmes on politics and traditional culture, the **government-run** national **TV** company, Doordarshan, has struggled to compete with the onslaught of mass access to cable and **satellite TV**. The main cable network in English is Rupert Murdoch's **Star TV**, which incorporates BBC World and otherwise dominates the schedules. Zee TV (with Z News) presents a progressive blend of Hindi-oriented chat, film, news and music programmes. Star Sports and ESPN churn out a mind-boggling amount of cricket with occasional forays into other sports – both broadcast Premier and Champions League football, for example. Others include CNN, the Discovery Channel, National Geographic, MTV, the immensely popular Channel V, hosted by scantily clad Mumbai models and DJs, and an increasing number of reasonable channels showing Indian and Western films, like Star Movies, HBO, Zee Studio and AXN.

At the last count, no less than 10 separate **regional TV channels** were transmitting out of Kerala: Doordarshan

Kerala, Asianet and its network partner Asianet News, Surya and Kiran from the Sun Network, the Malayalam-language Kairali TV, India Vision, Jeevan TV, Amrita TV by the Mata Amritanandamayi Math (Amma Ashram), Manorama News (from the top-selling Malayalam daily, *Malayala Manorama*) and Shalom TV, a lurid evangelical Christian channel.

Most of these can be accessed through hotel television sets, but exactly how many channels you receive in any given location is rather hit and miss (the BBC tends to be particularly elusive).

Festivals

Few places on the planet lavish as much time and creative energy on their festivals as Kerala. Every temple, mosque and church in the state stages its own annual celebration, featuring parades of elephants in gleaming golden headpieces, fireworks, feasting and performances of traditional arts such mohiniyattam dance and kathakali ritual drama.

Events vary in scale, but are always attended by huge crowds of locals, who respond to the old art forms with as much enthusiasm as their ancestors. Hundreds of thousands turn out for the largest events, like Thrissur's **Puram**, the mother of the state's Hindu temple festivals, and the famous **snake boat races**, held each monsoon in the backwaters, in which teams of over one hundred rowers and singers ride exquisite wooden longboats along palm-fringed canals. The year is also marked by more intimate, family-oriented rituals in the home, the best-loved of them **Onam**, the annual harvest festival, when relatives gather from far and wide for elaborate *sadya* feasts.

One of the most striking features of religious festivals in Kerala, both large and small, is the extent to which Hindu, Muslim and Christian celebrations resemble each other. Elephants handled by Hindu *mahouts*, dressed in traditional gold head ornaments (called *nettippattom* in Malayalam) feature both in Islamic celebrations and Hindu temple festivals (or *utsavam*), when the deities appear in processions outside the shrines, regaled by mass ranks of *chenda melam* drummers and brass trumpet players.

Even some Syrian-Christian feast days feature elephant parades and *chenda* drums; almost every festival culminates in a massive, raucous firework display.

Finding festivals is often a matter of chance. You might follow the sound of drumming though the palm grove behind your hotel to discover a temple ritual in full swing, complete with dancers and a crowd of rapt onlookers, or pass a poster advertising a thirty-elephant parade happening that night near where you're staying. Notices of forthcoming events across the region are listed daily in the state's main daily, *Malayala Manorama*, although you'll need a helpful local to translate them for you. Wherever you are, it's worth checking at local tourist information offices to find out what's on; they'll also be the people best placed to fill you in with precise dates and timings. In Ernakulam, the Tourist Desk at the Main Boat Jetty (see p.177) hands out monthly events rundowns and is a particularly good source of advice on festivals staged in more off-track areas, particularly the north. Kerala Tourism's website also hosts a detailed "Events Calendar", with dates running forward to 2010.

The following list covers only Kerala's **main festivals**; scores more are held at other temples, mosques and churches year round; consult the nearest tourist office for details. As for **national public holidays**, India only has four: January 26 (Republic Day), August 15 (Independence Day), October 2 (Mahatma Gandhi's birthday) and December 25 (Christmas Day). Most businesses also close on the major holidays of their own religion.

The solar **Malayali calendar** months are given in brackets below, as most of the festivals listed are fixed according to it. Their equivalent dates in the Gregorian calendar vary from year to year, which is why you'll have to check online or at tourist offices if you want to find more precise timings. Just to confuse matters, some national festivals, such as Diwali and Dussehra, are dated according to the lunar Hindu calendar, which has different months (also named in brackets after the specific listing where relevant).

Key: C=Christian; H=Hindu; M=Muslim; N=non-religious.

Aug–Sept (Chaingam)

(N) Nehru Trophy Snake Boat Race, Alappuzha (second Sat in Aug). The most spectacular of all Kerala's boat races, with longboats crewed by 150 rowers and singers. A grand procession precedes the start of the heats on Punnamada Lake. See p.146.

(M) Ramadan (first day: Sept 2, 2008; Aug 22, 2009; Aug 11, 2010). The start of a month during which Muslims may not eat, drink or smoke from sunrise to sunset, and should abstain from sex.

(H) Guru Deva Jayanti (Sept 3). Celebrations marking the birthday and *samadhi* of the spiritual leader and social reformer Shri Narayana Guru, staged at his former ashram on the outskirts of Varkala, and featuring processions of saffron-clad acolytes, cultural shows, community feasts and temple rituals. See p.128.

(H) Onam (Sept 12–22, 2008; Sept 2–12, 2009). Lasting ten days, Kerala's harvest festival is the most important religious and social event of the Hindu calendar, reuniting families in much the same way that Christmas does in the west. *Pookalam* – geometric floral decorations – are laid out in the courtyards of houses; special Onam songs (*ona paattuu*) are sung; and everyone dons splendid new clothes (*onakkodi*) for the great Onam feast, *sadya* (see p.41), which brings the celebrations to a close.

(H) Athachamayam, Thripunitra. Exponents of all Kerala's ritual and folk arts assemble to mark the start of Onam, with a colourful procession to the Royal Palace, accompanied by massive *chenda melam* drum orchestras.

(H) Pulikkali, Thrissur. Marking the fourth day of Onam, troupes of men cover their bodies in orange and black stripes, donning masks and belts of bells to perform surreal "tiger plays", accompanied by exuberant drumming – one of the state's more bizarre spectacles.

(N) Aranmula Snake Boat Race (Sept 16, 2008; Sept 6, 2009). Held on the Pamba River in central Kerala, this is among the more traditional of the state's famous rowing races. See p.146 & *Kuttanad backwaters* colour section.

Sept–Oct (Kanni)

(H) Dussehra (1–10 of Hindu month of Ashvina). Ten-day festival (usually two days' public holiday) associated with vanquishing demons, in particular Rama's victory over Ravana in the *Ramayana*, and Durga's over the buffalo-headed Mahishasura. Dussehra celebrations include performances of the *Ram Lila* (life of Rama).

(M) Id ul-Fitr (Oct 1, 2008; Sep 21, 2009; Sep 9, 2010). Feast to celebrate the end of Ramadan.

(N) Mahatma Gandhi's Birthday (2 Oct). Rather solemn commemoration of independent India's founding father.

(H) Vidyarambham (first week of Oct). In homes, temples, mosques and churches across the region, children between the ages of 3 and 5 are initiated into the world of learning – as many as 10,000 attend the ceremony in Kollam's Saravasti ("Goddess of Wisdom") temple.

(H) Snake festival, Mannarsala. Over a week in Kanni, hundreds of cobra deities from the famous snake grove at Mannarsala are paraded and presented offerings, led by the senior female priest, Valliamma. See p.149.

Oct–Nov (Thulam)

(H) Diwali (Deepavali) (15 of Hindu month of Kartika). Festival of lights, especially popular in northern India but increasingly celebrated in Kerala, to mark Rama and Sita's homecoming in the _Ramayana_. Festivities include the lighting of oil lamps and firecrackers, and the giving and receiving of sweets.

(C) Feast of Mar Thoma (Nov 21). A colourful procession of decorated carts leads to this ancient site where St Thomas first landed, at Kodungallur. See p.207.

(H) Arattu, Thiruvananthapuram. Ten days of festivities inside the Padanabhaswamy temple culminate in a procession through the streets of the capital. Led by the maharaja of Travancore, the deity is carried to the sea for ritual immersion, accompanied by traditional drum orchestras, a 21-gun salute and huge crowds. See p.98 & p.103.

Nov–Dec (Virchikam)

(H) Thiruvappana, Parassinikadavu, Kannur (Dec 1). The centrepiece of the Muthappam temple's annual festival is a spectacular _theyyam_ performance representing the four phases in the life of the deity. See p.247.

(M) Id ul-Zuha (Dec 9, 2008; Nov 28, 2009; Nov 16, 2010). Pilgrimage festival coinciding with the end of the _Haj_ to commemorate Abraham's preparedness to sacrifice his son Ismail. Celebrated with the slaughtering and consumption of sheep.

Dec–Jan (Dhanu)

(H) Kalpathy Ratholsavam, Kalpetta (Nov 13–15, 2008; Nov 13–15, 2009). Tamil Brahmins preside over this famous procession, in which temple deities are dragged by devotees along the main street of a brahmin colony on three huge, ornately carved and decorated _raths_ (giant wheeled chariots).

(C) Christmas (Dec 25). Paper star lanterns and fairy lights decorate Christian homes and feasts are held, reuniting families. Sweets are exchanged between households.

(N) Kochi Carnival (final week of the year). A week of revelry in the streets of Fort Cochin, with costumed processions, masked dances and elephant processions.

(N) Kerala Kalamandalam Festival, Cheruthuruthy. Annual festival of music and dance, featuring performances by graduates and staff of the renowned Kalamandalam Academy of Keralan performing arts. See p.209.

(H) Thiruvathira. Over the full moon of Dhanu, Keralan women keep all-night vigils for Lord Shiva, and dance around the family _nilavilakku_ lamp, dressed in beautiful white saris (_kasavu mundu_) edged in gold.

(M) Muharram (first day: Jan 10, 2008; Dec 18, 2009). Commemorates the martyrdom of the (Shi'ite) Imam, the Prophet's grandson and popular saint Hussain.

(N) Swathi Sangeetotsavam, Puttan Malika Palace, Thiruvananthapuram (usually first or second week of Jan). Carnatic and traditional Keralan music take centre stage for this dreamy annual festival in the grounds of the former Travancore royal palace, held in honour of "the Goddess" (Mahadevi). See p.98.

Jan–Feb (Makaram)

(N) Malabar Mahotsavam, Kozhikode (Jan 13–15). Northern Kerala's premier cultural festival showcases the best of the region's music, dance, martial and ritual arts and cuisine on stages at the city's central *maidan*.

(H) Pongala (14 Jan, 2008; 14 Jan, 2009). The harvest festival, known elsewhere in India as "Makar Sankranti", is celebrated in Kerala with the building of small makeshift stoves in the street, on which lines of Malayali women dressed in their best saris prepare special *payasam* puddings.

(H) Makara Vilakku, Sri Ayappan temple, Sabarimala (Jan 14). Culmination of the massive Ayappan pilgrimage, when the doors to the shrine are flung open to reveal the deity swathed in jewels, while a mysterious star, the "Makarajyothi", appears fleetingly on the horizon. See p.167.

(H) Shiva Temple Festival, Ernakulam. *Kathakali* and classical music recitals accompany the nine-elephant parades around modern Ernakulam's busy Shiva temple.

(H) Elephant Festival, Thiruvananthapuram. The capital's Shiva temple hosts a spectacular elephant procession.

(N) Nishangandhi Festival, Thiruvananthapuram (mid-Jan). Top-drawer classical music and dance artists from all over the country perform on two open-air stages at the Kanakakannu Palace, alongside a popular food festival. See p.98.

(C) Arthungal Perunnal (Jan 20). Devotees crawl on their hands and knees from one of Kerala's oldest churches to the sea for the culmination of the Feast of St Sebastian.

(N) Republic Day (Jan 26). Military parades are held in the capital.

Feb–March (Kumbham)

(H) Maha Shivratri (the moonless night, usually early March). Anniversary of Shiva's *tandav* (creation) dance and his wedding anniversary, marked by strict fasting. A *Shivalingam* rises out of the sands of the Periyar River at Alua, near Kochi, attracting tens of thousands of pilgrims.

(H) Holi (usually early March). This crazy spring festival, in which coloured dyes and powders are thrown liberally around, is a much bigger deal in North India, but it's started to catch on in Kerala, where the paint bombs make life at street level hard-going and bonfires marking the defeat of the demon Holika are lit in parks.

(H) Guruvayur Puram Festival, Guruvayur. Although the temple here is off-limits to non-Hindus, the big procession, featuring forty tuskers, and a spectacular elephant race, are well worth the visit.

(H) Kakkoor Kalavayal, near Piravom, Ernakulam District. A specially decorated bullock cart known as the *Rishabhavana* leads processions of caparisoned elephants, musicians and dancers around the temple, followed by dramatic bullock-cart races in newly harvested paddy fields.

(H) Ettumanur Temple Festival. The Mahadeva temple hosts the famous *ezhara ponnana* procession featuring "seven-and-a-half" statues of golden elephants. See p.156.

(C) Maramon Convention (Feb). Said to be the largest Christian gathering in South Asia, the ten-day Maramon Convention is held on the River Pamba at Kozhencherry.

(H) Kuttikkol Thampuratty, near Erinhipuzha (around third week of Feb). One of north Kerala's most visually impressive *theyyattam* festivals.

Principal Keralan festivals...*continued*

March–April (Meenam)

(H) Ramanavami (9 of Hindu month of Chaitra). Birthday of Rama, the hero of the *Ramayana*, celebrated with readings of the epic and discourses on Rama's life and teachings.

(C) Easter (Good Friday). The big feast day for Kerala's Christians.

(H) Bharani Festival, Kodungallur. Spirit possession trances, drinking and the singing of sexually explicit songs to the Goddess Bhagawati form the focus of this famous Tantric ritual. See p.205.

(H) Arattu Festival, Thiruvananthapuram. Second of the year's biennial Arattu (see p.98 & p.103).

(M) Chandanakudam Mahotsavam Beemapalli, near Thiruvananthapuram. Elephant processions, music, dance, traditional storytelling and swordplay mark the saint's day at the Beemapalli Dargah Shareef tomb – one of Kerala's main festivals.

April–May (Medam)

(H) Thrissur Puram Festival, Thrissur. Frenzied drumming and massive elephant parades, all in the blazing heat of early May. See p.202.

(H) Vishu (April 14). Malayalis believe that fortunes over the coming year depend on the first object that's seen on Vishu, so displays of auspicious items (such as rice, metal mirrors, *uruli* bell-metal utensils and *nilavilakku* lamps) are arranged in most Hindu households.

June–July (Mithunam)

(H) Champakulam Moolam Boat Race, Champakulam. To commemorate the installation of the local temple deity, this big snake boat race – said to be the oldest and most traditional in the state – is held at a lake near Alappuzha. See p.147.

July–Aug (Karkatakam)

(N) Independence Day (15 Aug). India's largest secular celebration, on the anniversary of its independence from Britain, is marked with parades and fireworks.

Sports and outdoor activities

Kerala is not a place that most people associate with competitive sports. However, football has a huge fan base in the state, while cricket has started to claim a passionate following among young Keralans. The most popular adventure activities with foreign visitors are trekking and, in the remote archipelago of the Lakshadweep Islands, scuba diving.

Sports

While the rest of the country is cricket-crazy, Keralans have traditionally favoured soccer as the sport of choice – a status quo which the spread of cable TV is fast overturning.

Football

Although **football** has long been the state's number one game, not a single Keralan club is represented in India's premier division, the

National Football League. While the state side has achieved some success in the prestigious Santosh Trophy, winning in 2001 and 2004, its top teams – Viva Kerala and FC Kochi (both based in Kochi's Jawaharlal Nehru Stadium) and State Bank of Travancore (based in Thiruvananthapuram's Chandrasekar Nair Stadium) seem forever trapped in the Second Division. Lack of sponsorship is the reason most often advanced for the moribund state of Keralan football. With national attention focused on cricket, the region's utilities and most profitable companies prefer to have their logos emblazoned over the shirts of high-profile batsmen and bowlers.

Check the local press or ⓦwww.indianfootball.com for details of local fixtures; you can usually get in to see a match on the day, with the cheapest tickets going for around Rs50, and swankier seats costing up to Rs500.

Cricket

Cricket is said to have been introduced to South India in the northern Keralan town of Thalassery (Tellicherry) by no less than Colonel Arthur Wellesley, the future Duke of Wellington. Since then, it's steadily grown in popularity and now looks to be overtaking soccer as the state's most popular game; you'll see it being played on open spaces all around the country – especially the beaches. Coverage of the Indian team's matches dominates sports channels, though international matches are rarely hosted in Kerala.

Inter-state cricket is, by contrast, easy to catch live. The most prestigious competition is the Ranji Trophy, whose games are usually held in the Municipal Cricket Ground at Thalassery (Tellicherry) Stadium; tickets can usually be purchased on the day.

Outdoor activities

Outdoor pursuits are only just starting to catch on in a state that's always been more into team sports, which tends to mean little in the way of infrastructure and facilities – all part of the appeal of regions such as the Western Ghat mountains, which offer some wonderful trekking possibilities. In the Lakshadweep Islands you can also **snorkel** and **scuba dive** in some of the world's clearest seas. For information on Kerala's **wildlife sanctuaries** and **national parks**, see the box in Contexts, p.308.

Trekking

With Kerala's trekking scene still in its infancy, expect few qualified guides and no waymarked routes, let alone dependable maps. That said, some magnificent walks await the adventurous around hill stations such as Periyar and Munnar, and in Wayanad to the north, where the rainforests of the Western Ghats give way to exposed grassy uplands that, in places, exceed 2500m – the height of a respectable Pyrenean peak.

In southern Kerala, **Munnar** is by far the best base to trek from, with a ring of superb mountain summits soaring above its picturesque tea gardens. Details of where to find guides and how to arrange permits for the ascent of South India's highest mountain, Ana Mudi (2695m) appear on p.216, along with tips on other less challenging day routes in the area.

The most obvious target for any trekking expedition in the north of the state is Chembra Peak (2100m), whose slopes dominate the region of **Wayanad**. Full coverage on how to tackle it appears on p.238.

The best time to trek is between late December and the end of January, when humidity levels are at their lowest and visibility best. It isn't necessary to have any specialized gear, but you'll need a lightweight waterproof, fleece layers for added warmth (it can get surprisingly chilly above 2000m, even in Kerala), strong boots, a headtorch, sleeping bag, sunblock and, of course, bottles or platypus hoser bags with a minimum capacity of three litres.

Scuba diving and snorkelling

The most promising destination for both scuba diving and snorkelling in the region is **Lakshadweep**, a classic coconut-palm-covered atoll 400km west of Kerala in the Arabian Sea. The shallow lagoons, extensive coral reefs and exceptionally good visibility make this a perfect option for both first-timers and more experienced divers. The catch is that permit restrictions mean foreigners are only allowed to visit a couple of islands and must stay in phenomenally expensive five-star resorts. See the box on pp.194–195 for more details.

As with other countries, qualified divers should take their current certification card and/or log book; if you haven't used it for one year or more, you may have to take a short test costing around Rs300.

Yoga and ayurveda

Yoga is taught all over Kerala, but particularly in the resorts of Kovalam and Varkala, and there are several internationally known centres where you can train to become a teacher. Kerala also hosts innumerable ashrams — communities where people work, live and study together, drawn by a common (usually spiritual) goal – the most famous and visited of them at Amritapuri in the backwaters, home of the "hugging Guru", Amma.

Details of teachers, courses and ashrams are provided throughout the Guide. Most places can enrol you at short notice, but some of the more popular ones listed opposite need to be booked well in advance.

Yoga and meditation

The word **"yoga"** literally means "union", the aim of the discipline being to help the practitioner unite his or her individual consciousness with the divine. This is achieved by raising awareness of the true nature of self through spiritual, mental and physical discipline.

Many texts and manuscripts have been written describing the practice and philosophy of yoga, but probably the best known are the *Yoga Sutras of Patanjali*, written by the sage Maharishi Patanjali in either the second century BC or the second or third century AD. He believed the path to realization of the self consisted of eight spiritual practices which he called the "eight limbs": these were *yama* (moral codes); *niyama* (self-purification through study); *asana* (posture); *pranayama* (breath control); *pratyahara* (sense control); *dharana* (concentration); *dhyana* (contemplation); and *samadhi* (meditative absorption). Of these eight limbs the first four are "external" in nature while the last four are "internal".

Today it is **asanas**, or the physical postures, that are most commonly identified as yoga, but these are just one element of what to many practitioners is a complete transcendental philosophy.

Types of yoga

A multitude of paths and practices exist to help the individual attain the ultimate goal of union with the divine. Hatha yoga is the term most commonly used for the physical and spiritual practices described above, and there are innumerable approaches to teaching it. Broadly speaking they all focus on a series of *asanas*, which stretch, relax and tone the muscular system of the body and also massage the internal organs. Each *asana* has a beneficial effect on a particular muscle group or organ, and although they vary widely in difficulty, consistent practice will lead to improved suppleness and health benefits.

Iyengar yoga is one of the most famous approaches studied today, named after its founder, B.K.S. Iyengar, a student of the great yoga teacher Sri Tirumalai Krishnamacharya. His style is based upon precise physical alignment during each posture. With much practice, and the aid of props such as blocks, straps and chairs, the student can attain perfect physical balance and, the theory goes, perfect balance of mind will follow. Iyengar yoga has a strong therapeutic element and has been used successfully for treating a wide variety of structural and internal problems.

Ashtanga yoga is an approach developed by Pattabhi Jois, who also studied under Krishnamacharya. Unlike Iyengar yoga, which centres on a collection of separate *asanas*, Ashtanga links various postures into a series of flowing moves called *vinyasa*, with the aim of developing strength and agility. The perfect synchronization of movement with breath is a key objective throughout these sequences. Although a powerful form, it can be frustrating for beginners as each move has to be perfected before moving on to the next one.

The son of Krishnamacharya, T.K.V. Desikachar, established a third major branch in the modern yoga tree, emphasizing a more versatile and adaptive approach to teaching, focused on the situation of the individual practitioner. This style became known as **Viniyoga**, although Desikachar has long tried to distance himself from the term. In the mid-1970s, he co-founded the Krishnamacharya Yoga Mandiram (KYM), now a flagship institute in Chennai, in neighbouring Tamil Nadu and, in 2006, an offshoot now steered by his son Kausthub, called the Krishnamacharya Healing and Yoga Foundation (KHYF).

The other most influential Indian yoga teacher of the modern era has been Swami Vishnu Devananda, an acolyte of the famous sage Swami Sivananda, who established the International Sivananda Yoga Vedanta Center, with more than twenty branches in India and abroad. **Sivananda**-style yoga tends to introduce elements in a different order from its counterparts – teaching practices regarded by others as advanced to relative beginners. This fast-forward approach has proved particularly popular with Westerners, who flock in their thousands to intensive introductory courses staged at centres all over India – the most renowned of them at Neyyar Dam, in the hills east of the Keralan capital, Thiruvananthapuram, (see pp.121–122).

Ashrams

Ashrams – centres where followers of a particular guru or spiritual discipline may gather to study – are dotted all around South India, and Kerala is no exception. Foreigners, however, tend to gravitate towards the state's two internationally famous institutions, both located in southern Kerala, within easy reach of its resorts and capital.

Mata Amritanandamayi Math Amritapuri, Vallikkavu, Kerala ✆ www.amritapuri.org. The ashram of the famous "Hugging Saint", Amma, is a sugar-pink, multi-storey affair looming out of the Keralan backwaters between Kollam and Alappuzha. Hundreds of thousands pass through annually for *darshan* and a hug from the smiley guru, whose charitable works have earned her near-divine status in the South. See pp.135–137 for a biography and account.

Sivananda Yoga Vedanta Dhanwantari Ashram 28km east of Thiruvananthapuram, Kerala ✆ 0471/229 0493, ✆ www.sivananda.org. An offshoot of the original Divine Life Society, a yoga-based ashram where *asanas*, breathing techniques (*pranayama*) and meditation are taught. They also run month-long yoga teacher-training programmes, but book well in advance. For more on the ashram and on Sivananda, see pp.121–122.

Ayurveda

Ayurveda, a Sanskrit word meaning the "knowledge for prolonging life", is a five-thousand-year-old holistic medical system widely practised in India, but especially in Kerala.

Ayurveda stems from the same period of Vedic philosophy as yoga, and places great importance on the **harmony** of mind, body and spirit, acknowledging the psychosomatic causes behind many diseases. The skin is seen as a mirror of our inner health and the body manifests everything that happens internally. Unlike the allopathic medicines of the West, which depend on finding out what's ailing you and then killing it, ayurveda looks at the whole patient: disease is regarded as a symptom of imbalance, so it's the imbalance that's treated, not the disease.

Ayurvedic theory holds that the body is controlled by three **doshas** (forces), themselves made up of the basic elements of space, fire, water, earth and air, which reflect the forces within the self. The three *doshas* are: *pitta*, the force of the sun, which is hot and rules the digestive processes and metabolism; *kapha*, likened to the moon, the creator of tides and rhythms, which has a cooling effect, and governs the body's organs and bone structure; and *vata*, wind, which relates to movement, circulation and the nervous system. People are classified according to which *dosha* or combination of them is predominant. The healthy body is one that has the three forces in the correct balance for its type.

To **diagnose** an imbalance, the ayurvedic doctor not only goes into the physical complaint but also into family background, daily habits and emotional traits. Once a problem is diagnosed it is then treated with a combination of strict diets (vegetarianism is advised for long-term benefits), massage with essential oils, spiritual practice and ancient herbal medicine. In addition, the doctor may prescribe various forms of yogic cleansing to rid the body of waste substances. Popular **treatments** include *abhyanga* (full body massage), *shirodhara* (head and neck massage followed by a gentle stream of warm medicated oil dripping onto the forehead), *shiro abhyanga* (head massage) and *sarvanghadhara*, a full ayurvedic oil massage followed by a selection of other treatments.

For more on ayurveda in Kerala, including a rundown of specific therapies and tips on how to find the best treatment centres, see pp.110–111.

Culture and etiquette

Cultural differences extend to all sorts of little things, and while allowances will usually be made for foreigners, visitors unacquainted with Keralan customs may need a little preparation to avoid causing offence or making fools of themselves. The list of dos and don'ts here is hardly exhaustive: when in doubt, watch what the Indian people around you are doing.

Eating and the right-hand rule

The biggest minefield of potential faux pas has to do with **eating**. You can ask for a fork, but this is usually done with the fingers (outside tourist resorts and hotel restaurants), and requires practice to get absolutely right. Rule one is: eat with your **right hand only**. In Kerala, as right across Asia, the left hand is for wiping your bottom, cleaning your feet and other unsavoury functions (you also put on and take off your shoes with your left hand), while the right hand is for eating, shaking hands, and so on. While you can hold a cup or utensil in your left hand, you shouldn't use it to pass food or wipe your mouth. The rule extends beyond food too: you should also accept things given you with your right hand, for example.

The other rule to beware of when eating or drinking is that your lips should not touch other people's food. When drinking out of a cup or bottle to be shared with others, don't let it touch your lips, but rather pour it directly into your mouth. This custom also protects you from things like hepatitis. It is customary to wash your hands before and after eating.

Temples and religion

Most **Hindu** temples in Kerala are closed to non-Hindus, but when visiting those that aren't you should dress conservatively (see opposite), and try not to be obtrusive. When entering, remove your shoes and leave them at the door (socks are acceptable) – the same applies to mosques and churches. If you're visiting a *dargah* (Sufi shrine) cover your head with a cap or cloth. Mosques will not normally allow you in at prayer time, and women are sometimes not let in at all.

Lastly, Hindus are very superstitious about taking **photographs** of images of deities and inside temples; if in doubt, resist. Do not take photos of funerals or cremations.

Dress

The most common cultural blunder committed by foreign visitors to Kerala concerns **dress**. People accustomed to the liberal ways of Western holiday resorts often assume it's fine to stroll around town in beachwear: it isn't, as the stares that follow tourists who walk through towns shirtless or in a bikini top demonstrate.

Ignoring local norms in this way will rarely cause offence, but you'll be regarded as very peculiar. This is particularly true for women (see "Women travellers", below), who should keep legs and breasts well covered in all public places. It's OK for men to wear shorts, but swimming togs are only for the beach, and you shouldn't strip off your shirt, no matter how hot it is. None of this applies to the beach, of course, except in the most remote coastal villages, where local people may not necessarily be used to Western sunbathing habits.

Other possible gaffes

Kissing and **embracing** are regarded in Kerala as part of sex: do not do them in public. In the larger, more cosmopolitan cities of Thiruvananthanpuram and Kochi it is increasingly common to see young married couples holding hands, and if you do the same you shouldn't attract too much attention. In conservative Moppila districts of northern Kerala, however, avoid any physical contact with your partner. Be aware, too, of your feet: when entering a private home, you should normally remove your shoes (follow your host's example) and when sitting avoid pointing the soles of your feet at anyone. Accidental contact with someone's foot is always followed by an apology.

Dealing with hassle

Although there is nothing like the same amount of aggressive **touting** on the streets of Kerala as there is elsewhere in the country, you will undoubtedly find yourself being offered unwanted services or goods, from guides, rickshaws and rooms to garlands, toys and illegal substances, on a fairly regular basis. Then, of course, there are **beggars** and mendicants just asking for baksheesh (see p.68). The wisest approach is not to get dragged into a dispute and certainly not to display anger, which is often not understood and encourages people to bait you further. It is better to say a single, firm "No thanks", avoid eye contact and walk on briskly. Most touts will not follow you but, if they do, ignore them by remaining silent; they will soon get bored and give up.

Meeting people

Like most Indians, Keralans are generally very **gregarious** and enjoy getting to know their visitors. You'll often be quizzed about your background, family, job and income by locals. Questions like these can seem baffling or intrusive to begin with, but such topics are not considered "personal", and it is completely normal to chat like this.

Things that Keralans are likely to find strange about you are: lack of religion (you could adopt one), travelling alone, leaving your family to come to India, being an unmarried couple (letting people think you are married can make life easier) and travelling second class or staying in cheap hotels when, as a tourist, you are relatively rich. You will probably end up having to explain the same things many times to many different people.

Asking questions back will not be taken amiss – far from it – so you could take it as an opportunity to ask things you want to know about Kerala. English-speaking Malayalis are usually extremely well informed and well educated and often far more *au fait* with world affairs than Westerners.

You should be aware that in the same way as Indian English can seem very formal, your English may seem rude to them. In particular, **swearing** is taken rather seriously in India, and casual use of the F-word is likely to shock.

Women travellers

Compared with other regions of India, Kerala is an easy-going destination for **women travellers**: incidents of sexual harassment are relatively rare, and opportunities to meet

Rape

Rape is probably less of a danger in Kerala than in most Western countries, but the number of sexual assaults on women travellers has seen a marked increase over the past decade. The few attacks on foreigners that have occurred have nearly all taken place at night.

It therefore makes sense to take the same precautions as you would at home: keep to the main roads when travelling on foot or by bicycle, avoid dirt tracks and unfrequented beaches unless you're in a group, and when you're in your hotel or guesthouse after dark, ensure that all windows and doors are locked.

local women frequent. At the same time, it is important to remember that significant cultural differences still exist, especially in those areas where tourism is a relatively recent phenomenon.

Problems, when they do occur, invariably stem from the fact that many travellers do a range of things that no self-respecting Keralan woman would consider: from drinking alcohol or smoking in a bar-restaurant, to sleeping in a room with a man to whom they are not married. Without compromising your freedom too greatly, though, there are a few common-sense steps you can take to accommodate local feelings.

The most important and obvious is **dress**. Western visitors who wear clothes that expose shoulders, legs or cleavage do neither themselves nor their fellow travellers any favours. Opt, therefore, for loose-fitting clothes that keep these areas covered. When travelling alone on public transport, it is also a good idea to sit with other women (most buses have separate "ladies' seats" at the front). If you're with a man, a wedding ring also confers immediate respectability.

Appropriate behaviour for **the beach** is a trickier issue. The very idea of a woman lying semi-naked in full view of male strangers is anathema to South Indians. However, local people in the coastal resorts have come to tolerate such bizarre behaviour over the past three or four decades and swimsuits and bikinis are no longer deemed indecent, especially if worn with a sarong. **Topless bathing**, on the other hand, is definitely out of the question. One very good reason to keep your top on is that it confounds the expectations of men who descend on places like Kovalam and Varkala expressly to ogle

women, enticed by the prospect of public nudity.

Not surprisingly, the beaches are where you're most likely to experience **sexual harassment.** Your **reaction** to harassment is down to you. Verbal hassle is probably best ignored, but if you get touched it's best to react: the usual English responses will be well enough understood. If you shout "don't touch me!" in a crowded area, you're likely to find people on your side, and your assailant shamed. Touching up a Keralan woman would be judged totally unacceptable behaviour, so there's no reason why you should put up with it either.

Tipping and baksheesh

As a well-off visitor, you'll be expected to be liberal with **baksheesh**, which takes three main forms. The most common is **tipping**: a small reward for a small service, which can encompass anyone from a waiter or porter to someone who lifts your bags onto the roof of a bus or keeps an eye on your vehicle for you. Large amounts are not expected – ten rupees should satisfy all the aforementioned. Taxi drivers and staff at cheaper hotels and restaurants do not necessarily expect tips, but always appreciate them, of course, and they can keep people sweet for the next time you call. Some may take liberties in demanding baksheesh, but it's often better just to acquiesce rather than spoil your mood and cause offence over trifling sums.

More expensive than plain tipping is paying people to **bend the rules**, many of which seem to have been invented for precisely that purpose. Examples might include letting you into a historical site after hours, finding you a seat or a sleeper on a train that is "full", or speeding up some bureaucratic process.

This should not be confused with bribery, a more serious business with its own risks and etiquette, which is best not entered into.

The last kind of baksheesh is **alms giving**. In a country without a welfare system, this is an important social custom. People with disabilities and mutilations are the traditional recipients, and it seems right to join local people in giving out small change to them. Kids demanding money, pens, sweets or the like are a different case, pressing their demands only on tourists. In return for a service it is fair enough, but to yield to any request encourages them to go and pester others.

Public toilets

There are precious few **public toilets** in the cities other than in railway stations and bus stands and those in the latter, especially, often leave much to be desired. If you get taken short, duck into a café, restaurant or hotel and ask to use their facilities – a request unlikely to be refused.

Smoking

In 2003 Kerala became the first state in India to **ban smoking** from all public places, including streets, parks and beaches. Unlike such laws in the West, though, the ban doesn't extend to restaurants or bars, where it remains at the owner's discretion. There's a Rs200 on-the-spot fine for offenders, though the law seems to be more strictly enforced in larger cities than rural areas. Of course, you won't receive a ticket if busted, so it's a handy extra source of baksheesh for the Keralan police.

Shopping

With Kerala enjoying a period of unparalleled economic prosperity, shopping has a major profile across the state. Gigantic hoardings tower over intersections, advertising the latest line in brocaded silk saris, sexily sequined tops, heavy gold jewellery and other expensive accoutrements for Malayali weddings. In the cities, brightly lit a/c malls host international chain stores and brands. The old bazaars are packed with more traditional treasures, from the elegant bell-metal lamps you see at the entrance to most Keralan homes to the resplendently gilded, cotton-fringed nettippattom used to adorn festival elephants. As with most things in Kerala, prices are low by Western standards and affording this shopping bonanza will probably be less of a problem than getting all the stuff you buy home at the end of your trip.

Where to shop

The backstreets of Fort Cochin and Mattancherry, in the city of Kochi, are traditionally where most visitors to Kerala do their **souvenir shopping**. After Independence, departing Jewish and British families offloaded many of their heirlooms into antiques warehouses here, from where they were sold to visitors on cruise-liner stopovers or to wealthy Indians looking for "ethnic art" to decorate their penthouse apartments in uptown Mumbai. A couple of large emporia – notably Alberts Arts, Heritage Arts, Neroth John Chandy & Co and the Lawrence Art Gallery – in the area retain some genuine pieces from this era (including, in one instance, an entire snake boat), but for the most part, the approaches to the Pardesi Synagogue and ground floors of the Fort's old Dutch mansions have been taken over by Kashmiri vendors selling generic Indian handicrafts made in the

B

BASICS | Shopping

B

distant north – at exorbitant prices. The same range of carpets, Himalayan curios, Hindu icons and mirror-inlaid Rajasthani wall-hangings crops up in the boutiques around the entrances to luxury resorts across the state, and along the beachfronts in Kovalam and Varkala. The stuff they stock is often eye-catching, but to buy any of it for a reasonable price you'll have to allow for at least half an hour of hard bargaining (some advice on which appears below).

Elsewhere, **markets** such as Chalai Bazaar and Connemara Market in Thiruvananthapuram (see p.101), and the main streets in central Kollam and Alappuzha, where local people do most of their shopping, offer more authentically Keralan items at more authentically Keralan prices. Often overlooked, another great source of souvenirs is the busy modern centre of Ernakulam, whose MG Road is lined with trendy fashion stores, silk emporia and malls, with merchandise at more or less fixed prices. In most sizeable towns, the Keralan government also operates a chain of handicraft and cottage industries, promoting local wood- and metalwork.

Bargaining

You will be expected to **haggle** over the price of almost all goods, with the exception of food, household items and cigarettes. Bargaining is very much a matter of personal style, but should always be light-hearted, never acrimonious. There are no hard and fast rules – it's really a question of how much something is worth to you. It's a good plan, however, to have an idea of how much you want, or ought, to pay. "Green" tourists are easily spotted, so try and look as if you know what you are up to, even on your first day, or put off purchases till later.

Don't take too much notice of initial prices. Some guidebooks suggest paying a third of the opening price, but it's a flexible guideline depending on the shop, the goods and the shopkeeper's impression of you. You may not be able to get the seller much below the first quote; on the other hand, you may end up paying as little as a tenth of it. If you bid too low, you may be hustled out of the shop for offering an "insulting" price, but this is all part of the game, and you'll no doubt be welcomed as an old friend if you return the next day.

Don't start haggling for something if you know you don't want it, and never let any figure pass your lips that you are not prepared to pay. It's like bidding at an auction. Having mentioned a price, you are obliged to pay it. If the seller asks you how much you would pay for something, and you don't want it, say so.

What to buy

Kerala is a paradise for **souvenir shopping**, as well as a great place to pick up clothes, jewellery and other items. **Things not to bring home** include ivory or anything else made from a rare or protected species, including snakeskin and turtle products. When it comes to **antiques** (more than 75 years old), if they really are genuine – and, frankly, that is unlikely – you'll need a licence to export them, which is virtually impossible to get.

Metalware and jewellery

No household in Kerala is considered complete without its **coconut-oil lamp**, or **nilavilakku**. You'll also see these distinctive brass-coloured columns, which rise from cylindrical bases to wick saucers topped by spikes or bird-like figures, at *kathakali* recitals and in the foyers of most smart hotels. Other kinds hang from chains or shine from niches in the walls of temples. They're made from an alloy of copper and tin known as **bell-metal** (because it gives a sonorous chime when struck) – as against brass, which is a blend of copper and zinc.

The same mix of metal is used to make traditional Keralan cooking and puja utensils too, including shallow bowls called *uruli* and water carriers with spouts known in Malayalm as *kindi*. Inferior, brass-coated steel versions are sold in bazaars across the state, but for the real thing you should travel to the village of **Nadavaramba** (see p.206), near Thrissur in central Kerala, where a family of traditional artisans maintains one of the last remaining bell-metal workshops in the region.

Another dying craft is the manufacture of metal **mirrors**, or **valkannadi** – a Keralan speciality nowadays confined to the village of **Aranmula**, in the south of the state. To make them, an alloy of copper, silver, brass, white lead and bronze is cast in wax – the so-called "lost wax" technique – before being laboriously finished by hand. Few places, however, sell them: enthusiasts travel to Aranmula to buy them direct from the workshops.

These traditional alloys may be on the decline, but the popularity of **gold** has never been stronger in Kerala – largely due to the deluge of Gulf dollars pouring into the state, which poorer Malayali families tend to put into jewellery rather than a savings account. Gold emporia are often the largest and most glittering shops in Keralan cities. Try Bhima (www.bhimajewellery.com), who have showrooms in Kochi, Thiruvananthapuram and Alappuzha, the House of Alapatt (www.houseofalapatt.com), one of the major landmarks in Kochi, or Josco Fashion Jewellers (www.joscogroup .com), who have a dozen or more branches around the state.

In the resorts, **silver** tends to be more popular with visitors, though it varies in quality. Run mostly by Kashmiri vendors, boutiques stock a bewildering array of earrings, necklaces, pendants and bracelets, often encrusted with semi-precious stones such as turquoise, amber, labradorite, carnelian and lapis lazuli. They're sold by weight, regardless of how much work has gone into them or how large the stones are, though expect to have to haggle hard over the final price.

Last, but by no means least, the ultimate metalwork souvenir from Kerala has to be a **nettippattom** – the gloriously golden caparisons draped over the foreheads of elephants during religious festivals. You'll find them on sale at top-drawer bell-metal shops in bazaars around the state. They're made in the village of Thiruvankulam, between Ernakulam and Thrissur in central Kerala.

Woodwork and stone carving

Deep-red **rosewood**, inlaid with lighter-coloured teaks or shell to create geometric patterns, is used for carving elephants and heavy furniture, samples of which are to be found at most state-run emporia. Rosewood and teak are also used to make Keralan

jewellery caskets, or **nettur petti**, which traditionally contained a woman's dowry goods and are embellished with ornate brass joints, clasps and corner pieces. Metal trunks have largely superseded them, but Keralan cabinet-makers still turn out reproductions for the tourist market.

Sandalwood, sourced in managed forests deep in the Western Ghat mountains, is an exquisite, but increasingly rare material that Keralan carvers use to fashion figurines of Hindu deities – particularly the elephant-headed Ganesh (or Ganapati).

In the resorts you'll also see numerous figures sculpted from soapstone. These will have come from the village of Mamallapuram, just south of Chennai in Tamil Nadu, renowned as India's **stone-carving** capital. Pieces range from larger-than-life-size icons for temples to pocket-size gods. Whatever their size, though, the figures are always precisely carved according to measurements meticulously set out in ancient canonical texts, which explains why little innovation has taken place over the centuries. The only recent developments in Mamallapuram's output in recent decades has been in the design of *chillums* (pipes), and small pendants, bought wholesale for export to the summer festival hippy market back in Europe.

Textiles and clothing

Homespun, handloom-woven, hand-printed cloth is called **khadi**, and is sold all over Kerala in government shops called Khadi Gramodyog. Methods of dyeing and printing this and other textiles vary from the tie-dyeing (*bandhini*) of Rajasthan to block printing and screen printing of calico (from Kozhikode), cotton and silk.

Saris for everyday use are normally made of cotton, although **silk** is used more frequently in Kerala than in the rest of India. It takes years of practice to carry wearing one off properly, but they're usually a good buy, provided you're sure the textile is genuine. The classic Keralan sari – a **kasavu** – is made of light, raw, unbleached cotton with a border woven on handlooms from golden thread. Modern versions sometimes add colour to the edging, or layer cotton and gold thread over one another to create a shimmering effect. Also available in the same traditional fabrics are shorter, narrower *mundu* – Keralan sarongs, worn by both men and women to weddings, festivals, naming ceremonies and other important events. Dependable Keralan *kasavu* specialists include Kasavukada in Kochi (🌐www.kasavukada.com) and Karalkada in Thiruvananthapuram (🌐www.karalkada.com).

For women, **salwar kamise**, the elegant pyjama suits worn by Muslims, Sikhs, unmarried girls and middle-class students, make ideal travel outfits, although in the sticky heat of Kerala you may find them too heavy. Long loose shirts – preferably made of *khadi* and known as *kurta* pyjama – are more practical. Tourist shops sell versions in various fabrics and colours. Block-printed bedsheets, as well as being useful, make good wall-hangings.

On top of this, with **tailoring** so cheap in India, you can choose the fabric you want and have it made into whatever you fancy. Kovalam and Varkala are packed with tiny hole-in-the-wall tailors holding shelves full of cheap cotton designed for the tourist market, though don't expect the garments to last all that long – the dye is particularly prone to leaching. Most tailors will also copy a piece of clothing you already have.

Carpets and rugs

South India is less renowned for its **carpets** than the north, although the Tasara Creative Weaving Centre, near Kozhikode (Calicut) is a little-visited spot with a lively handloom and weaving industry. For everyday domestic use, **rag rugs**, made from recycled clothing, are good buys. Available just about everywhere, they cost little enough in Europe and North America, but in Kerala are fantastically cheap; many visitors buy large ones and post them home by surface mail.

Of course, you don't have to go all the way north to buy a **Kashmiri** rug or carpet. Any of the Kashmiris who have set up shop in the tourist centres will be delighted to sell you one, though it is best to learn something about what you are trying to buy before you lay out a lot of cash. A pukka Kashmiri carpet should have a label on the back stating that it is made in Kashmir, what it is

made of (wool, silk or "silk touch", the latter being wool combined with a little cotton and silk to give it a sheen), its size, the density of knots per square inch (the more the better) and the name of the design. To tell if it really is silk, scrape the carpet with a knife and burn the fluff – real silk shrivels to nothing and has a distinctive smell. Even producing a knife should cause the seller of a bogus silk carpet to demur.

Keralan mural paintings

Mural painting is a traditional Keralan art developed between the fifteenth and nineteenth centuries, and is still widely studied and practised (see p.285). Rendered in rich, earthy reds, greens and yellows, mythological scenes – showing Vishnu reclining on the bed of serpents, or Krishna sporting with the *gopi* girls – are the most popular subject matter, and look superb when framed. Demand for large pieces to adorn the walls of temples and palaces having fallen off, mural artists these days turn out smaller works on paper for the tourist market. You can usually watch one or two at work in shops around Kovalam and Varkala. Prices vary according to the size and detail of the painting.

Books and music

Of course, not everything typically Indian is old or traditional. **CDs and audio cassettes** of Malayalam, Hindustani classical, Carnatic, Bhangra, *filmi* and Western music are available in most major towns and cities for a fraction of what you'd pay back home. Sargam and Music World (see p.193), both in Ernakulam, are Kerala's best-stocked CD stores.

Books are also excellent buys, whether by Indian writers (see Contexts, p.309) or authors from the rest of the English-speaking world. Once again, they are usually much cheaper than at home, if not always so well printed or bound.

Worth looking out for in tourist areas and bookshops around Thiruvananthapuram and Ernakulam are a series of DVDs showcasing traditional Keralan arts such as *kudiyattam*, *kathakali*, *mohiniyattam* and *Ottamthullal*. The series, published by Invis, captures some of the state's greatest performers in action, but at around Rs500 each, they're expensive by local standards.

Bamboo flutes are incredibly cheap, while other **musical instruments** such as tabla, sitar and *sarod* are sold in music shops in the larger cities. The quality is crucial; there's no point going home with a sitar that is virtually untuneable, even if it does look nice. A good place to start looking is Manuel Industries in Ernakulam (see p.193). For traditional Keralan drums, ask around the bazaar in Thripunitra, just outside Ernakulam (see p.193).

Travelling with children

Keralans adore kids, and if you're travelling with any in tow, you can expect to have them constantly picked up, pinched and photographed – especially if they're fair-haired. This can, admittedly, get to be a bit wearing after a while, but it's generally done in the best of spirits. If you're staying in a small, family-run hotel or guesthouse, meanwhile, contacts with other parents can be very rewarding.

The main problem with children, especially small ones, is their vulnerability. The most obvious thing to watch out for is the Keralan **sun**, which can roast young, sensitive skin at any time of the day or year. Come armed with sun hats and plenty of maximum-factor block, and keep skin covered as much as possible. Both Kovalam and Varkala beaches can be treacherous: always be wary of a strong **undertow**, which can arise at certain phases of the tide even in relatively shallow water.

Even more than their parents, children need protecting from unsafe drinking water, heat and unfamiliar food. All that chilli in particular may be a problem, even with older kids, if they're not used to it. Remember too, that **diarrhoea**, perhaps just a nuisance to you, could be dangerous for a child: rehydration salts (see p.54) are vital if your child goes down with it.

Make sure too, if possible, that your child is aware of the dangers of rabies; keep children away from **animals**, and consider a rabies jab. Bites and stings are, however, less of a problem than mosquitoes and the concomitant risk of malaria. Always ensure your kids are well protected by prophylactic tablets, or at the very least DEET-based repellent in the evenings, and that they're well covered by a net throughout the night. Special small nets for babies' cots are sold at local markets and may be available through your hotel or guesthouse.

Formula milk and jars of **baby food** are available at supermarkets in the main cities, but are not easy to get hold of elsewhere, and they will taste different from what your baby is used to. Therefore, dried baby food could be worth taking; mix it with hot (boiled) water – any café or chai-wallah should be able to supply you with some. You'll find international brands of **nappies** such as Pampers and Huggies fairly widely available but if you're getting off the beaten track you may want to consider going over to cotton ones – disposing of "disposables" can present major difficulties, even in the resorts, as there is no formal waste disposal provision in the state. A changing mat is another necessity.

For touring, hiking or walking, **child-carrier backpacks** are ideal; they start at around £50 ($100) and can weigh less than 2kg. If the child is small enough, a fold-up MacClaren-style buggy is also well worth packing, especially if they will sleep in it (while you have a meal or a drink), although the pavements can be uneven. If you want to cut down on long journeys by flying,

73

remember that under-2s travel for ten percent of the adult fare (or less in some cases), and under-12s for half price.

Most **hotels and guesthouses** will provide an extra bed for a small additional charge (usually less than 25 percent of the room rate). Bigger hotels are also likely to be able to provide cots, but check first (through your tour operator if you're on a package holiday).

 # Travel essentials

Costs

For visitors, India is still one of the **least expensive** countries in the world, and a little foreign currency goes a long way. You can be confident of getting good value for your money, whether you're setting out to keep your budget to a minimum or to enjoy the opportunities that spending a bit more brings.

What you spend depends on you: where you stay, how you get around, what you eat and what you buy. In the resorts at the height of the tourist season, you'll be hard pushed to find a double room for much under Rs750 (£9.00/$18.00), whereas in neighbouring towns, a night in a simple lodge can cost half that. Meals will rarely set you back more than Rs50 in a typical South Indian rice-plate restaurant, but in your average five-star can take a bite out of Rs1000.

Staying in one of the beach-side enclaves, such as Kovalam or Varkala, you'll be able to manage quite comfortably on a budget of around Rs1000 (£12.50/$25) per day if you stay somewhere basic, don't splurge on expensive seafood and beers every night, get around by rented bicycle rather than taxi, and don't indulge in too many ayurvedic massages or expensive yoga lessons. Double that, and you can expect to stay somewhere with more space and a good-sized sea-facing balcony, eat well and get around by car or rented scooter. If you're happy spending Rs3000–4000 (£37–50/$74–100) per day, however, you can really pamper yourself; to spend much more

than that, you'd have to be staying in five-star or boutique hotels and renting taxis for full days.

Crime and personal safety

Crime levels in Kerala are a long way below those of Western countries, and violent crime against tourists is extremely rare. Virtually none of the people who approach you on the street intend any harm: many want to sell you something, some want to practise their English, others (if you're a woman) to chat you up. As a tourist, however, you are an obvious target for the tiny number of thieves (who may include some of your fellow travellers), and it makes sense to take a few precautions.

Most tourists carry valuables in a **money belt**, though most hotels will also have a safe-deposit facility where you can store them. Budget travellers would do well to carry a **padlock**, useful both for securing the doors of cheap hotel rooms and for locking your bag to seats or racks in trains. The prime time for theft on buses and trains is just before you leave, so keep a particular eye on your gear then. Remember that routes popular with tourists tend to be popular with thieves too.

It's not a bad idea to keep an amount such as £100 or $200 separately from the rest of your money; it's also worth keeping a separate note of your travellers' cheque receipts, insurance policy number and phone number, and a photocopy of the pages in your passport containing personal data and your Indian visa. This will cover you in case you do lose all your valuables. When making a **credit-card** purchase, insist that the transaction is done in front of you, in order to prevent fraud.

If the worst happens and you get robbed, the first thing to do is **report the theft** as soon as possible to the local police. They are very unlikely to recover your belongings, but you need a report from them in order to claim on your travel insurance. If you **lose your passport**, the police will issue you with the all-important "complaint form" you'll need in order to travel around and check into hotels. Dress smartly and expect an uphill battle; city cops in particular tend to be jaded from too many insurance and travellers' cheque scams. Some even demand baksheesh to cooperate.

Illegal drugs

Drug offences generally carry much higher penalties in Kerala than they would at home, even possession of small quantities of marijuana.

Should you find yourself arrested under the 1985 Narcotic Substances Act, the first thing you should try to do is bribe your way out of the situation as quickly and discreetly as possible. Don't underestimate the seriousness of your predicament. Indian police routinely accept backhanders, but the amount will probably run into hundreds of dollars if you're caught in possession of some Keralan *ganja*, or thousands of dollars in the case of anything more serious. Should the situation escalate and you find yourself being formally charged in a police station, contact your nearest consul or high commission at the first possible opportunity.

Disabled travellers

For the **disabled traveller**, there is the advantage of social acceptance sometimes lacking in the West, as there are so many disabled Indians. On the other hand, you'll be lucky to see a state-of-the-art wheelchair or a loo for the disabled and the streets are full of all sorts of obstacles that would be hard for a blind or wheelchair-bound tourist to negotiate without help. Kerbs are often high, pavements uneven

and littered, and ramps non-existent. There are potholes all over the place and open sewers. Some of the more expensive hotels have ramps for the movement of luggage and equipment, making them accessible to wheelchairs, though this is more by accident than design.

Then again, Indian people are likely to be very helpful if, for example, you need their help getting on and off buses or up stairs. Taxis and rickshaws are easily affordable and very adaptable; if you rent one for a day, the driver is certain to help you on and off, and perhaps even around the sites you visit. If you employ a guide, they may also be prepared to help you with steps and obstacles.

For further information in India, contact the India Rehabilitation Co-ordination (℡040/2402 2143), a Mumbai-based support group.

Electricity

Voltage is generally 220V/50Hz AC, though direct current supplies also exist, so check before plugging in. Most sockets are triple round-pin, but accept European-size double round-pin **plugs**. British, Irish and Australasian plugs will need an adaptor, preferably universal; American and Canadian appliances will need a transformer, too, unless they are multi-voltage. Power cuts and voltage variations are very common, so voltage stabilizers should be used to run sensitive appliances such as laptops.

Entry requirements

Today, everyone except citizens of Nepal and Bhutan needs a **visa**. If you're going to Kerala on business or to study, you'll need to apply for a special student or business visa; otherwise, a standard tourist visa will suffice. These are valid for six months from the date of issue (not of departure from your home country or entry into India), and cost £30/US$60/Can$62/Aus$55/NZ$90.

Much the best place to get a visa is in your country of residence, from the embassies and high commissions listed on pp.76–77; you should be able to download forms from the embassy and consulate websites. As a rule, visas are issued in a matter of hours; in

Indian public holidays: a warning

Wherever you intend to get your visa from, bear in mind that your nearest high commission, embassy or consulate will observe **Indian public holidays** (as well as most of the local ones), and that it might therefore be closed. Always check opening hours in advance by phone, or via the website, beforehand.

the US, postal applications take a month as opposed to a same-day service if you do it in person – check with your nearest embassy, high commission or consulate.

In many countries it's also possible to pay a **visa agency** (or "visa expediter") to process the visa on your behalf, which in the UK costs £40–45 (plus the price of the visa). In Britain, try The Visa Service (℡0870 890 0185, ⊛www.visaservice.co.uk); or Visa Express (℡020 7251 4822, ⊛www .visaexpress.com). In North America, where you can expect to pay anywhere between US$150–280 to obtain a visa within two weeks, reliable expediters include Travel Document Systems (℡1-202-638-3800, ⊛www.traveldocs.com) and Visa Connection (⊛www.visaconnection.com) – the latter has offices in Vancouver, Calgary, Ottawa and Toronto, as well as in the US.

It is no longer possible to **extend a visa** in India, though exceptions may be made in special circumstances, such as illness. Most people whose standard six-month tourist visas are about to expire head for Bangkok or neighbouring capitals such as Colombo in Sri Lanka or Kathmandu in Nepal; however, in recent years this has been something of a hit-and-miss business, with some tourists having their requests turned down for no apparent reason. The Indian High Commission in Kathmandu is particularly notorious for this.

If you do stay more than 180 days you are supposed to get a **tax clearance certificate** before you leave the country, available at the foreigners' section of the income-tax department in every major city. They are free, but you should take bank receipts to show you have changed your money legally. In practice, tax clearance certificates are rarely demanded, but you never know.

For details of other kinds of visas – five-year visas can be obtained by foreigners of Indian origin, business travellers and even students of yoga – contact your nearest Indian embassy. Finally, in addition to a visa, **special permits** are required for travel to Lakshadweep (more information on how to obtain these appear on pp.194–195).

Indian high commissions, embassies and consulates abroad

Australia High Commission: 3–5 Moonah Place, Yarralumla, Canberra, ACT 2600 ℡02/6273 3999, ℮hcicouns@bigpond.com. Consulates: Level 27, 25 Bligh St, Sydney, NSW 2000 ℡02/9223 9500, ⊛www.indianconsulatesydney.org; 15 Munro St, Coburg, Melbourne, VIC 3058 ℡03/9384 0141, ⊛www.cgindiamel-au.org. Honorary Consulates: Level 1, Terrace Hotel, 195 Adelaide Terrace, East Perth, WA 6004, Australia (mailing address: PO Box 6118, East Perth, WA 6892, Australia) ℡08/9221 1485, ℮india@vianet.net.au.

Canada High Commission: 10 Springfield Rd, Ottawa, ON K1M 1C9 ℡1-613-744-3751, ⊛www.hciottawa.ca. Consulates: 2 Bloor St W, #500, Toronto, ON M4W 3E2 ℡1-416-960-0751, ℮cgitoronto.ca; 325 Howe St, 2nd floor, Vancouver, BC V6C 1Z7 ℡1-604-662-8811, ⊛www .cgivancouver.com.

The Netherlands Embassy: Buitenrustweg-2, 2517 KD, The Hague ℡070/346 9771, ⊛www .indianembassy.nl.

New Zealand High Commission: 180 Molesworth St, Wellington ℡04/473 6390, ⊛www.hicomind.org.nz.

Republic of Ireland Embassy: 6 Leeson Park, Dublin 6 ℡01/497 0843, ℮eoidublin@indigo.ie.

South Africa High Commission: The Terraces, 9th Floor, 34 Bree St, Cape Town ℡021/419 8110, ⊛www.india.org.za. Consulates: 1 Eton Rd, Parktown, Johannesburg ℡011/482 8492, ⊛www.indconjoburg.co.za; The Old Station Building, 4th Floor, 160 Pine St, Durban ℡031/304 7020, ⊛www.indcondurban.co.za.

Sri Lanka High Commission: 36–38 Galle Rd, Colombo 3 ℡011/232 7587, ⊛www.hcicolombo .org. Consulate: 31 Rajapihilla Mawatha, PO Box 47, Kandy ℡08/224563.

Thailand Embassy: 46 Soi 23 (Prasarn Mitr), Sukhumvit Rd, Bangkok 10110 ℡02/258 0300,

ⓦ www.embassyofindia-bangkok.org. Consulate:
113 Bumruangrat Rd, Chiang Mai 50000
ⓣ 053/243066, ⓦ www.indcon-chiangmai.com.
UK High Commission: India House, Aldwych, London
WC2B 4NA ⓣ 020/7836 8484, ⓦ www.hcilondon
.net. Consulates: 20 Augusta St, Jewellery Quarter,
Hockley, Birmingham B18 6GL ⓣ 0121 212 2782,
ⓦ www.cgibirmingham.org; 17 Rutland Square,
Edinburgh EH1 2BB ⓣ 0131 229 2144, ⓦ www
.cgiedinburgh.org.
USA Embassy of India (Consular Services): 2107
Massachusetts Ave NW, Washington DC 20008
ⓣ 1-202-939-7000, ⓦ www.indianembassy
.org. Consulates: 3 East 64th St, New York, NY
10021 ⓣ 1-212-774-0600, ⓦ www.indiacgny
.org; 540 Arguello Blvd, San Francisco, CA 94118
ⓣ 1-415-668-0683, ⓦ www.indianconsulate-sf.org;
455 North Cityfront Plaza Drive, Suite 850,
Chicago IL 60611 ⓣ 1-312-595 0405 (ext 22 for
visas), ⓦ chicago.indianconsulate.com; 201 St
Charles Ave, New Orleans, LA 70170 ⓣ 1-504-
582-8106; 2051 Young St, Honolulu, HI 96826
ⓣ 1-808-947-2618.

Gay and lesbian travellers

Homosexuality is not generally open or
accepted in India, and anal intercourse is a
ten-year offence under article 377 of the
penal code. Laws against "obscene
behaviour" are used to arrest gay men for
cruising or liaising anywhere that could be
considered a public place.

For **lesbians**, making contacts is
even more difficult; the Indian Women's
Movement does not readily promote lesbi-
anism as an issue that needs confronting.
The only public faces of a hidden scene
are the Mumbai-based organizations
listed below.

Gay and lesbian contacts

Bombay Dost ⓦ bombay-dost.pbwiki.com.
Wiki page of the (now defunct) Mumbai-based
Gay magazine Bombay Dost, featuring information
on its popular "Sunday High" club nights in the
Maharashtran capital.
Gay Bombay ⓦ www.gaybombay.org.
Humsafar Trust ⓦ www.humsafar.org. Website set
up to promote "a holistic approach to the rights and
health of sexual minorities".

Insurance

In the light of the potential health risks
involved in a trip to Kerala – see pp.50–56
– **travel insurance** is too important to
ignore. In addition to covering medical
expenses and emergency flights, it also
insures your money and belongings
against loss or theft. Before paying for a
new policy, however, it's worth checking
to see whether you are already covered:
some all-risks home insurance policies
may cover your possessions when abroad,
and many private medical schemes include
overseas cover. In Canada, provincial
health plans usually provide partial medical
cover for mishaps overseas, while holders
of official student/teacher/youth cards in
Canada and the US are entitled to – albeit
meagre – accident coverage and hospital
in-patient benefits. Students will often find
that their student health coverage includes
vacations and one term beyond the date of
last enrolment.

After exhausting the possibilities above,
you might want to contact a specialist **travel
insurance company**, or consider the travel
insurance deal offered by Rough Guides
(see box below). A typical travel insurance

Rough Guides travel insurance

Rough Guides has teamed up with Columbus Direct to offer you **travel insurance**
that can be tailored to suit your needs. Products include a low-cost **backpacker**
option for long stays; a **short break** option for city getaways; a typical **holiday
package** option; and others. There are also annual **multi-trip** policies for those who
travel regularly. Different sports and activities (trekking, skiing, etc) can usually be
covered if required.

See our website (ⓦ www.roughguides.com/website/shop) for eligibility and
purchasing options. Alternatively, UK residents should call ⓣ 08700 339988; US
citizens should call ⓣ 1-800-749-4922; Australians should call ⓣ 1300-669999. All
other nationalities should call ⓣ +44 8708 902843.

policy usually provides cover for the loss of baggage, tickets and – up to a certain limit – cash or cheques, as well as cancellation or curtailment of your journey. Most of them exclude so-called dangerous sports unless an extra premium is paid: in Kerala this can mean scuba diving, rafting, windsurfing and trekking with ropes, though probably not Jeep safaris. Many policies can be chopped and changed to exclude coverage you don't need – for example, sickness and accident benefits can often be excluded or included at will. If you do take medical coverage, ascertain whether benefits will be paid as treatment proceeds or only after return home, and whether there is a 24-hour medical emergency number. When securing baggage cover, make sure that the per-article limit – typically under £500 – will cover your most valuable possession. If you need to make a claim, you should keep receipts for medicines and medical treatment, and in the event you have anything stolen, you must obtain an official statement from the police.

Internet

All large cities and many tourist towns have places offering **Internet** and **email** access – these are usually cybercafés, but also include many hotels and some STD (standard trunk dialling) booths. Charges start at around Rs10 per hour, and can go up to as much as Rs120, but are most commonly Rs30–40 for reading mail and browsing, and extra for printing; most cybercafés offer membership deals which can cut costs if you'll be around for a while. In the main cities and resorts faster ISDN/broadband connections are the norm. Most places with a decent broadband connection also have webcams and microphones, allowing for VoIP chats via systems such as Skype. Internet cafés listed in the Guide are marked on the relevant maps.

Laundry

In India, no one goes to self-service laundries: if they don't do their own, they send it out to a **dhobi**. Wherever you are staying, there will either be an in-house *dhobi* or one very close by to call on. The *dhobi* will take your dirty washing to a *dhobi ghat*, a public clothes-washing area (the bank of a river, for example), where it is shown some old-fashioned discipline: separated, soaped and given a damn good thrashing to beat the dirt out of it. Then it's hung out to dry in the sun and, once dried, taken to the ironing sheds where every garment is endowed with razor-sharp creases and then matched to its rightful owner by hidden cryptic markings. Your clothes will come back from the *dhobi* absolutely spotless, though this kind of violent treatment does take it out of them: buttons get lost and eventually the cloth starts to fray.

Mail

Mail can take anything from four days to four weeks or even more to get to or from Kerala, depending largely on where exactly you are; ten days to a fortnight is about the norm. Most **post offices** are open Monday to Friday 10am to 5pm and Saturday 10am till noon, but big city GPOs, where the poste restante is usually located, keep longer hours (Mon–Fri 9.30am–6pm, Sat 9.30am–1pm). Stamps aren't expensive, and aerogrammes and postcards cost the same to anywhere in the world. You can also buy stamps at big hotels. Ideally, you should have mail franked in front of you.

Having parcels sent out to you in Kerala is not such a good idea – chances are they'll go astray. If you do have a parcel sent, have it registered. **Sending a parcel** out of India can be quite a performance. First you have to get it cleared by customs at the post office (they often don't bother, but check), then you take it to a tailor and agree a price to have it wrapped in cheap cotton cloth (which you may have to go and buy yourself), stitched up and sealed with wax. In big city GPOs, people offering this service will be at hand. Next, take it to the post office, fill in and attach the relevant customs forms (it's best to tick the box marked "gift" and give its value as less than Rs1000 or "no commercial value" to avoid bureaucratic entanglements), buy your stamps, see them franked, and dispatch it. Parcels shouldn't be more than a metre long or weigh more than 20kg. Surface mail is incredibly cheap, and takes an average of three months to arrive – although delivery times vary wildly, and it may take anything from six weeks to a year. It's a good way to dump excess baggage and souvenirs, but don't send anything fragile.

As in Britain, North America and Australasia, books and magazines can be sent more cheaply, unsealed or wrapped around the middle, as printed papers ("book post"). Alternatively, there are numerous **courier** services, although they're not as reliable as they should be, and there have been complaints of packages going astray – it's safest to stick to known international companies such as DHL or FedEx, which have offices in all the state capitals. Packages sent by air are expensive. Remember that all packages from India are likely to attract attention, and be searched or X-rayed on arrival: don't send anything dodgy.

Maps

Even allowing for a bit of bias here, we think you'll find the Rough Guide's **South India map** to be the most user-friendly on the market. Drawn at a scale of 1:1,200,000, it features clear modern mapping and bang up-to-date research, and is printed on plastic paper so it won't tear (and should even survive a dip in the Arabian Sea). It's also been tested and proofed on the road by the author of this guide. Another excellent map of South India is the Nelles India 4 (South) 1:1,500,000, which shows colour contours, road distances, inset city plans and all but the tiniest places.

Ttk, a Chennai-based company, publishes basic **state maps**, which are widely available in Kerala and in some specialized travel and map shops in the UK.

On the Internet, and much to the displeasure of the Indian government, **GoogleEarth**'s satellite coverage of Kerala at ⓦmaps.google.com is impressive. Though its street mapping remains rudimentary, you can use the satellite images for superb bird's-eye explorations of backwaters and beaches not covered on most published maps.

Money

India's unit of currency is the **rupee**, usually abbreviated "Rs" and divided into a hundred **paise** (pronounced *pi*-suh). Almost all money is paper, with notes of 10, 20, 50, 100, 500 and, more rarely, 1000 rupees; a few 5 rupee notes are still in circulation. Coins in practice start at 25 and 50 paise, and 1, 2 and 5 rupees, though you might still see the odd beaten-up 10 or 20 paise piece. For exchange rates, see box below.

Banknotes, especially lower denominations, can get into a terrible state. Don't accept **torn banknotes**, since no one else will be prepared to take them and you'll be left saddled with the things unless you can be bothered to change them at the Reserve Bank of India or large branches of other big banks. Don't pass them on to beggars; they can't use them either, so it amounts to an insult.

Large denominations can also be a problem, as **change** is usually in short supply. Many Indian people cannot afford to keep much lying around, and you shouldn't necessarily expect shopkeepers or rickshaw-wallahs to have it (and they may – as may you – try to hold onto it if they do). Larger notes – like the Rs500 note – are good for travelling with and can be changed for smaller denominations at hotels and other suitable establishments.

It is worth noting that certain numbers are referred to differently in India and Pakistan to anywhere else in the world: a hundred thousand is a *lakh* (written 1,00,000); ten million is a *crore* (1,00,00,000). The words "million", and "billion" are not in common use, being replaced by ten *lakh* or a hundred *crore*, respectively.

It is **illegal** to carry more than Rs5000 spending money into India, and you won't get them at a particularly good rate in the West anyway (though you might in Thailand, Malaysia or Singapore). It is also illegal to take over Rs5000 out of the country.

At the time of writing, the **exchange rates** were: Rs80.7 to GB£1; Rs40.7 to US$1; Rs39 to Can$1; Rs34.5 to Aus$1; Rs30 to NZ$1; Rs6 to ZAR1. Check ⓦwww.xe.com for up-to-the-minute exchange rates.

ATMs, cards and travellers' cheques

By far the easiest and most secure method of exchange is to make withdrawals from the increasingly ubiquitous **ATMs** in Kerala using your **debit card**; the flat transaction fee is usually quite small (typically 1.5 percent). Make sure you have a personal identification number (PIN) that's designed to work overseas. Not all ATMs are geared towards accepting Cirrus, though these are becoming increasingly rare. Most are open 24 hours.

A **credit card** is a handy backup, as an increasing number of hotels, restaurants, large shops and tourist emporia now take them. If you have a selection of cards, take them all in case one gets lost, stolen or chewed in a machine.

In addition to cash and card(s), carry some **travellers' cheques** to cover all eventualities, with a few small denominations for the end of your trip, and for the odd foreign-currency purchase such as tourist-quota rail tickets. US dollars are the easiest currency to convert, with pounds sterling a close second and euros third. Other hard currencies can be changed easily in tourist areas and big cities, but less so elsewhere. If you enter the country with more than $10,000 or the equivalent, you are supposed to fill in a currency declaration form.

Travellers' cheques aren't as liquid as cash, or as straightforward to use as cards, but are obviously more secure and you get a slightly better exchange rate for them at banks. Not all banks, however, accept them, and those that do can be quirky about exactly which ones they will change. Well-known brands such as Thomas Cook and American Express are your best bet, but in some places even American Express is only accepted in US dollars and not as pounds sterling. Both companies have branches in the major cities of South India; see the relevant accounts in the Guide and collect a full list when you purchase your traveller's cheques.

A compromise between travellers' cheques and plastic is **Visa TravelMoney**, a disposable prepaid debit card with a PIN which works in all ATMs that take Visa cards. You load up your account with funds before leaving home, and when they run out, you simply throw the card away. Up to nine cards can be purchased to access the same funds – useful for couples or families travelling together – and it's a good idea to buy at least one extra as a backup in case of loss or theft. The card is available in most countries from branches of Thomas Cook and Citicorp. For more information, check the Visa website, ⓦ www.usa.visa.com.

Changing money

Changing money in regular **banks**, especially government-run banks such as the State Bank of India (SBI), can be a time-consuming business, involving lots of form-filling and queuing at different counters, so change substantial amounts at any one time. You'll have no such problems, however, with **private companies** such as Thomas Cook or American Express. Major cities and main tourist centres usually have several **licensed currency exchange bureaux**; rates usually aren't as good as at a bank, but transactions are generally a lot quicker and there's less paperwork to complete.

Outside **banking hours** (Mon–Fri 10am–2/4pm, Sat 10am–noon), large hotels may change money, probably at a lower rate, and exchange bureaux have longer opening hours. Banks at Mumbai and Chennai airports stay open 24 hours, but neither is very conveniently located.

Wherever you change money, hold on to **exchange receipts** ("encashment certificates"); they will be required if you want to change back any excess rupees when you leave the country, and to buy air tickets and reserve train berths with rupees at special counters for foreigners. The State Bank of India now charges for tax clearance forms.

Opening hours

Standard **shop** opening hours in India are Monday to Saturday 9.30am to 6pm. Smaller shops vary from town to town, religion to religion and one to another, but usually keep longer hours. **India Tourism** offices are in principle open Monday to Friday 9.30am to 5pm, Saturday 9.30am to 1pm, though these may vary slightly; **state tourist offices** are likely to be open Monday to Friday 10am to 5pm, but sometimes operate much longer hours – see p.82 for more information on tourist offices.

For opening hours of post offices, see "Mail", p.78; for opening hours of banks, see "Changing money", p.80. For dates of **public holidays**, see the "Principal Keralan festivals" box, pp.59-62.

Phones

Privately run phone services with **international direct dialling** facilities are very widespread. Advertising themselves with the acronyms **STD/ISD** (standard trunk dialling/international subscriber dialling), they are extremely quick and easy to use, and some stay open 24 hours; some booths have fax machines too. Both national and international calls are dialled direct. Your bill, which you can see ticking over on the booth's meter, is calculated in seconds and usually rounded up to the nearest rupee.

Almost all such booths **charge** according to official government rates, which are around Rs10 per minute to most Western countries. "Call back" (or "back call", as it's often known) is possible at most phone booths, although check before you call and be aware that, in the case of booths, this facility rarely comes without a charge of Rs3–5 per minute.

Calling from hotel room phones is often not possible and is always more expensive when it is. Having somebody call you at your hotel, on the other hand, should present no problems (except the odd linguistic issue) and is never charged for. Internet joints in India's big metropolitan cities and tourist centres have started to offer **Net2Phone (or NetPhone)** services, which allow you to make telephone calls over the Web for incredibly low rates – typically Rs2–3 for calls to the UK and US. At the time of writing, services were limited to international calls. Keep your eyes peeled for the logo – the widespread iWay cybercafé franchise invariably has the facility.

Home country direct services are also available from any STD/ISD phone to the UK, the US, Canada, Ireland, Australia, New Zealand, South Africa and a growing number of other countries. These allow you to make a collect or telephone credit card call to that country via an operator there. If you can't find a phone with home country direct buttons, you can use any phone toll-free, by dialling 000, your country code and 17 (except Canada which is 000-127).

Mobile phones

Call charges to and from **mobile phones** are far lower in Kerala than in Western countries, which is why lots of foreign tourists opt to sign up to a local network while they're travelling. To do this you'll need to buy an Indian SIM card from a mobile phone shop; these cost around Rs300, plus the price of a top-up card (varying from Rs200–500). Your retailer will help you get connected. They'll also advise you on which company to use. Kerala is dominated by seven major companies: BSNL, Bharti Airtel, BPL Mobile, Hutch, Idea Cellular, Reliance and Tata Indicom. If you intend to stay inside their designated coverage area (ie within the state borders), charges for texts and calls are cheap (Rs1–2/min). However, once you leave Kerala you'll automatically be paying roaming charges (Rs3–5/min). Note that when roaming, you also pay for incoming calls.

We list mobile numbers in the Guide using the convention ☎mXXXXX XXXXX.

International dialling codes

	From India	To India
UK	☎00 44	☎00 91
Irish Republic	☎00 353	☎00 91
US and Canada	☎00 1	☎011 91
Australia	☎00 61	☎0011 91
New Zealand	☎00 64	☎00 91
South Africa	☎00 27	☎09091 91

Photography

Beware of pointing your camera at anything that might be considered "strategic", including airports, anything military and even bridges, railway stations and main roads. Remember too that some people prefer not to be photographed, so it is wise to ask before you take a snapshot of them. On the other hand, you'll get people, especially kids, volunteering to pose.

Most photo shops can now transfer **digital** images onto a CD – useful in order to free up memory space. **Camera film**, sold at average Western prices, is widely available in Kerala (but check the date on the box, and note that false boxes containing outdated film are often sold). It's fairly easy to get films developed, though they don't always come out as well as they might at home. Konica studios through South India have hi-tech equipment and process film in one hour (Rs200–250). If you're after **slide film**, buy it in the big cities, and don't expect to find specialist brands.

Time

Kerala, like the rest of India, is all in one time zone: GMT plus 5 hours 30 minutes. This makes it 5 hours 30 minutes ahead of London, 10 hours 30 minutes ahead of New York, 13 hours 30 minutes ahead of LA, 3 hours 30 minutes ahead of Johannesburg, 4 hours 30 minutes behind Sydney and 6 hours 30 minutes behind New Zealand; however, summer time in those places will vary the difference by an hour.

Tourist information

The Indian government maintains a number of **tourist offices** abroad, whose staff are usually helpful and knowledgeable. Other sources of information include the websites of Indian embassies and consulates, travel agents (though their advice may not always be totally unbiased), and the Indian Railways representatives listed on p.28.

Inside India, both national and the Kerala state government run **tourist information offices**, providing general travel advice and handing out an array of printed material, from city maps to glossy leaflets on specific destinations and activities. The Indian government's tourist department, India Tourism

(Ⓦ www.incredibleindia.org), has branches in most major Keralan cities. These, however, operate independently of the state-run Kerala Tourism's **information counters** (Ⓦ www .keralatourism.org), which offer a wide range of travel facilities, including guided tours, car rental and their own hotels. Also run by the Keralan government is the Kerala State Tourist Development Corporation, better known by its acronym, KTDC (Ⓦ www.ktdc .org), a commercial venture set up to promote the state-owned chain of hotels and tours.

Finally, besides our own extensive site on India (Ⓦ www.roughguides.com), the following are some useful websites on South India and Kerala, some with search engines, listings and news.

Travel advice

Australian Department of Foreign Affairs
Ⓦ www.smartraveller.gov.au.
British Foreign & Commonwealth Office
Ⓦ www.fco.gov.uk.
Canadian Department of Foreign Affairs
Ⓦ www.voyage.gc.ca.
Irish Department of Foreign Affairs
Ⓦ www.foreignaffairs.gov.ie.
New Zealand Ministry of Foreign Affairs
Ⓦ www.safetravel.govt.nz.
South African Department of Foreign Affairs
Ⓦ www.dfa.gov.za
US State Department Ⓦ www.travel.state.gov.

India Tourism offices overseas

Australia Level 2, Piccadilly, 210 Pitt St, Sydney NSW ☎ 02/9264 4855, info@indiatourism.com.au.
Canada 60 Bloor St (West), #1003, Toronto, ON M4W 3B8 ☎ 1-416-962-3787, Ⓔindiatourism @bellnet.ca.
South Africa Hyde Lane, Lancaster Gate, Johannesburg 2000 ☎ 011/325 0880, Ⓔ goito@global.co.za.
UK 7 Cork St, London W1X 2LN ☎ 020 7437 3677, Ⓔ info@indiatouristoffice.org.
USA 3550 Wilshire Blvd, Suite #204, Los Angeles, CA 90010 ☎ 1-213-380-8855, Ⓔ indiatourismla @aol.com; Suite 1808, 1270 Ave of Americas, New York NY 10020 ☎ 1-212 586 4901, Ⓔ rd@itonyc .com.

Other useful websites

Ⓦ **www.ananthapuri.com** Thiruvananthapuram portal, with links to a wide range of information

sites. Alternatives include: ⓦwww
.thiruvananthapuram.net and ⓦwww
.trivandrumonline.com.

ⓦ**www.indiamike.com** Popular travel forum
run out of a bedroom in New Jersey by inveterate
Indophile Mike Szewczyk. Lively chat rooms, bulletin
boards, photo archives and banks of members'
travel articles, as well as a daily news feed.

ⓦ**www.kerala.cc** Kerala portal pitched at
Non-Resident Keralans abroad, featuring lots of
background on the state and its culture.

ⓦ**www.kerala.com** The state's busiest
and best general portal, and the one with the
sturdiest links.

ⓦ**www.ktdc.com** Website of the state-run
tourism development corporation, acting as a
booking platform for its many hotels.

ⓦ**www.kerala.gov.in** Official portal of the Kerala
government, featuring a particularly good rundown
of the region's history.

ⓦ**www.keralatravels.com** Dependable Kerala-
based online travel agent.

ⓦ**www.malayalamcinema.com** All the latest
news and views from the world of Malayali cinema,
aka "Mallu Wood".

ⓦ**www.manoramaonline.com** English-language
version of Kerala's top-selling daily.

ⓦ**www.rediff.com** A leading India-wide portal
with great search facilities and a site plan that
stretches from news to travel.

ⓦ**www.travelintelligence.net/wsd/articles/
artbyplce_143.html** A huge selection of top-quality,
inspiring travelogues by India experts including
William Dalrymple, Sue Carpenter and Justine Hardy.

Guide

Guide

Southern Kerala

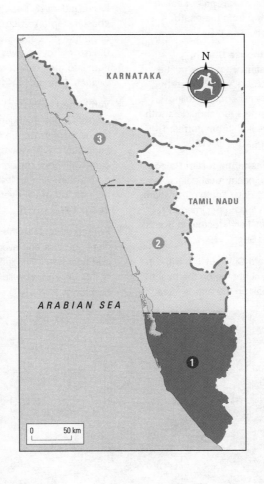

CHAPTER 1 # Highlights

* **Thiruvananthapuram** With its huge temple, royal palace, museums and traditional Keralan restaurants, the state capital makes an appealing day-trip from the nearby resorts. See p.93

* **Lighthouse Beach, Kovalam** The nerve centre of Kerala's busiest resort, where fishermen hauling hand-nets rub shoulders with sunseekers from northern Europe. See p.112

* **Padmanabhapuram Palace** This elegant royal palace, an hour's drive south of Kovalam, is the finest specimen of regional architecture in South India. See p.119

* **Varkala** Chill out in a cliff-top café, sunbathe on the beach or soak up the atmosphere around the town's busy temple tank. See p.123

* **The backwaters** Explore the beautiful waterways of Kerala's densely populated coastal strip on a rice barge or punted canoe, following the narrow, overgrown canals right into the heart of the villages. See pp.144–145

* **Vembanad Lake** Kerala's largest lagoon is ringed by resorts and wonderful homestays from where you can experience the area's backwaters without leaving the comfort of your verandah. See p.149 & p.155

* **Periyar** Wild elephants, bison, giant squirrels and even the odd tiger lurk in the jungles of this benchmark wildlife sanctuary. See p.159

△ Papanasam Beach, Varkala

Southern Kerala

Southern Kerala attracts a greater number of visitors than any other region in peninsula India. If you're travelling here on a package break, chances are it will be in one of the many hotels or self-contained holiday complexes lining the densely populated coastal strip of the far south, within an hour's bus ride of the capital, Thiruvananthapuram. It was here that beach tourism in general, and the whole concept of healthy, **ayurveda-based holidays** in particular, first took root in Kerala, and where you'll find the most sophisticated spas, five-stars and boutique hideaways. Interrupted only by the odd laterite headland and fishing harbour, sandy beaches fringe the entire coastline, against an unrelentingly green backdrop of coconut forest.

Villages cluster in an unbroken band under the palm canopy, forming what in Kerala is known as a "rurban belt", where the land is so jam-packed, and so evenly distributed into little plots (a legacy of communist land reform) that the outskirts of towns and cities merge imperceptibly with the countryside. Along with coconut and rice cultivation, **fishing** is the mainstay, and you'll find yourself sharing the sands with an assortment of local fishermen, whose early-morning polyphonic songs and perilously unstable *kettumaran* log rafts are among the south's defining features.

Inland, wooded hills and paddy fields ripple into the hazy outlines of the Western Ghats as they taper towards the tip of the Subcontinent at Kanyakumari, in neighbouring Tamil Nadu. The history of this intensely tropical end of the state is inextricably bound up with that of princely **Travancore**, which at its height in the eighteenth century stretched from Nagercoil, just across the Kerala–Tamil Nadu border, to beyond Kochi. It was the Travancore rajas who first developed Thiruvananthapuram as the region's capital, and whose patronage of education and the arts did much to shape the state's modern identity.

Thiruvananthapuram's massive temple, Shri Padmanabhaswamy, and its adjacent royal palace, Puttan Malika, are the capital's two principal sights, and the focus of its main **festivals**: Arattu (held biannually in March/April and Oct/Nov), and the harvest celebration of Onam (late Aug/Sept). Traditional arts also thrive here, with two of South India's major music events – Nishagandi (mid-Jan) and the Swathi Sangeetotsavam (Oct/Nov) – staged in the city, alongside regular monthly performances of *kathakali* and *kudiyattam* at the renowned Margi School.

The arcane world of ritual Keralan drama is a far cry from the holiday culture prevailing at nearby **Kovalam**, just over half-an-hour by road south of the capital. The resort is made up of four separate beaches, divided by low laterite headlands and backed by a tightly-packed band of low-rise concrete

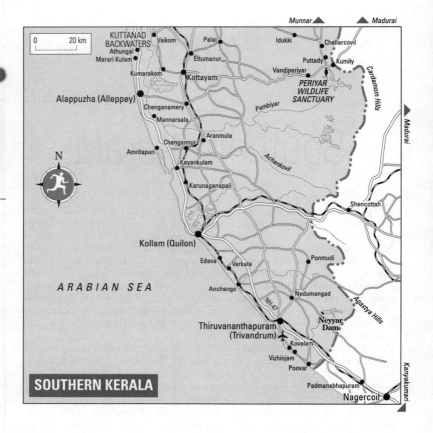

SOUTHERN KERALA

hotels, restaurants, cafés, ayurvedic massage centres, tailors' stalls and Kashmiri handicraft shops. Kovalam started out life in the 1980s as a budget travellers' resort, and while the scene has definitely grown more expensive, middle-aged and health-conscious over the past decade, the village still holds a wider choice of accommodation than the settlements huddled behind less-frequented coves to the south, beyond the ramshackle fishing port of **Vizhinjam**, where upscale hotels and luxury spas dominate.

Aside from Thiruvananthapuram's museums, bazaars and great-value restaurants, possible targets for forays **inland from Kovalam** include the splendid former royal palace at **Padmanabhapuram**, an hour or so south. Another fine specimen of traditional Keralan architecture, **Koikkal Kottaram**, stands just outside the capital at Nedumangad, which can easily be slotted in to a trip to the **Agastya Hills**, 25km northeast. The hub of this hill region, and only an hour's drive away from the coast, is the lakeside settlement of **Neyyar Dam**, where Kerala's most popular yoga ashram, the Sivananda Yoga Vedanta Dhanwantari, attracts devotees from all over the world. With a couple of days to spare, you could press on deeper into the mountains to overnight at the hill resort of **Ponmudi**, set amid fragrant tea and cardamom plantations at an altitude of just over 1000m.

North of Thiruvananthapuram, the Hindu pilgrimage village and budding tourist resort of **Varkala**, with its spectacular beach and cliff-top café scene, is an essential stop on the well-trodden trail between the far south of the state and Kerala's famous **backwaters** region, **Kuttanad**. The gateway to this watery world, best explored on an old-style, punted *kettu vallam* rice barge or canoe, is the market town of **Kollam** (Quilon) – a former dynastic capital and port boasting some unique heritage accommodation. Most of the canal traffic heading north from there pauses at **Amritapuri** for a hug from Kerala's world-renowned guru, Amma. But her ashram, a baby-pink pile of multi-storey concrete tower blocks rising above the palm trees, is only one among several sights reachable from the backwaters' main hub, **Alappuzha**. Others include a Tantric snake-worship temple at **Mannarsala**, and the beautiful royal palaces at **Kayamkulam**.

Heading inland from Alappuzha, ferries skirt the edges of **Vembanad Lake**, a vast, shimmering lagoon around whose shores dozens of resort complexes and homestays have sprung up in recent years. Access to the **Kumarakom Bird Sanctuary** on its eastern flank is via the bustling town of **Kottayam**, capital of a prosperous rubber-growing region dominated by Syrian Christians. Beyond a couple of ancient churches dating from the earliest days of Christianity in India, it offers little to detain travellers, but does serve as a convenient pit-stop on the long haul east into the Western Ghat range. Chief among the attractions of the so-called "Cardamom Hills" is the **Periyar Wildlife Sanctuary**, a former royal hunting reserve whose impressive rainforest is centred on a reservoir where wild elephant and other animals still congregate in healthy numbers. Safaris are conducted either on noisy diesel launches (which tend to scare any wildlife within earshot away) or on paddle-powered bamboo rafts – part of a ground-breaking eco-tourism initiative recently introduced by the local forest department.

Transport around the region is plentiful, with regular express trains running on the main Thiruvananthapuram–Kochi line, via Varkala and Kollam, and buses heading from the capital's chaotic KSRTC bus stand to all but the most remote villages. Services are most frequent along the busy NH-47 highway, which passes within a couple of kilometres of Kovalam, and which you can use to reach Padmanabhapuram Palace. Heading in the opposite direction, it cuts between the western edge of Thiruvananthapuram and the airport, and then winds in tandem with the rail line northwards along the coast. Ambassador **taxis** are ubiquitous in the resorts; prices are ostensibly fixed by the union, but in practice should always be open to negotiation.

Some history

Travancore was the last in a long line of princely states stretching back to the second century BC, when the **Ay** dynasty were the dominant political power in the far southwest of India. For centuries, the Ays formed a buffer between the mighty Pandyan dynasty to the east, which ruled most of what is now Tamil country, and the **Cheras** to the north, whose gradual imperial expansion began in the first centuries of the Christian era, from their capital, the port city of Muziris (near modern-day Kochi). By this time, Hinduism had asserted itself over Jainism and Buddhism as the prime religion, although tolerance of other faiths prevailed. From the Ays onwards, royal patronage financed the construction of major temple complexes, including Padmanabhaswamy in Thiruvananthapuram,.

Chera power was eroded by constant attacks from the south by the Pandyans and, after them, the powerful Cholas, but revived around 800AD under an illustrious line of kings who would become known as the **Kulasekharas**. Under their enlightened rule, during the so-called **Second Chera Empire**, southern Kerala enjoyed three centuries of stability and prosperity. This was the region's classical golden age, when literature, the arts and commerce thrived, and when Malayalam began to take shape as a language distinct from Tamil. The capital, **Mahodayapuram**, grew famous all over the ancient world as a centre of learning and culture, boasting South India's only observatory. Ships from China and Arabia filled the harbours of Vizhinjam and Quilon (modern Kollam).

However, in 999AD, the region plunged into a century of tumult as war once again erupted with the Chola empire. Foreign trade declined, temples were neglected, centres of learning were converted into military academies, the capital was burned to the ground and the second Chera empire slowly began breaking into smaller chiefdoms.

With the demise of the Kulasekharas, **Venad**, one of their former principalities, emerged as the most important *swaroopam*, or kingdom, in the south. On the back of brisk trade with China and Persia, Quilon, its main port, became a glittering city of many temples and paved roads, described in glowing terms by Marco Polo. Despite repeated invasions by the Nayaks of Madurai, its rulers grew steadily more wealthy and powerful. In 1312, after successfully conquering the Pandyan's former territory to the east, **Ravi Varma Kulasekhara** (1299–1314) crowned himself the "Emperor of the South". Over the coming four centuries, however, the rise of other regional dynasties gradually nibbled away at Venad's territory, pegging its kings back into a narrow belt between Thiruvananthapuram and the tip of India.

The modern history of Travancore as southern Kerala's major power begins with the accession in 1729 of **Raja Marthanda Varma**. By this time, what remained of Venad – now better known as "Thiruvitamkode" (later corrupted to Travancore) – was in rough shape: the priestly caste, in cahoots with the local nobility, controlled the workings of state; trade and taxation were dominated by competing European powers and the king's coffers were empty.

Having secured promises of financial and military support from former adversaries, the Nayaks of Madurai, along with the British East India Company, Marthanda Varma set about his policy of "blood and iron", crushing the power of the region's feudal lords and extending his territory northwards. In 1741, his campaign culminated in the dramatic defeat of the **Dutch East India Company** at the Battle of Colachen – the first time an Asian army managed to vanquish a European power in open combat. Thereafter, Travancore controlled the local pepper trade, profits from which financed the move from the Rajas' magnificent palace at Padmanabhapuram (now just across the Kerala–Tamil Nadu border, but included in this chapter) to the new capital at Thiruvananthapuram.

An invasion by Tipu Sultan, the legendary "Tiger of Mysore", was held at bay in the late eighteenth century, but only with more support from the British, an arrangement that ultimately led to Travancore becoming a Protectorate of the East India Company, with its own Resident and nineteen-gun salute. The peace dividend of Pax Britannica, however, enabled Travancore's rulers to fund the development of roads, schools, colleges, hospitals and artistic life in the region, whose population became one of the best educated in India. This widespread literacy is often regarded as having paved the way for the later **politicization** of the state's underclasses, not to mention its future economic prosperity.

For all its cultural advances, nineteenth century Travancore remained under the grips of a particularly oppressive caste system. Agitation against the old social order coalesced around the **Vaikom Satyagrahya**, or "Movement Against Untouchability" led by such luminaries as the sage Shri Narayana Guru (see p.269). Not until the landmark "Temple Entry Proclamation" of 1936, however, were the doors of the state's Hindu shrines finally thrown open to all.

These days the region, while retaining its unique ritual and art traditions, is at the forefront of innovation and commerce in Kerala. The prolific **Malayalam movie industry** is based on the outskirts of the capital, along with the **Vikram Sarabhai Space Centre** (VSSC), from where India's first satellite rocket was launched in 1963. Home to over one hundred blue-chip companies, including the software giant Infosys, it also hosts the country's largest IT campus, **Technopark**. More than twenty percent of the region's income, however, comes from expatriate workers in the Gulf and beyond. As a result, fancy modern mansions nowadays appear on the outskirts of nearly every village in southern Kerala.

Thiruvananthapuram (Trivandrum)

Kerala's capital, the coastal city of **THIRUVANANTHAPURAM** (still widely and more commonly known as **Trivandrum**), is set on seven low hills, 87km from the southern tip of India. Despite its administrative importance – demonstrated by wide roads, multi-storey office blocks and gleaming white colonial buildings – it's a decidedly easy-going city, with a mix of narrow backstreets and traditional red-tiled gabled houses, and palm trees and parks breaking up the bustle of its modern concrete centre.

Although it has few monuments as such, Thiruvananthapuram holds enough of interest to fill a day or two. The oldest and most interesting part of town is the **Fort** area in the south, around the **Shri Padmanabhaswamy temple** and **Puttan Malika Palace**, while the **Sri Chitra Art Gallery** and **Napier Museum**, showcases for painting, crafts and sculpture, stand together in a park in the north. In addition, schools specializing in the martial art *kalarippayattu* and the dance/theatre forms of *kathakali* and *kudiyattam* offer visitors an insight into the Keralan obsession with physical training and skill.

Most travellers choose to pass straight through Thiruvananthapuram, lured by the promise of Kovalam's palm-fringed beaches (see p.112). A mere twenty-minute bus ride south, Kerala's most popular resort is close enough to use as a base to see the city, although its booming package tourist trade means sky-high prices for food and accommodation, and a decidedly un-Keralan atmosphere.

Arrival

Connected to most major Indian cities, as well as Sri Lanka, the Maldives and the Middle East, **Beemapalli airport** (Ⓦ www.trivandrumairport.com) is 6km

---

The city of the snake Anantha

Thiruvananthapuram was the capital of the kingdom of Travancore from 1750 until 1956, when the state of Kerala was created. Its name – formally readopted to replace the anglicized version of "Trivandrum" – derives from *thiru-anantha-puram*, or "the holy city of Anantha", the **coiled snake** on which the god Vishnu reclines in the midst of the cosmic ocean.

Vishnu is given a special name for this non-activity – Padma-nabha (lotus-navel) – and is invariably depicted lying on the sacred snake with a lotus growing from his belly button. The god Brahma sits inside the flower, which represents the beginning of a new world era. Padmanabha is the principal deity of the royal family of Travancore and of Thiruvananthapuram's Shri Padmanabhaswamy temple.

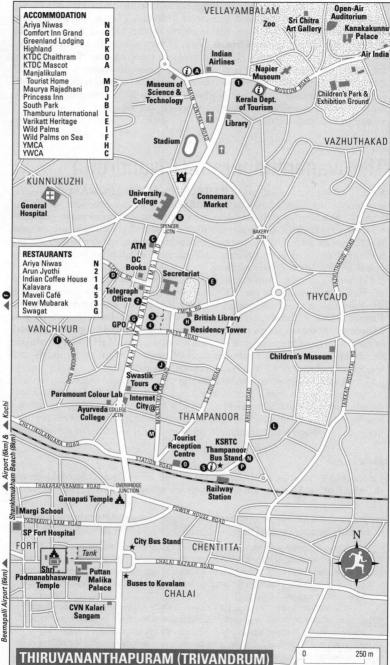

▲ *Kollam, Kochi & NH-47*

ACCOMMODATION
Ariya Niwas	N
Comfort Inn Grand	G
Greenland Lodging	P
Highland	K
KTDC Chaithram	O
KTDC Mascot	A
Manjalikulam	
Tourist Home	M
Maurya Rajadhani	D
Princess Inn	J
South Park	B
Thamburu International	L
Varikatt Heritage	E
Wild Palms	I
Wild Palms on Sea	F
YMCA	H
YWCA	C

RESTAURANTS
Ariya Niwas	N
Arun Jyothi	2
Indian Coffee House	1
Kalavara	4
Maveli Café	5
New Mubarak	3
Swagat	G

VELLAYAMBALAM

Zoo
Sri Chitra Art Gallery
Open-Air Auditorium
Kanakakunnu Palace
Air India

Indian Airlines

Napier Museum

Museum of Science & Technology

Kerala Dept. of Tourism

Children's Park & Exhibition Ground

Library

Stadium

VAZHUTHAKAD

KUNNUKUZHI

General Hospital

University College

Connemara Market

SPENCER JCTN

BAKERY JCTN

ATM
DC Books

Secretariat

Telegraph Office

GPO

British Library

Residency Tower

PRESS ROAD

THYCAUD

VANCHIYUR

YMCA RD

Children's Museum

Swastik Tours

Paramount Colour Lab

Internet City@

Ayurveda College

COLLEGE JCTN

THAMPANOOR

Tourist Reception Centre

KSRTC Thampanoor Bus Stand

STATION ROAD

CHETTIKULANGARA ROAD

Railway Station

THAKARAPARAMBU ROAD

OVERBRIDGE JUNCTION

Ganapati Temple

Margi School

SP Fort Hospital

FORT

POWER HOUSE ROAD

City Bus Stand

CHENTITTA

Tank

CHALAI BAZAAR ROAD

Shri Padmanabhaswamy Temple

Puttan Malika Palace

Buses to Kovalam

CVN Kalari Sangam

CHALAI

N

0   250 m

THIRUVANANTHAPURAM (TRIVANDRUM)

▼ *Kovalam & Kanyakumari*

MAIN CENTRAL ROAD

MUSEUM ROAD

MAHATMA GANDHI RD

STATI RD

VAZHUTHACAD ROAD

TAIKAD HOSPITAL RD

ARISTO ROAD

S.S. KOIL ROAD

MANJALIKULAM ROAD

MATHRUBHOOMI ROAD

Airport (6km) & Shankhumukham Beach (8km) ◀ Kochi

Beemapalli Airport (6km)

southwest of town and serviced by an airport bus and bus #14 to and from the City bus stand. Auto-rickshaws will run you into the centre for around Rs75 and there's also a handy prepaid taxi service, for which you pay a set fee before departure of Rs175 for the railway station, and Rs375 for Kovalam's Lighthouse Beach. A Kerala Tourism information booth and Thomas Cook foreign exchange facility are located just before the exit of the arrivals concourse.

The long-distance KSRTC **Thampanoor bus stand** and **railway station** face each other across Station Road in the southeast of the city, a short walk east of Overbridge Junction on MG Road. **Local buses** (including those for Kovalam) depart from **City bus stand**, in East Fort, ten minutes' walk south from the KSRTC and railway stations. **Auto-rickshaws** run to Kovalam for Rs100–150, while **taxis** charge around Rs250 – but beware of overcharging scams.

Information and tours

The **tourist information counters** at the **airport** (☎0471/250 1085) are open during flight times. Kerala Tourism also has a booth at the KSRTC **Thampanoor bus stand** (Mon–Sat 10am–5pm; ☎0471/232 7224), which is good for general information and maps, and at the **railway station** (☎0471/233 4470). Their main visitor ("tourist facilitation") centre is 150m south of the Napier Museum on Museum Road (open 24hr in theory; ☎0471/2321132, Ⓦwww.keralatourism.org).

Kerala Tourism (KTDC) also has a visitor reception centre, next to their *KTDC Chaithram* hotel on Station Road (☎0471/233 0031, Ⓦwww.ktdc.com), where you can book accommodation in their hotel chain and tickets for various **guided tours**. Most of these, including the city tours (daily: 8.30am–7pm, Rs130; half-day 8.30am–1pm or 2–7pm, Rs70/80), are far too rushed, but if you're really pushed for time and want to reach the tip of India, try the **Kanyakumari** tour (daily 7.30am–9pm; Rs250), which takes in Padmanabhapuram Palace (except Mon), Suchindram temple, and Kanyakumari.

Accommodation

Accommodation in all categories is a lot easier on the pocket in Thiruvananthapuram than at nearby Kovalam beach. That said, this is one city where budget travellers, in particular, should consider spending a couple of hundred rupees more than they might usually; with the exception of the YWCAs and *Greenland Lodging*, there's nowhere really worth bothering with for under Rs300, whereas in the Rs450–500 bracket you're spoiled for choice.

Close on a hundred **hotels** and lodges lie within ten minutes' walk of the railway and bus stations, in the district known as **Thampanoor** – the best of them up Manjalikulam Road, which runs due north from the main road outside the stations. As ever with state capitals and other large cities, it pays to book ahead, and reconfirm the day before checking in.

Inexpensive

Greenland Lodging Aristo Rd, Thampanoor ☎0471/232 8114. Large and efficient lodge with spotless en-suite rooms for Rs270. The best low-cost option in the vicinity of the bus stand and railway station. Book ahead or arrive before noon. ❷
Manjalikulam Tourist Home Manjalikulam Rd, Thampanoor ☎0471/233 0776. Don't be fooled by

the shining glass and marble ground floor – above lurks a basic budget place offering variously priced rooms, all of them clean and with good, comfy mattresses. ❹
Princess Inn Manjalikulam Rd, Thampanoor ☎0471/233 9150, Ⓔprincess.inn@yahoo.com. Well-scrubbed, respectable cheapie close to the

stations. One of the more welcoming and better-value small hotels in this busy enclave, though it's a bit more of a plod up the lane from Station Rd than some. ❸

🏃 **YMCA** YMCA Rd, near the Secretariat ☎0471/233 0059, ✉ymcatvm @sancharnet.in. Neat, smartly furnished rooms at bargain rates for the levels of comfort. The "luxury" options (Rs500) are enormous and have high ceilings, quiet fans, TVs and spacious bathrooms;

singles from Rs200; some a/c. Amazing value, though you'll probably need to book at least two weeks in advance. ❸–❹

YWCA Spencer Junction ☎0471/247 7308. Spotless en-suite doubles (from Rs350) on the fourth floor of a grubby, run-down office block. Friendly, safe and central, with some non-a/c rooms, but the place is locked at 10.30pm sharp. Primarily for women, although couples and men are welcome. ❸–❹

Mid-range and luxury

Ariya Niwas Aristo Rd, Thampanoor ☎0471/233 0789. Large, spotlessly clean, well-aired rooms with comfy beds and city views from upper floors. The best value in this bracket (Rs625–800; plus Rs500 for a/c) and only 2min walk from the railway station. A wonderful mural from Guruvayur is on display in the lobby, and the best "meals" restaurant in the state stands on the ground floor (see "Eating", p.104) . ❹–❺

Comfort Inn Grand opposite the Secretariat, MG Rd ☎0471/247 1286, ⓦwww.comfortinngrand.in. Smart new business hotel in the city centre, completely refurbished in 2005. The "standard" rooms are on the small side for two, but cool and quiet. The "executive" deluxe options on the top storey are larger and more plush, and have the best views. There's also a quality a/c veg restaurant on site. ❻–❼

KTDC Chaithram Station Rd ☎0471/233 0977, ⓦwww.ktdc.com. Big government-run tower-block hotel very close to the railway station and Thampanoor bus stand, holding a range of differently priced, spacious rooms (some a/c), restaurants, travel agent, car rental, beauty parlour, cybercafé, bookshop and bar. ❹–❻

KTDC Mascot Mascot Junction, near the Indian Airlines office ☎0471/231 8990, ⓦwww .ktdc.com. The city's only five-star, at the north end of town near the museums, is a state-run luxury hotel, patronized mainly by government flunkies (the Kerala State Legislature is close by). Opening onto long polished marble corridors lined with hardwood panels, the fancier "executive" and "suite" rooms occupy a wing built to house British officers in World War I; the "standard" ones are in a less attractive modern block. There's an open-air pool, bar and a/c restaurant. ❽–❾

Highland Manjalikulam Rd ☎0471/233 3200, ⓦwww.highland-hotels.com. The rooms in this dependable lower mid-range option fail to live up to the promise of the six-storey concrete and tinted-glass facade, but it's well managed, and only a short walk from the stations, and easy to find.

The "economy" non-a/c options are dowdy, but large enough for two. If it's full, try the *Highland Park* (☎0471/233 8800), a little further up the same street. ❹–❺

Maurya Rajadhani General Hospital Rd ☎0471/246 9469, ⓦwww.rajadhanihotels.com. Gleaming new, state-of-the-art business hotel, tucked away off MG Rd in a quiet backstreet, currently riding high after starring in the Bollywood hit movie *Fouj Mein Mauj*. It offers all the comforts you'd expect from a modern four-star – though there's no pool. ❼–❽

The South Park MG Rd ☎0471/233 3333, ⓦwww.thesouthpark.com. Award-winning Welcomgroup four-star presiding over the most hectic stretch of MG Rd. With 83 centrally air-conditioned rooms, lavish multi-cuisine restaurants, bars and conference halls, it's primarily a business hotel, though the odd tour group also stays here. ❽–❾

Thamburu International Aristo Junction, Thampanoor ☎0471/232 1974, ⓦwww.thamburu.com. This mid-range hotel lies within walking distance of the railway station and has more character than most in the area, with varnished wood-lined rooms (from Rs850) and views over the surrounding rooftops. It's perhaps a touch overpriced, but clean and quiet, with polite staff. ❹–❻

🏃 **Varikatt Heritage** Poonen Rd, near Cantonment Police Station, behind the Secretariat (look for the brown gates) ☎0471/233 6057, ⓦwww.varikattheritage.com. Trivandrum's only heritage homestay, run by the affable Col. K. K. Kuncheria (Gurkha Rifles, Rtd), is a real gem. It occupies a gorgeous 1830s Indo-Saracenic-style bungalow originally built by a lovesick British spinster, Miss Blanket, who followed a teaplanter out to India after the two had met on holiday in Yorkshire. Romance bloomed, but didn't last, and the house was eventually sold to a prominent local lawyer, in whose family it has remained ever since. The three front-side suites ($125), opening onto a high-ceilinged veranda where you can enjoy a *chota peg* under the hunting trophies after supper, retain their original rosewood furniture – and more period atmosphere than the much less appealing rear-side doubles ($95). **⑨**

Wild Palms Mathrubhoomi Rd, ☎0471/247 1175, ⓦ www.wildpalmsonsea.com. Plush guesthouse in a modern suburban house, 10min walk from MG Rd. Owners Hilda and Justin Pereira lived in the UK for years, and this is as much a labour of love as a homestay, though the place is large enough to afford a degree of privacy, and the en-suite rooms (Rs1100–2000) are very large for the price. They also run *Wild Palms on Sea* (see below). **⑤–⑦**

Wild Palms on Sea 20km west of town (or 16km from airport) at Puthenthope, ☎0471/275 6781, ⓦ www.wildpalmsonsea.com. Off-shoot of the Periera's town house: a compound of detached red-brick "cottages" next to a three-storey fusion building ranged around a curvi-form pool – all set in a coconut grove next to the beach. Half-board on request. **⑤**

The City

Thiruvananthapuram's centre can be explored easily on foot, though you might be glad of a rickshaw ride back from the museums and parks, close to the top end of MG Road. The historical and spiritual heart of town is the **Fort area**, at the southern end of **MG Road**, which encloses the Shri Padmanabhaswamy Vishnu temple. En route between the two you pass through the main shopping district, which is busy all day, and especially choked when one of the frequent, but generally orderly, political demonstrations converges on the grand colonial **Secretariat** building halfway along.

Shri Padmanabhaswamy

A Neo-Classical gateway leads from the Fort and City bus stands to the serene **Shri Padmanabhaswamy temple**, which is still controlled by the Travancore royal family. Unusually for Kerala, it's built in the Dravidian style of Tamil Nadu, with a tall, seven-tiered *gopura* gateway and high fortress-like walls. Non-Hindus are not permitted inside.

Most of Padmanabhaswamy's buildings date from the eighteenth century, added by Raja Marthanda Varma (1729–1758) to the much older shrine within.

△ Shri Padmanabhaswamy

According to legend, the temple was founded after Vishnu – disguised as a beautiful child – merged into a huge tree in the forest, which immediately crashed to the ground. There it transformed into an image of the reclining Vishnu, a full 13km long. Divakara, a sage who witnessed this, was frustrated by his limited human vision, and prayed to Vishnu to assume a form that he could view in its entirety. Vishnu complied, and the temple appeared.

The **deity** in the central sanctum is composed of 12,008 sacred stones, or *salagrams*, brought by elephant from the bed of the Gandhaki River in Nepal. A rare form of stucco known as *katusarkara yogam*, made according to an ancient ayurvedic recipe, forms the outer surfaces. To make offerings and perform *darshan*, or ritual viewing of the god, worshippers have to mount special stone platforms from which they can peer at different parts of the reclining Vishnu – feet, navel and face – through three openings in the floor, known as *vaayils*.

The main approach road to Shri Padmanabhaswamy, where devotees bathe in a huge tank, is lined with stalls selling religious souvenirs such as shell necklaces, *puja* offerings, jasmine and marigolds. It's an atmospheric area for a stroll – particularly in the early morning and at dusk, when devotees make their way to and from prayers (a closed iron gate bars the northern side, but everybody climbs through the gap). As recently as the turn of the last century, this was a "no-go" area for members of low-caste communities – possibly on pain of death.

Puttan Malika Palace

The **Puttan Malika Palace** (Tues–Sun 8.30am–12.30pm & 3–5.30pm; Rs20, camera Rs15) immediately southeast of the temple, became the seat of the

---

Festivals of Thiruvananthapuram

The annual **Nishagandi Dance and Music Festival** is held in the grounds of the **Kanakakunnu Palace**, just to the east of the public gardens, in mid-January. Originally built as a cultural venue for the maharajas of Thiruvananthapuram, the large, open-air amphitheatre where the event is staged makes an ideal venue for evening performances of classical dances and music. Over the past few years, the festival has gained in stature and now hosts some of India's best-known artists. A lively food and crafts fair springs up below it, and in the Childrens' Park, on the opposite side of Museum Road, a popular flower festival attracts large crowds. Ask at a KTDC tourist office for details.

The **Arattu** festival, centred on the Shri Padmanabhaswamy temple, takes place biannually, in Meenam (March/April) and Thulam (Oct/Nov). Each time, ten days of festivities inside the temple (open to Hindus only) culminate in a procession through the streets of the city, taking the deity, Padmanabhaswamy, to the sea for ritual immersion. Five caparisoned (decorated) elephants, armed guards and a *nagaswaram* (double-reed wind instrument) and *tavil* drum group are led by the maharaja of Travancore, in his symbolic role as *kshatrya*, the servant of the god. Instead of the richly apparelled figure that might be expected, the maharaja (whose rank is no longer officially recognized) wears a simple white *dhoti*, his chest bare save for the sacred thread. Rather than riding, he walks the whole way, bearing a sword. To the accompaniment of a 21-gun salute and music, the procession sets off from the east gate of the temple at around 5pm, moving at a brisk pace to reach Shankhumukham Beach at sunset, about an hour later. The route is lined with devotees, many of whom honour both the god and the maharaja. After the seashore ceremonies, the cavalcade returns to the temple at about 9pm, to be greeted by another gun salute. An extremely loud firework display rounds off the day.

Travancore rajas after they left Padmanabhapuram at the end of the nineteenth century. It was originally commissioned by Raja Ravi Thirunal Varma, who died at the tender age of 30, only a year after the palace was completed. To generate funds for much-needed restoration, the Travancore royal family opened the palace to the public a decade ago – for the first time in more than two centuries. Although much of it remains off-limits, palace guides show you around some of the most impressive wings, which have been converted into a **museum**. The cool chambers, with highly polished plaster floors and delicately carved wooden screens, house a crop of dusty Travancore heirlooms. Among the array of portraits, royal regalia and weapons are some genuine treasures, such as a solid crystal throne – a gift from the Dutch – and some fine murals. The real highlight, however, is the elegant Keralan architecture itself. Beneath sloping red-tiled roofs, hundreds of wooden pillars, carved into the forms of rampant horses (*puttan malika* translates as "horse palace"), prop up the eaves, and airy verandas project onto the surrounding lawns.

The royal family have always been keen patrons of the arts, and the open-air **Swathi Sangeetotsavam festival**, held in the grounds during the festival of Navaratri (Oct/Nov), continues the tradition. Performers sit on the palace's raised porch, flanked by the main facade, with the spectators seated on the lawn. Songs composed by Raja Swathi Thirunal (1813–1846), known as the "musician king", dominate the programme. For details, ask at the KTDC tourist office.

CVN Kalari

Around 500m southeast of the temple in East Fort, the red-brick **CVN Kalari Sangam** ranks among Kerala's top **kalarippayattu** gymnasiums (see box, p.100).

For ten days in March/April, Muslims celebrate **Chandanakuda Mahotsavam** at the Beemapalli Dargah Shareef tomb, 5km southwest of the city on the coastal road towards the airport. The Hindu-influenced festival commemorates the anniversary of the death of Bee Umma (aka "Beema Beevi"), a female descendant of the Prophet Mohammed revered for her piety and spiritual powers. On its first, most important, day, pilgrims converge on the mosque inside the complex carrying earthenware pots, or *chandana-kuddam*, covered in sandalwood paste and flowers, and containing money offerings. Activities such as traditional storytelling (*kathaprasangam*) and sword play (*daharamuttu*) take place inside the mosque, while outside there is dance and music. In the early hours of the morning, a flag is brought out from Beema Beevi's tomb and taken on a procession, accompanied by a *panchavadyam* drum and horn orchestra and two caparisoned elephants, practices normally associated with Hindu festivals. Once more, the rest of the night is lit up with fireworks.

The great Keralan festival of **Onam** (late August or September) takes place during the late-monsoon harvest period, when Keralans remember the reign of King Mahabali, a legendary figure who, it is believed, achieved an ideal balance of harmony, wealth and justice during his tenure. Unfortunately, the gods became upset and envious at Mahabali's success and Vishnu packed him off to another world. However, once a year the king was allowed to return to his people for ten days, and Onam is a joyful celebration of the royal visit. Families display their wealth, feasts and boat races are held and, in Thiruvananthapuram, there's a week-long cultural festival of dance and music culminating in a colourful street carnival in which thousands of local women prepare *payasam* (Keralan rice pudding) in earthen pots in the street – the greatest gathering forms on the road leading to the Shri Padmanabhaswamy temple. Again, the best source of precise dates are any of the KTDC offices dotted around the city.

It was founded in 1956 by C. V. Narayanan Nair, one of the legendary figures credited for the martial art's revival, and attracts students from across the world. From 6.30am to 8am (Mon–Sat) you can watch fighting exercises in the sunken *kalari* pit that forms the heart of the complex. Foreigners may join courses, arranged through the head teacher, or *gurukkal*, although prior experience of martial arts and/or dance is a prerequisite. You can also join the queues of locals who come here for a traditional **ayurvedic massage**, and to consult the gym's expert ayurvedic doctors (Mon–Sat 10am–1pm & 5–7.30pm, Sun 10am–1pm).

The Margi School

Thiruvananthapuram has for centuries been a crucible for Keralan classical arts, and the **Margi Theatre School** (℡0471/247 8806, ⓦwww.margitheatre.org), at the western corner of the Fort area, keeps the flame of the region's ritual theatre traditions burning brightly. **Kathakali** dance drama and the more rarely performed **kudiyattam** theatre form (see p.296) dominate the curriculum. By prior arrangement you can watch students being put through their paces. Foreigners are also welcome to attend introductory courses (Mon–Sat 10am–noon, Rs3000 for 20 days). However, the reason most visitors venture out here is to watch one of the authentic *kathakali* or *kudiyattam* performances staged in its small theatre, details of which are posted on the school's website.

To reach Margi, head to the SP Fort hospital on the western edge of Fort, and then continue 200m north; the school is set back from the west side of the main

Kalarippayattu

Practised in special earth-floored gyms and pits across the state, **kalarippayattu** is Kerala's unique martial art – a distinctive brand of acrobatic combat drawing heavily on yoga and ancient Indian knowledge of the human body. Its techniques of hand-to-hand fighting, weapon skills and healing were first formalized in the twelfth century by the bodyguards of medieval warlords and chieftains, though plenty of evidence exists to suggest the form derives from practices two or more thousand years old. Under guidance from their gurus, young boys (and sometimes girls) would be trained for years as specialist fighters, who in time would be employed to wage duels and settle disputes on behalf of landowners and chiefs. In the eighteenth century, *kalarippayattu* was banned by the British, but it has since made a strong comeback and now has numerous followers – Hindus, Christians and Muslims alike.

Two distinct **schools** survive – the southern and northern systems. Both, however, follow a similar progression. Once initiated, students are taught a complex set of strenuous exercises designed to render their bodies strong and flexible: kicks, jumps, animal postures, spins, step sequences and vigorous stretches, joined in increasingly long and complicated sequences. Sesame-oil massages, given with the feet and hands by teachers holding on to ropes suspended from the gym's rafters, are another essential part of the training. When the set moves have been mastered, students are eventually introduced to combat with weapons: the *udaval* (sword), *paricha* (shield), *kadaras* (dagger), *kuntham* (spear), *gadha* (mace) and *urumi* (a long flexible sword). The final stage, **verum kaythari**, focuses on barehanded combat against an armed enemy and is for advanced practitioners only.

Staged at gyms and tourist resorts across Kerala, *kalarippayattu* demonstrations are never dull, and injuries, although rare, do happen. As part of their advanced training, masters, known as *gurukkal*, are initiated into a system of physical therapy combining oil massage and ayurvedic herbal medicine, which is why famous *kalarippayattu* gyms, such as CVN Kalari in Thiruvananthapuram, double as traditional out-patient clinics. For details of places to learn *kalarippayattu*, see p.99 & p.103.

road in a large red-tiled and tin-roofed building, behind the High School (the sign is in Malayalam).

MG Road: markets and shopping

An assortment of **craft shops** along MG Road, north of Station Road, sells sandalwood, brass and Keralan bell-metal oil lamps (see box, p.206). The Gandhian Khadi Gramodyog, between Pazhavangadi and Overbridge junctions, stocks handloom cloth (dig around for the best stuff), plus radios and cassette machines manufactured by the Women's Federation. Natesan's Antique Arts, further up, is part of a chain that specializes in paintings, temple woodcarvings and so forth.

At first glance most of the **bookshops** in the area seem largely intended for exam entrants, but some stock a good choice of titles in English – mostly relating to India – and a fair selection of fiction too. DC Books, on Statue Road, on the first floor of a building above Statue Junction, stocks the city's best selection, with a separate area devoted to Kerala.

Almost at the top of MG Road, on the right-hand side, **Connemara Market** is the place to pick up odds and ends, such as dried and fresh fish, fruit, vegetables, coconut scrapers, crude wooden toys, coir, woven winnowing baskets and Christmas decorations.

Connemara also contains several tailors' workshops, but the main source of **textiles** in the city is **Chalai Bazaar**, the big market area centred on the road running east from Fort district, slicing past the bus stand. Jammed with little shops selling bolts of cloth, flowers, incense, spices, bell-metal lamps and fireworks, it's a great area for an aimless browsing.

The Napier Museum, Zoo and Sri Chitra Art Gallery

A minute's walk east from the north end of MG Road, opposite Kerala Tourism's information office, brings you to the entrance to Thiruvananthapuram's **Public Gardens**. As well as serving as a welcome refuge from the noise of the city – its lawns are usually filled with courting couples, students and picnicking families – the park holds the city's best museums. Give the dusty and uninformative Natural History Museum a miss and head instead for the more engaging **Napier Museum** of arts and crafts (Tues–Sun 10am–5pm; Rs5). Designed at the end of the nineteenth century by architect Robert Fellowes Chisolm (1840–1915), it was an early experiment in what became known as the "Indo-Saracenic" style, with tiled, gabled roofs, garish red-, black- and salmon-patterned brickwork, and, above the main entrance, a series of pilasters forming Islamic arches. The spectacular interior boasts stained-glass windows, a wooden ceiling and loud turquoise, pink, red and yellow stripes on the walls. Chisolm set out to incorporate Keralan elements into colonial architecture; the museum was named after his employer, Lord Napier, the governor of the Madras Presidency. Highlights of the collection include fifteenth-century Keralan woodcarvings from Kulathupuzha, minutely detailed ivory work, a carved temple chariot (*rath*), wooden models of Guruvayur temple and an oval temple theatre (*kuttambalam*), plus twelfth-century Chola and fourteenth-century Vijayanagar bronzes.

North of the museum, the spectacular trees of the former royal botanical gardens shade the city's famous **Zoo** (Tues–Sun 10am–5pm; Rs6), one of the largest and best equipped in India. Its collection of animals, covering 75 species from the Subcontinent and beyond, are housed in a mixture of modern, open-style enclosures and an extraordinary campus of quirky Raj-era structures, little changed since they were built in the 1850s: Grecian friezes of gorillas adorn the ape area, the giraffes inhabit an elegant Chinese pagoda and the barking

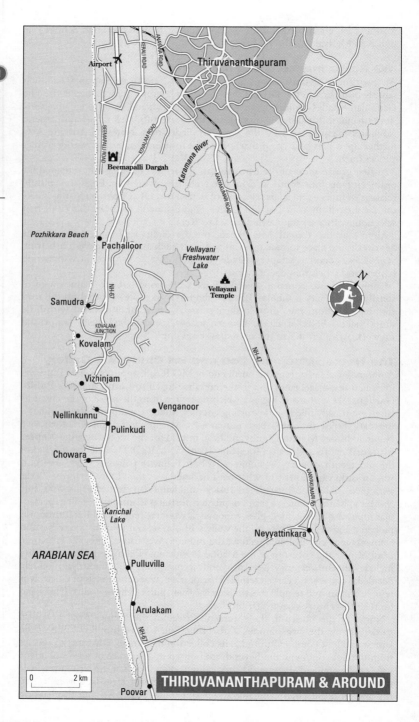

THIRUVANANTHAPURAM & AROUND

deer shelter beneath a roof of Mangalorean tiles. Founded by the Maharaja of Travancore, the zoo must be one of the few in the world to have earned a place in literary history, as the place novelist Yann Martel claimed inspired him to write his 2002 Booker-prize winning *Life of Pi* (the claim was later challenged after striking similarities were found between his book and Brazilian author Moacyr Scliar's *Max and the Cats*).

You have to pass through the main ticket booth for the zoo to reach the excellent **Sri Chitra Art Gallery** (Tues–Sun 10am–5pm; Rs50), which shows paintings from the Rajput, Moghul and Tanjore schools, along with pieces from China, Tibet and Japan. The meat of the collection, however, is made up of works by the celebrated Keralan artist, **Raja Ravi Varma** (1848–1906), who is credited with introducing oil painting to India. Varma's style was much criticized for its sentimentality and for showing a strong Western influence, but his treatment of Hindu mythological themes is both dramatic and beautiful. Also on view are a couple of minor Tagores, and some striking oils by the Russian artist-philosopher and mystic, **Nicholas Roerich**, who arrived in India at the turn of the twentieth century. His spiritually oriented, strongly coloured Himalayan landscapes reflect his love of the region. Roerich lived out his latter years in Nagar (in the Kulu valley), where he died in 1947.

Away from the centre

The **Chachu Nehru Children's Museum** (Tues–Sun 10am–5pm; free), in Thycaud in the east of the city, serves as a rather dusty testament to the enthusiasm of an anonymous collector back in the 1960s. One room contains ritual masks, probably from Bengal, Rajasthan and Orissa, while the rest of the place is taken up with stamps, health-education displays and over two thousand dolls featuring figures in Indian costume, American presidents, Disney characters and British beefeaters.

Also on the eastern side of town, visitors can, by arrangement, watch classes in the martial art of *kalarippayattu* (see box, p.100), at the P. S. Balachandran Nair Kalari **martial arts gymnasium**, Kalariyil, TC 15/854, Cotton Hill, Vazhuthakad (daily 6–8am & 6–7.30pm). Built of stone in 1992 along traditional lines, the *kalari* fighting pit is overlooked by a 4m-high viewing gallery. Students (some as young as eight) train both in unarmed combat and in the use of weapons. The school arranges short courses in *kalarippayattu*, and can also provide guides for forest trekking.

On Sunday evenings, half the city migrates to **Shankhumukham Beach**, 8km west of the centre, to stroll along the sand and watch the sunset. Fried-food stalls spring up on the roadside, and the *Indian Coffee House* does a roaring trade at its popular seafront branch. It occupies a building that once belonged to the royal family, where the Raja of Travancore used to preside over executions. A macabre painting displayed in the Puttan Malika Palace shows the cage of tigers used for this purpose: huge crowds would gather to gawp at the condemned criminals being torn limb from limb. These days, the main attraction, aside from the surf, is a huge sculpture of a curvaceous mermaid reclining on landscaped ground behind the *Indian Coffee House* – a work by the renowned Keralan artist Canai Kunuram.

Shankhumukham draws the biggest crowds of all during the biannual **Arattu** festival, when the Padmanabhaswamy deity is brought, amid much pomp, from the temple to be ritually immersed in the sea here (see p.98).

Eating

In common with most South Indian cities, Thiruvananthapuram has busy, hygenic places to eat on seemingly every street corner, serving freshly

Moving on from Thiruvananthapuram

Thiruvananthapuram is the main hub for traffic travelling along the coast. Towns within a couple of hours of the capital – such as Varkala, Kollam and Kanyakumari – can be reached by both bus and train, though it's always worth aiming for limited-stop services rather than much slower "local" or "passenger" ones. For longer hauls, you're invariably better off on the **train**, as buses tend to hurtle along the coastal highway at terrifying speeds; they're also more crowded. JAICO produces an excellent monthly guide with timetables and comprehensive travel details for Kerala and beyond; it's available from bookshops, Thampanoor bus stand and the railway station. For an overview of transport from Thiruvananthapuram, see "Travel details", p.168.

By air

Thiruvananthapuram's **Beemapalli airport**, 6km southwest of the city, offers international and domestic flights from a rapidly expanding list of carriers, several of whom have offices downtown (see p.106). For general advice on booking flights, see pp.28–29. "Travel details" at the end of this chapter includes a full rundown of who flies where, and how often.

As the roads to Beemapalli were recently upgraded, it's a comfortable enough journey by auto-rickshaw (around Rs75); taxis charge Rs175–200 from the railway station, and Rs375 from Kovalam's Lighthouse Beach.

By bus

Buses to **Kovalam** leave every 20 to 30min from the roadside in East Fort, just south of City bus stand (see map p.94). To reach anywhere else, you'll have to head for the grimy KSRTC **Thampanoor bus stand**. Services to **Varkala** leave from here at irregular intervals throughout the day from 7.25am – though it's worth noting that many of them are nail-bitingly slow, winding through dozens of villages and taking up to two-and-a-half hours instead of the one-and-a-half hours required by "super-fast" buses that follow the highway. For **Ponmudi**, there are departures at 5am and 8am. Heading **north** up the coast (to Kollam, Alappuzha, Ernakulam, Thrissur and Palakkad), the buses to aim for are the 6am or 5.30pm "super-deluxe a/c" specials, **tickets** for which – along with

---

cooked *dosas*, *iddli-vada-sambar* and other traditional *udipi* snacks. Wonderful Kerala-style thali "meals" are also widely available – the best places are listed below. For a quick pit-stop, the *Indian Coffee House* chain has several branches around the city, including the famous circular *Maveli Café* next to the KSRTC bus stand in Thampanoor, and another, larger cafeteria on Museum Road – handy for the public gardens. They also run a breezy terrace café at Shankhumukham beach where, on Sunday evenings, something of a funfair atmosphere prevails as thousands of city folk break out of the suburbs for a sunset stroll (see p.103).

Ariya Niwas *Ariya Niwas* hotel, Aristo Rd, Thampanoor. Top-class South Indian vegetarian thalis dished up on shiny green banana leaves in a scrupulously clean dining room on the hotel's ground floor. You buy your ticket first (Rs38 per head; "No Sharing"). Hugely popular with everyone from office workers to company directors and their families, and deservedly so: there's really nowhere better to eat in the city. The usual *udipi* menu, along with some North Indian and Chinese dishes, is served outside lunch hours (noon–3pm).

Arun Jyothi opposite the Secretariat on MG Rd. A delightfully old-fashioned "meals" restaurant that does unlimited red- or white-rice Keralan thalis (Rs28) from noon–3pm, including particularly delicious *avial*, an array of a half-dozen condiments and *payasam* for desert. *Dosas, uttapams* and other *udipi* fare are served through the rest of the day.

Kalavara Press Rd. One of the city's most popular multi-cuisine restaurants, down a

tickets for all other long-distance routes – may be purchased in advance at the reservations hatch on the main bus stand concourse (daily 6am–10pm). The Tamil Nadu bus company, TNSRTC, has its own counter on the same concourse. Numerous private bus companies also run inter-state services; many of the agents are on Aristo Road near the *Greenland Lodging*.

A full list of destinations reachable by bus from Thiruvananthapuram appears in "Travel Details" on p.168.

By train

Kerala's capital is well connected **by train** with other towns and cities in the country, although getting seats at short notice on long-haul journeys can be a problem. **Reservations** should be made as far in advance as possible from the efficient computerized booking office at the station (Mon–Sat 8am–2pm & 2.15–8pm, Sun 8am–2pm). Sleepers are sold throughout Kerala on a first-come, first-served basis, not on local stations' quotas.

The following trains are recommended as the **fastest** and/or **most convenient** from Thiruvananthapuram.

Recommended trains from Thiruvananthapuram

Destination	Name	Number	Frequency	Departs	Total time
Alappuzha	Netravati Exp*	#6346	daily	10am	2hr 50min
Ernakulam/ Kochi	Kerala Express	#2625	daily	11.30am	4hr
Kollam	Kerala Express	#2625	daily	11.30am	1hr 5min
Kottayam	Cape–Mumbai Express	#1082	daily	8.10am	2hr 20min
Kozhikode	Mangalore Exp	#6347	daily	8.45pm	9hr 30min

* via Kollam, Varkala, Ernakulam, Thrissur, Palakkad, Kozhikode, Kannur and Kasargode

sidestreet off MG Rd. You can eat in their dowdy first-floor dining room or, from 6.30pm onwards, on the more attractive rooftop terrace under a pitched-tile shelter. The furniture's plastic, but the food (mostly non-veg) is tasty and inexpensive: fish, beef, mutton and pork dominate the menu, plus they do fish curry "meals" from 12.30–2pm.

Maveli Café next to the bus station on Station Rd, Thampanoor. Part of the *Indian Coffee House* chain, this bizarre red-brick, spiral-shaped café (designed by the renowned expatriate British architect, Laurie Baker) is a Trivandrum institution. Inside, waiters in the trademark *ICH pugris* serve *dosas*, *vadas*, greasy omelettes, mountainous biriyanis and china cups of the usual (weak and sugary) filter coffee. An obligatory pit-stop, though a grubby one.

New Mubarak off Press Rd. Terrific little no-frills backstreet joint that's famed for its wonderful Malabari-Muslim dishes, especially

seafood. In addition to the usual masala-fry pomfret, kingfish, seer fish and pearlspot (*avioli*), you can order huge jumbo prawns, squid and crab, served with proper tapioca (*kappa*) curry and the famous house seafood pickle – at prices undreamed of in Kovalam (most mains Rs75–150). It's tricky to find: you have to squeeze down a narrow pedestrian alleyway off Press Rd (find your way to the *Residency Tower* hotel and ask there).

Swagat *Comfort Inn Grand*, MG Rd. Fine vegetarian Indian food served by black-tie waiters in a blissfully cool a/c dining hall, with tinted windows and discrete Carnatic music in the background – just the ticket if you've had enough of the heat and humidity outside. Their Rs100 "Swagat Special" thali is one for monster appetites, featuring green plantain in coconut, ladies' finger masala and tangy *rasam*. They also do full a multi-cuisine vegetarian menu, even during lunch hours.

Listings

Airlines Air India, Museum Rd, Vellayambalam Circle ☎0471/231 0310 (airport ☎0471/250 0585); Gulf Air, Ground Floor, Saran Chambers, Vellayambalam ☎0471/272 8003 (airport ☎0471/250 1205); Indian Airlines, Air Centre, Mascot Junction ☎0471/231 4781 (airport ☎0471/233 1063); IndiGo, 1st Floor, Krishna Commercial Complex, Bakery Junction ☎0471/233 0227; Jet Airways, 1st Floor, Akshaya Towers, Sasthamangalam Junction ☎0471/272 8864 (airport ☎0471/250 0710); KLM/Northwest, c/o Spencer Travel Services, Spencer Junction, MG Rd ☎0471/246 3531; Qatar Airways, Bela Vista,TC 30/1403, near SBT, Nalumukku, Pettah ☎0471/391 9091 (airport ☎0471/250 2548); SriLankan Airlines, 1st Floor, Spencer Building, Palayam, MG Rd ☎0471/247 1815 (airport ☎0471/250 1140).

Ayurveda The best dispensary in the city, where you can also consult doctors free of charge, is the Kottakkal Aryavaidya Sala, Karamana Junction, southeast of the centre on the national highway ☎0471/246 3439.

Banks and exchange A string of big banks along MG Rd – including HDFC, the SBI, UTI and ICICI – have ATMs and change traveller's cheques and currency. Thomas Cook maintains a foreign exchange counter at the airport and at its travel agency on the ground floor of the Soundarya Building (near the big Raymond's tailoring store), MG Rd (Mon–Sat 9.30am–6pm).

Hospitals SP Fort Hospital (☎0471/245 0540), just down the road from the Margi School in West Fort, has a 24hr casualty and specialist orthopaedic unit; the private Cosmopolitan Hospital, in Pattom ☎0471/244 8182 is also recommended. The Government-run General Hospital, 600m east of Statue Circle on MG Rd, is one of the busiest in the state.

Internet access Internet City on Manhalikulam Rd (see map p.94) charges Rs20/hr and is convenient if you're staying in Thampanoor. There's also a tiny, more cramped cybercafé to the rear of the *KTDC Hotel Chaithram*'s lobby, next to the bus stand (Rs30/hr).

Photography and printing The excellent Paramount Colour Lab on Ayurveda College Junction, MG Rd, has state-of-the-art digital printers, sells memory cards and will load data onto discs. In the bowels of the building below ground level there's also a counter specializing in business card printing (Rs1–2/card).

Post office The main post office, with poste restante (daily 8am–6pm), is just south of the Secretariat on MG Rd.

Yoga The Sivananda Yoga Ashram at 37/1929 Airport Rd, Palkulangara, West Fort (☎0471/245 0942 & 245 1398; ✺www.sivananda.org), holds daily classes at various levels. See also the box on p.122.

South of Thiruvananthapuram

Despite the fact that virtually the entire 550-kilometre length of the **Keralan coast** is lined with sandy beaches, rocky promontories and coconut palms, **Kovalam** is one of the only places where swimming in the sea is not considered eccentric by locals, and which offers accommodation to suit all budgets. To experience daily life away from the exploits of the Kovalam beach scene, you can take an easy wander through the toddy groves to villages such as **Pachalloor** and **Vizhinjam**. A finely preserved example of Keralan architecture is also within easy reach of Thiruvananthapuram: 63km to the south lies the magnificent palace of **Padmanabhapuram**, former capital of the kingdom of Travancore.

Kovalam

The coastal village of **KOVALAM** may lie just 14km south of Thiruvananthapuram but, as Kerala's most developed **beach resort**, it's a world away from the rest of the state. Each year greater numbers of Western visitors – budget travellers and package tourists alike – arrive in search of sun, sea and palm-fringed beaches.

Europeans have been visiting Kovalam since the 1930s, but no hotels were built until hippies started to colonize the place some thirty years later. As the resort's popularity began to grow, more and more paddy fields were filled and the first luxury holiday complexes sprang up. These soon caught the eye of European charter companies scouting for "undiscovered" beach hideaways to supplement their Goa brochures, and since the mid-1990s plane loads of package tourists have been flying here direct from Europe. This influx has had a dramatic impact, with rocketing prices and burgeoning numbers of ayurvedic massage centres, Kashmiri souvenir shops and pricy seafood restaurants packed into a narrow strip behind Lighthouse Beach.

Kovalam's metamorphosis has coincided with the rise, along the 20km of sandy coastline stretching south of neighbouring Vizhinjam, of a string of luxury resorts. Specializing in expensive "ayurveda-spa" treatments, these gated, high-walled campuses inhabit a separate universe from the poor fishing communities surrounding them.

Arrival, information and getting around

Buses leave from the roadside south of Thiruvananthapuram's City bus stand every twenty or thirty minutes for Kovalam, looping through the top of the village before coming to a halt outside the gates of the *Leela Kempinski*, on the promontory dividing Hawah and Kovalam beaches. If you don't intend to stay at this northern end of the resort, or at Samudra, get down a couple of hundred metres earlier, just past the *Blue Sea* hotel where the road bends – a lane branching to the left drops steeply downhill towards the top of Hawah Beach. The bus journey generally takes 30–45 minutes, but you can cover the 14km from Thiruvananthapuram more quickly by **auto-rickshaw** (Rs100–125) or **taxi** (Rs350–400).

Expect to be plagued by commission touts as you arrive; an approach via the back paths is a good way of avoiding them. The friendly **tourist office** (daily 10am–5pm, closed Sun in low season; ☎0471/248 0085, ⓦwww.keralatourism .org), just inside the *Leela Kempinski* gates, close to where the buses pull in, stocks the usual range of glossy leaflets on Kerala and can offer up-to-date advice about cultural events in the area.

There are plenty of places to **change money** in Kovalam, but private exchange rates can vary so it's best to check beforehand. The Central Bank of India has a branch at the *Kovalam Beach Resort* and the Andhra Bank at KTDC *Samudra*; but for an **ATM**, you'll have to travel up to **Kovalam Junction**, 3km inland, on the national highway (Rs80–100 return in an auto-rickshaw; see map, p.102).

Western Travels (daily 8am–8pm; ☎0471/248 1334) near the bus stand is a reliable agent for flight confirmations and ticketing, and can arrange **car rental**. Voyager Travels (☎0471/2481993), on the lane cutting uphill from the end of Hawah Beach, specializes in **motorbike rental**, at competitive rates: an Enfield Bullet is Rs350–500 per day; a scooter Rs250. You'll need to leave your driver's license or passport with them as security. **Surfboards** can be rented on Lighthouse Beach for an extortionate Rs250 per hour, or boogie boards for Rs50. Alternatively, for around Rs300 you can take a ride on a traditional **kettumaran** (*kettu* meaning tied; *maran* logs), which gave the catamaran its name. Widely used by the fishermen of Kovalam, the rudimentary boat consists of five logs lashed together with coir rope, and can feel disconcertingly vulnerable in even a slightly choppy sea: accept a lifejacket if it's offered.

Plenty of places offer broadband **Internet** access for Rs40 per hour. Kovalam doesn't have a major **bookshop**, but many of the tailors and clothes stalls supplement their trade by dealing in the usual hit-and-miss selection of secondhand books, and there's a decent selection on offer at a stall upstairs in *Waves (German Bakery)*.

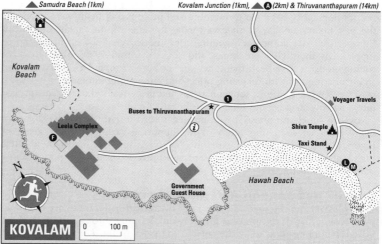

Samudra Beach (1km) — Kovalam Junction (1km), A (2km) & Thiruvananthapuram (14km)

Kovalam Beach

B

Voyager Travels

Buses to Thiruvananthapuram

Leela Complex

Shiva Temple

Taxi Stand

Hawah Beach

Government Guest House

KOVALAM   0   100 m

Accommodation

Although Kovalam is crammed with **accommodation**, decent rock-bottom rooms are hard to find, as all but a handful of the many budget travellers' guesthouses have been upgraded to suit the package tourists who flock here over Christmas and the New Year. This also means that hotels are often block-booked weeks in advance, so it's a good idea to make a reservation before you arrive, which also spares you from the tenacious touts who hang around the edges of the village.

Prices are extortionate compared with the rest of Kerala, almost doubling in peak season (Dec to mid-Jan), when you'll be lucky to find a basic room for less than Rs500. At other times, haggling should bring the rate down by twenty to fifty percent, especially if you stay for more than a week. The codes below are for high-season prices.

Budget

Moon Valley Cottage behind Lighthouse Beach ☎m94461 0029 1248, ✉sknairkovalam@yahoo .com. This simple budget guesthouse stands right next to the footpath leading from the rear of Lighthouse Beach to the Avaduthura Devi temple. Its rooms are really big for the price, have mozzie nets and quality bedding, and are pleasantly decorated. The best are hidden around the back of the building, which overlooks open fields. The same owner also offers a couple of similarly well-priced two-bedroom apartments in another building nearby. ❸–❹

Rockland Lighthouse Rd ☎0471/248 0588. *Rockland* is one of a cluster of three co-run budget hotels, sandwiched together just off the lane above the south end of Lighthouse Beach. It has the edge over its neighbours because its six comfortable rooms – all en suite and with balconies – look straight through coconut palms to the sea. Reasonable rates given the location. ❹

Sea Breeze behind Lighthouse Beach ☎0471/248 0024, ⊛www.seabreezeayurvedicresort.com. One of Kovalam's better-value budget choices: quiet, secluded, with large and sunny communal balconies overlooking a well-tended tropical garden. The rooms (Rs350–700) are clean and large for the price, and there's a yoga *shala* on the top floor where you can attend morning *ashtanga* classes. ❸–❹

Surya Lighthouse Beach ☎0471/248 1012, ✉ kovsurya@yahoo.co.in. Professionally run guesthouse down a narrow lane from the seafront. It's secure and quiet, with pleasant rooms for the price (a/c and non-a/c); some of the verandas look straight onto adjacent buildings, but there's lots of space inside, the beds are new, and the plumbing and electrics sound. One of the better budget options. If it's full, try the equally spruce *White House* (☎0471/248 3388; ❹) next door. ❹

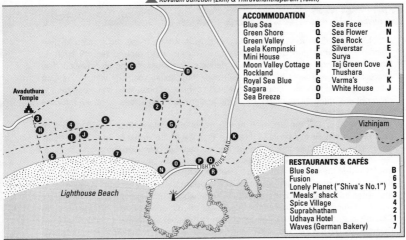

ACCOMMODATION

Blue Sea	B	Sea Face	M
Green Shore	Q	Sea Flower	N
Green Valley	C	Sea Rock	L
Leela Kempinski	F	Silverstar	E
Mini House	R	Surya	J
Moon Valley Cottage	H	Taj Green Cove	A
Rockland	P	Thushara	I
Royal Sea Blue	G	Varma's	K
Sagara	O	White House	J
Sea Breeze	D		

Avaduthura Temple

Vizhinjam

Lighthouse Beach

RESTAURANTS & CAFÉS

Blue Sea	B
Fusion	6
Lonely Planet ("Shiva's No.1")	5
"Meals" shack	3
Spice Village	4
Suprabhatham	2
Udhaya Hotel	1
Waves (German Bakery)	7

Mid-range

Blue Sea 100m before junction to Hawah Beach ☎0471/248 1401 & ☎m93499 91992, ⓦwww .hotelskerala.com/bluesea. Half-a-dozen quirky round buildings in the rear garden of a grand double-fronted colonial-era mansion overlooking the main road above Hawah Beach. Each contains three rooms, arranged on separate storeys around a (rather shabby) central pool; they're spacious, cool and good value, with plenty of outside balcony space. There are also a couple of older, more atmospheric rooms in the main house, furnished with antique carved wood beds and fronted by pillared verandas. An established favourite, and the owner-managers – brothers Sabu and Saji – are welcoming. ⑤–⑥

Green Shore Lighthouse Rd ☎0471/248 0106, ⓦwww.thegreenshore.com. Eight impeccably smart, well-furnished rooms in a modern building close to the lighthouse. It's is a bit boxed in, but the interiors are nicely done (glossy ceramic tiled floors, split-cane blinds, low twin-beds with thick mattresses, and fancy bedside lamps) and there are big common verandas to lounge on. Tariffs increase the higher up the block you go. A/c costs Rs600 extra. ④–⑤

Green Valley behind Lighthouse Beach ☎0471/248 0636, ⓔindira_ravi@hotmail.com. Set on the edge of the open land a couple of hundred metres or so from the beach, this is one of Kovalam's longest-established guesthouses. It holds a range of differently priced rooms, from dingy singles to spacious a/c options large enough for three people, but the building itself is an unsightly hotch potch and few of the balconies offer much privacy. ④–⑤

Mini House Lighthouse Rd ☎0471/248 0867, ⓔnaswara@hotmail.com. Six large, simply furnished, sea-facing non-a/c rooms in a prime spot on the rocks above a small cove, just under the lighthouse. The balconies catch uninterrupted breezes, though even allowing for the great location it's a bit overpriced. ⑤–⑥

Royal Sea Blue behind Lighthouse Beach ☎0471/212 7857, ⓦwww.royalseablue.com. Recently built three-storey block, well off the road in the palm groves. Fronted by a large garden that's big enough for kids to run around in, the rooms are sparkling, with polished marble floors, TVs, fridges and separate a/c units (Rs500 extra), and the location is very peaceful. ⑤–⑥

Sagara Lighthouse Beach ☎0471/248 1995, ⓦwww.sagarabeachresort.com. This is the kind of place that looks much better from the inside than out: a sprawling, multi-storey complex of 42 slightly worn a/c rooms, stacked up the hillside above Lighthouse Beach. The views are great, and there's a small pool and rooftop restaurant. Basically a charter hotel, but they accept walk-ins and offer good discounts for longer stays. ⑥

Sea Face Hawah Beach ☎0471/248 1835, ⓦwww.seaface.com. An ugly modern block slap on the beachfront, with three-star pretensions. Looking across a raised pool and café terrace to the sea, its rooms are fronted by little walled sun decks; each has its own fridge, cable TV and good-sized bathroom. ⑧–⑨

Keralan ayurvedic treatments

"Health tourism" is very much a buzz phrase in Kerala these days. International-standard hospitals and dental clinics have mushroomed around resorts such as Kovalam, catering for cost-conscious patients from abroad who've travelled here expressly for treatments, while no self-respecting luxury resort is without its own money-spinning "ayurvedic spa" or "wellness centre". Hippies who first came here to drop out are, three decades on, returning to detox and de-stress – and even for the odd hip replacement.

Synonymous with the boom in health travel is Kerala's close association with **ayurvedic medicine**. Ayurveda, literally "science of life" (described in more detail on p.65), is an ancient system of herbal healing practised throughout India. Nowhere, however, are its Sanskrit roots so strictly adhered to as in the far southwest of the country, where the great sage **Agasthya** is said to have developed the *siddha* form of medicine from which modern ayurveda evolved. Legend also attributes the discovery of the sacred Agashtyakooda mountain on the Tamil–Kerala border, famous as a source of medicinal herbs of unparallelled potency, to Agasthya. According to tradition, eighteen families were originally chosen by Lord Brahma to hold the secrets of ayurveda. Over time these dwindled to eight – known as the **Ashtavaidyas** – of whom only six still practise, mostly around the towns of Thrissur and Kozhikode (see opposite).

The Keralan approach to ayurveda has two distinct elements: first, the body is cleansed of toxins generated by imbalances in lifestyle and diet; secondly, its equilibrium is restored using herbal medicines, mainly in the form of plant oils applied using a range of different massage techniques. A practitioner's first prescription will often be a course of **panchakarma** treatment – a five-phase therapy during which harmful impurities are purged through induced vomiting, enemas, and the application of medicinal oils poured through the nasal cavity. Other less onerous components, tailored for the individual patient, may include: *dhara*, where the oils are blended with ghee or milk and poured onto the forehead; *pizhichi*, in which a team of four masseurs apply different oils simultaneously; and, the weirdest looking of all, *sirovashti*, where the oils are poured into a tall, topless leather cap placed on the head.

Alongside these, patients are prescribed special balancing foods, and given vigorous full-body **massages**, or *abhayangam*, each day. Some practitioners may also offer **marma chikitsa** foot massage, a Keralan speciality where pressure is applied to the body with the soles of the feet; to control how much weight he or she brings to bear, the masseur grips a knotted rope suspended from the ceiling. The technique, which focuses on key connective energy "*marma*" points, was originally developed by masters of the martial art, *kalarippayattu*; part of every fighter's training routine involves a gruelling oily rubdown before dawn, as does the beginning of a typical *kathakali* student's day.

Sea Flower ☏0471/248 0554, ⊛www .seaflowerbeachresort.com. You can't get closer to the sea than the orange-painted *Sea Flower*, which rises straight from the sand at the south end of Lighthouse Beach. Facing the surf, its spacious, breezy and comfortable rooms are spread over two storeys – the upper ones cost Rs350 extra, but are worth it for the views. **❹**

Sea Rock Hawah Beach ☏0471/248 0422. One of Kovalam's oldest hotels, right on the seafront and with a popular terrace restaurant. At identical prices to the *Sea Face* next door, the a/c rooms are perfectly aligned for the sunset views over the beach. It's a popular choice, requiring at least a fortnight's advance booking, despite the high tariffs and busy location. **❽**

Silverstar behind Lighthouse Beach ☏0471/248 2883, ☏m98956 73443, ⊛www .silverstar-kovalam.com. Owned by a welcoming German-Keralan couple, the *Silverstar* is a relative newcomer hidden away in the palm groves a couple of hundred metres inland from the beach. Centred

Where to go

Kerala's tourist resorts are full of places offering ayurvedic cures for every conceivable ailment. Few of them, however, are staffed by fully qualified practitioners, despite what the certificates displayed on their walls may suggest. Standards of both treatment and hygiene vary greatly, as do the prices – a significant factor if you sign up for a minimum three-week stint, as most places advise. Woman travellers also sometimes complain of sexual harassment at the hands of opportunistic male masseurs; cross-gender massage is forbidden in ayurveda, though the rule is routinely ignored in small, tourist-oriented centres. Dodgy oils that can cause skin problems is another risk you might be exposed to at a backstreet clinic.

The only sure-fire way to be guaranteed bona fide treatment is to splash out on somewhere that's been approved by the government. Kerala Tourism's **accreditation scheme** divides centres into **Green Leaf** establishments – which apply the highest standards of hygiene, employ only pukka staff, never allow cross-gender massage, and use top-grade oils and medicines – and **Olive Leaf** ones, which offer equally dependable treatments, but in more traditionally Keralan surroundings, with massage tables carved from medicinal hardwoods, beautiful earth-walled practice rooms, yoga *shalas* and steam baths on site. This is the kind of place generally referred to as an **ayurvedic spa** and will nearly always be attached to a posh seaside hotel or heritage resort, offering packages that include gourmet vegetarian meals, yoga lessons and cultural programmes in the evenings. We've listed many such places in this chapter, but have – with a handful of tried and tested exceptions – steered clear of smaller, less expensive clinics, whose credentials may be harder to verify.

For all the claims many make, most outfits around Kovalam and Varkala – even the pricey ones – should be regarded primarily as places to seek **rejuvenation** rather than cures for **serious medical conditions**. If you've come to Kerala in search of treatment for a chronic illness of some kind, then you'd do better to explore the possibility of a spell at one of the old *Ashtavaidya* **ayurveda hospitals** listed below, which are famous all over India for the quality of their doctors and medicines, produced on their own organic estates and in-house labs. You'll need to set aside a minimum of four weeks, and book at least nine months in advance.

Arya Vaidya Sala Kottakkal near Malappuram in northern Kerala (26km from Kozhikode airport) ☎0483/274 2216, ⓦwww.aryavaidyasala.com.

SNA Oushadhasala near Jubilee Museum, Thrissur ☎0487/242 0948, ⓦwww.thaikatmooss.com.

Vaidyaratnam Oushadhasala Thaikkattussen, 8km from Thrissur ☎0487/235 3610, ⓦwww.vaidyaratnammooss.com.

Regardless of the kind of treatment you go for, and where you go for it, bear in mind the **optimal season for ayurveda** is said to be during the monsoons (June–Oct), when the air is free of dust and the humidity promotes detoxifying perspiration.

---

on a well-shaded, beaten-earth courtyard, the location is tranquil by Kovalam standards, leafy and cool, and the rooms very large, with verandas or terraces out front, and new mozzie nets inside. **❼**
Thushara behind Lighthouse Beach ☎0471/248 1694, ⓦwww.hotelthushara.net. Small but slick hotel in the thick of the action, mostly given over to charter tourists. The rooms are large and comfortable, and have private balconies overlooking a central, well-maintained swimming pool. Rates include continental breakfast. **❻**

Varma's Lighthouse Rd ☎0471/248 0478, ⓔvarmabeach@hotmail.com. One of the few places in Kovalam that's tried to incorporate traditional Keralan architecture into its design (despite being Goan-owned). The result is an attractive blend of modern comforts and old-style Malabari wood and brass décor. All twelve rooms are sea-facing, tastefully fitted with block-printed textiles, and open onto secluded balconies. It's also well placed for the less frequented cove south of Lighthouse Beach. **❽**

Luxury

Taj Green Cove GV Raja Ratapara Rd, Samudra ⌖0471/248 7733, Ⓦwww.tajhotels.com. Taj Group's new luxury resort is spread over a lush, wooded hillside a kilometre back from Kovalam and Samudra beaches (over the headland from Hawah). Clad with local grey granite and elephant-grass thatch, its faux-rustique chalets are lined with polished teak and open onto lovely sea-facing verandas smothered in greenery. Golf buggies ("club cars") whisk guests from the lobby area, with its open-kitchen *Jasmine* restaurant,

infinity pool and bar billiards table, to a private fishing lagoon and sunbathing area next to the sea. Rooms from $340 per night. Ⓞ
Leela Kempinski Hawah-Kovalam ⌖0471/248 0101, Ⓦwww.theleela.com/kovalam. This "five-star-deluxe" resort, set in 44 acres of mature woodland which you navigate in golf buggies, sweeps down the hillside to its own exclusive end of Kovalam Beach. Wonderful views extend out to sea and up the coast from a pair of dreamy infinity pools. Rooms come in a range of categories, from around $300. Ⓞ

The beaches

Kovalam consists of four fairly small stretches of sand; the southernmost, known for obvious reasons as **Lighthouse Beach**, is where most visitors spend their time. It takes about ten minutes to walk from end to end, either along the sand or on the concrete pathway (patrolled by lots of touts) which fronts a long strip of resorts, guesthouses and restaurants. You can hire surfboards, venture out to sea in wooden *Kettumaran* (see p.107) or hire beach chairs and parasols for the day.

The red-and-white-striped **lighthouse**, on the promontory at the southern end of the beach, is the area's most prominent landmark. It opens for two hours each afternoon (daily 3–5pm; Rs5), when you can scale the 142 spiral steps and twelve ladder rungs to the observation platform: on clear days, views extend over the beach as far as Beemapalli mosque in one direction, and south to Poovar in the other.

South of the lighthouse, a tiny white-sand cove opens into a much larger beach, overlooked by a scattering of upmarket hotels, which you can reach by following the lane that peels off Lighthouse Road, before *Varma's Beach Resort* (see map, pp.108–109). Lots of tourists mistakenly believe this is a private area, but it isn't.

Heading in the opposite direction (northwards) from Lighthouse Beach, you round a small rocky headland to reach **Hawah Beach** – almost a mirror image of its busier neighbour, although it is backed for most of its length by empty palm groves. In the morning before the sunworshippers arrive, it functions primarily as a base for local fishermen, who hand-haul their massive nets through the shallows, singing and chanting as they coil the endless piles of rope.

North of the next headland, **Kovalam Beach** is dominated by the angular chalets of the five-star *Leela* above it. Home to a small mosque, it's shared by guests of the luxury resort and local fishermen in roughly equal measure; to get there, follow the road downhill past the bus terminus.

Only a short walk further north, **Samudra Beach** is very small, especially at high tide, and is backed by a cluster of package-tour resorts surrounding a tiny

Warning: swimming safety

Due to unpredictable rip currents and a strong undertow, especially during the monsoons, **swimming** from Kovalam's beaches is not always safe. The introduction of blue-shirted lifeguards has reduced the annual death toll, but at least a couple of tourists still drown here each year, and many more get into difficulties. Follow the warnings of the safety flags at all times and keep a close eye on children. There's a first-aid post midway along Lighthouse Beach.

The Kuttanad backwaters

An immense labyrinth of interconnecting canals, islets, paddy fields, glassy lagoons and inland lakes, the Kuttanad backwaters of central and southern Kerala encompass a landscape and way of life unique in India. Nowhere else will you encounter Orthodox Syrian-Christian bishops with Father-Christmas beards rushing to mass in speedboats, huge flocks of domestic ducks being shepherded by their owners from canoes, coir-makers punting rafts of coconut husks to market or crews of 150 bare-chested men racing medieval longboats against a backdrop of dense palm forest. Yet this ecologically fragile region is facing some serious challenges from land reclamation, pesticide pollution and – alarmingly – mass tourism.

Life below sea level

Kuttanad owes its distinctive geography to the proximity of the **Western Ghat mountains**, 100km inland, which block the advance of the monsoon clouds when they sweep in from the Arabian Sea in early June. The resulting rainfall – between three and nine metres in places – then drains across the coastal lowlands, dragging with it a deluge of alluvial silt. Managed by a complex system of sluices, pumps, dykes and dams, this annual flow is the key to the backwaters' fertility (Kuttanad has for centuries served as Kerala's rice bowl), but also means its inhabitants spend half their lives two metres below mean sea level.

Sustained by a bountiful supply of rice, coconuts and fish, Kuttanadis have adapted ingeniously to life in the floodwaters. **Canals** whose courses have been fixed for

Snake boat racing

Of all the craft native to the Kuttanad backwaters, none is more majestic than the mighty **snake boats** – *chundan vallam* – raced each year in around a dozen different locations at the start of the Onam harvest festival. Up to 130 rowers crew these slender, seventy-metre-long vessels, which are distinguished by their graceful cobra-shaped prows and beautiful brass studwork. The striking design evolved five centuries ago after a local ruler ordered a warship to be built that could absorb the recoil of a canon. Nowadays, the position of the big gun on the firing platform is occupied by two drummers whose job it is to beat out the rhythm for the oarsmen to follow, aided by a choir of 25 singers. The strongest rowers sit at the front to set the pace, while the boat is steered by six helmsmen at the rear.

Intense competition surrounds the **annual races**, with crews training for weeks ahead of the big events. Alappuzha's Nehru Trophy is the main meet of the year, but similar, more traditional races are held on waterways across the Kuttanad region for the duration of the monsoons.

centuries by carefully laid stone embankments serve as the region's main arteries. Views constantly change as you glide around them: narrow channels clogged with purple water hyacinth yield to mirror-like stretches of open water, where every now and then a whitewashed church tower or blast of film music will reveal the presence of a hidden village. Kingfishers and parakeets screech from the shadows, and fish eagles flap lazily past in search of prey.

▲ An egret in the backwaters

Whether you travel around in local diesel-powered ferries, converted rice barges or canoes, scenes of everyday domestic life on **riverbanks** are what linger longest in the memory: kids being paddled to school, their satchels piled high on the bows of slender dugouts; women soaping down babies or thumping piles of washing on the front steps of little red-tiled houses; fishermen diving for clams; and itinerant vegetable vendors haggling with travellers on the river.

Kettu vallam

Traditional boat-building may be declining in other parts of Kerala, but it remains a growth industry in Kuttanad, not least because of the exponential rise in tourist cruises over the past decade. Old-style *kettu vallam* **rice barges** were the backwaters' answer to trucks, hauling paddy, building materials and any other heavy goods to and from the towns. With the spread of roads across the coastal lowlands, these elegant old vessels, distinguished by their coir and palm-leaf canopies, looked as if they'd become redundant. Then local entrepreneurs started taking visitors out in them, adding bedrooms, dining rooms and viewing platforms scattered with cushions and lanterns. Now about five hundred ply the backwaters around Vembanad Lake, Kuttanad's largest lagoon, and the boatyards that make them have waiting lists a couple of years long.

Kettu vallam are still made by hand, using techniques that have altered little in hundreds, and possibly thousands, of years. Amazingly, no nails or any other artificial substances are used in the **construction process**. Seasoned planks of *anjili* ("angelin") wood, a local relative of the breadfruit tree, are lashed together using cotton and coir ropes soaked in resin before the hull is waterproofed with cashew oil. Then the trademark canopy is added, its vents made by moulding soaked bamboo mats into curves. It takes a team of three to six carpenters an average of six months to build a medium-sized *kettu vallam*.

◀ A *kettu vallam* barge

A disappearing world

Balanced for centuries by careful land and water management, the delicate ecosystem of the Kuttanad backwaters has started to buckle under the weight of recent environmental pressures. Nitrates from rice fields have promoted the growth of invasive plants and algae, which form a thick layer that clogs canals and has decimated the local fishing industry. Meanwhile, land-reclamation work has accelerated to keep up with a rapidly rising population, reducing the total water area of Kuttanad by two thirds in a little over a century. But from a visitor's perspective, by far the most noticeable encroachment of the modern era on this area's traditional atmosphere is the constant stream of motorized tourist traffic chugging around it, especially rice barges. Although they provide seasonal employment for some, the luxury boats are resented by many locals as an intrusion, and for the polluting slicks of oil and diesel left in their wake. There are, however, cleaner, more environmentally friendly alternatives; for some pointers, see p.145.

▼ Backwater traffic

temple. It holds little to recommend it during the day, but comes alive at night, when rows of restaurant tables spring up along the seawall.

To escape the beach scene altogether, head into the cool and shaded **coconut groves** behind Lighthouse Beach's hotel strip. Here, ladies gossip in shrill Malayalam while they wash clothes and children in the village tank, sewing machines whirr as tailors run up cheap cotton clothes for the tourists and kids play innovative versions of cricket with coconut shells and sticks. Bear in mind that although the sight of Westerners in skimpy bathing suits on the beach has become relatively normal for locals, it's polite to dress in a respectful manner when walking in the palm groves or near Kovalam Beach's mosque.

Ayurvedic centres

Kovalam is crammed with places offering all manner of ayurvedic treatments, ranging from grubby massage shacks in the palm grove behind Lighthouse Beach to fully accredited Olive Leaf clinics in the nearby five-star resorts complete with their own teak-lined steam rooms and beachside yoga *shalas*. See our box on ayurveda (p.110) for general advice on finding a reputable place.

One thoroughly dependable mid-scale centre worth singling out, both for the standard of its practitioners and overall ambience, is *Amruthamgamaya* (☏94478/56461), tucked away on the edge of Venganoor village, 4km inland from Kovalam. Equipped with traditional palm-thatch, mud-walled huts, as well as an open-sided yoga hall where clients may attend free classes, it offers the full gamut of ayurvedic treatments at fair prices. Phone ahead for directions, as not even the local rickshaw-wallahs know where to find it.

Eating, drinking and nightlife

Lighthouse Beach is lined with identikit cafés and restaurants specializing in **seafood**: you pick from displays of fresh fish such as blue marlin, sea salmon, barracuda and delicious seer fish, as well as lobster, tiger prawns, crab and mussels. They are then weighed, grilled over a charcoal fire or cooked in a tandoor (traditional clay oven), and served with rice, salad or chips. Meals are **pricey** by Indian standards – typically around Rs175–350 per head for fresh fish, and double that for lobster or prawns – and service is often painfully slow, but the food is generally very good and the ambience of the beachfront terraces convivial.

For **breakfast** you can choose from any number of cafés offering the usual brown bread, fruit salad and pancakes, or try a traditional Keralan breakfast at one of the local teashops near the bus stand. Freshly cooked, delicious Keralan *appam* and egg masala are also on offer at a makeshift shelter on the side of the pathway leading from Lighthouse Beach to the Avaduthura Devi temple. Further along the same path, on the right next to where it meets the surfaced lane, the locals enjoy tasty rice-plate thali **"meals"** for around Rs20 at a nameless, dingy shack. It's a rough and ready place, and you'll have to squeeze onto narrow tables to eat, but the food is delicious and probably more hygienic than most of the stuff served on the beach.

Nightlife in Kovalam is pretty laid-back, and revolves around the beach, where Westerners chill when the restaurants close. Beer and spirits are served in most cafés, albeit in discrete china teapots from under the table due to tight liquor restrictions. One or two places also run **movie nights**, screening pirate copies of just-released hits.

During your stay in Kovalam you may be offered marijuana, but bear in mind that cannabis is illegal in Kerala, as everywhere else in India, and that the local police occasionally conduct raids.

Blue Sea above Hawah Beach ☎0471/248 1401, ☏m93499 91992. Mouthwatering garlic prawns (Rs250) and tandoori chicken are the two specialities of this slightly off-beat restaurant at the top of the village. Meals are served at poolside tables in a quiet rear garden. Phone ahead, preferably in the morning, to book and pre-order.

🏃 Fusion Lighthouse Beach. Along with Waves, the funkiest place on Lighthouse Beach, with three innovative menus (Eastern, Western and fusion), served on a first-floor terrace overlooking the bay. Try the fish creole in orange vinaigrette with cumin potatoes, one of the Keralan seafood specialities, or home-made tagliatelle and chilli pesto. They also have fine selection of drinks, a hefty sound system playing Indo-Western music, and a toilet that has to be seen to be believed. Most mains Rs180.

Lonely Planet ("Shiva's No.1") behind Lighthouse Beach. Flanked by a pond that's alive with croaking frogs, the covered terrace of this large, family-run budget travellers' place is one of the most enduringly popular restaurants in the village, and a relaxed spot to while away an evening. Its menu of North and South Indian vegetarian standards is nothing to write home about, though inexpensive for Kovalam (most mains Rs50–80) and the food is well tempered for the sensitive Western palate. Wed evenings host a cultural show with all-you-can-eat buffet (7.30–9pm; Rs150; book in advance).

Spice Village behind Lighthouse Beach. In much the same mould as the nearby Lonely Planet, though smaller and run by a posse of local lads in snazzy shirts rather than a family, and it also serves cold Kingfishers.

Suprabhatham near the Silverstar. Simple, popular vegetarian café-restaurant in a well-shaded garden setting, where you can order inexpensive Indian breakfasts, fresh juices, lassis and shakes, as well as an extensive multi-cuisine menu: the "Bengali aubergine" and "chunky avocado salad" are popular specials. Evenings tend to end with the staff downing stiff whisky-and-soda slammers around 10.30pm, after which the service and cooking degenerate rapidly.

Udhaya Hotel near the bus terminus. Hidden away behind a tiny general store, this local teashop serves the best Keralan breakfasts for miles, in a narrow, blue-walled cafeteria lined with Hindu, Muslim and Christian religious pictures. Huge trays of steaming iddiappam (rice-flour vermicelli), puttu (rice rolls) and appam (steamed pancakes made from fermented rice flour) are brought at regular intervals down the wooden staircase from the kitchen on banana leaves, and served with tin plates of egg masala, spicy sambar and more-ish chickpea chana wada. The chai's delicious too. You'll be hard pushed to spend more than Rs25 per head here.

🏃 Waves (German Bakery) Lighthouse Beach. This rooftop terrace, shaded by a high tiled canopy, functions as a laid-back café during the daytime, where you can order light meals, snacks, German cakes and delicious, freshly ground coffee. After sunset, its atmospheric designer lighting makes a great backdrop for more sophisticated cooking: Thai and Kerala seafood curries, lobster in vodka, fish steaks with sesame and coriander crust, or steamed prawns with chilli and coconut milk. For desert, go for the Malabar fruit flambée. Most mains Rs175–200.

North of Kovalam: Pozhikkara and Pachalloor

If you need a break from the rampant commercialism of Kovalam, keep plodding north along Samudra Beach for around 4km, past a string of fishing hamlets, until you arrive at a point where the sea merges with the backwaters to form a salt-water lagoon.

Although only thirty or forty minutes' walk away, the sliver of white sand known as **Pozhikkara Beach** is a world away from the holiday culture of Kovalam. Here, the sands are used primarily for landing fish and fixing nets. **PACHALLOOR**, a quiet village sandwiched behind the lagoon and nearby highway, makes a good alternative base for the area, with two appealing places to stay. The British-run Lagoona Davina (☎0471/238 0049, Ⓦwww .lagoonadavina.com; ❾), a small, exclusive boutique hotel overlooking the river mouth, is the pricier of the pair, patronized mainly by well-to-do Brits. Costing around $160/Rs7000 per night in season, its rooms are small but individually styled, with carved wood four-posters, Indian textiles and animal paintings. They open onto a terrace where staff wearing cummerbunds and

△ Hand-net fishing near Kovalam

gold-edged saris serve a mixture of indifferent Keralan dishes and low-fat European cuisine (Rs700 for three courses).

The other guesthouse at Pachalloor, the *Beach and Lake Resort* (☎0471/238 2086, Ⓦwww.beachandlakeresort.com; Rs3500; Ⓞ), lies across the water from *Lagoona Davina* (you'll have to hail a boatman to reach it). It's an altogether more down-to-earth affair, with less inspired interiors, but an even better location closer to the surf and fishing beach. Opening onto a relaxing waterside terrace, the rooms are spacious, with correspondingly large bathrooms, and at around Rs3500 per night in season cost half of what you pay in *Lagoona*.

Both guesthouses organize guided **backwater trips** and offer ayurvedic massages and yoga classes. If you book in advance, drivers can be dispatched to meet you at the airport; otherwise take a taxi 6km along the highway towards Kovalam, and bear right along the "bypass" where the road forks, just after the Thiruvallam bridge. After another 1km or so, signboards on the right-hand side of the road point through the trees to the guesthouses.

South of Kovalam: Vizhinjam to Poovar

A tightly packed cluster of tiled fishers' huts, **VIZHINJAM** (pronounced "Virinyam"), on the opposite (south) side of the headland from Lighthouse Beach, was once the capital of the Ay kings, the earliest dynasty in south Kerala. During the ninth century the Pandyans fought to control it, and it was the scene of major Chola–Chera battles in the eleventh century. A number of simple small shrines survive from those times, and can be made the focus of a pleasant afternoon's stroll through coconut groves, best approached from the centre of the village rather than the coast road – brace yourself for the sharp contrast between hedonistic tourist resort and workaday fishing village.

A strikingly modern pink **mosque** on the promontory overlooks the Muslim quarter, home to around 3000 fishermen; the Christian area, with a population of around 7000, lies on the opposite side of the bay, beneath a large church. Tension between the two has frequently erupted into riots, and the village remains something of a communal flashpoint, a situation not helped by ongoing disputes over proposals to upgrade Vizhinjam harbour into a massive container

The price of fish

From the comfort of a sunbed in Kovalam, it's easy to be lulled by official tourist office rhetoric about Kerala being a "land of plenty". But you only have to stroll around the headland to neighbouring Vizhinjam to realize that for the **traditional fishing communities** who live and work on this stretch of coast, life is far from a beach.

Kerala's fishermen rank among the region's poorest groups, suffering levels of income, literacy and life expectancy well below the state average. Their one-room mud-brick, plastic-walled shacks are little more than slums, often without running water. Child mortality rates are high, and alcoholism and domestic violence all too common.

The roots of this enduring poverty, which has proved impervious to Kerala's much-touted communist reforms and trickle-down from the recent economic boom, are many and complicated. Barred until the 1930s from temples, churches and schools, local fishermen have always been trapped on one of the lowest rungs of the social hierarchy. For centuries they were obliged to sell their fish at rock-bottom rates to socially superior dealers, who often doubled as money-lenders. With interest rates fixed at a crippling ten percent per day, anyone who borrowed to buy a new boat or net would soon find himself bogged down in spiralling debt.

The problem was only compounded by the arrival on India's southwest coast of the Roman Catholic church. Francis (later "Saint Francis") Xavier and other Jesuit missionary priests who travelled here in the sixteenth century in search of converts found fertile pastures amid the disempowered, oppressed sub-castes of Malabar and Travancore. But the churches they left in their wake creamed a further ten percent off the income of their poor congregations – hence the large churches and tiny dwellings in many Christian quarters.

In the 1960s and 1970s, some progress was made when radicalized Marxist clergy, inspired by Latin-American-style **Liberation Theology**, attempted to unionize Kerala's fishing communities. **Cooperatives** were set up to buy and market the daily catch, enabling them to bypass middlemen and claim fairer prices for their fish, as well as access low-interest loans. However, the benefits of collective action were soon wiped out by a big government-led promotion of **mechanized trawler fishing** in the 1980s, which in the space of a few years decimated fish stocks and led to a fifty percent drop in yields for artisanal inshore fishers.

Among the consequences of the deepening poverty and resentment has been an upsurge in **communal tension**, as rival political parties seeking to exploit the discontent for short-term electoral gains stoke up hatred between opposing religious communities. In Vizhinjam, repeated – and often violent – clashes between Christians and Muslims have given rise to a bleak no-man's-land between the Muslim quarter, clustered around the large pink mosque on the north side of the harbour, and the larger Christian area, spread below the church on the opposite side of the bay. Communal divisions were further exacerbated by the **2004 Boxing Day Tsunami**, or more particularly the aid which arrived in its wake: most of the money came not from the government, but NGOs with religious or caste affiliations, and was spent accordingly.

The worst outburst in the recent spate of religious conflicts along the shoreline, however, occurred in 2005–6 at the northern Keralan fishing settlement of **Marada**, where a dozen people were killed after fighting erupted between Dheevara-caste Hindus and their Muslims neighbours. With party politics aggravating the age-old dividers of caste and religion, the prospects of peace and prosperity spreading from the tourist resorts to their adjacent fishing villages seem as remote as ever.

port. The plan was recently shelved in favour of a rival site in Tamil Nadu, but the recriminations rumble on.

On the far side of the fishing bay in the village centre, fifty metres down a road opposite the police station, a small unfinished eighth-century **rock shrine** features a carved figure of Shiva with a weapon. The **Tali Shiva** temple nearby, reached by a narrow path from behind the government primary school, may mark the original centre of Vizhinjam. The simple shrine is accompanied by a group of *naga* snake statues, a reminder of Kerala's continuing cult of snake worship, a survivor from pre-Brahminical times.

Toward the sea, ten minutes' walk from the village's main road along Hidyatnagara Road, the grove known as **Kovil Kadu** ("temple forest") holds a square Shiva shrine and a rectangular one dedicated to the goddess **Bhagavati**. Thought to date from the ninth century, these are probably the earliest structural temples in Kerala, although the Bhagavati shrine has been renovated.

Nellinkunnu, Pulinkudi, Chowara and Poovar

Golden-sand beaches fringe the shore stretching southwards from Vizhinjam, interrupted only by the occasional rock outcrop and tidal estuary. This dramatic coastline, with its backdrop of thick coconut plantations, can appear peaceful compared with Kovalam, but it's actually one of the most densely populated – and intensely political – corners of the state. Fishing villages, dominated by out-size churches and garishly painted Hindu temples, line the entire 25km of road that winds south along the shoreline. As in Vizhinjam, communal tensions often run high, and the sand remains primarily somewhere to defecate and work rather than swim off (the undertow can be treacherous) – not that this has in the least deterred the developers. Over the past decade, virtually every metre of land backing the prettiest stretches of coast has been bought up and built on. Five kilometres south of Kovalam, at **Nellinkunnu** and neighbouring **Pulinkudi**, low, terraced cliffs enfold a sequence of beautiful palm-backed coves, each overlooked by its own luxury resort complex. Nearly all of them follow the same formula, focusing on ayurvedic *panchakarma* treatments (see p.110), with accommodation provided in individual thatched, air-conditioned "cottages" or antique wooden houses relocated from Keralan villages.

It's worth renting a scooter and exploring the back lanes and secluded beaches of this distinctive area – a sometimes surreal mix of undeveloped Malayali fishing villages and sumptuous wellness retreats. One of the region's most memorable views can be enjoyed just north of **Chowara** village, 8km south of Kovalam, where an oddly-proportioned kneeling Christ statue surveys the sands from atop a rocky bluff. Beyond it, an endless sandy beach yawns south to the horizon, scattered with literally hundreds of wooden boats.

Chowara Beach peters out twelve kilometres further south at **Poovar**, where the Neyyar River flows into the sea. Before some cataclysmic event threw up a sandbar here, a harbour used to overlook the river mouth, which some historians claim may have been the port Orphyr – famous in the ancient world as a source of spices, slaves and gemstones. The backwaters behind the sandbar today shelter a cluster of luxury hideaways, only reachable by boat, and these make comfortable bases for forays beyond the tourist belt at the southern tip of Kerala. Non-guests may travel out to them, but will have to pay for the transfer (usually around Rs250).

Accommodation south of Kovalam

The twenty-kilometre stretch of coast between Kovalam and Poovar harbours more than thirty **luxury resorts** and **ayurvedic spas**, in addition to a handful of more homely **guesthouses**. The following, divided into areas, are the pick of the crop.

Nellinkunnu & Pulinkudi

Bethsaida Hermitage Pulinkudi ℡0471/226 7554, ⦿www.bethsaida-c.org. An "eco-friendly ayurvedic beach resort" with a difference. The comforts – huge, well-furnished rooms in brick cottages or an imposing new block, with a pool, à la carte restaurant and prime location right next to a beautiful cove – are standard for the area, but the profits support a church-run orphanage for 1700 boys and girls – a great initiative that's been doing a fine job for more than a decade; and at $126 per night, it's cheaper than most of the competition. ⑨

Karikkathi Beach House Pulinkudi ℡0471/240 0956, ⦿www .karikkathibeachhouse.com. Simplicity is the essence of this exquisite little bolthole, nestled amid the palm trees above a quiet cove, only a stone's throw from the surf. You pay more for the location than luxury, though the house – encircled by a low wall with two en-suite rooms opening onto a common, sea-facing veranda – has its own understated style: white walls, traditional terracotta tiles, wood furniture and window shutters set the tone. Staff are on hand to provide drinks and meals. One of the most desirable places to stay in South India, though such exclusivity comes at a price ($266 per double room, or $535 if you book the whole house – recommended for privacy). ⑨

Surya Samudra Pulinkudi ℡0471/248 0413, ⦿www.suryasamudra.com. The dreamiest of all the "heritage resorts" on this strip. An army of Keralan woodworkers and stone sculptors from Mammallapuram were drafted in to reconstruct its antique, gabled villas, scattered across a 21-acre promontory between a pair of quiet beaches. The stone carvings, oiled rosewood and bowls of floating hibiscus and marigolds glow to magical effect in the evening sunlight. Each room is individually styled with devotional statues and opulent textiles, and the pool, adapted from a former stone quarry, features underwater sculptures. $185–530. ⑨

Thapovan Nellinkunnu, Mullor PO ℡0471/248 0453, ⦿www.thapovan.com. This German-run heritage resort comprises two separate parts: one in a grove next to the seashore, and another higher up the hillside, on a cliff. The latter's elevated position and views across the palm canopy to Vizhinjam give it the edge, and the traditional teak chalets, set amid well-tended gardens, are lovely. Indian Classical concerts are a regular feature, plus the usual ayurvedic and yoga facilities are on site. Doubles from $115. ⑨

Chowara

Dr Franklin's Chowara ℡0471/248 0870, ⦿www.dr-franklin.com. Dr Franklin was among the first Keralan physicians to spot the tourism potential of ayurvedic medicine, and though his resort may not be as easy on the eye as some in this area, the *panchakarma* treatments it provides are of the highest quality. Accommodation comes in the form of "special" or larger "deluxe" rooms with tiled floors and patios, thatched mud huts (fully en suite) and swish new Western-style rooms. ⑥–⑦

Nikki's Nest Azhimala Shiva Temple Rd, Chowara ℡0471/226 8822, ⦿www.nikkisnest.com. Set on a steep slope with direct access to a hidden cove below, this family-run resort of Keralan-style structures (gable-roofed, wooden houses, a/c rooms and semi-detached cottages) blends traditional architecture with modern amenities. The campus centres on a multi-cuisine restaurant and good-sized pool, with uninterrupted views of the sea and beach. $115–230. ⑨

Somatheeram Chowara ℡0471/226 6501, ⦿www.somatheeram.org. *Somatheeram* established the model which countless ayurvedic health resorts have followed, packaging high-quality herbal therapies with accommodation in traditional-style Keralan houses fitted with a/c and other mod cons. When you're not being doused with medicinal oils, you can relax in a range of rooms – from budget stone cottages with thatched roofs and shared bathrooms to luxurious two-bedroomed wood *tharavadukal* sporting antique doors and pillared verandas – all stacked on terraces overlooking the beach. Sister concern *Manaltheeram* (℡0471/226 6222, ⦿www.manaltheeram.com), next door, offers more of the same, plus a pool (open for guests of *Somatheeram*). Doubles $100–250. ⑨

Travancore Heritage Beachfront ℡0471/226 7828, ⦿www.thetravancoreheritage.com. The centrepiece of this extravagant complex is a splendid 150-year-old mansion (serving now as the hotel reception), fronted by a kidney-shaped pool and sun terrace. Below it are set sixty relocated antique bungalows, some boasting alfresco garden bathrooms and their own plunge pools. At beach level, reached via a lift, there's a rather less inspiring modern block on two storeys, also with a big pool in front. Rooms $115–300. ⑨

Poovar Island

Estuary Island ℡0471/221 4355, ⦿www .estuaryisland.com. Formerly the *Poovar Island Resort*, this is the largest complex in the area, and the one with the least character. Its 46 luxury a/c rooms occupy a building inspired by the *Brunton Boatyard* in Fort Cochin, but lacking the same elegance. A row of bizarre floating wood rooms are its only distinguishing feature. Rooms $134–200. ⑨

🏃 **Friday's Place** ☎0471/293 3392, ⓦwww.kukimedia.com/fridaysplace. One of Kerala's more eccentric homestays: four beautifully made teak and mahogany "eco-cottages", set in an acre of palm and acacia gardens deep in the backwaters. Each has its own veranda, solar electricity supply, comfy rubber-mattress beds and attractive hand-loom textile decor. You're well cut off from the mainland (the river's not so much nearby as actually flowing through the plot via a network of little canals), but British-Sri Lankan owners Mark and Sujeewa are sociable hosts, offering fine organic South Indian cuisine, yoga tuition, and use of an 20cm telescope for stargazing. Doubles $200. ⑨

Isola di Cocco ☎0471/221 0008, ⓦwww.isoladicocco.com. Yet another large-scale "heritage resort", offering a/c rooms, antique Keralan cottages and suites spread over 30 acres, but with the distinction of being surrounded on all sides by water. Facilities include a big pool, billiards room and library. ⑨

Poovar House ☎0471/213 3533, ☎m99954 60368. British-owned homestay offering fully en-suite rooms (a/c or non-a/c) in a grand modern house with its own pool and Jacuzzi. Free Internet access and 3hr backwater excursions (Rs300) available on request. ⑦

Padmanabhapuram Palace

Although now officially in Tamil Nadu, **PADMANABHAPURAM**, 63km southeast of Thiruvananthapuram, was the capital of Travancore between 1550 and 1750, and maintains its historic links with Kerala, from where it is still administered. For anyone with even a minor interest in Keralan architecture, the small **Padmanabhapuram Palace** (Tues–Sun 9am–1pm & 2–4.30pm; Rs50 [Rs20], cameras Rs20), whose design represents the high point of regional building, is an irresistible attraction. It lies a pleasant ten- to fifteen-minute walk from the bus station: cross the main road outside the station, turn left and follow the road on the right. Once through the paddy fields, you'll emerge at a village that clusters around the imposing walls of the royal compound. It's worth avoiding weekends, when the complex is overrun with bus parties.

Set in neat, gravelled grounds against a backdrop of steep-sided hills, the palace's predominantly wooden exterior displays a perfect combination of clean lines and gentle angles, the sloping tiled roofs of its buildings broken by triangular projecting gables that enclose delicately carved screens.

In the **entrance hall** (a veranda), a brass oil lamp hangs from an ornate teak, rosewood and mahogany ceiling and is carved with ninety different lotus flowers. Beautifully ornamented, the revolving lamp inexplicably keeps the position in which it is left, seeming to defy gravity. The raja rested from the summer heat on the cool, polished-granite bed in the corner. On the wall hangs a collection of *onamvillu* (ceremonial bows) decorated with images of Padmanabha – the reclining form of Vishnu – which local chieftains would present to the raja during the Onam festival.

Directly above the entrance hall, on the first floor, the **mantrasala** (council chamber) is gently illuminated by light that filters through panes of coloured mica. Herbs soaking in water were put into the boxed bench seats along the front wall as a natural air-cooling system. The highly polished black floor is made from a now-lost technique using burnt coconut, sticky sugar-cane extract, egg whites, lime and sand.

The oldest part of the complex is the **Ekandamandapam**, or "lonely place". Built in 1550, it was used for rituals for the goddess Durga and typically employed elaborate floor paintings known as *kalam ezhuttu*. A loose ring attached to a column is a *tour de force* of the carpenter's art: both ring and column are carved from a single piece of jackwood. Nearby is a *nalekettu*, a four-sided courtyard found in many Keralan houses, open to the sky and surrounded by a pillared walkway. A trapdoor once served as the entrance to a secret passageway leading to another palace, since destroyed.

The Pandya-style stone-columned **dance hall** stands directly in front of a shrine to the goddess of learning, Saraswati. The women of the royal household had to watch performances through screens on the side, and the staff through holes in the wall from the gallery above. Typical of old country houses, steep, wooden ladder-like steps, ending in trapdoors, connect the floors. Belgian mirrors and Tanjore miniatures of Krishna adorn the chamber, forming part of the **women's quarters**, where a swing hangs on plaited iron ropes, while a four-poster bed, made from sixteen kinds of medicinal wood, dominates the **raja's bedroom**. Its elaborate carvings depict a mass of vegetation, human figures, birds and, as the central motif, the snake symbol of medicine, associated with the Greek physician deity Asclepius. The **murals** for which the palace is famous – alive with detail, colour, graceful form and religious fervour – adorn the walls of the **meditation room** directly above the bedroom, which was used by the raja and the heirs apparent. Unfortunately, this is now closed to preserve the murals, which have already been damaged by generations of hands trailing along the walls.

Further points of interest in the palace include a **dining hall** intended for the free feeding of up to two thousand Brahmins, and a 38-kilo stone which, it is said, every new recruit to the raja's army had to raise above his head 101 times.

Practicalities

Frequent **buses** run to Padmanabhapuram from Thiruvananthapuram's Thampanoor station; hop on any service heading south towards Nagercoil or Kanyakumari and get off at **Thakkaly** (sometimes written Thuckalai). You can flag the same buses down from the side of the highway at Kovalam Junction (3km inland from the beaches). To see Padmanabhapuram and Kanyakumari in one day, aim to leave early, arriving when the palace opens at 9am. Heading back, two express buses leave Thakkaly at 2.30pm and 3.30pm for Thiruvananthapuram. Alternatively, sign up for KTDC's Kanya-kumari tour from Thiruvananthapuram (daily 7.30am–9pm; Rs250), which calls at the palace en route.

The small stalls inside the outer walls of the palace are the best place to get **snacks** and **drinks**, as the area around the bus station is noisy and dirty.

North of Thiruvananthapuram

When it gets too hot at sea level, **Ponmudi** and the **Peppara Wildlife Sanctuary**, just northeast of Thiruvananthapuram, make a refreshing overnight break: in a couple of hours you can be walking through rubber and cardamom plantations and endless slopes of green tea bushes in cool air. Alternatively, the richly forested **Agastya Hills** lie 25km northeast of the capital. Accessible as a day-trip, they form a beautiful backdrop to the **Neyyar Dam**, on the banks of which stands the world-famous **Sivananda Yoga centre**. Just before you turn off to the Agastya Hills, it's well worth pausing to visit **Koikkal Kottaram palace** at Nedumangad – as fine an example of traditional Keralan architecture as you'll find anywhere in the state, with the added attraction of an excellent little museum devoted to local archeology, history and coinage.

If you want to stick to the coastline, head for **Varkala**, Kerala's number two resort and an important Hindu pilgrimage site. A little further north, the busy town of **Kollam** serves as the main departure point for boat trips through the unforgettable Keralan **backwaters**.

Koikkal Kottaram

The stately palace of **Koikkal Kottaram** (Tues–Sun 10am–5pm; Rs3, cameras Rs10), 18km northeast of Thiruvananthapuram, sits on the outskirts of **Nedumangad**, a busy market town near the turning to the Neyyar Dam and Agastya Hills. Considering its proximity to Kovalam and the capital, the monument sees surprisingly few visitors, yet it represents one of the highpoints of regional architecture, and its museum outstrips any other in the state. The Archaeological Survey of India maintain the building, providing knowledgeable (and obligatory) guides to show visitors around the collections and exhibits; their services are free but a tip is always appreciated.

The palace was originally constructed for Umyamma Rani, a local queen who reigned from 1677 until 1684. It retains all the distinctive features of traditional Keralan architecture: a bowed, triangular-gabled roof made of terracotta tiles, intricately carved teak features, cool stone floors and dark rooms that open onto a private central courtyard for the ladies. In common with other royal buildings in Travancore, it was cooled by a wonderfully effective natural air-conditioning system using sloping wooden slats. There is also a secret passage, leading out from the courtyard, that the queen could use as an escape when her enemies laid siege to the palace, a common military tactic in seventeenth-century Kerala.

The **ground-floor** rooms contain a vast coin collection – one of India's finest – which charts the development of international trade along the Malabar coastline. Most of the coins were discovered during archeological excavations in the area, and include Roman finds, punch-marked pieces issued by local rajas and silver rupees from the Victorian period. Other rooms around the courtyard contain Keralan household and farming implements dating from the eighteenth and nineteenth centuries, as well as three ornamental palanquins for carrying the royal ladies.

Upstairs, the make-up and costumes for *kathakali*, *Ottamthullal* and *theyyattam* dance performances are displayed on ferocious-looking models, and there is an exquisite *kettuvialaku* (platform) for the goddess Durga, which is carried around town during local spring festivities. Also displayed are the musical instruments and implements used in temple rituals, such as iron weaponry representing aspects of deities and the elaborate jewellery worn by priests.

Practicalities

Regular **buses** run to Nedumangad from Thiruvananthapuram's Thampanoor stand, taking around 45 minutes. If you want to refuel before heading back or onwards to the hills, try the air-conditioned *Ponmudi* **restaurant** inside the swish *Hotel Surya* on Surya Road, which serves sumptuous Keralan meals at lunch time (Rs100) in addition to a full multi-cuisine menu.

Agastya Hills and Neyyar Dam

Within easy distance of Kovalam, 25km to the northeast and feasible as a daytrip, the jagged, forested **Agastya Hills** form a verdant backdrop to the **Neyyar Dam**, which interrupts the flow of three major rivers to form a large reservoir. Standing on its banks is the world famous **Sivananda Yoga Vedanta Dhanwanthari Ashram**, one of the country's leading yoga centres (see box, p.122). Among locals, however, the spot is better known as a picnic destination:

Sivananda Yoga Vedanta Dhanwantari

Located amid the hills and tropical forests of the **Neyyar Dam**, 28km east of Thiruvananthapuram, the **Sivananda Yoga Vedanta Dhanwantari** (@www.sivananda.org) was founded by Swami Sivananda – dubbed the "Flying Guru" because he used to pilot light aircraft over war-stricken areas of the world, scattering flowers and leaflets calling for peace – as a centre for meditation, yoga and traditional Keralan martial arts and medicine. Sivananda was a renowned exponent of Advaitya Vedanta, the philosophy of non-duality, as espoused by the Upanishads and promoted later by Shankara in the eleventh century.

Aside from training teachers in advanced raja and hatha yoga, the ashram offers **introductory courses** for beginners. These comprise four hours of intensive tuition per day (starting at 5.30am), with background lectures. During the course, you have to stay at the ashram and comply with a regime that some Western students find fairly strict (no sex, drugs, rock'n'roll or smoking, pure-veg diet and early morning starts), as well as join in Hindu devotional worship. Some people have also noted strained relations with the local villagers, whom ashramites are discouraged from mixing with or even buying goods from. For more details, contact the ashram itself (℡0471/229 0493), or their branch in Thiruvananthapuram at 37/1929 Airport Rd, West Fort (℡0471/245 0942).

streams of bus parties pour through on weekends to stroll around the ornamental gardens at the water's edge, dotted with garishly painted plaster images of gods and heroes, and get a glimpse of the lions at the tiny **safari park**. Buses depart from the Wildlife Interpretation Centre for the half-hour trip (Rs20) around the site, home to a pride of seven rare Asian lions. You can also hire boats from the centre for excursions to an island in the reservoir said to be inhabited by elephants, bison and deer – though few are ever spotted. Sightings of crocodile, by contrast, are guaranteed, thanks to the presence of a small **Crocodile Breeding Park** near the interpretation centre.

The only way to enter the 12,000-hectare **Neyyar Dam Wildlife Sanctuary** proper, however, is through the Forest Department, who will, on request, organize a boat and an obligatory guide. To **trek** in the park, you'll need a guide and prior permission from the Forest Department offices at **Vazhuthakad** in Thiruvananthapuram. The local Forest Department range officer at the Neyyar Dam also issues permits, if approached through the manager at the tourist bungalow, KTDC *Agastya House* (see below).

Practicalities

Buses from the KSRTC Thampanoor bus stand in Thiruvananthapuram depart every hour or so for the Neyyar Dam. The only **accommodation** worthy of note is the KTDC *Agastya House* (℡0471/227 2160; ❹), which has huge rooms and verandas (with views), and a decent restaurant serving excellent South Indian meals and snacks. During the weekend, avoid the rooms upstairs as the popular beer bar below gets noisy.

Ponmudi and Peppara Wildlife Sanctuary

The hill station of **PONMUDI** lies in the tea-growing region of the **Cardamom** (or Ponmudi) **Hills**, about 60km northeast of Thiruvananthapuram and 77km from Kovalam. Located 1066m above sea level, on the top of a hill commanding breathtaking views out across the range as far as the sea, it comprises a range of cottages, rooms and a restaurant. The main reason to come up here is that Ponmudi serves as the only practical base for visits to the 53 square kilometres of forest set aside as the **Peppara Wildlife Sanctuary**, which protects elephants, *sambar*, lion-tailed macaques, leopards and other assorted wildlife. Although Peppara is theoretically open all year, the main season is from January until May.

The beautiful drive up, via the small towns of Nedumangad and Vithura, runs along very narrow roads past areca nut, clove, rubber and cashew plantations, with first the River Kavakulam and then the River Kallar close at hand. The bridge at **Kallar Junction** marks the start of the real climb. Twenty-two hairpin bends (numbered at the roadside) lead slowly up, starting in the foothills, heading past great outcrops of black rock and thick clumps of bamboo (*iramula*), then through the Kallar teak forest. Finally you wind into the tea plantations; the temperature is noticeably cooler and, once out of the forest, the views across the hills and the plains below become truly spectacular – on a clear day you can see as far as the coast. There really is very little to do up here, but the high ridges and tea estates make good rambling country.

Practicalities

Six daily **buses** run from Thiruvananthapuram to Ponmudi, via Vithura, the first at 5.30am and the last at 3.30pm. The nearest **tourist office** is currently in Thiruvananthapuram, where information on Ponmudi is readily available. The *Government Guesthouse* (☎0472/289 0230; ❸–❺) has 24 rooms and seven cottages, all with attached bathrooms and hot water. The simple, inexpensive and delicious meals have to be ordered a couple of hours in advance; otherwise the cold drinks and snack shop is open daily until 4pm, or you can walk down the road to the teashop on the bend (400m from the hotel). The main building, which originally belonged to the raja of Travancore, has lost any charm it may once have possessed, but the views across the hills and misty valleys from the terrace make up for it. Weekends get lively (to say the least), thanks to the beer parlour (daily 10am–6pm).

If your budget can stretch to it, the best place to sidestep Ponmudi's noisy daytrippers, and make the most of its beautiful woodland, is ⚜ *Duke's Forest Lodge* (☎0472/285 9273, ⓦwww.dukesforest.com; ❾) at Anapara, 51km from Thiruvananthapuram. Situated on the edge of a 130-acre rubber plantation, this family-run resort has five beautiful pool villas, designed in traditional Keralan style with high, pitched-tiled roofs and deep verandas that look straight into the trees, set in landscaped gardens. Each stands on stone pillars, and spiral staircases wind from the upper floors to secluded Jacuzzi terraces below, screened by roll-down cane blinds. There's also a big, sunny main pool, and a restaurant area in front of which recitals of music, dance and ritual theatre (including *theyyattam*) are held. Rates range from $100 to 150.

Varkala

Long renowned by Hindus as a place of pilgrimage, **VARKALA**, 54km northwest of Thiruvananthapuram, with its spectacular sands and red cliffs, is these days a considerably more appealing beach destination than Kovalam. Centred on a clifftop row of budget guesthouses and palm-thatch cafés, the tourist scene is still relatively low key, although the arrival in recent years of the first charter groups and luxury hotels may well be the harbinger of full-scale development: building inland and at both ends of the beach is already proceeding apace.

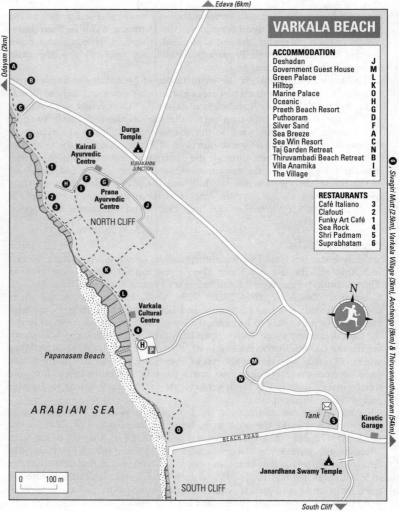

▲ *Edava (6km)*

◄ *Odayam (2km)*

VARKALA BEACH

ACCOMMODATION
Deshadan	J
Government Guest House	M
Green Palace	L
Hilltop	K
Marine Palace	O
Oceanic	H
Preeth Beach Resort	G
Puthooram	D
Silver Sand	F
Sea Breeze	A
Sea Win Resort	C
Taj Garden Retreat	N
Thiruvambadi Beach Retreat	B
Villa Anamika	I
The Village	E

RESTAURANTS
Café Italiano	3
Clafouti	2
Funky Art Café	1
Sea Rock	4
Shri Padmam	5
Suprabhatam	6

Durga Temple

Kairali Ayurvedic Centre

KURAKANNI JUNCTION

Prana Ayurvedic Centre

NORTH CLIFF

Varkala Cultural Centre

Papanasam Beach

ARABIAN SEA

N

Tank

Kinetic Garage

BEACH ROAD

Janardhana Swamy Temple

SOUTH CLIFF

South Cliff ▼

6, Sivagiri Mutt (2.5km), Varkala Village (3km), Anchengo (9km) & Thiruvananthapuram (54km) ►

0   100 m

Arrival and information

Varkala beach lies 4km of west of Varkala village proper, which is grouped around a busy market crossroads. The village's mainline railway station, served by express and passenger **trains** from Thiruvananthapuram, Kollam and most other Keralan towns, stands 500m north of this central junction. While some **buses** from Thiruvananthapuram's Thampanoor stand, and from Kollam to the north, continue on to within walking distance of the beach and clifftop area, most terminate in Varkala village, where you'll have to pick up an auto-rickshaw for the remaining five-minute ride (around Rs40–50) to the seashore.

If you can't get a direct bus to Varkala, take any "superfast" or "limited stop" bus running along the main NH-47 highway to **Kallamballam**, 15km east, from where slower local mini bus services (Rs10), auto-rickshaws (Rs80–100) and taxis (Rs150–175) will transport you to the beach.

Motorcycles are available for rent everywhere in Varkala for around Rs250–300 per day (or Rs350–400 for an Enfield), but if you're after something dependable just to potter around the lanes on, start your hunt at the Kinetic Garage, near Temple Junction, whose scooters are kept in top condition.

There are numerous places to **change money** on the clifftop: City Tours and Travels, in front of the *Hilltop Beach Resort*, exchange currency and traveller's cheques, and offer advances on visa cards for a small commission. The nearest **ATMs** are at the banks up in Varkala village, just off the crossroads. The many **Internet** centres in Varkala charge Rs40/hr.

Accommodation

Varkala offers a wide choice of accommodation, from five-star luxury at the *Taj Garden Retreat* to no-frills travellers' guesthouses. Being pitched almost exclusively at foreigners, none are cheap by Indian standards, but they're always clean and usually have some kind of outside space attached, whether a veranda or garden. The hotels up on the clifftop are most people's first choice, with more inspiring views than those lining the road to the beach. Auto-rickshaws from the railway station and village tank go as far as the helipad or round the back to North Cliff; it's worth stopping on the way to see if the *Government Guesthouse* has vacancies. Pressure on beds is acute in **peak season** (late Nov–mid-Feb, the period to which the rates quoted below refer), when it's a good idea to book in advance. For options further north up the coast, see "Accommodation north of Varkala" on p.130.

Budget

Government Guesthouse Cliff Rd ☎0470/260 2227, @www .keralatourism.org. Five minutes' walk north of the temple, behind the *Taj* hotel, this former maharajah's holiday palace has been converted into a charming guesthouse. The two en-suite rooms in the original building are enormous and fantastic value; the others (all en suite) occupy a modern block in the same grounds and are much less inspiring. Meals available on request. ②–③

Oceanic North Cliff ☎0470/229 0373, @oceanicresidence@yahoo.co.in. Very pleasant rooms, with flowering climbers trailing from its balconies, close to the thick of things on the clifftop. Café noise is sometimes a problem at night, but this ranks among the better-run, better-value budget options close to the strip. ④–⑤

Sea Win Resort North Cliff ☎0470/260 1084, ☎m98950 83950. One of several swanky modern buildings to have sprung up recently at the end of the cliff on the back of Saudi riyals. The colour schemes are a bit off-beat, but the rooms themselves are enormous, with quality double and twin beds, fridges, a spacious common veranda on one side and large private sitouts on the other where you can crash out on cane furniture and watch the sea only a stone's throw away. ④–⑤

Silver Sand North Cliff ☎m98468 26144 or ☎m98464 78432. This budget guesthouse, 200m back from the cliff edge behind the *Funky Art Café*, offers unbeatable value: its eight marble-clad, simply furnished rooms are large and comfortable for the price, with thick mattresses and doors opening to a sociable common veranda. ④

Villa Anamika North Cliff ☎0470/260 0095, @www.villaanamika.com. A welcoming homestay, 200m from the cliff, run by Keralan artist Shobhana (aka "Chicku") and her German husband Frank. Their five, variously priced rooms are all light, airy, cool and attractively furnished, with block-printed bedspreads and paintings by the hostess. Guests get the run of a beautiful rear garden, and breakfasts feature home-made German bread and jams. Best of all, the plot opposite serves as a grazing ground for one of Varkala's resident elephants. ④–⑤

Mid-range and luxury

Deshadan North Cliff ☎m98460 31005, ⓦwww
.deshadan.com. The smartest and most efficiently
run of several new, small-scale resort complexes,
pitched primarily at the package trade but which
welcomes walk-in clients when there are
vacancies. Centred on a clean swimming pool, its
twelve individually themed rooms ("Asam",
"Rajasthan", "Malabar", etc) are "designed for
maximum aesthetic impact" and offer international-standard comforts. ⓼

Green Palace North Cliff ☎0470/261 0055,
ⓦwww.greenpalacevarkala.com. Currently the
swishest place on the clifftop: a double-storey
block built in 2006, buffered from the main path by
a lawn where you can lounge in the shade. Its
dozen sea-facing rooms (seven with a/c) have
shiny marble floors, TVs, quality beds and individual
sitouts overlooking the garden – though the
"standard" options on the ground floor lack sea
views and are quite dark. ⓺–⓼

Hilltop North Clifftop ☎0470/260 1237, ⓦwww
.hilltopvarkala.com. Long-established hotel in a
prime location, right on the rim of the cliff looking
out to sea. It offers three categories of en-suite
rooms: "deluxe" (with breezy balconies and uninterrupted sea views; Rs2000); "standard" (the same,
but without views; Rs1200); and "economy" (older
options to the rear ground floor; Rs800). ⓸–⓺

Marine Palace off Beach Rd ☎0470/260 3204.
The "regular" and "deluxe" rooms in this complex
close to the beachfront are way overpriced and
poorly maintained, but the brand new Keralan-style
apartments (Rs3000 per night) are some of the
nicest places to stay in Varkala, with huge wood-
lined bedrooms, self-catering kitchenettes and
verandas with sea views. ⓻–⓼

Preeth Beach Resort North Clifftop area,
off Cliff Rd ☎0470/260 0942, ⓦwww
.preethbeachresort.com. Large, well-maintained
two-star complex set 5min back from the cliff in
a shady palm grove. Grouped around a kidney-
shaped pool and sun terrace, its accommodation
ranges from no-frills economy rooms to spacious
a/c cottages with generous verandas. An
additional attraction is the top-notch "Prana"

ayurvedic clinic – one of the few in Varkala with
a fully qualified doctor. ⓸–⓻

Puthooram North Cliff ☎0470/320 2007,
☎m98952 32209. Snug chalet-cottages made
entirely of polished wood, some with traditional
Keralan railings and thatched roofs, opening onto a
trim little garden, right on the cliff edge. Their
published rates are high, but you can usually
haggle hefty discounts later in the day. Courteous
management, and there's a quality in-house
ayurvedic centre ("Santhigiri"). ⓸–⓻

Sea Breeze North Cliff ☎0470/260 3257,
☎m98460 04243. Set back in a coconut grove
behind a small tidal beach, this rather grand new
building is currently the northernmost guesthouse in
Varkala proper – only 5min walk from the bright
lights of the clifftop area, but in a peaceful position.
Its rooms are large for the price, opening onto a big
common veranda that's strung with hammocks and
catches the breezes straight off the surf. ⓹–⓻

Taj Garden Retreat Cliff Rd ☎0470/260 3000,
ⓦwww.tajhotels.com. Not the most alluring of Taj
Group's five-star hotels (the architecture owes
more to the Costas than Kerala) but the most
luxurious option in Varkala: thirty plush a/c rooms
and suites (sea- or garden-facing), opening onto
private balconies and lawns, with direct access to
a large curvi-form pool. Tariffs (from $250 per
night) include breakfast and dinner buffets in the
Cape Comorin restaurant. ⓽

Thiruvambadi Beach Retreat North Cliff
ⓦwww.thiruvambadihotel.com ☎0470/260 1028.
This idiosyncratic, family-run guesthouse at the far
(quiet) end of the cliff has fifteen rooms, the best of
them split-level a/c suites boasting big, sea-facing
balconies and over-the-top Mughal-kitsch decor
(cusped Islamic arches and elaborately carved
wooden doors). The rooftop restaurant is a great
place to relax, looking straight out to sea. ⓺–⓼

The Village North Cliff ☎m99471 55442. Three
newly built, handsomely furnished octagonal cottages
set back from the road in a small garden; each has
its own private sitout and kitchenette. A good choice
for families, as the rooms are especially large and
can accommodate extra beds for kids. ⓺–⓻

The beach and village

Known in Malayalam as Papa Nashini ("sin destroyer"), Varkala's beautiful
white-sand **Papanasam Beach** has long been associated with ancestor worship.
Devotees come here after praying at the **Janardhana Swamy Temple** (said to
be over 2000 years old), to bring the ashes of departed relatives for their "final
rest". Non-Hindus are not permitted to enter the inner sanctum of the shrine
but are welcome in the grounds.

△ View from the clifftop, Varkala

Backed by sheer red laterite cliffs and drenched by rolling waves off the Arabian Sea, the coastline is imposingly scenic and the beach relatively relaxing – although its religious associations do ensure that attitudes to public nudity (especially female) are markedly less liberal than other coastal resorts in India. Western sun-worshippers are thus supposed to keep to the northern end of the beach (away from the main puja area reserved for the funerary rites) where they are serviced by a non-stop parade of local "hallo-pineapple-coconut?" vendors. Whistle-happy lifeguards ensure the safety of swimmers by enforcing the no-swim zones beyond the flags: be warned that the undercurrent is often strong, claiming lives every year. **Dolphins** are often seen swimming quite close to the coast, and, if you're lucky, you may be able to swim with them by arranging a ride with a fishing boat. Sea otters can also occasionally be spotted playing on the cliffs by the sea.

Few of Varkala's Hindu pilgrims make it as far as the **clifftop area**, the focus of a homespun but well-established tourist scene that's grown steadily over the past ten or twelve years, and now accommodates fortnighting winter sunseekers as well as long-haul travellers. Bamboo and palm-thatch cafés, restaurants and souvenir shops jostle for space close to the edge of the mighty escarpments, which plunge vertically to the beach below in a dramatic arc, most beautiful at sunset, when their laterite tint glows molten red. Several steep flights of steps cut into the rock provide fast routes from the sand, and you can also get there via the gentler path that starts behind the *Marine Palace* restaurant, or along the metalled road winding its way up from the village, built to service the helipad in advance of Indira Gandhi's visit in 1983. She came here to inaugurate a small government "nature cure" hospital, set up to take advantage of the sea air and three natural springs whose healing waters still bubble out of the rocks.

Countless private **ayurvedic centres** and **yoga schools** have followed in its wake, benefiting from the same salubrious location and a constant turnover through the winter months of well-off foreigners. As in Kovalam, many non-qualified practitioners have jumped on the bandwagon, so it's wise to look around, and get other travellers' recommendations before going for a treatment

Nanoo Swami

Varkala is inextricably linked in the popular Indian imagination with the philosopher, poet and social reformer **Shri Narayana Guru**, who founded an ashram – the famous **Sivagiri Mutt** – on a hilltop near the town. Pilgrims travel from all over the Subcontinent to pay their respects at his *samadhi*, where the guru's remains are enshrined, and at the Shree Sarada Saraswati temple he founded on the site. Both Gandhi and the Bengali poet and thinker Tagore came here during the sage's lifetime, claiming the great man's teachings had influenced their own political and religious ideas.

Born into a Ezhava (low-caste) family near Thiruvananthapuram in 1854, "Nanoo Swami", as he became known to his devotees, followed a well-trodden route to sainthood, leaving his family while still in his twenties to seek enlightenment amid the hills, forests, remote beaches and temples of southern India. This itinerant *sannyasi* phase lasted five years, during which he not only studied yoga under a renowned guru, Ayyavu Swami, but also grew increasingly troubled by the treatment of low-caste communities in his homeland. Kerala was (and remains to a great extent) one of the regions of the country where caste divisions were most rigidly upheld: Untouchables were not allowed in any temples, and had to keep a distance of at least ninety feet from Brahmins. Until 1914, women from the very lowest castes were not permitted to wear sari tops, or educate their children, and no low-caste person could legally travel on any roads.

The great watershed in the Swami's life came in 1888, at his cave hermitage in **Arrivippuram**, on the Neyyar River in south Kerala, where he had begun to attract a band of acolytes and admirers. On the night of Shivratri, while bathing in the river, he pulled a rock from the water and with it consecrated a Shiva temple – held to be a heinous crime by Brahmins, who considered *prathishta* (the act of installing a temple deity) the exclusive right of high-caste priests.

Nanoo Swami's heresy electrified his followers and over the coming years, dozens more Shiva temples were opened in South India, open to all regardless of caste. Later, the Shiva idols would be replaced by mirrors, intending to demonstrate to worshippers that "God lay inside every person". The religious rebellion eventually coalesced into a much broader social movement which, with support from other great reformers of the day, would result in the gradual removal of caste bars.

From 1904 until the end of his life in 1928, the guru based himself and the SNDP (the organization he founded for the promulgation of his "One Caste, One Religion, One God" philosophy), at a 20-acre site on **Sivagiri** hill, 3km inland from Varkala beach. In keeping with his inclusive ideas, this is one holy place in Kerala which anybody can visit. Its centrepiece is a three-tiered, circular, cream-and red-painted tower, which stands on high ground above the sage's former residence, where an exhibition of his few personal possessions is displayed.

For the full story, go to ⓦwww.sivagiri.org.

(see p.110). Two clinics that stand out are *Kairali* (☎0470/329 4660, ⓦwww .kairalivaidhyamadomvarkala.com), near the *Silver Star* guesthouse behind the *Funky Art Café* and *Prana*, in the *Preeth Beach Resort* (☎0470/260 0942). For yoga, one teacher receiving consistently high praise from readers is Vasu, who works from a shala at the north end of the clifftop, behind *Papaya* restaurant. You can pick up medicinal oils and other health-oreinted produce, such as herbs and handmade soaps, as well as books on yoga, meditation and massage, at the Prakrithi Stores on the clifftop.

Nearby, and aimed unashamedly at the tourist market, the **Varkala Cultural Centre** (☎0470/608793), behind the *Sunrise* restaurant on North Clifftop, holds daily **kathakali** and **bharatanatyam** dance performances (make-up 5–6.45pm; performance 6.45–8.15pm; Rs150). Using live musicians instead of a recorded soundtrack, it's a pleasant and authentic-enough introduction to the two types of dance, especially if you're not going to make it to Kochi (see p.187). For anyone with a more serious interest in the classical arts, the centre also offers short courses on *kathakali* make-up and dance, *bharatanatyam*, devotional song (*bhajan*) and Carnatic percussion (*mridamgan*).

Eating

Seafood lovers will enjoy Varkala's crop of clifftop **café–restaurants**, which specialize in locally caught seafood – seer fish, shark, marlin, kingfish and jumbo prawns – prepared in a variety of styles: tandoori, masala-fried or simmered Keralan-style in spicy coconut-based gravies. You'll also find plenty of pasta and pizza, and German baked treats. Prices are fairly high: expect to pay Rs75 or more for a simple veggie curry, Rs100–150 for pizza or pasta, and Rs100–200 for a fresh fish dish. Service can be very slow, but the superb location more than compensates, especially in the evenings, when the sea twinkles with the lights of distant fishing boats.

Due to Kerala's antiquated licensing laws, which involve huge amounts of tax, a lot of cafés choose to serve **beer** discreetly; a teapot-full costs Rs80–100.

Café Italiano North Clifftop. Authentic Italian menu featuring pizza and pasta dishes in a variety of sauces (Rs120–200) – the house speciality *fruite di mare* is hard to beat.

Clafouti North Clifftop. Nepali-run restaurant serving, somewhat disappointingly given the Gallic promise of the name, the usual generic German-bakery cakes, in addition to fresh seafood dishes, Mexican and Thai specials, a crowd-pleasing steak Chateaubriand – and delicious expresso. It's right on the cliff edge, and has great sea views.

Funky Art Café North Clifftop. The naffest name but still the hippest spot on the cliff, with full tables from sunset until the small hours. It serves a predictable traveller-oriented menu, but most people come here to lounge, drink, smoke and socialize over the gut-thumping sound system.

Sea Rock Clifftop, next to the helipad. As well as a fairly standard range of Indian and Continental food, this place serves tasty South Indian *iddli-vada*

breakfasts and masala *dosas* from 8.30am–3pm. In the evenings, fresh local fish takes over, followed by DVD screenings.

Shri Padmam Temple junction. This dingy-looking café on the temple crossroads serves freshly made, cheap and tasty South Indian veg food (including Rs25 "meals" and lunchtime). You can walk through the front dining room to a large rear terrace affording prime views of the tank – particularly atmospheric at breakfast time.

Suprabhatam Varkala village, 4km east of the beach. The cheapest and best pure-veg joint in Varkala, situated just off the main crossroads in a dining hall lined with coir mats and grubby pink walls. Their *dosas* and other fried snacks aren't up to much, but the lunchtime "unlimited" rice-plate "meals" (noon–3pm; Rs20), featuring the usual *thoran*, *avial*, dhal, *rasam*, buttermilk, curd, papad and red or white rice, pull in streams of locals and foreigners alike.

Around Varkala

Head along the coast in either direction from Varkala and the tourist scene soon starts to feel a world away. With a scooter, motorbike or taxi, one feasible target for a short foray **south** is the former British outpost of **Anchengo Fort**, 9km south of Varkala. In 1684, faced with the *zamorin* of Calicut's reluctance to grant trading rights to Europeans, the East India Company obtained permission from the Rani of Attingal to site a "factory", or trading post, on a sandy beach near Varkala. Fortified walls were erected a decade later, and it wasn't long before Anchengo started to flourish as a colonial spice port, second only to Bombay. Indeed, it might well have overtaken its sibling had not a dispute broken out: irritated by the colonial traders' manipulation of pepper prices, an irregular Indian force from the surrounding area massacred a column of 140 British troops and merchants as they marched to present annual tribute gifts to the Rani of Attingal in 1721. Anchengo Fort was besieged but held out for six months until reinforcements arrived from Tellicherry. The British were handsomely compensated for their losses, with a grant from the Rani to the East India Company of a full monopoly over the region's lucrative pepper trade, as well as permission to build factories. Thus it was that Anchengo played a pivotal role in the development of colonial power in India – not that you'd know it from the building today. Hemmed in by a poor Christian fishing settlement, its bleached, sloping walls rise neglected and forlorn behind the beach, enclosing a half-hearted garden and couple of rusting canons.

North of Varkala the shoreline is a lot less densely populated, though more ostentatiously wealthy, with many out-size Gulf returners' houses dotted around its hinterland of leafy lanes and palm groves. You can comfortably walk the 2km from the north end of Varkala cliff to **Odayam**, a mixed Hindu and Muslim village where a cluster of modest guesthouses has sprung up to service the small black-sand beach. Beyond, a paved walkway winds for another three or four kilometres over low cliffs to the next settlement, **Edava**, a busier place cut through by the main train line, whose fringes hold a couple of idyllic, empty coves and more low-key accommodation (reviewed below). Shimmering north from there, one vast, unbroken, white-sand beach arcs almost to the horizon, backed by a lagoon and totally empty save for the odd fishing boat.

Accommodation north of Varkala

If you're happy to watch the bright lights of Varkala's clifftop from a distance, the coast further north has a lot to recommend it, offering better-value **accommodation** and access to a wild and windy shoreline where tourism has, thus far, made very little impact.

Ashthamay 10/107 East Odayam ☎0470/266 3613, ⊛www.asthamay.com. Half-a-dozen attractive semi-detached bungalows, with red-tiled roofs and pink walls, set in a garden only a few metres from the waves. It's an efficient place, and open year round – a great spot to be during a monsoon storm. The restaurant's recommended for sunny breakfasts of fresh bread and coffee on the terrace, but not for evening meals, which are overpriced. ⑤

Kadaltheeram Edava ☎0470/266 4218, ☎94951 688574, ⊛www.kadaltheeram.com. Friendly new twelve-room resort and ayurvedic spa, in neo-Keralan style, situated next to a lovely little beach that's deserted most of the time. It offers three types of rooms, all neat, clean and spacious, with good-sized balconies looking over the hotel's well-tended gardens to the sea; they're differently priced according to the views. If it's free, book #107. ⑦–⑧

Kattil Beach Resort Odayam ☎0470/266 2226, ☎m98955 82740. The best-value economy option in this area, offering a choice of en-suite rooms in three different wings, all on high ground above the beach, with pleasant views from private or common verandas. The ones in the block called *Sona* are the pick of the crop, looking through the palm groves to the nearby stream gulley and beach. ③–④

Munna Edava ☎m98955 28150, ☎edavasasheer@yahoo.com. This no-frills budget

guesthouse, situated on a palm-shaded terrace that's open to the sea breezes on one side, is the northernmost mark of tourism in the Varkala area, and an absolute steal, with rooms from only Rs400. They're very basic, but those on the upper floor share a common veranda looking straight out to sea. If you're happy with simple amenities and can sort out transport (Edava's a bit cut off), you'll probably end up staying for weeks. ③

Oasis Odayam ☎0470/266 0063, ☎m99462 01214, ☎oasisodayam@yahoo.co.in. Simple, clean, pleasant rooms – the best of them on the rooftop looking south – though a notch pricier than the competition. ⑤

Paddy Fields Odayam ☎m98473 97504, ☎paddyfields6@yahoo.co.in. A cosy B & B, just behind *Asthamay* and only a stone's throw from the sea, run by a friendly family. They've a range of different rooms, with prices varying according to views, space and orientation. ③–④

Royal Palm Odayam ☎0470/266 0750, ☎m98958 83884, ☎royalpalm_beachresort @yahoo.com. Big, new, white-painted rooms (all non a/c and en suite) at a breezy spot on a bluff looking out to sea. Edged by turned-wood railings, its large sitouts make the most of the idyllic views. The same owner also has cheaper budget rooms just below in a beige-coloured block called *Crystal Palace* (☎m99951 06089; ③). ④

Kollam (Quilon)

One of the Malabar Coast's oldest harbours, **KOLLAM** (pronounced "Koillam", and previously known as Quilon), 74km northwest of Thiruvananthapuram and 85km south of Alappuzha, was once at the centre of the international spice trade. The port flourished from the very earliest times, trading with the Phoenicians, Arabs, Greeks, Romans and Chinese. It finds mention in the Persian *Book of Routes and Kingdoms* compiled by Ibn Khurdadhibh in 844–848, and again in the fourteenth-century journals of the Moroccan traveller, Ibn Battuta, who saw Chinese junks loading pepper here in the 1330s. Two hundred years later, the Portuguese writer Duarte Barbossa described Quilon as a "very great city with a right good haven" visited by "Moors, Heathen and Christians in great numbers".

Nowadays, Kollam is chiefly of interest as one of the entry or exit points to the **backwaters of Kerala** (see box, pp.144–145), and most travellers simply stay overnight en route to or from Alappuzha.

Arrival and information

Kollam's busy mainline **railway station** lies east of the clocktower which marks the centre of town. Numerous daily trains run from Ernakulam and Thiruvananthapuram and beyond. The helpful **District Tourism Promotion Council** (DTPC) has a tourist office across town (daily 9am–6pm; ☎0474/274 5625, ⓦwww.dtpckollam.com) at the **boat jetty** on the edge of Ashtamudi Lake, where you can book tickets for the daily tourist backwater cruises (see pp.144–145); they'll also help arrange taxis for trips around the area, and can advise on local ferry transport. The local **Alappuzha Tourism Development Council** office (ATDC; daily 7am–9pm; ☎0474/276 7440), on the opposite side of the road, offers comparable services.

The jetty and KSRTC **bus stand** are close together on the edge of Ashtamudi Lake. Bookable express **buses** leave for Thiruvananthapuram (1hr 45min) and Kochi (3hr) via Alappuzha (2hr) every fifteen minutes or so; as ever, the express services are much better than the "limited stop" buses. Note that most Thiruvananthapuram-bound **trains** do not stop in Varkala.

Useful **facilities** such as exchange bureaux, ATMs and Internet outlets can be found in the smart Bishop Jerome Nagar shopping mall, just south of the main road between the jetty and the clocktower. The efficient UTI bank also has a dependable and secure ATM north of the clocktower near the *Shah International Hotel*; and there's another convenient, cheap Internet place, Cyber. Com, just south of the clocktower on the first floor of Yeskay Towers, charging just Rs20/hr.

The town

Kollam **town** itself, sandwiched between the sea and Ashtamudi ("eight inlets") Lake, is less exciting than its history might suggest. It's a typically sprawling Keralan market hub, with a central bazaar of old tiled wooden houses and winding backstreets, kept busy by the local trade in coir, cashew nuts (a good local buy), pottery, aluminium and fish.

The one monument worth going out of your way to see is the former **British Residency**, a magnificent 250-year-old mansion on the shores of the lake, now used as a *Government Guesthouse* (see review, p.134). Overlooking the balding expanse of the old *maidan* (parade ground) it's one of only a handful of monuments surviving from the early days of the Raj,

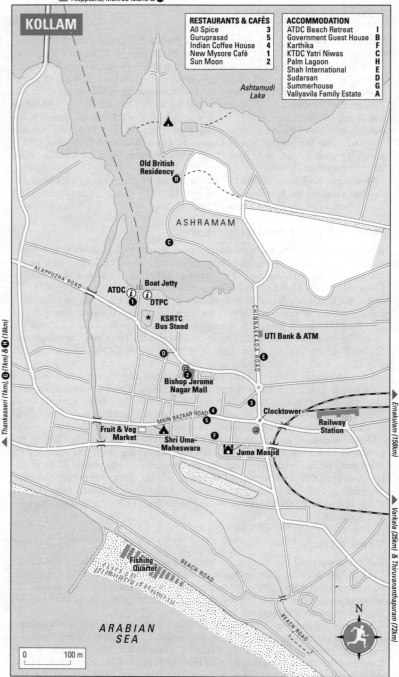

▲ *Alappuzha, Monroe Island &* Ⓐ

KOLLAM

RESTAURANTS & CAFÉS	
All Spice	3
Guruprasad	5
Indian Coffee House	4
New Mysore Café	1
Sun Moon	2

ACCOMMODATION	
ATDC Beach Retreat	I
Government Guest House	B
Karthika	F
KTDC Yatri Niwas	C
Palm Lagoon	H
Shah International	E
Sudarsan	D
Summerhouse	G
Valiyavila Family Estate	A

Ashtamudi Lake

Old British Residency
Ⓑ

ASHRAMAM

Ⓒ

ALAPPUZHA ROAD

Boat Jetty
ATDC ⓘ ⓘ
❶ **DTPC**

★ **KSRTC Bus Stand**

CHINNAKKADA ROAD

UTI Bank & ATM
Ⓔ

Ⓓ
@❷
Bishop Jerome Nagar Mall

❸ **Clocktower**

Railway Station

MAIN BAZAAR ROAD

❹
❺

Fruit & Veg Market
Shri Uma-Maheswara
Ⓕ
@
🕌 **Jama Masjid**

Fishing Quarter

BEACH ROAD

BEACH ROAD

ARABIAN SEA

N

0   100 m

◀ *Thankasseri (1km),* Ⓖ *(1km) &* Ⓗ *(18km)*

▶ *Ernakulam (158km)*

▶ *Varkala (35km) & Thiruvananthapuram (72km)*

▼ Ⓘ

and perfectly epitomizes the openness to indigenous influences that characterized the era, with typically Keralan gable roofs surmounting British pillared verandas. Inside, palatial rooms retain their original early Georgian furniture, giant Chinese pickle jars and floor-to-ceiling shuttered windows, while the walls sport antique East India Company lithographs of Wellesley storming "Srirangapatnam". Much of the structure is literally falling apart, but you're welcome to visit: there are no set hours – just turn up and ask the manager if you can have a look around.

A few kilometres southwest of the centre, on the seaward side of town, the district of **Thankasseri** holds fading remnants of other eras, when the bay it overlooked would have been filled with ships bound for Europe, southeast Asia and China. Encircling the modern, red-and-white-striped lighthouse are the partly collapsed walls of an early sixteenth-century **Portuguese fort**, while the **Church of St Thomas**, now a pile of rubble inside, may well have been one in which St Francis Xavier (see pp.263–264) attended mass during his evangelical mission to the Malabar coast in the 1540s.

Other buildings in the area surviving from the Portuguese period include the **Church of Infant Jesus**, and the chapel attached to the **Bishop of Quilon's palace** – both five minutes' walk north of the old fort. Throughout the British period, Thankasseri was a primarily Anglo-Indian district, but after Independence most of its elegant old bungalows were sold off as residents emigrated to the UK and Canada. Many now lie empty and in states of evocative dereliction, languishing in overgrown gardens.

To the east of Thankasseri lies one of the town's two main fishing quarters, lined by hundreds of painted boats (the other is due south of the centre; see map opposite). They're scattered over what must, four or five centuries ago, have been Kollam's fabled harbour. As ever, if you walk on the beach, remember it's used as a public toilet in the mornings.

Backwater cruises from Kollam

DTPC and ATDC's popular **cruises from Kollam to Alappuzha** (Rs300) operate on alternate days, departing at 10.30am and taking eight hours, with stops for lunch and tea. Tickets for both can be bought on the day from the tourist offices at the boat jetty on Ashtamudi Lake (see map, pp.144–145), and at some of the hotels. DTPC and ATDC also offer exclusive overnight *kettu vallam* cruises (see box, p.144 for details), while the DTPC runs half-day trips to nearby **Monroe Island** (daily 9am–1pm & 2–6.30pm; Rs300), which provide a fascinating glimpse of village life in this unique – and very scenic – waterlogged region.

Tourist cruises are a real money spinner for the local tourist offices, but you may find that you get a far better impression of backwater life by hopping between villages on the very cheap **local ferries**, tickets for which are sold on the boats themselves. Consult DTPC or ATDC for timetable and route information.

Accommodation

Considering the numbers of foreign tourists that pour through during the season, accommodation is in surprisingly short supply in Kollam – book in advance if you're arriving late in the day. Reservations, however, cannot be made in the place that should be the first choice of any traveller interested in Kerala's colonial history: in the converted British Residency on the edge of town, Kollam's *Government Guesthouse* offers a unique chance to stay in one of the Raj's first, and grandest, civic buildings, at prices comparable with the grungy lodges opposite the station.

The one place to avoid unless you're desperate is the KTDC *Yatri Niwas*, close to the *Government Guesthouse* on the shores of Ashtamudi Lake: as with most in the chain, it's lapsed into an awful state of disrepair and no longer merits its rates.

ATDC Beach Retreat 3km south of centre ☏ 0474/275 276 3793, ⓦ www.atdcalleppey .com. Typical government-run place with smudged walls and average-sized rooms (some a/c), situated directly across the road from the beach and good value. It's also quiet in the evenings, has a rooftop restaurant with sea views, and an untypically enthusiastic and helpful young staff. Station pick-up (Rs50) on request. ❸–❹

🏃 **Government Guesthouse** Ashtamudi Lake, 2km northeast, ☏ 0474/274 3620. Sleeping in this grand 250-year-old building, the former British Residency (see p.131), feels like overnighting in a museum. Full of original furniture and fixtures, the rooms are gigantic for the price (go for an a/c one on the first floor if it's offered), but, as with most *Government Guesthouses*, you'll have to try for a vacancy on spec as they rarely accept advance bookings. Breakfast and dinner available. ❷–❸

Karthika off Main Rd, near the Jama Masjid mosque ☏ 0474/275 1821. Large and popular budget hotel in a central location offering a range of acceptably clean, plain rooms (some a/c) ranged around a courtyard in which the centrepiece is, rather unexpectedly, three huge nude figures. ❷

Palm Lagoon Vellimon West ☏ 0474/254 8974, ⓦ www.palmlagoon.com. See map on p.136. Keralan-style bungalows, with tiled roofs and painted pillared verandas, in a lush six-acre plot on Ashtamudi Lake, 18km from town. There's a pool, plus a swimming enclosure in the lake itself. Good ayurvedic treatment facilities are available, and they can arrange bike, boat and fishing trips in the surrounding backwaters. One of the few affordable resorts of this kind in Kerala, with rooms from only Rs1800, plus Rs375 for full board. ❻

Shah International Chinnakkada Rd ☏ 0474/274 2362, ⓔ hotelshah@hotmail.com. A modern tower block hotel close to the centre of town, holding

differently priced rooms, from large, clean economy doubles to full a/c suites with plasma-screen TVs and views over the town. Hardly the most atmospheric choice, but a dependably comfortable one. ❸–❻

Sudarsan Parameswar Nagar ☏ 0474/274 4322, ⓦ www.hotelsudarshan.com. Central and popular, though definitely not as palatial as the posh foyer would lead you to believe. Describing itself (somewhat ominously) as a "hospitalized zone that will charm your brain", the building has a range of rooms: all are the same size, but the a/c ones are cleaner, more recently refurbished and lie on the quiet side of the building. In addition to a standard multi-cuisine restaurant and bar, they've a themed diner, "Night Flight", decked out like the interior of an aircraft, where the waiters all wear camp flight-crew gear. ❹–❺

🏃 **Summerhouse** Thirumallawaram and Thankasseri ☏ 0474/279 4518, ☏ m98956 62839, ⓔ contactsummerhouse @hotmail.com. Run by the amiable Mr Shashi, this trio of suburban homestays offers simple, characterful accommodation on the northwestern edge of town near, or next to, the sea. Pick of the bunch is "No.3", a cosy wood cabin with only two rooms (book both for privacy), opening onto a wonderful veranda enfolded by palm trees, slap on the sea wall. "No.1" is an older structure, also next to the waves, but more spartan. "No.2" is a former family house, large enough for a group, with its own garden, 5min walk from the shore in a leafy residential area. ❹

Valiyavila Family Estate Panamukkom, Kureepzha, Ashtamudi Lake ☏ 474/270 1546, ⓦ www.kollamlakeviewresort.com. The local tourist offices tend to plug this place but it's a dud. The location, on a wooded *presqu'ile* that you can only reach by boat, is certainly romantic, but the garishly coloured rooms are not all that well maintained and ridiculously overpriced. ❻–❼

Eating

All of the hotels, resorts and guesthouses listed above provide meals, but if you'd prefer to eat out, try one of the following dependable options in and around the centre of town.

All Spice near the main bazaar. This determinedly Western, brightly lit fast food joint, above a bakery, is where the town's middle classes come for family evenings out, and where foreign tourists come to escape the heat – and get away from Indian food. The a/c certainly hits the spot, but the burgers, pizzas and fried chicken turn out to be less appealing than the main North Indian and Chinese dishes (Rs100–150).

Guruprasad Main Bazaar. Cramped and sweaty, but wonderfully old-school "meals" on the market's main street: blue walls, framed ancestral photos and Hindu devotional art provide the typical backdrop for pukka pure-veg rice plates and *udipi*-style snacks.

Indian Coffee House Main Bazaar. Typical *ICH* fare – limp *dosas*, oily biryanis, toast, omelettes, pot-chai and filter coffee – served on regulation chipped china by waiters wearing ice-cream-fan *pugris*.

New Mysore Café boat jetty, opposite KSRTC Bus Stand. This is the most popular of the "meals" joints clustered around the bus stand and boat jetty area, serving delicious "all-you-can-eat" rice plates for only Rs19 at lunchtime, then the usual *udipi* snacks through the rest of the day. A convenient option if you've time to kill before catching onward transport.

Sun Moon Top Floor, Bishop Jerome Nagar Mall ☎ 0474/301 3000, Ⓦ www.zeez.info. Traditional Keralan cooking – *karimeen pollichathu* (white fish steamed in banana leaf) and masala-fried calamari, as well as Continental dishes and a big multi-cuisine buffet – served in a blissfully cool, a/c rooftop restaurant, against a backdrop of carved stone temple brackets and woodwork. The food's the best in town, and so are the panoramic views. Count on Rs300 for three courses.

Between Kollam and Alappuzha

Most visitors travelling north between Kollam and Alappuzha, or southwards in the opposite direction, do so by **boat** through the Kuttanad backwaters, either on local tourist-office cruisers or privately chartered *kettu vallam* rice barges. But if you're pushed for time and opt to cover this backwater stretch by the somewhat less scenic **NH-47** or its adjacent **railway** line, you've the option of pausing at several landmarks along the way.

Karunaganapali

In **KARUNAGANAPALI**, 23km north of Kollam on NH-47, it's possible to see traditional **kettu vallam**, or "tied boats", being built and repaired. These long cargo vessels, a familiar sight on the backwaters, are built entirely without nails. Each jackwood plank is sewn to the next with coir rope, and then the whole is coated with a caustic black resin made from boiled cashew kernels. With careful maintenance they last for generations. If you want to buy a *vallam* you'll need between ten and twenty *lakh* (one or two million) rupees; a far cheaper alternative is to hire the boats (see p.145).

Regular **buses** pass through Karunaganapali on the way to Alappuzha. One daytime **train**, #6525, leaves Kollam at 2.15pm, arriving in Karunaganapali half an hour later. On reaching the bus stand or railway station, take an auto-rickshaw 1km north along the national highway, then turn left into a lane for 4km to the riverside village of **Alumkattaru**, and the boatyard of the *vallam asharis*, the boat carpenters, who are generally friendly and happy to let visitors watch them work. In the shade of palm trees at the edge of the water, some weave palm leaves, others twist coir strands into rope and craftsmen repair the boats. Soaking in the shallows nearby are palm leaves, used for thatch, and coconut husks for coir rope.

The Mata Amritanandamayi Math

The **Mata Amritanandamayi ("MA") Math**, or Amritapuri as it's more familiarly known, is the home ashram of Kerala's most famous living spiritual

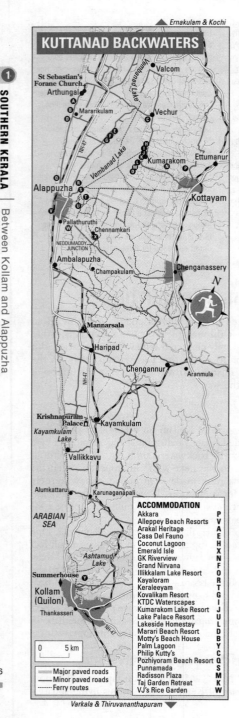

KUTTANAD BACKWATERS

▲ Ernakulam & Kochi

Valcom

St Sebastian's
Forane Church
Arthungal
Mararikulam

Vechur

Vembanad Lake

Kumarakom
Ettumanur

Alappuzha
Kottayam

Pallathuruthi
Chennamkari
NEDDUMADDY
JUNCTION
Ambalapuzha
Champakulam
Chenganassery

N

Mannarsala

Haripad

Chengannur
Aranmula

Krishnapuram
Palace
*Kayamkulam
Lake*
Kayamkulam

Vallikkavu

Alumkattaru
Karunaganapali

*ARABIAN
SEA*

*Ashtamudi
Lake*

Summerhouse

Kollam
(Quilon)

Thankasseri

0   5 km

Varkala & Thiruvananthapuram ▼

ACCOMMODATION	
Akkara	P
Alleppey Beach Resorts	V
Arakal Heritage	A
Casa Del Fauno	E
Coconut Lagoon	H
Emerald Isle	X
GK Riverview	N
Grand Nirvana	F
Illikkalam Lake Resort	O
Kayaloram	R
Keraleeyam	T
Kovalikam Resort	G
KTDC Waterscapes	I
Kumarakom Lake Resort	J
Lake Palace Resort	U
Lakeside Homestay	L
Marari Beach Resort	D
Motty's Beach House	B
Palm Lagoon	Y
Philip Kutty's	C
Pozhiyoram Beach Resort	Q
Punnamada	S
Radisson Plaza	M
Taj Garden Retreat	K
VJ's Rice Garden	W

══ Major paved roads
── Minor paved roads
----- Ferry routes

136

figure, "Amma". It stands in the village of **VALLIKKAVU**, 10km northwest of Karunaganapali – a striking vision of pink tower blocks, capped with concrete domed cupolas, rising incongruously above the palm canopy on a sliver of land between the sea and the backwaters. Thousands of visitors and residents may be here at any given time, but numbers swell considerably when Amma herself is in residence – January to April and August to mid-November are the best times to catch her.

Amma offers her famous hugs to visitors during Darshan sessions, held on Wednesdays, Thursdays and Fridays from noon, and from 10am on weekends. After 5pm, *bhajans*, or devotional songs, precede a more formal Bhava Darshan ritual, in which Amma dons the garb of Krishna and Devi (Goddess) and removes successive layers to reveal "a glimpse of the Divine beneath". Quite how this squares with Amma's repeated assertions that she does not wish to be seen as a Goddess is a matter that frequently gets debated in the Indian media, but it's a popular event for her devotees. Other more low-key activities visitors are welcome to attend include various ceremonial chants, meditation sessions, spiritual discussions and scripture classes facilitated by senior ashramites throughout the day and evening.

For those wishing to stay, **accommodation** is available in simple rooms (visitors are expected to put in a couple of hours' voluntary service). Free vegetarian meals are served three times daily. A few house rules apply: celibacy, modest dress and soft speech are mandatory; and drugs, alcohol and non-vegetarian food are forbidden.

The hugging saint

On Sept 27, 2003, an extraordinary birthday celebration was staged at Kochi's Jawaharlal Nehru Stadium. Around a half a million people from 91 countries turned up for the party, among them the Indian president and deputy prime minister. The queue of well-wishers spiralled out of the ground and across the city. At the head of it, embracing each one in turn, stood a small, round, 50-year-old Keralan lady wrapped in a white sari with an even whiter smile on her dark face.

Mata Amritanandamayi ("Mother of Immortal Bliss") – or just plain "Amma" ("Mum") to her devotees – is one of India's all-time spiritual megastars. To call her a guru would be both an understatement and distortion, for although Amma does occasionally speak to her followers, she's regarded less as a teacher than an "embodiment of pure, selfless Love" – which she imparts primarily, and most famously, through the simple act of a hug.

Born in 1953 to a low-caste fishing family, "Sudhamani", as she was first called, showed signs of being special from an early age. While still a child she would spend hours in deep meditation, composing emotionally charged *bhajans* to Krishna, having strange visions and caring for elderly or sick neighbours.

After her 21st birthday she left her family to escape an unwanted arranged marriage and made a vow of celibacy. Gradually, devotees began to gather around her; in May 1981, a small ashram was founded in the Kuttanad backwaters, in her home village of Parayakadavu. Thereafter, Amma's fame rapidly spread far beyond Kerala, inspiring a mass following in Europe and the States. In the process, her ashram, the **Mata Amritanandamayi ("MA") Math**, expanded into a huge complex of sugary-pink skyscrapers, with a permanent population of 1800 and a transient one of many times more.

When she's not receiving visitors at home, Amma is out on the road, taking her trademark embrace on tour to the organization's 33 centres worldwide. Over the past few decades it's been estimated that she's hugged a staggering 30 million individuals, which explains why her rate has speeded up from one to five people per minute in recent years. Yet most of those who experience an Amma hug claim to be filled with a vivid, powerful feeling of love, as if she's somehow managed to tap into their own emotional core. "Her presence heals," declared Deepak Chopra, one of many high-profile fans, among whom number CEOs of some of the world's most successful multinationals.

The years of hugging, backed up by some well-focused marketing and merchandizing in the US and Europe, have made Amma and her aides very wealthy indeed. No one can say for sure how much money the MA trust turns over, but the ashram spends vast sums on charitable works: hospitals, free food programs, schools, medical camps, grants for poor students, pensions for widows, and 25,000 new homes for the needy each year, all receive generous funding by the *Math*. Amma's most public donation, however, was her pledge of $25 million to help tsunami victims in 2003. The district in which her ashram is located was badly hit by the Boxing Day waves, and the MA trust was quick to respond, providing disaster relief in Kerala, Tamil Nadu and the Andaman Islands.

Her much publicized generosity has seen a massive upsurge in Amma's popularity of late. You'll see her photograph beaming from roadside hoardings, taxi dashboards and hotel receptions all over Kerala, especially in the backwaters area. But Amma has her detractors, too, principally among Kerala's Christian and Muslim minorities, who accuse her of pedalling a form of Hinduism with links to right-wing political groups.

Whether such claims are based on communal paranoia or actual fact, it's undeniable that Amma, who lives a modest existence in a one-bedroom flat in her ashram, has created an effective form of wealth redistribution, channelling huge amounts of cash from her wealthy supporters to the needy across India.

For more on visiting her ashram, the MA Math, see pp.135–136.

Kayamkulam

KAYAMKULAM, served by local buses from Kollam and Alappuzha, was once the centre of its own small kingdom, which after a battle in 1746 came under the control of Travancore's king, Marthanda Varma. In the eighteenth century, the area was famous for its spices, particularly pepper and cinnamon. The French Renaissance social reformer and traveller Abbé Reynal claimed that the Dutch exported some two million pounds of pepper each year, one fifth of it from Kayamkulam. At this time, the kingdom was also known for the skill of its army, made up of 15,000 Nair (Kerala's martial caste). These days, NH–47's endless through traffic dominates the town's ailing economy, together with the local backwater coir and fishing industries. One vestige of Kayamkulam's former glory, however, survives.

Set in a tranquil garden on the outskirts of town, just off the main highway, the eighteenth-century **Krishnapuram Palace** (Tues–Sat 10am–4.30pm; Rs5, camera Rs15) is imbued with Keralan grace, constructed largely of wood with gabled roofs and rooms opening out onto shady internal court-yards. Inside, a small museum displays coins, puja ceremony utensils and oil lamps, some of which are arranged in an arc known as a *prabhu*, placed behind a temple deity to provide a halo of light. Fine miniature *panchaloha* ("five-metal") bronze alloy, with gold as one ingredient) figures include the water god Varuna, several Vishnus and a minuscule worshipping devotee. Small stone columns carved with serpent deities were recovered from local houses.

The prize exhibit, however, is a huge **mural** of the classical Keralan school, in muted ochre-reds and blue-greens, which covers more than fourteen square metres. It depicts **Gajendra Moksha** – the salvation of Gajendra, king of the elephants. In the tenth-century Sanskrit *Bhagavata Purana*, the story is told of a Pandyan king, Indrayumna, a devotee of Vishnu cursed by the sage Agastya to be born again as an elephant. One day, while sporting with his wives at the edge of a lake, his leg was seized by a crocodile whose grip was so tight that Gajendra was held captive for years. Finally, in desperation, the elephant called upon his chosen deity Vishnu, who immediately appeared, riding his celestial bird-man vehicle, Garuda, and destroyed the crocodile. The centre of the painting is dominated by a dynamic portrayal of Garuda about to land, with huge spread wings and a facial expression denoting *raudra* (fury), in stark contrast to the compassionate features of the multi-armed Vishnu. Smaller figures of Gajendra in mid-trumpet, and of his assailant, are shown to the right. As with all paintings in the Keralan style, every inch is packed with detail. Bearded sages, animals, mythical beasts and forest plants surround the main figures. The outer edges are decorated with floriate borders, which at the bottom form a separate triptych-like panel showing Balakrishna, the child Krishna, attended by adoring women.

Alappuzha (Alleppey)

Roughly midway between Kollam (85km south) and Kochi (64km north), **ALAPPUZHA** once ranked among the wealthiest ports along the Malabar Coast, acting as a clearing house for spices, coffee, tea, cashews, coir and other produce shipped from the backwaters. Unlike its rivals elsewhere in the region, however, the town – known in colonial times, and still commonly referred to, as "Alleppey" – didn't see its heyday until the mid-1800s, by which time the main canal scything through its heart, linking the waterways with the Arabian Sea, was lined with factories and warehouses. Alappuzha prospered to such an extent that the successful British traders who had settled here during the Raj were loath to leave at Independence. A sizeable community of expats remained after 1947, but their luck ran out ten years later, when the newly elected communist government clamped down on private businesses and they were forced to return to Britain.

With its trading history and interconnecting **canals**, tourist literature is fond of referring to Alappuzha as the "Venice of the East". Don't expect too much of a resemblance, though: cut through by the main national highway, the busy centre is as ramshackle and chaotic as any mid-sized Keralan town, although it does boast some quiet and leafy suburbs sporting rows of old colonial-era wharfs and bungalows.

The town is still a major hub in the coir industry, which accounts for much of the water-borne traffic chugging to and from the nearby lakes. However, the big bucks these days are being made from **houseboat cruises**. Around five hundred *kettu vallam* barges operate in the Kuttanad area – four hundred of them out of Alappuzha itself. The resulting congestion has proved a major challenge for the ecosystem of the backwaters (see box, p.144). It's possible to explore the area ethically, though, and Alappuzha provides plenty of scope for day-trips into the network of narrow canals around the town, which you can cover on environmentally friendly man-powered punts or canoes, as well as offering some of the state's best-value accommodation – much of it in characterful homestays.

Arrival and information

The KSRTC **bus stand**, served by regular buses to and from Kollam, Kottayam, Thiruvananthapuram, Ernakulam and most other major Keralan towns, stands at the northeast edge of town. Close to its north exit, the main boat jetty on **Vadai Canal** is where the daily tourist ferry to and from Kollam, and local boat connections with Kottayam, arrive and depart. The **railway station,** on the main Thiruvananthapuram–Ernakulam line, lies 3km southwest across town, on the far side of Alappuzha's main waterway, **Commercial Canal**.

The town has several rival **tourist departments**, all of them eager to offer advice and book you onto their respective houseboat tours. The most conveniently situated – at the jetty itself on VCSB (Vadai Canal South Bank) Road – are the DTPC **tourist reception centre** (daily 7.30am–9pm; ☎0477/225 1796) and adjacent Kerala Tourism office (Mon–Sat 10am–5pm; ☎0477/226 0722, ⓦwww.keralatourism.org). On the opposite side of the canal on the corner of Mullackal and Vadai Canal North (VCNB) Road, ATDC's main information office (daily 8am–8pm; ☎0477/224 346 or "Shambhu" ☎m98950 10833, ⓦwww.atdcalleppey.com) is more tucked away, on the second floor of the Municipal Shopping Complex. Both ATDC and DTPC sell tickets for their ferries, backwater cruises and charter boats, and can help you fathom the intricacies of local ferry timetables.

You can **change money** at the efficient UTI bank on Mullackal Road (Mon–Sat 9.30am–4.30pm). Both it and the State Bank of India directly opposite have reliable ATMs. **Internet** access is widely available for Rs30–40 per hour, with several outlets along the road facing the boat jetty; Mailbox on VCSB Road, five minutes' walk west of Mullackal Road, boasts the town's fastest connection.

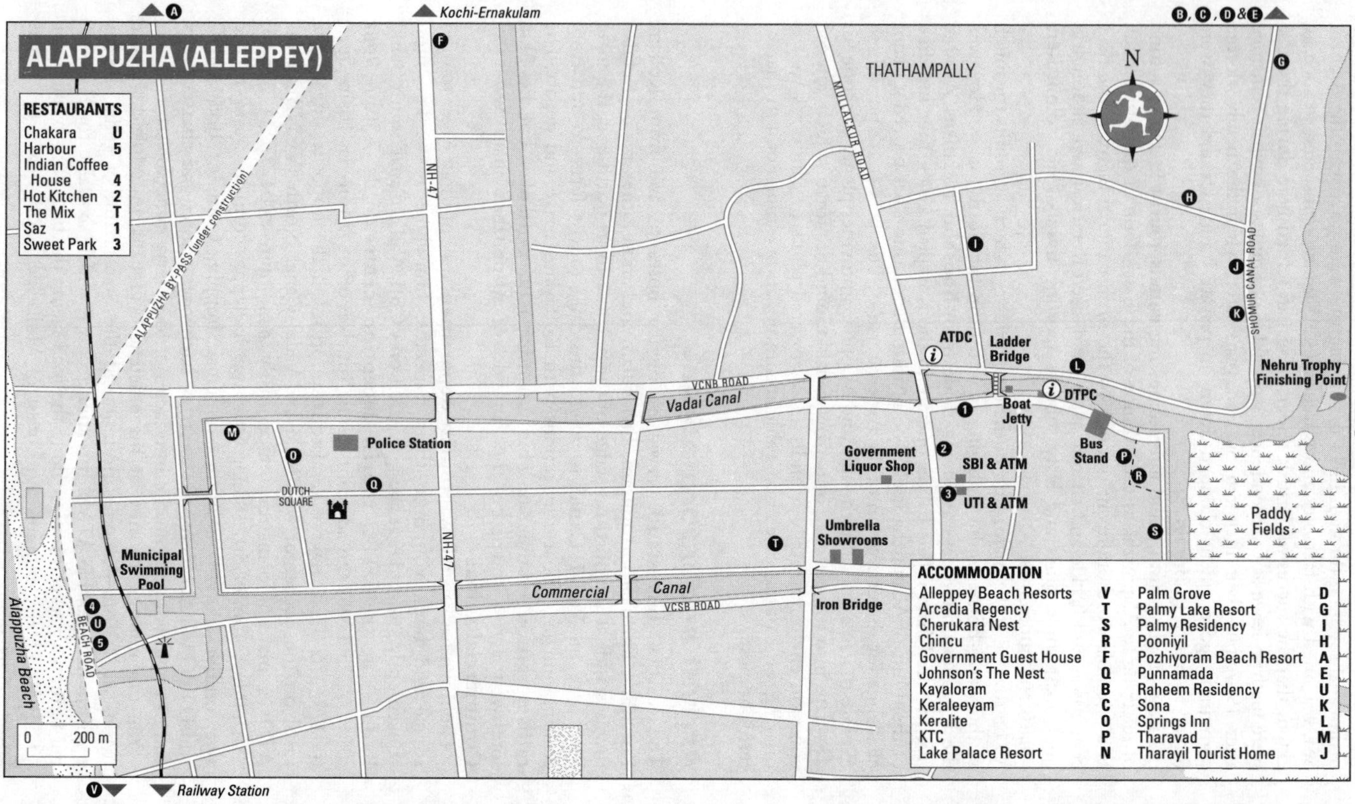

ALAPPUZHA (ALLEPPEY)

RESTAURANTS

Chakara	U
Harbour	5
Indian Coffee House	4
Hot Kitchen	2
The Mix	T
Saz	1
Sweet Park	3

ACCOMMODATION

Alleppey Beach Resorts	D
Arcadia Regency	G
Cherukara Nest	I
Chincu	H
Government Guest House	F
Johnson's The Nest	Q
Kayaloram	B
Keraleeyam	C
Keralite	O
KTC	P
Lake Palace Resort	N
Palm Grove	V
Palmy Lake Resort	T
Palmy Residency	S
Poonyil	R
Pozhiyoram Beach Resort	A
Punnamada	E
Raheem Residency	U
Sona	K
Springs Inn	L
Tharavad	M
Tharayil Tourist Home	J

Nehru Trophy Finishing Point

Paddy Fields

SHOMUR CANAL ROAD

THATHAMPALLY

MULLACKUR ROAD

Kochi-Ernakulam

NH-47

NH-47

ALAPPUZHA BY-PASS (under construction)

BEACH ROAD

Railway Station

Alappuzha Beach

Municipal Swimming Pool

DUTCH SQUARE

Police Station

Commercial Canal

VCSB ROAD

Canal

VCSB ROAD

Iron Bridge

Umbrella Showrooms

Government Liquor Shop

Vadai Canal

VCNB ROAD

SBI & ATM

UTI & ATM

Boat Jetty

Ladder Bridge

ATDC

DTPC

Bus Stand

0   200 m

Accommodation

The choice of **places to stay** in the town centre is fairly uninspiring, but there are some great possibilities in all brackets if you are willing to travel to the outskirts and pay a little more. In the suburb of **Thathampally**, on the fringes of the Punnamada Lake, a string of ultra-luxurious resorts soak up the tour group and honeymoon custom in campuses of reassembled Keralan wooden houses, located on the water's edge.

Nearly everywhere, whatever its bracket, has some kind of tie-in with a houseboat operator: good-natured encouragement tends to be the order of the day rather then hard-sell tactics, but you may be able to negotiate a reduction on your room tariff if you do end up booking a backwater trip. In Alappuzha, as elsewhere in the state, rates tend to increase by 25–30 percent between mid-December and mid-January. Whenever you come, and wherever you chose to stay, though, brace yourself for clouds of **mosquitoes**.

All the hotels listed below are marked on, or arrowed off, the main Alappuzha map opposite; places further out of town also appear on the Kuttanad map on p.136.

Budget

Chincu near KSRTC bus stand ⊕0477/223 6687, ⊕m98951 06817, ⊛www.arcadiaregency.com. Three impeccably clean attached rooms in a converted portion of a small family home, hidden down a narrow alleyway close to (but beyond earshot of) the bus stand. If it's booked up, the slightly less appealing, but cheaper *KTC* ⊕0477/225 4275, ⊕m98461 15553; ②–③) is up the same lane. ②–③

Government Guesthouse next door to KTDC *Yatri Niwas*, on NH-47 ⊕0477/224 6504. Like its namesakes in other Keralan towns, this place is basically set up for the benefit of visiting officials, but they'll accommodate tourists if there are vacancies (though you'll probably have to call in person on the day). Ranged on two floors above a central courtyard, the rooms are plain and a touch institutional, but fantastic for the price (Rs220 non-a/c or Rs450 for much nicer a/c), with big, clean bathrooms. ②–③

Johnson's The Nest Lalbagh, Convent Square, 2km west of the centre ⊕m 09961 466399, ⊛www.johnsonskerala.com. Friendly, sociable homestay on a quiet suburban street, popular mainly with young backpackers. Its six individually themed en-suite rooms are large, with Barbie-pink mosquito nets, and most have funky little sitouts fitted with cane swings. Money exchange, laundry and meals available – and they offer enjoyable day-trips to a quiet beach north of Alappuzha. ②–④

Keralite Vadakekalam House, north of Dutch Square ⊕0477/224 3569, ⓔalice_t@rediffmail.com. Opening onto a broad sand courtyard filled with pot plants, the heart of this delightful 100-year-old house is a high-ceilinged salon where hostess Alice Thomas serves traditional Syrian-Christian meals under the watchful eye of ancestral portraits. Comfortable antique beds furnish the guest rooms, which have lots of period atmosphere; the only catch is that some lack en-suite bathrooms – hence the bargain rates. ③–④

Palmy Residency North of DTPC tourist office, beyond Ladder Bridge ⊕0477/223 5938, ⊕m94476 67888, ⊛www.palmyresort.com. Up a sidestreet 5min walk from Main Canal, this well-run guesthouse (an off-shoot of the excellent *Palmy Resort*) is situated in a quiet neighbourhood. It has six rooms in total – the two cheaper ones around the back of the building are great no-frills budget options, with mozzie nets and attached bathrooms; an extra Rs250 buys you more space and a TV. ③–④

Pooniyil Thathampally, 1km north of the boat jetty ⊕0477/223 2593, ⊕m98471 09074. Annexe of three simple rooms, plus a curious palm-leaf and wood "cottage" (worth the Rs100 extra), in a sandy compound off the Punnamada Rd; they're a bit spartan and not all that big, but impeccably clean, and there's a long north-facing veranda to laze on. Comfortable and pretty good value, with some of the cheapest a/c options in Alappuzha. ③–④

Springs Inn Nehru Trophy Rd ⊕m98477 50000. Three simple en-suite rooms with white walls, wood ceilings and red-oxide tiled floors, fronted by a shady veranda. A bit boxed in by the neighbouring block, but clean and well placed for the boat jetty. Tariffs include Mrs Kumar's fragrant Keralan breakfasts. ③

Mid-range

Alleppey Beach Resorts Beach Rd ☎ 0477/226 3408, ⊚ www.thealleppeybeachresorts.com. See map on p.136. Eccentric, slightly Fawlty-Towers-esque hotel offering Alappuzha's only beachside rooms. Opening onto common verandas with great sea views, they're huge (the non-a/c "deluxe" on the first floor are vast) and a bit overpriced, but many will consider the relaxing, breezy location worth the extra. Moreover, the food gets rave reviews from guests. ➅–➆

Arcadia Regency Near the Iron Bridge ☎ 0477/223 0414, ⊚ www.arcadiaregency.com. A gleaming, multi-storey tower block clad in white-painted concrete and tinted windows. Hardly the most sympathetic addition to the town's historic centre in recent years, but it offers good-value three-star accommodation: modern rooms, a multi-cuisine restaurant, 24hr coffee shop and splendid rooftop pool. ➄

Cherukara Nest 9/774 Cherukara Bldgs ☎ 0477/225 1509, ☎ m99470 59628. Nineteenth-century "heritage" home, run by the welcoming Mr Tony John, on a quiet canal road only a short walk around the corner from the KSRTC bus stand. The cheaper of his four rooms are light with high ceilings; those to the rear, in converted teak-lined granaries, are gloomier but possess more Keralan character. Breakfast is served in an old courtyard. Eco-friendly houseboat cruises are a sideline. ➃–➄

Palm Grove Lake Resort Punnamada Kayal, 3.5km north of boat jetty ☎ 0477/223 5004, ☎ m98474 30434, ⊚ www.palmgrovelakeresort .com. Situated at a tranquil spot close to where the canal meets Punnamada Lake, this relaxed resort actually overlooks the water – a perfect spot from which to watch the snake boat races. Shaded by areca and coconut palms, its quaint bamboo cottages have gabled tile roofs, private outdoor showers and sitouts opening onto the garden. *Palm Grove* isn't in the same league as the luxury places up the lane, but is a lot more affordable. ➄–➅

Palmy Lake Resort Thathampally, 2km north of boat jetty ☎ 0477/223 5938, ☎ m94476 67888, ⊚ www.palmyresort.com. Spacious, neatly painted red-tiled "cottages" (a/c and non-a/c), grouped behind a modern family home on the northeastern limits of town. Despite the name, it isn't actually on the lake, but offers exceptional value for money. You get loads of space for the price: all rooms have private pillared verandas opening onto a restful garden. Owners Biggi and Mercy Matthews are smiling hosts,

providing delicious home-cooked Keralan meals. Phone ahead for free pick-up. ➃–➄

Pozhiyoram Beach Resort 5km north of Alappuzha town ☎ 0477/325 6238, ☎ m93878 27235, ⊚ www.pozhiyorambeachresort.com. See map on p.136. Only a 10min drive up the coast road, but a world away from the bustle of Alappuzha town, on the edge of a small lagoon and white sand beach. Its accommodation comprises four simple "beach view" rooms, with sea-facing sitouts right next to the sand, and more comfortable, pricier "Kerala cottages" further back in the palm grove, sporting gabled roofs and little verandas. Traditional Kuttanad meals are served in a little restaurant overlooking the waterfront, featuring seafood straight off the nearby fishing boats. ➅–➆

Sona Shomur Canal Rd, Thathampally ☎ 0477/223 5211, ⊚ www.sonahome.com. Elegant old Keralan home, with a graceful gabled roof, set back from the road to the lake. The four rooms in the original house, run by an elderly owner who loves to share his knowledge of the town and its backwaters, are far more attractive (and cheaper) than the three cheekily squeezed-in new ones in the garden. This place gets mixed reviews, but ranks among the least expensive heritage homestays within easy reach of the jetty. Meals, houseboat rental and ayurvedic treatments available. ➃–➄

Tharavad West of North Police Station, Sea View Ward ☎ 0477/224 4599, ⊚ www .tharavadheritageresort.com. Few of Alappuzha's heritage properties retain as pukka a feel as this former doctor's mansion, which rests in the shade of an old mango tree on the quiet west side of town. Entered via a typically colonial-era veranda, its interior holds polished eggshell and teak floors, carved rosewood furniture and antique bell-metal curios collected by successive generations. The differently priced rooms (ranging from singles to family suites) are all large and well aired, the only concessions to the modern era being their bathrooms. Meals available. ➃–➆

Tharayil Tourist Home Shomur Canal Rd, Thathampally ☎ 0477/223 3543, ⊚ www .tharayiltouristhome.com. In a 1980s building on the edge of town, this modest, family-run guest-house soaks up most of the overspill from nearby *Sona*. It has 8 simple a/c and non-a/c rooms; they're spacious, well ventilated and nicely furnished, with comfy modern beds and individual balconies. A row of four recently added "cottages" outside are fancier but not such good value. ➃–➄

Luxury

Kayaloram Punnamada Kayal ☎ 0477/223 2040, ⓦ www.kayaloram.com. See map on p.136. Twelve antique Keralan wood *tharavadukal*, complete with luxurious interiors and private "open-to-sky" bathrooms, dotted around an immaculate palm garden running right to the lakeside. The location is sublime, offering uninterrupted views across the water, and there's a good-sized pool and open-sided restaurant if you tire of relaxing on your own terrace. *Kayaloram* claims to have been the first resort to make use of relocated period houses, and it's still one of the most congenial of its type. Rates include boat transfer from the Nehru Trophy jetty. From $235. ⑨

Keraleeyam Nehru Trophy Rd, Thathampally ☎ 0477/223 1468, ⓦ www.keraleeyam.com. See map on p.136. This small-scale backwater resort, run by a famous ayurveda outfit, is centred on one of most beautiful period houses in the Alappuzha area, facing the Punnamada canal close to where it runs into the lake, near the start of the snake boat race. Capped with a picture-postcard twin-gabled roof, the old building has a few rooms; the palm-leaf huts in the garden, which open straight onto the water's edge and are perfectly placed to watch the houseboats chug past, are much better value. ⑦–⑧

Lake Palace Resort 4km across Vembanad Lake ☎ 0477/223 9701, ⓦ www.lakepaceresort.com. See map on p.136. Owned by a local politician, the *Lake Palace* is the most recent, and ostentatiously grand, of Alappuzha's upscale resort complexes, though it lacks the traditional style of smaller places closer to town. The 50-acre site is centred on a private lagoon and offers three types of accommodation, the flashiest of them "Jumbo-Sized Water Villas" on stilts. Access is by boat transfer from a jetty near the KSRTC bus stand. Rates start at Rs10,5000/$250. ⑨

Punnamada 4km north, on Punnamada Lake ☎ 0477/223 3690, ⓦ www.punnamada.com. See map on p.136. Large, formulaic five-star resort, sprawling over landscaped gardens and more than a kilometre of its own exclusive water frontage. The rooms come in four categories, the nicest of them "lake-facing" and double-storeyed "duplex villas", which both have their own private alfresco showers and pebble gardens. From $145. ⑨

🏃 **Raheem Residency** Beach Rd ☎ 0477/223 9767, ⓦ www.raheemresidency.com. The glossiest of Alappuzha's heritage hotels occupies a grand 140-year-old mansion on the beachfront. Sumptuously restored from near dereliction by its Indian-Irish owners, the building encloses half-a-dozen spacious, richly furnished a/c rooms, equipped with carved four-posters (some of which you need a step to climb into) and original wood and glass window shutters. For outside lounging space, you've a gorgeous imported French swimming pool, hammocks on a roof terrace and a breezy open-sided restaurant. $200–300. ⑨

The town, lakes and beach

Alappuzha tends to be eclipsed by the backwaters that unfold from its eastern flank, but it's definitely worth setting aside an afternoon to sample the town's own idiosyncratic charms. Thanks to recent efforts by the local council to clean up the canals, some of the older sidestreets, with their colonial-era factories and warehouses, are a lot more pleasant than they used to be. The best way of **getting around** them is to rent a bicycle. There's usually someone in front of the DTPC tourist office with a couple of rattly old Heros to spare: if not, ask inside and they'll help you find one.

Because of the intense traffic pouring through it, you're more likely to want to browse the main bazaar, **Mullackal Road**, on foot. It's crammed with a typically Keralan assortment of shops, from gold jewellery emporia to bell-metal and fishing hardware suppliers. Beyond its southern side (on the north bank of the canal; see map, p.140), is another quintessentially South Indian sight: a row of snazzy a/c **umbrella showrooms**, stocking every conceivable colour and size of brolly, whether smart monsoon-grade ones with lacquered handles or the faintly ridiculous plastic parasols backwater canoeists strap on their heads.

You might well want to invest in a sunshade for trips out to **Alappuzha's lakes**: Punnamada and Vembanad. Reaching them from town is most

Kuttanad: the backwaters of Kerala

One of the most memorable experiences for travellers in India is the opportunity to take a boat journey on the **backwaters of Kerala**. The area, known as **Kuttanad** (see map, p.136) stretches for 75km from Kollam in the south to Kochi in the north, sandwiched between the sea and the hills. This bewildering labyrinth of shimmering waterways, composed of lakes, canals, rivers and rivulets, is lined with dense tropical greenery and preserves rural Keralan lifestyles that are completely hidden from the road.

Views constantly change, from narrow canals and dense vegetation to open vistas and dazzling green paddy fields. Homes, farms, churches, mosques and temples can be glimpsed among the trees, and every so often you might catch the blue flash of a kingfisher, or the green of a parakeet. Pallas fishing eagles cruise above the water looking for prey and cormorants perch on logs to dry their wings. If you're lucky enough to be in a **boat** without a motor, at times the only sounds are birds chattering and occasional film songs drifting across from distant radios. Some families live on tiny pockets of land, with just enough room for a simple house, yard and boat. They bathe and wash their clothes – sometimes their buffaloes, too, muddy from ploughing the fields – at the water's edge. Traditional Keralan longboats, *kettu vallam*, glide along, powered by gondolier-like boatmen with poles, the water often lapping perilously close to the edge. Fishermen work from tiny dugout canoes and long rowing boats, and operate massive Chinese nets on the shore.

Coconut trees at improbable angles form shady canopies, and occasionally you pass under simple curved bridges. Poles sticking out of the water indicate dangerous shallows. Here and there basic drawbridges can be raised on ropes, but major bridges are few and far between; most people rely on boatmen to ferry them across the water to connect with roads and bus services, resulting in a constant crisscrossing of the waters from dawn until dusk – a way of life beautifully represented in the visually stunning film *Piravi*, by Keralan director Shaji.

Threats to the ecosystem

The **African moss** that often carpets the surface of the narrower waterways may look attractive, but it is actually a menace to small craft traffic and starves underwater life of light. It is also a symptom of the many serious **ecological problems** currently affecting the region, whose population density ranges from between two and four times that of other coastal areas in southwest India. This has put growing pressure on land, and hence a greater reliance on fertilizers, which eventually work their way into the water causing the build-up of moss. Illegal land reclamation, however, poses the single greatest threat to this fragile ecosystem. In a little over a century, the total area of water in Kuttanad has been reduced by two-thirds, while mangrove swamps and fish stocks have been decimated by pollution and the spread of towns and villages around the edges of the backwater region. Tourism is now adding to the problem, as the film of oil from motorized ferries and houseboats spreads through the waters, killing yet more fish, which has in turn led to a reduction of over fifty percent in the number of bird species found in the region. Some of the tourist agencies are trying to lessen the impact of visitors by introducing more eco-friendly vessels (see p.146).

Tourist cruises

The most popular excursion of all in the Kuttanad region is the full-day journey between **Kollam** and **Alappuzha**. All sorts of private hustlers offer their services, but the principal boats are run on alternate days by the Alleppey Tourism Development Co-op (ATDC) and the District Tourism Promotion Council (DTPC) – see p.139 for contact details. The double-decker boats leave from both Kollam and Alappuzha daily, departing at 10.30am (10am check-in); tickets cost Rs300 and can be bought in advance or on the day at the ATDC/DTPC counters, other agents and some hotels. Both companies make three stops during the eight-hour journey, including one for lunch, and another at the **Mata Amritanandamayi Math** at Amritapuri (see p.135), around three hours north of Kollam.

Although it is by far the main backwater route, many tourists find Alappuzha–Kollam too long, with crowded decks and intense sun. There's also something faintly embarrassing about being cooped up with a crowd of fellow tourists, madly photographing any signs of life on the water or canal banks, while gangs of kids scamper alongside the boat screaming "one pen, one pen".

One alternative is to charter a four- or six-seater motorboat, which you can do through DTPC and ATDC for around Rs300/hr. Slower, more cumbersome double-decker country boats are also available for hire from Rs250/hr.

Village tours and canoes

Quite apart from their significant **environmental impact**, most houseboats are too wide to squeeze into the narrower inlets connecting small villages. To reach these more idyllic, remote areas, therefore, you'll need to charter a punted **canoe** (see p.146). The slower pace means less distance gets covered in an hour, but the experience of being so close to the water, and those who live on it, tends to be correspondingly more rewarding. Individual guides have their own favourite itineraries. You'll also find more formal **"village tours"** advertised across the Kuttanad area, tying together trips to watch coir makers, rice farmers and boat builders in action with the opportunity to dine in a traditional Keralan village setting.

Kettu vallam (houseboats)

Whoever dreamed up the idea of showing tourists around the backwaters in old rice barges, or **kettu vallam**, could never have imagined that two decades on, five hundred or more of them would be chugging around Kuttanad waterways. These **houseboats**, made of dark, oiled jackwood with canopies of plaited palm thatch and coir, are big business, and almost every mid- and upmarket hotel, guesthouse and "heritage homestay" seems to have one. An estimated four hundred work out of Alappuzha alone, the flashiest fitted with a/c rooms, silk cushions on their teak sun decks, imported wine in their fridges and Jacuzzis that bubble away through the night. One grand juggernaut (called the *Vaikundan*, based near Amma's ashram in Kollam district) holds ten separate bedrooms and won't slip its lines for less than Rs25,000 ($580). At the opposite end of the scale are rough-and-ready transport barges with gut-thumping diesel engines, cramped bedrooms and minimal washing facilities.

What you end up paying for your cruise will depend on a number of variables: the **size** and **quality** of the boat and its fittings; the number and standard of the **bedrooms** (a/c will bump up the price by around 50–75 percent); and, crucially, the **time of year**. Rates double over Christmas and New Year, and halve off-season during the monsoons. In practice, however, Rs4500–8000 is the usual bracket for a trip on a two-bedroom, non-a/c boat with a proper bathroom (or Rs11,000–14,000 for a/c), including three meals, in early December or mid-January. The cruise should last a minimum of 22 hours, though don't expect to spend all of that on the move: running times are carefully calculated to spare gas. From sunset onwards you'll be moored at a riverbank, probably on the outskirts of the town where the trip started.

You'll save quite a lot of cash, and be doing the fragile ecosystem a big favour, by opting for a more environmentally-friendly punted *kettu vallam*. This was how rice barges were traditionally propelled, and though it means you travel at a more leisurely pace, the experience is silent (great for wildlife spotting) and altogether more relaxing.

Houseboat operators work out of **Kollam**, **Karunaganapali** and **Kumbakonam**, but by far the highest concentration is in **Alappuzha**, where you'll find the lowest prices – but also the worst congestion on more scenic routes. Spend a day shopping around for a deal (your guesthouse or hotel owner will be a good first port of call) and always check the boat over beforehand. It's also a good idea to get the deal fixed on paper before setting off, and to withhold a final payment until the end of the cruise in case of arguments.

Local ferries

Kettu vallam may offer the most comfortable way of cruising the backwaters, but you'll get a much more vivid experience of what life is actually like in the region by jumping on one of the local **ferries** that serve its towns and villages. Particularly recommended is the trip from **Alappuzha to Kottayam** (5 daily; 2hr 30min; Rs12), which winds across open lagoons and narrow canals, through coconut groves and islands. The first ferry leaves at 7.30am; arrive early to get a good place with uninterrupted views.

There are also numerous other local routes that you can jump on and off, though working your way through the complexities of the timetables and Malayalam names can be difficult without the help of the tourist office. Good places to aim for from Alappuzha include **Neerettupuram**, **Kidangara** and **Champakulam**; all three are served by regular daily ferries, but you may have to change boats once or twice along the way, killing time in local cafés and toddy shops (all of which adds to the fun, of course). Whatever service you opt for, take a sun hat and plenty of water.

straightforward by water. For short cruises, it's possible to charter diesel-powered **motorboats** (Rs250/hr) or more sedate, twin-decked **country boats** (Rs300/hr) from ATDC/DTPC. Better still, dispense with engines altogether and opt for a guided **village tour** in a hand-paddled canoe. Aside from being more "green", these allow you to penetrate narrow waterways beyond the range of the other tourist boats. DTPC offer their own punted tours, carrying two people for Rs150/hr. One commendable private operator who's been ferrying tourists around Alappuzha's off-track backwaters for years is Mr K.D. Prasenan (☏m93888 44712), based at the *Palm Grove Lake Resort* on the Punnamada Kayal, 3.5km north of the boat jetty. In a slender ten-metre boat, he offers five- and nine-hour trips (Rs1250/2200 respectively, for two people) via routes connecting the Holy Padma River and Punnamada Lake – both get consistently glowing reviews from readers.

In the opposite direction, on the west side of town, you pass through Alappuzha's formerly affluent, colonial-era suburbs, which gradually open out as you approach the town **beach**. Although unsuitable for swimming and sunbathing, the wide, gleaming white sands stretch out of sight in both directions and provide a welcome blast of fresh air. A British-built **pier** extends a kilometre into the surf from its centre. Dating from 1862, the jetty once supported three separate railway lines that fanned out to wharfs around the town. These days, however, its stark silhouette receives scant attention, except during Kerala Tourism's annual **beach festival** in late-December, when it serves as a surreal backdrop for various cultural events and a procession of fifty caparisoned elephants.

The snake boat races

Alappuzha really comes alive on the second Saturday of August, in the middle of the monsoon, when it serves as the venue for one of Kerala's major spectacles – the **Nehru Trophy snake boat race**. This event, first held in 1952, is based on the traditional Keralan enthusiasm for racing magnificently decorated longboats, with raised rears designed to resemble the hood of a cobra. Each boat carries 25 singers, and 100–130 enthusiastic oarsmen power the craft along, all rowing to the rhythmic *Vanchipattu* ("song of the boatman"). There are a number of prize categories, including one for the women's race; sixteen boats compete for each prize in knock-out rounds. Similar races can be seen at Aranmula (p.156), and at Champakulam, 16km by ferry from Alappuzha (p.147). The ATDC information office (see p.139) will be able to tell you the dates of these other events, which change every year.

Eating

Aside from the **restaurants** listed below, most of Alappuzha's homestays and guesthouses provide meals for guests, usually delicious, home-cooked Keralan food that's tailored for sensitive Western tastes. Many of them also serve cold beers, albeit discreetly, in little china pots. For **take-outs**, you can join the scrum that forms each evening outside the government "beverages" shop, just off Mullackal Road in the main bazaar (see map, p.140).

Chakara *Raheem Residency*, Beach Rd ☏ 0477/223 0767. "Chakara" means "bumper catch of fish" in Malayalam, and the accent in this, Alappuzha's classiest restaurant, is firmly on seafood, with specialities ranging from local-style fish curry (their signature dish) to seer fish simmered in flavoursome *moillee* coconut gravy, and crunchy masala-fried prawns to calamari – all fresh off the boats and prepared with minimal oil. They also have plenty of tempting, healthy continental alternatives, courteously served on a raised terrace looking across the beach. Count on Rs650 for a fixed 4-course menu; or a bit more à la carte.

Harbour Beach Rd. All the food served in this gleaming little seafront restaurant is prepared in the kitchens of the swanky *Raheem Residency* next door, so quality and freshness are assured. You can order grilled prawns, Alappuzha-style chicken curry, Kuttanadi fish, chilli chicken or a range of light continental meals, snacks and sandwiches, dished up in a dining hall with bare laterite walls under an old-style tiled roof. For dessert, there's fruit salad with ice cream and coconut. Most mains are under Rs100.

Indian Coffee House Beach Rd. The usual smudged cotton uniforms and insipid *ICH* menu of *udipi* snacks and rice-based meals, but under a traditional pagoda-shaped shelter on the beachfront. The food may not be up to much, but the coffee is okay and the location pleasantly breezy in the afternoons.

Hot Kitchen Mullackal Rd. The most reputed pure-veg South Indian "meals" restaurant in town, run by a Tamil family that has been here for genera-tions. The masala *dosas*, *vadas* and other fried snacks aren't so great, and the dining hall's seen better days, but the lunch-time thalis (also available in the evening) are deservedly popular.

The Mix *Arcadia Regency*, near Iron Bridge, NH-47 ☎0477/223 0414. Modern multi-cuisine restaurant in Alappuzha's only Western-style business hotel, noteworthy as much for its strident red decor as its good-value, "all-you-can-eat" buffets (Rs125), featuring a huge range of Chinese and North Indian, as well as Keralan specialities.

Saz VCSB Rd, near Ladder Bridge. This no-frills non-veg place on Vadai Canal does a roaring trade at lunchtime with its fish-curry rice plate "meals" (Rs30), while in the evenings half the tourist population of Alappuzha pours in for the succulent flame-grilled barbeque and tandoori chicken, served at a brisk pace by black-tie waiters. They also have a full-on kebab counter outside, and offer a range of typical Kuttanadi "specials", chalked on a board on the wall. It's a bit grubby, but hygienic enough and cheap, with most mains Rs80–130.

Sweet Park next to UTI Bank, Mullackal Rd. The perfect pit-stop in the main bazaar, serving freshly baked macaroons, chilli and cashew cookies, samosas, veg cutlets and flaky prawn patties, with hot coffees and teas, in an open-sided café overlooking one of the main crossroads in the market area.

Around Alappuzha

With so much congenial accommodation on offer in Alappuzha, you might be tempted to stay in the town for a couple of extra days, making short trips to outlying areas by boat, taxi or bus. The following accounts cover some of the more obvious destinations, but there are dozens of similar sites scattered around the Kuttanad area, best explored by means of local ferries from the boat jetty near the DTPC tourist office, which can help with route planning (see p.139).

South of Alappuzha

CHAMPAKULAM, 14km southeast of Alappuzha in the middle of the backwaters, is home to the **Church of St Mary's,** erected in 1579 by the Portuguese on the remains of a chapel believed to have been one of the seven founded by St Thomas the Apostle. Now a centre of Syrian-Christian worship, it boasts an extravagantly decorated Rococo interior, dripping with gold leaf and elaborate murals – some fusing elements of Hindu and Christian iconog-raphy. The church rises from the bank of a broad river where each year, in the Hindu month of Midhunam (June–July), the Champakulam boat race attracts large crowds. The village's own crew recently won the big Nehru Trophy race three years in succession, and the magnificent forty-metre-long **snake boat** they competed in is stored at a shed on the outskirts, ten minutes' walk from St Mary's. Head to the riverbank behind the church, turn right and follow the lane for 400m past the bazaar and boat jetty until you reach a stepped footbridge; instead of crossing it, keep going straight on until the next bridge and cross that, following the path as it skirts some houses, by which time you'll have the boat

Moving on from Alappuzha

As Alappuzha isn't on the main railway network, but on a branch line, the choice of **trains** servicing the town is limited. There are, however, train connections to Thiruvananthapuram and Kollam in the south, and to Kochi/Ernakulam, Thrissur, Palakkad and other points in the north. **Bus** connections are adequate, especially to Kochi/Ernakulam, where there is a greater choice of trains to northern destinations and Tamil Nadu. Although buses travel to Kollam, **boats** offers a more scenic, leisurely way of getting there. Regular ferry services connect Alappuzha to Kottayam, from where you can catch buses to Periyar, as well as several destinations along the coastal highway. For more on public transport from Alappuzha, see "Travel details", p.168.

By bus

The filthy KSRTC bus stand, on the east side of town and a minute's walk from the boat jetty, is served by regular buses to **Kollam** (2hr), **Kottayam** (1hr 30min), **Thiruvananthapuram** (3hr–3hr 30min) and **Kochi/Ernakulam** (1hr 30min). For Fort Cochin, catch any of the fast Ernakulam services along the main highway and get down at **Thoppumpady** (7km south of the city), from where local buses run the rest of the way.

By boat

Tourist boats travel regularly to **Kollam**, with the ATDC and DTPC boats operating a similar schedule, departing at 10.30am and arriving in Kollam at 6.30pm. From the jetty just outside the KSRTC bus stand, much cheaper local **ferries** travel to **Kottayam** (service P380; 2hr 30min; Rs12), with five departures between 7.30am and 2pm, and a constellation of satellite villages in the backwaters. Regular services run to Champakulam, where you pick up less frequent boats to Neerettupuram and Kidangara, and back to Alappuzha again. This round route ranks among Kuttanad's classic trips, but you'll need some help from one or other of the tourist offices to make sense of the timetables.

By train

As the backwaters prevent trains from continuing directly south beyond Alappuzha, only a few major daily services and a handful of passenger trains depart from the railway station, 3km southwest of the jetty. For points further north along the coast, take the Jan Shatabdi Express and change at Ernakulam, as the afternoon Alleppey–Cannanore Express (#6307), which runs as far as **Kozhikode** and **Kannur**, arrives at those destinations rather late at night. It is, however, a good service if you only intend to travel as far as Thrissur.

The following trains are recommended as the **fastest** and/or **most convenient** from Alappuzha.

Recommended trains from Alappuzha

Destination	Name	Number	Frequency	Departs	Total time
Ernakulam/ Kochi	Jan Shatabdi Exp.	#2076	daily	8.40am	1hr 10min
	*Alleppey–Chennai Exp.	#6042	daily	4.10pm	1hr 20min
Thiruvananthapuram	Ernakulam–Trivandrum Exp.	#6341	daily	7.20am	3hr 5min
	Jan Shatabdi Exp.	#2075	daily	6.33pm	2hr 48min
Thrissur	*Alleppey–Chennai Exp.	#6042	daily	4.10pm	3hr

* This train also travels to Irinjalakuda and Palakkad.

in your sights. If you get lost, ask for the *vallam* and someone will wave you in the right direction. Champakulam is connected to Alappuzha by regular **ferries** (every 30min; 30min).

The curved sterns of Kerala's traditional racing boats are said to imitate the unfurled hood of a cobra, and at **MANNARSALA**, near the village of **Haripad**, 25km south of Alappuzha on NH-47, 30,000 carved stones of rearing snakes were inspired by the same form. Dusted in turmeric and vermillion powder, they litter a leafy forest glade attached to the state's principal **Nagaraja temple**, dedicated to the "God of Serpents". Uniquely in Kerala, the shrine is officiated over by an elderly female Namboordiri priestess, "Valliamma", who leads processions and pujas from her adjacent house each morning and evening. It is particularly popular with childless couples: on Sundays, many come to propitiate the deity with offerings of turmeric and salt, holding a brass urn (*uruli*) upside down if they've just made their petition, or carrying it right-side up if their wish has been fulfilled.

Accommodation south of Alappuzha

See map on p.136.

Emerald Isle Kanjooparambil–Manimalathara ⌀0477/270 3899, ⌀m94470 77555, ⌨www.emeraldislekerala.com. For once, the real deal: an authentic, 150-year-old *tharavadu*, still occupied by the owners and in its original location deep in the backwaters, sandwiched between a river and acres of rice paddy. Under an exquisite traditional Kuttanadi roof, four teak rooms have been converted for use by guests, with antique doors, lustrous carved-wood furniture and private outdoor bathrooms. Cookery lessons, fishing and canoeing trips are all on offer, and there's a beautiful garden to the rear. *Emerald Isle* is, however, fiendishly hard to find. Head east down the Kottayam highway for 13km to Neddumaddy junction, turn left and keep going until you hit the backwater, where boatman Babu will be waiting

with his dugout. Tariffs (Rs4000–4800) include all meals. ⑨

VJ's Rice Garden Pallathurthy, 6km from Alappuzha ⌀0477/270 2566, ⌀m91944 611 8931, ⌨www.ricegardenkerala.com. If you'd like to be marooned in the backwaters but can't afford any of the heritage resorts, give this quirky little guesthouse a try. Its rooms – a couple of simply furnished doubles and a larger "bamboo cottage" – hold less appeal than the romantic location, on a slither of riverbank backed by miles of rice fields. You can reach it by boat, or by taking an auto-rickshaw along the Kottayam road for 5km as far as a big concrete bridge (with a KTDC hotel below it); cross over to the other side and turn immediately right, keeping to the footpath along the bank for another 1km, where you'll be met by a boatman who'll paddle you across. ④

North of Alappuzha

Some of Kerala's most bijou resorts occupy prime spots on the western shores of **Vembanad Lake** – a vast, 200-square-kilometre expanse of shimmering lagoon that reaches its widest point at the village of **MUHAMMA** (you can get there either via NH-47, turning off at **Kanjikudi**, or via the more scenic backroad closer to the lake shore). For reviews of accommodation in the area, see p.150.

West of Muhamma, the wedge of densely populated coconut plantation dividing Vembanad from the sea comes to an abrupt end at **MARARIKULAM**, on whose fringes a string of small resort hotels has sprung up, nestled under the palm trees behind an endless golden-sand beach strewn with fishing boats. For the time being, villagers far outnumber tourists along this peaceful stretch of coast, and if you can afford the high tariffs, these places offer idyllic stopovers on the journey between Alappuzha and the Keralan capital (Ernakulam airport lies less than a couple of hours' drive north on NH-47).

The one noteworthy sight is **St Andrew's Forane Church** (popularly known as **St Sebastian's**) at **ARTHUNGAL**, 4km north of Mararikulam. Catholics who have recovered from serious illness or accidents make a pilgrimage here, hobbling on their knees from the altar to the beach via a path lined with crosses and candle stands. Curiously, it's also a popular stop on the Sabarimala trail (see p.167), and during the season hundreds of Hindu men in black *lunghis* pour through to pay their respects. Behind the main nineteen–century Gothic church a much older chapel built in the 1590s by Portuguese Jesuits stands virtually forgotten. The best time to visit Arthungal is on Sunday evenings (around sunset), when a congregation of hundreds spills in to the main square for Mass.

Accommodation north of Alappuzha

See map on p.136.

Arakal Heritage Mararikulam-North, 3km north of *Marari Beach Resort* ☎0478/286 5545, ☎m9847 268661, ⓦwww.arakal.com. This is one of those rare homestays that manages to provide all the comforts you could wish for of a beachside hideaway while retaining an authentic Keralan village atmosphere. Dotted around a sandy plot close to the sea, the five 200-year-old houses come complete with beautiful gabled roofs, traditional railings and original antique furniture. All have shady verandas and hidden outdoor bathrooms – "Mango" even has a tree growing through the middle of it. Hosts Abi and Mini can help arrange bicycle, elephant and boat rides in the area, as well as cookery lessons and ayurvedic treatments. One of the loveliest places to stay in the state, and well worth splashing out on for a night or two if it's above your normal budget. From Rs3500 (plus Rs800 for a/c). ❽

Casa del Fauno Muhamma ☎0478/286 0862, ⓦwww.casadelfauno.com. If Fellini had ever made a film in Kerala, its set might have looked like this dream villa on the shores of Vembanad Lake, created by Italian designer Maria Angela Fernhof. The fusion architecture blends polished marble and fragments of old Tamil stone sculpture to stunning effect (you approach the house via a mock acropolis of temple brackets), and the guest rooms inside are light, cool and exquisitely furnished. Authentic Italian (and Vietnamese) meals are served alfresco in a secluded inner courtyard, on shabby-chic granite tables. ❽

Grand Nirvana Jana Sakthi Rd, Muhamma ☎0478/286 1970, ⓦwww.grandnirvana.com. Imposing new five-star luxury resort on the western shore of Vembanad Lake, conceived in grand Dutch colonial style. All the rooms boast uninterrupted views across the water. Facilities include an über-luxury *kettu vallam* with its own Jacuzzi, and floating deck where guests are encouraged to join sunrise yoga sessions. Rooms start at $430. ❾

Kovalikam Muhamma ☎0478/286125, ⓦwww.ananyahillresorts.com. Newly built campus of *tharavadu*-style houses with majestic tiled roofs, red-oxide floors and pillared verandas that catch the breezes blowing off the lake. The modern interiors aren't as characterful, but offer international-standard comfort, while the open-sided multi-cuisine restaurant makes the most of the tranquil location. ❽

Marari Beach Resort Mararikulam-North ☎0478/286 3801, ⓦwww.cgearth.com. Gated resort complex, enclosing 52 a/c thatched "fisherman's huts", each with a low raised veranda and a little tap to wash the sand off your feet. The 25-acre plot also boasts a large curvy pool, starred restaurant and lotus ponds with ducks splashing around. Security guards are, of course, on hand to prevent the real fishermen from wandering through and spoiling the idyll. ❾

Motty's Beach Houses Marari Beach ☎0477/224 3535, ☎m98470 32836. Kerala has very few attractive small houses to rent as close to the beach as this, and the traditional architecture of the relocated wooden dwellings is as beautiful as the location, amid the palms of a busy fishing community. From their verandas, cusped arches and lathe-turned pillars frame views through the trees to the sea. Not all of the houses are of the same standard (or price), however, nor as nicely situated or private (one is divided in two by a thin wall). Full details available on booking.

Kottayam

Some 76km southeast of Kochi and 37km northeast of Alappuzha, **KOTTAYAM** is a compact, busy Keralan town strategically located between the backwaters

△ Cheriapalli, one of Kottayam's Syrian-Christian churches

to the west and the forests and mountains of the Western Ghats to the east. Most visitors come here on their way somewhere else – foreigners take short boat trips to nearby Vembanad Lake or Alappuzha, or set off to Periyar Wildlife Sanctuary, while Ayappan devotees pass through en route to the forest temple at Sabarimala (see pp.167–168).

For Keralans, the town is synonymous with **money**, both old and new. The many **rubber plantations** around it, first introduced by British missionaries in the 1820s, have for more than a century formed the bedrock of a booming local economy, most of it controlled by landed **Syrian Christians**, for whom Kottayam is something of a heartland. Younger sons and their families not in line for a slice of the estate have tended for generations to leave home and seek their fortunes abroad, and signs of the resulting remittance wealth are everywhere, from adverts for foreign banks to the huge hoardings erected by gold merchants.

Aside from rubber and its famously well-educated workforce (this was the first town in India to achieve 100 percent literacy), Kottayam's other main export is the state's number-one newspaper, the *Malayala Monorama*, which is the largest of five dailies edited in the town. Boasting a readership of 1.5 million, the *Manorama* (literally "Entertainer") has been in circulation since 1890 and has had a chequered history. Fearing the rise of its Christian-minority backers, the Raja of Travancore once closed the paper down, and its owners have been embroiled in several major financial controversies since, most recently in 2006 after the collapse of a banking firm with which the *Manorama* was connected. These days, however, it's going stronger than ever: check out the English edition at Ⓦwww.manoramaonline.com.

Kottayam's long history of Syrian-Christian settlement is reflected by the presence of two thirteenth-century churches on a hill 5km northwest of the centre, which you can get to by rickshaw. Two eighth-century Nestorian stone crosses with Palavi and Syriac inscriptions, on either side of the elaborately decorated altar of the **Valliapalli** ("big") church, are among the earliest solid traces of Christianity in India. The visitors' book contains entries from as far back as the 1890s, including one by the Ethiopian king, Haile Selassie, and a British viceroy. The interior of the nearby **Cheriapalli** ("small") church is covered with lively paintings, thought to have been executed by a Portuguese artist in the sixteenth century. If the doors are locked, ask for the key at the church office (9am–1pm & 2–5pm).

Practicalities

Kottayam's KSRTC **bus stand**, 500m south of the centre on TB Road (not to be confused with the private stand for local buses on MC Road), is an important stop on routes to and from major towns in South India. Four of the frequent buses to Kumily/Periyar (3–4hr) continue daily on to Madurai in

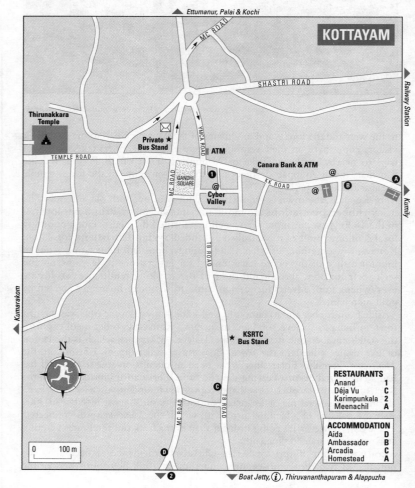

Ettumanur, Palai & Kochi

KOTTAYAM

Railway Station

SHASTRI ROAD

MC ROAD

Thirunakkara Temple

Private Bus Stand

YMCA ROAD

ATM

TEMPLE ROAD

MC ROAD

GANDHI SQUARE

Canara Bank & ATM

KK ROAD

Kumily

Cyber Valley

A

B

TB ROAD

KSRTC Bus Stand

Kumarakom

N

0   100 m

MC ROAD

TB ROAD

C

D

RESTAURANTS	
Anand	1
Déja Vu	C
Karimpunkala	2
Meenachil	A

ACCOMMODATION	
Aida	D
Ambassador	B
Arcadia	C
Homestead	A

Boat Jetty, (i), Thiruvananthapuram & Alappuzha

Tamil Nadu (7hr), and there are regular services to Thiruvananthapuram, Kollam and Ernakulam. The **railway station**, 2km north of the centre, sees a constant flow of traffic between Thiruvananthapuram and points north, while **ferries** from Alappuzha and elsewhere dock at the weed-clogged jetty, 2km south of town.

DTPC maintain a tiny **tourist office** at the jetty (daily 9am–5pm; ☎0481/256 0479). The best place to **change money** is the Canara Bank on KK Rd, which also has one of several **ATMs** around the main square. **Internet** facilities are available at Intimacy (Rs30 per hour), also on KK Rd, just north of the KSRTC Bus Stand.

Accommodation

Accommodation in Kottayam is very limited for a town of its size. Those travellers that do pause here tend to do so in one of the resorts or homestays in the surrounding area (see p.158), although the following places in the town centre are fine for a night.

Aida TB Junction, MC Rd ☎0481/256 8391, ⓦwww.hotelaidakerala.com. Large 1980s hotel on the south side of town with a wide range of dowdy, brown rooms, including some with a/c (only Rs150 extra), plus reasonably priced singles. There's a quiet restaurant (not recommended) and bar. ❹

Ambassador KK Rd ☎0481/256 3293, ⓦwww .fhrai.com. Solid, old-fashioned economy place on the northeast side of town that's worn around the edges but well scrubbed. A/c costs only Rs50 extra, but the air coolers are noisy. ❷–❹

Arcadia TB Rd ☎0481/256 9999, ⓦwww .arcadiahotels.net. The town's top hotel, occupying its tallest building – a towering, white, angular monster block just south of the centre. Its rooms look much nicer from the inside, however, and are very good value (especially the "standard doubles"); there's also a fantastic rooftop pool on the 14th floor, as well as a restaurant (*Déja Vu*, see below) and bar (*Fahrenheit*). ❻–❼

Homestead KK Rd ☎0481/256 0467. The best mid-price option: "your key to a soft pillow" goes their slogan, though the beds in the economy rooms are rock hard and it's well worth shelling out an additional Rs130 for a "deluxe" with more space, better furniture and thicker mattresses. ❸–❻

Eating

Kottayam may not be a particularly alluring destination in itself, but it has a handful of very good **places to eat**.

Anand *Anand Lodge*, KK Rd, just off the main square. If you're only passing through and want a delicious, freshly cooked pure-veg thali, look no further than here. Of its two adjacent wings, the a/c family hall is the more relaxing (the meals only cost Rs10 more and it's blissfully cool inside). In addition to traditional "keep-it-coming" rice plates (Rs30) with three or four vegetables, *rasam*, buttermilk and all the trimmings, they also do excellent *udipi* snacks, including embarrassingly large paper-roast *dosas* over a metre in length.

Déja Vu *Hotel Arcadia*, TB Rd. Swish rooftop restaurant on the 14th floor of a business-oriented three-star. In a smart dining hall with polished marble floors, starched white napkins and wonderful panoramic views over the town, you can order from an exhaustive multi-cuisine menu (North and South India, continental and Chinese); most mains Rs85–150.

Karimpunkala 6km south on the MC Rd, at Nattakom-Palam. This roadside place, which you'll need to catch an auto-rickshaw or taxi to reach if you don't have your own transport, is legendary in Kottayam for its sumptuous, village-style seafood *sadyas*, featuring *karimeen polli-chathu* (spiced *karimeen* fish steamed in a banana leaf), *kakairachi* (oysters) and proper *kappa* (tapioca), as well as moreish, crusty-edged *appam*. Count on Rs100–150 for the works.

Meenachil *Homestead Hotel*, KK Rd. Quality non-veg Keralan food – Kuttanadi chicken curry, *karimeen pollichathu* – plus Punjabi-style tandoori and Chinese duck dishes, served in a popular little hotel restaurant close to the centre. It's a/c, the service is speedy and the rates restrained (with most mains Rs75–100). They also do set Keralan "meals" (Rs45 for veg; Rs58 non-veg).

Arundhati Roy

In 1997, the sleepy village of Aymanam, a few kilometres outside Kottayam in southern Kerala, suddenly found itself the subject of intense international media attention after a novel set in it, *The God of Small Things*, won the Booker Prize for fiction. Its Kerala-raised author, **Arundhati Roy**, who'd grown up in Aymanam and whose family still lived in the area, became the first *pukka desi* ("non-expatriate") writer – and the only Indian woman ever – to bag the award. The decision wasn't without its detractors (a former chairperson of judges said at the time she thought the novel "an execrable book"), but *The God of Small Things* went on to sell more than six million copies worldwide, earning its author considerable acclaim and no small fortune – quite an achievement for a debut novel of only 350 pages.

In language that is by turns hauntingly poetic, playful and incantatory, *The God of Small Things* recounts the tragic turn of events surrounding the visit of an English girl, "Sophie Moll", to the home of her twin cousins, Esther and Rahel, in the backwaters of Kerala. The Syrian-Christian household around which the story revolves consists of a couple of dour, elderly sisters, the twins' divorced mother and their uncle Chacko, who'd returned to his home village to take over the family pickle firm after his marriage to an English woman he'd met while an undergraduate in Oxford broke down.

Seen through the eyes of its child-protagonists, the narrative – ingeniously broken into a collage of interlocking flashbacks – pitches the innocence of childhood against the bitterness of the world of the twins' grown-up relatives, with all its disappointments, caste prejudices, politically motivated myopia and, ultimately, terrifying fragility.

While the sad events at the heart of the book derive from the novelist's own imagination, the setting closely mirrors the circumstances of her own life. Like the twins, Arundhati Roy was born in the northeastern hill region of India to an alcoholic Bengali tea-planter father and young Keralan Christian mother (later the well-known social activist and educator, Mary Roy) who fled her violent marriage to settle in the family homestead back in Kottayam. There, in the shadow of their mother's perceived shame, her children led a slightly feral life, "on the edge of the community", as Arundhati later described it. "I didn't have a caste, and I didn't have a class, and I had no religion, no traditional blinkers, no traditional lenses on my spectacles, which are very hard to shrug off. I sometimes think I was perhaps the only girl in India whose mother said, 'Whatever you do, don't get married'."

When she was only sixteen, Arundhati left home and travelled to **Delhi**, where she lived in a squatter's colony on the margins of the city, infamously scraping a living by

Around Kottayam

Some of Kerala's most attractive backwater scenery lies within easy reach of Kottayam. Probably the ideal destination for a day-trip (although it also has some wonderful accommodation), the beautiful **Kumarakom Bird Sanctuary** lies on the shore of Vembanad Lake to the west. **Aranmula**, to the south, is one of the last villages still making *kannadi* metal mirrors, and has a Krishna temple which organizes a ritual "non-competitive" boat race. The Mahadeva temple at **Ettumanur**, a short way north of Kottayam, is known to devotees as the home of a dangerous and wrathful Shiva and to art lovers as a sublime example of temple architecture, adorned with woodcarvings and murals (some of which, for once, are viewable by non-Hindus). Frescoes of a very different kind, dating from the eighteenth century, adorn one of the region's oldest churches at **Palai**, a fifteen-minute drive northeast of Ettumanur in an area that sees very few visitors.

selling empty beer bottles. After a spell in the capital's school of architecture, she disregarded her mother's advice and did get married, to the (now internationally famous) architect Gerard de Cunha. The couple bummed around Goa for a while hawking home-made cakes on the beaches to tourists, but the marriage ended after only three years.

A couple of movie and drama scripts (including one with second husband, director Pradeep Krishen) were the first unpromising steps of her **literary career**. But it wasn't until Arundhati wrote a much-publicized condemnation of the film *Bandit Queen*, whose makers she attacked for distorting the facts of its heroine, Phoolan Devi's life, did she gain public notoriety. In the wake of the ensuing controversy, Roy retreated out of the public eye and, while working part-time as an aerobics instructor at home in Delhi, began writing what would, five years later, see the light of day as *The God of Small Things*.

Since its publication in 1996, the novel has caused some controversy back in Kerala. Communist politicians, including a former chief minister and the veteran leader E.M.S. Namboodiripad, publicly objected to its unflattering portrayal of party officials; and lawyers horrified by the cross-caste sexual content tried to get the book banned on the grounds that it was "obscene" and likely to "deprave the minds of readers". Arundhati, meanwhile, has devoted much of her time and money to **campaigning** on issues such as the Narmada dam scheme, India's nuclear arms race, globalization and the American-led "War on Terror". She still lives with husband Pradeep in Delhi, but is a frequent visitor to the Kottayam district, where her mother is the head teacher of the experimental Pallidoodam (formerly "Corpus Christi") School.

Fans of *The God of Small Things* occasionally turn up in Aymanam searching for **real-life landmarks** featured in the novel. One that can easily be located is the main "Ayemenem house", actually an amalgam of two properties: Puliyampallil House and Shanti House, at the end of a path leading from from the Reverand Rao Bahadur John Kuriyan School at Aymanam Junction. "Paradise Pickles" was a barely disguised version of the real family business, "Palat Pickles", which is still run by Arundhati Roy's Anglophile uncle Isaac (the "Chacko" of the novel), complete with the same slogan: "Emperor in the Realm of Taste". The "History House" of British planter and ghost "Kari Saippu" also exists – though not in Aymanam. It was inspired by the old residence of missionary Henry Baker, later converted into a luxury five-star hotel by Taj Group (see p.158).

Kumarakom

KUMARAKOM, 10km west of Kottayam, is spread over a cluster of islands on Vembanad Lake, surrounded by a tangle of lush tropical waterways and low-lying paddy fields. It was here that the British missionary **Henry Baker** chose to reclaim land to make a small rubber and fruit farm in the 1820s, which was subsequently expanded by his descendants into a full-blown plantation. After Independence, the estate and its main house were ceded to the government, who designated the core area abutting the lakeside as a nature reserve. Due to its easy accessibility by road from Kottayam, this has since become the focus of a boom in backwater tourism, with a row of large luxury resorts lined up along the water's edge. Baker, meanwhile, became immortalized as the "Kari Saippu" (Black Sahib) of Arudhati Roy's *The God of Small Things* – the author grew up in a nearby village – while his house, featured as the ghostly "History House" in the novel, has been converted into a luxury hotel by Taj Group (see p.158).

Kumarakom can be reached quite easily by bus (every 20–30min) from Kottayam, which lies 15km to the east. The best time to visit the **Bird Sanctuary** (daily dawn–dusk; Rs45), occupying the westernmost island of Baker's former estate, is between November and March, when it serves as a winter home for many migratory birds, some from as far away as Siberia. Species include the darter or snake bird, little cormorant, night heron, golden-backed woodpecker, crow pheasant, white-breasted water hen and tree pie. Dawn is the quietest and best time for viewing. Although the island is quite small, a guide is useful; you can arrange one through any of the hotels.

Birds, or representations of them, feature prominently in the area's most bizarre visitor attraction, the **Bay Island Driftwood Museum** (open daily 10am–6pm; Rs50; ⓦwww.bay-island-museum.com), just off the main road on the outskirts of Kumarakom. While out on rambles along the shoreline of the distant Andaman Islands, schoolteacher Raji Punnoose used to collect lumps of driftwood, twisted and worn into shapes resembling animals, birds, fish and people. Once finishing touches had been applied with a chisel and varnish, these were shipped home to form the basis of a curious exhibition. Raji guides visitors through the highlights with a breathless commentary that's as idiosyncratic and entertaining as the pieces themselves. Allow at least an hour for the full tour.

Aranmula

The village of **ARANMULA** offers another appealing day-trip from Kottayam (start early), 30km to the south. Its ancient temple is dedicated to Parthasarathy, the divine name under which Krishna acted as Arjuna's charioteer during the bloody Kurekshetra war (recorded in the *Mahabharata*), and the guise in which he expounded the Bhagavad Gita. About 1800 years old, the temple is a major site on the Vishnaivite pilgrimage trail in Kerala, and, as Vishnu is represented here in the form of Annadanaprabhu ("One Who Gives Food"), it is said that no pilgrim worshipping at the temple will go hungry. Each year, towards the end of the Onam festival (Aug/Sept), a **Snake Boat Regatta** is celebrated as part of the temple rituals, and crowds line the banks of the Pampa River to cheer on the thrusting longboats (similar to those seen at Alappuzha; see *Kuttanad backwaters* colour section).

Aranmula is also known for the manufacture of extraordinary *kannadi* **metal mirrors** (called Aranmula *valkannadi*), produced using the "lost wax" technique with an alloy of copper, silver, brass, white lead and bronze. Once a prerequisite of royal households, these ornamental mirrors are now exceedingly rare; only a handful of master craftsmen and their families still make them. The most modest models cost around Rs300–400, while custom-made mirrors can cost Rs50,000.

The **Vijana Kala Vedi Cultural Centre** in Aranmula offers ways of "experiencing traditional India through the study of art and village life". Set up in 1977 by a French scholar, Louba Schild, it stages daily classes in *kathakali*, *mohiniyattam* and *bharatanatyam* dance, woodcarving, mural painting, cooking, *kalarippayattu*, ayurvedic medicine and several Indian languages. Courses (five hours each day) cost $230 per week, decreasing on a sliding scale the longer you stay (to $430 per month for a course of seven months or more). They also do shorter intensives on yoga, ayurveda and *kathakali*. For further details, go to ⓦwww.vijnanakalavedi.org.

Ettumanur

The magnificent Mahadeva temple at **ETTUMANUR**, 12km north of Kottayam on the road to Ernakulam, features a circular shrine, fine woodcarving and one of the earliest and most celebrated of Keralan **murals**. The deity is Shiva in one of his most terrible aspects, described as *vaddikasula vada*, "one who takes his dues with interest" and is "difficult to please". His predominant mood is *raudra* (fury). Although the shrine is open only to Hindus, foreigners can see the sixteenth-century courtyard murals, which may be photographed after obtaining a camera ticket (Rs20; video Rs50) from the counter on the left of the main entrance gateway (the priests may try to charge you considerably more, but if you insist on seeing a printed tariff will drop the price to the official one).

The murals are spread over two four-metre panels flanking the rear side of the main doorway. The most spectacular depicts Nataraja – Shiva – executing a cosmic *tandava* dance, trampling evil underfoot in the form of a demon. Swathed in cobras, he stands on one leg in a wheel of gold, with his matted locks fanning out amid a mass of flowers and snakes, while devotees gather round. Musical accompaniment is provided by Krishna on flute, three-headed Brahma on cymbals and, playing the ancient sacred Keralan *mizhavu* drum, Shiva's special rhythm expert Nandikesvara. Another noteworthy feature of the Ettumanur temple is its *valia vilakku*, a giant oil lamp at the entrance to the main shrine. Fed by constant streams of sesame oil donated by worshippers, it is supposed to have remained lit for over 450 years.

Ettumanur's ten-day **annual festival** (Feb/March) reflects the wealth of the temple, with elaborate celebrations including music. On the most important days, the eighth and tenth, priests bring out the temple's golden elephants – seven large specimens, each fashioned from 95 kilos of gold, and a smaller one half the weight – which were presented in the eighteenth century by Marthanda Varma, the raja of Travancore.

Palai

The small town of **PALAI** 30km northeast of Kottayam, is home to the **Church of St Thomas**, renowned for its beautiful eighteenth-century **frescoes**. Buses from Kottayam and Kochi pull in frequently at the KSRTC **bus stand** next to the bell tower in the centre of town. From here, the church is a two-kilometre walk or auto-rickshaw ride east along the main road and over a small bridge; turn right into a lane which leads to St Thomas's.

Rebuilt several times (most recently in the eighteenth century), the church has a Portuguese-style white ornamental facade, with a squat spire and nave. Inside, a bizarre spiral pulpit carved from a single piece of teak stands under ceilings richly painted with gold leaf. The *pièce de résistance*, however, lies hidden behind the altar – you'll need to ask the resident caretaker for a candle. Extraordinarily well preserved in the darkness, a wall of exquisite frescoes rendered in earthy vegetable pigments depicts the life of St Thomas and Jesus as the Lamb of God.

The larger, more modern **church** alongside was built in 1981. A finger-bone relic of St Thomas is kept here and brought out for public viewing once a year on the Feast of the Magi (mid-October).

Accommodation around Kottayam

With a couple of exceptions, Kumarakom's **resort complexes** are resolutely upscale and exclusive, screened by the waters of Vembanad Lake on one side and by high walls and uniformed Gurkhas on the other. However, smaller, authentic **homestays** are also starting to mushroom in the backwaters and rubber plantations further from the lakeside, the majority of them in landed Syrian-Christian households.

Kumarakom's lakeside resorts

See map on p.136.

Coconut Lagoon Kumarakom ☏0481/252 4491, ⓦwww.cghearth.com. The original, and still the most stylish of the grand-scale luxury resorts in this area, reached by boat from Kavaratikara jetty, just north of the *Taj* (see p.136). The launch glides right into the heart of the complex: a miniature village of red-tiled "heritage bungalows" grouped around a transplanted 1860s mansion on the lakeshore. Although fitted with mod cons, the rooms have a traditional feel, with old wood, open-roofed bathrooms and some antique fixtures. A beautiful ayurvedic centre, *kalari* pit and butterfly garden complete the picture. From around $300. ⑨

Illikkalam Lake Resort Karottukayal, Kumarakom ☏0481/0252 3282, ⓦwww.kumarakomtourism.org. A nice little mid-price option: eight simple, spacious chalets (a/c or non-a/c) right on the waterside with waves lapping against the garden walls. Each has its own lake-facing sitout (with great views), and extra room to the rear side for children. The owner, a lawyer from Kottayam, stays on site, but this is more anonymous than a homestay, which some will prefer; meals available. ⑥–⑦

Lakeside Homestay Kumarakom ☏0481/316 3332. A single cottage, recently built in traditional style with gabled roof and verandas, right on the lakeshore at an idyllic, breezy spot: all you can hear are the lapping waves and rustle of palms. A much more congenial option than many of the nearby resorts, at a fraction of the price (Rs1500 per double), with meals on request. The only catch is it's hard to find: turn off 4km before the *Taj*, when you see the *Shree Chitra Tourist Home* next to a small bridge. Advance booking is essential as there are only two rooms. ⑥

KTDC Waterscapes Kumarakom ☏0481/252 5861, ⓦwww.ktdc.com. This state-run resort sits right on the lake and consists of comfortable a/c cottages (from Rs6200) on stilts; few have a decent view over the lake and the ugly metal walkways further detract, but it's significantly cheaper than its competitors and convenient for the bird sanctuary. ⑨

Kumarakom Lake Resort Kumarakom ☏0481/252 4900, ⓦwww.klresort.com. One of India's top spa resorts, built on a similarly opulent scale to *Coconut Lagoon*, with relocated "heritage villas" ranged around a huge pool and network of canals, right on the lakeside – though it feels very artificial. Rates from $300–1000. ⑨

Radisson Plaza Karottukayal, Kumarakom ☏0481/252 7290, ⓦwww.radisson.com. Newest of the mega-resorts in this area, on a sprawling 18-acre site that aims, according to its publicity bumpf, to be a "Paradise City". Most of the villas overlook a central lagoon, and there's a very snazzy spa complete with sabai stone therapists, Thai masseurs and ayurvedic treatment wing. Starting at around $400, rates are top-whack, even by Kumarakom's standards. ⑨

Taj Garden Retreat Kumarakom ☏0481/252 4377, ⓦwww.tajhotels.com. The Baker family's Edwardian mansion – the "History House" of Arundhati Roy's *The God of Small Things* – stands as the nucleus of this five-star resort. Its old wooden floors, high ceilings and verandas have been extensively refurbished but retain much period character, though the plush a/c villas and cottages dotted around the grounds, with their pool and private lagoon, possess much less charm. From around $325. ⑨

Homestays and boutique hotels

Akkara Mariathuruthu ☏0481/251 6951, ☏m91944 771 6951, ⓦwww.akkara.in. Set on a bend in the Meenachil River, 5km northwest of Kottayam, this homestay is a model backwater B&B, offering an idyllic, typically Keralan setting, traditional architecture, comfortable rooms full of 1930s–1950s period furniture, wonderful Syrian-Christian cuisine and an easy-going atmosphere. Hostess Mrs Shanta Kurian provides warm hospitality while giving her guests plenty of space to enjoy the peace and quiet. Phone ahead for directions; access is by dugout canoe. ⑦

GK's Riverview Thekkakarayil, Kottaparambil, near Pulikkuttssery, 4km by water from Kumarakom ☏0481/259 7527, ☏m94471 97527,

ⓦwww.gkhomestay-kumarakom.com. Award-winning homestay, buried deep in the watery wilds between Kottayam and Kumarakom. The accommodation comprises four comfortable guest rooms in a separate block behind a family home, overlooking paddy fields. There's a garden and hammocks to lounge in, and host George Kutty takes visitors out in a canoe to look at the local snake boat and other sights. Delicious home-cooked food is also available. Phone ahead from Kottayam to be picked up (free if you stay two or more nights). ⑥

Philip Kutty's Pallivathukal, near Ambika Market, Vechoor, 20km northwest of Kottayam ☏04829/276529, ☏m98950 75130, ⓦwww.philipkuttysfarm.com. Luxury homestay on a working island farm, 40min drive from Kottayam in the remote backwaters of Vembanad Lake. Five beautifully furnished villas, built in traditional style with whitewashed walls, tiled roofs, antique doors and open-plan interiors, offer private hideaways set back from the main farmhouse but close to the water's edge. Owner Anu, her son Philip and mother-in-law Aniamma create a welcoming family atmosphere, leading cookery classes and walking tours of the 50-acre plot where nutmeg, bananas, cocoa and pepper are grown organically. From $230–280 in season. ⊙

Serenity at Kanam Estate 20km east of Kottayam on the Kumily/Periyar (KK) Rd at Payikad, near Vazhoor ☎ 0481/245 6353, ⊛ www.malabarescapes.com. If your budget can stretch to it, this stylish boutique hotel, part of the German-run Malabar Escapes chain, makes the perfect stopover en route to the hills. Situated on a hilltop deep in a belt of rubber plantations and spice gardens, the dreamy 1920s bungalow holds six rooms, designed in eclectic style blending antique furniture with chic original art; all have sit-outs or verandas. Facilities include a pool surrounded by cocoa trees, gym, yoga *shala*, ayurvedic spa and mountain bikes. You're also invited to spend a day with the resident elephant. From $240 per double. ⊙

Periyar and around

One of the largest and most visited wildlife reserves in India, the **Periyar Wildlife Sanctuary** occupies 777 square kilometres of the Cardamom Hills region of the Western Ghats. The majority of its visitors come in the hope of seeing **tigers** and **leopards** – and most leave disappointed, as the few that remain very wisely keep their distance, and there's only a slight chance of a glimpse even at the height of the dry season in April and May, when water shortages force the animals to congregate around the lakeshore. However, plenty of other animals survive in healthier numbers: elephant, *sambar*, Malabar giant squirrel, gaur, stripe-necked mongoose, wild boar and over 323 species of birds, including Nilgiri wood pigeon, purple-headed parakeet, tree pie and flycatchers. See pp.299–308 for more on wildlife.

Located close to the Kerala–Tamil Nadu border, only a few kilometres off the national highway, Periyar makes a convenient place to break the long journey across the Ghats between Madurai and the coast. It's also a good base for day-trips into the Cardamom Hills, with a couple of tea factories, spice plantations, the trailhead for the Sabarimala pilgrimage (see pp.167–168), and numerous viewpoints and forest waterfalls within striking distance.

In addition, the park has a particularly enlightened conservation policy. Instead of earning their livelihoods through poaching and illegal sandalwood extraction, local Manna people in the Periyar area are employed by the Forest Department to protect vulnerable parts of the sanctuary. **Eco-tourism** initiatives such as the "Border Hiking", "Tiger Trail" and "Jungle Patrol" tours, in which visitors accompany the tribal wardens on their duties, both serve to promote community welfare and generate income for conservation work. Indigenous villagers also act as guides for forest walks and bullock cart rides and staff the government-run *Bamboo Grove* hotel (reviewed on p.163).

Getting to Periyar

The base for exploring Periyar is the village of **Kumily**, a kilometre or so north of the main park entrance (known as **Thekkady**). The road that winds up through the undulating hills from Ernakulam and Kottayam makes for a slow drive but provides wonderful views across the Ghats. The route is dotted with churches and roadside shrines to St Francis, St George and the Virgin Mary – a charming Keralan blend of ancient and modern. Once you've climbed through

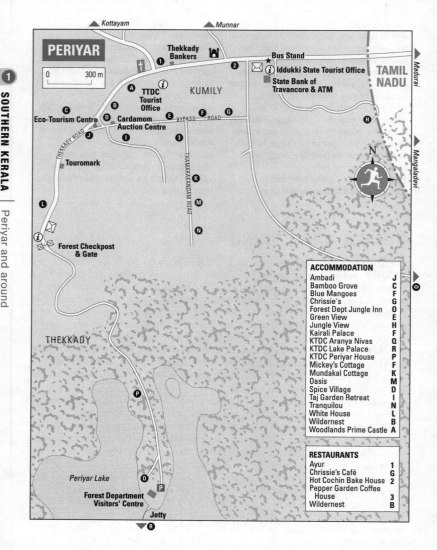

PERIYAR

0   300 m

▲ Kottayam   ▲ Munnar   ▲ Madurai

TAMIL NADU

KUMILY

THEKKADY

Thekkady Bankers

Bus Stand

Iddukki State Tourist Office

State Bank of Travancore & ATM

TTDC Tourist Office

Eco-Tourism Centre

Cardamom Auction Centre

BYPASS ROAD

THEKKADY ROAD

THAMARAKANDAM ROAD

Touromark

Mangaladevi

N

Forest Checkpost & Gate

Periyar Lake

Forest Department Visitors' Centre

Jetty

ACCOMMODATION

Ambadi	J
Bamboo Grove	C
Blue Mangoes	F
Chrissie's	G
Forest Dept Jungle Inn	O
Green View	E
Jungle View	H
Kairali Palace	F
KTDC Aranya Nivas	Q
KTDC Lake Palace	R
KTDC Periyar House	P
Mickey's Cottage	F
Mundakal Cottage	K
Oasis	M
Spice Village	D
Taj Garden Retreat	I
Tranquilou	N
White House	L
Wildernest	B
Woodlands Prime Castle	A

RESTAURANTS

Ayur	1
Chrissie's Café	G
Hot Cochin Bake House	2
Pepper Garden Coffee House	3
Wildernest	B

the rubber-tree plantations into Idukki District, the mountains become truly spectacular, and the wide-floored valleys are carpeted with lush tea and cardamom plantations.

Buses from Kottayam (every 30min; 4hr), Ernakulam (10 daily; 6hr) and Madurai in Tamil Nadu (at least hourly; 5hr 30min) pull in to the scruffy bus stand east of Kumily's bazaar. **Auto-rickshaws** will run you from the bus stand to the visitor centre inside the park for around Rs40–50, stopping at the park entrance at Thekkady for you to pay the fee. The gates close at 6pm, after which you will have to show proof of an accommodation booking before they will let you in. If you are staying at the KTDC *Lake Palace* (see p.166), the last boat is officially at 4pm but the hotel will arrange a boat during daylight hours.

Kumily

As beds inside the sanctuary are in short supply, most visitors stay in nearby **KUMILY**, a typical High Range town centred on a busy roadside bazaar. In recent years, hotels and Kashmiri handicrafts emporia have spread south from the market area to within a stone's throw of the park, and tourism now rivals the spice trade as the area's main source of income. That said, you'll still see plenty of little shops selling local herbs, essential oils and cooking spices, while in the busy **cardamom sorting yard** behind the *Spice Village* resort, rows of Manna women sift through heaps of fragrant green pods using heart-shaped baskets.

Idduki District **tourist office** (Mon–Sat 10am–5pm; ☎04869/222620) stands just south of the bus stand. Besides offering information on the district itself, they organize tours, including a "spice valley" trip (6.30am–9.30pm; Rs250), which takes in Munnar and several spice plantations. To book any of the Periyar Tiger Reserve's own **eco-tourism tours** (see p.162), you'll have to walk down the Thekkady Road to the Eco-Tourism Centre on Ambadi Junction (daily 8am–6pm, last tickets sold at 5.30pm; ☎04869/224571).

Both the State Bank of Travancore, near the bus stand, and the Thekkady Bankers in the main bazaar can **change currency and traveller's cheques**; there's an ATM at the former. **Internet** facilities are available around Thekkady Junction for about Rs40 per hour.

Tours and treks around Kumily

As well as the attraction of the wildlife sanctuary, **tea factory** and **spice plantation tours** are offered by almost every hotel and tourist agency in Kumily. Unfortunately, many places have become heavily commercialized, so it's worth shopping around; often the best way to organize a tour is to ask at your hotel – most of the staff will have a relative who has a good plantation. The only certified organic spice garden in the area is the Aroma at Muthuplackal, 2km west of Kuily on the Kottayam road; for more details, contact the owner, Mr Sebastian, on ☎m94953 67837. Most of the plantations charge around Rs300–500 per person for a three-hour tour with guide and vehicle.

A popular excursion for families is to **Elephant Junction** (daily 9am–6pm; ☎04869/320474), on the outskirts of Kumily just off the Murikkady road, where you can enjoy elephant rides, help with feeding and washing sessions in the river, and watch timber-dragging demonstrations. In addition, most winters see at least one baby tusker added to the resident herd – a child-friendly photo opportunity.

The windy, grassy ridgetops and forests around Periyar afford many fine **trekking** possibilities, with superb views over the High Range guaranteed. Ex-park wardens and other local people made redundant by the recent Eco-Tourism initiative (which reserved jobs for Manna tribal people) offer their services as guides through guesthouses, hotels and restaurants, and it can be worth employing someone for a day or more to show you the paths to the best viewpoints; check out their letters of recommendation and follow up tips from fellow visitors. One half-day route that's straightforward to attempt on your own is the 90-minute hike up **Kurusamalai**, the prominent peak towering to the northwest of Kumily, whose summit is crowned with a Holy Cross. Follow the Kottayam road out of the main bazaar for just over fifteen minutes, until you see a turning to the left (just before the *Holiday Homestay*). From here, a track leads uphill through a string of small Manna villages to the peak, steepening the higher you climb. The owner of the *Green View* homestay in Kumily (see p.162) hands out photocopies of a roughly drawn map that will help with route finding.

Although hilly, this area is also good **cycling** territory; **bicycle rental** is available from several stalls in the market. For more physical trips into the mountains, Touromark (℡04869/224332, ⓦwww.touromark.com), midway between Kumily and Thekkady, have imported 21-speed **mountain bikes** for rent. They also offer guided trips, ranging from four-hour/fifteen-kilometre hacks through local spice gardens, coffee plantations and woodlands to longer expeditions, such as the three-night/four-day ride across the Cardamom Hills from Periyar to Munnar.

From the Eco-Tourism Centre at Ambadi Junction, the Forest Department run **village tours** (6am–2.30pm; Rs750) to a remote tribal settlement on the Tamil Nadu side of the mountains bordering Periyar. You're transported 10km by taxi to the start of the route, which is covered by **bullock cart** and **coracle** through a variety of different habitats and farmland. Profits go to the development of the local community.

Accommodation

Kumily has **accommodation** to suit all pockets, offering particularly good value in lower price brackets, thanks to the recent proliferation of small homestay guesthouses on the fringes of the village. At the opposite end of the scale are some truly gorgeous colonial-era hideaways deep in the mountains which you'll need a car and driver to reach, but which provide atmospheric bases for explorations of less visited corners of the High Range. For accommodation in the sanctuary, see p.166.

Budget

Blue Mangoes Bypass Rd ℡04869/224603, ℡m98951 87789. Simple en-suite rooms (with sitouts and balconies) in an impeccably clean modern block. Rock-bottom rates, but good bedding and a quiet location. Owner Bobby speaks excellent English. ❷–❸

Green View Bypass Rd ℡04869/211015, ℡m94474 32008. One of Kumily's most popular homestays, in a newish house just off the Thekkady Rd. Offers 17 differently priced rooms, from basic Rs200 options with bucket hot water to large en-suite ones equipped with solar-heated showers and balconies looking across the valley to Kurusmalai mountain. A lovely rear garden attracts lots of wild birds. If it's full, try the identically priced *Rose Garden* next door (℡04869/223146). ❸–❻

Jungle View on the eastern edge of town ℡04869/223582, ℡m94461 36407. The best-value budget homestay in Kumily, a 10min plod (or Rs15-auto-rickshaw ride) from the bus stand – literally on the Tamil Nadu–Kerala border. The clean, bright, attached bedrooms are all comfortably furnished; those on the upper storey are larger, opening onto a deep, marble-floored veranda only metres away from jungle. Nocturnal wildlife-spotting walks into the adjacent forest are offered as a complimentary extra. ❹–❺

Kairali Palace Bypass Rd ℡04869/224604, ℡m98951 87789. Outstandingly attractive homestay in a fusion building that blends traditional and modern styles, with gabled roofs, and wooden railings wrapped around the airy first-floor terrace. Its en-suite rooms are all well furnished for the price. ❸–❺

Mickey's Cottage Bypass Rd ℡04869/222196, ℡m94472 84160. One of the oldest guesthouses in Kumily, whose smiling owner, Sujata, offers a range of differently priced rooms and cottages, all with balconies or sitouts littered with relaxing cane furniture. The more expensive ones are larger and come with more outside space. ❸–❹

Mundakal Cottage Thamarakandam Rd ℡04869/223317, ℡m94479 80924. Philip and Mariyamma Mundakal's new budget travellers' homestay, up a side lane off Bypass Rd, comprises six squeaky-clean rooms in a peaceful spot well away from the bustle of the bazaar, the best of them inside a brand new block fitted with comfy wooden beds, quality mattresses and shiny tiled floors. ❸–❹

Oasis Thamarakandam Rd ℡04869/223544, ℡m94479 07890, ⓔoasisthekkady@yahoo.com. Large, new rooms sharing common verandas that look out across the treetops on the village's eastern fringes. Meals are served on the ground floor in a sunken lounge area, next to a kitchen which guests are welcome to use for self-catering. Clean, quiet, secure and good value. ❸–❹

Tranquilou Thamarakandam Rd ℡04869/223269, ℡m94476 12149. Sunny south-facing budget rooms, or shadier, more snugly furnished "deluxe" ones with wood ceilings, in a modern house right on the edge of the forest. Comforts include piped hot water and cane swings to lounge on. ❸–❹

White House Thekkady Rd ☎04869/222987. A mixed but very good-value bag of bamboo huts, tree houses and rooms, handily placed for the park gates and run in a very welcoming fashion by owner Mrs Lily Joseph. Pick of the bunch are her two rear-side doubles, whose balconies have lovely green views into the sanctuary. ❷–❸

Mid-range

Ambadi Ambadi Junction, Thekkady Rd ☎04869/222193, ⓦwww.hotelambadi.com. Wood and red bricks dominate the architecture of this hotel, packed higgledy-piggledy onto the side of the road to the park. It offers three categories of rooms, all excellent value and with lots of Keralan character. Best are the "duplexes", which have beds on mezzanine floors and balconies sporting old-style pillars overlooking woodland. The location's busy during the day, but quiet in the evenings. ❺–❻

Bamboo Grove ☎04869/224571, ⓦwww .periyartigerreserve.org. Part of the Forest Department's Eco-Tourism project, this eco-lodge situated between Kumily bazaar and the park gates is certainly well meaning – its spacious en-suite huts are made of renewable, natural materials and the staff are drawn from local *adivasi* minorities. But ultimately, you pay well over the odds for basic accommodation, lackadaisical service and a location that's not nearly as remote and inspiring as the brochure shots suggest. Rates include breakfast, jungle treks and boat trips. ❼

△ *Spice Village*, Periyar

Chrissie's Bypass Rd ☎04869/224155, ☎m94476 01304, ⊛www.chrissies.in. Smart new four-storey hotel below the bazaar, run by expats Chrissie (from the UK) and Adel (from Egypt). It's pricier than most homestays in the area, but you get more privacy and better views, and relaxing, homely interiors featuring throws in warm colours, beds carved from local wood and watercolours of Dorset hanging on the walls. There's also a great yoga *shala* on the rooftop, and popular little café-restaurant on the ground floor (see below for review). ❺–❻

Wildernest Thekkady Rd ☎04869/224030, ⊛www.wildernest-kerala.com. *Wildernest*'s ten quirkily designed rooms are the most appealing option in this bracket, despite their proximity to the main road. With high, slanted ceilings, red oxide floors and white walls, they're more like little maisonettes: wood staircases wind up to terraces overlooking the central courtyard, and French windows open onto secluded, private gardens. Rates include generous breakfasts. ❼

Woodlands Prime Castle Thekkady Rd ☎04869/223469, ⓔprimecastle@sify.com. Large, efficiently managed mid-scale hotel with a striking Chinese-pagoda-style roof, close to the bazaar. It holds differently priced options on three storeys, varying in size but all immaculately clean; some have rear balconies as well as front verandas. A dependable option if you prefer the anonymity of a hotel to a homestay. ❺

Luxury

Green Mansions Gavi ☎04869/224571. Deep in the tropical forest lining the state border, this remote, Forest Department-run eco-lodge stands on a low hillock overlooking Gavi Lake. Its bungalow accommodation, reached via a bone-jarring 30km Jeep ride from Kumily, is simple, bordering on institutional, but perfectly comfortable and well placed for jungle trekking and wildlife-spotting trips. Tariffs (from \$100 per person) include obligatory full board. Book through the Eco-Tourism Centre in Kumily. ❾

Shalimar Spice Garden Murikaddy, 6km from Kumily ☎04869/222132, ⊛www.shalimarkerala.net. Teak huts in traditional Keralan style, on the edge of an old cardamom and pepper estate, with elephant-grass roofs, whitewashed walls, chic interiors and verandas looking straight onto forest. Facilities include a beautiful ayurveda centre, outdoor pool set amid the trees and an open-sided restaurant where you can fine dine off rough-hewn granite tables. Rates from \$180–220. ❾

Spice Village Thekkady Rd ☎04869/222514, ⊛www.cghearth.com. Part of the green-conscious CGH earth chain, this campus of mock-tribal huts is the first choice of most luxury tour groups. Its wooden thatched cottages (from \$275) are dotted around substantial landscaped gardens planted with spices and flowering trees. There's also a smart restaurant, a pool, and special wildlife resource centre where guests can attend daily lectures on Periyar's flora and fauna. ❾

Taj Garden Retreat Amalambika Rd ☎04869/222401, ⊛www.tajhotels.com. Yet another resort of luxurious, pseudo-tribal dwellings (from \$235), on stilts overlooking a coffee plantation, with a/c and access to a pool. ❾

Eating

You're more likely to take meals at your guesthouse or hotel than eat out in Kumily, but for a change of scene the following are the best options within walking distance of the bazaar.

Ayur west side of the main bazaar. Quality South Indian thali "meals" (Rs50), freshly made each day and served on banana leaves from a buffet. It's more hygienic (and less manic) than the competition further down the main street. *Ginger*, upstairs, is a swisher a/c alternative offering an exhaustive Indian-Chinese-Continental menu.

Chrissie's Café Bypass Rd. This relaxing expat-run café, on the ground floor of a hotel of the same name, pulls in a steady stream of foreigners throughout the day and evening for its delicious pizzas and pasta bakes (Rs120–160), made with Kodai mozzarella; check out the specials board. They also do healthy breakfasts of muesli with fresh fruit, crunchy cereal, toast with home-made bread and cakes, with proper coffee. Count on Rs250 per head.

Hot Cochin Bake House main bazaar. The best of a pretty unimpressive batch of "meals" places on the east side of the main street, close to the bus stand. Most people come at lunchtimes for the tasty fish curry thali, with optional *avioli* (pearlspot) masala fry, served on china plates instead of the usual tin trays or leafs.

Pepper Garden Coffee House Thamarkandam Rd. In a garden filled with cardamom bushes behind a prettily painted blue-and-green house, a former park guide and his wife whip up tempting travellers' breakfasts (date and raisin pancakes, porridge with jungle honey, fresh coffee and Nilgiri tea), in addition to home-cooked lunches of veg fried rice, curry and dhal, using mostly local organic produce. Mains Rs20–75.

Wildernest Thekkaday Rd. Filling continental buffet breakfasts (fruit, juices, cereals, eggs, toast, peanut butter, home-made jams and freshly ground coffee; Rs100) served on polished wood tables in the ground-floor café of a stylish small hotel. In the afternoons they also do tea and cakes (including a particularly delicious, very British warm plum cake).

The sanctuary

Centred on a vast artificial **lake** created by the British in 1895 to supply water to the drier parts of neighbouring Tamil Nadu, the **Periyar Wildlife Sanctuary** lies at altitudes of between 900m and 1800m, and is correspondingly cool: temperatures range from 15°C to 30°C. The royal family of Travancore, anxious to preserve favourite hunting grounds from the encroachment of tea plantations, declared it a forest reserve, and built the Edapalayam Lake Palace to accommodate their guests in 1899. It expanded as a wildlife reserve in 1933, and once again when it became part of **Project Tiger** in 1979 (see Contexts, p.303).

Seventy percent of the protected area, which is divided into core, buffer and tourist zones, is covered with evergreen and semi-evergreen forest. The **tourist zone** – logically enough, the part accessible to casual visitors – surrounds the lake, and consists mostly of semi-evergreen and deciduous woodland interspersed with grassland, both on hilltops and in the valleys. Although excursions on the lake (either by diesel-powered launch or paddle-powered bamboo raft) are the standard ways to experience the park, you can get much more out of a visit by **walking** with a local guide in a small group away from the crowd. However, avoid the period immediately after the monsoons, when **leeches** make hiking virtually impossible.

The **best time to visit** is from December until April, when the dry weather draws animals from the forest to drink at the lakeside.

Park practicalities

The **entrance fee** is Rs150 for foreigners (Rs12 for Indians) for the first day, and Rs50 on subsequent days. If you're staying inside the park you must buy a new pass for each day you stay, either from the entrance gate or from the Forest Information Centre by the jetty. KTDC's hectic and uncomfortable **weekend tours** to Periyar from Kochi, calling at Kadamattom and Idukki Dam en route (Sat 7.30am–Sun 8pm), are not recommended unless you're really pushed for time.

Boat trips

KTDC's **boat trips** on the lake (daily at 7am, 9.30am, 11.30am, 2pm & 4pm; 2hr; Rs45 for the lower deck, Rs100 for the upper deck, which is less cramped and has a better view) are in large double-decker launches with noisy engines. The Forest Department also runs its own boats (9.30am, 11.30am, 2pm and 4pm; Rs35); they're smaller and shabbier, but can get closer to the banks of the lake (and thus the wildlife). Tickets for both services are sold through the Forest Department hatch just above the main **visitor centre** (daily 7am–6pm; ℡04869/222027) at the end of the road into the park.

It's unusual to see many animals from the boats – engine noise and the presence of a hundred other people make sure of that – but if you're lucky you might spot a group of elephants, wild boar and *sambar* grazing by the water's edge. To maximize your chances of wildlife sightings, take the 7am service (wear warm clothing) and try for a ticket on the upper deck if there are any left (most tend to be block-booked by the luxury hotels).

Better still, sign up for one of the Forest Department's excellent **bamboo rafting trips**, which start with a short hike from the boat jetty at 8am and return at 5pm, with a minimum of three hours spent on the water. The rafts carry four or five people and, because they're paddled rather than motor-driven, can approach the lakeshore in silence, allowing you to get closer to the grazing animals and birds. Tickets cost Rs1000 per person and may be booked in advance from the Eco-Tourism Centre on Ambadi Junction.

Walks and treks

Although you can – leeches permitting – trek freely around the fringes of Periyar, access to the sanctuary itself on foot is strictly controlled by the Forest Department. Their community-based Eco-Tourism Programme offers a variety of structured **walking tours**, ranging from short rambles to three-day expeditions, all guided by local Manna tribal wardens. Tickets should be booked in advance from the Eco-Tourism Centre on Ambadi Junction, where you can also pick up brochures and leaflets on the trips.

The **Nature Walk** (7am, 11am & 2pm; Rs100 per person) is the least demanding option, covering 4–5km of level evergreen and moist deciduous forest. Groups of up to five people are led by a single guide who identifies trees, plants and wildlife. You can also do a similar walk at night: the **Jungle Patrol** (7–10pm & 10pm–1am; Rs500) is loaded with atmosphere and the sounds of the forest, though you probably won't get to see much more than the odd pair of eyes picked out in a torch beam. For scenery, a better option is the full-day **Border Hiking** tour (8am–5pm; Rs1000 per person), which takes you into grassland and thick jungle at altitudes of between 900m and 1300m. Finally, the **Periyar Tiger Trail** (Rs3000–5000) is the one for committed trekkers. Guided by former poachers, the itinerary lasts for one night and two days, or two nights and three days. Armed guards equipped with walkie-talkies accompany the group, trekking through 35km of hill country, thick forest and grassland to top wildlife-spotting sites in the Periyar Sanctuary, sleeping outdoors in tent camps and eating vegetarian food prepared on kerosene stoves and open fires.

Accommodation and eating in the sanctuary

For the *Lake Palace*, *Periyar House* and the *Aranya Nivas* you should book in advance at the KTDC offices in Thiruvananthapuram or Ernakulam – essential if you plan to come on a weekend, a public holiday, or during **peak season** (Dec–March), when rooms are often in short supply.

Forest Department Jungle Inn 3km east of Kumily at Kokkara, off the Mangaladevi Temple road. Located an hour's walk (3km) into the park, this simple "forest cottage" sits in a glade frequented by langur monkeys and giant tree squirrels. It's cramped and overpriced, though the location is serene and does allow you to be in position early for the wildlife. Tariffs include half-board; check-out is 9am. Book through the Eco-Tourism Centre at Ambadi Junction ❼

KTDC Aranya Nivas Near the boat jetty, Thekkady ☎04869/222282, ⊛www.ktdc.com. Plusher than *Periyar House*, this colonial old manor has some huge rooms ($100–150), a pleasant garden and pool, multi-cuisine restaurant, bar and plenty of marauding wild monkeys to keep you entertained. Full-board and upper-deck tickets for two boat trips are included in the tariff. ❽–❾

KTDC Lake Palace Across the lake from the visitor centre ☎04869/222023, ⊛www.ktdc.com. The sanctuary's most luxurious hotel, with six suites in a converted maharajah's game lodge surrounded by forest. Wonderful views extend from the charmingly old-fashioned rooms and lawns – this has to be one of the few places in India where you stand a chance of spotting tiger and wild elephant while sipping tea on your own veranda. Full-board only at $210 per double room. ❾

KTDC Periyar House Midway between the park gates and the boat jetty, Thekkady ☎04869/9222026, ⊛www.ktdc.com. Close to the lake, with a restaurant, bar and balcony overlooking the monkey-filled woods leading down to the waterside. Not as nice a location as the neighbouring *Aranya Nivas*, but a lot cheaper. Ask for a lake-facing room. ❺–❼

Around Periyar and Kumily: the Cardamom Hills

Periyar and Kumily are convenient springboards from which to explore Kerala's beautiful **Cardamom Hills**. Guides will approach you at Thekkady with offers of trips by Jeep; if you can get a group together, these can be good value. Among the more popular destinations is the **Mangaladevi Temple**, 14km east. The rough road to this ancient ruin deep in the forest is sometimes closed due to flood damage, but when it is open the round trip takes about five hours. With a guide, you can also reach remote waterfalls and mountain viewpoints offering panoramic views of the Tamil Nadu plains. Rates vary according to the season, but expect to pay around Rs500–600 for a Jeep-taxi, and an additional Rs200 for a guide. An easy day-trip by bus (or as part of a local plantation tour) from Kumily, the grand viewpoint of **Chellarcovil** is right on the edge of the

The Ayappan cult

During December and January, Kerala is packed with huge crowds of men wearing black or blue *dhotis*; you'll see them milling about railway stations, driving in overcrowded and gaily decorated Jeeps and cooking a quick meal on the roadside by their tour bus. These men are all pilgrims on their way to the Sri Ayappan forest temple (also known as Hariharaputra or Shasta) at **Sabarimala**, in the Western Ghat mountains, around 200km from both Thiruvananthapuram and Kochi. The **Ayappan devotees** can seem disconcertingly ebullient, chanting "*Swamiyee Sharanam Ayappan*" ("give us protection, god Ayappan") in a call-and-response style reminiscent of English football fans.

Ayappan – the offspring of a union between Shiva and Mohini, Vishnu's beautiful female form – is primarily a Keralan deity, but his appeal has spread phenomenally in the last thirty years across South India, to the extent that this is said to be **the second largest pilgrimage in the world**, with as many as a million devotees each year. Pilgrims are required to remain celibate, abstain from intoxicants, and keep to a strict vegetarian diet for a period of 41 days prior to setting out on the four-day walk through the forest from the village of **Erumeli** (61km, as the crow flies, northwest) to the shrine at Sabarimala. Less keen devotees take the bus to the village of Pampa, and join the five-kilometre queue. When they arrive at the modern temple complex, pilgrims who have performed the necessary penances may ascend the famous eighteen **gold steps** to the inner shrine. There they worship the deity, throwing donations down a chute that opens onto a subterranean conveyor belt, where the money is counted and bagged.

The pilgrimage reaches a climax during the festival of **Makara Sankranti** when massive crowds of over 1.5 million congregate at Sabarimala. On January 14, 1999, 51 devotees were buried alive when part of a hill crumbled under the crush of a stampede. The devotees had gathered at dusk to catch a glimpse of the final sunset of *makara jyoti* ("celestial light") on the distant hill of Ponnambalamedu.

Although **males** of any age and even of any religion can take part in the pilgrimage, **females** between the ages of nine and fifty are barred. This rule, still vigorously enforced by the draconian temple oligarchy, was contested in 1995 by a bizarre court case. Following complaints to local government that facilities and hygiene at Sabarimala were substandard, the local collector, a 42-year-old woman, insisted she be allowed to inspect the site. The temple authorities duly refused, citing the centuries-old ban on women of menstrual age, but the High Court, who earlier upheld the gender bar, was obliged to overrule the priests' decision. The collector's triumphant arrival at Sabarimala soon after made headline news, but she was still not allowed to enter the shrine proper.

For advice on how to visit Sabarimala, via a back route beginning at Kumily near the Periyar Wildlife Sanctuary, see pp.167–168.

mountains, with the endless green plains of Tamil Nadu falling away below. To get here, take a bus or Jeep to the village of Anakkara, 15km north of Kumily, and jump on a rickshaw for the last 4km through the paddy fields to Chellarkovil; hang onto your driver if you don't want to walk back to the bus.

Sabarimala

The other possible day-trip from Kumily, though one that should not be undertaken lightly (or, according to Hindu lore, by pre-menopausal women), is to the Sri Ayappan forest shrine at **Sabarimala** (see pp.167–168). This remote and sacred site can be reached in a long day-trip, but you should leave with a pack of provisions, as much water as you can carry and plenty of warm clothes in case you get stranded. Jeep-taxis wait outside Kumily bus stand to transport pilgrims to the less frequented of Sabarimala's two main access points at a windswept mountaintop 13km above the temple (2hr; Rs50 per person if the Jeep is carrying ten passengers). Peeling off the main Kumily–Kottayam road at **Vandiperiyar**, the route takes you through tea estates to the start of an appallingly rutted forest track. After a long and spectacular climb, this emerges at a grass-covered plateau where the Jeeps stop. You proceed on foot, following a well-worn path through superb old-growth jungle, complete with hanging creepers and monkeys crashing through the high canopy, to the temple complex at the foot of the valley – a surreal spread of concrete sheds and walkways in the middle of the jungle. Allow at least two hours for the descent, and an hour or two more for the climb back up to the roadhead – the cars wait till sunset. The alternative route from Kumily to Sabarimala involves a Jeep ride on a forest road to **Uppupara** (42km), with a final walk of 6km through undulating country. Given the very real risks involved with missing the last Jeep back to Kumily (the mountaintop is prime elephant and tiger country), it's advisable to get a group together and rent a 4WD for the day (about Rs900 including waiting time).

Travel details

For details of ferry services on the backwaters – primarily between Alappuzha and Kollam – see p.145.

Trains

Thiruvananthapuram to: Alappuzha (3–5 daily; 2hr 40min–3hr 15min); Kochi/Ernakulam (12–16 daily; 4hr–5hr 20min); Kollam (13–16 daily; 55min–1hr 30min); Kottayam (9–10 daily; 2hr–2hr 45min); Kozhikode (3–5 daily; 9hr–10hr 30min); Thrissur (10–12 daily; 5hr 45min–7hr); Varkala (12–13 daily; 45–55min).

Buses

Alappuzha to: Kochi/Ernakualm (every 30min; 1hr 30min); Kollam (every 45min; 2hr); Kottayam (every 30min; 1hr 30min–2hr); Kumily (1 daily; 6hr); Thiruvananthapuram (5 daily; 3–4hr).
Kumily to: Alappuzha (daily; 6hr); Kochi/Ernakulam (10 daily; 6hr); Kottayam (every 30min; 4hr); Munnar (4 daily; 4hr); Thiruvananthapuram (6 daily; 8–9hr).

Thiruvananthapuram to: Alappuzha (5 daily; 4hr); Chennai (4 daily; 18hr); Kanyakumari (9 daily; 2hr 30min); Kochi/Ernakulam (every 2hr; 5–6hr); Kollam (every 2hr; 1hr 30min–2hr); Kottayam (every 30min; 4hr); Kozhikode (8 daily; 11–12hr); Kumily (1 daily; 9hr); Munnar (3 daily; 9–10hr); Nedumangad (hourly; 45mins–1hr); Neyyar Dam (hourly; 1hr 15min); Ponmudi (6 daily; 2hr–2hr 30min); Thrissur (hourly; 8–9hr); Varkala (10 daily; 1hr 30min–2hr 30min).

Flights

For a list of **airline websites**, see pp.22–23. In the listings below AD is Air Deccan, AI Air India and AIE Air India Express.
Thiruvananthapuram to: Kochi (AD, AI, AIE 1–2 daily; 30min); Kozhikode (AI, AIE 1–3 daily; 50min).

Central Kerala

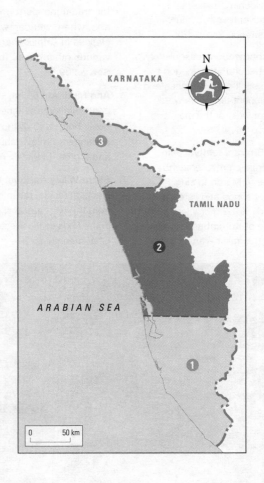

KARNATAKA

N

TAMIL NADU

ARABIAN SEA

0 50 km

CHAPTER 2 # Highlights

※ **Fort Cochin** No better-preserved crop of early colonial monuments survive in Asia than those lining Fort Cochin's sixteenth- and seventeenth-century backstreets. See p.182

※ **Lakshadweep** An exquisitely remote coral atoll, fringed by white shell-sand beaches and translucent turquoise water, 400km west of the mainland. See pp.194–195

※ **The Bharani festival** Join the drunken revellers who gather in March to sing bawdy songs and listen to sword-wielding oracles at the shrine of Kurumba Bhagavati at Kodungallur – an intense

Tantric ritual, even by Keralan standards. See p.205

※ **Kerala Kalamandalam** The state's premier academy for the traditional performing arts, where you can watch classes in *kathakali* and various other dance forms. See p.209

※ **Ana Mudi** At 2695m, peninsula India's highest peak: homeland of the endangered Nilgiri tahr goat, and a great trek. See p.216

※ **Silent Valley National Park** A jungle paradise, recently saved from the dam builders, hidden in the folds of the Western Ghat mountains. See p.220

△ Cycling in Fort Cochin

Central Kerala

The plains of **central Kerala**, stretching from coastal backwaters to the mountains inland, and north as far as the mighty Krishna temple at Guruvayur, once formed the heartland of the princely state of **Kochi**, whose rulers traced their lineage back to the Chera kings. Its capital, the port of **Muziris**, ranked among the wealthiest in the ancient world, attracting streams of ships from Egypt, Greece, Rome, Persia, China and the Arabian peninsula. When a massive flood destroyed the harbour in 1341, the court moved south to **Cochin** (now called Kochi), on the mouth of the Periyar River, and the new docks soon became the focus of the rapidly expanding trade with Europe: first the Portuguese, and later the Dutch and British, left their mark on a city already awash with foreign influences, leaving a cosmopolitan legacy that continues to attract visitors to the region.

In the city's colonial district, **Fort Cochin**, Lusitanian churches, Dutch mansions and stately Raj-era bungalows rise from a waterfront lined with red-tiled *godown* warehouses. Despite the crowds and commercialism surrounding its monuments, the old quarter holds enough atmosphere to warrant a stay of at least a couple of days. Once you've admired the church where Vasco da Gama was buried and watched the Chinese fishing nets in action on the promenade, there's isn't a great deal to see, but plenty of funky little cafés and courtyard restaurants offer inspirational spots to catch up on some leisurely postcard writing.

After the unhurried pace of life in the fort, the brightly lit malls and hectic traffic of its big-city counterpart across the water, **Ernakulam**, can come as a shock. Epitomizing the prosperous modern face of the state, Ernakulam is central Kerala's business capital and main transport hub and, as such, impossible to avoid – though its twenty-first-century shopping and swanky restaurants may tempt you onto a ferry if you've been buried deep in the backwaters for a couple of weeks.

Whether in heritage hotels in Fort Cochin or somewhere less touristy in the modern city, the plentiful **accommodation** on offer in Kochi makes it a convenient base from which to explore the wealth of **traditional Keralan culture** surviving in outlying districts. Temple festivals, featuring drum orchestras, elephant processions and performances of ritual theatre, are common throughout the region during the winter months, although the most splendid of all – the famous **Puram** at **Thrissur** – takes place in the stifling heat of May. You'll have to pass through Thrissur, an hour or two's train ride north, to reach **Guruvayur**, one of South India's most revered Hindu pilgrimage centres, where an elephant sanctuary stands as a popular sideshow to the religious intensity of the main Krishna temple. Thrissur is also the springboard

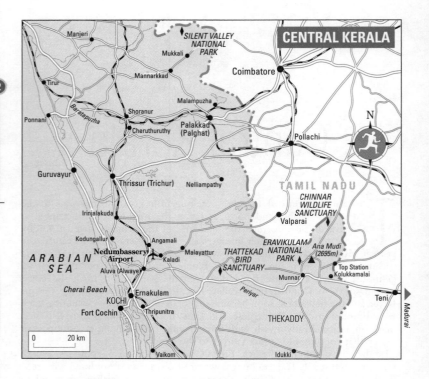

for **Cheruthuruthy**, home of the world-renowned Kalamandalam academy of Keralan performing arts, where you can watch young students of *kathakali*, *kudiyattam* and *mohiniyattam* being put through their paces – a vivid taste of the awesome physical and spiritual dedication required to keep the torch of Kerala's home-grown art forms burning.

Inland, the greenery becomes more intense and the skies bluer and clearer as you head from the humid, waterlogged paddy and rubber forests of the plains towards the **Western Ghats**. Rising to well over 2500m, the wooded mountains dividing Kerala from Tamil Nadu offer optimal conditions for tea and coffee cultivation, as the British were quick to discover. Vast swathes of virgin teak forest were clear-felled in the late nineteenth century to make way for plantations, and the hillsides of central Kerala's **High Range** still support a giant patchwork of tea estates, interspersed with fragrant coffee and cardamom groves. One of the best introductions to the unique ambience of the tea-growing region is the hill station of **Munnar**, four hours by road east of Kochi. Around the town, some of South India's highest plantations carpet the lower flanks of spectacular peaks such as Ana Mudi (2695m), whose grassy uplands make ideal trekking terrain, and hold a couple of excellent **wildlife sanctuaries** populated by wild elephants and the delightfully gregarious Nilgiri tahr.

Further north, the town of **Palakkad**, strategically sited on the main highway through the hills, acts as the transport hub for an even more pristine wilderness area, the **Silent Valley National Park**, one the last strongholds of the lion-tailed macaque. Another off-track destination reachable from Palakkad, and one which sees surprisingly few visitors given the beauty of its scenery, is the tiny hill station of **Nelliampathy**. Affording superb views across the central Keralan plains, the bone-jarring journey to it repays the effort of the diversion alone, but an added incentive is the presence amid the forests and tea estates of the surrounding hills of some bijou homestay and plantation retreats, from where you can trek to viewpoints and tiny temples lost in the jungle.

The ultimate tropical hideaway accessible from central Kerala, however, are the **Lakshadweep Islands**, a coral atoll of palm-fringed islets scattered over a wide area between 200km and 400km off the coast. A single Indian Airlines plane makes the journey daily from Kochi airport, but only holds twelve seats, and when you get there accommodation (for non-Indians, at least) is limited to a single, extremely expensive eco-resort of luxury huts. Yet, for those whose budgets can stretch to it, Lakshadweep's crystal clear waters – ideal for snorkelling and scuba diving – offer an exclusive, Maldives-style beach experience unique in India.

Some history

For more than two thousand years, central Kerala's prosperity has rested on the maritime trade passing through its ports. Spices grown on the forested hillsides of the interior originally drove this lucrative commerce, which lured traders from as far afield as Greece and Rome to the quaysides of **Muziris**, whose precise location archeologists continue to debate, but which must have lain somewhere close to modern Kodungallur, 38km north of modern Kochi. In *Periplus Maris Erythraei* ("Voyage Around the Erythraean Sea"), an anonymous Alexandrian text written on papyrus in the first century AD, it is recorded that the Romans sailed here with holds full of "flowered robes, eye-liner . . . mica and wine", returning laden with "spices, monkeys, tigers and elephants". **Pepper**, however, was always the prime commodity. Pliny the Elder (23–73 AD) famously complained that trade in the coveted "Malabar Gold" was draining the imperial coffers of silver – a claim backed up by the hordes of Roman coins that have come to light over the years in central Kerala. It was via Muziris that local tradition asserts **St Thomas the Apostle** introduced Christianity to the Subcontinent in 52 AD and where India's first major influx of Jewish refugees settled following the destruction of the temple in Jerusalem.

After the decline of Rome, **Arab merchants** used their exceptional navigational skills to monopolize the spice trade. They well understood the power of central Kerala's heavy laterite-laden river silt to calm the surf that blocked most other South Indian ports through the monsoons. But build-ups of sand also cause catastrophe, as in 1341 AD, when a wave of river mud flowed seaward and blocked the harbour mouth of Muziris.

Half a century later, the local rulers and their merchants decamped to the only tributary of the Periyar River still open to the sea, establishing a new capital at Cochin in 1405. **Vasco da Gama**, whose appearance off the Keralan coast in 1498 was to change the world map for ever, was the first European to spot its potential and in 1503 the **Portuguese**, by exploiting the raja of Cochin's long-standing rivalry with the *zamorin* of Calicut, obtained permission to erect a fortified trade post on a headland to the west, which was christened "Fort Manuel" – the forerunner of Fort Cochin. Several bloody encounters with Calicut followed as the Portuguese fought to break the Arab hold over the spice trade – the *zamorin* lost 32,000 troops in a single encounter in 1504. But over time the Portuguese lost out to the superior naval strength and organizational powers of the **Dutch** who, in alliance with Calicut, took control of Cochin in 1613. They in turn were ousted by Raja Marthanda Varma of Travancore after the Battle of Colachen in 1741, after which the **British** gradually asserted control of the area and its sea trade.

A massive upgrade of the port in the 1920s saw Cochin emerge as the most dependable and richest harbour in South India. After Independence, however, its fortunes declined sharply. Economic stagnation set in and lasted until the liberalizing economic reforms of the 1990s. Since 2000, the service sector has boomed in central Kerala. Kochi now prides itself on being a major centre of gold trading, IT, health care, shipbuilding and spices, as well as tourism, which has transformed the formerly dilapidated, forlorn streets of Fort Cochin into one of India's busiest visitor attractions.

Kochi and around

Kochi may not be the state capital, but the high-rise, neon-lit, traffic-choked mayhem of its main roads remind you that it is far and away Kerala's biggest city – a status underlined by the size of its new airport at Nedumbassery, 26km north of the centre. Most travellers arriving in Kerala do so here and few rush straight off. Aside from holding the remarkably well-preserved vestiges of India's first major European trading post, the twin districts of **Fort Cochin** and **Mattancherry**, clustered on the tip of a peninsula on the opposite side of the harbour from the modern half of the city, **Ernakulam**, boast some memorable places to stay, eat and drink, many of them in four- or five-hundred-year-old buildings with original teak floors and beams. In addition, several theatres dotted around Kochi lay on tourist-friendly introductions to **Keralan ritual arts** – worth attending if you're hoping to experience the real thing, at an all-night recital in one of the temples further afield.

Top-notch *kathakali* performances feature alongside processions of fifteen or more elephants and drum troupes in the annual *utsavam* festival held every October or November at **Thripunitra**, a twelve-kilometre auto-rickshaw or bus ride southeast of Ernakulam – just one of many similar events hosted by villages and towns **around Kochi** throughout the winter months. Even if your visit doesn't coincide with the event, it's worth visiting Thripunitra to see its distinctive, colonial-style hill palace, now an eclectic museum.

To escape the confines of the city, you could travel up the coast to **Cherai**, the most promising beach within easy reach of Fort Cochin. Further southwest, just off the main highway to Munnar, **Thattekkad** is Kerala's number one bird sanctuary, served by a better-than-average selection of resorts and homestays at beautiful rural locations.

Finally, Kochi also serves as the springboard for the archetypal paradise archipelago of the **Lakshadweep Islands** – where CGH Earth's *Bangaram Island Resort* offers the country's ultimate luxury beach break.

Kochi (Cochin)

The venerable city of **KOCHI** (long known as Cochin) is Kerala's prime tourist destination, spreading across islands and promontories in an imperious location between the Arabian Sea and the backwaters. Its main sections – modern

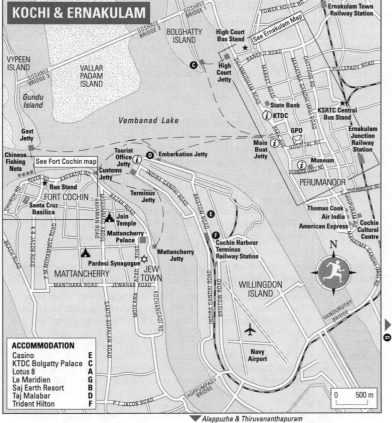

KOCHI & ERNAKULAM

Nedumbassery Airport (26km), **A** & **B**

Goshree Bridge 1

Goshree Bridge 2

Ernakulam Town Railway Station

POWER HOUSE RD

See Ernakulam Map

High Court Bus Stand

BOLGHATTY ISLAND

High Court Jetty

BANERJI ROAD

SHANMUGHAM ROAD

MARKET ROAD

MAHATMA GANDHI ROAD

CHITTOOR RD

PULLEPADY ROAD

VYPEEN ISLAND

VALLAR PADAM ISLAND

GOSHREE BRIDGE 3

State Bank

KTDC

KSRTC Central Bus Stand

Gundu Island

Vembanad Lake

GPO

HOSPITAL RD

Ernakulam Junction Railway Station

Govt Jetty

Main Boat Jetty

Museum

Ernakulam Junction Railway Station

Chinese Fishing Nets

Tourist Office Jetty

See Fort Cochin map

Customs Jetty

Embarkation Jetty

DURBAR HALL RD

PERUMANOOR

OVERBRIDGE RD

RIVER RD

KALVATHI RD

BAZAR ROAD

RAHAMAN ROAD

INDIRA GANDHI ROAD

BRISTOW ROAD

Terminus Jetty

Thomas Cook
Air India
American Express

Cochin Cultural Centre

Bus Stand

FORT COCHIN

CHURCH RD

Santa Cruz Basilica

Jain Temple

Mattancherry Palace

Mattancherry Jetty

Cochin Harbour Terminus Railway Station

B B JACOB ROAD

BEACH ROAD

P M MOHAMMED ROAD

Pardesi Synagogue

JEW TOWN

N

MATTANCHERRY

MANTHARA ROAD

JEWAHAR ROAD

MULLAHRD

KOCHANGADI RD

INDIRA GANDHI ROAD

BRISTOW ROAD

WILLINGDON ISLAND

VANDURUTHY BRIDGE

SANTO GOPALAN ROAD

THOPPUMPADY BRIDGE

Navy Airport

G

ACCOMMODATION

Casino	E
KTDC Bolgatty Palace	C
Lotus 8	A
Le Meridien	G
Saj Earth Resort	B
Taj Malabar	D
Trident Hilton	F

P T JACOB ROAD

0   500 m

Alappuzha & Thiruvananthapuram

Ernakulam and the old peninsular districts of **Mattancherry** and **Fort Cochin** to the west – are linked by a complex system of ferries, and distinctly less romantic bridges. Although some visitors opt to stay in the more convenient Ernakulam, the overwhelming majority base themselves in Fort Cochin itself, where the city's complex history is reflected in an assortment of architectural styles. Kochi is also one of the few places in Kerala where you are guaranteed **kathakali** dance performances, both in authentic and abridged tourist versions.

Kochi sprang into being after the silting up of Muziris harbour forced the royal family to move here in 1405. The name probably derives from *kocchazhi*, meaning the new, or small, harbour. **European** involvement in the rapid expansion of the town was characterized by constant blockades and clashes, as the Portuguese, Dutch and British competed to control the port and its lucrative spice trade. In 1800, the state of Cochin became part of the British Madras Presidency, and from 1812 until Independence in 1947 it was administered by a succession of *diwans*, or finance ministers. In the 1920s, the British expanded the port to accommodate modern ocean-going ships, and Willingdon Island, between Ernakulam and Fort Cochin, was created by extensive dredging.

Arrival and local transport

Kochi's **international airport** (@www.cochinairport.com) – one of India's most modern and efficient – is at Nedumbassery, near Alwaye (Aluva), 26km to the north of Ernakulam. A prepaid taxi into town costs around Rs400 and takes 30–40 minutes, traffic permitting – travelling by bus is more trouble than it's worth. There are two main **railway stations**, Ernakulam Junction, near the centre, and Ernakulam Town, 2km further north. No trains run to Fort Cochin or Mattancherry, while the Cochin Harbour Terminus, on Willingdon Island, serves the island's luxury hotels.

The KSRTC **central bus stand** (☎0484/237 2033), beside the rail line east of MG Road and north of Ernakulam Junction, is for state-run long-distance services. There are also two stands for private services: the **Kaloor stand** (rural destinations to the south and east) is across the bridge from Ernakulam Town railway station on the Alwaye Road; while the **High Court stand** (buses to Kumily, for Periyar Wildlife Reserve, and north to Thrissur, Guruvayur and Kodungallur) is opposite the High Court ferry jetty. The **Fort Cochin bus terminus** serves tourist buses and local services to Ernakulam.

Although **auto-rickshaws** are plentiful and reliable in Ernakulam, expect to pay well over the odds across the water in Mattancherry and Fort Cochin.

Kochi by ferry

Half the fun of visiting Kochi is getting about on the cheap **local ferries**, which depart from the four jetties marked on the map on p.175. A pamphlet giving exact ferry times is available from the ticket hatches by the jetties and from the helpful tourist desk at the Main Boat Jetty in Ernakulam.

Ernakulam to Bolghatty Island
From Ernakulam (High Court Jetty). Six per day; 6.30am–9pm; journey time 10min. There are also speedboat taxis (only for guests of the *Bolgatty Palace* hotel).

Ernakulam to Fort Cochin
From Ernakulam (Main Jetty) to Fort Cochin (Customs Jetty). Every 20–55min; 5.55am–9.30pm; journey time 15min. A less frequent express service runs from Ernakulam's High Court Jetty to Government Jetty in Fort Cochin.

Ernakulam to Mattancherry
From Ernakulam (Main Jetty) via Fort Cochin (Customs Jetty) and Willingdon Island (Terminus Jetty) to Mattancherry (Mattancherry Jetty). Every 1hr 30min; 5am–5.45pm.

Ernakulam to Vypeen
From Ernakulam (Main Jetty). This service has two routes: one to Willingdon Island (Embarkation Jetty; 25min), and a fast one to Vypeen (Government Jetty; 15min). Every 30min–1hr; 7am–9.30pm.

Fort Cochin to Vypeen
From Fort Cochin (Government Jetty) to Vypeen (Government Jetty). Every 10min; 6.30am–9pm; journey time 10min.

Willingdon Island to Fort Cochin
From the Willingdon Island (Tourist Office Jetty) to Fort Cochin (Customs Jetty). Every 30min; 6.30am–6.15pm; journey time 10min.

Kochi's excellent **ferry system** (see box opposite) provides a relaxing way to reach the various parts of town. **Bicycles** can be rented from many of the hotels and guesthouses in Fort Cochin.

Tours and backwater trips

KTDC's half-day **Kochi boat cruise** (daily 9am–12.30pm & 2–5.30pm; Rs100) is a good way to orient yourself but doesn't stop for long in either Mattancherry or Fort Cochin, so give it a miss unless you're pushed for time. Departing from the Sealord Jetty on Shanmugham Road, Ernakulam, it calls at Willingdon Island, the synagogue, Mattancherry Dutch Palace, St Francis Church, the Chinese fishing nets and Bolghatty Island. Book at the KTDC Reception Centre on Shanmugham Road (℡0484/235 3234).

The KTDC tourist office and a couple of private companies also operate popular all-day **backwater trips** out of Kochi. Taking in a handful of coir-making villages north of the city, these offer a leisurely and enjoyable way to experience rural Kerala from small hand-punted canoes. KTDC's daily tours cost Rs350, including the car or bus trip to the departure point, 30km north, and a knowledgeable guide. Better value, however, are the trips run by the private **tourist desk** (see below) at the Main Boat Jetty in Ernakulam (daily 8.30am–5pm; Rs550), which include hotel pick-up, transfer, a morning cruise (in a motorized boat) on the open backwaters, a village tour, a Keralan lunch buffet on board the *kettu vallam* and an afternoon trip through narrow waterways in a much smaller punted canoe.

Information

India Tourism's main office, providing reliable information and qualified guides for visitors, is situated on Willingdon Island (Mon–Fri 9am–5.30pm, Sat 9am–noon; ℡0484/266 8352, ⓦwww.india-tourism.com), between the *Taj Malabar Hotel* and Tourist Office Jetty; they also have a desk at the airport. KTDC's **reception centre**, on Shanmugham Road, Ernakulam (daily 8am–7pm; ℡0484/235 3234, ⓦwww.ktdc.com) reserves accommodation in their hotel chain and organizes sightseeing and backwater tours (see above); they too have a counter at the airport. For general advice, the two most convenient sources are the **Kerala Department of Tourism's** office next to the Government Jetty in Fort Cochin (Mon–Sat 10.15am–5pm; no phone, ⓦwww.keralatourism.com), and the tiny, independently run **Tourist Desk** (daily 8am–6.30pm; ℡0484/237 1761, Ⓔtouristdesk@satyam.net.in) at the entrance to the Main Boat Jetty in Ernakulam. Both hand out maps of the town and backwaters, but you'll probably find the latter more helpful when it comes to checking ferry and bus times. The Tourist Desk, located directly opposite the improbably named "Ken Livingstone Tea Stall" (named after the controversial Mayor of London), is also *the* place to obtain information on ritual theatre and temple festival dates around the state. In addition, they arrange daily boat tours and accommodation on houseboats, and take bookings for two excellent guesthouses in northern Kerala (one near Kannur and the other in Wayanad). Over in Fort Cochin, you can call at their subsidiary office on Tower Road (same hours; ℡0484/221 6129).

A useful local **publication** is the monthly *Jaico Timetable* (Rs10), which lists comprehensive details of bus, train, ferry and flight times. Both KTDC and the Tourist Desk publish free walking-tour maps and guides to Fort Cochin.

Accommodation

Most foreign visitors opt to stay in **Fort Cochin**, which, with its uncongested backstreets and charming colonial-era architecture, holds considerably more appeal than the mayhem of modern Ernakulam. Dozens of period buildings have been turned over to heritage hotels and homestays in recent years. There are, however, drawbacks: room rates are grossly inflated (especially over the Christmas and New Year period), with few options at the budget end of the scale, and there is a disconcertingly high concentration of tourists. **Ernakulam** may lack historic ambience, but it's far more convenient for travel connections, and offers lots of choice in all categories and far better value for money; however, its hotels do tend to fill up early in the day, so book well in advance – particularly if you're planning to be here on a weekend, when vacancies are like gold dust. Another alternative to Fort Cochin are the luxury and heritage places on **Bolghatty and Willingdon Islands**, which range from the three-star, government-run *Bolgatty Palace*, housed in a wonderful old Dutch mansion, to more formulaic five-stars. There are also a couple of new business-class hotels out at the **airport**.

Places to stay in Ernakulam and Fort Cochin are marked on their respective maps (p.188 & p.183); those on Willingdon and Bolghatty islands appear on the main Kochi/Ernakulam map (p.175).

Ernakulam

Budget

Biju's Tourist Home Corner of Cannonshed and Market roads ☎0484/238 1881, ⓦwww.bijustouristhome.com. The pick of the budget bunch: a friendly, efficiently run block only 2min walk from the boat jetty, with thirty spotless, well-aired and generously sized rooms ranged over four storeys. It has its own clean water supply and offers a cheap same-day laundry service. All in all, unbeatable value. For telephone reservations, ask to speak in person to the manager, Mr Thomas Panakkal. ❹

Broadway Tower TD West Rd ☎0484/236 1645, ⓦwww.broadwaytowers.com. Situated in the thick of Ernakulam's busy textile bazaar, this recently built, well-scrubbed little economy hotel occupies the second and third storeys of a modern block. Its rooms offer great value for money (including the cheapest a/c rooms in town); there's even a dorm (Rs75), and a nice little veg "meals" place on the ground floor. ❸–❹

Cochin Tourist Home Chavar Rd ☎0484/237 7577. Cleanest of the cheap hotels lined up outside Ernakulam Junction station, but often full of noisy families and pilgrim groups. The basement holds a dingy organic vegetarian restaurant. ❸

Maple Guest House XL/271 Cannonshed Rd ☎0484/235 5156. Best of the few rock-bottom options in the streets immediately east of the Main Boat Jetty, with cheap, clean non-a/c rooms close to the city centre – though it's not nearly as pleasant as *Biju's*. ❷–❸

Modern Guest House XL/6067 Market Rd ☎0484/235 2130. Popular economy lodge in the main bazaar. The rooms are pretty standard, but inexpensive and clean for the price. If it's full, ask if they have vacancies in either of their two (slightly less appealing) sister hotels nearby. ❷–❸

Saas Tower Cannonshed Rd ☎0484/236 5319, ⓦwww.saastower.com. Since its refit, this tower block hotel, with 72 well-furnished rooms, has begun to rival nearby *Biju's* for quality and price at the upper end of the budget category. Singles from Rs300, and also some a/c options. ❸–❹

Mid-range

Abad Plaza MG Rd ☎0484/238 1122, ⓦwww.abadhotels.com. Very comfortable business-oriented high-rise bang on Ernakulam's main street, with eighty centrally a/c rooms, multi-cuisine and Keralan speciality restaurants, 24hr coffee shop and pool. ❼–❽

Excellency Nettipadam Rd, Jos Junction ☎0484/237 8251, ⓦwww.hotelexcellency.com. Smart, modern mid-range place, offering better value than most options in the city centre. The majority of its 49 rooms are a/c, and there's a 24hr coffee shop and quality multi-cuisine restaurant. ❹–❺

Government Guesthouse Marine Drive ☎0484/236 0502. The maharaja of Kerala's great-value Government Guesthouse, in a shiny new eight-storey tower overlooking the harbour. Centred on a vast atrium lobby, with acres of brass hand rails and polished marble, its rooms offer comfort comparable to a four-star business-class hotel, only at amazingly low rates (and they do single occupancy). Advance reservation, as with all Kerala state guesthouses, can be hit-and-miss, with priority given to government officials; if they have any free, ask for a sea-facing room at the top of the building. ❺

Grand MG Rd ☎0484/238 2061. This is the most classically glamorous place to stay in central Ernakulam. Spread over three floors of a 1960s building, its relaxing a/c rooms are done out in retro-colonial style, with varnished wood floors and split-cane blinds. Surprisingly low tariffs given the level of comfort and location. **❼**–**❽**

Metropolitan Chavar Rd ☎0484/237 5285, ⓦwww.metropolitancochin.com. Smart business hotel near Ernakulam Junction station – well placed for late-night arrivals and early-morning departures – with the usual multi-cuisine restaurant, 24hr coffee shop and bar. **❼**–**❽**

Sealord Shanmugham Rd ☎0484/238 2472, ⓦwww.sealordhotels.com. The high-rise *Sealord*, near the High Court Jetty, has been an institution in the city for four decades and, with its handsome new interiors, offers excellent value for money. Their "standard" rooms are the best deal (ask for one on the top floor), and there's a relaxing rooftop terrace restaurant (see p.190) and bar. **❺**–**❻**

Yuvarani Residency Jos Junction, MG Rd ☎0484/237 7040, ⓦwww.yuvaraniresidency.com. Comfortable, central and well-managed three-star hotel with a choice of carpeted or tiled rooms – and especially good showers in their bathrooms. The popular Keralan seafood restaurant hosts live music recitals daily (except Tues), and there's a bar and a coffee shop. **❺**–**❼**

Luxury

Avenue Regent 39/2206 MG Rd ☎0484/237 7977, ⓦwww.avenueregent.com. Slick four-star Best Western affiliate, close to the railway station and main shopping area, with a couple of restaurants, 24hr coffee shop and bar. Expect only the highest standards, as this place doubles as a well-respected hotel-management training college. **❽**–**❾**

Le Meridien Maradu ☎0484/270 5777 (See main "Kochi and Ernakulam" map, p.175). Luxury five-star on the southern outskirts of the city centre, popular mainly with business clients, flight crews and tour groups. In addition to 223 rooms overlooking the backwaters, the complex holds glitzy shopping arcades, an ayurveda spa and a wide choice of food and beverage outlets. Charmless by comparison with places across the water, but efficient. $240–850. **❾**

Taj Residency Marine Drive ☎0484/237 1471, ⓦwww.tajhotels.com. Ernakulam's most established business hotel, in a prime location overlooking the harbour, with luxury a/c rooms, an impressive greenhouse-like café (see p.189), and several quality restaurants, but no pool. $135–270. **❾**

Fort Cochin

Budget

Adam's Old Inn 1/430 Burgher St ☎0484/221 7595. Ropey old budget travellers' lodge that's been here for years but recently came under new management. Plans are afoot to upgrade the hard coir mattresses and phase out the rooftop dorm (**❶**), but for time being this is still one of Fort Cochin's few rock-bottom cheapies. **❹**

Elite Princess St ☎0484/221 5733. Several floors of basic, but clean and inexpensive, non-a/c rooms (plus a few a/c options), stacked around a central gallery. It's a bit humid inside, but the rooms and landings are repainted annually, and the bathrooms are well scrubbed. On our last visit, a terrace restaurant was nearing completion on the rooftop. **❹**

Leelu Queiros St ☎0484/221 5377, ☎m98460 55377, ⓦwww.leeluhomestay.com. A very welcoming little homestay, tucked away down a quiet lane in a former family home that's been completely modernized. Its cheerfully decorated guest rooms are spacious, with squashy mattresses, huge bathrooms and optional a/c (Rs500 extra). Landlady Mrs Leelu Roy also offers popular daily cookery classes (non-guests welcome). Especially recommended for women travellers. **❹**–**❺**

Orion 926 KL Bernard Rd ☎0484/321 9312, ☎m98955 24797, ✉mail@orionhomestay.com. Impeccable little homestay in a new house on the quiet south side of town. Rates vary according to size of rooms, which don't all have balconies, but are all kept shining and neat. **❹**–**❺**

Santa Cruz Peter Celli St ☎0484/221 6250, ☎m98475 18598. Half of the rooms in this small guesthouse behind St Francis' Church have windows opening onto an enclosed corridor, but the others are well ventilated – and they're all impeccably clean, neatly tiled and freshly painted throughout, with new beds. Good value. **❸**–**❹**

Mid-range

Ballard Bungalow River Rd ☎0484/221 5854, ⓦwww.cochinballard.com. Eighteenth-century Dutch mansion, later used as the residence of the British Collector of Cochin, now converted into a good-value mid-range hotel run by the local Diocese. With their garish 1980s-style bedroom furniture, the ecclesiastical owners haven't quite grasped the heritage concept, but the original wood floors have come through the renovation unscathed and the place retains plenty of period atmosphere. Friendly, helpful staff. **❺**–**❼**

Bernard Bungalow 1/297 Parade Rd ☎0484/221 6162, ☎m98474 2799, ⓦwww.bernardbungalow.com. Half-a-dozen large, airy en-suite rooms, some with lovely new teak floors, in a 300-year-old Dutch house run by a welcoming couple. Despite some heavy-handed renovation, lots of historic atmosphere remains, and the accommodation is comfortable for the price. ⑤–⑥

Chiramel Residency 1/296 Lilly St ☎0484/221 7310, ⓦwww.chiramelhomestay.com. A great seventeenth-century heritage homestay, with welcoming owners and five lofty and carefully restored non-a/c rooms set around a fancily furnished communal sitting room. All have big wooden beds, teak floors and modern bathrooms. ⑥

Delight Ridsdale Rd, opposite the parade ground ☎0484/221 7658, ⓦwww.delightfulhomestay .com. Occupying an annexe tacked onto a splendid 300-year-old Portuguese mansion, David and Flowery's homestay holds seven spacious, comfortable and well-aired rooms, all equipped with new bathrooms and quiet ceiling fans; some open onto a lovely courtyard garden; another has a long veranda overlooking the parade ground; and there's a high-ceilinged salon with original teak floors to lounge in. Breakfast available. ④–⑦

🏃 **Fort House** 2/6A Calvathy Rd ☎0484/221 7103, ⓦwww.forthousecochin.com. Stylishly simple rooms ranged along the sides of a sandy courtyard littered with pot plants and votive terracotta statues, cooled by breezes blowing straight off the waterfront. Those in the much preferable original block (#1–5) have white walls and red-oxide floors, comfy king-sized beds and good showers in their chic little wet-room bathrooms – though the a/c units can be noisy. Avoid the en-suite "bamboo huts" (#6–9): they're well set up but have embarrassingly thin walls. Rates include breakfast, and there's a good waterside restaurant on site (see p.190). ⑥

Kapithan Inn 1/931 KL Bernard Rd ☎0484/221 6560, ⓦwww.kapithaninn.com. Clean, pleasant rooms in a friendly homestay behind Santa Cruz Basilica, plus some posh new a/c cottages to the rear. A touch overpriced, but it usually has vacancies. ⑤–⑦

Napier House Napier Lane, off Napier St ☎0484/221 5715, ☎m98953 33622, ⓦwww .napierhouse.com. Relaxing, low-key guesthouse in a 120-year-old Dutch house. The interiors have been done in a somewhat anodyne Western style, but they're comfortable and some have bathtubs. The one outstanding room is the suite, which has preserved its original teak floorboards and opens onto a private balcony overlooking the street. Breakfast (included in the rate) is served on a pleasant common terrace. ⑥–⑧

🏃 **The Old Courtyard** 1/371–2 Princess St ☎0484/2216302, ⓦwww.oldcourtyard .com. A gem of a heritage hotel, whose eight rooms flank a photogenic seventeenth-century courtyard framed by elegant Portuguese arches and bands of original *azulejos* tiles. For once the decor and antique furnishings (including romantic four-posters) are in keeping with the building – though some may find them dark and lacking modern refinements. Ask for one on the upper storey as it's less disturbed by noise from the courtyard restaurant (see p.191). ⑧–⑨

Raintree 1/618 Peter Celli St ☎0484/325 1489, ☎m98470 29000, ⓦwww.fortcochin.com. Five outstandingly smart rooms furnished in modern style (two of them with tiny balconies) in a cosy guesthouse that's within easy walking distance of the sights, but still tucked away. The really nice thing about this place is its plant-filled roof terrace, which has panoramic views over the Basilica and the old Portuguese and Dutch houses of the neighbourhood. ⑥

Spencer Home 1/298 Parade Rd ☎0484/221 5049. Warm-toned wood pillars and gleaming ceramic tiled floors line the verandas fronting this Portuguese-era house's eleven immaculate rooms, which open onto a painstakingly kept garden. Peaceful and good value for the area. A/c costs Rs600 extra. ④–⑥

Walton's Homestay Princess St ☎0484/221 5309, ☎m92497 21935, ⓔcewalton@rediffmail .com. Among Cochin's most characterful homestays, run by philosopher and local historian Mr Christopher Edward Walton, in a centuries-old Dutch house. Try to book the "garden cottage", which opens onto a delightful garden busy with birdlife. Facilities include a book-swap library and in-house yoga classes; breakfast (not included in tariff) is served on a communal terrace. ⑤–⑥

Luxury

Brunton Boatyard Bellar Rd, next to Fort Cochin Government Boat Jetty ☎0484/221 8221, ⓦwww.cghearth.com. Luxury chain hotel, built on the site of an eighteenth-century boatyard. The architecture and furnishings set out to replicate the feel of the British era, with antique *punkah* fans dangling from the lobby ceiling, portraits of old worthies and Dutch charts on the walls, and a billiards table set against Keralan carved wood and whitewash. Three types of room are offered, all of them overlooking the harbour (you get sea views from your bathtub) – though avoid the ones on the jetty side of the complex, which are plagued by traffic noise, at all costs.

Facilities include three speciality restaurants (see p.190), an ayurveda centre and a waterside pool. $225–325. ❾

Koder House Tower Rd ☏0484/221 8485, Ⓦwww.koderhouse.com. One of the Fort's newest boutique hotels, in a converted 200-year-old house that originally belonged to a prominent Jewish merchant (poets, painters and visiting dignitaries used to attend the Koder family's legendary Sabbath suppers in the early 1900s). The imposing red, double-fronted facade is less alluring than its interiors, with their long, dark wood floors, original art and antique furniture. Six sumptuous suites are on offer, from around $300; there's a restaurant and ayurvedic spa. ❾

Malabar House 1/268 Parade Rd ☏0484/221 6666, Ⓦwww.malabarhouse.com. Fort Cochin's original and most stylish boutique hotel is set in a historic eighteenth-century mansion at the bottom of the parade ground. Crammed with antiques and contemporary Keralan art, the German-designed interiors present a mix of traditional charm and European chic, centred on a serene temple-style courtyard pool. Tariffs ($270–460) include breakfast. ❾

🏃 **The Old Harbour** 1/328, Tower Road ☏0484/221 8006, ☏m98470/29000, Ⓦwww.oldharbourhotel.com. This 300-year-old former Portuguese hospice, later occupied by a firm of British tea brokers, was recently restored under the direction of German architect Karl Damschen (of *Brunton Boatyard* and *Surya Samudra* fame). A storehouse of graceful Lusitanian arches, lathe-turned wood pillars and teak floors, it now accommodates one of Kerala's top heritage hotels, at a prime location close to the Chinese fishing nets. The thirteen individually styled rooms either have private balconies facing an internal courtyard or open onto the garden and large pool, and there are also a handful of separate "cottages" in the grounds, each with roofless bathrooms and verandas. $115–230. ❾

Trinity House Ridsdale Rd, parade ground ☏0484/221 6666, Ⓦwww.malabarhouse.com. The last word in heritage-boutique chic: three uncompromisingly modern designer apartments, occupying the old headquarters of the Dutch East India Company. An off-shoot of the *Malabar House* across the road, its three exclusive suites ("red", "blue" and "yellow") share a living room and communal mezzanine area, and would thus better suit a family or group, though at $175–275 apiece, you'd have to have money to burn to block-book the lot. ❾

Willingdon and B̶ islands

Casino Willingdon Island, 2km from Navy, close to Cochin Harbour Terminus railway sta ☏0484/266 8221, Ⓦwww.cghearth.com. The first venture of the now-extensive CGH Earth chain, but utterly characterless and shut in by the grey docks. With its courtyard pool, multi-cuisine restaurants, ayurveda spa and shops, it's popular primarily with tour groups and often booked up, and also books flights for the Lakshadweep Islands. $150–245. ❾

KTDC Bolgatty Palace Bolghatty Island ☏0484/275 0500, Ⓦwww.ktdc.com. Extensively renovated palace in a beautiful location, a short hop from High Court Jetty. The main building, built by the Dutch in 1744 and later home of the British Resident, is now a three-star hotel with twenty deluxe rooms; there are also six "honeymoon" cottages on stilts right at the water's edge. Reserve through any KTDC tourist office and come armed with mosquito repellent. At weekends, the adjacent KTDC canteen and bar is noisy with day-trippers. $125–240. ❽–❾

Taj Malabar Willingdon Island, by Tourist Office Jetty ☏0484/266 6811, Ⓦwww.tajhotels.com. Pink-orange tower block in a superb location on the tip of the island with sweeping views of the bay; the old "heritage" wing, waterfront gardens and pool have been extensively refurbished, and the whole place oozes *Taj* style and quality. $220–275. ❾

Trident Hilton Bristow Rd, Willingdon Island ☏0484/266 9595, Ⓦwww.trident-hilton.com. Despite the bleak dockyard environs, this is the most intimate of the five-stars around the island port, with interesting displays of Keralan tribal and household artefacts, a pool in a tropical oasis, a restaurant, a bar and a range of luxurious rooms. Officially $120–170, but discounts are often available online. ❾

Near the airport

🏃 **Lotus 8** opposite Nedumbassery Airport ☏0484/261 0640, Ⓦwww.lotus8hotels .com. Gleaming tinted-glass and concrete tower block directly opposite the main terminal. The rooms are just what you'd expect from an international-standard business hotel, with big king-sized beds, separate living-room areas and direct Internet access, but the real selling point here is that they take bookings for less than 24hr (Rs920 for 5hr/Rs1500 for 8hr/Rs3500 for 24hr), making this a great option if you're in transit and only need a room for a short while. ❽

Nedumbassery
ww.sajhotels.com.
sort close to the airport
ional style, with
gs and screens, focused
some have their own

private Jacuzzis and plunge pools. You enter through a spectacular reception structure designed to resemble a temple, and are whisked from there to the chalets in electric golf buggies. The multi-cuisine restaurant's enclosed in a glass-sided atrium, and has a fashionable open kitchen. $235–350. ⑨

O..   thumb-shaped peninsula whose northern tip presides over the entrance to ... city's harbour, formed the focus of European trading activities from the sixteenth century onwards. With high-rise development restricted to Ernakulam across the water, its twin districts of **Fort Cochin**, in the west, and **Mattancherry**, on the headland's eastern side, have preserved an extraordinary wealth of early-colonial architecture, spanning the Portuguese, Dutch and British eras – a crop unparalleled in India. Approaching by ferry, the waterfront, with its sloping red-tiled roofs and ranks of peeling, pastel-coloured *godowns* (warehouses), offers a view that can have changed little in centuries.

Closer up, however, Old Kochi's historic patina has started to show some ugly cracks. The spice trade that fuelled the town's original rise is still very much in evidence: scores of shops lining the narrow streets of Mattancherry enjoy a brisk turnover of Malabari cardamom, chillies, turmeric and ginger, while the famous Pepper Exchange has boomed since it went online a couple of years back. But over the past decade, an extraordinary rise in visitor numbers has had a major impact on the town. Thousands of free-spending foreign tourists pour through daily during the winter, and with no planning or preservation authority to take control, the resulting rash of new building threatens to destroy the very atmosphere people come here to experience. Whereas old Portuguese arches and Dutch wood verandas used to dominate the streets of Fort Cochin, now garish signboards and the glass fronts of air-conditioned Kashmiri handicraft emporia are more likely to draw the eye. That said, tourism has also brought some benefits to the area, inspiring renovation work to buildings that would otherwise have been left to rot. Quite a few splendid old mansions across the town have been restored to accommodate high-end **heritage hotels**, where you can savour the 300-year-old architecture from the comfort of an antique four-poster or courtyard plunge pool.

Fort Cochin

The district where tourism has made its most discernible impact is **Fort Cochin**, the grid of venerable old streets at the northwest tip of the peninsula, where the Portuguese erected their first walled citadel, Fort Immanuel. Only a few fragments of the former battlements remain, crumbling into the sea beside Cochin's iconic Chinese fishing nets. But dozens of other evocative Lusitanian, Dutch and British monuments survive, ranging from stately tea brokers' bungalows to Bishops' palaces, spice traders' mansions and the gabled facade of the oldest church in Asia.

A good way to get to grips with Fort Cochin's many-layered history is to pick up the free **walking-tour maps** produced by both Kerala Tourism and the privately run Tourist Desk, available from their respective offices and counters (see p.177). The routes outlined in them lead you around some of the district's more significant landmarks, including the early-eighteenth-century Dutch Cemetery, Vasco da Gama's supposed house and several traders' residences.

Fort Cochin also has a small but active **arts scene** based around the popular *Kashi Art Café* (daily 8.30am–7.30pm) on Burgher Street (reviewed on p.190).

Willingdon Island & ▲Ernakulam   ▲Mattancherry

Customs Jetty

State Bank of India

ACCOMMODATION
Adam's Old Inn	H
Ballard Bungalow	C
Bernard Bungalow	P
Brunton Boatyard	A
Chiramel Residency	R
Delight	N
Elite	I
Fort House	B
Kapithan Inn	T
Koder House	E
Leelu	L
Malabar House	O
Napier House	S
The Old Courtyard	F
The Old Harbour	D
Orion	U
Raintree	M
Santa Cruz	J
Spencer Home	Q
Trinity House	K
Walton's Homestay	G

Al Bayan Mosque

Rhythms Centre (Greenix)

KALVATHI ROAD

Jama Masjid

① B

Vypeen Island

RIVER ROAD

ASHWALL JUNCTION

P M MOHAMMED ROAD

Government Boat Jetty

Taxi ★Stand

Bus Terminus

G A

PILLIPPALATH RD

YMCA ROAD

P M MOHAMMED ROAD

KUNNUMPIRAM JUNCTION

ICICI Bank & ATM

P M MOHAMMED ROAD

Syrian Orthodox Church

FOSSE ROAD

PULLUPALAM ROAD

Federal Bank & ATM

KUNNUMPIRAM ROAD

RISDALE BRANCH ROAD

Chinese Fishing Nets

Tourist Desk

K B JACOB ROAD

Football Pitch

San Mike Tours (Motorcycle Rental)

① ②

④ ③

TOWER ROAD

BURGHER STREET

PRINCESS STREET

Santa Cruz Basilica

⑥

K B JACOB ROAD

Childrens Park

Idiom Bookshop

D E

Café de Net @

PETER CELLI STREET

LILY STREET

Riverside Beach

RIVER ROAD

ROSE STREET

BASTION STREET

Vasco da Gama's House

⑤

DUTCH STREET

⑦

K B BERNARD ROAD

SANTA CRUZ ROAD

T U

N

CHURCH ROAD

Cochin Club

Church of St Francis

Parade Ground

RIDSDALE ROAD

BASTION STREET

K B J

RIDSDALE ROAD

M

PARADE ROAD

Dutch Cemetery

⑧

O

P R

S

NAPIER STREET

LILY STREET

ELPHINSTONE ROAD

Indo-Portuguese Museum (Bishop's) Palace

PATTALAM ROAD

BEACH ROAD

Seaside Beach

N

RESTAURANTS & CAFÉS
Addy's	8
Brighton Café	2
Chariot Beach	3
Elite Bakery	1
Fort House	A
The History	4
Kashi Art Café	4
Malabar House	F
The Old Courtyard	D
The Old Harbour	D
Salt 'n' Pepper	2
Teapot Café	7
Upstairs	6
Vasco Café	5

100 m

0

For **kathakali** and other traditional forms of ritual dance and drama, you've a choice of venues staging daily tourist shows (see box, p.187). The Fort's pair of **beaches**, on the northwest edge of the peninsula, are certainly not places you'd wish to swim from or sunbathe on, with slicks of dubious coloured pollution washing over them periodically – although Riverside Beach (the northernmost of the two) is a good spot for viewing the Chinese fishing nets. The nearest decent seaside destination is Cherai Beach, 35km north (see pp.194–195).

△ Carnival in Kochi

Chinese fishing nets

The huge, elegant **Chinese fishing nets** lining the northern shore of Fort Cochin add grace to the waterfront view, and are probably the single most familiar photographic image of Kerala. Traders from the court of Kublai Khan are said to have introduced them to the Malabar region. Known in Malayalam as *cheena vala*, they can also be seen throughout the backwaters further south. The nets, which are suspended from arced poles and operated by levers and weights, require at least four men to control them. You can buy fresh fish from the tiny market here and have it grilled with sea salt, garlic and lemon at one of the ramshackle stalls nearby.

St Francis Church and around

South of the Chinese fishing nets on Church Road (the continuation of River Road) is the large, typically English **Parade Ground**, where generations of colonial troops were drilled in the merciless heat, and on which local lads now brush up their cricketing skills after school.

Overlooking it is the **Church of St Francis**, (daily 8.30am–6.30pm) the first built by Europeans in India. Its exact age is not known, though the stone structure is thought to date back to the early sixteenth century; the land was a gift of the local raja, and the title deeds, written on palm leaf, are still kept inside. The facade, meanwhile, with its multi-curved sides, became the model for most Christian churches in India. Vasco da Gama was buried here in 1524, but his body was later removed to Portugal. Under the Dutch, the church was renovated and became Protestant in 1663, then Anglican with the advent of the British in 1795; since 1949 it has been attached to the Church of South India. Inside, various tombstone inscriptions have been placed in the walls, the earliest of which is from 1562. One hangover from British days is the continued use of *punkahs,* large swinging cloth fans on frames suspended above the congregation, operated by a *punkah-wallah.*

East of St Francis Church, the interior of the twentieth-century **Santa Cruz Basilica** will delight fans of a colourful, gaudy Indo-Romano-Rococo style of decoration. The building dates from 1887, and was constructed on the site of a much older Portuguese one demolished by the British a century earlier.

The Indo-Portuguese Museum

At the southern end of Ridsdale Road, the grand Bishop House of 1557 has been converted into the **Indo-Portuguese Museum** (Tues–Sun 9am–1pm & 2–6pm; Rs25 [Rs10]), hosting a none-too-impressive assortment of Catholic relics, altarpieces and other religious paraphernalia. Some minimal ruins of the fort's foundations can be seen in the basement.

Mattancherry

Mattancherry, the old district of red-tiled riverfront wharfs and houses occupying the northeastern tip of the headland, was once the colonial capital's main market area – the epicentre of the Malabar's spice trade, and home to its wealthiest Jewish and Jain merchants. Like Fort Cochin, its once grand buildings have lapsed into advanced states of disrepair, with most of their original owners working overseas. When Mattancherry's Jews emigrated en masse to Israel in the 1940s, their furniture and other non-portable heirlooms ended up in the **antique shops** for which the area is now renowned – though these days genuine pieces are few and far between. Kashmiris have taken over the majority of them, selling handicrafts and curios at inflated prices to the tour groups and cruise-ship visitors who stream through daily during the winter.

The sight at the top of most visitors' itineraries is **Mattancherry Palace** (10am–5pm; closed Fri; Rs2), on the roadside a short walk from the Mattancherry Jetty, a kilometre or so southeast of Fort Cochin. Known locally as the Dutch Palace, the two-storey building was actually erected by the Portuguese, as a gift to the raja of Cochin, Vira Keralavarma (1537–61) – though the Dutch did add to the complex. While its squat exterior is not particularly striking, the interior is captivating.

The **murals** that adorn some of its rooms are among the finest examples of Kerala's underrated school of painting. Friezes illustrating stories from the *Ramayana*, on the first floor, date from the sixteenth century. Packed with detail and gloriously rich colour, the style is never strictly naturalistic; the treatment of facial features is pared down to the simplest of lines for the mouths and characteristically aquiline noses. Downstairs, the women's bedchamber holds several less complex paintings, possibly dating from the 1700s. One shows Shiva dallying with Vishnu's female form, the enchantress Mohini; a second portrays Krishna holding aloft Mount Govardhana; another features a reclining Krishna surrounded by *gopis*, or cowgirls. His languid pose belies the activity of his six hands and two feet, intimately caressing adoring admirers. While the paintings are undoubtedly the highlight of the palace, the collection also includes interesting Dutch maps of old Cochin, coronation robes belonging to past maharajas, royal palanquins, weapons and furniture. Without permission from the Archeological Survey of India, **photography** is strictly prohibited.

A few hundred metres west of the palace, on Gujarati Road, lies the peaceful **Jain temple**, boasting a pair of airy marble sanctuaries with some delicate carving. The temple's serene atmosphere is broken daily at noon when one devotee rings a bell loudly to announce the feeding of the local pigeons. At this point the courtyard turns into a mini-Trafalgar Square, and anyone around is encouraged to help dish out grain to the hungry birds.

Jew Town

The road heading south from Mattancherry Jetty leads into the district known as **Jew Town**, where N.X. Jacob's tailor shop and the offices of J.E. Cohen, advocate and tax consultant, serve as reminders of a once-thriving Jewish community. The area is now dominated by Kashmiri shopkeepers selling mostly fake antiques, Hindu and Christian wood carvings, oil lamps, masks, spice boxes and other bric-a-brac, plus some tempting coffee-table books; one showroom even houses a full-size snake boat.

In the heart of Jew Town, the **Kochi International Pepper Exchange** once housed a noisy trading floor, packed with dealers shouting the latest prices and clinching deals by means of arcane sign language. Recently, however, the market was superseded by the India Pepper and Spice Trade Association (IPSTA) and converted to online trading (Ⓦwww.ipsta.com), since when the building has seen fewer sacks of actual pepper pass through its doors than do the majority of spice shops further north in the main bazaar, where trucks and handcarts loaded with jute sacks of the Malabar's "black gold" routinely block the narrow lanes.

A right turn at the old Pepper Exchange brings you into Synagogue Lane, at the end of which stands the famous **Pardesi (White Jew) Synagogue** (10am–noon & 3–5pm; closed Sat; Rs2). Founded in 1568 and rebuilt in 1664, the building is best known for its interior, an attractive, if incongruous hotchpotch paved with hand-painted eighteenth-century blue and white tiles from Canton. Each of the tiles is unique, depicting a love affair between a

Kathakali in Kochi

Kochi is the only city in the state where you are guaranteed the chance to see live **kathakali**, Kerala's unique form of ritualized theatre (see p.294). Whether in its authentic setting, in temple festivals held during the winter, or at the shorter tourist-oriented shows that take place year-round, these mesmerizing dance dramas – depicting the struggles of gods and demons – are an unmissable feature of Kochi's cultural life.

Four venues in the city hold daily shows, each preceded by an introductory talk at around 6.30pm. You can watch the dancers being made up if you arrive an hour or so beforehand, and keen photographers should turn up well before the start to ensure a front-row seat. Tickets, costing Rs100–150, can be bought at the door.

Most visitors only attend one performance, but you'll gain a much better sense of what *kathakali* is all about if you take in at least a couple. The next step is an all-night recital at a temple festival, or one of the performances given by the top-notch **Ernakulam Kathakali Club**, which stages night-long plays once each month, either at the TDM Hall in Ernakulam (see map, p.188) or at the Ernakulathappan Hall in the city's main Shiva temple. For further details contact the tourist desk at the Main Boat Jetty, Ernakulam. The four principal venues are listed below.

Art Kerala, Kannanthodathu Lane, Valanjambalam ☎0484/237 5238 ✉art_kerala@ satyam.net.in. Next door to the See India Foundation, the *kathakali* performances here have proved popular with large tour groups, so expect a crowd. Make-up starts at 6pm, the performance at 7pm.

Dr Devan's Kathakali, See India Foundation, Kalathiparambil Cross Rd, near Ernakulam Junction railway station ☎0484/236 6471. The oldest-established tourist show in the city, introduced by the inimitable Dr Devan, who starts the show with a lengthy discourse on Indian philosophy and mythology. From 6.45–8pm (make-up at 6pm).

Kerala Kathakali Centre, opposite *Brunton Boatyard*, Fort Cochin. Popular performances by a company of graduates of the renowned Kalamandalam academy. You usually get to see three characters, and the music is live.

Rhythms Theatre (Greenix), opposite *Fort House*, Fort Cochin. Costing Rs450, this is the priciest show, but combines excerpts from *kathakali* plays with displays of *mohiniyattam* dance, *kalarippayattu* martial art and, on Sundays, *theyyattam*, set against a combination of live and pre-recorded music. Performances aren't of the highest standard, but the evening is more likely to appeal to kids as costumes and acts change in quick succession.

mandarin's daughter and a commoner. The nineteenth-century glass oil-burning chandeliers suspended from the ceiling were imported from Belgium. Above the entrance, a gallery supported by slender gilt columns was reserved for female members of the congregation. Opposite, an elaborately carved Ark houses four scrolls of the *Torah* (the first five books of the Old Testament), encased in silver and gold, on which sit gold crowns presented by the maharajas of Travancore and Cochin, testifying to good relations with the Jewish community. The synagogue's oldest artefact is a fourth-century copperplate inscription from the raja of Cochin.

An attendant is usually available to show visitors around and answer questions; his introductory talk features as part of the KTDC guided tour (see p.177). Outside, the streets surrounding the synagogue are crammed with **antique emporia**, run by Kashmiris to relieve wealthy cruise-ship passengers of their spending money.

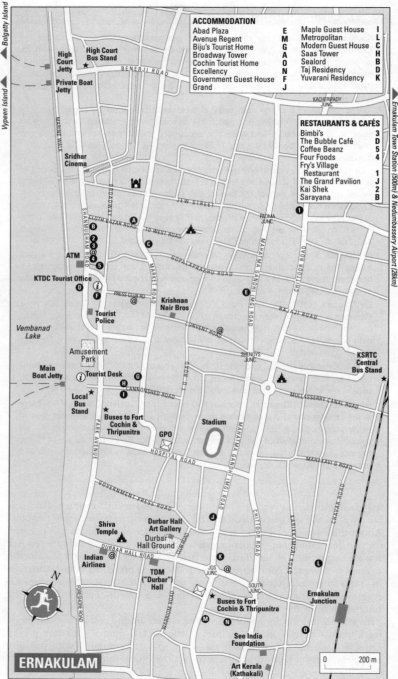

ACCOMMODATION

Abad Plaza	E
Avenue Regent	M
Biju's Tourist Home	G
Broadway Tower	A
Cochin Tourist Home	O
Excellency	N
Government Guest House	F
Grand	J

Maple Guest House	I
Metropolitan	L
Modern Guest House	C
Saas Tower	H
Sealord	B
Taj Residency	D
Yuvarani Residency	K

RESTAURANTS & CAFÉS

Bimbi's	3
The Bubble Café	D
Coffee Beanz	5
Four Foods	4
Fry's Village Restaurant	1
The Grand Pavilion	J
Kai Shek	2
Sarayana	B

Bolgatty Island

Vypeen Island

High Court Jetty

Private Boat Jetty

High Court Bus Stand

BENERJI ROAD

Sridhar Cinema

MARINE WALK

BROADWAY

SHANMUGHAM ROAD

CLOTH BAZAR ROAD

JEW STREET

KACHERIPADY JUNC.

Ernakulam Town Station (500m) & Nedumbassery Airport (26km)

PADMA JUNC.

ATM

KTDC Tourist Office

PRESS CLUB RD

Krishnan Nair Bros

TD WEST ROAD

MARKET ROAD

GOPALAPRABHU ROAD

MAHATMA GANDHI (MG) ROAD

CHITTOOR ROAD

RAJAJI ROAD

Vembanad Lake

Tourist Police

Amusement Park

Tourist Desk

CONVENT ROAD

SHENOYS JUNC.

KSRTC Central Bus Stand

Main Boat Jetty

Local Bus Stand

Buses to Fort Cochin & Thripunitra

CANNONSHED ROAD

PARK AVENUE

GPO

Stadium

MULLASSERRY CANAL ROAD

HOSPITAL ROAD

MAHATMA GANDHI (MG) ROAD

MAHAKAVI G ROAD

GOVERNMENT PRESS ROAD

Shiva Temple

Durbar Hall Art Gallery

Durbar Hall Ground

DURBAR HALL ROAD

Indian Airlines

TDM ("Durbar") Hall

CHITTOOR ROAD

KARIKKAMURI ROAD

THAYAR ROAD

Ernakulam Junction

JOS JUNC.

SOUTH JUNC.

See India Foundation

N

FORESHORE ROAD

Buses to Fort Cochin & Thripunitra

Art Kerala (Kathakali)

0   200 m

ERNAKULAM

Cochin Cultural Centre

Ernakulam and south of the

ERNAKULAM presents the modern face o. [...] feel than Thiruvananthapuram. Other than the [...] the small **Durbar Hall Art Gallery** (daily 11a [...] Road, there's little in the way of sights. Along the [...] **Gandhi (MG) Road**, which more or less divides [...] activities are shopping, eating and movie-going. Here [...] emails and phone calls, and choose from an assortme [...] Keralan food. This area is particularly good for clo [...] selection of colours; whatever the current trend in *lunght* [...] year, you'll get it on MG Road.

An eight-day annual **festival** (Jan/Feb) at the Shiva temp [...] Road, features elephant processions and *panchavadyam* (dr [...] groups) out in the street. The festival usually includes night [...] ances of **kathakali**, and the temple is decorated with an am [...] electric lights.

The village of **Netoor**, 10km southeast of the centre, is home [...] Kalari school of **kalarippayattu** (℡0484/270 0810, Ⓔenskalari [...] one of the leading centres of the Keralan martial art form (see box, p.1 [...] well-organized centre, established in 1954, is unusual in that it blends b [...] northern and the southern systems of *kalarippayattu*. Twice-daily tra [...] sessions start early at 4am; visitors are welcome to attend demonstrat [...] (6–7pm) and the open session on Sundays (3–7pm). Alternatively, you c [...] enrol on one of their *kalarippayattu* certificate courses, which run from on [...] week to one year and are tailored to the needs of the student. The centre also offers lessons in the unique **Uzhichil massage** – a treatment derived from ayurvedic medicine, designed as a cure to *kalari*-related injuries, which concentrates on the lymph glands to improve tone and circulation. To get to the school take a bus from the KSRTC or the Kaloor bus stands to the Netoor INTUC bus stand, and walk down the road for half a kilometre; the school is opposite the Mahadevar Temple.

Eating

Kochi offers an outstanding choice of places to eat, from the rustic fish-fry stalls next to the Chinese nets to fine dining with harbour views. As with accommodation, restaurants in Ernakulam tend to be cheaper but less atmospheric than those in Fort Cochin. If you're dining across the water from your hotel, make sure you are familiar with the ferry timings back (see box, p.176).

Unless otherwise stated, restaurants under the "Ernakulam" and "Fort Cochin" headings are marked on their relevant maps (see p.188 & p.183).

Ernakulam

Bimbi's Shanmugham Rd. This modern South Indian fast-food joint, in midtown near the Sealord boat jetty, is hugely popular locally for its inexpensive *udipi*, North Indian and Chinese snacks and meals. Their *vada-sambars* are the tangiest in town, and there's an exhaustive range of cooling ice cream and shakes to round your meal off.

The Bubble Café *Taj Residency*, Marine Drive. Luxury coffee shop in a vast, a/c glass-roofed conservatory close to the waterfront, serving pricey chilled snacks (such as prawns with papaya and mint timbale), multi-cuisine main courses and a particularly good range of Western cakes (Dundee, plum, palmettes and fudge).

Coffee Beanz Shanmugham Rd. Trendy a/c cappuccino bar, patronized mainly by well-heeled students shrieking into their mobiles over a full-on MTV soundtrack. The din notwithstanding, it's a good spot to beat the heat and grab a quick meal (burgers, fries, grilled sandwiches, *dosas*, fish

mosas). The coffee's freshly
s, though the service is far less
fast-food uniforms.

hanmugham Rd. Busy, clean and
dside restaurant serving veg and non-
including generous thalis, fish dishes
d-value "dish of the day". For dessert, try
mbai-style *faloodas*, vermicelli steeped in
ith dried fruits and ice cream.

Fry's Village Restaurant Chittoor Rd, next
to Mymoor Cinema). *Fry's* was the first place
e city to offer the kind of proper Keralan meals
ple would eat in their home towns and villages.
busiest at lunch times, when workers pour in
the excellent value thalis (veg Rs35; non-veg
s40). You can also order mountainous Moppila-
Muslim-style biryanis (veg, prawn, mutton or
chicken; Rs30–40), steaks of deliciously fresh
masala-fried kingfish and the full range of traditional Keralan steamed rice cakes: *iddiappam*,
pootu, etc. A comfortable, hygienic and cheap place
to sample quality local cooking.

The Grand Pavilion MG Rd ☏ 0484/238
2061. An Ernakulam institution, famous
for its gourmet Keralan dishes, especially the
karimeen pollichathu with *appam*, which draws
crowds on Sun evenings. They also do a huge
range of Far Eastern, North Indian and Continental options, served on white table cloths by a
legion of brisk waiters wearing black ties and
waistcoats. The prices are restrained, too: count
on Rs500–600 for three courses. Reservation
recommended.

Kai Shek Penda Shopping Mall, Shanmugham Rd.
Dimly lit Chinese, with a much brighter, family a/c
floor upstairs. Specialities include ginger chicken,
chilli prawns and roast duck – though there are
plenty of fried rice options for veggies. Mains from
Rs80–120.

Sarayana *Sealord* hotel, Shanmugham Rd.
Reasonably priced rooftop restaurant serving good
Chinese, Indian and sizzlers. The harbour view is
not what it was since the shopping centre opposite
was built, but it's still a pleasant enough spot for a
cold beer.

Fort Cochin

Addy's 1/286 Elphinstone Rd. Ramshackle, atmospheric and friendly, this family-run place near the
Indo-Portuguese Museum occupies the ground
floor of a late-eighteenth-century Dutch house. In a
dining room with peeling pink plaster walls, you
can enjoy homely Keralan dishes, the most
tempting of them local seafood specialities
steamed in banana leaves or pan-fried over a low
flame on a proper *thava* griddle iron. Try the squid

chootu porachathu, grilled seer fish with garlic and
black pepper sauce or chicken *molee*. Most mains
Rs165–210.

Chariot Beach Princess St. Unassuming terrace
café-restaurant on one of the Fort's main crossroads, which really comes into its own in the
evenings – it's one of only a handful of places
serving beer (Prohibition-style from little china
jugs), and stays open until midnight. The menu is a
standard multi-cuisine, foreigner-oriented mix, with
lots of seafood and Chinese options, and a tandoori
churns out hot naan breads to go with the tasty
flame-grilled chicken kebabs.

Elite Bakery Ground Floor, *Elite Lodge*, Princess
St. One of very few bona fide locals' cafés left in
Fort Cochin, and a dependable option if you're
travelling on a budget. They serve Keralan and
Western breakfasts, filling, freshly prepared veg
and non-veg thalis at lunchtime, and Anglo-Indian
snacks such as flaky pastry puffs (veg, beef or
egg), fried potato cutlets, spring rolls and patties
throughout the day and evening.

Fort House *Fort House Hotel*, 2/6A Calvathy
Rd. One of the fort's hidden gems: carefully
prepared Keralan specialities – including delicious
karimeen pollichathu or a grilled fish steak –
served on a romantic, candle-lit jetty jutting into
the harbour. The food is consistently good, and not
too pricey (most mains Rs175–245), and the
location's perfect for watching the ships chugging
in and out of the docks.

The History *Brunton Boatyard*, Bellar Rd, next to
Fort Cochin Government Boat Jetty. Renowned
Keralan chef Jerry Matthew delved into the culinary
traditions of Fort Cochin to devise the *History's*
eclectic menu. Served on a breezy raised terrace
looking across the water to Vypeen Island, favour-
ites include the Anglo-Indian "First-Class Railway
Lamb Curry", Portuguese "Fernandes roast pork"
and Syrian-Christian "Kuttanadi *tharavu* roast
duck". Count on Rs750–850 for three courses, or
more if you hit the (Indian) wine list.

Kashi Art Café Burgher St. Chichi art gallery
café, patronized almost exclusively by Westerners,
and with a menu to match. Fragrant, freshly
ground espresso coffee is the big draw, along
with the *Kashi's* famous house cakes (their
chocolate gateau is legendary among travellers),
but they also do a selection of light meals and
savoury snacks through the day: check out the
specials board.

Malabar House *Malabar House Hotel*, 1/268
Parade Rd ☏ 0484/221 6666, ⊛www
.malabarhouse.com. Gourmet fusion cuisine, made
from market-fresh ingredients and served on a
chic garden dining terrace in one of Kerala's most

stylish boutique hotels. Their signature dish is the seafood platter (Rs980), featuring juicy local lobster, tiger prawns, calamari and choice cuts of fish from the lagoon, but they offer a range of more sensibly priced Italian and South Indian alternatives, both veg and non-veg (Rs250–450). For dessert, try the chocolate samosas. The menu can be viewed online.

The Old Courtyard 1/371–2 Princess St. Few places capture the feel of old-world Cochin as vividly as this courtyard restaurant, where candle-lit tables are laid out beneath Portuguese vaulted arches. The food is as fine as the location (hallmark dishes include baked seafood spaghetti and fish grilled with coriander butter) – and the *patronne-chef* is a dessert wizard. Most mains Rs200–275.

Salt 'n' Pepper/Brighton Café Tower Rd. This pair of terrace cafés, spread under the rain trees along the north side of Tower Rd, fill up after sunset and stay open until the small hours during the season. Both serve simple snacks, but the main attraction is the beer – surreptitiously poured out of china pots to rows of bored foreign budget tourists.

Teapot Café Peter Celli St. With its massive collection of teapots from around the world, shabby-chic colour-washed wood floors, tea-chest tables and funky little mezzanine floor, this backstreet tearoom has been giving the *Kashi* some much-needed competition over the past few seasons. Quality teas and coffees are its mainstay, but there's also a selection of light meals and delicious home-made cakes on offer (including a stupendous "death by chocolate").

Upstairs Santa Cruz Rd. Currently the backpacker's favourite: a hip little *trattoria* run by a young Indian-Italian couple in a quirky, blue-and-white-painted first-floor dining room opposite the Basilica. The food's simple, fresh and authentically Italian, down to the imported olive oil and parmesan: green leaf salad (Rs70); tasty bruschettas (Rs130); crisp-edged pizzas (Rs160–220); fresh pasta bakes and *lasagna al forno* (Rs260); and for dessert, rum-soaked pears or melt-in-the-mouth *zuccotto* (moist sponge filled with home-made ice cream).

Vasco Café Bastion St. Tiny budget travellers' breakfast joint in the heart of the tourist enclave, with relaxing wood tables and a huge bell-metal bowl in its barred window. The food – toasties, omelettes, muesli, fruit salad with curd, pancakes juices and the like – is prepared to order, tasty and inexpensive.

Listings

Airlines, domestic Air Sahara, airport ☎0484/261 1340; Indian Airlines, Durbar Hall Rd ☎0484/237 114, airport ☎0484/261 0101; Go Air, c/o UAE Travel Services, Chettupuzha Towers, PT Usha Rd Junction ☎0484/235 5522; Jet Airways, 39/4158, Elmar Square Bldg, MG Road ☎0484/235 9212, airport ☎261 0037; Kingfisher Airlines, K.B. Oxford Business Center, 39/4013, Free Kandath Rd, MG Rd ☎0484/235 1144; Paramount Airways, airport ☎0484/261 0404.

Airlines, international Air Arabia XXVII/3202-A Kunnalekat Building, Atlantis Junction, MG Road ☎484/235 9601; Air India, Collis Estate, MG Rd ☎0484/235 1295, airport ☎0484/261 0040; Air India Express, Collis Estate, MG Rd ☎0484/238 1885, airport ☎0484/261 0050; Emirates, Plot No. 696-A, opposite Wyte Fort Hotel, NH-47 Bypass, Maradu ☎0484/238 9999, airport ☎0484/261 1194; Gulf Air, c/o Jet Air, Atlantic Junction, MG Rd ☎0484/235 9242, airport ☎0484/261 1346; Kuwait Airways, 39/6823 Polachirackal Mansions, Ravipuram, MG Rd; airport ☎0484/261 0252; Qatar Airways, Hotel Le Meridien, Mezzanine Floor, Maradu ☎0484/3017350, airport ☎0484/261 1302; Saudi Arabian Airlines, airport ☎0484/261 1286; Silk Air, Aisha Manzil, Ravipuram, MG Rd ☎0484/ 236 1666, airport ☎0484/261 0157; SriLankan Airlines, Trans Lanka Ltd, MG Rd ☎0484/236 1215, airport ☎0484/261 1313.

Banks Branches on MG Rd in Ernakulam include: ANZ Grindlays; State Bank of India (which also has a branch opposite the KTDC Tourist Reception Centre); and Andhra Bank. To exchange travellers' cheques, the best place is Thomas Cook (Mon–Sat 9.30am–6pm), near the Air India Building at Palal Towers, MG Rd; they also have a branch at the airport. ATMs can be found all over the centre of Ernakulam. In Fort Cochin, the Canara Bank has an ATM on Kanumpuram Junction (see map, p.183). The Wilson Info Centre and Destinations, both on Princess St (daily 9am–9pm) change cash and travellers' cheques at rates slightly above Thomas Cook, but are much more conveniently located.

Bookshops The two branches of Idiom (opposite the Dutch Palace, Jew Town, Mattancherry; and on Bastion St near Princess St, Fort Cochin) are wonderful places to browse for books on travel, Indian and Keralan culture, flora and fauna, religion and art; they also have an excellent range of fiction.

Cinemas Sridhar Theatre (☎0484/ 235 2529), Shanmugham Rd, near the *Sealord hotel*, screens

Moving on from Kochi/Ernakulam

For an overview of travel services to and from Kochi/Ernakulam, see "Travel details" on p.222.

By air

The international airport (℡484/261 0113, ⒲www.cochinairport.com) at **Nedumbassery**, near Alwaye (aka Aluva), is 26km north of Ernakulam and serves as Kerala's main gateway to and from the Gulf. A full list of domestic airlines, and the destinations they fly to from Nedumbassery, appears on p.222. For flights to the **Lakshadweep Islands** contact *Casino Hotel*, Willingdon Island (see p.181). Recommended travel agents are listed on the page opposite.

By bus

Buses leave Ernakulam's KSRTC Central bus stand for virtually every town in Kerala; most, but not all, are bookable in advance at the bus station. A full list appears in "Travel Details" at the end of this chapter, on p.222.

By train

Kochi lies on Kerala's main broad-gauge line and sees frequent trains down the coast to Thiruvananthapuram via Kottayam, Kollam and Varkala and north to Thrissur.

Although most long-distance express and mail trains depart from **Ernakulam Junction**, a couple of key services leave from **Ernakulam Town**. To confuse matters further, a few also start at Cochin Harbour station, so be sure to check the departure point when you book your ticket. The main reservation office, good for trains leaving all three stations, is at Ernakulam Junction; availability, fares and timetables can be checked online at ⒲www.indianrail.gov.in.

The trains listed below are recommended as the fastest and/or most convenient services from Kochi. If you're heading to **Alappuzha** for the backwater trip to Kollam, take the bus, as the only train that can get you there in time invariably arrives late.

Recommended trains from Kochi/Ernakulam

Destination	Name	Number	Station	Frequency	Departs	Total time
Kozhikode (Calicut)	Netravati Express	#6346	EJ	daily	2.15pm	4hr 45min
Thiruvananthapuram	Parasuram Express	#6350	ET	daily	1.30pm	5hr 5min
Varkala	Parasuram Express	#6350	ET	daily	1.30pm	3hr 50min

EJ = Ernakulam Junction
ET = Ernakulam Town

English-language movies daily; check the listings pages of the *Indian Express* or *Hindu* (Kerala edition) to find out what's on. For the latest Malayalam and Hindi releases, head for the Saritha Savitha Sangeetha (℡0484/ 236 6183), at the top of Market Rd.

Dentist The Emmanuel Dental Centre, Noble Square, Kadavanthara (℡0484/220 7544, ⒲www .cosmeticdentalcentre.com) is an international-standard practice that does routine dental procedures as well as more advanced cosmetic work.

Hospitals The 600-bed Medical Trust Hospital on MG Rd (℡0484/235 8001,

⒲www.medicaltrusthospital.com) is one of the state's most advanced private hospitals and has a 24hr casualty unit and ambulance service. Also recommended is the Ernakulam Medical Centre, NH Bypass, Paalarivattom (℡0484/280 7101, ⒲www.emccochin.com).

Internet access *Café de Net* on Bastion Rd, Fort Cochin, has nine machines and charges Rs30/hr; if it's full, try any of the smaller places off the bottom of Princess St nearby. In Ernakulam, convenient options include Net Park on Convent Rd and Mathsons on Durbar Hall Rd (both Rs30/hr).

Music shops Sargam, XL/6816 GSS Complex, Convent Rd, opposite the Public Library, stocks the best range of music in the state, mostly Indian (Hindi films and lots of Keralan devotional music), with a couple of shelves of Western rock and pop. Music World, MKV Building, near Shenoy's Theatre on MG Rd is Kochi's answer to a music superstore, with Western pop, classical, compilations, world music and Indian *filmi* music. Sound of Melody, DH Rd, near the Ernakulam Junction station, has a good selection of traditional South Indian and contemporary Western music.

Musical instruments Manuel Industries, Banerji Rd, Kacheripady Junction, is the best for Indian classical and Western instruments. For traditional Keralan drums, ask at Thripunitra bazaar (see below).

Police The city's tourist police have a counter at Ernakulam Junction railway station. There is also a counter next to the KTDC Tourist Office at the southern end of Shanmugham Rd.

Post office The GPO is on Hospital Rd, not far from the Main Jetty; the city's poste restante is at the post office behind St Francis Church in Fort Cochin.

Tour and travel agents For air tickets, Kapitan Air Travel and Tours at 1/430 Burgher St in Fort Cochin (on the ground floor of *Adam's Old Inn*) is the Fort's only IATA-bonded agent. Wild Kerala Tours, at VI/480 KVA Bldgs on Bazaar Rd, Mattancherry (℡ 0484/309 9520, ℡ m98461 62157, ⩊ www .wildkeralatours.com) is recommended for wildlife and adventure safaris to some of Kerala's wildest corners, guided by local experts. If you'd like to book shorter backwater cruises by motorboats and canoes in the area, go to the Tourist Desk at the Main Jetty in Ernakulam (℡ 0484/237 1761), who also book accommodation for small hotels in beautiful locations in northern Kerala.

Around Kochi

Within easy distance of Kochi are **Thripunitra**, a small suburban town and former royal seat, and a three-kilometre stretch of sand called **Cherai Beach**, which offers a taste of both beach- and backwater life. On the road to Munnar, in an area dotted with some outstanding farmstays and heritage accommodation, the bird sanctuary of **Thattekkad** makes an ideal spot to break the journey into the hills. Visitors to Kochi and Ernakulam who really want to get away from it all, however, and have time and a lot of money to spare, could do no better than to head from here for **Lakshadweep** (see pp.194–195), the "one hundred thousand islands", which lie between 200km and 400km offshore, in the deep blue of the Arabian Sea.

Thripunitra

Some 12km southeast of Ernakulam and a short bus or auto–rickshaw ride from the bus stand just south of Jos Junction on MG Road, the small suburban town of **THRIPUNITRA** is worth a visit for its dilapidated colonial-style **Hill Palace** (Tues–Sun 9am–5pm; Rs10), now an eclectic museum. The royal family of Cochin at one time maintained around forty palaces – this one was confiscated by the state government after Independence, and has slipped into dusty decline over the past decade.

One of the museum's finest exhibits is an early seventeenth-century wooden *mandapa* (hall) removed from a temple in Pathanamthitta, featuring excellent carvings of themes from the *Ramayana*, including the coronation of the monkey king Sugriva. Of interest too are the silver filigree jewel boxes, gold and silver ornaments, and ritual objects associated with grand ceremonies. The **epigraphy gallery** contains an eighth-century Jewish Torah, and Keralan stone and copperplate inscriptions. Sculpture, ornaments and weapons in the **bronze gallery** include a *kingini katti* knife, whose decorative bells belie the fact that it was used for beheading, and a body-shaped cage in which condemned prisoners would be hanged while birds pecked them to death. Providing the place isn't crowded with noisy school groups, you could check out the nearby **deer park**;

there are peaceful spots to picnic beneath the cashew trees in the garden behind the palace.

Performances of theatre, classical music and dance, including consecutive all-night **kathakali** performances, are held over a period of several days during the annual festival (Oct/Nov) at the **Shri Purnatrayisa Temple** on the way to the palace. Inside the temple compound, both in the morning and at night, massed drum orchestras perform *chenda melam* in procession with fifteen caparisoned elephants. At night, the outside walls of the sanctuary are covered with thousands of tiny oil lamps. The temple is normally closed to non-Hindus, but admittance to appropriately dressed visitors is usually allowed at this time.

Cherai Beach

The closest decent beach to Kochi is **Cherai**, 35km to the north. It shelters a backwater and supports an active fishing community, some of whom use Chinese fishing nets (see p.185). The **Sri Goureeswara Temple**, closed to non-Hindus, is dedicated to the deity Sri Subramanya Swami and holds its annual nine-day festival (*utsavam*) in January or February every year. The *utsavam* is a great time to see traditional dance, including *kathakali* performances, but the

The Lakshadweep Islands

Visitors to Kerala in search of an exclusive tropical paradise may well find it in **LAKSHADWEEP** (@www.lakshadweep.nic.in), the "one hundred thousand islands" which lie between 200km and 400km offshore in the deep blue of the Arabian Sea. The smallest Union Territory in India, Lakshadweep's 27 tiny, coconut-palm-covered **coral islands** are the archetypal tropical hideaway, edged with pristine white sands and surrounded by calm lagoons where average water temperature stays around 26°C all year. Beyond the lagoons lie the coral **reefs**, home to sea turtles, dolphins, eagle rays, lionfish, parrotfish, octopus, barracudas and sharks. Devoid of animal and bird life, only ten of the islands are inhabited, with a total population of just over 50,000, the majority of whom are Malayalam-speaking Sunni Muslims said to be descended from seventh-century Keralan Hindus who converted to Islam.

The main sources of income are fishing and coconuts. Fruit, vegetables and pulses are cultivated in small quantities but staples such as rice have always had to be imported. The Portuguese, who discovered the value of **coir rope**, spun from coconut husk, controlled Lakshadweep during the sixteenth century; when they imposed an import tax on rice, locals retaliated by poisoning some of the forty-strong Portuguese garrison, and terrible reprisals followed. As Muslims, the islanders enjoyed friendly relations with Tipu Sultan of Mysore, which naturally aroused the ire of the British, who moved in at the end of the eighteenth century and remained until Independence, when Lakshadweep became a Union Territory.

Visiting Lakshadweep

Concerted attempts are being made to minimize the ecological impact of tourism in Lakshadweep. At present, accommodation is available for **non-Indians** on only two of the islands – Bangaram and Kadmat. Indian tourists are also allowed to visit the neighbouring islands of Kavaratti and Minicoy (both closed to foreigners).

All visits to **Kadmat** must be arranged in Kochi through the Society for Promotion of Recreational Tourism and Sports (SPORTS) on IG Road, Willingdon Island (@0484/266 8387, @www.lakshadweeptourism.com). They offer a five-day package **cruise** to Kavaratti, Kalpeni and Minicoy islands ($225–375 per person) on one of their ships. Meals are included, and permits taken care of.

highlight of the festival is on the seventh day, when eighteen caparisoned elephants take to the streets in a spectacular procession.

To get there, you can either jump on the ferry across to Vypeen Island from Fort Cochin and transfer onto the hourly bus, or catch one of the more frequent buses from opposite the High Court Jetty in Ernakulam.

Thattekkad Bird Sanctuary

Kerala's number one bird sanctuary, **THATTEKKAD** occupies a 25-square-kilometre wedge of former rubber plantation between two branches of the Periyar River. Lying just off the highway between Munnar and Kochi, it offers a tranquil stopover on the journey from the mountains and the coast. When the world-renowned ornithologist Salim Ali visited the site in the 1930s, he described it as the "richest bird habitat in peninsula India". Since then much of the area's forest has been felled, but what remains gives you some idea of phenomenal avian diversity that once characterized the Keralan lowlands. A total of 275 species have been sighted here, most of them endemics. On an average day, visitors can expect to see between eighty and one hundred, including rarities such as the crimson-throated barbet, grey-headed fishing

The uninhabited, teardrop-shaped half-square-kilometre islet of **Bangaram** welcomes a limited number of foreign tourists at any one time, and expects them to pay handsomely for the privilege. CGH Earth's *Bangaram Island Resort* (@www .cghearth.com; ⑨), bookable through the *Casino Hotel* in Kochi (see p.181), accommodates up to thirty couples in thatched cottage rooms, each with a veranda. Cane tables and chairs sit outside the restaurant on the beach, and a few hammocks are strung up between the palms. There's no a/c, TV, radio, telephone, newspapers or shops, let alone discos. Facilities include scuba diving (again expensive at $85 per day plus $40 per dive, or $70 for two), glass-bottomed boat trips to neighbouring uninhabited islands, and deep-sea fishing (Oct to mid-May; $65–90). Kayaks, catamarans and a sailing boat are available free, and it's possible to take a day-trip to Kadmat.

A British-run diving firm based in Goa also operates diving holidays in Lakshadweep; a full rundown of prices and booking conditions appears online at @www .goadiving.com.

Getting to the islands
At present, the only way for foreigners to reach Bangaram are the expensive flights on small 12-seater aircraft run by Indian Airlines out of **Kochi** (one daily except Sun; 1hr 35min), bookable through the *Casino Hotel* on Willingdon Island (see p.181). Foreigners pay around $300 for the round trip; the journey takes an hour and a half. Flights arrive in Lakshadweep at the island of **Agatti**, 8km southwest of Bangaram; the connecting boat journey to Bangaram takes two hours, picking its way through the shallows to avoid corals. During the monsoon (May 16–Sept 15) helicopters are used to protect the fragile coral reefs that lie just under the surface. All arrangements, including flights, accommodation and the necessary entry permit, are handled by the *Casino Hotel*, Willingdon Island, Kochi (☎0484/266 8221, ©casino@vsnl.net). Some foreign tour operators, however, offer all-in packages combining Lakshadweep with another destination, usually Goa.

Theoretically, it's possible to visit Lakshadweep all year round; the hottest time is April and May, when the temperature can reach 33°C; the **monsoon** (May–Sept) attracts approximately half the rainfall seen in the rest of Kerala, in the form of passing showers rather than a deluge, although the seas are rough.

eagle and Malabar grey hornbill. Larger animals, from flying lizards to elephants, also put in occasional appearances.

Practicalities

National Highway #49 runs to within 15km of Thattekkad; the turning off the main road is at the town of **Kothamangalam**, connected by infrequent buses to Ernakulam (55km; 2hr) and Munnar (120km; 3hr 30min). If you find yourself faced with a long wait for a service, catch one of the more frequent buses to **Muvattupuzha**, to the southwest, and change there. Once you're in Kothamangalam, you shouldn't have any problem finding a local bus for the remaining half-hour leg to the sanctuary. Pending the completion of a new road bridge (under construction at the time of writing), the crossing of the Periyar River to reach Thattekkad is achieved by means of an extraordinary *jangar* ferry, consisting of three dugouts lashed together; the bus drives onto a wooden platform on top of them – a white-knuckle affair if you happen to be stuck inside a vehicle. The nearest railway station is inconveniently situated 48km away at Aluva.

Private boat operators are also on hand to ferry birders to the sanctuary and daytrippers to Boothathanketu Lake further upriver – though don't expect international safety standards. In February 2007, fifteen school children and three of their teachers died on an excursion when the boat they were travelling in capsized.

The sanctuary itself is open daily from 9am to 5pm; admission costs Rs20. Early morning, between 6 and 7.30am, is the best time for bird-watching.

Accommodation

With the exception of the *Hornbill Inspection Bungalow*, **accommodation** within range of Thattekkad tends to be pitched at well-heeled foreign bird-watchers, and correspondingly pricey, set on plantations or close to the riverside for early safari departures. The only place to stay inside the sanctuary itself is a three-storey, double-bedded **watchtower** on stilts (❹) surrounded by a 360-degrees open window and, at ground level, an electric fence (solar powered) to keep out the elephants. You can book it through the Assistant Wildlife Warden in Kothamangalam (see review for *Hornbill Inspection Bungalow* for contact details).

Haritha Farms ("The Pimenta") Kadalikad, off the Muvattupuzha–Thodupuzha Rd, 38km southwest of Thattekkad ☎04865/260216, ⓦwww.harithafarms.com. This homestay, on a mixed organic farm hidden in the central lowlands 14km east of Muvattupuzha, was one of Kerala's eco-tourism pioneers when it opened its doors to guests in the early 1990s. Thanks to its magical setting and the warm hospitality of the Mathew family, it's still going strong, with four self-contained cottages for rent. When you tire of lazing on the veranda watching the birds and butterflies flit past, host Jacob can arrange visits to local places of interest (including a truck-painting centre and elephant training camp). Delicious organic home-cooked food is included in the rates, and cooking classes are available. ❽

Hornbill Camp book through Kalypso Eco Lodges and Camps, G-307 Panampilly Nagar, Kochi ☎0484/209 2280, ⓦwww.thehornbillcamp.com. Luxury camp, at a beautiful site slap on the banks of the Periyar River opposite the sanctuary. Each of the tents is furnished with comfy twin beds, a toilet and wash basin; shower facilities are in a common block. Home-cooked Keralan meals are served in a high thatched gazebo, and as well as arranging birding tours they also lay on kayaking trips in the area. From Rs3000 per day, full board. ❾

Hornbill Inspection Bungalow Book through the Assistant Wildlife Warden, Nyayapilly PO, Kothamangalam ☎0485/258 8302. No-frills government inspection bungalow close to the sanctuary gates, with simple, attached double rooms. It's a bit cheerless, and decidedly overpriced (at Rs950 per person), but still cheaper than the alternatives this close to the reserve. Book as far in advance as possible as it's popular. ❻

Mundackal Estate Pindimana PO, Kothamangalam ☎0485/257 0717, ☎m93886 20399, ⓦwww.mundackalhomestay.com. Swish homestay in the imposing Western-style home of welcoming local aristos Jose and Daisy

Mundackal, on their working rubber, coconut and pepper plantation. It's within easy range of the sanctuary and Kothamangalam bus stand, 7km southwest. The Keralan–Christian cooking gets rave reviews (Daisy runs courses by prior arrangement). Doubles from $125. ⑨
Periyar River Lodge book through 31/1027-A Friends Avenue, Vyttila Kochin ☎0484/2207173, ☎m94477 07173, ⓦwww.periyarriverlodge.com.

This handsome teak-built lodge sits on the riverbank next to the Thattekkad Sanctuary, centred on a traditional *nalukettu* sunken courtyard. A spacious lounge separates its two en-suite bedrooms, also wood-lined and tastefully furnished, and the entire building is surrounded by a veranda on which you can enjoy the river views from a cane swing chair. Rates (Rs3200 per double or Rs5200 for the whole house) include full board. ⑧

Thrissur and around

If you've come to Kerala in search of traditional arts, you could do a lot worse than start your hunt in **Thrissur**. As the home of several performance arts academies, the town is the state's pre-eminent cultural capital, a role it has enjoyed since Maharaja Sakthan Thampuram rebuilt his capital after its destruction at the hands of Tipu Sultan's army in the Mysore wars of the late eighteenth century. Recitals of *kathakali*, *kudiyattam*, *mohiniyattam* and other more obscure ritual forms feature prominently in the annual **Puram festival**, held in May, whose processions of massed elephants and drum orchestras are the largest and most fervently celebrated of their kind anywhere in the state. During the rest of the year, the large, circular *maidan* surrounding the Vaddukanatha Temple, where this extravagant event unfolds, plays host to a constant round of rallies and trade union meetings.

△ Thrissur's grand festival, Puram

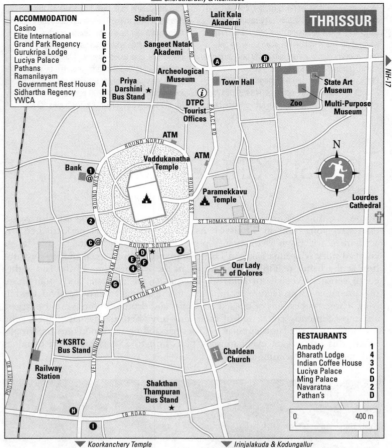

▲ *Cheruthuruthy & Kozhikode*

THRISSUR

ACCOMMODATION
Casino	I
Elite International	E
Grand Park Regency	G
Gurukripa Lodge	F
Luciya Palace	C
Pathans	D
Ramanilayam	
Government Rest House	A
Sidhartha Regency	H
YWCA	B

Stadium

Lalit Kala Akademi

Sangeet Natak Akademi

Archeological Museum

Priya Darshini ★ Bus Stand

Town Hall

State Art Museum

Multi-Purpose Museum

Zoo

DTPC Tourist Offices

ATM

Vaddukanatha Temple

ATM

Bank

Paramekkavu Temple

ST THOMAS COLLEGE ROAD

Lourdes Cathedral

Our Lady of Dolores

KSRTC Bus Stand

Railway Station

Chaldean Church

Shakthan Thampuran Bus Stand

RESTAURANTS
Ambady	1
Bharath Lodge	4
Indian Coffee House	3
Luciya Palace	C
Ming Palace	D
Navaratna	2
Pathan's	D

0   400 m

▼ *Koorkanchery Temple*   ▼ *Irinjalakuda & Kodungallur*

If Thrissur is the crucible of central Kerala's cultural and political life, then its hinterland serves as its main storehouse, dotted with towns and villages where both contemporary party politics and ancient art traditions are pursued with great enthusiasm, despite the disruptive impact on local life of mass out-migration (expatriate earnings form the mainstay of the district's economy, and nearly every family has one or more of its male relatives absent in the Gulf). At **Irinjalakuda**, a half-hour bus ride from Thrissur, one of the region's most acclaimed acting families has set up a centre to document some of their less frequently performed traditional arts, including shadow puppetry, female mono-acting and mime. Old-style crafts are another feature of life here, and at a village just outside Irinjalakuda you can watch Nadavaramba bell-metal oil lamps being cast and finished.

Nearby **Kodungallur**, site of the former port of Muziris, holds no traces of its historical role in the international spice trail, but does play host to one of Kerala's most outlandish and dramatic Tantric rituals, the **Bharani festival**, in which low-caste villagers cavort drunkenly around the local temple singing obscene songs for the Goddess. By contrast, the pilgrimage scene at **Guruvayur**, Kerala's most important Krishna shrine, is more sober, but no less fervent. The main temple is closed to foreign visitors, but the precinct around it buzzes with ritual activity, and is worth visiting for a stroll around adjacent elephant sanctuary. The one site you shouldn't miss in this area, though, is at **Cheruthuruthy**, 32km north of Thrissur, where the renowned **Kalamandalam academy** allows visitors to watch classes in traditional performing arts such as *kathakali* and *mohiniyattam*. Time your visit to coincide with the annual **Thauryathrikam festival** in January, and you'll be treated to recitals by the top students and their masters in the school's beautiful *kuttambalam* auditorium, replicating those found in the area's temples (most of which, as elsewhere in the state, remain closed to non-Hindus).

Thrissur

THRISSUR (Trichur), a bustling market hub and temple town roughly midway between Kochi (74km south) and Palakkad (79km northeast) on the NH-47, is a convenient base for exploring the cultural riches of central Kerala. Close to the Palghat (Palakkad) Gap – an opening in the natural border made by the Western Ghat mountains – it presided over the main trade route into the region from Tamil Nadu and Karnataka. For years Thrissur was the capital of Cochin State, controlled at various times by both the *zamorin* of Kozhikode and Tipu Sultan of Mysore.

The modern town dates from the eighteenth century, when Raja Rama Varma, the ruler of Travancore, developed the city, laying out roads and establishing markets with which Christian merchants were invited to trade. Although a Hindu himself, the raja helped further ensure the welfare of the Christian communities by establishing enclaves for them to the east and south of the city centre.

Today, Thrissur derives most of its income from remittance cheques sent by expatriates in the Gulf – hence the predominance of ostentatious modern houses in the surrounding villages. The state's largest temple, **Vaddukanatha**, is here too, at the centre of a huge open park that hosts all kinds of public gatherings, not least Kerala's most extravagant, noisy and sumptuous festival, **Puram**.

Arrival and information

The principal point of orientation in Thrissur is the **Round**, a road (subdivided into North, South, East and West) which circles the Vaddukanatha Temple complex and *maidan* in the town centre. On the mainline to Chennai and other points in neighbouring Tamil Nadu, and with good connections to Kochi and Thiruvananthapuram, the **railway station** is 1km southwest, opposite the **KSRTC long-distance bus stand. Priya Darshini bus stand** (also known as "North", "Shoranur" and "Wadakkancheri" stand), close to Round North, serves Shoranur (for the Kalamanadalam academy). The **Shakthan Thampuran bus stand**, on TB Road, just over 1km from Round South, serves local destinations south such as Irinjalakuda, Kodungallur and Guruvayur.

The DTPC **tourist office** (Mon–Sat 10am–5pm; ☎0487/232 0800) is on Palace Road, opposite the Town Hall (five minutes' walk off Round East). Run by volunteers, its primary purpose is to promote the Puram elephant festival, but staff also give out maps of Thrissur. The best place to **change money** and travellers' cheques is the UTI Bank in the City Centre Shopping building (Mon–Fri 9.30am–3.30pm, Sat 9.30am–1.30pm) on Round West. The UAE

Exchange & Financial Services (Mon–Sat 9.30am–6pm, Sun 9.30am–1.30pm) in the basement of the *Casino Hotel* building also changes currency and travellers' cheques. Both of the above, and a dozen or so other banks around the centre, have ATMs. The **main post office** is on the southern edge of town, near the *Casino Hotel*, off TB Road. **Internet** facilities are available at Hugues Net on the top floor of the City Centre Shopping building and SS Consultants next to the *Luciya Palace* hotel; rates are around Rs20 per hour.

Accommodation

Thrissur has a fair number of mid-price **hotels**, but only a couple of decent budget places – the best of them the splendid *Ramanilayam Government Guesthouse*. Almost everywhere follows a 24hr checkout policy. If you're planning to be here during **Puram**, book well in advance and bear in mind that room rates soar – some of the more upmarket hotels charge up to ten times their normal prices.

Casino TB Rd, near the railway station ☏0487/242 4699, ⊛www.casinotels.com. Formerly the town's poshest hotel, now in decline; the rooms (non-a/c and a/c) are all en suite and presentable enough, if a little rough around the edges. There's a multi-cuisine restaurant, cocktail bar, lawn and kiddies park, and foreign exchange (residents only). ④–⑤

Elite International Chembottil Lane, off Round South ☏0487/242 1033, ©mail @hoteleliteinternational.com. Pronounced "Ee-light", this mid-range place in the centre of town has rooms opening onto corridors, some with balconies overlooking the green. The staff are very friendly and helpful, and there's a good restaurant and relaxing garden. Rates include breakfast. ④–⑥

Grand Park Regency Mullassery Tower, Kuruppam Road ☏0487/242 8247, ⊛www .grandparkregency.com. Gleaming, efficient business hotel in a pink-coloured multi-storey block bang in the town centre, close to the bus stand, railway station and temple green. Its rooms are modern and centrally a/c. Facilities include a fitness centre and roof garden. ⑤–⑥

Gurukripa Lodge Chembottil Lane ☏0487/242 1895. Run with great efficiency by the venerable Mr Venugopal, the *Gurukripa*, just off Round South, offers a variety of simple en-suite rooms, (including several great-value singles) ranged around a long, pleasant inner courtyard. Some a/c. ②–③

🏃 **Kadappuram Beach Resort** Nattika Beach, 30km southwest ☏0487/239 7588, ⊛www.kadappurambeachresorts.com. Exclusive, eco-friendly wellness resort located on a tranquil stretch of Nattika Beach. Scattered under a shady palm grove criss-crossed by narrow tidal canals, its ten bamboo and coconut-leaf cottages are panelled with aromatic herbs; each has two double rooms and attached bathrooms, and there's a top-notch

Green Leaf ayurveda centre, *Chikilsalayam*. The whole 4-acre site is blissfully quiet (no TVs or telephones in the huts) and the beach is only 200m away. From $130 for a double room (including obligatory full board). ⑨

Luciya Palace Marar Rd ☏0487/242 4731, ©luciyapalace@hotmail.com. Slightly overpriced mid-range option, with uninspiring doubles and suites, whose redeeming feature is a secluded rear garden. ④–⑥

Pathans Round South ☏0487/242 5620. Its basement entrance is none too promising, but the good-sized rooms in this conveniently central hotel, with its lavishly carved teak and rosewood furniture, have an appealing colonial feel and are good value. ③–④

🏃 **Ramanilayam Government Guesthouse** Palace Rd ☏0471/233 2016. Star-hotel comfort at economy lodge rates, in palatial suites with balconies, or smaller doubles (some a/c), set in manicured gardens on the northeast side of town near the zoo and museum. As with all Government Guesthouses, officials get priority (even at the last minute), which can make a mockery of advance bookings. ②–③

Sidhartha Regency Veliyannur Rd, Kokkalai ☏0487/242 4773, ⊛www.hotelsidhartharegency .com. In the southwestern corner of town near the railway station, this good-value, modern three-star ranks among the most welcoming and comfortable options within walking distance of the centre. The seven-storey block holds a swimming pool (set in lawns to the rear), multi-gym, health club, multi-cuisine restaurant, bar and gardens. ⑤–⑥

YWCA Museum Rd, Chembakabu ☏0487/232 2528. Women-only hostel opposite the town zoo and museum, popular mainly with long-staying students (both young and not so young). Its clean en-suite doubles (non-a/c) are a bargain. ②

The Town

At the centre of the Round, the **Vaddukanatha Temple** (closed to non-Hindus) is a walled complex of fifteen shrines, dating from the twelfth century or earlier, the principal of which is dedicated to Shiva. Inside, the grassy compound is surprisingly quiet and spacious, with a striking apsidal shrine dedicated to Ayappan (see box, p.167). Once an essential ingredient of the temple's cultural life, but now under-used and neglected, the long, sloping-roofed **kuttambalam theatre** (closed to non-Hindus), with carved panels and lathe-turned wooden pillars, serves as a venue for the ancient Sanskrit performance forms of *chakyar kuttu* and *kudiyattam*.

The **State Art Museum** (Tues–Sun 9am–6.30pm; Rs8) stands on Museum Road, ten minutes' walk from the Round in the northeast of town. Collections of faded local bronzes, jewellery, fine woodcarvings of fanged temple guardians and a profusion of bell-metal oil lamps make up the bulk of its collection. Next door, the **zoo** (same hours as museum; free) is a predictably sad, run-down affair. In the same compound, the **Multi-Purpose Museum** (same hours; free) is home to an odd hoard of skeletons, stuffed animals, minerals, weapons and costumes.

A five-minute rickshaw ride away, opposite the Priya Darshini bus stand, the **Archeological Museum** (Tues–Sun 9.30am–1pm & 2–4.30pm; Rs10) occupies the 200-year-old Shaktan Thampuran Palace, the former residence of the Kochi royal family. Beautifully decorated throughout with intricate wood- and tile-work, the building is centred on a colonnaded patio. Exhibits include fifteenth- and eighteenth-century hero stones, a fearsome selection of beheading axes, and a massive iron-studded treasury box still in its original place (presumably because no one has ever managed to shifts its 1500kg dead weight). The real highlight, however, is the royal *palliyara*, or bedchamber, boasting a traditional carved wood four-poster and vibrant ceramic tiles. Visits wind up at the **Heritage Garden**, where you can cool off in the shade next to a delightful lily pond, with exotic birds and butterflies flitting through the greenery.

Also on the northern side of the centre, on Stadium Road, the **Sangeet Natak Akademi** (℡0487/233 2134, ⓦwww.sangeetnatak.org) features a large auditorium that hosts occasional music and dance concerts as well as contemporary Keralan theatre, which has an enthusiastic following and tends to be heavily political. Around the corner stands the **Lalit Kala Akademi** (Mon–Fri 11am–7pm; ℡0487/233 3773, ⓦwww.lalitkala.gov.in), where you can see exhibitions of international artists as well as contemporary Indian art.

One of the most important churches for Thrissur's large Christian population is the Syrian-Catholic **Lourdes Cathedral**, along St Thomas College Road, 1km east of the Round, where daily masses serve a regular congregation of nine hundred. Like many of Kerala's Indo-Gothic churches, the exterior of dome and spires is more impressive than the interior, with its unadorned metal rafters and corrugated iron ceiling. Steps lead down from the altar to the crypt, a rather dilapidated copy of the grotto in Lourdes. The 80-metre **Bell Tower** is also open to visitors (Tues–Fri 10am–1pm & 2–6pm; Sat & Sun 10am–1pm & 2–7.30pm; Rs15); you can climb the 350 steps or take the lift to the top, from where views extend across the palms to the foothills of the distant Ghats. Those who walk can pause for breath at the permanent exhibition of artwork depicting the life of Jesus which lines the tower staircase, ranging from beautifully detailed stained-glass windows to garish frescoes and woodcarvings.

Our Lady of Dolores, just south of the Round, is another important Catholic shrine, boasting neo-Gothic spires and the largest interior of any

Puram

Thrissur is best known to outsiders as the venue for Kerala's biggest annual festival, **Puram**, which takes place on one day in May (ask at a tourist office for the exact date). Inaugurated by Shaktan Tampuran, the Raja of Cochin between 1789 and 1803, Puram is the most extreme example of the kind of *utsavam* celebration seen on a smaller scale at temples all over Kerala, whose main ingredients invariably include **caparisoned elephants**, **drum music** and **fireworks**.

On this day, at the hottest time of year, the centre of Thrissur fills to capacity, and a sea of people gravitate towards Round South, where a long wide path leads to the southern entrance of the **Vaddukanatha Temple** complex. Two majestic processions, representing the Tiruvambadi and Paramekkavu temples in Thrissur, compete to create the more impressive sights and sounds. They eventually meet, like armies on a battlefield, facing each other at either end of the path. Both sides present fifteen tuskers sumptuously decorated with gold ornaments, each ridden by three Brahmins clutching objects symbolizing royalty: silver-handled whisks of yak hair, circular peacock-feather fans and colourful silk umbrellas fringed with silver pendants. At the centre of each group, the principal elephant carries an image of the temple's deity. Swaying gently, the elephants stand still much of the time, ears flapping, seemingly oblivious to the crowds, the bomb-like firework explosions and the huge orchestra that plays in front of them.

Known as **chenda melam**, this quintessentially Keralan music, featuring as many as a hundred loud, hard-skinned, cylindrical *chenda* drums, crashing cymbals and wind instruments, marks the progress of the procession. Each kind of *chenda melam* is named after the rhythmic cycle (*tala* or, in Malayalam, *talam*) in which it is set. Drummers stand in ranks, the most numerous at the back often playing single beats. At the front, a line of master drummers, the stars of Keralan music, try to outdo each other with their speed, stamina, improvisational skills and showmanship. Facing the drummers, musicians play long double-reed, oboe-like *kuzhals* (similar to the North Indian *shehnai*) and C-shaped *kompu* bell-metal trumpets. The fundamental structure is provided by the *elatalam* – medium-sized, heavy, brass hand-cymbals that resolutely and precisely keep the tempo, essential to the cumulative

church in South India. Slightly further south, the **Chaldean Church** (services Mon–Sat 7–9am & Sun 7.30–9.30am), dedicated to Mary, is the most ancient of all Keralan Christian centres and the focal point of the **Nestorian Syrian** community, which also runs a school here. Not much of the original structure remains, as the church was extensively renovated in the nineteenth century. Owing to this renovation, the gabled facade is the most remarkable part of what remains of the original structure.

Shopping

Thrissur is a good place to pick up Keralan **crafts**, and its main shopping area is on the Round. On Round West, the **Kerala State Handicraft Emporium** specializes in wood; a one-minute walk from Round East at the top of Palace Road, **Co-optex** sells a good range of hand-loom cloth. At **Chemmanur's** on Round South, near the *Elite Hotel*, you'll find the usual carved wooden-elephant-type souvenirs, and, on the ground floor, a high-kitsch Aladdin's Cave of nodding dogs, Jesus clocks, Mecca table ornaments and parabolic nail-and-string art. **Alter Media** at Utility Building, Nehru Bazaar, Nayarangadi is a small but interesting bookshop devoted to women's studies, while **Cosmos**, on Round West, is a treasure trove of novels, academic tomes and books on art, drama and culture.

effect of the music. Over an extended period, the *melam* passes through four phases, each twice as fast as the last, from a grand and graceful dead slow through to a frenetic pace.

At the arrival of the fastest tempo, those astride the elephants stand, manipulating their feather fans and hair whisks in coordinated sequence, while behind, unfurled umbrellas are twirled in flashes of dazzling colour, their pendants glinting silver in the sun. The cymbals crash furiously, often raised above the head, requiring extraordinary stamina (and causing nasty weals on the hands). The master drummers play at their loudest and fastest, frequently intensified by surges of energy emanating from single players, one after another; a chorus of trumpets, in ragged unison, accompanies the cacophony, creating a sound that has altered little since the festival's origins.

All this is greeted by tremendous firework explosions and roars from the crowd; many people punch the air, while others are clearly *talam branthans*, rhythm "madmen", who follow every nuance of the structure. When the fastest speed is played out, the slowest tempo returns and the procession edges forward, the *mahouts* leading the elephants by the tusk. Stopping again, the whole cycle is repeated. At night, the Vaddukanatha Temple entrances are a blaze of coloured lights and a spectacular firework display takes place in the early hours of the morning.

If you venture to Thrissur for Puram, be prepared for packed buses and trains. Needless to say, accommodation should be booked well in advance. An umbrella or hat is recommended for protection from the sun. Unfortunately, Puram has become an excuse for groups of Indian men to get very drunk; women are advised to dress conservatively and only to go in the morning, or to watch with a group of Indian women.

Similar but much smaller events take place in town, generally from September onwards, with most during the summer (April and May). Enquire at a tourist office or your hotel, or ask someone to check a local edition of the newspaper, *Mathrabhumi*, for local performances of *chenda melam*, and other drum orchestras such as *panchavadyam* and *tyambaka*.

For an eclectic selection of Indian music, try **Melody Corner**, at the junction of Round South and Kuruppam Road. Its shelves are stacked with classical Hindustani and Carnatic albums, devotional and *panchavadyam* (Keralan temple festival music) compilations and Hindi and Malayalam film songs.

Kuruppam Road, which leads south towards the railway station from the western end of Round South, is one of the best spots in Kerala to buy **bell-metal** products, particularly oil lamps made in the village of Nadavaramba, near Irinjalakuda (see p.206). The friendly **Nadavaramba Krishna & Sons** is a good place to start browsing. Continuing south on Kuruppam Road to the next junction with Station Road, cheap Christian, Muslim and Hindu devotional pictures etched on metal are the main stock in trade, along with festival accessories such as medallion-fringed umbrellas similar to those used for Puram (see box, p.202).

Eating and drinking

With so many hotels and busy "meals" joints lining the Round, there's no shortage of dependable places to eat in Thrissur. From 8.30pm onwards, you can also join the auto-rickshaw-wallahs, hospital visitors, itinerant mendicants, Ayappa devotees and student revellers who congregate at the popular **thattu-kada** hot food market on the corner of Round South and Round East,

Chembuthra Puram

If you're in the area in late January or early February, it's well worth checking the precise dates of the spectacular **Chembuthra Puram** temple festival, held in the nearby village of **CHEMBUTHRA**, 13km north of Thrissur. Second only in its scale and extravagance to Thrissur's own annual Puram, the event features no less than **46 elephants**, flaming firebrands attached to their trunks, and accompanied in their slow marches by the usual cacophony of drum orchestras and fireworks. Processions reach their climax as they converge on the village *maidan*, watched by ecstatic and noisy crowds.

Buses to Chembuthra leave from Thrissur's Priya Darshini stand, dropping passengers at the junction on the NH-17 highway, a kilometre's pleasant walk from the temple.

opposite the Medical College Hospital. The rustic Keralan cooking – omelettes, *dosas*, *parottas*, *iddiappam*, bean curries and egg masala – is always freshly prepared, delicious and unbelievably cheap.

Ambady Restaurant Round West. Down a lane and away from the Round traffic noise. Good selection of Keralan staples as well as lunchtime thalis and dozens of milkshakes and ice creams.
Bharath Lodge Chembottil Lane, 50m down the road from the *Elite Hotel*. Piping hot South Indian *vada-sambar* and *iddli* breakfasts, as well as "all you can eat" Keralan meals (Rs24–35) at lunchtime.
Indian Coffee House Round South. The usual cheap and popular *ICH* range of South Indian snacks, as well as strong chai and weak coffee, served by waiters whose serious demeanour is undermined by their old-school ice-cream fan turbans and curry-stained tunics.
Luciya Palace Marar Rd, just off the southwest corner of the Round. Hotel restaurant serving Indian and Chinese dishes in a pleasant garden illuminated by fairy lights.

Ming Palace Pathan Building, Round South. Inexpensive "Chindian" with dim lighting, cheesy muzak and a menu of chop suey, noodles and lots of chicken and veg dishes.
Navaratna North Indian Restaurant Round West. Inexpensive Keralan and North Indian veg and non-veg menus as well as Chinese noodles and fish soup. With a hefty air-con system, it's a great spot to cool down, and the compartment-style layout allows for greater privacy than most places.
Pathans Round South. Deservedly popular veg restaurant, with a cosy a/c family annexe and a large canteen-like dining hall. Generous portions and plenty of choice, including *koftas*, kormas and lots of tandoori options, as well as Keralan thalis and wonderful Kashmiri naan.

Around Thrissur

The chief attraction of the area **around Thrissur** is the opportunity to get to grips with Kerala's cultural heritage. Countless festivals, at their peak before the monsoon hits in May, enable visitors to catch some of the best drummers in the world, **kathakali** dance-drama and **kudiyattam**, the world's oldest surviving theatre form.

Irinjalakuda

The village of **IRINJALAKUDA**, 20km south of Thrissur, is the site of the unique **Koodal Manikiyam Temple**, dedicated to **Bharata**, the brother of Rama. It boasts a superbly elegant tiled *kuttambalam* **theatre** within its outer courtyard, built to afford an unimpeded view for the maximum number of spectators (drawn from the highest castes), and known for its excellent acoustics. A profusion of painted woodcarvings of mythological animals and stories from the epics decorate the interior. On the low stage, enclosed by painted wooden columns and friezes of female dancers, stand two large copper *mizhavu* drums for use in the Sanskrit drama **kudiyattam** (see p.296), permanently installed in wooden frames into which a drummer climbs to play. Traditionally, *mizhavus* were considered sacred objects; Nandikeshvara, Shiva's rhythm-man, was said to reside in them. The drama for which they provided music was a holy ritual, and traditionally the instrument was never allowed to leave the temple and was only played by members of a special caste, the Nambyars. Since then, outsiders have learned the art of *mizhavu* playing, although the orthodox authorities do not allow them to play inside.

Around 500m from the Bharata temple (turn left as you leave), **Natana Kairali** (Mon–Sat 11am–1pm & 3–7pm) is an important cultural centre dedicated to the documentation and performance of Kerala's lesser-known theatre arts, including *kudiyattam*, *nangiarkoothu* (female mono-acting), shadow and puppet theatres. The centre is based in the home of one of Kerala's most illustrious acting families, Ammanur Chakyar Madhom (say this name when you ask for directions). Natana Kairali's director, Shri G. Venu (☏0488/282 5559, ✉venuji@satyam.net.in), is a mine of information about Keralan arts, and can advise on forthcoming performances. In addition, his wife Nirmala Paniker, also an acclaimed scholar, founded **Natana Kaisiki,** a research centre on the same site dedicated to the preservation of traditional dance and theatre traditions of Keralan women: *mohiniyattam*, *nangiarkoothu* and *thiruvathirakali*. A selection of books on the region's performing arts, by Dr Venu, Nirmala Paniker and other academics, is sold inside.

Irinjalakuda is best reached by **bus** from the Shakthan Thampuran stand in Thrissur rather than by train, as the railway station is an inconvenient 8km east of town. If you need to stay, the *Udupi Woodlands Hotel* (☏0488/282 0149; ❸–❹), near the bus stand on the Bharata temple road, has clean, spacious double rooms – most of them with marble floors and powerful fans.

Kodungallur

Virtually an island surrounded by backwaters and the sea, **KODUNGALLUR** (Cranganore), 35km south of Thrissur, is rich in Keralan history. The relative obscurity of the unexceptional modern town contrasts with tales of its illustrious past. Kodungallur has been identified as the site of the ancient cities of **Vanji** (one-time capital of the Chera kingdom), and **Muziris**, described in the first century AD by the Roman traveller Pliny as "*primum emporium Indiae*", the most important trading post in India. Other accounts describe the harbour as crowded with great ships, warehouses, palaces, temples and *yavanas* (a generic term for foreigners) who brought gold and left with spices, sandalwood, teak, gems and silks. The Romans are said to have built a temple in Kodungallur, and while nothing remains, their presence has been shown through finds of coins, the majority of which date between the reigns of Augustus to Nero (27 BC–68 AD). Its life as a great port was curtailed in 1341 by floods that silted up the harbour, leading to the development of Kochi (Cochin). Today, travellers will find that most of Kodungallur's sights require some imagination to appreciate. The town is best visited in a day-trip by **bus** from Thrissur's Shakthan Thampuran stand (1hr 30min), or on a combined visit to Irinjalakuda, only 7km away.

Standing on a large piece of open ground at the centre of Kodungallur, the ancient and typically Keralan **Kurumba Bhagavati Temple** is the site of an extraordinary annual event that some residents would prefer didn't happen at all. The **Bharani festival**, held during the Malayalam month of Meenom

(March/April), attracts droves of devotees, both male and female, mainly from low-caste communities previously excluded from the temple. Their devotions consist in part of drinking copious amounts of alcohol and taking to the streets to sing Bharani *pattu*, sexually explicit songs about, and addressed to, the goddess Bhagavati, which are considered obscene and highly offensive by many other Keralans. On Kavuthindal, the first day, the pilgrims run en masse around the perimeters of the temple three times at breakneck speed, beating its walls with sticks. Until the mid-1950s, chickens were sacrificed in front of the temple; today, a simple red cloth symbolizes the bloody ritual. An important section of the devotees are the crimson-clad village oracles, wielding scythe-like swords with which they sometimes beat themselves on the head in ecstatic fervour, often drawing blood. Despite widespread disapproval, the festival draws plenty of spectators.

Cheraman Juma Masjid, 1.5km south of Kodungallur centre on NH-17, is thought to be the oldest mosque in India, founded in the seventh century by **Cheraman Perumal**, the legendary Keralan king who converted to Islam, abdicated and emigrated to Mecca. The supposed site of his palace, Cheraman Parambu, is today nothing more than a few broken columns on open ground. The present building, which dates from the sixteenth century, was predominantly made of wood, in a style usually associated with Keralan Hindu temples. Unfortunately, due to weather damage, it has been partly rebuilt, and the facade, at least, is now rather mundane, with concrete minarets. The wooden interior remains intact, however, with a large Keralan oil lamp in the centre. Introduced five centuries ago for group study of the Koran, the lamp has taken on great significance to other communities, and Muslims, Christians and Hindus alike bring oil on the auspicious occasion of major family events. In an anteroom, a small mausoleum is said to be the burial place of Habib Bin Malik, an envoy sent from Mecca by Cheraman Perumal. Women are not allowed into the mosque at any time, but interested male visitors should contact the assistant *mukhari* (*imam*, or priest), K.M. Saidumohamed, who lives directly opposite and will show you around.

Nadavaramba bell-metal oil lamps

Keralan nights are made more enchanting by the use of **oil lamps**. The most common type, seen everywhere, is a slim, free-standing metal column topped by a spike that rises from a circular receptacle for coconut oil, with cloth or banana-plant fibre wicks. Every classical theatre performance keeps a large lamp burning centre-stage all night. The special atmosphere of temples is also enhanced by innumerable lamps, some hanging from chains; others, *deepa stambham*, are multi-tiered and stand metres high.

The village of **Nadavaramba**, 5km from Irinjalakuda on the Kodungallur road, is an important centre for the manufacture of oil lamps and large cooking vessels, known as *uruli* and *varppu*. **Bell-metal** alloys are made from copper and tin – unlike brass which is a blend of copper and zinc – and give a sonorous chime when struck. One of the best places to buy is the *Bellwics Handicrafts Cooperative*, just north of Nadavaramba Church, where you can watch the various stages of the casting process, from the making of sand and wax moulds to the pouring of molten metal, labour-intensive filing and polishing. The largest independent manufacturer in Kerala, *Bellwics* produce an array of bell-metal utensils: fourteen different kinds of lamp, ayurvedic treatment utensils, cooking vessels of every conceivable size and temple decorations. Prices depend on the weight of the object, starting at Rs600 per kilogram.

Less than 500m south from the Cheraman Juma Masjid, past a bend in the main highway (NH-17), a wide avenue leads past tall lamps to the **Thiruvanchikkulam Mahadeva Temple**, dedicated to Shiva. Located in a peaceful setting with a backdrop of tall coconut trees, it's a fine example of traditional Keralan temple architecture. Access to the outer courtyard is via a majestic gateway with a sloping roof and carvings of elephants, gods and goddesses. Inside the enclosure, past a large multi-tiered metal lamp, a porch with carvings dedicated to the heroes of the great Hindu epic, the *Ramayana*, marks the furthest point non-Hindus are allowed. Within the restricted enclosure, an impressive columned hall shelters Shiva's ever-faithful bull Nandi, while the inner sanctum houses a plain stone *lingam*. Despite the restriction, low retaining walls allow a good view of the extensive complex, which is well worth the short detour.

The **Mar Thoma Pontifical Shrine**, fronted by a crescent of Neoclassical colonnades at Azhikode (pronounced "Arikode") Jetty (6km), marks the place where the Apostle Thomas is said to have arrived in India in 52 AD. Situated on the backwaters, it's a tranquil spot with a promenade and stalls selling religious paraphernalia, but hardly warrants a detour unless you're desperate to see the shard of the saint's wrist-bone enshrined within the church (daily 9am-6pm). Frequent buses from Kodungallur stop at Azhikode Jetty, at the end of the promenade past the fishing boats.

The *Hotel Indraprestham* (☎0480/280 2678; ❸–❹), close to the town centre, has standard non-a/c and a/c **rooms** as well as a cheap "meals" restaurant, an a/c "family" restaurant and bar.

Guruvayur

Kerala's most important Krishna shrine, the high-walled temple of **GURUVAYUR** (3am–1pm & 4.30–10pm; closed to non-Hindus), 29km northwest of Thrissur, attracts a constant flow of devotees, second only in volume to Ayappa's pilgrimage at Sabarimala (see box, pp.167–168). Its deity, **Guruvayurappan**, has inspired numerous paeans from Keralan poets, most notably Narayana Bhattatiri, who wrote the *Narayaniyam* in the sixteenth century, when the temple, whose origins are legendary, seems to have first risen to prominence.

Guruvayur is one of the richest temples in Kerala and is constantly awash with **pilgrims**, dressed in their best white and gold-trim clothes. The market outside is noisy and intense, with stalls full of glitter and trinkets and a palpable air of excitement, particularly when events inside spill out into the streets. A temple committee stall outside the main gates auctions off the donations, including bell-metal lamps, received at the shrine – according to superstition, if you buy any of these items they must be returned to the temple as gifts.

Of the temple's 24 annual **festivals**, the most important are Ekadashi and Ulsavam. The eighteen days of Ekadashi, in the month of Vrischikam (Nov/Dec), are marked by processions of caparisoned elephants outside the temple, while the exterior of the building is decorated with the tiny flames of innumerable oil lamps from sunset onwards. Performances staged in front of the temple (check dates with a KTDC office) attract the cream of South Indian classical music artists.

During Ulsavam, in the month of Kumbham (Feb/March), Tantric rituals are conducted inside, an **elephant race** is run outside on the first day, and elephant processions take place during the ensuing six days. On the ninth day, the Palivetta, or "hunt" occurs; the deity, mounted on an elephant, circumnavigates the temple accompanied by men dressed as animals, representing human

△ Punnathur Kotta Elephant Sanctuary, Guruvayur

weaknesses such as greed and anger, and are vanquished by the god. The next night sees the image of the god taken out for ritual immersion in the temple tank; devotees greet the procession with oil lamps and throw rice. It is considered highly auspicious to bathe in the tank at the same time as the god.

When not involved in races and arcane temple rituals, Guruvayur's tuskers are chained at the **Punnathur Kotta Elephant Sanctuary** (daily 8am–6pm; Rs5, cameras Rs25), 4km north of town. Around fifty elephants, aged from 8 to 95, live here, munching for most of the day on specially imported piles of fodder and cared for by their three personal *mahouts*, who wash and scrub them several times a week in the sanctuary pond. Only approach an elephant if a *mahout* allows you, as they can be unpredictable and dangerous.

The animals are considered the personal possessions of Lord Guruvayur, given to the temple by wealthy donors from as far afield as Bihar and Assam. All of them – apart from the most elderly, who are allowed an honourable retirement – are gainfully employed appearing at temple festivals. The standard daily charge is Rs3500 per elephant, but the prettiest pachyderms are often the subject of heated auctions, with rival villages bidding up to Rs75,000 for a single animal.

Practicalities

Buses from Thrissur (40min) arrive at the main **bus stand** at the end of East Nada Street, five minutes' walk from the temple, and the home of most of the **accommodation**. The town is crammed with strictly vegetarian **restaurants**, and there's an *Indian Coffee House* on the southern side of East Nada Street.

KTDC Mangalya near the entrance of the Krishna temple, by Devaswom Book Stall, ☎ 0487/255 4061. Large, acceptably clean en-suite rooms for up to six people, plus a rock-bottom six-bed dorm. There's also a popular vegetarian restaurant on the ground floor. ❶

KTDC Nandanam near the railway station, ☎ 0487/255 6266. Massive terracotta-coloured block surrounded by tall palm trees. It's been recently refurbished but retains a pleasantly old-fashioned look. The bright and airy rooms are terrific value and the staff helpful. ❸–❹

Sopanam Heritage 500m west of railway station on East Nada, ℡0487/255 5244, ⓦwww .sopanamguruvayoor.com. Business hotel made of shining tinted glass and concrete, holding 72 smart, centrally a/c rooms on five storeys. A bit bland, but secure, efficient and good value for the level of comfort. Their a/c multi-cuisine restaurants – *Agarsala* (veg) and *Rasoi* (non-veg) – are the swankiest in town, and there's a bar serving Indian liqueurs and cocktails. ❹–❻

Cheruthuruthy

The village of **CHERUTHURUTHY** is internationally famous as the home of **Kerala Kalamandalam**, the state's flagship training school for *kathakali* and other indigenous Keralan performing arts. Some 32km north of Thrissur, and within range of an easy day-trip, it stands close to the banks of Kerala's longest river, the **Bharatapuzha** (pronounced "bharatapura"), considered holy by Hindus, but sadly depleted by dams recently built around its headwaters in the Ghats. Although of little consolation to locals, the demise of the once mighty river, now a shimmering expanse of pale yellow-brown sand, has produced a landscape of incomparable beauty.

The academy was founded in 1927 by the revered Keralan poet Vallathol (1878–1957). At first patronized by the raja of Cochin, the school has benefited from funding by both state and national governments and has been instrumental in the large-scale revival of interest in *kathakali* and other unique Keralan art forms. Despite conservative opposition, it followed an open-door recruitment policy, based on artistic merit, which produced "scheduled caste" Muslim and Christian graduates along with the usual Hindu castes, something that was previously unimaginable. Kalamandalam artists perform in the great theatres of the world, many sharing their extraordinary skills with outsiders, including luminaries of modern theatre such as Jerzy Grotowski and Peter Brook. Nonetheless, many of these trained artists are still excluded from entering – let alone performing in – temples, a popular venue for Hindu art forms, especially music.

Non-Hindus are welcome to attend performances of *kathakali*, *kudiyattam* and *mohiniyattam* performed in the school's wonderful **theatre**, which replicates the style of the wooden, sloping-roofed traditional *kuttambalam* auditoria found in Keralan temples. You can also sit in on classes, watch demonstrations of mural painting, and visit exhibitions of costumes by signing up for the fascinating **"a day with the masters"** cultural programme (Mon–Sat, starts 9.30am, ends 1.30pm, $20 per person, including lunch). Try to coincide your visit with the annual, week-long **Thauryathrikam festival** in January. Held at the *kuttambalam* auditorium and at Kalamandalam's original riverside campus amongst the trees, the event presents all the art forms taught at the academy and is free. A short walk past the old school building leads to a small but exquisite **Shiva temple** in classic Keralan style. The exterior is lit by candles during the early evening puja, a particularly rewarding time to visit.

A handful of foreigners also come to the Kalamandalam academy each year to study full-time **courses**: one-month introductions, three-to-six month intensives, and full vocational training from four to six years. Applications may be made from abroad (full details on the website), but it's a good idea to visit before committing yourself, as the training is rigorous. For information contact the school office (℡04884/262418) or check out the Kalamandalam website, ⓦwww.kalamandalam.com.

Note that photography is not allowed anywhere in the Kalamandalam site without prior purchase of a **photography permit**, which will set you back Rs500 (for ten images only). This does not affect participants of the "a day with the masters" tour, whose cost includes the photo fee.

Practicalities

Cheruthuruthy's **accommodation** is limited, with some students staying as guests in private accommodation or in the school hostel near the main campus at Vallathol Nagar (☎04884/262418 for details). For a touch of a/c luxury, head for the *River Retreat Heritage Ayurvedic Resort* (☎04884/262244; Ⓦwww .riverretreat.in; ❼–❽), 2km from Kalamandalan. The former palace of the raja of Cochin, the three-star heritage hotel and ayurvedic spa occupies an idyllic position on the banks of the Bharatapuzha River on Palace Road. Despite some heavy-handed renovation work, its rooms are elegantly furnished with fine teak furniture; some have private terraces facing the river. In the lawned garden, a crystalline pool, partly shaded by coconut palms, also looks across to the Bhara-tapuzha. Other than the *River Retreat*, the only places to **eat** here are the simple *dhabas* in the centre of the village, such as the vegetarian *Mahatma*.

Buses heading to Shoranur from Thrissur's Priya Darshini (aka "Wadakkancheri") stand pass through Cheruthuruthy; the nearest mainline **railway station** is Shoranur Junction, 3km south, served by express trains to and from Mangalore, Chennai and Kochi.

The hills

The hill tract of central Kerala starts roughly 50km inland, where the paddy fields, lakes and backwaters of the coastal strip blister up into low, rolling ridges carpeted in rubber plantations, and thick forests of huge buttressed-root trees and liander creepers line the river valleys. From there, the profile of the Western Ghat range surges steeply to the horizon. Peaking between 80km and 100km from the coast, the Ghats are the southernmost extension of a vast range stretching 1200km down the southwest seaboard of India. In Kerala, they reach their dramatic climax at Ana Mudi (2695m), the peninsula's highest mountain, before rippling into the sea just short of Kanyakumari.

Dividing the humid, tropical climes of the Keralan coast from the drier, boulder-studded Tamil plains, the interior mountains form a wall that breaks up the rain-laden monsoon clouds as they blow eastwards off the Arabian Sea in early June, forcing them to deposit three to four metres of moisture in less than six months (in some areas, the figure can rise to nearly nine metres). This vast rainfall then drains back through the forests cloaking the range's western flank, and on to the densely populated backwaters. Around sea level, the woodlands, dominated by 30-metre-tall teak trees, are perennially moist, sticky, hot and green. Higher up, cooler and wetter montane rainforest takes over, ceding eventually to stunted deciduous trees and open expanses of savannah grassland.

Kerala's sweltering tropical latitudes and plentiful supply of rain have combined to create some of the planet's richest eco-systems: 4000 of the 15,000 or so plant species present in India grow in the southern portion of the Ghats – 1800 of them are endemic, and 1600 can't be seen anywhere else. Seven large mammals, including elephant, tiger, leopard, and bison, also survive here, along with around 300 types of bird.

Threats to this extraordinary biodiversity have come in recent decades in the form of giant dam projects: the one blocking the Parambikulam River in Palakkad district is the largest in India, and one of the ten biggest dams in the world (it's also a source of ongoing controversy between Kerala and its neighbour, Tamil Nadu, which reaps an unfair proportion of the water, resulting in the destruction of paddy fields lower down). But a much more devastating blow to the forest came towards the end of the nineteenth century, when the British clear-felled millions of acres for **tea plantations**. Despite the downturn in world consumption, Kerala's estates, the majority of them owned by the Indian multinational Tata, continue to churn out quantities of "CTC" ("cut, curl and trimmed") tea powder for the voracious domestic market, and the central portion of the mountains – known as the **High Range** region – is still dominated by neatly cropped tea gardens. The centre of the industry in the state is the hill station of **Munnar**, from whose riverside bazaar you can walk through vast hillsides wrapped in tea bushes and dotted with cosy British-era bungalows to reach the grasslands cloaking some of the Ghats' highest peaks. A couple of wildlife sanctuaries around the town protect some of the area's rarest flora and fauna, most notably the **Niligir tahr**, an unusually placid kind of mountain goat, as well as wild elephants that trudge with characteristic insouciance through the forests lining the state border.

Munnar is most easily accessed from the south via Periyar or the west along the main highway from Kochi. To reach the other wild parts of central Kerala's hill country, however, you'll probably have to pass through **Palakkad**, a busy market town presiding over the lowest gap through the range – a point of strategic military importance for many centuries. Apart from its sprawling fort, the main incentives to stop here are some outstanding ayurvedic resorts and homestays occupying former aristocratic seats – bastions of traditional Keralan architecture, healing sciences and performing arts.

From Palakkad, a further day's journey into the mountains brings you to the beautiful **Silent Valley National Park**, an area of exceptionally pristine forest recently saved from the dam-builders bulldozers, although still not, as yet, well set up for visitors. The same can't be said of **Nelliampathy**, a bijou tea station high in the hills where you can stay in high style amid the greenery of tea and coffee estates, with sweeping views down to the plains – at a fraction of the cost of similar places elsewhere in the state.

Munnar

MUNNAR, 130km east of Kochi and 110km north (4hr 30mins by bus) of the Periyar Wildlife Sanctuary, is the centre of Kerala's principal tea-growing region. A scruffy agglomeration of corrugated-iron-roofed cottages and tea factories, its centre on the valley floor fails to live up to its tourist office billing as a "hill station", but there's plenty to enthuse about in the surrounding mountains, whose lower slopes are carpeted with lush tea gardens and dotted with quaint old colonial bungalows. Above them, the grassy ridges and crags of the High Range offer superlative trekking routes, many of which can be tackled in day-trips from the town.

It's easy to see why the pioneering Scottish planters who developed this hidden valley in the 1870s and 1880s felt so at home here. At an altitude of around 1600m, Munnar enjoys a refreshing climate, with crisp mornings and sunny blue skies in the winter – though as with all of Kerala, torrential rains

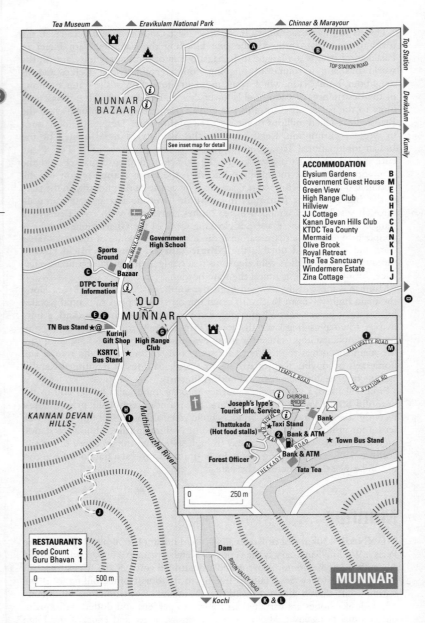

ACCOMMODATION
Elysium Gardens	B
Government Guest House	M
Green View	E
High Range Club	G
Hillview	H
JJ Cottage	F
Kanan Devan Hills Club	C
KTDC Tea County	A
Mermaid	N
Olive Brook	K
Royal Retreat	I
The Tea Sanctuary	D
Windermere Estate	L
Zina Cottage	J

RESTAURANTS
Food Count	2
Guru Bhavan	1

MUNNAR

descend during the monsoons. When the mists clear, the mountain summits form a wild backdrop to the carefully manicured tea plantations below.

Munnar's greenery and cool air draw streams of well-heeled honeymooners and weekenders from the metropolitan cities of South India. However, increasing numbers of foreign travellers are stopping here for a few days too, enticed by the superbly scenic bus ride from Periyar, which takes you across the high ridges and lush tropical forests of the Cardamom Hills, or for the equally spectacular climb across the Ghats from Madurai. Recent seasons have also seen the emergence of some wonderful **heritage** and **homestay accommodation,** much of it in restored British bungalows, where you can sip High Range tea on lawns against vistas of rolling estates and mountains.

The Town

Clustered around the confluence of three mountain streams, Munnar town is a typical hill bazaar of haphazard buildings and congested market streets, which you'll probably want to escape at the first opportunity. The one sight of note is the **Tea Museum** (Tues–Sun 9am–4pm; Rs50), 2km northwest of the centre on Nallathany Road, which houses various pieces of old machinery and an exhibition of photos of the area's tea industry, from the 1880s pioneers to the modern Kanan-Devan era under the Tata tea conglomerate.

The social hub of the colonial period, and an important cultural icon in Munnar, the famous **High Range Club** is perched on a balcony overlooking the river on the southeastern edge of town. Indians were only officially permitted to enter the premises as recently as 1948, but these days non-members of any race are welcome to visit the typically Raj-era building for a round of golf, or to enjoy and gin and tonic served on the lawns by liveried retainers. The clock seems to have stopped ticking somewhere in the late-1940s at the men-only bar, whose walls are hung with rows of hunting trophies and topees. The old hats were signed and dated by planters who had survived thirty years of service in the High Range tea estates. Aside from the ban on women in the bar, stiff-upper-lipped dress codes apply: no T-shirts or sandals, and after 7pm on Saturdays, men are required to don a dinner jacket and tie.

Practicalities

Munnar can be reached by **bus** from Kochi, Kottayam, Kumily and Madurai. State-run and private services all pull into the town bus stand in the modern main bazaar, near the river confluence and Tata headquarters; state ones continue through town, terminating at the bus stands nearly 3km south. For most hotels you should ask to be dropped off at **Old Munnar,** 2km south of the centre, near the ineffectual DTPC **tourist office** (daily 8.30am–7pm; ☎04865/231516). A better source of **information** on transport, accommodation and day-trips, including to Eravikulam, is the helpful **Joseph Iype,** who runs the **Tourist Information Service** (no set hours; ☎04865/231136, ☎m94471 90954) from a small office in the main bazaar. Immortalized in Dervla Murphy's *On a Shoestring to Coorg* and more recently by Booker-prize winning Arundhati Roy, this self-appointed tourist officer has become something of a legend. He has some useful **maps** and newspaper articles, can arrange **transport** for excursions, and will doubtless bombard you with background on the area. A few metres north is the **Munnar Tourist Information Centre** (daily 10am–8pm; ☎04865/230552), a government-sponsored body whose primary concern appears to be to promote its own guided tour (daily 9am–5pm; Rs250). Designed mainly for Indian tourists, the whistlestop tour takes in a spice plantation, boating, a dairy farm, viewpoints and Top Station in the morning, and Rajmalai Wildlife Sanctuary, waterfalls, an amusement park in the afternoon and sunset at a viewpoint.

You can **change money** at the State Bank of Travancore, the State Bank of India or at numerous ATMs around the town. **Internet** access is available from a couple of places around town, such as Alpha Computer Centre (Rs50 per hour), next to the Tamil Nadu bus stand.

Accommodation

The cost of Munnar's **accommodation** is significantly higher than elsewhere in the High Range region, reflecting the pressure on beds caused by the town's popularity with middle-class tourists from the big cities. Rooms at the low end of the scale are in particularly short supply; the few we found were blighted by constant racket from the bus stand and bazaar, and are thus not listed below. On the plus side, the hill station does possess a couple of wonderfully genteel Raj-era places to stay, still redolent of the Empire in its twilight days, while further afield in the hills around Munnar, the tea plantations and cardamom groves harbour several beautiful heritage bungalows and homestays overlooking some of the most magnificent mountain scenery in South India.

Budget

Green View Shri Parvati Amman Kovil St, near the KSRTC bus stand ☏04865/230189, ☏m94478 25447, ⊛www.greenviewmunnar.com. Clean and friendly budget guesthouse on the valley floor, down a side road just off the main drag, with rooms of various sizes – the best of them #402, a tiny double on the rooftop that has big windows and hill views. Pitched squarely at foreign backpackers, it's run by an enthusiastic, competent young crew who do a sideline in guided day treks. ●–●

JJ Cottage Shri Parvati Amman Kovil St, near the KSRTC bus stand ☏04865/230104. Next door to *Green View*, and very much in the same mould, though it's been open longer, charges higher rates and tends to get booked up earlier in the day. Like its neighbour, the nicest of its clean, differently sized rooms is the one at the top (frontside), which has wood-panel walls and fine views. ●–●

Kanan Devan Hills Club Kanan Devan Hills Rd ☏04865/230252, ⊜kdhclub@rediffmail.com. The budget traveller's answer to the *High Range Club*: a typical colonial bungalow, actually built in 1983 but in Raj style with corrugated roofs, wooden verandas and coir carpets; the attached rooms are good value for Munnar. ●

🏃 **Zina Cottage** Kad ☏04865/230349, ☏m94471 90954. Gorgeous British-era stone bungalow, nestled amid tea gardens high on the hillside above Munnar. Its flower-filled front terrace has magnificent views across the town to Ana Mudi, and host Joseph Iype (see p.213) will fill you in on local walks over flasks of hot tea in his sitting room. The rooms themselves lack outlook and are basic and gloomy, and you'll probably need a pile of blankets at night, but all have their own entrances and bathrooms. This is somewhere you'd stay more for the atmosphere than creature comforts, and it has plenty of it. ●

Mid-range

Elysium Gardens Top Station Rd ☏04865/232620, ⊛www.elysiumgarden.com. Large, white-painted motel on the outskirts of town. Its "standard" rooms are clean and functional; the "executive" ones boast a larger sitting area; and the detached "cottages" have spacious living rooms and verandas. ●–●

Government Guesthouse Matupatty Rd ☏04865/230385. On the far side of the river, around the hillside from the main bazaar, this former British bungalow stands in its own grounds looking across the valley. It has just six rooms, lined up in an annexe just above the main reception and dining room area. They're large and dowdy, and lack outside space, but have big bathrooms. Meals by arrangement. ●

🏃 **High Range Club** Kanan Devan Hills Rd ☏04865/230253, ⊜hrcmunnar@sify.com. This old Raj-era club, founded by local British planters in 1909, must have been a nightmare of stuffiness and racism in its heyday. But now the faded colonial ambience, with turbaned bearers politely greeting guests in lounges filled with 1940s furniture and moth-eaten hunting trophies, feels undeniably quaint. Knock back a *chota-peg* of gin in the ("Men-Only") bar, play billiards and tennis, enjoy a round of golf on the nine-hole course, or just laze with a book on the immaculate lawns. The club's guest wing holds three kinds of rooms and cottages, varying in size and comfort. Rates include obligatory full board. ●–●

Hillview Kanan Devan Hills Rd ☏04865/230567, ☏m94477 40883, ⊛www.hillviewhotel.com. A big red block on the southern edge of town. It's not much to look at from the outside, but the interiors boast stripped wood floors and traditional carved wall panels. Some rooms are much darker than others. A dependable mid-range choice, despite its rough edges. ●–●

Mermaid Nadayar Rd ☏ 04865/232320, ⊛ www
.milmermaid.com. Former British PWD Inspection
Bungalow, now run (rather unconvincingly, and with
no frills) as a "heritage hotel". Rooms in the original
100-year-old block (there's a less attractive modern
annexe attached to it) are huge and retain some
colonial-era feel, with worn coir rugs and cream-
painted walls, but don't have any outside space and
are overpriced, even by Munnar's standards. ⑥
Olive Brook PO Box 62, Pothamedu
☏ 04865/230588, ⊛ www.olivebrookmunnar.com.
Delightfully old-fashioned homestay, run by a
schoolteacher, in the thick of a cardamom estate on
a hillside overlooking the southern end of Munnar.
The five rooms, spread over two blocks, all have
wonderful views, and the home-cooked food is
excellent. Rates include full board, cookery classes,
trekking, evening barbecues and campfires. ⑧
Royal Retreat Kanan Devan Hills Rd
☏ 04865/230240, ⊛ www.royalretreat.co.in.
Pleasant, efficiently run motel on the roadside at the
south end of town. Go for one of its "super-deluxe"
rooms if there are any free: they're south-facing,
have brick fireplaces and cane furniture, and are
fronted by a cheerful little flower garden. ⑥

Luxury

KTDC Tea County Off Matupatty Rd
☏ 04865/230460, ⊛ www.ktdc.com. The poshest

address in Munnar town is a rather anodyne,
government-run "four-star deluxe" resort offering a
range of luxurious chalet-style rooms and suites
($120–150) stacked along a hilltop. There's a good
multi-cuisine restaurant and beer parlour. ⑨

The Tea Sanctuary KDHP House
☏ 4865/230141, ⊛ www.theteasanctuary
.com. A selection of five former planters'
bungalows, scattered across the Kanan Devan Hill
Plantations Company's 240 square kilometres of
tea gardens. Situated on prime viewpoints amid
well-tended gardens, each has been sensitively
restored to its original state – with ivy-covered
exteriors and cosy open fireplaces indoors – and is
staffed by a liveried *chowkidar* and cook. If you're
hoping to experience the pre-war gentility of the
High Range, book a couple of nights in "Chockanad
East", 4km beyond the High Range Club. $130 per
night for two, including full board. ⑨

Windermere Estate PO Box 21,
Pothamedu ☏ 04865/230512, ⊛ www
.windermeremunnar.com. Alpine-style chalet
lodges, perched high on a hilltop above the town in
cardamom and tea groves, with glorious views over
the Chithirapuram Valley. Accommodation is offered
in a converted farmhouse, plantation home and
various garden cottages, all beautifully furnished
and decorated with natural wood and stone and
warm-coloured textiles. ⑨

Eating

If your hotel, homestay or guesthouse package doesn't include meals, your best
option will either be one of the popular local places reviewed below, or the
thattukada (hot food stall market) just south of the main bazaar, opposite the
taxi stand. This place gets into its stride around 7.30pm and runs through the
night, serving delicious, piping hot Keralan food – *dosas, parottas, iddiappam,*
green-bean curry, egg masala – ladled onto tin plates and eaten on rough wood
tables in the street. As with all *thattukadas*, taxi drivers and single Malayali men
working away from home make up most of the clientele, as the food is homely
and cheap (you'd be hard pushed to spend Rs30).

Food Count Ground Floor of the *Munnar Inn*, main
bazaar. Shiny, glass-sided café serving samosas,
veg cutlets, sandwiches and light meals. The most
hygienic option down in the main bazaar.
Guru Bhavan Matupatty Rd, Ikka Nagar. The most
dependable of Munnar's local South Indian "meals"

joints. It's a ten-minute plod north of the main
bazaar, but worth the walk, with a menu of
delicious Keralan vegetarian dishes that changes
daily, in addition to hot *parottas*, stupendously
crunchy paper *dosas* and other *udipi* snacks.
Recommended for local breakfasts, too.

Around Munnar

Munnar bazaar may not be the most inspiring spot in the High Range, but it
serves as a useful hub for explorations of the spectacular mountain region
surrounding it. Several of the summits towering above the town may be reached
on day treks through the tea gardens, and buses wind their way up to the aptly
named Top Station, a hamlet famed for its views and meadows of **Neelakurunji**

plants, and to the more distant nature sanctuaries of Eravikulam and Chinnar, where you can spot Nilgiri tahr, elephant and many other wild animals. To reach the most remote attractions hereabouts, however, you might want to hire a taxi for the day (easily done through your hotel, Joseph Iype, or at the taxi stand in the bazaar. Rates are a standard Rs6–7/km).

Walks and treks

Given the stupendous scenery rearing on all sides of Munnar, the **hiking** scene is surprisingly undeveloped. You can ramble at leisure through the tea estates, watching local Muthuvan pluckers at work (contact Joseph Iype at his office in the bazaar for route suggestions; see p.213). For anything more ambitious, it makes sense to employ the services of a guide. A good first stop is the *Green View* guesthouse, on the south side of town (see map, p.214), whose owner, Deepak (☏m94478 25447), heads up a team of enthusiastic young guides who've devised a menu of interesting hiking trails in the area. Drop by at the guesthouse to see a computer slideshow of their scenic highlights. Trips cost Rs600–800 per person per day (or Rs100/hr), with transport to and from the trailheads included.

For the **ascent of Ana Mudi**, South India's highest peak, you'll need to obtain a permit from the Forest Officer in Munnar, Mr Roy P. Thomas (☏m94479 79093). At his office (Mon–Fri 10am–1pm & 2–5pm) just above the taxi stand he'll arrange all the necessary paperwork and guides. With a pre-dawn start, the climb can be accomplished in a long day. Permits are not, however, granted during the mating season of the tahr in late January and February.

Top Station and Kolukkamalai

One of the most popular excursions from Munnar is the 34km climb through some of the Subcontinent's highest tea estates to **TOP STATION**, a tiny hamlet on the Kerala–Tamil Nadu border which, at 1600m, is the highest point on the interstate road. Pack ponies still labour up the endless switchbacks to the site, which takes its name from the old aerial **ropeway** that used to connect it

△ The view from Top Station, Munnar

with the valley floor, the ruins of which can still be seen in places. Apart from the marvellous views over the Tamil plains, Top Station is renowned for the very rare **Neelakurunji plant** (*Strobilanthes*), which grows in profusion on the mountainsides but only flowers once every twelve years, when huge crowds climb up here to admire the cascades of violet blossom spilling down the slopes (the next flowering is due in Oct/Nov 2018). Top Station is accessible by **bus** from Munnar (10 daily starting at 5.30am; 1hr 30min), and Jeep-taxis do the round trip for Rs850. To catch the best views, try to get here before the mist builds up at 9am.

Top Station sees streams of visitors during the season, but you can sidestep the crowds completely, and see even more awesome scenery, at the remote **Kolukkumalai estate**, 23km out of Munnar. At an altitude of 2400m, it's officially India's highest tea plantation, producing leaves prized for their delicate flavour. The only way to reach it is by Jeep, via the **Chinnakkanal Suryanelly Estate**. An old bridleway drops down the east flank of the mountain from here to the Tamil plains, visible in the distance – a popular local trekking route.

Eravikulam National Park and Chinnar Wildlife Sanctuary

Encompassing 100 square kilometres of moist evergreen forest and grassy hilltops in the Western Ghats, the **Eravikulam National Park** (daily 7am–6pm; Rs200 [Rs15]; ⓦwww.eravikulam.org), 13km northeast of Munnar, is the last stronghold of one of the world's rarest mountain goats, the **Nilgiri tahr**. Its innate friendliness made the tahr pathetically easy prey during the hunting frenzy of the colonial era. On a break in his campaign against Tipu Sultan in the late 1790s, the future Duke of Wellington reported that his soldiers were able to shoot the unsuspecting goats as they wandered through his camp. By Independence the tahr was virtually extinct; today, however, numbers are healthy, and the animals have regained their tameness, largely thanks to the efforts of the American biologist Clifford Rice, who studied them here in the early 1980s. Unable to get close enough to observe the creatures properly, Rice followed the advice of locals and attracted them using salt, and soon entire herds were congregating around his camp. The tahrs' salt addiction also explains why so many hang around the park gates at **Vaguvarai**, where visitors – despite advice from rangers – slip them salty snacks.

Although it borders Eravikulam, the **Chinnar Wildlife Sanctuary** (daily 6am–7pm; Rs100 [Rs10]; ⓦwww.chinnar.org) is much less visited, not least because its entrance lies a two-hour drive from Munnar along 58km of winding mountain roads. The reserve, in the rain shadow of the High Range and thus much drier than its neighbour, is one of the best spots in the state for bird watching, with 225 species recorded to date. But the real star attractions are the resident **grizzled giant squirrels**, who scamper in healthy numbers around the thorny scrub here, and the near-mythical "**white bison of Manjampatti**", thought to be an albino Indian gaur. Supported **treks** through the reserve are run by the excellent Wild Kerala Tour Company (☎0484/236 9121, ⓦwww.wildkeralatours.com), based in Kochi.

To reach Chinnar you have to pass through the small bazaar town of **MARAYOOR**, 42km east of Munnar, where it's worth stopping to admire Kerala's only **sandalwood forest**. The 92-square-kilometre reserve, a couple of kilometres out of town, holds an estimated 60,000 trees, whose wood currently sells for $1000–1500 per kilo on the international market. Wardens are on hand to shepherd visitors around the heavily protected zone which, despite its high fences and the death in 2004 of arch-smuggler Veerapan, continues to haemorrhage illegally felled sandalwood; they'll also show you **prehistoric rock-art** sites for which this area is famous. A collection of stone-capped **burial chambers**, known locally as the Munniozens, litter the land around the old Thenkasinathan Temple at the hamlet of **Kovilkadavu**, on the banks of the River Pambar.

Palakkad and around

Surrounded by paddy fields, **PALAKKAD** (Palghat) lies on NH-47 between Thrissur (79km) and Coimbatore in Tamil Nadu (54km), and on the railway line from Karnataka and Tamil Nadu. Due to the natural twenty-kilometre-wide gap through the Western Ghats here, this area has always been an important entry point into the Malabar region. The town itself doesn't particularly warrant a stop other than to break a journey, though its beautiful environs do harbour some of Kerala's most appealing heritage homestays and ayurvedic resorts. Further north, the **Silent Valley National Park** and the hill station of **Nelliampathy** are off-track destinations you might have to pick up transport here to reach.

With its imposing ramparts and moat, Palakkad's square **fort** (daily 8am–6pm; free), the best-preserved in Kerala, is the town's main sight. It was built by Haider Ali of Mysore in 1766, and witnessed a bloody skirmish a couple of decades later when the British stormed it on behalf of their ally, the *zamorin* of Calicut. These days, it's besieged every weekend by streams of local school groups and picnickers. Just outside the citadel, **Vatika Gardens** are another favourite family destination (daily 11am–8pm, Rs5), second only in popularity to the amusement park at **Malampuzha**, 10km north (daily 11am–9pm; Rs80, includes all rides), renowned locally for its cable car or "ropeway" and fantasy rock garden created by the artist Nek Chand of Chandigarh fame; on Saturday and Sunday nights the site is illuminated (although it still closes at 9pm).

Many travellers in search of **kathakali** performances also find themselves directed to Palakkad as, in April and May particularly, hundreds of one-off events take place in the area. The local Government Carnatic Music College has an excellent reputation, and a small open-air amphitheatre next to the fort often hosts first-class music and dance performances. Ask at the tourist office (see below) for details.

Practicalities

Palakkad is well connected to the rest of Kerala and most of the express trains travelling through to Chennai, Bangalore and points further north stop at the mainline **railway station**, 6km to the northeast. The KSRTC **bus stand** is right in the middle of town.

DTPC's helpful **tourist office**, around the corner from the *Hotel Indraprastha* (see opposite) at Fort Maidan (Mon–Sat 9.30am–5pm; ☎0491/253 8996), is a good source of advice on local festivals and cultural events. Both the *Indraprastha* and the *Fort Palace* have residents-only foreign exchange facilities, and you can **change money** and travellers' cheques at the State Bank of India, next door to the *Indraprastha*, where there's also a 24hr ATM.

Accommodation and eating

Palakkad's small but adequate crop of **hotels** is pitched primarily at business clients passing through. Further afield, a handful of more upscale, foreigner-oriented heritage **homestays** and ayurvedic **spas** are desirable destinations in their own right, with lots of traditional Keralan character and potential for trips into the less-frequented rural corners of the state.

For an inexpensive pit-stop in the town centre, look no further than the pure-veg *Kapilavasthu*, next to the KSRTC bus stand, which does fresh fruit juices and cool shakes in addition to the usual selection of South Indian snacks and rice-based meals – though you'll need to bring your own bottled water. A slicker, slightly pricier alternative is the *Hotel Omega,* near the *Ammbadi* hotel, which serves good-value pan-Indian veg and non-veg dishes.

Ammbadi TB Road ☏0491/253 1244. Plain, clean and comfortable rooms opposite the town bus stand, with a restaurant attached serving Chinese and Indian food. ❹

🏃 **Ayurveda Manna** Peringode, Kootanadu, Palakkad District ☏0466/237 0660, ⓦwww.ayurvedamana.com. One of the state's top ayurvedic resorts, set in the ancestral home of a famous Namboodiri Brahmin family long associated with Keralan healing sciences. Fronted by a pillared veranda, their "heritage rooms" in a nineteenth-century palace are handsomely furnished, with original tiled floors, Keralan mural paintings on the walls and large windows. Most people come for expert medical treatments and *kalarippayattu* training, with packages ranging from a full-board single day stay with one massage ($85) to courses of a month or more (from $135 per day). ❾

Fort Palace 1km from bus stand on West Fort Rd ☏0491/253 4621, ⓦwww.fortpalace.com. Situated opposite the fort, this mid-range hotel, built in humorous mock-citadel style complete with crenellations and coloured flags flying from its walls, offers a choice of polished, very good-value a/c and non-a/c rooms, all en suite, as well as a bar and huge garden restaurant. ❸–❹

Indraprastha English Church Rd ☏0491/253 4641, ⓦwww.hotelindraprastha.com. Palakkad town's poshest hotel is a well-managed place with spacious, modern, centrally a/c rooms. There's a lovely lawn and a dim but blissfully cool multi-cuisine restaurant, a well-stocked bar and a 24hr vegetarian coffee shop built in traditional Keralan style. The rooms are often block-booked by visiting government honchos, so reserve in advance. ❺–❼

🏃 **Kalari Kovilakom** 20km south of Palakkad at Kollengode ⓦwww.kalarikovilakom.com. Occupying the former residence of the Vengunad dynasty, *Kalari Kovilakom* is part palace hotel and part ayurvedic spa, and quite simply one of the most exquisite places to stay in South India. Accommodation is offered either in a 1920s "guest wing", with its typically British furnishings and decor, or the more traditionally Keralan,

zenana-style "palace wing". Guests are encouraged not to leave the premises during their stay, which is no great chore as the whole place, set in substantial grounds, is an architectural feast: colonnaded walkways lead to open *nadumuttam* courtyards, hidden bathing pools and wood-lined interiors, lit by louvred windows and slatted screens. The food served in the strictly vegetarian restaurant is tailored to fit individual treatment regimes; alcohol and tobacco are forbidden. Prices start at a hefty $8500 full-board for two sharing, for a 14-day stay. ❾

Kandath Tharavad Thenkurussi ☏04922/284124, ⓦwww.tharavad.info. Idyllic heritage homestay, in a 200-year-old ancestral seat set on the edge of a sleepy village 10km south from Palakkad. Surrounded by rice paddy, the mansion's most striking feature is the raised, colonnaded *purathalum* veranda at the front, whose bulbous pillars are capped by carvings of elephants, snakes and dragons. Host Mr Bhagwaldas and his offspring, the fifth and sixth generations to live here, offer six simply furnished guest rooms, and activities ranging from guided birding and trekking to bullock cart and cycle rides, cookery classes and even toddy tapping trips. From $100 (includes full-board). ❽

Olappamanna Mana Vellinezhi, 43km northwest ☏0466/2285797, ☏m9847 764532. ⓦwww.olappamannamana.com. This stately Namboordiri *mana* (feudal mansion), resting on sandstone embankments in a clearing at the heart of a palm grove, possesses a certain mystique. Its traditional owners were renowned patrons of local arts, particularly Carnatic music and Sanskrit literature, and during your stay here you can take short "orientation courses" in *kathakali* (Vellinezhi was one of the cradles of the dance form and retains an extraordinary 300-year-old temple-theatre, which guests are welcome to visit). The family also regularly perform *kalam ezhuttu* powder pattern rituals in the house. Strictly Brahmin-vegetarian food; no alcohol. Doubles from $100, full-board. ❽

Silent Valley National Park

High up in the watershed of the Western Ghats, the **Silent Valley National Park**, 75km by road northwest from Palakkad on the Tamil border, may not be Kerala's best-known nature reserve, but its 90 square kilometres of rainforest rank among the most pristine in the Subcontinent. Some 966 species of flowering plant (including 100 different orchids) were recently identified in its moist evergreen woodlands, along with 211 different kinds of bird and 128 types of butterfly. Its enigmatic name derives from the apparent absence of cicadas remarked upon by British engineers when they explored the valley in the 1840s. The calls of plenty of other creatures resound through the tree cover, however, not least that of the rare **lion-tailed macaque**; Silent Valley holds one of the last viable breeding populations of this highly endangered primate, in addition to gaur, sloth bears, three species of jungle cats and vestigial numbers of tigers.

Barely 7km from east to west, and 12km from north to south, the park is drained by **Kunthipuzha River**, one of only two major streams in these mountains, rising and flowing through totally uninhabited, unpolluted regions. In 1973 it became the subject of a fierce environmental controversy when the Indian government announced plans to erect a dam across it. Faced with international pressure, Indira Gandhi dropped the project, and the whole zone was declared a national park in 1986. However, Silent Valley is still not entirely out of the woods. A second hydro scheme proposed in 2001 continues to be debated, with strong support from the current chief minister of Kerala, V.S. Achuthanandan. Another threat to the forest hereabouts is posed by illegal **ganja cultivation**. Under the auspices of local mafia groups, the indigenous minorities who live in the area abutting the park – the Irula and Mudugar – are the prime source of Kerala's famed grass, for which land is illegally cleared each year.

Park practicalities

The **best season** to visit Silent Valley is between December and March; in April and May the park may be closed due to forest fires. **Access** is strictly controlled by the Forest Department. You first have to obtain a **permit** from the main Silent Valley National Park office in **Mannarkkad** (☎04924/222056, Ⓔwlwsvnpmkd@sancharnet.in), 32km short of the main entrance and served by regular buses from Palakkad. Private vehicles can press on another 9km as far as **Mukkali** (reachable by local bus from Mannarkkad) but from there on only authorized Jeeps are allowed. These should be booked at the office of the Assistant Wildlife Warden, currently Mr Kunjumou (☎04924/253225), in Mukkali. Return trips depart from 8am to noon, last for five hours and cost Rs600 per vehicle; visitors must report back to the office by 6pm. The entrance fee is Rs210 per person – plus an extra Rs25 per camera and Rs250 per group for the compulsory guide. The only **accommodation** option in Mukkali is the basic National Park guesthouse (book through the Assistant Wildlife Warden; ❹), 100m beyond the ticket office, where beds cost Rs800 per person; meals are also available on request.

At the time of writing, a new paved road was nearing completion from Mukkali to the Silent Valley Visitors Centre at **Sairandhri**, 23 winding kilometres further north, where there's an observation tower giving a panoramic view over the park. With a standard day pass, you're permitted to follow a 2km trail down the steep side of the valley to the Kunthipuzha River, spanned by a suspension bridge, but not press on any further.

Some 80km of superb **trekking** trails also radiate out of Sairandhri, served by a chain of five camps; to follow any of them you'll need to obtain permission and arrange guides through the warden at Mukkali or the forest office in Mannarkkad, who'll also be able to fill you in with route options. Trekking permits cost a stiff Rs900 per day, plus the Rs250 per day guide fee and a nominal amount for meals. If you'd like a dependable firm of experts to make all the necessary arrangements on your behalf, contact the Wild Kerala Tour Company, at VI/480 KVA Buldings, Mattancherry, Kochi (℡0484/309 9520, Ⓦwww.wildkeralatours.com).

Nelliampathy

Surrounded by teak forests and estates where tea, coffee, cardamom and oranges grow in profusion, the village of **NELLIAMPATHY**, 75km south of Palakkad, is Kerala's least-known hill station. Only in the past decade or so have visitors started to venture up to the settlement, spread over undulating terrain at an altitude of a little above 1500m. The grandiose scenery surrounding it and refreshingly cool climate make it a delightful break from the humidity of the coastal plains, while the journey itself, winding up a succession of mountain spurs, ranks among the most scenic in the state. In addition, the scattering of small-scale plantation homestays and resorts that have sprung up here are, on the whole, much less pricey than their counterparts in Munnar. Nelliampathy holds neither wildlife sanctuaries nor any conventional sights, beyond a string of viewpoints reachable via forest paths, but the high country around it has plenty of trekking potential.

Sporadic KSRTC **buses** run to Nelliampathy from Palakkad, although you'll probably get there quicker by jumping on one of the more frequent services from Palakkad town bus stand to **Nemmara**, from where shared Jeeps cover the onward 26km leg. Skirting the Pothundi reservoir and dam before it begins its vertiginous ascent via a series of ten hairpin bends to the hill station, the road is scenic from start to finish.

After the spectacular climb, buses terminate at Nelliampathy's **Kaikatty** cross-roads, where there's a small NTPC **tourist office** (daily 9am–5pm; ℡949/513 6463) and a fleet of local **Jeeps** waiting to ferry arrivals to their respective hotels and guesthouses. Prices depend on the number of people and whim of the driver; expect to pay around Rs10–20 per kilometre.

Accommodation

If the following established **places to stay** are fully booked, try the NTPC tourist office at Kaikatty for details of newly opened homestays in the area – though given the long slog up here, you'd be ill advised to arrive without some reservation in the bag. As with all hill stations, rooms tend to be in shorter supply on weekends.

Ciscilia Heritage Ranimedu Estate, 6km from Kaikatty ☎04923/206283, Ⓦwww .cisciliaheritage.com. An affordable option in a secluded, remote setting high up on the hills behind Kaikatty. Its rooms come in the form of quaint wooden huts overlooking tea gardens, with teak linings and solar-powered hot water. Your alfresco dinners will be accompanied by a cacophony of exotic animal noises emanating from the pristine shola forest just behind the resort which, due to its far-flung location, tends to have vacancies when places nearer Kaikatty are full. ❹

Green Land Farmhouse 9km from Kaikatty in Palapagandi ☎04923/246245. At a superbly isolated position amid mature coffee plantations, this simple farmstay offers great views and value for money. Optional full board only costs Rs200 extra. ❹
ITL Holiday Resorts Kaikatty ☎04923/246357, Ⓔpgt_itl@sancharnet.in. A well-set-up budget lodge close to Kaikatty, and one of the cheapest options in the area, with dorm beds (Rs225) in addition to attached non-a/c rooms. Reserve well in advance as tour groups frequently block-book the whole place. ❹–❻

Tropical Hill Resorts 4km from Kaikatty in Padagiri ☎04923/246238. Accommodation to suit all pockets – from dorm beds and tents for budget travellers to luxurious, cosy British-era bungalows with fireplaces and wood verandas – on a 2.5-square-kilometre, picture-postcard coffee estate. Closed at the time of writing for renovation work, but scheduled to re-open in early 2008. ❸–❼

Whistling Thrush Bungalow 6km from Kaikatty on the Poothundu Plantation, Padagiri ☎04923/324 6235, ☎m9447 144921, ⓦwww.nelliampathy .com. Three smartly furnished guest rooms in a modern bungalow, surrounded on three sides by reserve forest, and on the other by a working tea, cardamom, coffee and vanilla plantation. Rates include obligatory full board. ❽

Travel details

Trains

Kochi/Ernakulam to: Alappuzha (5–7 daily; 1hr 10min–1hr 40min); Kanyakumari (2–3 daily; 7hr 25min–10hr); Kollam (Quilon) (12–15 daily; 2hr 50min–4hr 25min); Kottayam (9–11 daily; 1hr–1hr 20min); Kozhikode (4–6 daily; 4hr 45min–5hr 30min); Thiruvananthapuram (11–15 daily; 5hr–5hr 35min); Thrissur (15–18 daily; 1hr 15min–2hr 30min).
Thrissur to: Kochi/Ernakulam (15–17 daily; 1hr 30min–2hr 10min); Thiruvananthapuram (10–12 daily; 5hr 55min–7hr 10min).

Buses

Kochi/Ernakulam to: Alappuzha (every 30min; 1hr 30min); Kanyakumari (6 daily; 9hr); Kollam (every 30min; 3hr); Kottayam (every 30min; 1hr 30min–2hr); Kozhikode (hourly; 5hr); Kumily (10 daily; 6hr); Munnar (6 daily; 4hr 30min–5hr); Periyar, see "Kumily"; Thiruvananthapuram (every 2hr; 5–6hr); Thrissur (every 30min; 2hr).
Munnar to: Kochi/Ernakulam (6 daily; 4hr 30min–5hr); Kottayam (5 daily; 5hr); Kumily (4 daily; 4hr); Thiruvananthapuram (5 daily; 8–9hr).

Thrissur to: Guruvayur (10 daily; 40min); Kochi/Ernakulam (every 10min; 2hr); Kozhikode (every 30min; 2hr 30min); Mysore (5 daily; 8hr); Palakkad (every 20min; 2hr); Thiruvananthapuram (every 20min; 7–8hr).

Flights

For a list of airline websites, see pp.22–23. In the listings below IA is Indian Airlines, AI Air India, AIE Air India Express, JA Jet Airways, SA Sahara Airlines, AD Air Deccan, KA Kingfisher, IG IndiGo, GA Go Air, SJ SpiceJet and PA Paramount Airways.
Kochi/Ernakulam to: Bangalore (Bengaluru) (AD, SA, KA, JA, GA, IA 8–10 daily; 1hr 15min–2hr 15min); Chennai (DA, PA, KA, JA 6–7 daily; 1hr 30min); Coimbatore (AD 1 daily; 30min); Hyderabad (AD, SA 2 daily; 1hr 30min); Kozhikode (AIE 1 daily; 35min); Lakshadweep (IA 6 weekly; 1hr 35min); Mumbai (Bombay) (AD, AIE, IA, GA, KA, JA 9–12 daily; 1hr 45min–2hr 30min); Goa (AI, KA 1–2 daily; 1hr 10min); Thiruvananthapuram (AD, AIE, AS, IA 4 daily; 30min).

Northern Kerala

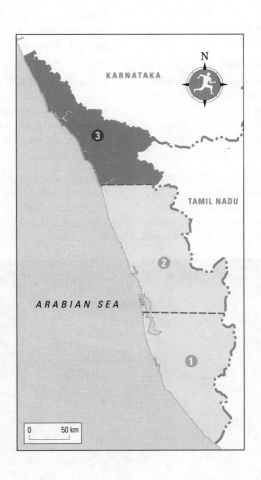

CHAPTER 3   # Highlights

✳ **Kuttichira mosques** A collection of beautiful wooden mosques, built between 700 and 1100 years ago in distinctive Malabari style, the last vestiges of Kozhikode golden age as a spice port. See p.232

✳ **Moppila food** Enjoy one of the most hybrid, delicious regional cuisines of the south, a legacy of Arab influence in the region. Two authentic restaurants in Kozhikode are *Zains* and *Paragon*. See p.234

✳ **Wayanad** Trek through dense rainforest, past waterfalls and remote Hindu temples, to the green summits of the Western Ghats in one of Kerala's most beautiful mountain regions. See p.236

✳ **Theyyattam** Otherworldly spirit possession rituals, involving elaborate masks, make-up and costumes, take place throughout the region between November and March. See p.245

✳ **Costa Malabari** This small hotel near Kannur (Cannanore) is perfectly placed for explorations of remote beaches and *theyyam* rituals. See p.247

✳ **Valiyaparamba** Explore the "northern backwaters" – a less touristy alternative to Kuttanad – on a *kettu vallam* rice barge. See p.248

△ Tholpetty Wildlife Sanctuary, Wayanad

Northern Kerala

N orthern Kerala, where the state tapers into the hilly coastal belt of Karnataka, lies more than 600km from the capital, Thiruvananthapuram, and in many respects feels like a region apart. From the thirteenth century, its dominant rulers, the *zamorins* of **Calicut** and the **Kolathiri** rajas of neighbouring Cannanore (modern day Kannur), formed their own distinct centre of gravity, beyond the reach of distant Travancore. International commerce flourished in the ports of what came to be known as the "Malabar coast", visited by ships from as far afield as China, Africa and the Middle East. Still grown in the hinterland, pungent "Malabari black" pepper was the commodity most came in search of, along with cardamom, cinnamon, timber and printed "calico" cotton (named after its principal source, the *chaliyan* weavers' workshops of Calicut). Tax raked off this brisk trade filled the coffers of the Malabar's kings with unprecedented wealth, giving rise to one of South Asia's most refined and sophisticated societies.

Over time, **Calicut** (or "Kozhikode" as it's now officially called) emerged as the undisputed capital of northern Kerala, its trade monopolized by a class of Arab merchants whose business acumen, political nous and treasuries proved invaluable to successive *zamorins*. Under the umbrella of their tolerant reign, **Islam** – spread through intermarriage between the local population and Arab merchant families, and the voluntary conversion of disenfranchised lower-caste Hindus – flourished as it never quite did anywhere else in Kerala, developing its own hybrid style of architecture and cuisine. All but a handful of the old wooden mosques of the Malabar have now been replaced by contemporary Mecca-style *masjids*, but the Muslim community – known as **Moppilas** – retain a distinctive presence in northern Kerala.

Muslims enjoy a particularly high profile in **Kozhikode** (Calicut) city itself, whose economy owes its current buoyancy to the flow of remittance *riyals* and *dinars* posted home each month by Malayalis working in the Gulf states. Kozhikode's lack of sights – not to mention its heavily congested and polluted centre – have long acted as a disincentive to tourism, but its outlying districts hold some of the region's finest old Moppila mosques, and around the busy markets of the centre are dotted many excellent restaurants, old-fashioned cafés and *halwa* shops, where you can sample the Malabar's famously spicy, Arab-tinged cuisine.

Moppila influence peters out as you head inland towards the mountains, where *adivasi* tribal people form the most conspicuous minority in a region still extensively covered in rainforest. The prospect of treks to waterfalls and across the grassy uplands of the Western Ghats' watershed peaks is beginning to tempt travellers up to **Wayanad**, one of Kerala's most scenic hill districts. A scattering

of swanky eco-resort hotels nestle under the canopy, providing accommodation in luxury tree houses or romantic teak *tharavadukal*, with views over coffee plantations from their verandas. Wild elephant and gaur bison still inhabit the surrounding forest and are the star attractions of the **Wayanad National Park**, divided into two separate portions: **Muthanga** and **Tholpetty**.

Further north, the former colonial trading ports of **Mahé** and **Thalassery (Tellicherry)**, dominated by salt-worn bastions and bustling little harbours, serve as stepping stones on the long haul up to **Kannur (Cannanore)**, the centre of a district renowned for the extraordinary masked spirit possession dances held through the winter in its scattered villages. Known as **theyyam** or **theyyattam**, each of these four hundred or so rituals has its own elaborate set of traditional costumes and mythological associations, harking back thousands of years to an era before Brahmanical Hinduism spread to the fringes of peninsula India.

Beyond Kannur, you enter a still-more traditional corner of the state, well off the tourist trail, where traditional in-shore fishing and rice cultivation (along with remittance money) dominate the local economy. Edged by stands of palm and casuarina trees, deserted beaches and sandbars line a shoreline broken only by occasional river mouths and hidden lagoons.

The largest **backwater** area in the far north centres on the island of **Valiya-paramba**, which you can explore on one of only four rice-barge cruise boats operating in the area, from a far-flung jetty outside the town of **Nileswaram** on the main coastal highway. Few travellers make it as far as **Bekal Fort**, the most northerly and impressive of Kerala's coastal strongholds, but those that do are rewarded with a stupendous panorama of empty golden sand and palm forest.

Some history

Prior to the rise of colonial Cochin in the sixteenth century, Kozhikode's rulers, the *zamorins*, were the dominant force along the Malabar coast. It was to their court that Vasco da Gama first appealed for permission to trade in 1498, and their eventual demise enabled the Dutch and British to flex their imperial muscles in the region.

Kozhikode's emergence as a major port began in the twelfth century, after the decline of the Kulasekhara empire. The seat of the Polatiri dynasty, it was conquered by the **Eradis** of the Nediyiruppu kingdom to the east. The Eradis shifted their capital to the newly acquired seaport and set about constructing a large fortified palace, or *koyil kotta* – whence "Kozhikode" (later corrupted by the British into "Calicut").

The new kingdom was named **"Nediyiruppu Swaroopam"** and its rulers the "samuris", or "zamorins". Ibn Battuta, the Chinese-Muslim traveller Ma Huan and Nicolo de Conti were among the many foreigners who applauded the town's splendid buildings and tolerant regime in the fourteenth and fifteenth centuries. By declaring it a free port and espousing a liberal attitude to other religions, the Hindu *zamorins* were able to entice whole communities of Chinese and Arab merchants to their capital. Ultimately, it was the Arabs who would triumph in the struggle for control of Malabar's spice trade. Arab ships, horses, arms and soldiers formed the backbone of successive *zamorins'* military campaigns in the region, which by the eve of Da Gama's arrival had seen Calicut's territory extend from Cochin in the south to Cannanore, the domain of the Kolathiri rajas, in the north.

At the height of its power, Calicut was one of Asia's most prosperous and cultured cities. As well as powerful warlords, the *zamorins* were passionate sponsors of the arts, particularly literature. The magnificence of their court impressed Vasco da Gama's **Portuguese** delegation when it limped into the city after discovering the sea route around the Cape of Good Hope in 1498. The *zamorin* was less enthralled by the lacklustre presents offered by the European visitors, which some historians have suggested explains his refusal to grant requests from the Lusitanian navigator to site a trading post on the Malabar. The real root of the cool welcome was, however, probably the influence over the *zamorin* of his close Arab advisors, who were quick to recognize the threat to their monopoly posed by the sudden appearance of the vehemently anti-Muslim "Franks".

The second Portuguese expedition, under Pedro Alvarez Cabral in 1501, succeeded in levering trade concessions from the Calicut court. But in the course of the visit, relations with the city's Arab merchants degenerated badly, unleashing a series of violent attacks and counter-attacks that would leave an indelible mark on the history of the Malabar.

Trouble started after Cabral's men bombarded an Arab ship in the harbour and put its crew to the sword. Trapped on shore, the remaining Portuguese were soon massacred by an angry mob. Retribution came in 1502, when Da Gama sailed into Calicut harbour at the head of a fleet of fifteen war ships and eight hundred men. After the *zamorin* refused to expel all Muslims from the capital, the Portuguese turned their cannons on the city. Malabari sailors captured on rice barges standing to in the port were mutilated and their body parts blasted over the rooftops.

This proved the first of many bloody encounters between the *zamorin* and the Portuguese, who pursued their commercial ambitions on the Malabar by allying with Calicut's enemies, principally Cochin. Clashes, blockades and battles between the two rumbled on through the first decade of the sixteenth century. A treaty granting full trading rights and annual tribute to the Portuguese finally settled matters a decade later, but not before the *zamorin's* palace had been reduced to ruins and the city set ablaze.

Over the coming centuries, Calicut's influence steadily waned as its traditional enemies, the houses of Cochin and Kolathiri, gained the upper hand. Meanwhile, the **French East India Company** and its British counterpart fought for supremacy on the northern Malabar, establishing outposts at Mahé and Tellicherry respectively, from where they exported pepper, cardamom, cinnamon, timber and calico cotton. With the defeat of Tipu Sultan in the Mysore wars of the late seventeenth century, the region finally became absorbed into the Raj's **Madras Presidency** in 1800.

Civil disturbances directed by the region's Muslim Moppilas at their Hindu landlords (or Janmis) saw riots, killings and the desecration of temples erupt throughout northern Kerala between 1836 and 1856. The roots of the so-called **Moppila Riots** continue to be debated, but almost certainly lay in the consequences of ill-thought-out British tax reforms.

A second, more carefully orchestrated Muslim uprising exploded in 1921, and this time directly targeted symbols of British authority. Dubbed the **Malabar Rebellion**, it later took the form of communal attacks on Hindus, before being brutally suppressed. The most infamous episode of the rebellion, whose ringleaders were rounded up and shot and followers imprisoned or deported to the Andaman Islands, was when 61 Moppila prisoners suffocated to death while being transported by train across the Ghats. The so-called "**Black Hole of Podanar**" left a legacy of enduring hatred in the Malabar region, playing a key part in the formation of the "Muslim League", which since Independence has held the balance of power in this fifty-percent Muslim region.

Emigration has been the prime shaping force of life in northern Kerala over recent decades. Hundreds of thousands of mostly Muslim Malabaris now work in the Gulf states, and the impact of the money they send home is more evident in the north than in any other area in the state.

Kozhikode (Calicut)

Formerly one of Asia's most prosperous trading capitals, the busy coastal city of **KOZHIKODE** (Calicut), 193km by rail north of Kochi, occupies an extremely important place in Keralan legend and history. After Vasco da Gama landed at nearby Kappad in 1498, he and his fellow sailors were surprised to find themselves in a sophisticated, cosmopolitan city already inhabited by communities of Jewish, Arab and Chinese merchants, as well as Christians who'd been here since the time of St Thomas. Gem dealers and gold shops lined the bazaars en route to the *zamorin's* palace, where they were received in halls hung with gold and silk brocade.

Nowadays, with the exception of a crop of splendid **Moppila mosques**, precious few remnants survive of the city's illustrious past, and the small number

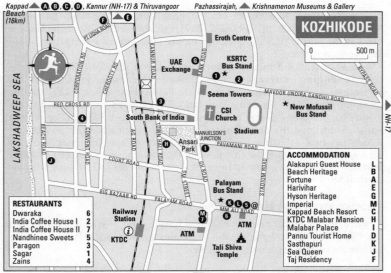

of foreigners that find their way here tend only to be breaking longer journeys to somewhere else. Even so, it's a strikingly upbeat, prosperous place, riding high on a tide of remittance cheques from the Gulf and expanding rapidly in all directions: the city and its surrounding district receives more income per capita from abroad than any other in the state, hence the striking number of huge gold emporia and silk shops in its bazaars.

Arrival and information

The **railway station** (☎0495/270 1234), close to the centre of town, is served by coastal expresses, slower passenger trains, and superfast express trains from Kochi and Thiruvananthapuram. There are three **bus stands**. All government-run services from destinations outside the city pull in at the **KSRTC bus stand** on Mavoor Road (aka Indira Gandhi Road). Private long-distance – mainly overnight – buses stop at the **New Mofussil private stand**, 500m away on the other side of Mavoor Road – there's a row of agents for booking tickets on these along MM Ali Road. The **Palayam bus stand**, off MM Ali Road, just serves the city.

Kozhikode's **airport** (⊛www.calicutairport.com), at Karippur, 23km south of the city, is primarily a gateway for emigrant workers flying to and from the Gulf, but also has flights to Kochi and Thiruvananthapuram. A taxi from the airport into town will cost around Rs300, but you can save a few rupees by taking an **auto-rickshaw** to the Kozhikode–Palakkad highway and then catching a bus. Flight tickets can be bought through PL Worldways, on the 3rd Floor of Seema Towers, Bank Road, just north of the CSI Church. Indian Airlines (Mon–Sat 10am–1pm & 1.45–5.30pm; ☎0495/276 6243) and Air India (Mon–Sat 9.30am–5.30pm; ☎0495/276 0715) are both at the Eroth Centre, opposite Hyson Heritage on Bank Road. The rest of the carriers (listed on p.250) all have counters at the airport.

KTDC's **tourist information** booth (officially daily 9am–7.30pm; ☎0495/270 0097) at the railway station has info on travel connections and sites around Kozhikode, but opening hours are erratic. The main KTDC tourist office (☎0495/272 2391), in the KTDC *Malabar Mansion* hotel at the corner of SM Street, can supply only limited information about the town and area.

With so much Gulf money floating around, you shouldn't have any difficulty **changing currency** in Kozhikode. Recommended places for exchanging cash or travellers' cheques are PL Worldways (see p.229) and the spanking new UAE Exchange on Bank Road, next to Hyson Heritage (Mon–Sat 9.30am–1.30pm & 2–6pm, Sun 9.30am–1.30pm). The Union Bank of India and the State Bank of India, opposite each other on MM Ali Road, are two of many large branches with ATMs. **Internet** access is available at the Hub, on the first floor of the block to the right of *Nandhinee Sweets*, MM Ali Road, and at Internet Zone, near *KTDC Malabar Mansion* (both Rs30/hr).

Accommodation

Kozhikode's reasonably priced city-centre **hotels**, most of which operate 24hr checkout, often fill up by noon; the beach area and Kappad, 16km north, offer quieter alternatives with more character.

Budget

Imperial Kallai Rd ☎0495/270 1291. Large budget lodge built around a courtyard with basic, very cheap rooms and a branch of *India Coffee House* on the ground floor. ❷

KTDC Malabar Mansion SM St ☎0495/272 2391, ⓦwww.ktdc.com. A favourite with backpackers, although the stuffy rooms and occasional dodgy "guides" hanging around reception add little to its appeal. On the plus side, there's a beer parlour and a good South Indian restaurant. ❸

Pannu Tourist Home 16km north at Kappad Beach ☎0496/268 8634. Set back only 100m from the seafront (look for the signboard opposite the rock temple), this simple guesthouse offers quiet, simple attached rooms with large balconies looking onto a palm plantation. Not in the same league as the nearby *Beach Resort*, but correspondingly less pricey. ❸–❹

Sasthapuri MM Ali Rd ☎0495/272 3281, ⓦwww.sasthapuri.com. Compact budget place, close to the Palayam bus stand and market, with well-maintained, nicely furnished rooms (including some of the city's cheapest a/c options), a funky little roof garden restaurant sporting ersatz tribal murals, and a bar. Very good value. ❶–❹

Mid-range

Alakapuri Guest House MM Ali Rd, near the railway station, 1km from KSRTC bus stand ☎0495/272 3451. Built around a courtyard, the a/c rooms in this dependable mid-range place have huge bathtubs, polished wood and easy chairs; the

cheaper, non-a/c options are rather spartan. There's a bar, restaurant and a relaxing lawn, and single rates are available. ❹–❺

Beach Heritage 3km north of the centre on Beach Rd ☎0495/236 5363, ⓦwww.beachheritage.com. Dating from 1890, the premises of the colonial-era Malabar English Club, with its closely cropped lawns and high-pitched tiled roofs, now house a delightfully eccentric heritage hotel, whose white walls, dark-wood furniture and original tiled floors retain plenty of period feel. It's the kind of place you'd expect to see Somerset Maugham sipping a gin sling on the veranda – which indeed he did; Chester Bowles and Jawaharlal Nehru also stayed here in the 1950s. There are only six rooms and two suites, all with a/c, balconies or private patios, ceiling fans, and mod cons such as TVs and CD players. Best of all, the tariffs are amazingly restrained by Keralan standards. ❹–❺

Hyson Heritage Bank Rd, near the KSRTC bus stand ☎0495/276 6423, ⓦwww.hysonheritage.com. Another gleaming, blissfully cool a/c business hotel close to the centre, but with much lower tariffs than the *Fortune*: their "budget" non-a/c rooms are especially good value. ❹–❺

Kappad Beach Resort 17km north of the centre ☎0496/268 8777, ⓦwww.renaissancekappadbeach.com. If you can face the 45min trip and afford its high rates, this former government place, now run by the Kochi-based Renaissance chain, is Kappad's most appealing option. Situated slap on the beach, the site holds four separate cottages, each with four rooms (two on the upper, and two on the lower floors) – the best of them have breezy rear balconies with uninterrupted sea views. There's a swimming pool, a multi-cuisine restaurant with garden terrace and a small ayurveda centre. **⑦–⑧**

Malabar Palace Manuelsons Jn ☎0495/272 1511, ⓦwww.malabarpalacecalicut.com. Ritzy four-star bang in the city centre. Ranged over six storeys, its rooms are lavishly furnished with luxurious beds, thick burgundy carpets and polished-wood writing desks; those to the rear have great views over the palm grove. There is also a quality restaurant, offering Rs125 buffet lunches. **⑥–⑧**

Sea Queen Beach Rd ☎0495/236 6604. Ageing mid-range hotel overlooking a rather grim part of the beach and lorry park. Best to splash out on a "deluxe" room since the lower-priced ones are rather grubby. **④–⑤**

Luxury

Fortune Kannur Rd, 3km north of the centre ☎0495/276 8888, ⓔfortunecalicut@hotelskerala .com. Business-oriented four-star, with plush rooms and central a/c, plus a rooftop swimming pool,

fitness suite and sauna, foreign exchange facilities, bar, 24hr coffee shop and Indian restaurant. The tariff includes a buffet breakfast. **⑥**

Harivihar 4km north of the centre in the suburb of Bilathikulam ☎0495/276 5865, ⓦwww.harivihar.com. Ancestral home of the Kadathanadu royal family, converted into a particularly wonderful heritage homestay. Set in beautiful gardens landscaped with herb beds, lotus ponds and an original laterite-lined bathing tank (which guests are welcome to use), the mansion is a model of traditional Keralan refinement: white-washed, high-ceilinged rooms filled with antique furniture open onto pillared walkways inside, where you can follow short courses in yoga, astrology, cookery and Indian mythology. There's also a top-grade Green Leaf-accredited ayurvedic treatment centre on the premises. **⑧**

Taj Residency PT Usha Rd ☎0495/276 5354, ⓦwww.tajhotels.com. The swankiest hotel in the city, northwest of the centre close to the seafront, though it lacks the usual *Taj* grandeur. There's a pool, coffee shop, multi-cuisine restaurant, and health and ayurvedic centre. From $150. **⑨**

The City

Barely any trace remains of the model fourteenth-century city laid down by the *zamorins*, which followed a Hindu grid formula based on a sacred diagram containing the image of the cosmic man, Purusha. The axis and energy centre of the diagram was dictated by the position of the ancient **Tali Shiva temple** (closed to non-Hindus), just south of MM Ali Road, which survives to this day. Everything, and everybody, had a place. The district around the port in the northwest was reserved for foreigners: the Chinese community lived in and around Chinese Street (now Silk Street) and the Portuguese, Dutch and British later occupied the area. Keralan Muslims (Moppilas) lived in the southwest. The northeast of the city was a commercial quarter, while the southeast housed the Tali temple, royal palace and fort; all but a couple of the military *kalaris* (martial art gymnasiums) that stood around the perimeter have now gone.

Kozhikode beach and Palayam market

Locals enjoy walking along the **city beach,** 3km west of the centre, in the late afternoon and early evening – especially on weekends. Although not suitable for swimming, it's a relaxing place, where you can munch on freshly roasted peanuts while scanning the sea for dolphins. The northern end towards the pier is distinctly more attractive than the southern stretch, which doubles as a lorry park. After dark it's difficult to find an auto-rickshaw to take you back into town, but there are regular buses.

Another good place for an aimless wander – if you can get there during the coolest, busiest time of day from 7am to 9am – is the fresh produce market in **Palayam**, next to the Palayam bus stand. Spilling into the backstreets around the **Mohiudeen Masjid**, it's a typically hectic north Keralan fruit and veg bazaar, with porters scurrying around balancing impossibly heavy loads of bananas, breadfruit, coconuts and watermelons on their heads.

The Kuttichira mosques

In pre-colonial times, the Malabar's maritime trade lay largely under the control of a class of wealthy Moppila merchants, originally descended from Arabian and Middle Eastern immigrants whom successive *zamorins*, in return for the weapons and horses they supplied to their armies, afforded protection. Tucked away in the Muslim quarter of the city, a cluster of traditional wooden mosques are the sole surviving monuments from this golden age. Unlike most of their counterparts elsewhere in the state – and in spite of Da Gama's repeated bombardments in the fifteenth and sixteenth centuries – they have retained their multi-tiered roofs, distinguished by gracefully angled teak beams, slatted screens and typically Keralan carved gables. Few foreigners ever set eyes on them, but Kozhikode's Moppila mosques rank among some of the most handsome antique buildings in southern India.

The three most impressive specimens lie off a backroad running through the **Kuttichira** quarter of **Thekkepuram**, 2km southwest of the *maidan* (all the auto-rickshaw-wallahs will know how to find them). Start at the 1100-year-old **Macchandipalli Masjid**, at the southern end of the lane leading from Francis Road to Kuttichira tank, whose ceilings are covered in beautiful polychrome stucco and intricate Qur'anic script. An engraved stone inside recounting the history of the thirteenth-century *zamorins* provided a valuable chronology for the region's historians. A couple of hundred metres further north, the **Juma Masjid**'s main prayer hall, large enough for a congregation of 1200 worshippers, dates from the eleventh century and holds another elaborately carved ceiling. The most magnificent of this trio of mosques, however, is the **Mithqalpalli** (aka **Jama'atpalli**) **Masjid**, at the northern end of the lane, hidden behind Kuttichira tank. Resting on 24 wooden pillars, its four-tier roof and turquoise exterior were built over 700 years ago. Opposite the eastern wall is a small information centre where you can obtain a leaflet about the neighbourhood and its monuments.

The museum and art gallery

The **Pazhassirajah and Krishnamenon Museum** (Tues–Sun 9am–4.30pm; Rs10) and **Art Gallery** (10am–5pm; free) stand together 5km north of the centre on East Hill, fringed by palm groves and lawned gardens that provide a breezy, shaded escape from the heat of the day. Copies of murals, coins, bronzes and models of the umbrella-shaped stone megalithic remains peculiar to Kerala dominate the museum's collection. The Art Gallery displays memorabilia associated with the left-wing Keralan politician V. K. Krishnamenon, along with works by Indian artists.

The building itself, named after the martyred local leader of the 1805 revolt against the East India Company, originally served as the residence of colonial Calicut's British Collector. In the Moppila uprising of 1921, it was the scene of a brutal murder when four of the revolt's ringleaders killed the local magistrate, H. V. Connolly.

CVN Kalari

Calicut district is renowned for its **kalarippayattu** gymnasiums, the most illustrious of which, CVN Kalari Sangan (☎0495/276 9114, ⓦwww.cvnkalarikerala.com), stands in the suburb of Nadakkavu, 2km north of the city centre. Established over fifty years ago by the father of the current Master, the centre enjoys

△ *Kalarippayattu* in action

an international reputation, with members regularly performing in Europe, the Middle and Far East. CVN Kalari's great claim to fame, however, is that it choreographed the combat scenes for the film *The Myth*, starring martial-arts supremo Jackie Chan. Visitors are welcome to watch demonstrations and lessons (details posted on the CVN website), though you'll have to get up at the crack of dawn to catch the more worthwhile of the two daily training sessions, held in the morning from 6am to 9am; evening sessions are for beginners and children. The centre also offers three- and six-month residential courses for those interested in learning the basics of the martial art and *marma chikitsa*, the specialist ayurveda massage technique used for *kalari* practitioners.

Shopping

What Kozhikode lacks in monuments it more than makes up for in **shops** – a consequence of the vast number of Gulf *riyals* and *dinars* flowing through the town. Around SM Street, a plethora of fabric and ready-made clothes shops sell locally produced cotton *lunghis*, many in unbelievably jazzy styles and shades. You cannot fail to be dazzled by the sheer number of gold jewellery emporia, full of ladies spending lavishly ahead of family weddings. This district is also a good place to try the local *halwa* sweets, especially popular with the large Moppila community. The **Kerala State Handicrafts** on MM Ali Road, next to the *Alakapuri Guest House*, stocks the usual collection of ordinary brass, bell metal and woodcarvings.

A more promising source of souvenirs is the **Tasara Creative Weaving Centre**, in Beypore North, 7km south of Kozhikode, just off the Kozhikode–Beypore Road. In a compound full of tropical flowers and plants, rugs, bedspreads and wall hangings are hand-woven in vibrant, contemporary designs that are refreshingly different from the traditional patterns found elsewhere in Kerala. Finely spun, non-violent silks (produced without killing the worm) are another speciality. Visitors are welcome to watch the artists at work, to view the art gallery (daily 9am–6pm; free) and buy the finished goods – prices range from $15 to $1000. You can study handloom techniques here, and try your hand at dyeing, batik and printing, under the tutelage of Mr Vasudevan Balakrishanan (☎0495/241 4832, Ⓦwww.tasaraindia.com). Short "Weaver Bird" courses last for five nights and four days, and cost $275; or you can stay for a month as an "artist in residence" for $1100. Prices include all meals, and accommodation in a stylish designer guesthouse with open-plan stairs and simple, high-ceilinged rooms off a central atrium.

Eating

Kozhikode is famous for its **Moppila cuisine**, which has its roots in the culinary traditions of the city's former Arab traders. Fragrant chicken biriyanis and seafood curries with distinctive Malabari blends of spices crop up on most non-veg restaurant menus, but to sample the definitive versions you should aim to have a least one meal in *Paragon* or *Zains* (or preferably both). **Mussels** are also big news here; deep-fried in crunchy, spicy millet coatings, they're served everywhere during the season, from October to December (if you order them at any other time, they'll have been imported and won't be as fresh). A great place to sample them, and other local snacks, is the *thattukada* market on Beach Road, a row of gas-lit Keralan fast-food stalls that whip up cheap meals through the night from 9pm until 4am. Finally, no Kozhikode feast is considered complete without a serving of the city's legendary **halwa**: a sticky Malabari sweet made from rice flour, coconut, *jaggery* (sugar cane) and ghee. It comes in a dazzling variety of Day-Glo colours and flavours. *The* place to try it has always been Mithai Theruvu, or **SM ("Sweet Market") St**, near the Palayam bus stand – though the survival of this atmospheric bazaar was in doubt after a devastating fire destroyed most of its businesses in April 2007; if the area's still not up and running, try *Nandhinee Sweets*, reviewed on below. For a quick pit-stop, there's also the perennially popular *Indian Coffee House*, which has two branches: one near the KSRTC bus stand on Mavoor (Indira Gandhi) Road; and the other further south, diagonally opposite the Palayam bus stand.

Dwaraka opposite *Sasthapuri Hotel*. A busy, down-to-earth non-veg diner where you can order inexpensive fresh mussels as well as masala-fried fish and local seafood curries.

Nandhinee Sweets MM Ali Rd. This is a hygienic place to sample the joys of Malabari *halwa*, nuts and savoury snacks; they also do great fresh fruit cocktails, *badam* milk and *falooda* shakes.

🏃 **Paragon** off the Kannur Rd. A short auto-rickshaw ride from the *maidan*, *Paragon* has been a city institution since it opened in 1939. Don't be put off by the uninspiring setting beneath a flyover or the somewhat hectic atmosphere: both are well worth enduring for the superb Malabari cooking. In a high-ceilinged dining hall with cast-iron columns, you can tuck into steaming plates of tamarind-tinged fish *moillee* or *the* house special, fish *kombathu*, mopped up with deliciously light *appam*, *parotta* and crumbly *pootu*. They also do plenty of veg options. Most mains Rs70–125.

Sagar next to the KSRTC stand, Mavoor Rd. Another old favourite of Calicut's middle classes, buried amid the high-rises and traffic mayhem of Mavoor Road. Ignore the generic North Indian-Chinese multi-cuisine menu; everyone orders proper Malabari dishes such as egg roast, fish korma and, best of all, the flavour-packed chicken *porichathu* – boneless chicken pieces marinated in ginger, garlic, green chillies and curry leaves, and then crisp fried.

🏃 **Zains** Convent Cross Rd. An unassuming, faded, pink-coloured family house in the west end of town is hardly what you'd expect the Holy Grail of Moppila cooking to look like, but the food served here is second to none. For the benefit of the uninitiated, the dishes of the day are displayed on a central table. There's generally a choice of biriyanis (fish, chicken or mutton), various fiery seafood curries, and a range of different *pathiris* – the definitive Malabari rice-flour bread, which can be steam-cooked, and flavoured with fish, shallow fried, dipped in egg or layered with coconut. Most mains Rs100–125.

Around Kozhikode

A couple of minor attractions – one to the north of town, one to the south – offer welcome respite from the traffic of central Kozhikode. Both **Kappad Beach**, a long, empty stretch of sandy coast that's changed little since Vasco da Gama first stepped onto it in 1498, and the **boatyards** of **Beypore**, where you can watch sea-going ships being built by hand out of wood, are accessible by bus from the city – though you'll reach them quicker if you can bear the bumpy ride by auto-rickshaw.

Kappad

KAPPAD BEACH, also known locally as Kappakadavu, a long stretch of golden sand and crashing surf 16km north of Kozhikode, is where – on May 27, 1498 – Vasco da Gama and his 170-strong crew made their first landfall in India after discovering the sea route around the Cape of Good Hope. This momentous event in the history of the Subcontinent is commemorated by a small plaque. Its historic associations aside, Kappad's refreshing breezes offer a pleasant escape from the mayhem of the city, and it's only a 45-minute journey away. **Buses** leave from Kozhikode's new Mofussil stand (platforms 8 or 9); you have to jump on one bound for Badagam, and get off at **Pookkal**, where local services and auto-rickshaws are on hand for the remaining 2km. The beach itself sees more fishermen than bathers, but it's safe for swimming and as yet relatively undeveloped, with only a handful of modest guesthouses and resorts providing food and accommodation to the few visitors (reviewed on pp.230–231).

Beypore

The coastal village of **BEYPORE**, 11km south of Kozhikode at the mouth of the Chaliyar River, is famous throughout Kerala for its ancient **shipyard** – one of only two in India where large, ocean-going vessels are still hand-made out of wood using traditional methods (the other is in Mandvi, Gujarat). Known in Malayalam as *paikappal* and in Arabic as *uru*, the ships are almost identical to those which transported *Haj* pilgrims, horses and trade goods across the Arabian Sea and down the east coast of Africa. These days, the few that are built here each year tend to be sold to wealthy Gulf Arabs as pleasure *dhows* or floating casinos. Visitors are, by prior arrangement, welcome to look around any that may be under construction in the handful of family-run workshops still open; contact Bichu & Co, 15/2093 South Beach Rd, Beypore, ✆ bichco@s.mail.com

More astonishing even than the industry's survival into the modern era is that the entire construction process, which can take anywhere from six months to two years depending on the size of the ship and number of shipwrights employed to build it, is seen through without any recourse to written plans. All the calculations are carried in the head of the yard master, or *maistri*, while the work – in typically Keralan fashion – is done by hand using skills and tools handed down through generations.

One of the great spectacles of the Malabar region is the sight of a newly finished *paikappal* being launched into the Chaliyar. Teams of specialist *khalasi* porters assemble for the task, which is completed by means of winches, pulleys, levers, lengths of steel and coir rope, and lots of shouting – an amazing achievement, given that an average ship put to sea from here will have required between 250 and 300 cubic metres of heavy jackwood, along with more than a tonne of nails and 100kg of brass fixtures.

The technical expertise of Beypore's *khalasis* was called upon under tragic circumstances on July 21, 2001, after a train bound for Chennai plunged off the nearby **Kadalundi Bridge** into the monsoon-swollen waters of the Chaliyar. Four carriages derailed and three were left dangling in the air, killing 64 people and injuring 300 more. The *khalasis* teamed up with navy divers to haul the wreckage from the river.

Wayanad

The hill district of **Wayanad**, situated 70km inland from Kozhikode at the southern limits of the Deccan Plateau, is one of the most beautiful regions of Kerala. Spread over altitudes of between 750m and 2100m, its landscapes vary from lush riverine rice paddy to semi-tropical savannah grasslands, from spice, tea and coffee plantations to steep mountainsides smothered in jungle. The few towns tend to be typically ramshackle Indian hill bazaars, which serve widely scattered satellite villages whose 200,000 or so inhabitants are mainly *adivasi* tribal peoples, dependent on low-paid seasonal crop picking, smallholding and wild food gathering. Due to the relative isolation and lack of decent roads, these minority communities – who include the Kurumbas, Adiyas, and Paniyas – have so far managed to preserve their traditional identities, despite the gradual intrusion of modernization.

The region's only formal visitor attraction is the **Wayanad Wildlife Sanctuary** – a park split into two separate zones, **Muthanga** and **Tholpetty**, both of which hug the Tamil border and form part of the sprawling Nilgiri Biosphere. For those with a little time on their hands, Wayanad makes a rewarding base from which to explore Kerala's northern hill tract, and one that's far less frequented than the Cardamom Hills around Periyar and Munnar further south.

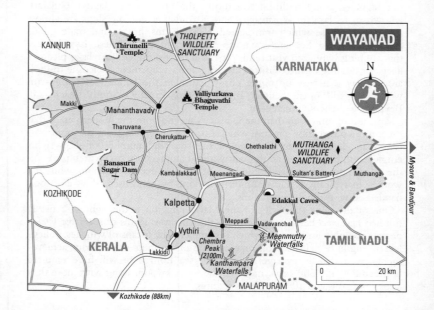

Travelling the 70km east from Kozhikode, a beautiful but tortuous road climbs a series of hairpin bends up the Southern Ghats through unspoiled forests, where macaques forage along the roadside, impervious to the groaning, diesel-belching trucks and buses going past. As the road arrives at the lip of the great plateau there are sweeping views back towards the coast of lush, green cover, and you can glimpse the sea in the hazy distance. On the highway to Mysore and Ooty, **Kalpetta**, the district headquarters, makes a good base from which to discover most of Wayanad, but **Mananthavady**, 27km from Kalpetta, is more convenient for exploring the northern jungles.

Kalpetta and around

Surrounded by plantations and rolling hills, the district's capital, **KALPETTA**, 72km east of Kozhikode, is a quiet market town with little to commend it except its pleasant location on the edge of the Muthanga Wildlife Sanctuary. Along with the settlement of **Vythiri**, 12km to the southwest, Kalpetta provides ample amenities and excellent walking country, including the spectacular **Chembra Peak** (2100m), the highest mountain in Wayanad.

The state **bus stand** in the centre of Kalpetta has connections to Kozhikode (72km; 2hr) and Mananthavady (27km; 1hr). **Auto-rickshaws** and **Jeeps** are available for local destinations. **Internet access** is available at Net World (Rs25/hr) next to the *Udupi Restaurant*, while the **Kerala Tourism Office** (Mon–Sat 10am–5pm, closed second Sat of each month; ☏04936/204441) is in Kalpetta North, 1km from the bus stand, in a building sharing space with the local DTPC information desk. The staff are extremely helpful and can assist with hiring **forest guides** (Rs50/day), and Jeeps (Rs8/km plus the Rs100 vehicle entrance fee) for those going to the wildlife sanctuary independently. The Mysore bus passes the **entrance** to Muthanga Sanctuary, near the scruffy town of **Sultan's Battery**.

Muthanga Wildlife Sanctuary

The southern portion of the Wayanad reserve, located 40km east of Kalpetta, is known as the **Muthanga Wildlife Sanctuary** (daily 6–10am & 3–5pm; Rs100, camera Rs25). Like nearby Bandipur National Park, in neighbouring Karnataka, the reserve, with its dry deciduous forests, is noted for elephants and also shelters deer, wild boar, bear and tiger. **Trekking** in the sanctuary is only allowed during the morning slot; hiring a (mandatory) guide for the three-hour official route costs Rs150. If you opt for the two-hour-long, 22-kilometre Jeep trip, you'll still have to pay for a guide (Rs100) as well as the Jeep rental (Rs250) and the vehicle's entry fee (Rs100).

The highway from Kalpetta to Mysore and Bandipur (via **Sultan's Battery**) passes through part of the sanctuary, and provides an opportunity, if you're lucky, to see wild elephants crossing the road on ancient migratory trails. **Buses** bound for Mysore and Bangalore (Bengaluru) run past the park gates, as do local services heading in the direction of Ponkuzhy.

Tholpetty

Forming the northern sector of the Wayanad reserve, **Tholpetty Wildlife Sanctuary**, 25km northeast of Mananthavady, is one of the best parks in South India to see elephants, as well as plentiful bison, boar, *sambar*, spotted deer, macaques and langurs; tigers also inhabit the park, though they are rarely spotted. The forest department lays on two-hour **Jeep safaris** into the park (daily 7–9am & 3–5pm), costing Rs300 for up to five people, with an additional Rs200 for the obligatory guide. You can also join guided treks (daily 8am–1pm;

Rs750 for up to four people). Taxis charge Rs300 for the trip from Manantha-vady to Tholpetty, or you can save a few rupees by taking one of the frequent KSRTC buses to Kutta, which will drop you off at the sanctuary entrance. Buses back to Mananthavady run until 8.45pm.

Accommodation is available just outside the park at *Pachyderm Palace* (book through the tourist desk in Kochi on ☏0484/237 1761; ⑦), a traditional Keralan bungalow with five comfortable rooms rented on an all-inclusive basis; the authentic Keralan cuisine is delicious, and a friendly welcome guaranteed.

Thirunelli and around

One of Wayanad's most celebrated temples, **Sree Thirunelli**, lies in a remote part of the district 32km north of Kalpetta, off the Kogadu road, in the hamlet of Thirunelli. Set in a serene mountain landscape with sweeping views, the temple is an unusual mix of Keralan tiled roofs and North Indian-style pillared halls. It is dedicated to the god Vishnu and is considered to be a *tirtha*, or crossing, between the mundane world and the divine. Devout pilgrims bathe in the nearby **River Papanasini**, which is said to absolve them of their worldly sins. Behind the temple you can see the end of a small stone aqueduct resting on beautifully carved pillars – part of an ingenious system which brings spring water from the nearby mountains.

More interesting still is the **Valliyurkava Bhagavathi temple**, an unassuming Keralan-style shrine dedicated to the goddess Durga, 8km east of Mananthavady. It serves as the principal shrine for Wayanad's *adivasi* (tribal) inhabitants, who gather here in numbers each year for a goddess festival in March/April – the event served as a major slave trade market until well into the twentieth century. The inner sanctum is closed to non-Hindus. **Accommodation** is available at the brand new, excellent-value *Panchatheertham Rest House* (☏04935/210055; ①) opposite the temple, which holds simple, clean and spacious rooms. A dozen buses daily connect Mananthavady to Thirunelli, either direct or via the village of Kartikulam. Mananthavady itself is a one-hour bus ride away from Kalpetta on KSRTC buses. Jeeps charge Rs400 for the run from Kalpetta.

Chembra Peak

At 2100m, **Chembra Peak** is the highest point in the Wayanad region, dominating the landscape for miles around. Carpeted on one side by soaring ridges and grassland and on the other by dense tropical forests, the massif can be tackled in around ten hours – a stiff physical challenge given the heat and humidity, but one that's amply rewarded with a stupendous view over Wayanad and, on clear days, out to the distant coast. The springboard for the climb is the small town of **Meppadi**, 18km south of Kalpetta and reachable on southbound buses passing through the main KSRTC stand (30min). Permission for the trek has to be applied for in advance at the Forest Range Office, 1km west of Meppadi. The permit is free, but you have to pay Rs10 to access the trailhead, situated on the Chembra Tea Estate, 7km away along a paved road, and arrange for one of the two forest rangers to accompany you (Rs200). Auto-rickshaws will do the trip to the trailhead for about Rs75–100. The recommended start time is 6am and all necessary arrangements should ideally be made a couple of days in advance.

Edakkal Caves

One of this region's more off-beat sights are the remote **Edakkal Caves** (daily 9am–5pm; Rs10), a prehistoric rock-art site lost in the forests adjoining the Tamil border. To get there by public transport you have to first head to Sultan's Battery,

△ Chembra Peak, Wayanad

24km east, and change there to a bus bound for Ambalavayal, which passes the turning for Edakkal. A mixture of auto-rickshaws (for the first 400-metre paved section) and Jeeps (for the remaining 2km) shuttle visitors to and from the ticket office. From here on, metal ladders and some exposed scrambling have to be negotiated on the climb up the cliff to the cave site – best undertaken in the morning while the route is still in shade. After all the excitement of the approach, the "caves" themselves come as something of an anti-climax. Gouged onto the inner flanks of two massive boulders wedged into the rock face, the much-photographed etchings comprise a mixture of geometric shapes and wild-haired anthropomorphic figures, thought to have been carved five thousand years ago. The only **accommodation** in the area is the *Edakkal Hermitage* (see p.240).

Meenmuthy and Kanthampara waterfalls

If the caves at Edakkal fail to live up to the promise of their dramatic approach, the same can't be said of the **Meenmuthy waterfalls**, 23km east of town off the Ooty road. Buses from Meppadi (see p.238) pass through the village of **Vadavanchal**, where you can pick up an auto-rickshaw for the fifteen-minute run out to the start of an enjoyable four-kilometre walk – the first 1500m of it an easy amble though picturesque coffee and tea plantations. The remaining leg follows an exhilarating, and at times steep, jungle path requiring strong shoes, plenty of drinking water and, in damp conditions, a stick of some kind. Allow an hour for the descent and two or three times that for the climb back. Crashing down 300m of grey-black granite in three distinct phases, the falls themselves are a thrilling sight and well worth the trek.

A softer and more accessible – but correspondingly less impressive – alternative to Meenmuthy are the **Kanthampara waterfalls,** a popular local picnic spot 22km southeast of Kalpetta. Buses from Meppadi will drop you at the turning, from where auto-rickshaws shuttle visitors to the car park at the head of the falls – although it's an easy and pleasant downhill stroll along tarmac, with fine views across coffee groves to the surrounding mountains. A footpath drops 250m from the car park to the falls themselves. At the bottom, you can also cross the river by means of three precarious-looking rope and bamboo footbridges to explore some beautiful forest on the far bank.

Accommodation and eating

Kalpetta and the nearby villages of **Vythiri** and **Lakkidi**, on the Kozhikode road, are fast emerging as low-key hill **retreats** in their own right, with a clutch of mostly upscale resorts and plantation stays catering for well-heeled metropolitan Indians and foreigners. Picking up on a trend that's paying dividends elsewhere in the mountains of the South, most are avowedly "green", though their much-touted eco-credentials don't always bear much scrutiny.

All of them provide quality regional **cuisine** along with accommodation, but if you're just passing through Kalpetta and in search of a pit-stop, the *Indian Coffee House*, opposite the tourist office, serves the usual South Indian snacks, rice-based meals and so-so filter coffee. The *Hotel New Palace*, south of the bus stand with its kitchen open to the street, is a favourite among Kalpetti families for its mainly non-veg North Indian dishes, vegetable biriyanis and delicious ghee rice; they also do rich Malabari-style curries made with local quail (*kada*).

Edakkal Hermitage near Edakkal Caves, Ambalavayal ☏04936/221860, ⓦwww .edakkal.com. Half-a-dozen pleasantly furnished cottages, with old floorboards and quality bathrooms, well spaced on small rock platforms overlooking a lawned garden to the valley, with breathtaking views down to the plains. An even more amazing panorama is to be had from their tree house, accessed via a rickety bamboo ladder, which literally sways in the wind as you sleep – an adventure in itself. The candle-lit restaurant occupies a man-made cave. ⑧

Green Gates TB Rd, Kalpetta North ☏04936/202001, ⓦwww.greengateshotel.com. Modern three-star hotel, tucked away in its own lush grounds 300m north of the tourist office, offering variously sized, differently priced rooms in the main multi-storey block, or more private cottages to its rear. There's a pool, plenty of chill-out space in the gardens, and an ayurveda centre. ⑦–⑧

Green Magic Vythiri book through: ☏0495/652 1163, ⓦwww.jungleparkresorts.com. Kerala's ultimate eco-resort, on a 500-acre site deep in the forest that's only accessible by 4WD (with the final 1.5km on foot). Dotted around the woods are various cottages and "villa rooms", but the benchmark accommodation is in luxury treehouses (from $250) nestled 20m off the ground under a lush rainforest canopy – you're winched to them on counterweight-pulley lifts. Energy sources include solar power and *gobar* (cow-dung) gas, and meals (included in the rates) are prepared from organically grown vegetables. Several forest trails lead out from the resort offering plenty of opportunities for guided walks; tours of the sanctuaries can also be arranged. ⑨

Harita Giri Emily Rd ☏04936/203145, ⓦwww .hotelharitagiri.com. A conventional hotel offering six

different grades of room (including singles), from budget to deluxe a/c suites; the site also contains a garden, restaurant, bar, rooftop terrace and good-sized pool. Rooms nearer the staircase tend to be noisier, particularly during weekends. ⑤–⑦

Rain Country Resort Lakkidi, 22km from Kalpetta ☏04936/251 1997, ☏m94470 04369, ⓦwww .raincountryresort.com. A 3km track takes you from the main road to a secluded pocket of greenery overlooking the Lakkidi valley, where eight beautifully reconstructed antique Keralan *tharavadukal*, culled from locations around the state, are scattered over a clearing in the forest. In front of them, pillared verandas equipped with cane furniture face a spring-fed pond, though the views are restricted by a natural balcony. There are plenty of walks in the immediate surroundings – staff are happy to accompany you. ⑧

Vythiri Resort booking at Kochi office ☏0484/4055250, ⓦwww.vythiriresort.com. Set in a lovely seven-acre woodland plot with three boulder-strewn mountain streams flowing through it, *Vythiri Resort* feels like a small jungle-hill village, down to the terracotta roofs, wood pillars and cable suspension bridge. Accommodation comes in three forms: cottages with private sitouts; beautifully refurbished plantation workers' rooms, with stone-lined plunge pools; and deluxe rooms in little double-floored blocks. Guided walks and visits to a nearby tea factory number among the complimentary extras, and there's a pool. Rates include full board. ⑧–⑨

Woodlands Kalpetta ☏04936/202547, ⓦwww.thewoodlandshotel.com. Comfortable, modern rooms (some a/c) at reasonable tariffs in a smart roadside hotel, conveniently located on a road just north of the bus stand. Courteous staff, ample parking and separate veg and non-veg restaurants. ⑤–⑦

The far north

A seemingly endless succession of near-deserted beaches, backed by palm-fringed lagoons and low, wooded hills spreads **north from Kozhikode**. This was one of the first parts of the Malabar to be targeted by early colonial prospectors, and wind-worn seventeenth- and eighteenth-century laterite forts punctuate the coast at regular intervals, dating from an era when the Portuguese, Dutch, British and various local rulers were vying for control of the pepper trade.

Typically Malabari fishing harbours, markets and Moppila mosques comprise the workaday charms of these former trading posts, the liveliest of them **Mahé**, an erstwhile French colony, and **Thalassery**, the first British garrison and port in the area. The main reason most tourists venture this far north, however, is to experience *theyyam* or *theyyattam*, the extraordinary masked spirit possession rituals staged in villages across the region between November and May. A couple of nights is all most visitors manage, but you'll considerably increase your chances of tracking down one or more rituals by staying a week. **Kannur**, another former colonial outpost, makes much the most appealing base, with a wider choice of accommodation than anywhere else in the area, including some beachside guest houses. Taxis are on hand in the town for the early morning departures to and from the remote villages where the ceremonies tend to be held, and to whisk visitors out to nearby **Parassinikadavu**, the only temple in Kerala hosting daily *theyyattam*.

Beyond Kannur, sights become thinner on the ground as the coastal highway and rail line approach the Karnatakan border. In this conservative, predominantly Moppila corner of the state, the rambling ruins of **Bekal Fort** are the number one weekend destination for locals, with laterite ramparts affording panoramic views of the gloriously empty beaches stretching away on both sides of it. To the south, the **Valiyaparamba backwaters** comprise a tangle of largely uninhabited creeks, islets and winding rivers served by a mere handful of houseboats.

Mahé

Clustered on a broad spit of land at the mouth of the Mayyazhi River, **MAHÉ**, 58km north of Kozhikode, became the French East India Company's first foothold on the northern Malabar Coast in 1721. The British factors at nearby Tellicherry were dismayed by the appearance on their doorstep of their Gallic rivals, and encouraged the local rulers to resist the incursion. But the French dug in and – by means of the timely arrival in 1725 of Admiral de Padaillon and his fleet, and some clever political manoeuvring – managed to hold on to the fort they erected overlooking the river mouth.

Opinion is divided over whether the town was renamed after **Bertrand François Mahé La Bourdonnais** – the legendary naval commander who served under de Padaillon during the 1725 recapture of Mahé and who later went on to play a vital role in the establishment of French interests in South India – or whether the commander added the name of the colony to his own in honour of the victory. Either way, it remained a French protectorate until 1954, since when the six-square-kilometre enclave has been administered as a Union Territory from France's principal former possession, Pondicherry, on the opposite coast of India in Tamil Nadu.

Mahé's colonial past is visible in the tumbledown remains of a fort, a handful of nineteenth-century Gothic churches and administrative buildings, and a statue of Marianne, symbol of the French Republic, in a park on the waterfront. But the most conspicuous legacy of French rule are the distinctive *képis* (military caps) still worn by local policemen, and an overwhelming number of **liquor shops** – Mahé's Union Territory status means lower excise duties on booze and fuel than the rest of Kerala. As a consequence, bus-loads of whisky-swilling men tend to inundate the town on weekends. The busiest time of year, however, is first fortnight of March when the area's temples stage exuberant *theyyattam* ceremonies during the annual **Puthalam Festival**.

The Town

Fringed on one side by dense palm groves and on the other by a white-sand beach (which is not safe for swimming), Mahé's most picturesque quarter fronts the river on the north side of town, where well-groomed public gardens line a waterside walkway from where you can watch the comings and goings of local boat traffic. Three-hour **dolphin-spotting trips** (daily 9am–6pm; Rs350) operate out of the government-run **Water Complex**, a kilometre or so stroll upriver, just before the big railway bridge. Tickets cost Rs350 for a minimum of ten passengers, or you can charter the whole boat for Rs350.

Barely discernible beneath its mantle of overgrowth, the ruined French East India Company's **St George's Fort** crowns a hillock on the north side of the river. The crumbling remains barely warrant the effort, but if you're determined, ask an autorickshaw to take you up to the TV relay station, from where one of the locals will lead you through a backyard to view the lone turret and fragment still standing.

En route, you could pay a visit to the **Malayala Kalagramam** (℡0490/223 2961; ⓦwww.malayalakalagramam.com), a renowned school of traditional performing arts 100m upriver from the town bridge. With prior permission from the Director, M.V. Devan – himself a nationally famous artist and critic – visitors are welcome to watch classes in dance, music, sculpture, mural painting, Malayali graphics and yoga. The centre, started in 1994 by a wealthy Chennai-based benefactor, also hosts a small art gallery and auditorium where performances by students and staff are occasionally staged.

Practicalities

Mahé is easily reachable by regular **buses** from Kannur and Kozhikode via NH-17, although there's no bus stand as such – services pull up at various points along the main street, Church Road. The **railway station**, 1500m southeast of the centre, lies on the main line and is served by seventeen daily express trains in both directions.

Accommodation options are limited, to say the least, and most visitors end up staying in nearby Thalassery. The best-presented and most welcoming of a pretty uninspiring bunch is *Zara Resorts* (℡0490/233 2503; ❹), on Railway Station Road, midway between the station and town centre, which has a choice of variously priced, recently upgraded rooms (some a/c) set in a laterite walled compound. There's a small family restaurant and an a/c bar on site. Cheaper fallbacks closer to the centre include the *Ashwathi Guest House* (℡0490/233 4475; ❷–❹), just off Maidan Road near the Syndicate Bank, which has mostly basic non-a/c doubles, and the similarly basic *Hotel Arena*, around the corner on Maidan Road (℡0490/233 7084; ❷–❹), 200m from the beach and riverfront.

Thalassery (Tellicherry)

THALASSERY, or "Tellicherry" as it was known in colonial times, was the linchpin of early British trade in pepper, cardamom and timber in the northern

Malabar, and the site of many a skirmish between the East India Company and its European rivals, not to mention their local Indian adversaries, the **Kolathiri** rajas. Built in 1708, the square **fort** erected by the British on a rocky bluff overlooking the waterfront still dominates the town. Its slanting ramparts witnessed particularly fierce action during the Mysore Wars at the end of the eighteenth century, and in the Pazhassi Revolts of the early nineteenth, when among the young defenders who distinguished themselves in battle was one Colonel Arthur Wellesley, the future Duke of Wellington. Aside from the old British stronghold, there's little here to warrant a detour, although the busy **fishing harbour** and an antique Moppila mosque – the stalwart **Odathil Palli Masjid** – hold plenty of local atmosphere. If you overnight here, you can also enjoy traditional hospitality and some famous regional cooking at the *Ayesha Manzil*, one of Kerala's top heritage homestays.

The Town

The massive walls of **St Joseph's Fort** (daily 8am–6pm; free) lord it over the fishing port and beach on the far western edge of town, a fifteen-minute walk west of the railway station. Visitors may wander around the gardens and (disused) lighthouse inside, and clamber over the ramparts for a view of the jetty below. But a better spot from which to appreciate the scale of the structure is the encircling path to the rear (follow the dirt path running anti-clockwise around the fort from its main gateway, past St Joseph's Boys School). In the old British cemetery behind stands the grave of Edward Brennan, an Englishman who was swept ashore after a shipwreck in the nineteenth century and liked the town so much he decided to stay. The school he eventually founded, Brennan College, now ranks among the Malabar's foremost educational institutions.

Thalassery's other illustrious expatriate was the German missionary **Dr Herman Gundert** (1814–93), credited with compiling the first ever English–Malayalam dictionary, and the publisher of Kerala's first newspaper. A scruffy little park next to the municipal stadium, behind the fort, holds a statue of the scholar, less well-known these days for his linguistic achievements than for being the grandfather of Nobel-Prize-winning novelist Herman Hesse.

The one other noteworthy monument in town, the **Odathil Palli Masjid**, is a striking Moppila mosque designed in typical hybrid Malabari style, with multi-tiered copper and tiled roofs, turquoise-painted slatted screens wrapped around its eaves and a gold-covered conical dome crowning its apex. The building, erected by a family of wealthy local Moppila merchants, the Keyis, stands in a palm-filled, walled enclosure close to the old bus stand at the bottom of town, just off the busy junction behind the fishing harbour.

Thalassery has long been an important centre of **kalarippayattu**, Kerala's own martial art (see p.100) and at the prestigious **CVN Kalari Kalarippay-attu** gymnasium in the suburb of Chirakava, 3km southeast of the fort near the Shri Rama Swami temple, you can (by prior arrangement) watch daily training sessions take place in a traditional earth-floored pit. During the dry season, these are held from 6.30am to 9am, while in the monsoons they run from 4.30pm to 9pm. Contact Mr Devadas, the *kalari gurukkal* (master), on ☎0490/232 0030 the day before your intended visit. A small donation of Rs50–100 for the students is welcome.

Practicalities

Thalassery is well connected by rail and road to Kozhikode and Kannur, and to most major towns in central and southern Kerala via the main Thiruvananthapuram–Mangalore line. Both the **railway station** and new

Narangapuran bus stand, where you'll be dropped if you arrive from Kozhikode or Kannur, lie on the east side of town, just over 1km northeast of the fort and beach. The usual welcoming committee of khaki-clad auto-rickshaw-wallahs is on hand at both to speed you down the hill, although you can cover the distance to the fort and fishing harbour on foot in around fifteen minutes.

Travellers' cheques and currency may be changed at the UAE Exchange (Mon–Sat 9.30am–6pm & 1.30–2pm, Sun 9.30am–1.30pm) on the first floor of the Sahara Centre, opposite Alukkas jewellery shop on A.V.K. Nair Road, a short rickshaw-ride or walk from the new bus stand or fort. The HDFC Bank **ATM** is in the same building. Cyber Guyz (Rs30/hr), near the *Paris Presidency* on Logan's Road, offers **Internet access**: to find it, turn right out of the *Paris Presidency* (see below), head east for 50m and take the first right – the centre is on the first floor of the large building immediately on your right-hand side.

For authentic non-veg Moppila **food**, including Thalassery's famous biriyanis and freshly fried *kallmakaya* (mussels), try the rough-and-ready *Paris Hotel*, down a lane off Logan's Road. It's almost next door to the *Paris Presidency*, whose a/c dining hall is the poshest place to eat in the town centre, serving North Indian, Chinese and continental main courses from around Rs75–200. Traditional Keralan rice-plate meals are served at the *Hotel Adhitya* on Gundert Road, opposite the fort. The *Indian Coffee House* near the old bus stand is another popular, dependable vegetarian option, as is the slightly smarter *Udipi* at the top of Logan's Road, not far from the new bus stand, which serves the usual range of tasty South Indian snacks and meals.

Accommodation

Accommodation in Thalassery is plentiful and good value, although, with the exception of the *Ayesha Manzil*, few places see more than the occasional tourist.

Ayesha Manzil Court Rd, opposite Sea View Park, ℡0490/234 1590, ⓔcpmoosa@rediffmail.com. Former British bungalow, built in the 1860s by an East India Company trader and cinnamon exporter atop a hillock on the outskirts of town, and later converted by its present Moppila owners into a splendid heritage homestay. Filled with carved wood furniture and other family heirlooms, the rooms (all attached) are huge, airy and comfortable. Host Mr C. P. Moosa and his wife, Malabari cooking expert Faiza, enjoy sharing their knowledge of the area and its culture with guests: come for a week and you can follow Faiza's famous cookery course. Tariffs ($200 for two full-board) include the use of a temple-style swimming pool, free transfers to nearby Muzhipirangad beach and superb local cuisine, served on a garden terrace looking out to sea. ❻

Paris Presidency Logan's Rd ℡0490/234 2666, ⒻR0490/234 3666, ⓦwww.parispresidency .com. Dependable mid-range option, bang in the centre of town just off busy Logan's Road, within easy walking distance of the fort. The rooms are large, though slightly worn – those at the back are quieter. ❸–❺

Pearl View Regency Kannur Rd ℡0490/232 6702, ⓦwww.pearlviewregency.com. The smartest hotel in Thalassery and the first choice of local business clients, with 52 rooms, ranging from compact standard doubles to large pool-facing "cottages", spread over six storeys and landscaped gardens on the edge of town. Ask for one with a view of the beautiful Kuyani River to the rear. ❺–❻

Kannur (Cannanore)

KANNUR (Cannanore), a small, run-of-the-mill market town 92km north of Kozhikode, was for many centuries the capital of the Kolathiri rajas, who prospered from the thriving maritime spice trade through its port. India's first Portuguese Viceroy, Francisco de Almeida, took the stronghold in 1505, leaving in his wake an imposing triangular bastion, **St Agnelo's Fort**. This was annexed in the seventeenth century by the Dutch, who sold it for one *lakh* rupees a hundred or so years later to the Arakkal rajas, Kerala's only ruling Muslim dynasty. They in turn were ousted by General Abercrombie's East India Company troops, who besieged the citadel in 1790, forcing the Arakkals' female ruler, Ali Raja Beebi, to sign a treaty of dependency.

These days, the town sees very little through-traffic, but makes a pleasant place to stopover on the northern Malabar, not least because it holds one of the region's most pleasant guesthouses, *Costa Malabari* – an ideal base from which to venture into the hinterland in search of *theyyattam* rituals.

The Town

Kannur town has two main centres of gravity: the area of busy streets and shops outside the railway and bus stations, where most travellers arrive; and "Moppila Bay", a kilometre or so to the south, dominated by the

Theyyattam around Kannur

Theyyattam (or *theyyam*), the dramatic spirit possession ceremonies held at village shrines throughout the northern Malabar region in the winter months, rank among Kerala's most extraordinary spectacles. Over four hundred different manifestations of this arcane ritual exist in the area around Kannur, each one with its own distinctive costumes, make-up, music and atmosphere.

Increasing numbers of visitors are making the journey up to Kannur to experience *theyyattam*, but **finding it** can be a hit-and-miss affair, requiring time, patience and, because many of the ceremonies run through the night, considerable stamina. The best source of advice is the local tourist information centre at the railway station (see p.246), who will be able to consult the daily *Malayala Manorama* on your behalf: notices of forthcoming performances are listed at top left of page two. Alternatively, stay at *Costa Malabari* (see p.247), whose management are *theyyattam* experts. Anyone pushed for time might also consider a trip out to **Parassinikadavu** (see p.247), where a form of *theyyattam* is staged daily.

Wherever you end up travelling to watch this uniquely Keralan phenomenon, it's worth bearing in mind that for local people, *theyyattam* rituals are far more than mere theatre. *Theyyams* are considered actual manifestations of gods or goddesses, and their appearance in the ritual arena, in front of a rapt crowd, is always an event of great religious intensity and significance. As a foreigner, you'll usually be welcome to attend, but should conduct yourself as you would on any other sacred occasion: dress respectfully, with legs, shoulders and arms covered (no shorts or knee-length skirts); never smoke or eat in the presence of the deity or around the temple or shrine; and refrain from drawing attention to yourself by talking loudly, moving around or pointing (if you turn up in a group, it can also be a good idea to disperse and blend in rather than stay bunched together).

Theyyattam ceremonies always have one main coordinator (usually seated at a table), and on arrival it's a good idea to ask him where the best place is for you to position yourself during the performance. Certain key areas exist where non-Hindus, in particular, will be less than welcome, and these might not be obvious to the uninitiated. The coordinator will also be able to tell you if it's OK to photograph the *theyyams* – it generally is, but bear in mind that flashes can be very distracting. If you have a digital camera, use high ISO settings instead.

Finally, try to **stay until the end**. As *theyyattam* rituals invariably last all night, culminating at dawn, this isn't always easy, but it will demonstrate that you appreciate the religious importance of the event. Leaving a **donation** (of Rs50–100) will also be much appreciated as *theyyattam* ceremonies can be expensive to organize. For more background on the tradition, see "Contexts", p.297.

fishing harbour and its adjacent citadel. Accessed through a gateway on its northern side, **St Agnelo's Fort** (daily 8am–6pm) remains in good condition and is worth visiting to scale the massive laterite ramparts, littered with British cannon, for views over the town's massive Norwegian-funded fishing anchorage.

The small **Arakkal Museum** (Tues–Sun 10am–6pm; Rs25), on the seafront opposite the entrance to the "Moppila Bay" fishing anchorage, below the fort, displays documents, weapons, various pieces of 400-year-old rosewood furniture and other heirlooms relating to the family's history – though the building itself, with its high-beamed ceilings and original floorboards, is more engaging than the exhibition. Other remnants of the Arakkals' former palace survive in the heritage district to the rear, **Arakkal Kettu,** many of whose dilapidated, red-tiled *tharavadukal* are fronted by long, pillared verandas and intricately carved doors. Five times daily, the *muezzin* reverberates from the prayer tower of the former royal mosque, the **Arakkal Masjid**, immediately behind the museum (not open to visitors).

A gentle half-hour walk around the headland to the northwest of St Agnelo's fort brings you to quiet **Baby Beach**, behind the *Government Guesthouse* in the army's cantonment area (daily access 9am–5pm), where a leafy seaside promenade (Rs2) leads to a lighthouse (open daily 3–5pm; Rs5), with fine views of the rocky coastlines and distant beaches. However, the most popular destination among local people for a stroll and splash in the surf is **Payyam-balam Beach**, a long stretch of white sand 4km north of town. The crowds that converge here on evenings and weekends can be sidestepped by walking further north: the empty sands come to an end after 4km at a headland, on the far side of which lies grim **Meankunnu Beach**.

Practicalities

Straddling the main coastal transport artery between Mangalore and Kochi/Thiruvananthapuram, Kannur is well connected by **bus** and **train** to most major towns and cities in Kerala, as well as Mangalore in Karnataka. The **railway station** is just over five minutes' walk southwest of the bus stand. The State Bank of India on Fort Road will **change money** and travellers' cheques, as will UAE Exchange in the City Centre Shopping complex (Mon–Sat 9.30am–1.30pm & 2–6pm), 500m east of the bus stand. There's a helpful **tourist information centre** at the railway station (Mon–Sat 10am–5pm; ☎0497/270 3121) where you can find out about impending *theyyattam* rituals. **Internet access** is widely available; try the air-conditioned Padinharakandy (Rs30/hr), 150m south of the pink City Centre Shopping building on Fort Road, or MetroNet (Rs20/hr), opposite in the Metro Hyper-market centre.

For inexpensive **food** there's an *Indian Coffee House* in Fort Road, 50m south of City Centre Shopping. Just behind the City Centre Shopping building, the trendy *Can Café* has a good selection of biriyanis as well as other inexpensive Malabari chicken and fish dishes. Like Kozhikode, Kannur is also famous for its **sweet shops**; local specialities sold in the many outlets dotted along Station Road include *kinnathappam* and *kalathappam* cakes, made with rice flour and *jaggery*.

Accommodation

Travellers hoping to track down *theyyattam* tend to stay at *Costa Malabari* while they're in this part of state, but there are plenty of other good options in town if it's full or beyond your budget.

Costa Malabari 10km south near Tottada village; book through the tourist desk in Kochi: ⊕0484/237 1761, ⓦwww.costamalabari .com. Hidden deep in cashew and coconut groves, this welcoming guesthouse, run by one of the region's most knowledgeable *theyyam* afficionados, has five airy and comfortable rooms. Five pristine beaches lie within 10min walk, and guests are plied with huge portions of excellent Keralan food (included in the rate). They also run good off-track backwater and wildlife trips in the region. Pick-up from Kannur (Rs150) by prior arrangement. ❺

Government Guesthouse Cantonment area ⊕0497/270 6426. Superb-value government-run place on a clifftop at the edge of town, with huge, simple a/c and non-a/c rooms whose huge balconies have uninterrupted sea views; it's primarily for visiting VIPs but usually has a few vacancies. Advance booking can be a problem; ring ahead when you arrive. Inexpensive vegetarian meals on request. ❷–❹

Malabar Residency Thavakkara Rd ⊕0497/276 5456. Smart, central hotel with comfortable attached a/c rooms, two restaurants, including the multi-cuisine *Grand Plaza*, and a 24hr coffee shop. ❺

Mascot Beach Resort 300m before Baby Beach ⊕0497/270 8445, ⓦwww.mascotresort.com. Perched on the rocky shoreline, offering large a/c rooms and cottages with views across the cove to the lighthouse. Facilities include a swimming pool, foreign exchange and a good restaurant – but no bar. ❺–❼

Meridian Palace Bellard Rd ⊕0497/270 1676, ⓦwww.hotelmeridianpalace.com. Only two blocks from the station, this compact hotel has a wide range of comfy, clean rooms and a popular little restaurant serving veg and local seafood meals. ❷–❺

Sweety International 200m north of railway station, near Munisheeran Kovil ⊕0497/270 8283. Standard economy high-rise with ordinary, "executive" and a/c rooms, all pretty decent value. ❷–❸

North of Kannur

The only place in Kannur district where you can be almost guaranteed a glimpse of *theyyattam* is the village of **Parassinikadavu**, half-an-hour's drive north, where temple priests don elaborate costumes, dance and make offerings to the God Muthappan each morning and evening. Heading further up the coast, two other spots that might tempt you to break a long journey towards the border with Karnataka include the beautiful backwaters of **Valiyaparamba**, whose lagoons remain almost untouched by tourism, and **Bekal Fort**, where you can walk along some impressive ramparts overlooking miles of empty coast.

Parassinikadavu

The **Parassini Madammpura** temple in the village of **PARASSINIKA-DAVU**, 20km north of Kannur beside the River Valapatanam, is visited in large numbers by Hindu pilgrims for its *theyyattam* rituals, enacted twice daily (6.30–8.30am & 5.45–8.30pm) before assembled worshippers by the resident priest, or *madayan*. Elaborately dressed and accompanied by a traditional drum group, he becomes possessed by the temple's presiding deity – Lord Muthappan, Shiva, in the form of a *kiratha*, or hunter – and performs a series of complex offerings. The two-hour ceremony culminates when the priest/deity dances forward to bless individual members of the congregation – all in all, an extraordinary spectacle, even for Kerala.

Regular local **buses** leave Kannur for Parassinikadavu from around 7am, dropping passengers at the top of the village. If you want to get there in time for the dawn *theyyam*, however, you'll have to splash out on one of the Ambassador taxis that line up outside Kannur bus stand (around Rs400 round trip). Cabbies sleep in their cars, so you can arrange the trip on the spot by waking one up; taxis may also be arranged through most hotels. Either way, you'll have to leave around 4.30am. Alternatively, stay in the conveniently located *Thai Resort* (⊕0497/278 4242; ❺–❻) 80m from the temple (to the left as you face the entrance). Shaded by coconut trees, seven circular stone cottages are dotted around a well-kept garden, with cool, comfortable rooms. If you've come for the morning performance and have a few hours to spare afterwards, one possibility for an excursion is to take a bus from Parassinikadavu to **Trichambaram temple**, a magnificent piece of traditional architecture dedicated to Krishna, with tiered clay roofs and slatted wooden walls. A smaller temple nearby, no more than a puja room surrounded by a water moat, is devoted to Durga Devi. Buses from Parassinikadavu take fifteen minutes, and drop you at a junction 800m from the temple complex.

Valiyaparamba

For the ultimate antidote to the traffic fumes and crowded streets of the Malabar's market towns and cities, press on 50km north of Kannur to one of the quietest stretches of coast in the state. Edged by a thin sliver of white sand and coconut trees, the **Valiyaparamba backwaters** – often misleadingly dubbed "the northern backwaters" – centre on a small, thirty-kilometre delta fed by four rivers whose various bands and tributaries form a tangle of inland lakes, creeks and winding lagoons speckled with tiny islets. Kuttanad it most assuredly isn't: Valiyaparamba holds comparatively few permanent dwellings and traffic on its waterways largely consists of country fishing boats. All the same, it makes a wonderful region for off-track explorations, not least because of the almost total absence of other tourists.

At present, only one firm runs **houseboat cruises** in the area. Based on the northern edge of the backwaters area, Bekal Boat Stay (℡0467/228 2633, Ⓦwww.bekalboatstay.com) has a total of four canopied *kettu vallam* for hire, with bed space for a maximum of four passengers. Prices start at Rs4000 for a day-cruise, or Rs6000 for 24 hours, inclusive of all meals. Shorter sunset and dinner trips are also available.

Practicalities

The most convenient springboard for independent forays into Valiyaparamba is the boat jetty at **Kottapuram**, a hamlet on the riverside 2km south of **NILESWARAM** village, 60km north of Kannur on the national highway. Buses from Kannur and Kozhikode stop at **Nileswaram**, a crossroads bazaar just east of the main road, more frequently than do trains – the nearest station for express rail services is Kasaragode 40km further north. Auto-rickshaw-wallahs wait around the bus stand to shuttle arrivals to the riverside jetty at Kottapuram, from where sporadic local ferries and canoes fan out to islands further afield. A 300-metre **footbridge** – the longest of the kind in the state – connects Kotta-puram with the island of Acham Thuruthi opposite.

Apart from the *Gitanjali Heritage* near Bekal (see opposite), the only **accommodation** in this area to speak of is the *Nalanda Resorts* (℡0467/228 2662; ❺–❼) in Nileswaram. Comprising five traditional-style cottages (a/c and non-a/c) set in a couple of acres of landscaped gardens, the riverside resort enjoys an idyllic setting, only slightly marred by the proximity of the highway and road bridge. The rooms themselves, with terracotta-tiled floors, wood-panelled ceilings and little verandas facing the river, are smart and comfortable, and there's a restaurant on site serving local specialities in addition to the usual multi-cuisine menu.

Bekal

Just 7km north of the town of Kanhangad, **BEKAL** is popular amongst Indians as a destination for a weekend day-trip, with a **fort** (daily 8am–5pm; Rs100) standing on a promontory between two long, classically beautiful

△ Bekal Fort

palm-fringed **beaches** (swimming is safe, but dress in suitably modest gear to avoid causing offence). Although this is one of the largest fortresses in Kerala and has been under the control of various powers including Vijayan-agar, Tipu Sultan and the British, it's nothing to get excited about. Heat haze permitting, the bay views from the bastion are impressive enough, but the vast *maidan* inside the walls is a hot and dry wasteland – hardly deserving of the stiff admission fee.

A short walk beyond the main entrance to the fort, you'll find the friendly *Bekal Resorts Development Corporation (BRDC)* **tourist office** (Mon–Sat 9.30am–5pm; ℡0944/779 3815), which can point visitors in the direction of local *theyyattam* performances and houseboat hire in the nearby Valiyaparamba backwaters area.

A lovely homestay in this area is the *Gitanjali Heritage* (℡0467/223 4159, ⓦwww.gitanjaliheritage.com; $100 per person full-board, ⑨), 7km inland (to the southeast) from Bekal in the sleepy village of Panayal. Tucked away in a coconut grove near the 2000-year-old Shiva temple, the 70-year-old house has three simple rooms, furnished in traditional Keralan style, with bent-cane chairs, wooden ceilings and slatted windows. The organic vegetable garden supplies owner Mr Jaganath's kitchen with fresh produce year round. This is also a good base from which to experience the area's *theyyattam* rituals.

Travel details

Buses

Kozhikode to: Kannur (every 30min; 2–2hr 30min); Kochi/Ernakulam (hourly; 5hr); Mysore (2 daily; 9–10hr); Thiruvananthapuram (12–15 daily; 11–12hr); Thrissur (hourly; 3hr 30min–4hr).

Thrissur to: Guruvayur (10 daily; 40min); Kochi/Ernakulam (every 10min; 2hr); Kozhikode (every 30min; 2hr 30min); Palakkad (every 20min; 2hr); Thiruvananthapuram (every 20min; 7–8hr).

Flights

For a list of airline websites, see pp.22–23. In the listings below IA is Indian Airlines and AIE Air India Express.

Kozhikode to: Kochi/Ernakulam (IA, AIE 2–3 daily; 30min); Thiruvananthapuram (IA, AIE 1–2 daily; 50min).

NORTHERN KERALA | Travel details

Contexts

Contexts

History

The most radical upheavals in Indian history have always tended to emanate from the far northwest. The Khyber Pass, dividing the steppes of central Asia from the fertile Gangetic plains, served time and again as a gateway to invaders who transformed the societies they conquered with new religions, weapons, art forms, languages and sensibilities. These influences did, over the centuries, percolate southwards, crossing the Deccan plateau and the Vindhya mountains to reach the tropical tip of the peninsula. But they tended to do so slowly, by a process of gradual absorption rather than at the point of the sword.

Insulated by distance, the Dravidian culture that held sway in the distant region now known as Kerala evolved along its own distinct trajectory. What major changes did come invariably blew in from the ocean. For thousands of years, merchants, adventurers, religious refugees and colonizers crossed the Arabian Sea to trade in spices and settle on the so-called "**Malabar Coast**", giving rise to one of the most heterogeneous cultures in the ancient world. The ways of life they imported, however, over-layered an indigenous society with amazingly resilient roots – roots that can be traced back not just to the earliest phases of recorded history in India, but, in some cases, to the very beginnings of Asian civilization itself.

Prehistory

Archeologists are still debating the chronology of the Keralan **Prehistoric** period. **Megalithic monuments** – dolmen burial chambers, cists, "umbrella" standing stones and rock-cut caves – litter the state, grouped mostly in the mountains. But they probably date from a much more recent era than their appearance would suggest. Most, including the elaborately decorated **Edakkal Caves** in Wayanad (see p.238), could only have been made with the help of iron implements, which came comparatively late to the far south of the Subcontinent: around the middle of the second millennium BC.

It is, however, widely agreed that there were hunter-gatherers in southwest India long before the arrival of metal tools, and that their descendants are the aboriginal *adivasi* tribals who live to this day in the forested areas of the Western Ghats. The physical appearance of some of these tribes, such as the Kadar, Mutuvans and Iralis of Wayanad district, suggests Asian-Negrito origins. Quite how aboriginal travellers with primitive technologies were able to cross the Andaman Sea tens of thousands of years ago remains a matter of conjecture, but cross the ocean they did – genetic research on some of the indigenous peoples of the Andaman Islands, who share similar black skin and peppercorn hair, have shown ancestral connections with Papuan and aboriginal Japanese populations.

Metal, and knowledge of **rice cultivation**, were probably first imported into South India from the northwest, where the sophisticated civilization of the **Indus Valley** – the region straddling the present-day India–Pakistan border – was already well established by 3000 BC. Paleo-botanical studies have shown that a sharp rise in rainfall occurred around this time, which probably explains why farming was able to flourish and cities emerge. The inhabitants of **Harappa** and **Mohenjo Daro**, large urban centres which reached their peaks between

2300 and 1800 BC, were certainly experts in the management of water. Huge communal granaries stored the surplus grain that underpinned a flourishing foreign trade, and the existence of palaces and spacious houses shows that this was a highly stratified society, with its own script and formalized religion.

Current archeological thinking holds that prolonged drought, rather than invasions, caused the eventual decline of the Indus Valley civilization. Over time, as rainfall decreased and agricultural output dropped, the impoverished inhabitants of the Indus plains drifted southward in search of more fertile land, taking their tools, language and religious beliefs with them.

The Dravidians

Some historians have advanced this migration theory to account for the origins of the **Dravidians**, who are believed to have colonized the southwest of India around 1800 BC – the same time the Indus Valley civilization went into decline. The most compelling evidence that the Dravidians originated in the northwest – and were, in fact, descended from the peoples of the Indus Valley – is linguistic. Malayalam and Tamil – the principal modern languages of South India – have completely different roots from the main languages of the North, which derive from the Indo-Aryan group, brought to India by invaders from central Asia, and are based principally on Sanskrit. Over the years, some wild comparisons have been made between Dravidian and other Asian tongues (notably Japanese), but the only surviving Asian language with definite Dravidian antecedents is Brahui, spoken by the nomadic people of the Baluchistan uplands on the Iran–Pakistan border. This suggests that the Dravidians almost certainly came from the Baluchi grasslands in the fourth or third millennium BC, via the Indus Valley, where they developed the metalwork and

The Rig Veda

Between 1800 and 1700 BC, after the disappearance of the Indus Valley cities, a wave of chariot-riding invaders, calling themselves the **Aryas** or **Aryans**, swept onto the Gangetic plains of northern India from the northwest. Most of what is known about these aggressive newcomers derives from an extraordinary body of literature called the **Rig Veda**, a vast compendium of 1028 hymns, epic chants, spells, songs and instructions for religious rituals composed between 1500 and 900 BC, and transmitted orally until they were set down in writing in the medieval era.

The Aryans' sacred scriptures contain a wealth of detail about their daily life, philosophical ideas and religious practices. Frequent references to Agni, the "God of Fire", and Indra, the "Fort Breaker", are indicative of violent encounters with the indigenous inhabitants of northern India, known as **Dasa** or **Dasyus**, literally "dark-skinned ones" or "slaves". They were "rich in cattle", knew how to work gold, built forts and towns and spoke a different language from the Aryans, who evidently disapproved of the fact they were also *sisna-devi*, "phallus worshippers". The *Rig Veda* implies a long spell of intermingling between the Aryans and Dasa, but over time the latter were swept aside as the invaders expanded eastwards in the middle of the second millennium BC. These conquests were facilitated by the Aryans' use of horse-drawn, spoke-wheeled **chariots**, an incomparably fast and effective way of crossing the dry plains.

By the dawn of the **Iron Age** early in the first millennium BC, the dominion of the Aryans, by now a loose confederacy of tribes who fought each other as much as their indigenous enemies, stretched south as far as the Vindhya Range and the rich soils of the Deccan Plateau. Beyond lay the wild unexplored territory of **Dakshinapatha**, "the Way South" – the route taken by the Dravidian peoples the Aryans had displaced.

farming techniques that subsequently allowed them to establish permanent settlements in the far south.

One Hindu myth often interpreted as some kind of transmission from this distant age is the story of **Parasurama**, the axe-wielding sixth incarnation of the God Vishnu. As a reward for defeating the Kshatriya warrior caste, it is said that Varuna, God of the Oceans, and Bhumidevi, Goddess of the Earth, granted Parasurama any land that could be encompassed by a throw of his axe from Kanyakumari, India's southernmost point. From the place where the axe fell, the waters receded and Parasurama Kshetra ("Parasurama's Country") was formed. The legend may well reflect the massive elevation of southwest India's seaboard that occurred sometime between 12,000 and 10,000 BC, and the intensive reclamation, drainage work and forest clearance carried out in its wake (*parasura* means "axe") by the first farmers of the Malabar Coast.

Early trade and the Ay Kingdom

The essentially agrarian economies of the Dravidians were, like their Harappan forerunners in the northwest, supplemented by trade in **luxury goods** such as shells, precious stones and pearls. Teak found in the third- and second-millennium BC ruins of the Mesopotamian city of Ur, in present day Iraq, almost certainly came from the Malabar Coast and both the ancient Egyptians and Phoenicians crossed the Arabian Sea to acquire sandalwood, pepper, cinnamon and other spices. In the Old Testament, King Solomon is said to have sent ships every three years to the port of Orphyr (thought have been at Poovar, south of modern day Kovalam) to buy silver, gold, ivory, monkeys and peacocks.

This maritime trade expanded steadily over the centuries, enabling the region's chiefs to extend their rule inland and create larger settlements away from the coast. Among the first dynasties to emerge as overlords in the region were the **Ay Kings**, whose domain stretched from the backwaters region of Kuttanad down to the tip of peninsula India, where they waged constant wars with the Pandya rulers of the Tamil lowlands to the east. Ancient Pandyan texts say their adversaries' lands, administered from their capital at Vizhinjam (where some Ay rock carvings survive; see p.115) were "fertile and teemed with elephants". One of the Ay's most illustrious rulers, Antiran, was the first of many Keralan rajas to use the elephant as his royal emblem.

The Sangam age: 00–500AD

A huge storehouse of historical detail relating to the early kingdoms of Kerala has survived in a remarkable body of classical Tamil poetry known as the **Sangam**, composed between the first and third centuries AD in the literary academies (*sangam*) of Madurai, in modern-day Tamil Nadu. The texts, which were only rediscovered in the nineteenth century, refer to an era when the indigenous Dravidian culture of the deep south was being transformed by Sanskritic influences from the North. Nevertheless, they vividly demonstrate that some of the most distinctive characteristics of Keralan civilization – including yoga, Tantra, the cult of the god Murugan and goddess worship – were almost certainly indigenous to the South, and widespread well before the arrival of the Aryans.

The first five centuries of the Christian Era, known to Indian historians as the **Sangam Age**, were dominated by a dynasty whose lineage would ripple in various incarnations across more than a thousand years of Keralan history: the **Cheras**. From their capital **Vanchimutur**, or **Vanchi**, in the watery lowlands of Kuttanad, these expansionist kings spread their rule east into the mountains and northwards up the Malabar Coast. Their well-equipped armies comprised infantry, cavalry, chariots and elephant brigades, backed up by a formidable fleet of warships. Roads crisscrossed their territories, which were patrolled by a prototypical police force of watchmen. Under the patronage of successive Chera kings and their regional tributaries, the arts also flourished, particularly poetry, dance and music, as did private property ownership, agriculture and knowledge of herbal medicine. Although different classes existed within society, caste was non-existent, and the status and freedoms accorded women were high.

As for **religious practices**, the *Sangam* makes it clear that the people of ancient Kerala followed old Dravidian forms of worship, venerating totemic gods and spirits residing in trees, rivers, hills and other natural features of the landscape. It is likely that *theyyattam* and other similar rituals still practised in many parts of Kerala, and now absorbed into Brahmanical Hindu mythology, are vestiges of these.

Other more formal religions, however, are known to have co-existed with the indigenous Dravidian traditions. From the third century BC, India – with the exception of the unconquered South – was controlled by the **Mauryan empire**, whose state religions were first **Jainism** and, later, **Buddhism**. Evidence that both took root in Kerala survives in many Sangam texts and in the region's architectural heritage. Many Hindu temples seem to have been built over foundations of Jain or Buddhist monasteries, and sculpture fragments dating from Chera times are scattered across the region to this day. Only with the spread of Brahmanical Hinduism across the South from the seventh century onwards did these two great faiths go into decline; in modern Kerala they've since died out altogether.

The expansion of trade

The prosperity of the Sangam era under the Cheras – and cultural flowering that flowed from it – were stimulated not merely by the spoils of military conquest, but by a rapid growth in **maritime trade**, from which the kings raked handsome taxes. Only a few kilometres inland from the Chera capital, Vanchi, lay one of the richest ports in the ancient world, **Muziris**. As well as Phoenician and Arab merchants, the Cheras' harbour supplied fleets of **Roman** ships. After a century of relentless civil war, peace had returned to Rome by the middle of the first century BC, bringing with it renewed demand in the imperial capital for luxury goods such as pearls, spices, perfumes, precious stones and silk. Augustus's conquest of Egypt (opening up the Red Sea) and Hippalus's discovery that the monsoon winds would blow a ship across the Arabian Sea in forty days brought the means to supply this appetite within the Romans' grasp.

A vivid picture of the boom that ensued has survived in an extraordinary mariners' manual entitled the *Periplus of the Erythraean Sea*, written in the middle of the first century AD by an anonymous Alexandrian merchant-adventurer. Featuring meticulous descriptions of the trade, ports and capital cities of India's far south, it reveals that Muziris was the main trading point for valuable foreign goods – notably Chinese silk and oil from the Gangetic basin – and the principal warehouse for locally grown spices, including pepper, ginger, turmeric, cardamom and cinnamon. So great were the sums spent by the Romans on

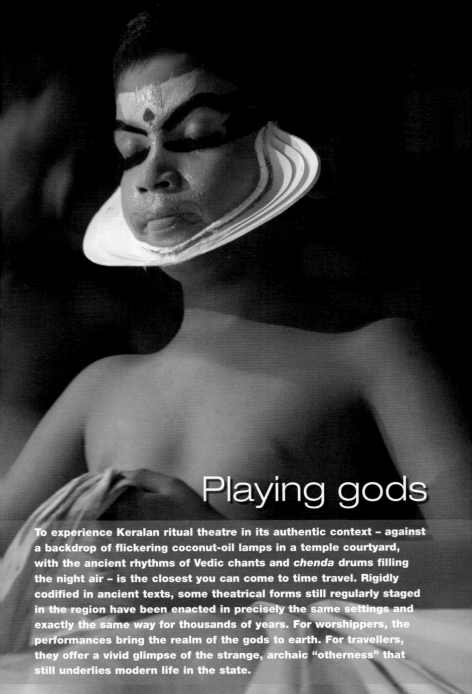

Playing gods

To experience Keralan ritual theatre in its authentic context – against a backdrop of flickering coconut-oil lamps in a temple courtyard, with the ancient rhythms of Vedic chants and *chenda* drums filling the night air – is the closest you can come to time travel. Rigidly codified in ancient texts, some theatrical forms still regularly staged in the region have been enacted in precisely the same settings and exactly the same way for thousands of years. For worshippers, the performances bring the realm of the gods to earth. For travellers, they offer a vivid glimpse of the strange, archaic "otherness" that still underlies modern life in the state.

Epic theatre

▲ Students at the Kalamandalam Academy, Cheruthuruthy

The adventures of god-heroes and their demonic adversaries – as told in epics such as the *Mahabharata* and *Ramayana* – are the most common subjects of **kathakali** story-plays, Kerala's most popular and best known ritual art form. Whether goodies, baddies, superheroes with special powers or female consorts, each of the four main character types wears instantly recognizable, and equally outlandish, costumes. Ridge-like masks of rice paper, decorative headgear set with red and green stones and voluminous skirts and jewellery adorn the "green" (*pacha*) heroes. Audiences, however, tend to most enjoy the antics of the villainous, lustful, greedy and violent "knife" (*katti*) anti-heroes, with their fangs and red-and-black faces.

Kathakali originated in the temples patronized by the region's rulers in the sixteenth and seventeenth centuries, when its costumes, core repertoire and complicated lexicon of gestures were fixed in writing. These cornerstone texts still form the basis of the arduous ten-year training young actors have to endure, starting at the tender age of eight, in academies such as Kalamandalam and the Margi School.

Kathakali, however, was merely a modern elaboration of much **older ritual theatre forms** traditionally performed as offerings for temple deities. Quite when and where these first arose is a matter of conjecture, but some – such as *kudiyattam* – are referred to in Sanskrit texts dating back more than two thousand years. Still taught in a school in Thiruvananthapuram and regularly performed at various temples around the state, *kudiyattam* is thought to be the world's oldest surviving theatre form.

▶ A "green" *kathakali* hero

Patronage

One explanation for the emergence and survival in Kerala of so many extraordinary temple arts is the prolonged peace which prevailed between the ninth and twelfth centuries under the **Kulasekhara** kings. Instead of squandering taxes on military campaigns, rulers were able, for over three centuries, to foster religious theatre – a tradition which continued until the communist reforms of the 1950s dismantled ancestral estates, forcing aristocratic families to dispense with the troupes of professional actors they formerly maintained to perform in their shrines. Since then, state patronage has kept some going, but many more are on the verge of extinction as younger generations take up more lucrative types of employment.

Spirit possession

As well as the formal types of ritual theatre sponsored by the upper castes and nobility, Kerala also has its own **grass-roots forms**, deriving from traditions thought to pre-date the arrival in the region of Brahmanical Hinduism. Known in northern Kerala as *theyyattam* or *theyyam*, they're held for all kinds of reasons: to celebrate the safe return of a son from the Gulf, the construction of a new house or as part of a temple feast. And they come in an amazing number of different shapes and sizes, each with its own distinctive make-up, costume and outlandish masks.

In villages around Kannur (Cannanore) in the north, some *theyyam* performers don huge headdresses made of crimson-painted papier-maché, metal studwork and tassles, framing meticulously painted faces and bodies loaded with jewellery and heavy costumes. Flickering in the firelight, such apparitions seem from another realm – precisely the effect intended. For unlike in *kathakali* and *kudiyattam*, where the actors are seen as mere representations of the gods, in *theyyattam* the bodies of performers are believed to be literally possessed by the deities themselves. As the god or goddess moves among the crowd, its spirit glares through the performer's bloodshot eyes, animating his every move and gesture like a puppet.

It's hard to convey the electric mix of terror and adoration such visions invoke among onlookers. Despite having been outlawed, age-old **caste restrictions** are still often upheld in more conservative rural parts of Kerala, barring those at the lower end of the caste hierarchy from access to the region's most revered Tantric shrines – which only adds to the intensity of these local rituals. Whether staged for a small family-sponsored puja or a full-on temple festival with thousands in attendance, *theyyattam* are always super-charged events.

▲ A *theyyam* deity

▲ *Theyyam* ritual near Kannur, northern Kerala

Where to find ritual theatre

Truncated, simplified versions of ritual theatre forms are staged at tourist shows in resorts and cities all over Kerala – especially in Fort Cochin and Ernakulam – but they're no replacement for the real thing.

Temple festivals (*utsavam* in Malayalam) are where you'll most often find proper all-night *kathakali*. Recitals generally start around 10pm and run uninterrupted until dawn, when audiences are treated to the final, dramatic disembowelling of the demon, followed by a restorative cup of chai at the temple gates.

In Thiruvananthapuram, the acclaimed **Margi School** (see p.100) lays on monthly shows of both *kathakali* and the more rarely performed *kudiyattam*. If you venture further north of Kochi, be sure to visit the **Kalamandalam Academy** at Cheruthuruthy (see p.209), Kerala's foremost performing arts college, to watch classes of students being put through their paces; the academy also hosts top-drawer shows in its traditional-style auditorium.

Tracking down *theyyattam* involves a bit more commitment. To improve your chances of seeing something really special, set aside at least a week and base yourself in the town of **Kannur** (**Cannanore**) (see p.244), where most guesthouse owners and the local tourist office will be able to point you in the right direction.

Finally, for other more obscure ritual art forms, including shadow puppetry and female mono-acting, the place to head is **Natana Kairali Cultural Centre** at Irinjalakuda (see p.205), near Thrissur. If you'd like to try your hand at learning some of the basics yourself, the **Vijana Kala Vedi Cultural Centre** in Aranmula (see p.156) runs short introductory courses for beginners.

"Malabar gold" (as they nicknamed pepper), that the chronicler Pliny the Elder (23–73 AD) famously complained that trade was fast emptying the imperial coffers – a remark substantiated by the hordes of Roman coins that have come to light over the years in central Kerala. It was also through Muziris that **St Thomas the Apostle** reportedly brought Christianity to India after the Resurrection in 52 AD, and where the first major influx of **Jewish refugees** settled following the destruction of the temple in Jerusalem.

The post-Sangam era

The stormy relations between the Cheras and the **Cholas** and **Pandyas**, across the mountains in Tamil Nadu, is a constant theme in Sangam literature. Throughout the first half of the first millennium AD, these three rival powers were frequently at war with each other, or with the rulers of neighbouring Sri Lanka. Ultimately, however, they all seem to have succumbed to an enigmatic fourth dynasty, the **Kalabhras**, about whom the Sangam poems say very little other than that they were "bad kings" (*kaliarasar*). Buddhist texts from a later period suggest they were originally hill tribes who swept down from the Deccan Plateau to harass the inhabitants of the river valleys and coastal areas, and who later took up Jainism and Buddhism.

Whatever their origins, the arrival of the Kalabhras – coupled with the decline of trade with Rome and resulting demise of Muziris – brought an end to five or more centuries of Chera rule in the southwest of India, ushering in a kind of "**dark age**" in the far southwest of the peninsula. From around 500 AD onwards, the region was repeatedly overrun by armies from the east, principally the Chalukyas and Pallavas. Little detail has survived about the regional chiefdoms that must have existed under them in the former Chera homelands.

The Brahmanization of the South

The "long historical night", as Keralan historians characterize the turbulent period between the sixth and eighth centuries, drew to a close with a silent revolution brought about by the rise to prominence of the **Brahmin** caste, descendants of the Aryans who had conquered the northern plains more than a thousand years before. No one is exactly sure when these paler-skinned priests started migrating south, but Sangam texts record that "Vedic sacrifices" were performed under the patronage of successive Chera rulers, and that Brahmin quarters existed in major towns and ports from at least the third century BC. However, from the seventh century AD onwards, the in-migration of Brahmins intensified, probably because they were encouraged to settle on lands newly conquered by kings from the Deccan, who were already adherents of Brahmanical tradition.

Along with their Sanskrit verses, Vedic rituals and philosophies, the Brahmins introduced radically new concepts of social order to Kerala. Precisely how notions of **caste** permeated the more egalitarian society of the tropical southwest remains a matter of debate among social historians. But the most likely explanation is that by controlling the large tracts of land they were gifted, and through their role as spiritual and political advisors to local rulers, the Brahmins – or **Namboodiris** as the uppermost strata of priests became known in Kerala – were able to impose the four-fold **Chaturvarnya** hierarchy which prevailed in their native north.

As the intermediaries between the people and their gods, the Brahmins occupied the topmost layer of this rigid system. Under them came the **Ambalavasis**, or temple servants, and the **Kshatriyas**, or "Warriors" – a position of high status which the Brahmins conferred on the ruling elite of Kerala in return for patronage. Unlike in northern India, there was no middle portion of the pyramid, as the positions of merchants, traders and shopkeepers (corresponding to the mid-ranking Vaishya castes of northern India) were dominated by Syrian-Christians, Muslims and Jews.

The **Nairs**, or martial caste, were technically near the bottom of the pile, employed in periods of peace as clerks and accountants by the nobility, though over time many prominent Nair families rose to become powerful landlords in their own right. Below them were manual labourers, field workers and servants, such as the **Tiyyas**, whose traditional role was the plucking of coconuts. At the base itself sat the so-called "polluting castes", the largest of which were the **Ezhavas**, or landless farmers. Finally, there were also out-castes, aka "**slaves**" or "Untouchables" – basically anyone who performed activities deemed highly polluting such as fishing, butchery, clothes washing, street sweeping or toilet emptying.

Ideas of **ritual pollution** in Kerala developed to an extraordinary degree. Namboodiris, for example, had to perform purifying rites if they so much as set eyes on a member of a slave caste, or if their shadow touched a Nair. An Ezhava had to keep forty paces behind a Nair, and an Untouchable sixty-six.

By the end of the eighth century AD, 32 separate Brahmin settlements, or *gramam*, had sprung up in Kerala and the caste system was well entrenched. Vedic philosophies promulgated by the new priesthood formed the religious bedrock of the region's many chiefdoms and larger principalities. Alongside temples, Namboodiris controlled education, and exercised great influence over the local rulers.

Bhakti and the poet-saints

One of the great driving forces behind the spread of Brahmanical Hinduism across the South was **bhakti**, a popular religious movement that blossomed in Tamil Nadu and quickly spread west across the mountains into Kerala. A devotional form of Hinduism encouraging individual devotees to forge a highly personal relationship with a chosen god (*ishtadevata*), *bhakti* was an approach that would revolutionize Hindu practice in the region forever.

Its great champions were the **poet-saints** of Kerala and Tamil Nadu, who were often said to have "sung" the religions of Jainism and Buddhism out of South India. Although in practice a variety of deities were worshipped, the movement had two strands: the **Nayanmars**, devoted to Shiva, and the **Alvars**, faithful to Vishnu. Collections of their poetry, the greatest literary legacy of South India, remain popular today, and the poets themselves are almost deified, featuring in carvings in many temples.

All the poems tell of the ecstatic response to intense experiences of divine favour, an emotion frequently described in terms of conjugal love, and expressed in verses of great tenderness and beauty. They stress selfless love between man and god, claiming that such love alone can lead to everlasting union with the divine. Devotees travelled the length and breadth of the South, singing, dancing and challenging opponents to public debates.

By emphasizing the importance of the individual's devotion to a particular god or goddess, *bhakti* inspired a massive upsurge in popular worship and, inevitably, a proliferation of shrines to accommodate worshippers. This process went hand in hand with the assimilation of important regional deities into the Hindu pantheon. In time, the same happened to lesser local gods and village deities, until innumerable cult centres across Kerala and beyond became bound in a complex web of interconnections. The institution of **pilgrimage**, linking local and distant deities, emerged as an essential element of Hinduism for the first time during the era of the poet-saints, and has remained an important unifying force in India ever since. It is no coincidence that some of the most defining texts of the *bhakti* movement are the *Mahatmyas*, oral chants intoned by Brahmins that elucidate the significance of individual temples and their relationship to other shrines.

The Kulasekharas and Second Chera Empire: 800–1102 AD

Against this backdrop of mounting religious fervour, a lineage of Keralan chiefs descended from the old Chera kings emerged as the region's overlords. Under the **Kulasekharas**, Kerala experienced three centuries of unprecedented peace and prosperity, during which the Malayalam language and many of the ritual art forms that characterize the state today took shape.

The founding father of the so-called **Second Chera Empire** was **Kulasekhara Varma** (ruled 800–820 AD) who, under the *nom de plume* of Kulasekhara Alwar, became one of only two Keralan poet-saints among the seventy-five immortalized in *bhakti* tradition. A Vaishnava (devotee of the God Vishnu), he composed some of the most celebrated Sanskrit and Tamil songs ever written in praise of Rama and Krishna, verses still regularly sung in Keralan temples. His successor, the Shaivite (Shiva-worshipping) **Rajasekhara Varman** (ruled 820–844 AD), achieved sainthood under the name of Cheraman Perumal.

In the course of the Kulasekhara rule over the ninth and tenth centuries, the spice trade with China and the Arab world revived the fortunes of the Malabar harbours, and the dynasty's capital, **Mahodayapuram** – which some scholars think was established on the site of the ancient Chera port of Muziris, near present-day Kodungallur – became one of the wealthiest cities in South Asia. Profits from the pepper trade financed the construction of Kerala's first large-scale **temples**, including Padmanabhaswamy in Thiruvananthapuram. These, in turn, served as crucibles for ritual art forms such as *kudiyattam* and *mohiniyattam* dance, as well as classical music, mural painting and sculpture. Vedic colleges, or *salais*, attached to the shrines, meant Namboodiri boys could study philosophy, Sanskrit grammar, calligraphy, law and theology in libraries filled with thousands of palm-leaf manuscripts. Ayurvedic dispensaries also proliferated in the sacred precincts, staffed by Namboodiri-Brahmin families whose descendants still run hospitals and clinics across Kerala today.

The Chera—Chola Wars

The Kulasekhara's "Golden Age" ground to an abrupt halt in 999 AD with the outbreak of war against the Tamil **Cholas**. The conflict, one of the bloodiest in Keralan history, would last for more than a century and leave a devastating legacy in the region. Temple building ceased almost overnight. *Salais* were converted into military academies and with the end of royal patronage the temple arts went into sharp decline. Generations of Keralan youths from the Nair caste – both men and women – were called up for compulsory training in a chain of *kalari* gymnasiums, where the martial art of **kalarippayattu** (see p.100) was taught. Some went on to enlist in **Chaver-Pada suicide squads**, whose bravery would eventually help turn the tide of the war.

Another consequence of the Chera–Chola conflict was a gradual increase in the power of the Namboodiris. Large areas of agricultural land were handed over as endowments by wealthy philanthropists to the temples – both to avoid the increased tax they generated, and to ensure their protection from pillage by the enemy (temple land was considered inviolable). But instead of ploughing the land revenues back into the war effort, the Namboodiris charged with their management often pocketed the profits. The upshot was the emergence of a new class of super-rich Brahmin landlords, known as the **Janmis**, and a system of feudal exploitation that would not be overturned until the communist era of the 1950s.

After nearly a century of conflict, the last Kulasekhara king, **Rama Varma Kulasekhara** (ruled 1090–1102 AD) rallied his army for a final push against the Cholas in the far south. Large sections of his forces transformed themselves into *Chaver-Pada* brigades and managed to repulse the aggressors once and for all. The war eventually petered out, but not before Mahodayapuram had been burnt to the ground and its palaces destroyed. With the royal treasury exhausted, Rama Varma moved south to Quilon (modern Kollam) and the Kulasekhara era drew to a close.

The age of the Naduvazhis

Over the three centuries of Kulasekhara rule, Kerala's regions – or *nadus* – were administered by viceroys with the title of **Naduvazhis**, who were responsible for the collection of taxes and recruitment of men to fight in the army. When the Second Chera empire declined at the end of the Chola wars, it was these regional chiefs who stepped into the power vacuum to assert their independence from the centre, giving rise to four distinct kingdoms, or *swaroopam*.

In the south, **Venad** encompassed the territory of the former Ay kings. Its chief port, **Quilon**, grew wealthy on the spice trade with Arabia and China, blossoming into a splendid city filled with temples, grand mansions and paved roads. Marco Polo was one of many foreigners dazzled by its splendour in the thirteenth century, when the harbour was crammed with vast, multi-decked Chinese junks. By this time, successive Venad kings had, in spite of waves of attacks by the Nayaks of Madurai, to the northeast, expanded their domain across the border into Tamil territory, and in 1312, **Ravi Varma Kulasekhara** (1299–1314) finally defeated the Pandyas, crowning himself the "Emperor of the South".

Further north, a lineage descended from the Cheras ruled much of central Kerala from what remained of the old capital, Mahodayapuram. Known as **Perumpadappu Swaroopam**, and later as the **Kingdom of Cochin**, it drew its wealth from trade through a harbour on the Periyar River, probably on, or close to, the site of ancient Muziris. But when floods swept a massive bar of silt across its entrance to the sea in 1341, the Cochin rajas were forced to relocate further south to a new site – the port that would eventually become Cochin.

The spice trade also enriched the Kolathiri rajas, who ruled the far north of Kerala – **Kolathunad** – from the fourteenth century onwards. They, however, were little more than tributaries of a much more powerful state to their immediate south. **Nediyiruppu Swaroopam** and its capital, **Kozhikode (Calicut)**, was the domain of the Eradi dynasty, whose kings called themselves the "samuris", later corrupted to "**zamorins**". By running its harbour as a free port, the *zamorins* encouraged communities of able Chinese and Arab merchants to settle. The Arabs, in particular, proved generous allies, donating ships, horses, arms and soldiers for military campaigns, and acting as wily advisors in political and economic matters. With their wealth and wiliness allied to the *zamorins'* military ambitions, Calicut had risen to become one of the world's most prosperous and sophisticated cities by the fifteenth century. As well as building splendid forts and palaces, the *zamorins* were passionate sponsors of the arts, particularly literature, holding an annual competition that attracted bards from across South India.

The Portuguese and Dutch

With the Moors ousted from the Iberian peninsula and Christendom established in the North African port of Ceuta, the crusading **European superpowers** began to seek fresh pastures in which to exercise their proselytizing zeal. The Americas, recently discovered by Columbus, provided the Spanish with potentially rich pickings, while the rival Portuguese turned their sights towards the African Gold Coast and beyond. Their initial goal had been to spread Christianity and locate the mythical Christian ruler Prester John, whom the Portuguese hoped would aid them in their quest against Islam in Africa. Later, however, the lure of cheap silk, pearls and, above all, Malabari spices overshadowed other motives, particularly after Bartolemeu Dias rounded the Cape of Good Hope in 1488, making a route across the Indian Ocean at last seem within reach. If this route could be opened up, it would bypass the much slower trans-Asian caravan trail, threatening the old Venetian-Muslim monopoly on Indian luxury goods and providing direct access to the spice ports of the Malabar Coast – all of which meant potentially vast profits for any nation able to maintain maritime dominance.

As a result, the Portuguese were quick to throw their Spanish rivals off the scent, informing them that the Cape lay a good ten degrees further south than it did. This ruse made the voyage around the tip of Africa seem a lot less viable as a short cut to the spice islands, and contributed in no small part to the **Treaty of Tordesillas** of 1494, in which the Spaniards relinquished any claims to territories east of a dividing line set at 370 leagues west of the Cape Verde Islands, off the coast of West Africa.

Once rights to the world's seas had been carved up between the two Iberian nations, the way was open for the Portuguese to capitalize on their earlier efforts along the rim of the Indian Ocean. Aside from Dias' pioneering expedition, several secret voyages, of whose existence historians have only recently learned from old naval records, probed up the east coast of Africa.

Vasco da Gama

By the close of the fifteenth century, the scene was thus set for the entry onto the world stage of **Vasco da Gama**, dispatched from Lisbon in July 1497 by the king of Portugal to find a sea route to the Indies. With the help of an expert Arab navigator, **Ibn' Masjid**, whom he hired at Malindi on the east coast of Africa to help him cross the Arabian Sea, Da Gama and his fleet of three *caravelas* took just under ten months to reach Calicut. However, news of atrocities committed by the Portuguese en route had preceded their arrival, and the *zamorin*, **Mana Vikrama**, briefly imprisoned Da Gama before allowing him to fill his holds with pepper and leave – an insult the proud Portuguese admiral would never forget.

The entire cost of Da Gama's expedition was recouped sixty times over by the profit from the spices it carried back to Lisbon, and barely a year elapsed before a fleet of 33 ships set sail to Calicut, under the command of **Pedro Àlvares Cabral**. Cabral was able to extract more concessions from the *zamorin* than did his predecessor, gaining permission to site a warehouse outside the city. However, relations with local merchants quickly degenerated. Fearing (with some justification, as it turned out) that the Portuguese intended to usurp their monopoly over the Malabar's spice trade, Arab advisors close to the Calicut king successfully lobbied against the Europeans. Cabral retaliated by rounding up Arab vessels standing off Calicut harbour and massacring their crews. On land, a mob stormed the Portuguese factory, putting all 53 of its inhabitants to the sword.

This last bloody episode was at the forefront of Vasco da Gama's mind when he returned in 1502. He waylaid a Muslim ship en route from Mecca and burned alive all seven hundred of its passengers and crew, then set about bombarding Calicut. While the cannonade rained down on the city's temples and houses, Da Gama ordered the crews of a dozen or so trade ships anchored in the harbour to be rounded up. Before killing them, he had the prisoners' hands, ears and noses hacked off and the pieces sent ashore piled in a small boat.

Leaving Calicut in flames, Da Gama sailed south to **Cochin**, where a mixture of gifts and threats was enough to make the local raja fill his holds with pepper and cardamom at favourable prices. More pepper was purchased at Quilon from the rulers of Venad before the admiral began his return voyage, slipping past the waiting navy of the angry *zamorin*.

Da Gama's tactics unleashed turmoil on the Malabar. Within months a major offensive was launched by the *zamorin* to punish the raja of Cochin for his collusion. After some initial success, the invasion was forestalled by the monsoons. It then foundered completely after a Portuguese naval squadron sailed to Cochin's aid in September 1503. The grateful raja responded by granting the Portuguese permission to build a fort at the mouth of his capital's harbour: erected in 1504, **Fort Manuel** – the nucleus of Fort Cochin – would be the first ever colonial stronghold on the Indian coast.

A second, and much more desperate attack was ordered by the *zamorin* shortly after, involving 280 ships, 4000 sailors and 60,000 land troops. But after a five-month campaign, it too ended in failure: 19,000 infantrymen lost their lives in a single action trying to cross Cochin harbour, and a further 13,000 died of cholera during the siege.

A treaty was eventually signed between the Portuguese and Calicut in 1513, but not before the *zamorin*'s city had been reduced to rubble. Notwithstanding, maverick Muslim commanders from his navy – the **Kunjali Marakkars** – took up the fight and further hostilities rumbled through the 1520s until finally, Vasco da Gama was brought back from retirement to resolve matters. His viceroyalty, however, was only to be short lived. On December 24, 1524, Da Gama died, probably from malaria, in Cochin's Fort Manuel, only three months after his third arrival on the Malabar.

The rise of the Dutch

Over the coming decades, the Portuguese – based at their capital city, Goa, to the north – extended their trade along the Malabar by exploiting enmities between the region's rulers. At the same time, conflicts regularly erupted between them and the *zamorins*, while at sea, the Kunjali Marakkars were playing havoc with Portuguese shipping. The Kunjalis' naval supremacy enabled an expedient coalition between the Kolathiri raja and *zamorin* of Calicut to take Fort St Agnelo at Cannanore in 1564, and Chaliyam seven years later – losses which marked the beginning of the end of Portuguese power on the Malabar.

It was the **Dutch**, however, who would bring an end to Lusitanian trade in Kerala. Determined not to allow its Roman Catholic rivals free reign in Asia, the Protestant Dutch East India Company – founded in 1592 – systematically took control of the international spice trade in the early seventeenth century, relieving the Portuguese of Quilon in 1598 and Colombo in 1663. An appeal from a prince of the Cochin royal family to intervene in a succession struggle gave them the excuse they needed to annexe the lynchpin of Portuguese operations, **Fort Cochin**, which they did after a fierce battle in 1663.

Yet Dutch supremacy on the Malabar – underpinned by their more manoeuvrable *fluyt* ships, which easily outsailed the more old-fashioned, ungainly *caravelas* from Lisbon – was to last for only a century. French and British trading posts started to pop up in the region soon after their triumph at Cochin, and their arms, munitions and military know-how enabled local rulers such as the rajas of Travancore to wage effective attacks against Dutch interests.

Colonial influence

Ultimately, it was the Portuguese rather than the Dutch who would leave the most lasting legacy on the Malabar Coast. Corruption and self-interest among colonial officials, and some gratuitous acts of cruelty, may have prevented them from establishing an effective system of government in the territories they acquired. But the Portuguese policy of holding the power of *zamorins* in check while reducing the status of the Cochin rajas to that of de facto vassals accelerated the rise of **minor principalities** elsewhere, and thus political disunity across the entire region. This, in turn, provoked constant wars and disrupted agriculture. Massacres and the repeated destruction of temples and mosques by the Portuguese further demoralized a civilian population already impoverished by deep economic recession – a result of the new foreign-imposed trade monopoly, which forced down the prices of local produce such as pepper and cloth.

In response, the Malabaris turned with renewed fervour to religion, especially the devotional **bhakti cults**. Writing in Malayalam, poet-scholars such as **Tunchat Ezhuthacan** and **Puntanam Namboodiri** did much to revive the mystical adoration of Vishnu in the region, in particular his incarnations as Rama and Krishna. It was during this era that Kerala's most revered Krishna shrines at Guruvayur and Ambalapuzha acquired the prominence they enjoy today.

At the same time, **Roman Catholicism**, spread by Jesuit Missionaries in the sixteenth century, claimed around 60,000 converts, mostly from the oppressed lower castes of Hinduism. Churches founded during the Portuguese period continue to have a high profile in Kerala, particularly among fishing communities along the coast. Finally, the Portuguese also introduced numerous novelties which were enthusiastically adopted in the Malabar and whose use spread rapidly across the rest of the Subcontinent: gunpowder (which made the Nair soldiers and their *kalarippayattu* martial arts redundant), tobacco, the practice of distilling coconut sap to make alcohol, cashew nuts (now one of Kerala's major exports), custard apples, pineapples, papaya and, not least, chilli peppers.

Travancore and Marthanda Varma

From the highpoint of Ravi Varma Kulasekhara's reign as "Emperor of the South" in the early fourteenth century, Venad – which later became known as "**Thiruvitamkode**" (corrupted by the British to **Travancore**) – had steadily declined as a regional power, its domain whittled away to a narrow band in the far southwest. A succession of kings and regents struggled unsuccessfully to hold at bay the invading armies of both the **Nayaks of Madurai** and the **Vijayanagar rajas**, who descended at regular intervals to exact tribute. One of the largest attacks launched by the Vijayanagars, the last and most powerful Hindu empire to rule over southern India, was in the 1540s, ostensibly to curb the proselytizing activities of Jesuit missionary, Francis Xavier. The emperors were displeased with the liberal stance of Thiruvitamkode's rulers towards the spread of Christianity along the Malabar Coast – less an act of genuine tolerance on the part of the Malabari kings than a placatory gesture towards the Portuguese, who aggressions were by now wreaking havoc in the Calicut region.

Instability in the far south was further compounded by conflicts with the high-ranking temple trustees (or Yogakkar) from the priestly Namboodiri caste who, in cahoots with the local Nair nobility, exercised increasing control over the kingdom's politics and finances. Over time, a mega-aristocracy emerged called the **Pillamar**, or "Eight Lords", who grew to pose a major threat to the authority of Travancore's rulers. The kingdom's coffers, meanwhile, were gradually emptying following the Dutch capture of its chief port, Quilon, in 1598.

Travancore would have to wait until the accession of **Marthanda Varma** in 1729 before it could regain its former glory. **Marthanda** (ruled 1729–58) made peace with the Nayaks of Madurai, and with financial support from them and the British East India Company, who by now ran a trading post out of his territory at Vizhinjam, managed to assemble a powerful army. Once he'd crushed the power of the Pillamar, Marthanda began advancing northwards. A succession of minor princedoms, including Quilon, were recaptured before the culmination of the campaign in 1754, when the Travancore army finally defeated the Dutch at **Colachen** – the first time an Asian army ever vanquished European forces in battle.

Marthanda Varma marked his military successes with an extraordinary gesture. On January 3, 1750, the raja went to the Padmanabhaswamy temple in Thiruvananthapuram (Trivandrum), his new capital, and, in a lavish ritual, handed over ownership of his recently expanded kingdom to the tutelary deity enshrined inside it. The sacrifice – known as **Trippatidanam** – played a symbolic role in preventing future rebellions across Travancore territory: henceforth, any uprising against the state would also, in effect, be an act of sacrilege against the God Vishnu.

The British

The **British East India Company**, formed two years before its Dutch counterpart in 1600, made its first tentative forays into the Malabar's spice trade in the early 1630s, while the Dutch were chipping away at Portugal's maritime empire. Permission to export pepper out of Cochin was granted by the Portuguese in 1636, and eight years later the raja of Travancore allowed

△ Vizhinjam, site of the first British factory on the Malabar

the Company to erect a small factory at **Vizhinjam** (next to modern Kovalam), where spices and cloth could be stored awaiting annual shipment to London. It wasn't until 1690, however, that the first British fort appeared in the region. **Anchengo**, just south of Varkala, provided a perfectly placed stronghold from which to extend the Company's influence on the Malabar. But its presence – or, more accurately, the manipulation by its factors of the area's pepper prices – soon enraged the local Pillamar. In 1721, a series of violent clashes culminated in the massacre of 150 British troops, attacked while marching to present tribute to the Rani of Attingal (on whose lands Anchengo was sited). The rebels besieged the fort for six months, but were defeated by the eventual arrival of British reinforcements.

As compensation for the outrage, Attingal paid reparations and granted the Company a full monopoly over the local spice trade with, crucially, the power to fix prices – an agreement that was further consolidated by a fully fledged treaty with Marthanda Varma, the raja of Travancore. In return, the British offered military and financial support for Marthanda's campaign against the Pillamar and rival states further north. The Company, who came initially to pursue nothing more than "a peaceful trade", were thus drawn into regional conflicts between the Malabar's rulers – the thin edge of a long wedge that would, within a century and a half, see them overlords of the entire peninsula of India.

Anglo-French conflict

In the northern Malabar, British trade, based at the newly constructed fort at **Tellicherry**, was hampered by the 1721 arrival of the **French** at **Mahé**, only a few kilometres to the south. Armed conflict between the two was expressly forbidden by their respective governments, but this didn't stop the factors from scheming with local chiefs to launch attacks against each other's forts – often with support from the companies' own troops. Remarkably, the uneasy standoff held firm throughout the War of the Austrian Succession in 1740, during which

British and French armies and their respective local allies slogged it out on the plains of Tamil Nadu to the east. Twenty-one years later, however, after the eight-month siege of Pondicherry (the French capital in India) ended in victory for the British, Mahé fell to the East India Company.

The Mysorean interlude: 1766–1792

Following the fall of Pondicherry, the French were certainly down, but they were not yet quite out, thanks to the one remaining thorn in the side of British territorial ambitions in South India: the Muslim warlord **Haider Ali**. A former general of the maharaja of Mysore, Haider had usurped his master's throne in 1761 and within a short time managed to conquer virtually the entire southeast of the peninsula. The secret of his success lay in his readiness to learn from the Europeans, in particular the French, whose military tactics he emulated, and who provided him with officers to train his infantry.

To feed his voracious military machine Haider Ali needed a dependable flow of arms through the northern Malabar, at this time embroiled in regional conflicts between the *zamorin* of Calicut and his neighbours, backed by the competing European powers. Haider saw in this political turmoil just the opportunity he needed to march across the Western Ghats and annexe Mahé. In the event, however, the smash-and-grab campaign would grind on for some twenty-six years and, ultimately, deliver the Malabar into the hands of the very enemy his military adventures were intended to expel from the Subcontinent.

The first **Mysore invasion** got under way in 1766. Ahead of a 16,000-strong army, bolstered by 8000 militiamen mustered by his Muslim ally Ali Raja of Cannanore, Haider Ali swarmed into northern Kerala. After taking a string of minor princedoms, he turned his attention to Calicut, where he offered the *zamorin* terms of surrender not even the richest king on the Malabar could afford. Having packed his family off to the hills for safety, the *zamorin* blew up his palace and committed ritual self-immolation.

With Calicut subjugated and the monsoons about to break, Haider returned to his base across the mountains at Coimbatore, leaving his newly conquered territory under the stewardship of his ally Ali Raja and local Moppila leaders. When news spread of his departure, however, Nairs throughout the Malabar rose up to attack Mysorean garrisons, prompting Haider's swift return with reinforcements. This pattern was repeated several times over following decade, until Haider finally set his sights on the British fort at **Tellicherry**. Assisted by the Kolathiri rajas, Mysorean forces laid siege to the East India Company's stronghold for eighteen months, but the attack failed.

Mysore's defeat at Tellicherry and the demise of Haider, who died shortly after in 1782, turned the tide of the Mysorean invasions, inspiring further uprisings by the Nairs; and it took several major offensives in the region before Haider's son, **Tipu Sultan** – dubbed the "Tiger of Mysore" by his enemies – could reassert control. In the end, however, it was the declaration of war by Great Britain on Mysore rather than local rebellions that brought the episode to a definitive close. Led by Lord Wellesley and his brother Arthur (later the Duke of Wellington, of Waterloo fame), East India Company troops stormed the Mysorean capital, **Srirangapatnam**, in 1792. Tipu died defending a breach in his walls (a story that later inspired Wilkie Collins's novel, *The Moonstone*), and through the resulting treaty, the British found themselves masters not only of the Malabar, but of the whole of South India.

Besides ushering in East India Company rule, the Mysorean interlude had lasting **consequences** for the southwest. Agriculture had been decimated by the mass flight of peasants into the forests and hills to escape Mysorean atrocities; pepper cultivation was especially badly hit, leaving the region's trade in the doldrums. Even the monolithic Keralan caste system was severely shaken up: Haider and Tipu's Muslim troops had shown scant respect for the higher caste Namboodiris, while the Nairs were all but wiped out in many areas as punishment for their repeated insurrections. Many Naduvazhi and Janmis landlords were also deprived of their estates, and administration of the region was taken on by a more centralized government.

The Madras Presidency and Pazhassi Revolts

Following the victory at Srirangapatnam, the British consolidated all their southern territory into a single unit, the **Madras Presidency**. It started life as a "hands-off" regime, with vast administrative districts on which colonial officers could make very little impact. But resentment at British rule bubbled up on several occasions, precipitating a series of bloody encounters on the Malabar in the late eighteenth and early nineteenth centuries.

The roots of the so-called **Pazhassi Revolts**, which troubled much of central and eastern Kerala between 1793 and 1805, lay in the imposition of harsh new taxes by the British on farmers in the Kottayam area. Marshalled by their ruler, **Raja Kerala Varma Pazhassi**, local people refused to pay taxes demanded by the colonial authorities. The Company responded by ordering its troops to occupy the Pazhassi palace, but the raja had by then already fled to the jungles of the Western Ghats where, for the next twelve years, he masterminded a guerilla-style insurrection against British rule. Thousands of Nairs joined the rebellion, whose most infamous episode was the slaughter of 1100 Company troops as they crossed the Periyar Pass in 1797.

The Pazhassi raja was eventually flushed out of his forest hideaway and shot dead in 1805, but another major rebellion erupted four years later – this time organized by the disgruntled former chief ministers of Travancore and Cochin. However, the two-pronged attack met with little success, serving merely to tighten the British grip on the Malabar's ruling houses.

Under the Madras Presidency, Kerala was divided into **three districts**. In the south and centre, Travancore and Cochin retained their traditional royal houses, but were administered by a British "Resident-Dewan" (effectively a prime minister) who maintained ultimate responsibility for revenue collection, law, order and the functions of state. From 1810 until 1819, the position of Dewan in both Travancore and Cochin was occupied by **Colonel** (later Major-General) **John Munro**. During his tenure, significant steps forward were made in the fields of health and education. Hospitals, colleges and free schools were opened; slavery was abolished (the first step on the road to the total abolition of "untouchability"); greater civic rights were accorded to members of disadvantaged castes; unjust taxes were repealed; and various land reforms initiated, enabling tenant farmers to lease land off feudal lords at fairer rates. The legal system was also remodelled along British lines, corruption stamped out in the civil service and a major programme of improvements to infrastructure begun. The reign of **Maharaja Swathi Thirunal** (ruled 1813–1846) also saw a renaissance of the traditional arts, notably music – a legacy that endures in the annual festival held in the grounds of his former palace in Thiruvananthapuram (see p.99).

In the north, the erstwhile kingdoms of the Calicut *zamorins* and Kolathiri and Ali rajas, run directly by the British as the district of Malabar, fared less well. Some progress was made in the areas of communication, social reform and education. But from 1836, civil unrest among the region's Muslims, the **Moppilas**, became a source of growing concern for the region's colonial rulers. Directed mainly at Hindu temples and upper-caste Janmis landlords, the riots were initially dismissed as mere "religious fanaticism", but after a special police force set up to deal with them failed to halt the disturbances, a judicial enquiry concluded that they were more probably the result of a failure in taxation policy. Unlike in the southern districts, where land reform had improved the lot of tenant farmers, in the Malabar the Moppilas enjoyed few rights and were subject to systematic exploitation by the Janmis. Laws were introduced to protect tenants from eviction, and improved employment opportunities under the colonial administration – in the army, on spice plantations and on the railways – further soothed Muslim anger. But the seeds of a deeper militancy had been sown, and would re-emerge to dog the British over the coming decades.

The "Home Rule" movement

Across the north of the country, increasing discontent at British rule erupted in 1857 in the Uprising (or "Great Mutiny" as it was dubbed by the Raj). Although its shock waves never reached the far south, which was enjoying considerable prosperity and civic improvements during the Pax Britannica, calls for freedom from the yoke of colonial suzerainty grew over the next five decades, culminating in the Home Rule movement, which coalesced after World War I around the **Indian National Congress**.

With the accession of Mahatma Gandhi to its leadership in 1920, the nationalist struggle found expression in the strategy of **Swadeshi** ("self-sufficiency"), which called for a boycott of imported goods, in particular British textiles, and the revival of India's own production techniques. *Swadeshi* soon spread across southern India, and Congress committees were formed all over Travancore and Cochin. Up in the Malabar, however, opposition to British rule focused more on the **Khilafat movement**, a mainly Islamic political campaign set up to protest against the British government's treatment of the Ottoman Empire in the wake of World War I. Both Gandhi and his colleague, Khilafat leader Maulana Shaukat Ali (who would later split with Congress to co-found the pro-Partition Muslim League) visited the Malabar to lend their support to demonstrations.

The swelling ranks of the Khilafat in northern Kerala provoked a knee-jerk clampdown on political activity by the British. All public meetings were banned, Khilafat leaders were rounded up and imprisoned without trial, and mosques raided. This, in turn, triggered violent clashes between Moppilas and the Indian police, which eventually snowballed into a full-blown insurrection – the so-called **Malabar Rebellion** of 1921. Following a series of bloody riots, martial law was declared and extra troops drafted in, leading to many deaths on both sides. The defining episode of the revolt, still commemorated in the region on November 20 each year, was the "**Wagon Tragedy**", in which 61 Moppila prisoners being transported by rail suffocated in a closed carriage.

Caste agitation and the Temple Entry campaign

While violent disturbances wracked the Muslim-majority Malabar district in the first decades of the twentieth century, Gandhian principles of non-violent protest were being adopted to overturn some of the more egregious iniquities of the old Hindu caste order further south.

Until the 1930s, caste in Kerala functioned as a kind of **apartheid**. Different sets of laws and punishments applied to different groups in society (Brahmins, for example, were exempt from the death penalty), and age-old economic inequalities, fixed since the "Brahmanization" of the far south of India a thousand years or more ago, were perpetuated through systems of education and land tenure.

Caste divisions were most stark in rural areas where, even at the end of the nineteenth century, a form of bonded **slavery** still prevailed. Landless peasants could be bought and sold by their Janmis. They were forbidden from owning milking cows, roofing their huts with clay tiles (only thatch was allowed) and using metal utensils. They were also obliged to pay punitive taxes for the right to carry umbrellas, ride in palanquins and, bizarrely, grow moustaches. Most insulting of all, though, was the ban on wearing sari blouses imposed on women: in more conservative districts, female members of some sub-castes were even expected to uncover their breasts if they passed within sight of a person of rank.

It was this particularly offensive symbol of caste oppression that sparked Kerala's first explicitly anti-caste campaign, the so-called "**Breast Cloth Agitation**". In defiance of local custom, women of the low-caste Shannar community in southern Travancore, recently converted to Christianity by Anglican missionaries, started wearing sari tops and shoulder scarves (*neryathu*), in the same way as Brahmin women. This provoked attacks from upper-caste traditionalists but, in 1859, forced a proclamation from the government abolishing all caste dress restrictions in the state.

Fifty years later, state-wide movements against caste inequality began to take shape around leaders such as **Shri Narayana Guru** (see box, p.128), a Shaivite holy man from the low Ezhava caste, who outraged Brahmins in Kerala by consecrating temples for his followers – hitherto an exclusive right of Namboodiri priests. The doors of Hindu shrines were at this time still firmly closed to all the lower castes; even the approach roads to them were strictly off-limits. In 1924, however, the **Vaikom Satyagraha**, a campaign of direct non-violent action supported in person by Gandhi, obliged the authorities at Vaikom temple near Cochin to open the roads around its shrine to all, irrespective of caste. This paved the way for the famous **Temple Entry Proclamation** of 1936, in which the maharaja of Travancore, before a huge crowd in the capital, announced that "henceforth there should be no restriction placed on any Hindu by birth or religion on entering and worshipping in temples" in his domain. Gandhi hailed the declaration as "a miracle of modern times".

The Salt Satyagraha and Congress split

Meanwhile, in North India the *Swadeshi* independence movement was gathering momentum too. Gandhi's "**Salt Satyagraha**" – in which the Mahatma marched at the head of a mass demonstration to his native Gujarat to harvest salt in defiance of a British-imposed monopoly – inspired similar acts in Kerala. At Calicut beach in May 1930, thirty salt *satyagrahis* were wounded in police charges, leading to the arrest and imprisonment of all the region's Congress leaders.

To increase pressure on the British government, campaigns of civil disobedience intensified all over the country through the early 1930s. Boycotts of the courts, schools, colleges and shops selling foreign goods led to widespread arrests. But when Gandhi called a temporary halt to the boycott in 1934 it provoked a three-fold **split** in the Keralan Congress party. "Rightist" moderates who supported Gandhian principles were squeezed out of the leadership by "Leftist" radicals such as **E. M. Sankaram Namboodiripad** (aka "**EMS**") and

P. Krishna Pillai. In the Malabar, non-violence as a weapon in the fight for self rule was rejected outright by extremist Muslims who – once formed into the more militant **Muslim League** – had started to agitate for a separate Islamic state called Pakistan.

By the time the British finally relinquished power to Congress on August 15, 1947, after feverish negotiations coordinated by Louis Mountabatten, India's last British Viceroy, the schisms that would dominate Keralan politics for decades had already become entrenched.

Post-Independence

In comparison with the North, where Partition unleashed a mass exchange of populations and the massacre of hundreds of thousands of people, Indian Independence passed off smoothly in Kerala. Travancore and Cochin were merged, while Malabar became part of Madras State. Nine years later, the States Reorganization Act of 1956 combined all three to form a single unit whose boundaries were drawn along linguistic lines, grouping together all the districts in the southwest where Malayalam was the majority language. A new **Legislative Assembly** also came into being, for which elections were held in 1957. These returned a **Communist government** – one of the first in the world to be democratically elected – with E. M. S. Namboodiripad, now the head of Kerala's Communist Party, as its Chief Minister.

Born into a Namboodiri-Brahmin family in Palakkad district in 1909, EMS turned his back on his aristocratic roots to become the great ideologue of Keralan communism. **Land reform** was top of the agenda in his self-styled "Liberation struggle" (*Vimochana Samaram*). But the "peaceful transition" to a better deal for the peasantry envisaged by EMS was anything but: within a year, fierce resistance to his coalition's plans from landowners and the Church had descended into widespread riots, assassinations and famine. Kerala was teetering on the brink of total anarchy in 1959, when Prime Minister Jawaharlal Nehru intervened to impose **President's Rule** from New Delhi.

Fresh elections the following year voted a Congress-led coalition to power, but in 1967, EMS and his party were back at the helm again – this time heading up a coalition dominated by a communist party that had split into two rival factions: the Communist Party of India and the Communist Party of India (Marxist) – the CPI (I) and CPI (M).

EMS adopted a more restrained approach in his second term, causing a rift with the party's backers in Beijing, who labelled his tactics "parliamentary cretinism". But it proved much more fruitful, pushing through the radical **Land Reform Amendment Act**, by means of which Keralan tenants became virtual owners of the land they farmed. No family was allowed to possess more than eight hectares; the remainder was apportioned between those who traditionally worked it, benefiting around one-and-a-half million landless families.

Kerala today

The past four decades of political life in the state have seen innumerable twists and turns, as smaller parties jostle for power in larger coalitions dominated either by Congress or the communists. Since the 1980s, the **Left Democratic Front** (LDF), led by the two communist parties, has alternated with the **United Democratic Front** (UDF), led by the largest of no less than five separate Congress factions.

In common with the rest of the country, each of these sub-groups tends to draw its support from a core community or caste, whose wider interests it is then expected to pursue when in government. Thus, the Congress represents mainly Christian and Nair groups, and the communists the state's various lower castes, while the Indian Union Muslim League (IUML) is the party of north Kerala's Moppila population.

The region's ever-changing political landscape and the exploits of its flamboyant leaders provide the main topics of conversation in thousands of tea shops across the state each morning, where men gather to read the paper and engage in debate. If Kerala is one of the most religious places on earth, it's also one of the most political. Rarely a day passes without some strike or flag-waving demonstration paralyzing traffic in the capital.

The "Kerala Model"

An exceptionally high **literacy** rate is one of the notable legacies of communist rule, and the century or so of missionary schools and state-funded education that preceded it. Some 91 percent of Malayalis, including those from the poorest of backgrounds, read and write. Coupled with this are some impressive health and welfare statistics: a birth rate 40 percent lower than the national average; life expectancy at 74 and rising – comparable with the US; infant mortality at a mere 14 per 1000 (compared with 91 for most developing countries); and a gender balance of 1040:1000 in favour of women – about right by international standards, but well above the figure for India as a whole, where female infanticide is a growing trend.

In spite of its extraordinary achievements in the field of human development, however, Kerala has suffered severe **economic stagnation** since Independence – an unusual combination often dubbed "**the Kerala Model**" by economists. GDP and annual growth lag well below the national norm, largely because more than half of Malayalis live off small-scale farming.

Investment levels are also comparatively low: potential employers tend to be wary of Kerala's politicized work force, preferring to locate to states with more flexible labour laws. The result has been perennially high unemployment, and thus a spiralling budget deficit.

The popular response to Kerala's economic lassitude since the 1970s has been a mass **exodus to the Gulf states**: some 20 percent of GDP derives from remittance cheques sent home by relatives from abroad, and in parts of the Muslim north the figure is far higher.

Much of the rest of the country suffered similar economic problems prior to the 1990s, but under Rajiv Gandhi and successive prime ministers, India has managed to liberalize its economy, attracting major foreign investment and turning around its balance of payments. The boom seemed to have passed Kerala by completely, until a sudden upturn in the service sector in 2000 saw a new **prosperity** emerge in urban centres. Thanks mainly to steady rises in the prices of major cash crops such as rubber, spices and vanilla, and a surge in the number of IT jobs available locally, middle-class Keralans these days have plenty of money to spend. The state accounts for only 3 percent of India's population, but currently consumes about 15 percent of the nation's total retail goods, and buys more **gold** per head of population than anywhere else in the country.

By contrast, the lot of Kerala's most disadvantaged citizens has improved little – a reason often advanced for **the rise of communal tension** across poorer parts of the state. The Moppila riots of the 1920s excepted, Kerala has witnessed relatively little conflict between its Muslim and Hindu populations. But in recent years, fishing communities along the entire length of the coast have been riven by violent clashes. The worst occurred in 2005–6 at **Marada**, in northern Kerala, where a dozen people were killed after fighting erupted between Dheevara-caste Hindus and their Muslim neighbours.

Some of the state's poorest fishing villages bore the brunt of the 2004 Boxing Day **tsunamis**. Kollam district was the area worst affected, with thousands of houses destroyed and 130 people killed. Around forty thousand Malayalis were forced to flee their homes across the state and settle temporarily in refugee camps. Aid was, however, quick to materialize. Itself flooded by the waves, Amma's ashram at Amritapuri (see p.135) donated $23 million dollars to the relief effort. Rehabilitation efforts focused on rebuilding houses and replacing the boats, nets and tools destroyed in the disaster. Today, all the coastal settlements devastated by the tsunamis are back on their feet again, but the disparity between rich and poor is as striking as ever.

Religion

Kerala is one of the most intensely religious places on earth. Ritual permeates nearly every aspect of life, from the daily ceremonies conducted inside private homes to the large-scale festivals associated with every temple, mosque and church in the state. Hinduism, the predominant religion, has its own distinct style and traditions in Kerala, and an extraordinary feature of the region is the extent to which these have been soaked up by the more recent faiths of Islam and Christianity. You'll see examples everywhere: from garlands of marigolds adorning Madonna icons to the *chenda melam* drummers and Hindu temple elephants that appear at Muslim saints' day celebrations. The results are forms of worship in all religions that are as identifiably Keralan as they are representative of their own faith. Moreover, adherence to one creed in Kerala does not necessarily preclude a person's involvement in acts of worship staged by another. Several mosques and Christian churches feature on the Hindu Sabarimala pilgrimage circuit, and Christians and Muslims mingle easily among the crowds of enthusiastic devotees at elephant parades, *kathakali* recitals and *panchavadyam* orchestra performances held during Hindu temple festivals.

Hinduism

Unlike Islam and Christianity, **Hinduism** has no orthodoxy. Rather, India's greatest faith – practised by a little under sixty percent of the state's population – is a loose agglomeration of thousands of different beliefs and practices which, over several millennia, have been bound into an overarching mythological

△ Vaikom Temple, near Kottayam

framework. Involving a plethora of gods, goddesses, shrines, cults and customs, it nevertheless binds the nation together: pilgrims from all over India travel to Kerala to worship in the region's major temples, and Malayali Hindus venerate shrines as far away as the Himalayas.

At the same time, there exist in Kerala forms of Hinduism that are unique to the southwest – a consequence of its geographical isolation. Hinduism as most people recognize it today derived largely from the traditions of the Aryans, who colonized northern India from around 1500 BC. Having absorbed many indigenous cults, these "Vedic" religious forms (the term derives from the Aryans' most sacred texts, the Vedas) gradually made their way southwards, finally arriving in Kerala in the middle of the eighth century AD, where they were spread by Brahmin priests among the local Dravidian population.

Rather than wipe out the older Dravidian traditions it encountered, however, Brahmanical Hinduism incorporated them into its own mythology. Thus the nature spirits worshipped in the far south three or more thousand years ago – trees, animals, features of the landscape and other elemental forces – re-emerge in the modern era as part of the Hindu pantheon. The nomenclature may have altered, but the essence of these ancient rites remains intact in a multitude of local religious traditions.

Tantra and snake worship

One of the most pervasive of these forms is worship of the Mother Goddess, or **Mahadevi** – often referred to by the names of her many associated deities: Bhagawati, Badrakali and Ottakkali, among others. Hindus regard goddesses as repositories of divine female energy, or **shakti**, the power from which the visible world emanates, and which drives the universe forwards. In Kerala, more than anywhere else in India, numerous so-called **Tantric** forms of goddess worship survive in which the object of ritual is to appropriate and channel *shakti* into one's own self – to attain magical powers, overcome illnesses, promote fertility or just to bring good luck. Tantra is often associated with transgressional acts of worship involving sex and blood sacrifice, but in Kerala it more often takes the form of spirit possession, where the body of a ritual specialist is inhabited by the goddess invoked. This is the essence of *theyyattam* – a particularly dynamic and theatrical ritual form still prevalent in northern Kerala (see p.245). It is also the animating principle of the famous **Bharani festival** of Kodungallur (see p.205), where long-haired, crimson-clad oracles beat themselves with swords, watched by a drunken crowd singing sexually explicit songs dedicated to the goddess Bhagawati.

The Bharani festival, whose participants are drawn exclusively from the lower castes, vividly demonstrates another important feature of Tantricism as it exists in Kerala. Unlike temple-based Brahmanical rituals, which are mediated by priests, Tantric practices are accessible to all, without distinction of caste or gender.

Another example of Tantricism is the popular tradition of **snake worship** – again, an aspect of pre-Vedic, non-Brahmanical Hinduism that remains especially strong in the state. When the first settlers cleared the region's woodland to make fields for agriculture, they set aside small areas of virgin forest known as *kaavus* – "sacred groves" – where no flower was ever picked, plant disturbed or, most importantly, snakes harmed. Many of these centres of nature worship still exist across the state, often filled with roughly carved *naga* (cobra) stones dusted with propitious turmeric or vermillion powder. The largest and most famous of them is the one at Mannarsala, in Alappuzha district (see p.149), which is run by a lineage of female Namboodiri priestesses.

Temples

Temple worship, as practised across the rest of India, came relatively late to Kerala. Only with the arrival of Brahmanical Hinduism and the emergence of the devotional **bhakti** tradition during the Second Chera (Kulasekhara) empire in the ninth century AD (see p.258), did local rulers start to sponsor the building of large, permanent shrines. Made of wood, laterite and clay tiles, they're generally low-rise and low-key compared with those of neighbouring Tamil Nadu – sometimes indistinguishable from their surrounding structures save for the presence of a ceremonial brass flagstaff (*dwajastambha*). The complex is set out according to the traditional **pancha prakara** layout of five interlocking courtyards, next to which is a stepped water tank for ritual ablutions. At the centre of the temple, the deity and its accessory gods and goddesses are enshrined in an enclosed sanctum, called the *shreekovil*.

Temple ceremonies, or **pujas**, are conducted in the *shreekovil* in Sanskrit by Namboodiri-Brahmin **pujaris**, sometimes called shantis. The shantis tend the image of the deity (**darshan**) in daily rituals that symbolically wake, bathe, feed and dress the god, and finish each day by preparing him or her for sleep. The most elaborate is the evening ritual, *aarti*, when lamps are lit, blessed in the sanctuary, and passed around devotees amid the clanging of drums, gongs and cymbals. Worshippers attend for a ritual glimpse of the *darshan*. They'll also leave personal offerings of flowers, coconuts and packets of incense, in return for which the priests will hand them special food (usually small sweets), which has been blessed as **prasad** by the deity and thus infused with its energy.

Communal worship is celebrated with *kirtan* or *bhajan*, the singing of hymns or verses in praise of Krishna taken from the Bhagavad Gita, or repetitive cries of "Jay Shankar!" ("Praise to Shiva"). In many villages, shrines to *devatas*, village deities who function as protectors and may bring disaster if neglected, are more important than temples.

Popular Hindu gods and goddesses

The Hindu pantheon is presided over by three principal deities: **Vishnu** (the Preserver), **Brahma** (the Creator) and **Shiva** (the Destroyer). Most of the rest of the gods and goddesses commonly worshipped in Kerala are either incarnations of these three, or else of their consorts or offspring. There are also numerous regional cults following gods of local origin.

Vishnu

The chief function of **Vishnu**, the "Preserver", is to keep the world in order. Blue-skinned and with four arms holding a conch, discus, lotus and mace, he is often either shaded by a serpent or resting on its coils, afloat on an ocean. He is usually seen alongside his steed, the half-man-half-eagle Garuda. Vaishnavites, distinguishable by two vertical lines on their foreheads, recognize Vishnu as the supreme lord, and believe that he has manifested himself on earth nine times. These incarnations, or **avatars**, have been as fish (Matsya), tortoise (Kurma), boar (Varaha), man-lion (Narsingh), dwarf (Vamana), axe-wielding Brahmin (Parasuram), Rama, Krishna and Balaram (though some say that the Buddha is the ninth avatar). Vishnu's future descent to earth as Kalki, the saviour who will come to restore purity and destroy the wicked, is eagerly awaited.

The most important avatars are **Krishna** and Rama, star of the epic *Ramayana*. Krishna is the hero of the Bhagavad Gita, in which he proposes three routes to salvation (*moksha*): selfless action (*karmayoga*), knowledge (*jnana*) and devotion to the gods (*bhakti*). Krishna explains that *moksha* is attainable in this life, even without asceticism and renunciation. This appealed to all castes, as it denied the necessity of ritual and officiating Brahmin priests, and evolved into the popular *bhakti* cult that legitimized love of God as a means to *moksha*. Through *bhakti*, Krishna's role was extended, and he assumed different faces (though he is always blue). Most popularly he is the playful cowherd who seduces and dances with cowgirls (*gopis*), giving each the illusion that she is his only lover. At other times he is also pictured as a chubby, mischievous baby, known for his butter-stealing exploits, who inspires tender motherly love. A third popular version shows Krishna dancing and playing the flute.

In Kerala, Vishnu is worshipped most fervently in the form of Lord Krishna at **Guruvayur**, near Thrissur (see p.207). The main Krishna shrine in southern Kerala is at **Ambalappuza**, just south of Alappuzha in the backwaters.

Brahma

Despite being the Creator god of Hinduism, **Brahma** has only a handful of temples dedicated to him in India. Two of these are in Kerala, at Thirunavaya and Kotakkal. In mythological art, Brahma is generally depicted as having four arms and four faces; his vehicle is a swan.

Shiva

Shaivism, the cult of Shiva, was also inspired by *bhakti*, requiring selfless love from devotees in a quest for divine communion, but Shiva has never been incarnate on earth. He is presented in many different aspects, such as **Nataraja**, "Lord of the Dance", **Mahadev**, "Great God", and **Maheshvar**, "Divine Lord" and source of all knowledge. Though he does have several terrible forms, his role extends beyond that of destroyer, and he is revered as the source of the whole universe.

Shiva is often depicted with four or five faces, draped with serpents, holding a trident and bearing a third eye in his forehead. In temples, he is identified with the *lingam*, or phallic symbol, resting in the *yoni*, a representation of female sexuality. Whether as statue or *lingam*, Shiva is guarded by his bull steed, Nandi, and often accompanied by a consort, who assumes various forms and is looked upon as the vital energy (**shakti**) that empowers him. Their erotic exploits – a legacy of ancient Tantricism – were a favourite sculptural subject between the ninth and twelfth centuries AD.

Shiva is the object of popular veneration all over India; devotees are identifiable by the horizontal lines (between one and three) painted on their foreheads. In particular, Shaivite ascetics worship Shiva in the aspect of the terrible **Bhairav**. These ascetics renounce family and caste ties and perform extreme meditative and yogic practices. Many smoke *ganja*, Shiva's favourite herb; all see renunciation and realization of Shiva as the key to *moksha*. Some ascetic practices enter the realm of **Tantricism**, in which confrontation with all that is impure, such as alcohol, death and sex, is used to merge the sacred and the profane, and bring about the realization that Shiva is omnipresent.

Mahadevi: the mother goddess

Female deities worshipped in Kerala are all manifestations of the supreme mother goddess, Mahadevi. She's most often venerated in her wrathful, destructive aspect as **Kali**, the "black one", but frequently appears as **Bhagawati** (the "fortunate" or "adorable"), Bhadrakali (the "virtuous" and "radiant"), or Durga. Other less common incarnations include Nagakali (Kali with a serpent), and the demoness Chamunda. As Shiva's consort, Parvati, or Uma, Mahadevi is remarkable for her beauty and fidelity. In whatever form, however, she incarnates *shakti*, the divine energy that animates the universe.

Ayyappan

Lord Ayyappan is Kerala's most popular deity, the subject of a pilgrimage that for a couple of months each year sees the state swarming with millions of bare-chested male devotees dressed in black *lunghis* en route to his principal shrine, situated deep in the forests of the Western Ghats. Legend tells that he was born of a union between Shiva and Vishnu in his female form, Mohini, and as such symbolizes a synthesis of the two main strands in Brahmanical Hinduism ("Ayya" means Shiva and "Appan" means Vishnu). Another explanation for his current popularity is that his temples have always been open to members of all castes.

Ganesh (Vingishwara)

The elephant-headed **Ganesh** (*Vingishwara* in Malayalam) is the first son of Shiva and Parvati. Tubby and smiling, he's invoked before every major undertaking (except funerals) and you'll see his image, seated on a throne or lotus, placed above temple gateways, in shops and in houses. In his four arms he holds a conch, a discus, a bowl of sweets (or club) and a water lily, and he is always attended by his vehicle, a rat. Credited with writing the *Mahabharata* as it was dictated by the sage Vyasa, Ganesh is regarded by many as the god of learning, success, prosperity and peace.

Murugan

Pictured as a triumphant youth bedecked with flowers, **Murugan**, also known as Kartikeya or Subramanyam, is the second son of Shiva and Parvati. The god of war, he has a huge following in neighbouring Tamil Nadu, where his cult probably predates the arrival of Brahmanical Hinduism in the south by a couple of millennia. Murugan's symbols are the peacock (his sacred vehicle) and a bow; his battle standard bears the emblem of a rooster.

Hanuman

India's great monkey god, **Hanuman** features in the *Ramayana* as Rama's chief aide in the fight against the demon king Lanka. He wields a mace and is the deity of acrobats and wrestlers, but is also seen as Rama and Sita's greatest devotee, and an author of Sanskrit grammar. As his representatives, monkeys find sanctuary in temples across southern India.

Saraswati

The most beautiful Hindu goddess, **Saraswati**, the wife of Brahma – with her flawless milk-white complexion – sits or stands on a water lily or peacock, playing a lute, sitar or *vina*. A goddess of purification and fertility, she is also revered as the inventor of writing, and the goddess of eloquence and music.

Lakshmi

The comely goddess **Lakshmi**, usually shown sitting or standing on a lotus flower, and sometimes called Padma (lotus), is the embodiment of loveliness, grace and charm, and the goddess of prosperity and wealth. Vishnu's consort, she appears in different aspects alongside each of his avatars; the most important are Sita, wife of Rama, and Radha, Krishna's favourite *gopi*. In many temples she is shown as one with Vishnu, in the form of Lakshmi Narayan.

Practice

A Hindu has three aims in life: **dharma**, fulfilling one's duty to family and caste, and acquiring religious merit (*punya*) through right living; **artha**, the lawful making of wealth; and **karma**, desire and satisfaction. The primary concern of most Hindus is to reduce bad *karma* and acquire *punya*, by honest and charitable living within the restrictions imposed by caste and worship, in the hope of attaining a higher status in rebirth.

These goals are linked with the four traditional **stages in life**. According to ancient custom, the life of a high-class Hindu man progressed through these four distinct phases – *brahmachari* (celibate), as a child and student devoted to learning; *grhastha* (householder), providing for a family and raising sons; *vanaprashta* (forest dweller), a period of self-isolation and meditation; and finally, *sanyasi*

Adi Shankara

Religious history in India tends to stress the transforming influence of northern, Brahmanical traditions on the Dravidian south. But in the middle of the eighth century, at a time when Hinduism was splintering into dozens of different sects, a philosophical movement spread from Kerala that would unify the competing strands of the Subcontinent's most ancient religious tradition, and in the process save it from near-extinction.

The movement's core philosophy was that of **advaita** – literally "not-two"-ness – and its chief exponent was a Brahmin guru called **Adi Shankara** (788–820 AD). The essence of his teaching, refined from ancient Vedic texts called the *Upanishads*, held that the soul (*atman*) was indivisible from the supreme creator being, Brahman. "Brahman is the only truth," he wrote. "The world is illusion and there is ultimately no difference between Brahman and individual self."

A precocious intellect from an early age, Shankara is said to have mastered Sanskrit, one of the world's most complex languages, while only three, and left home at eight in search of a guru. By the time he was sixteen, he'd written commentaries on the *Upanishads*, the Bhagavad Gita and other Vedic texts that would turn Hindu philosophy on its head. Travelling around India on foot, he engaged in debates with the greatest thinkers of the era and succeeded in convincing them of the truth of *advaita*.

Before his death at the age of 32, Shankara founded four major monasteries, or *mathas*, across India. These are still in existence today and stand as hubs on an extensive pilgrimage network that the guru did much to popularize in his lifetime. *Bhajans*, or devotional hymns, composed by him are also regularly sung in Hindu homes to this day.

Shankara's greatest legacy, however, lies in the emphasis he placed on meditation and the individual's quest for truth over Brahmanical ritual. All the sects of modern Hinduism remain to some extent influenced by his philosophies, and many scholars have argued that without his rigorous collation of Vedantic thought, Hinduism itself might never have outlived the threat to its survival posed by state-sponsored Buddhism and Jainism in the first five hundred years AD.

(a renunciate) - renouncing all possessions to become a homeless ascetic, hoping to achieve the ultimate goal of *moksha*. However, in practice, few now follow this course and the *vanaprashta* is no more; in general, life is meant to progress along ordered lines from initiation (for high-caste Hindus) through to education, career and marriage. A small number of Malayalis who follow the ideal life, including some women, assume the final stage as *sanyasis*, saffron-clad *sadhus* who wander throughout India, begging for food and retreating to isolated caves, forests and hills to meditate. They are a common feature in most Indian towns, and many stay for long periods in particular temples. Not all have raised families: some assume the life of a *sadhu* at an early age as a *chella* (pupil or disciple) to an older *sadhu*.

However, strict rules still apply to the *dharmic* principles of **purity** and **pollution**, the most obvious of them requiring high-caste Hindus to limit their contact with potentially polluting lower castes. All bodily excretions are polluting. Above all else, **water** is the agent of purification, used in ablutions before prayer, and revered in all rivers, especially Ganga (the Ganges).

Each of the great stages in life – birth, **initiation**, marriage, death and cremation – are marked by fervent prayer, energetic celebration and feasting. The most significant event in a Hindu's life is **marriage**, which symbolizes ritual purity, and for women is so important that it takes the place of initiation. Feasting, dancing and singing among the bride and groom's families, usually lasting for a week or more before and after the marriage, are the norm all over Kerala. The actual marriage is consecrated when the couple walk seven times round a sacred fire, accompanied by sacred verses read by an officiating Brahmin. Today, most Hindu marriages traditionally involve the parents, who negotiate the match; love marriages are increasingly common, especially in urban areas, but still tend to depend on parental consent and collusion.

The age-old Malayali tradition of giving **dowry**, a gift of money, jewellery and goods from the bride's family to the groom's, is now officially illegal, but still widely demanded and invariably given, for fear that a daughter's welfare will be in jeopardy if it is withheld. Dowry is prevalent in both Hindu and Christian communities, and is as much practised by the upper and middle classes as it is by the poor, but for the latter it can represent an endless cycle of saving and debt with each new generation. Among more wealthy and cosmopolitan families, scooters, TVs and holidays are now the essential elements of a modern dowry. As it is a "gift", dowry is undeclared income, and the groom's family can place relentless pressure on the bride's family to continue providing "gifts" long after the wedding.

For Hindus, **death** is an essential process in an endless cycle of rebirth in the grand illusion (*maya*) until the individual attains enlightenment and freedom (*moksha*) from *samsara* (transmigration). Hindus cremate their dead, except for young children, whom they bury or cast into a river. The eldest son is entrusted to light the funeral pyre and the ashes are scattered, usually on a sacred river, or at sites on the coast associated with funerary rituals (the main one is Varkala Beach; see p.126). Rites after death can be lengthy and complicated according to each Hindu community, and the role of the *purohit* (priest) is indispensable. Widows traditionally wear white.

Islam

Muslims make up around a quarter of Kerala's total population. They form a significant presence in almost every town, city and village, but especially in coastal parts of the north of the state, where they're known as **Moppilas** (also written as "Mapillas"). In most of India, Islam was spread by force during the Turkish and Mongol invasions of the medieval era, but in Kerala it took root peacefully, introduced by Arab traders who settled in the region from the eighth century AD onwards. Local Muslims played a pivotal role in the trade that underpinned the Kulasekhara empire, and the rise of Calicut in the fourteenth and fifteenth centuries. Moppila naval expertise, and their considerable wealth, also placed them at the forefront of efforts to resist European colonialism, from the Portuguese to the British.

Despite the great differences in their religious beliefs, dress and dietary laws, Kerala's Hindus and Muslims coexisted harmoniously for over a thousand years. Only at the end of the nineteenth century, when taxes and exploitative land laws provoked clashes between the Moppilas and their Janmis landlords, did communal violence erupt. Recent decades have seen a worrying rise in communalism, mirroring a nationwide trend, but the violence has never approached the scale seen in parts of northern India.

More than anywhere else in the region, the Muslim districts of northern Kerala depend on **remittance money** sent by relatives working in the Persian Gulf. The mass out-migration to Saudi Arabia and the Gulf Arab states has not only increased prosperity among Keralan Muslims, but also had an impact on their religious practices. Over more than a thousand years, the Moppilas evolved an extraordinarily hybrid culture, evident in their dress, cuisine and architecture. Their mosques, sporting temple-like gables and slatted wood eaves, were heavily influenced by local Hindu style. Now, however, the Gulf phenomenon has injected a much more sober dye into the Moppila mix, and the old mosques have nearly all been torn down to be replaced by more modern, Mecca-style structures with domes and minarets.

Origins and development of Islam

Islam, "submission to God", was founded by **Mohammed** (570–632 AD), who is regarded as the last in a succession of prophets and who transmitted God's final and perfected revelation to mankind through the writings of the divinely revealed "recitation", the **Qur'an**. The Qur'an is the authoritative scripture of Islam that sets down the tenets of Islamic belief: that there is one god, Allah (though he has 99 other names), and that Mohammed is his prophet. The beginning of Islam is dated at 622 AD, when Mohammed and his followers, exiled from **Mecca**, made the *hijra*, or migration, north to Yathrib, later known as Medina, "City of the Prophet". The *hijra* marks the start of the Islamic lunar calendar; the Gregorian year 2008 is for Muslims 1429 AH (Anno Hijra).

From Medina, Mohammed ordered raids on caravans heading for Mecca, and led his community in battles against the Meccans, inspired by jihad, or "striving" on behalf of God and Islam. This concept of holy war was the driving force behind the incredible expansion of Islam – by 713 AD Muslims had settled as far west as Spain and as far east as the banks of the Indus. When **Mecca** surrendered peacefully to Mohammed in 630 AD, he cleared the sacred shrine, the Ka'ba, of idols, and proclaimed it the pilgrimage centre of Islam.

Mohammed was succeeded as leader of the *umma*, the Islamic community, by Abu Bakr, the prophet's representative, or caliph, the first in a line of caliphs who led the orthodox community until the eleventh century AD. However, a schism soon emerged when the third caliph, Uthman, was assassinated by followers of Ali, Mohammed's son-in-law, in 656 AD. This new sect, calling themselves **Shi'as**, "partisans" of Ali, looked to Ali and his successors, infallible imams, as leaders of the *umma* until 878 AD, and thereafter replaced their religious authority with a body of scholars, the *ulema*.

By the second century after the *hijra* (ninth century AD), orthodox, or **Sunni**, Islam had assumed the form in which it survives today. A collection of traditions about the prophet, **Hadith**, became the source for ascertaining the *Sunna* (customs) of Mohammed. From the Qur'an and the Sunna, seven major **articles of belief** were laid down: belief in one God; in angels as his messengers; in prophets (including Jesus and Moses); in the Qur'an; in the doctrine of predestination by God; in the Day of Judgement; and in the bodily resurrection of all people on that day. Religious practice was also standardized under the Muslim law, *Sharia*, in the **Five Pillars of Islam**. The first "pillar" is the confession of faith, *shahada*, that "There is no god but God, and Mohammed is his messenger". The other four are: prayer (*salat*) five times daily, almsgiving (*zakat*), fasting (*saum*), especially during the month of Ramadan, and, if possible, pilgrimage (*Haj*) to Mecca, the ultimate goal of every practising Muslim.

Christianity

When Vasco da Gama stepped ashore in Calicut in 1498, he was amazed to find the city already full of Christians – although somewhat less thrilled to discover that they were not Roman Catholics, but adherents to an obscure eastern Orthodox tradition. Today, Christians account for around 21 percent of the total population in Kerala, with a history dating back to the first century AD, some three centuries before the faith received official recognition in Europe.

No less than five main denominations exist, alongside a bewildering assortment of sects and sub-sects: **Nestorians** (confined mainly to Thrissur and Ernakulam), **Roman** or **Latin Catholics** (found throughout Kerala), the **Syrian Orthodox Church** (previously known as the Jacobite Syrians), **Marthoma Syrians** (a splinter group of the Syrian Orthodox Church) and the Anglican **Church of South India**.

Some history

Local legend asserts that the **Apostle Thomas** ("Doubting Thomas") arrived in Kerala in 54 AD to convert itinerant Jewish traders living in the flourishing port of Muziris. Traditional accounts from Jews who later arrived there in 68 AD state that they encountered a community of Christians known as **Nazranis**, or "followers of the Nazarene" (Jesus). The Nazranis encountered little opposition to their religion from their Hindu hosts, and absorbed many indigenous practices into their worship.

There are numerous tales of the miracles performed by "**Mar Thoma**", as St Thomas is known in Malayalam. One tells of how he approached a group of Hindu Brahmins in Palur, who were trying to appease the gods by throwing water into the air; if the gods accepted the offerings, the droplets would hang above them. St Thomas also threw water in the air, which miraculously remained suspended, leading to the on-the-spot conversion of the assembled Brahmins to Christianity.

By oral tradition, the church he founded in India is the **oldest Christian denomination** in the world. Concrete documentary evidence of Christian activity in the Subcontinent, however, can only be traced back to the fourth century AD, when immigrant Syrian communities, belonging to seven tribes from Baghdad, Nineveh and Jerusalem under the leadership of the merchant **Knayi Thoma** (Thomas of Cana), were granted settlement rights along the Malabar coastline by royal charter. As they built Christian churches, the Syrians introduced architectural conventions from the Middle East, and so incorporated the nave and chancel with a gabled facade, which resulted in a distinctive style of Keralan church. They also adopted architectural traits from the Hindu–influenced Nazranis, retaining the *dwajastamba* (flag mast), the *kottupura* (gate house) and the *kurisuthara* (altar with a mounted cross).

A significant faction of the Syrian-Christian community, the **Nestorians** (after Nestorius, the patriarch of Constantinople) were the dominant Christian group in Kerala after the sixth century AD and at one stage had centres in various parts of India. However, the assertive spread of **Roman Catholicism**, led by the Jesuit missionary Francis Xavier out of Portuguese Goa in the sixteenth century, later reduced the Nestorians to a small community, which survives today mainly in Thrissur.

Kerala's early Christians followed a liturgy in the **Syriac language** (a dialect of Aramaic). Latin was introduced by missionaries who visited Kollam in the Middle Ages, and once the Portuguese appeared on the scene in the 1530s, a large community of **Roman** or **Latin Catholics** developed, particularly on the coast, and came under the jurisdiction of the pope. In the middle of the seventeenth century, with the ascendancy of the **Dutch**, part of the Church broke away from Rome, and local bishops were appointed through the offices of the Jacobite patriarch in Antioch.

The **British** initially took the attitude that the Subcontinent was a heathen and polytheistic civilization waiting to be proselytized. Their brand of Anglicanism particularly appealed to members of the lower castes and sub-castes, who converted en masse in some districts to form the **Church of South India**. At the same time, elements in the Syrian Church advocated the replacement of Syriac with the local language of Malayalam. The resultant schism led to the creation of the new **Marthoma Syrian Church**.

Today, numerous large and popular churches, as well as roadside shrines known as *kurisupalli*, or "chapels of the cross", bear witness to the continuing strength of the Christian communities throughout the state. **Christmas** is an important festival in Kerala; during the weeks leading up to December 25, star-shaped lamps are put up outside shops and houses, illuminating the night and identifying followers of the faith.

Practice

Christian practice in Kerala has, over the centuries, absorbed many elements of Hindu worship. **Festivals** are highly structured along "caste" lines and, like their Hindu brethren, some communities never eat beef or pork, which are considered to be polluting. In many churches across the state, you will see devotees offering the Hindu *arati* plate of coconut, sweets and rice, and women wearing a *tilak* dot on their forehead. Christians carry plates of food to the graves of their ancestors on the anniversary of their death, in much the same manner that a Hindu family will share a feast on such a day.

Pilgrimage is considered an integral part of faith, and Keralan Christians of all denominations tend to visit churches where there is a relic, such as a shard of finger bone alleged to have belonged to St Thomas. These relics are brought out on special feast days, and huge crowds will jostle to catch a sight of the tiny bit of yellowing bone lying in a casket.

The Jews of Kerala

Until their mass departure to Israel in the 1950s, **Jews** formed a significant minority in Kerala for a thousand years or more, acting as prominent merchants and bankers to the region's rulers. Tradition holds that the first Jewish arrivals on the Malabar Coast were fleeing the occupation of Jerusalem by Nebuchadnezzar in 587 BC. Another legend claims they came 1500 years previously as part of King Solomon's trading fleet. However, the first concrete evidence of their presence in the region dates from around 1000 AD, in the form of a couple of inscribed copper plates, now stored in the Pardesi Synagogue in Mattancherry, detailing the privileges granted to one Joseph Rabban by Raja Bhaskara Ravi Varma. According to the Tamil inscriptions, the ruler gave to Rabban and his community the village of Anjuvannan, near Cranganore, and all proceeds deriving from it, in perpetuity; he was also permitted to ride in a palanquin and carry a parasol – rights generally accorded to only the highest-ranking individuals in society.

Rabban's Jews, and the waves of other Jewish immigrants who seem to have travelled to the Malabar from across northern Africa, Egypt, Persia and the Middle East in the first millennium AD, became known as **Meyhuhassim** (literally "privileged") – or **"Black Jews"**. They were joined by Sephardic Jews fleeing the Spanish and Portuguese inquisitions in the sixteenth and seventeenth centuries, who later became known as the **"Pardesi"** (literally "foreign") – or **"White Jews"**. Both groups also had slaves who converted and were later freed to become the so-called **Meshu-hararim** ("released"). These slaves formed the lowest-ranking group, the **"Brown Jews"**.

The largest settlements of Jews on the Malabar, including Anjuvannan, were around Kodungallur (Cranganore), near the ancient port of Muziris. However, persecution in the Portuguese era, when houses and synagogues were routinely destroyed and Jews packed off to the Inquisition's dungeons in Goa, led to mass migration to **Cochin**, where the local raja set aside a parcel of land for the Jews in 1567. The new Jewish community centered on Mattancherry, still known as Jew Town, thrived under the more tolerant regimes of the Dutch and British; and by the end of the seventeenth century there were ten synagogues and around five hundred Jewish families in Cochin. Wealthy Jews, such as the Koders (whose splendid old mansion nowadays serves as one of the state's premier heritage hotels; see p.181) rose to occupy important positions of influence and authority.

Today, only fifty (mostly elderly) White Jews remain in Cochin, occupying faded family houses around the Pardesi Synagogue in Mattancherry; the rest departed for Israel in the 1940s and 1950s. Other synagogues survive around the state, but the Pardesi (see p.186), despite having been completely destroyed by the Portuguese and rebuilt under the Dutch, remains the one in best condition and is still in use.

Christians in Kerala have never adopted the practice of giving or receiving **dowry** on the occasion of marriage, although in an arrangement similar to Hindu practice, a Christian **marriage** tends to take place between members of the same denomination or sect. In most cases, the parents of the couple play a central role in the selection process, paying particular attention to the social status and education of the prospective bride or groom. If a woman becomes a **widow**, she is not socially ostracized as a Hindu woman would be, but is instead encouraged to remarry.

The sacred arts

Since the beginning of Indian history, art and religion have been inextricably linked. Paid for by royal patrons, the finest expressions of human creativity – whether sculpture, painting, music, dance or drama – were always reserved for temples. Sometimes they were deployed for decorative effect, to intensify the act of worship. Other forms of art, notably dance and ritual drama, were conceived as acts of worship in themselves: ritualized performances that served both as offerings for the resident deities and as entertainment for the higher castes permitted to enter their shrines.

In Kerala, the great temples erected during the "golden age" of the Kulasekhara empire were where the region's trademark sacred arts were refined, over three or more centuries of **patronage** from kings, nobility and wealthy pilgrims. Later, between the sixteenth and eighteenth centuries, regional dynasties such as the *zamorins* of Calicut and rajas of Cochin acted as enthusiastic patrons of newer, emerging forms – including *kathakali* – which drew on the older traditions fostered in the temples.

Meanwhile, in the villages, lower-caste communities preserved their own **folk art forms** as rituals outside shrines. Stretching back to Kerala's distant Dravidian past, the roots of these in many cases predate not just the arrival of Europeans, but also Brahmanical Hinduism itself. Kerala's localized, village-based, low-caste arts are the repositories of India's last thriving **Tantric** tradition, barely veiled by a cloak of Vedic mythology, and based around worship of the Mother Goddess, Mahadevi. In contrast to the sacred arts of the great temples, the object of Tantric rituals was not to amuse or praise the deity, but manifest the god's power in a tangible form that worshippers could tap into.

Whether a frenzied Tantric *theyyam* dance at a shrine in the remote north of Kerala or a stately *kathakali* recital in one of the royal temples of Kochi, the region's sacred arts can provide unforgettable experiences – even if you don't have any grasp of their arcane symbolic languages. Drawing on traditions set down in writing more than two millennia ago, they hold the power to transport audiences in ways that defy cultural boundaries.

The rundown that follows is far from complete. Covering only the most common types of sacred art prevalent in Kerala, it sets out the bare bones of traditions that have innumerable variations, sub-branches and sects. One of the most rewarding pleasures of travelling around the state is discovering styles of dance, music and ritual theatre you've never heard of and could not possibly have imagined yourself. Coming across them is largely a matter of chance, but you'll increase the odds by attending as many **festivals** – at as many different locations – as possible during your stay.

For more serious study, foreigners are welcome to visit the **academies** set up to preserve Kerala's performing and sacred arts in Thrissur (see p.201), Irinjalakuda (see p.205) and Cheruthuruthy (see p.209). Details of major **arts festivals** – such as Malabar Mahotsavam in Kozhikode (see p.61) and Nishagandi and Swathi Sangeetotsavam in Thiruvananthapuram (see p.99) – are given in Basics on pp.58–61, and in the relevant accounts throughout the Guide.

Murals

One of the best-kept secrets of South Indian art are the unique **Keralan murals** found at Mattancherry Palace in old Kochi (see p.186) and at around sixty other locations in the state. Most are on the walls of functioning temples; they are not marketable, transportable, or indeed even seen by many non-Hindus. Few date from before the sixteenth century, though their origins may go back to the seventh century, probably influenced by the Pallava style of Tamil Nadu, but only traces in one tenth-century cave temple survive from the earliest period. Castaneda, a traveller who accompanied Vasco da Gama on the first Portuguese landing in India, described how he strayed into a temple, supposing it to be a church, and saw "monstrous-looking images with two-inch fangs" painted on the walls, causing one of the party to fall to his knees exclaiming, "if this be the devil, I worship God".

Technically classified as **fresco-secco**, Kerala murals employ vegetable and mineral colours, predominantly ochre reds and yellows, white and blue-green, and are coated with a protective sheen of pine resin and oil. Their ingenious design incorporates intense detail, portraying human and celestial figures with clarity and dynamism; subtle facial expressions are captured with the simplest of lines, while narrative elements are always bold and arresting. In common with all great Indian art, the murals posses a complex iconography and symbolism.

Non-Hindus can see fine examples in Kochi's Mattancherry Palace, Padmanabhapuram (see p.119), Ettumanur (see p.156) and Kayamkulam (see p.138). Visitors interested in how they are made should head for the Mural Painting Institute at Guruvayur. A paperback book, *Murals of Kerala*, by M.G. Shashi Bhooshan serves as an excellent introduction to the field.

Also worthy of mention are Kerala's **Christian murals** – the finest examples of which are preserved in the Church of St Thomas in Palai, near Kottayam in southern Kerala (see p.157).

Temple sculpture

Hindu sculpture saw its finest flowering in the stone workshops of neighbouring Tamil Nadu, whose giant temples are encrusted with elaborate carvings and painted stucco figures. By comparison, Keralan shrines are more restrained, but they still contain some extraordinary stonework, principally in the form of carved pillars and doorways, but also the deities themselves, many of which are hewn from rare coloured granites or black basalt. Even if you are not able to enter the innermost confines of Hindu temples in the region, this sacred art can still be admired at a distance: from the courtyards, it's usually possible to peek inside the soot- and ghee-covered interior chambers, and at the colonnaded walkways surrounding the complexes.

All sacred sculpture in South India follows the strictest rules of iconography, originally set down in ancient canonical texts called the **Shilpa Shastras**. When it comes to creating images of gods and goddesses, measurement always begins with the proportions of the artist's own hand and the icon's resultant face-length as the basic unit. The overall scheme is allied to the equally scientific rules applied to classical music, specifically *tala* or rhythm. Human figures total eight face-lengths, eight being the most basic of rhythmic measures. Figures of deities are *nava-tala*, nine face-lengths.

Like their counterparts in medieval Europe, South Indian sculptors remained largely anonymous. Even though the most talented artists may have been known to their peers – in some rare cases earning renown in kingdoms at opposite ends of the Subcontinent – their names have become lost over time. An explanation often advanced for this is the *Shastras'* insistence that the personality of an individual artist must be suppressed in order for divine inspiration to flow freely.

Some fine examples of Hindu temple sculpture, most of them made in the stone-carving town of Mamallapuram in Tamil Nadu, are displayed in Kerala's top handicrafts shops, such as Natesan's in Thiruvananthapuram and around the antique emporia of Mattancherry. You'll also see some superb specimens in the lobbies of five-star hotels, where they're often placed amid pools of water and floating flowers.

Kalam ezhuttu

The tradition of **kalam ezhuttu** (pronounced "kalam-*erroo*-too") – detailed and beautiful ritual drawings, in coloured powder, of deities and geometric patterns (*mandalas*) – is very much alive all over **Kerala**, although few visitors to the region even know of its existence. The designs usually cover an area of around thirty square metres, often outdoors and under a *pandal* – a temporary shelter made from bamboo and palm fronds. Each colour, made from rice flour, turmeric, ground leaves and burnt paddy husk, is painstakingly applied using the thumb and forefinger as a funnel. Three communities produce *kalams*: two come from the temple servant (Ambalavasi) castes, whose rituals are associated with the god Ayappan (see p.277) or the goddess Bhagavati; the third, the

△ *Kalam ezhuttu*

Pullavans, specialize in serpent worship. Iconographic designs emerge gradually from the initial grid lines and turn into startling figures, many of terrible aspect, with wide eyes and fangs. Noses and breasts are raised, giving the whole a three-dimensional effect. As part of the ritual, the significant moment when the powder is added for the iris or pupil, "opening" the eyes, may well be marked by the accompaniment of *chenda* drums and *elatalam* hand-cymbals.

Witnessing the often day-long **ritual** is an unforgettable experience. The effort expended by the artist is made all the more remarkable by the inevitable destruction of the picture shortly after its completion; this truly ephemeral art cannot be divorced from its ritual context. In some cases, the image is destroyed by a fierce-looking *vellichapad* ("light-bringer"), a village oracle who can be recognized by shoulder-length hair, red *dhoti*, heavy brass anklets and the hooked sword he brandishes either while jumping up and down on the spot (a common sight), or marching purposefully about, controlling the spectators. At the end of the ritual, the powder, invested with divine power, is thrown over the onlookers. *Kalam ezhuttu* rituals are not widely advertised, but check at tourist offices.

Music

India is most famous for its Hindustani music, as played in the north of the country by maestros such as Ravi Shankar and Ustad Bismillah Kahn, but the South has its own, very different – and considerably more ancient – classical form, known as **Carnatic**, which enjoys a huge following in Kerala. In addition, Kerala preserves a uniquely Malayali style of devotional song called Sopana *sangeetham*, developed in the region's temples as accompaniment for ritual dramas. These, and the immensely popular percussion of **chenda melam**, can still be heard at religious festivals all over the state during the winter.

Carnatic music

The **Carnatic music** of South India might be labelled "classical", but it's nothing like classical music anywhere else in the world. Rather than being the domain of an urban elite, it's an explosion of colour, sound and popular Hindu worship – part of the warp and weft of the region's culture. The other major difference is that, lacking written notation, the form is learned by ear or – in the case of its highly sophisticated rhythmic system – taught by a marvellous, mathematical structure of "finger computing" which enables a percussionist to break down a complex *thaalam* (rhythmic cycle) into manageable units. The music and the faith which inspired the Carnatic genre have remained inseparable. You'll hear it performed outside temples and during major cultural festivals in Kerala, for which top artists from Tamil Nadu and other southern states travel to the region.

While devotional and religious in origin, Carnatic music is as much a vehicle for education and entertainment as for spiritual elevation. **Kritis**, a genre of Hindu hymn, are hummed and sung as people go about their daily business. Tuneful and easily recognizeable, they hold a similar position in popular culture to the Christian hymn in Western societies.

In performance, Carnatic musicians will distil the essence of a *ragam* – the melody – into six to eight minutes. In part this is because a *kriti*, the base of many recitals, is a fixed composition without improvisation. Carnatic musicians'

Thiruvananthapuram is the place you're most likely to hear top-notch Carnatic music. The capital hosts two major classical festivals each year: **Swathi Sangeetotsavam**, held in the first or second week of January in the grounds of the Puttan Malika palace; and the **Nishagandi Festival**, staged a couple of weeks later at the open-air auditorium next to Kankakannu palace. See pp.98–99 for more details of these.

creativity lies in their ability to interpret a piece faithfully while shading and colouring the composition appropriately. The words of a *kriti* affect even non-vocal compositions: instrumentalists will colour their interpretations as if a vocalist were singing along; the unvoiced lyric determines where they place an accent, a pause or melodic splash.

Improvisation has its place too, most noticeably in a sequence known as **ragam-thanam-pallavi**. This is a full-scale flowering of a Carnatic *ragam* and is every bit the equal of a Hindustani performance, although it is employed more sparingly, tending to be the centrepiece or climax of a Carnatic concert.

Whereas Carnatic music generally breaks down into three strands – temple music, temple dance-accompaniment, and music for private devotional observance – paying concert performances have somewhat blurred these distinctions. Concert-giving led to other changes, too, and **microphones** came into use during the 1930s. They lent soft-voiced instruments such as members of the *vina* family (see below) a new lease of life, and replaced full-tilt vocal power with greater subtlety. Nowadays, concerts will typically feature a named principal soloist (either vocal or instrumental) with melodic and rhythmic accompaniment and a *tanpura* or drone player. Percussionists of standing are often included in concert announcements and advertising as they are attractions in their own right. Female musicians involved in a principal role tend to be vocalists, *vina* players or violinists. Male musicians have access to a wider range of musical possibilities as well as outnumbering female principal soloists or accompanists by roughly three to one.

Carnatic instruments

The **vina** (or *veena*) is the foremost Carnatic **stringed instrument**, the southern equivalent (and ancestor) of the sitar. A hollow wooden fingerboard with 24 frets is supported by two resonating gourds at each end. The *vina* has seven strings, four used for the melody and the other three for rhythm and drone. The **chitra vina** (or *gotuvadyam*) is an unfretted 21-string instrument with sets for rhythm and drone as well as sympathetic strings. It has a characteristically soft voice which, before amplification, meant it was best suited to intimate surroundings.

As in the North, the transverse bamboo flute goes under the name of **bansuri** or **venu**, although it is typically shorter and higher in pitch than the Hindustani instrument. The **nadaswaram** is a piercing double-reed oboe-like instrument. It's longer and more deep-toned than the Hindustani *shehnai*, is associated with weddings, processions and temple ceremonies and is often paired with a drone. Besides its ceremonial functions – and it is perhaps best heard in the open air – it is sometimes employed in formal classical concert settings.

The Carnatic counterpart to the tabla is the **mridangam**, a double-headed, barrel-shaped drum made from a single block of jackwood. Both heads are constructed from layers of hide and can be tuned according to the *ragam* being performed. Other percussion instruments include the **tavil**, a folk-style barrel drum commonly found in ceremonial *nadaswaram* ensembles, and the **ghatam**, a clay pot tuned by firing. The latter is frequently found in South Indian ensembles and, unlikely as it may seem, in the hands of a top player can contribute some spectacular solos. The **morsing** (or *morching*) is a Jew's harp, often part of the accompanying ensemble, although it is frequently dropped when groups tour to save on the air fare. The **jalatarangam** (or *jalatarang*) is something of a curiosity: a melodic percussion instrument comprising a semi-circle of water-filled porcelain bowls. It can create a sound of extraordinary beauty as the lead melody instrument in a typical Carnatic ensemble with violin, *mridangam* and *ghatam*.

From the nineteenth century, Carnatic music began to appropriate **Western instruments**, notably the violin and clarinet, and more recently the mandolin and saxophone. The violin is played sitting on the floor with its body against the upper chest and the scroll wedged against the ankle, leaving the left hand free to slide more freely up and down the strings. South India's child prodigy, **U. Srinivas**, popularized the mandolin as a Carnatic instrument. He is a very devout musician and his performances usually have a devotional ingredient.

The **saxophone** is another recent import, and its champion, Kadri Gopalnath, is one of South India's most popular musicians, with dozens of recordings to his credit. Gopalnath demonstrates Carnatic music's particular ability to be ancient and modern at the same time. When he plays the Carnatic *ragams*, the powerful sound of the saxophone echoes the ancient *nadaswaram*, but with a distinctively contemporary tone and attitude.

Sopana and kathakali sangeetham

Whereas Carnatic music nowadays tends to be staged in concert halls, the context of Kerala's own classical vocal tradition, **Sopana sangeetham**, remains primarily the Hindu temple – specifically the steps leading to the central shrine. Sopana is always sung by a soloist, accompanied by the hour-glass-shaped *ettaka* drum, whose pitch can be shifted to shadow the vocals. The origins of the form are obscure. Thought to have started as the accompaniment to Tantric rituals, such as the making of *kalam ezhuttu* powder patterns for the goddess Kali (see p.286), it was later taken up by the **bhakti cult** – the distinctive structure of Sopana, which was supposed to reflect the ascent of devotees to ecstatic bliss, lent itself well to the intensely fervent atmosphere of Krishna worship, as popularized from the ninth century in temples such as Guruvayur, under patronage from the Kulasekhara rajas. During the cultural renaissance of the nineteenth century, however, Sopana was shunned by the salons of kings like Swati Thirunal – one of the great patrons of Carnatic music in the region – because it was deemed too "rustic".

Although you might not get a chance to hear Sopana performed in its authentic setting, you'll hear something pretty close to it sung during *kathakali* recitals. *Kathakali sangeetham* is similar to Sopana in terms of vocal technique, but it employs additional percussion of small cymbals (*kaimani*), gongs (*chengila*) and large, double-sided *chenda* drums. Here, the *ettaka* is deployed when female characters take the stage, its sing-song sound creating a feel that complements the drama.

The state's principal music colleges, where you can sit in on classes of *kathakali sangeetham* and Carnatic singing, are the Keralam Kalamandalam academy at Cheruthuruthy (see p.209), and Kerala Sangeetha Nataka Akademi, Thrissur (see p.201).

Chenda melam: Keralan ritual percussion

The noisiest, rowdiest and most intense phase of any Keralan temple festival is the one presided over by the local drum orchestra, or **chenda melam**, whose ear-shattering performances accompany the procession of the deity around the sacred precinct and into the shrine. As impressive for their mental arithmetic as percussion technique and showing enormous stamina in the intense heat, the musicians play an assortment of upright barrel drums (*chenda*) supported over the shoulder, bronze cymbals and wind instruments – the oboe-like *kuzhal* and the spectacular C-shaped brass trumpets (*kombu*), which emphasize and prolong the drum beating.

Performances invariably begin with an impressive "*ghrr*" and "*dhim*" produced on the drums. This is said to symbolize a lion's roar and was probably once performed in support of a lion hunt. After this mighty introduction, the drums drop the tempo and the music builds up like a pyramid, starting slowly with long musical cycles before working up to a short, fast, powerful climax. During the performance, an elephant, musicians and the crowd process round the temple precinct, until, after more than two hours, the excited crowd and sweating musicians celebrate the conclusion and follow the elephant and deity into the **inner temple**.

The first stage broadly symbolizes the ordinary life of men, while the peak of the last stage shows the ideal human or divine aspect of reality. The music must please the god on top of the elephant and, of course, the assembled temple crowd. While the main beats are provided by hitting the underside of the *chenda*, the skilled solo *chenda* players create intricate patterns over the top. Different

Yesudas

You can't go anywhere in Kerala, not even the remotest backwaters, without hearing the honey-toned voice of Yesudas drifting out of a *chayakada* or toddy shop. For Malayalis the world over – as well as tens of millions of Tamils – his songs provide the soundtrack to everyday life as well as important rites of passage. From the instant a bus driver slots one of his albums into the dashboard cassette player, dozens of eyes will mist over, recalling loved ones in the Gulf, a scene from a forgotten Bollywood movie or memories of last Onam's *sadya* feast.

Kattassery Joseph Yesudas was born in 1940, the son of a poor Christian family in Kochi. His father, a singer-actor on the local stage, trained him in Carnatic vocals from the age of three, but it wasn't until 1961 that the star had his first breakthrough as a playback artist in a Tamil film, singing four lines from a poem by his spiritual hero, Shri Narayana Guru. It's hard to imagine a more appropriate start to a career that would, in less than a decade, see him become a household name in India, performing songs from all the major faiths in more than twenty different Indian languages.

Narayana Guru's message of "One Caste, One Religion, One God" has always been particularly close to the heart of the vocalist. One of his best-loved hits is a track whose title translates as "I Will Pray at the Guruvayur Temple One Day" – an ironic reference to the fact that, as a Christian, Yesudas has never been permitted to enter Kerala's most hallowed Hindu shrine.

Yesudas's **devotional songs** to Lord Ayyappan blare from pilgrim coaches all over the state in January and February, and accompany millions of black-*mundu* wearing devotees on their way to and from Sabarimala each year – just a small part of a repertoire covering an estimated 30,000 recordings. In spite of his success, however, Kerala's most high-profile musician has remained as famous for his level-headedness and humility as his vocal talent, attributing his meteoric stardom to "Love of God".

players may gather for each event, but they are capable of playing together perfectly with no rehearsal – the concept is more like a big jazz band than a European classical orchestra.

A **typical setup** for a medium-sized temple festival kicks off with a turn from the *panchavadyam* orchestra, comprising three types of drums, cymbals and the *kombu* trumpets. A conch is blown three times, symbolizing the holy syllable "Om", and the performance begins its first stage with a slow, 1792-beat rhythmic cycle. The cycles speed up and contract into 896, 448, 224 and 112 beats, ending with a 56-beat cycle. Fireworks, a large crowd and elephants trumpeting support the ecstatic climax.

For the evening, performances of *tayambaka*, *keli* and *kuzhal pattu* are announced. Each is a solo performing style, with players from the *chenda melam* and *panchavadyam* orchestras. *Tayambaka* is the main attraction, an improvised *chenda* solo played with a small ensemble of accompanying treble and bass *chenda* and cymbals. The other solo styles, *keli* (with a soloist on the *maddalam*, a horizontally slung barrel drum) and *kuzhal pattu* (oboe), precede the midnight performance of the last *chenda melam*.

Dance

Among the most magical experiences a visitor to South India can have is to see one of the dances that play such an important part in the region's cultural life. India's most prevalent classical style, **bharatanatyam**, originated in the Chola temples of neighbouring Tamil Nadu and still fills concert arenas in cities today, as does the more uniquely Keralan form, **mohiniyattam**.

The Natya Shastra

All forms of Indian dance share certain broad characteristics and can be traced back to principles enshrined in the **Natya Shastra**, a Sanskrit treatise on dramaturgy dating from the first century BC. The text covers every aspect of the origin and function of **natya**, the art of dance-drama, which combines music, stylized speech, dance and spectacle, and characterizes theatre throughout South Asia. The spread of this art form occurred during the centuries of cultural expansion from the second century BC to the eighth century AD, when South Indian kings sent trade missions, court dancers, priests and conquering armies all over the region. Even in countries that later embraced Buddhism or Islam, dances continue to show evidence of Indian forms, and Hindu gods and goddesses still feature, mixed with indigenous heroes and deities.

South Indian dance and dance-dramas are divided into two temperaments: **tandava**, which represents the fearful male energy of Shiva, and **lasya**, representing the grace of his wife Parvati. *Kathakali* is *tandava* and *bharatanatyam* is *lasya*, while some other forms combine the two elements. Equally, they include in differing degrees the three main components of classical dance: **nritta**, pure dance in which the music is reflected by decorative movements of the body; **natya**, which is the dramatic element of the dance and includes the portrayal of character; and **nritya**, the interpretive element, in which mood is portrayed through hand and facial gestures and the position of the feet and legs.

The term **abhinaya** describes the resources at the disposal of a performer in communicating the meaning of a dance; they include costume and make-up, speech and intonation, psychological understanding and, perhaps the most distinctive and complex element, the language of gestures. Stylized gestures are prescribed for every part of the body – there are seven movements for the eyebrows, six for the nose and six for the cheeks, for example – and they can take a performer years of intensive training to perfect.

Once complete control of the body has been mastered, a performer will have a repertoire of several thousand meanings. In combination with other movements, a single hand gesture, with the fingers extended and the thumb bent for example, can be used to express heat, rain, a crowd of men, the night, a forest, a flight of birds or a house. Similarly, up to three characters can be played by a single performer by alternating facial expressions.

Despite frequent feats of technical brilliance, performers are rarely judged by their skill in executing a particular dance, but by their success in communicating certain specific emotions, or **bhava**, to the audience. This can only be measured by the quality of **rasa**, a mood or sentiment, one for each of the nine *bhavas*, which the audience experiences during a performance.

Bharatanatyam

The best-known Indian classical dance style is **bharatanatyam**, a composite term made up of **bharata**, an acronym of "*bhava*" (expression), "*raga*" (melody) and "*tala*" (rhythm) and **natyam,** the Tamil word for "dance". It is a graceful form, rich in gesture, performed only by women. A popular subject for temple sculptures throughout South India (especially in Tamil Nadu), it originated in the dances of the **devadasis**, temple dancing girls. Usually "donated" to a temple by their parents, the young girls were formally "wedded" to the deity and spent the rest of their lives dancing or singing as part of their devotional duties in the great Tamil shrines. Later, however, the *devadasis* system became debased, and the dancers, who formerly enjoyed high status in Hindu society, became prostitutes controlled by the Brahmins, whom male visitors to the temple would pay for sexual services.

In the latter half of the nineteenth century, four brothers set themselves the task of saving the dance from extinction and pieced together a reconstruction of the form through study of the *Natya Shastra*, the images on temple friezes and information gleaned from former *devadasis*. Although the dance today is largely based on their findings, this was only the first step in its revival, as *bharatanatyam* continued to be confined to the temples and was danced almost exclusively by men – the only way, as the brothers saw it, of preventing its moral decline. Not until the 1930s, when **Rukmini Devi**, a member of the Theosophical Society, introduced the form to a wider middle-class audience, did *bharatanatyam* begin to achieve popularity as a secular art form.

As ward of the nineteenth-century British rebel **Annie Besant**, Devi had greater exposure to foreign arts than many women of her generation. She developed an interest in Western dance while accompanying her husband, George Arundale, former principal of the Theosophical Society's school in Adyar, Chennai, on lecture tours and had studied under Pavlova, among others. In 1929, however, after witnessing a performance of the dance, she dedicated her life to its revival. The dance school she founded at Adyar is now known as Kalakshetra, and continues to develop some of the world's most accomplished exponents.

In her determination to make the art form socially respectable, Devi eliminated all erotic elements and was authoritarian in her views about how *bharatanatyam* should be danced. Many ex-pupils have gone on to develop their own interpretations of the style, but the form continues to be seen as

△ *Bharatanatyam*

an essentially spiritual art. Its theme is invariably romantic love, with the dancer seen as a devotee separated from the object of her devotion. In this way, she dramatizes the idea of **sringara bhakti**, or worship through love.

As with other classical dance forms, training is rigorous. Performers are encouraged to dissolve their identity in the dance and become instruments for the expression of divine presence. Performances – which last about two hours and are divided into nine stages - are preceded by a *namaskaram*, a salutation to the gods, offered by the stage, musicians and audience; a floral offering is made to a statue of the presiding deity, which stands at the right of the stage. The pivotal part of the performance is **varnam**, which the preceding three phases (*alarippu*, *jatiswaram* and *sabdam*) build up to through *nritta* (pure dance based on rhythm), adding melody and then lyrics. In *varnam*, every aspect of the dancer's art is exercised through two sections, the first slow, alternating *abinhaya* with rhythmic syllables, and the second twice the pace of the first, alternating *abinhaya* with melodic syllables. In the following two phases (*padams* and *javalis*) the emphasis is on the expression of mood through mime, and in the penultimate phase, the *tillana*, the dancer reverts again to the pure rhythm which began the dance. A *mangalam*, or short prayer, marks the end of a performance.

Mohiniyattam

A semi-classical form that originated in Kerala, **mohiniyattam**, like *bharatanatyam*, grew out of the temple dances of the *devadasis*. It, too, was revived through the efforts of enthusiastic individuals, first in the nineteenth century by Swati Thirunal, the raja of Travancore, and again in the 1930s, after a period of disrepute, by the poet Vallathol. *Mohiniyattam* ("the dance of the enchantress") takes its name from the mythological maiden **Mohini**, who evoked desire and had the ability to steal the heart of the onlooker. Usually a solo dance performed by women, it is dominated by the mood of *lasya*, with graceful movements distinguished by a rhythmic swaying of the body from side to side. The central theme is one of love and devotion to god, with Vishnu or Krishna appearing most frequently as the heroes.

Dancers of *mohiniyattam* wear realistic make-up and the cream-white, gold-bordered Kasavu sari of Kerala. The music which accompanies the dancer is Sopanam-inflected Carnatic, with lyrics in Malayalam.

Ritual theatre

Various forms of ritualized theatre have always been performed in Indian temples, both as visual sacrifices to the deities and as entertainment. If you're lucky enough to catch an authentic recital *in situ* during a temple festival you'll never forget it: the stamina of the performers and the spectacle of an audience sitting up all night to see the finale of a dance-drama at dawn is utterly remarkable.

Kathakali

Here is the tradition of the trance dancers, here is the absolute demand of the subjugation of body to spirit, here is the realization of the cosmic transformation of human into divine.

Mrinalini Sarabhai, classical dancer

The image of a **kathakali** actor in a magnificent costume with extraordinary make-up and a huge gold crown has become Kerala's trademark. There are still many traditional performances, which take place on open ground outside a temple, beginning at 10pm and lasting until dawn, illuminated solely by the flickers of a large brass *nilavilakku* oil lamp centre stage. Virtually nothing about *kathakali* is naturalistic, because it depicts the world of gods and demons. Both male and female roles are played by men.

Standing at the back of the stage, two musicians play driving rhythms, one on a bronze gong, the other on heavy bell-metal cymbals; they also sing the dialogue. Actors appear and disappear from behind a handheld curtain and never utter a sound, save the odd strange cry. Learning the elaborate hand gestures, facial expressions and choreographed movements, as articulate and precise as any sign language, requires rigorous training that can begin at the age of eight and last ten years. At least two more drummers stand left of the stage; one plays the upright **chenda** with slender curved sticks, the other the **maddalam**, a horizontal barrel-shaped hand drum. When a female character is "speaking", the *chenda* is replaced by the hourglass-shaped **ettaka**, a "talking drum" on which melodies can be played. The drummers keep their eyes on the actors, whose every gesture is reinforced by their sound, from the gentlest embrace to the wildest sword fight.

Although it bears the unmistakeable influences of *kudiyattam* and indigenous folk rituals, *kathakali*, literally "story-play", is thought to have crystallized into a distinct theatre form during the seventeenth century. The plays are based on three major sources: the *Mahabharata*, the *Ramayana* and the Bhagavata Purana. While the stories are ostensibly about god-heroes such as Rama and Krishna, the most popular characters are those that give the most scope to the actors – the villainous, fanged, red-and-black-faced *katti* ("knife") anti-heroes. These types, such as the kings Ravana and Duryodhana, are dominated by lust, greed, envy and violence. David Bolland's handy paperback *Guide to Kathakali*, widely available in Kerala, gives invaluable scene-by-scene summaries of the most popular plays and explains in simple language a lot more besides.

When attending a performance, arrive early to get your bearings before it gets dark, even though the first play will not start much before 10pm. Members of the audience are welcome to visit the dressing room before and during the performance, to watch the **masks** and **make-up** being applied. The colour and design of these, which specialist artists take several hours to apply, signify the personality of each character. The principal characters fall into the following seven types.

Pacca ("green" and "pure") characters, painted bright green, are the noble heroes, including gods such as Rama and Krishna.

Katti ("knife") are evil and clever characters such as Ravana. Often the most popular with the audience, they have green faces to signify their noble birth, with upturned moustaches and white mushroom knobs on the tips of their noses.

Chokannatadi ("red beard") characters are power-drunk and vicious, and have black faces from the nostrils upwards, with blood-red beards.

Velupputadi ("white beard") represents Hanuman, monkey son of the wind god and personal servant of Rama. He always wears a grey beard and furry coat, and has a black and red face and green nose.

Karupputadi ("black beard") is a hunter or forest-dweller and carries a sword, bow and quiver. He has a coal-black face with a white flower on his nose.

Kari ("black") characters, the ogresses and witches of the drama, have black faces, marked with white patterns, and huge breasts.

Minnukku ("softly shaded") characters are women, Brahmins and sages. The women have pale yellow faces sprinkled with mica and the men wear orange *dhotis*.

Once the make-up is finished, the performers are helped into their costumes – elaborate wide skirts tied to the waist, towering headdresses and long silver talons fitted to the left hand. Women, Brahmins and sages are the only characters with a different style of dress: men wear orange, and the women wear saris and cover their heads. The transformation is completed with a final prayer before the performance begins.

Visitors new to *kathakali* will undoubtedly get bored during such long programmes, parts of which are very slow indeed. If you're at a village performance, you may not always find accommodation, so you can't leave during the night. Be prepared to sit on the ground for hours, and bring some warm clothes. Half the fun is staying up all night to witness, just as the dawn light appears, the gruesome disembowelling of a villain or a demon *asura*.

Kudiyattam

Three families of the Chakyar caste and a few outsiders perform the Sanskrit drama **kudiyattam**, the oldest continually performed theatre form in the world. Until recently, it was only staged inside temples, and then only in front of the uppermost castes. Visually, it is very similar to its offspring, *kathakali*, but its atmosphere is infinitely more archaic. The actors, eloquent in sign language and symbolic movement, speak in the bizarre, compelling intonation of the local Brahmins' Vedic chant, unchanged for more than two millennia.

A single act of a *kudiyattam* play can require ten full nights; the entire play forty. A great actor, in full command of the subtleties of gestural expression, can take half an hour to do such a simple thing as murder a demon, berate the audience, or simply describe a leaf falling to the ground. Unlike *kathakali*, *kudiyattam* includes comic characters and plays. The ubiquitous Vidushaka, narrator and clown, is something of a court jester, and traditionally has held the right to openly criticize the highest in the land without fear of retribution.

To the uninitiated, the costumes look like pared down versions of those worn in *kathakali*, with mask-like make-up featuring rice-paper borders, heavy jewellery and pleated white skirts of starched fabric. Versions of just such outfits, including heavy gold headdresses, appear in ancient Indian murals, decorating the rock-cut caves of Ajanta in Maharashtra.

The ideal place to watch *kudiyattam* is at one of the purpose-built **kuttambalam** theatres in Keralan temples – beautiful works of art in their own right, with carved panels and lathe-turned wooden pillars. Entrance to them is often restricted to Hindus, but during festivals at major shrines in towns such as Thrissur, Irinjalakuda and Guruvayur non-Hindus may be allowed in during festivals (you'll increase your chances of admission if you're dressed correctly, in a white *mundu* or sari). Otherwise, you can always catch authentic performances by some of Kerala's top actors at the Margi School in Thiruvananthapuram's East Fort district (see p.100; ☎0471/247 8806, ⊛www.margitheatre.org), which stages monthly shows. The Natana Kairali Institute at Irinjalakuda (see p.204) also holds an annual *kudiyattam* festival in the first fortnight of January.

For real aficionados, nothing beats the 41-day ritual cycle of **Chakyar koothu**, a solo form of *kudiyattam*, staged in September and October in Thrissur's Vaddukanathan temple. While men and women percussionists of the Nambiyar caste create complex rhythms on the *elathalam* (cymbals) and the *mizhavu*, a large copper drum, the Chakyar stands on a platform wearing special headgear, starched white cloths bound around the waist and distinctive clownlike make-up. *Koothu* means "dance", but this is a bit of a misnomer as there's little body movement involved; rather, facial and hand expressions convey the narrative, which usually follows one of the Hindu epics, but with lots of comic asides criticizing contemporary events and personalities. The greatest exponent of *koothu* was **Mani Madhava Chakyar** (1889–1990), a Sanskrit scholar and ritual artist from Kozhikode district, who was especially renowned for his mastery of *rasa-abhinaya* (enacting sentiment through facial expression) and *netrabhinaya* (beautiful eye movements). His wife, **P. K. Kunjimalu**, was one of Kerala's greatest exponents of *nagiarama*, an all-female form of *kudiyattam* (unlike in *kathakali*, women rather than men play women's roles).

Ottamthullal

Ottamthullal is another form of solo mime, but one that's performed in less rarefied atmosphere than Chakyar *koothu*. Often dubbed the "poor man's *kathakali*", it's commonly staged in temple courtyards during festivals, where it serves as a kind of ritualized stand-up comedy. From atop small raised platforms, actors sing, dance and recite simple rhythmic verses in Malayalam (rather than the stylized Sanskrit of Chakyar *koothu*), swaying to and fro, accentuating their story with hand and arm movements. *Thullal* compositions were usually based on well-known Puranic stories, only incorporating asides that satirized local rulers, courtiers, Namboodiri-Brahmins, and other prominent people. The costumes can be wonderfully elaborate, featuring gilded, mirror-inlaid crowns and breastplates with woollen tassels and matching epaulettes, colourful starched and pleated skirts, and striking face make-up.

The man credited with inventing the form was **Kunchan Nambiar** (1705–70), an eighteenth-century actor-poet who is said to have fallen asleep during a long performance of Chakyar *koothu* and dreamed of a simplified, more accessible (and humorous) version.

Theyyattam

The most visually exciting of all Kerala's ritual arts is a form of spirit possession practised in villages in the far north of Kerala around Kannur (Cannanore). Its name – **theyyam** or **theyyattam** – derives from the Malayalam word for god, *deivam*. Unlike in *kathakali* and *kudiyattam*, where actors impersonate goddesses or gods, or characters from mythology, here the performers actually become the deity being invoked, acquiring their magical powers for the duration of the ceremony. These allow them to perform superhuman feats, such as rolling in hot ashes, remaining impervious to flames (while dressed in highly inflammable palm-leaf cloaks), or dancing with a crown that rises to the height of a coconut tree. By watching the *theyyam* enact legends associated with his or her life, members of the audience believe they can partake of the magical powers – to cure illness, conceive a child or get lucky in a business venture.

Traditionally staged in small clearings (*kaavus*) attached to village shrines, *theyyattam* rituals are always performed by members of the lowest castes; Namboodiri and other high-caste people may attend, but they do so to venerate the deity – a unique inversion of the normal social hierarchy. Each *theyyam* has its own distinctive **costume**, made of elaborate jewellery, body paints, intricate face make-up and, above all, gigantic headdresses (*mudi*) weighing many kilos.

Performances generally have three distinct phases: the *thottam*, where the dancer, wearing a small red headdress, recites a simple devotional song accompanied by the temple musicians; the *vellattam*, in which he runs through a series of more complicated rituals and slower, elegant poses; and the *mukhathezhuttu*, the main event, when he appears in full costume in front of the shrine. From this point on until the end of the performance, which may last all night, the *theyyam* is manifest and empowered, dancing around the arena in graceful, rhythmic steps that grow quicker and more energetic as the night progresses, culminating in a frenzied outburst just before dawn, when it isn't uncommon for the dancer to be struck by a kind of spasm.

The complicated series of moves of the rituals take up to a decade of regular training to acquire. From the age of eight or nine, boys follow courses of *kalaripayattu*, Kerala's martial art (see p.100), to build up the necessary strength. Performances are also usually preceded by a period of rigorous fasting.

Four hundred or more different forms of *theyyam* exist in the hinterland of Kannur. Most are manifestation of the Mother Goddess (Mahadeva) such as Bhadrakali or Bhagawati; others are spirit folk heroes and legendary characters from the epics. These days, they may be held for a family celebration or temple feast. But with each passing year, as younger generations of *theyyam* families move away from home or take up wage labour, performances are getting rarer and many of the *theyyams* danced a couple of decades ago have died out.

Our boxed feature "*Theyyattam* Around Kannur" on p.245 gives pointers that will help you track down the rituals, and how to behave during them. Notices for most events are listed in the "What's On" page of *Malayala Manorama*, although you'll probably need help to translate them.

Further south from Kannur, the area between Ernakulam and Kottayam in central Kerala is the heartland of another kind of Tantric ritual theatre form whose roots, like those of *theyyattam*, stretch back to Dravidian times. **Mutiyettu** is based on re-enactments of mythic combats between the Goddess Bhadrakali and the demon Darika. Again, they feature dazzling headdresses, costumes, and make-up, and usually a larger cast of performers than *theyyam*. Another interesting aspect of the rituals is that they're preceded by the making of large *kalam ezhuttu* powder paintings, which the actors later destroy by dancing over them.

Puppetry

Traditional **shadow puppetry**, or *tholpabavakoothu*, is a dying art form based in the Palakkad district of central Kerala, where it is staged in temples. The puppets, representing over 130 different divine and mythological characters, are made of deerskin and are manipulated against a large, 12-metre-long screen of white cotton, back-lit by as many as 21 different oil lamps. Musical accompaniment comes from *chenda* drums, with occasional blasts from a conch, whistle or pipe. Performances typically span a continuous period of between twelve and twenty-one nights and tell the story of the *Ramayana*, from the birth of Rama to his coronation – ostensibly for the benefit of the Goddess Bhadrakali, who is believed to have missed Rama's big tussle with the demon Ravava because she was herself grappling with another devil, Darika. Bhadrakali's presence is symbolized by cloth drapes, removed from her shrine and suspended within view of the puppets.

The Natana Kairali Institute in Irinjalakuda (see p.204) is the best place to go to watch Keralan **glove puppetry**, or *pavakathakali*. Its director, Gopal Venu, is one of the form's finest exponents. Like *tholpabavakoothu*, however, its traditional heartland is Palakkad district, where it is thought to have been introduced in the eighteenth century by itinerant puppeteers from Andhra Pradesh. Stories from the *Mahabharata*, *Ramayana* and Puranas provide the narratives for shows, which resemble *kudiyattam* and *kathakali* recitals in miniature: the puppets, skillfully carved from wood and decorated with gilded, jewel-inlaid headdresses, colourfully painted faces and elaborate cloth costumes, appear from behind an appliqué curtain, illuminated by flames from a sacred *nilavilakku* oil lamp. Only one sculptor, Ravi Gopalan Nair from Nedumangad near Thiruvananthapuram, still makes traditional *pavakathakali* puppets.

Wildlife

A fast-growing population and the rapid spread of industries have inflicted pressures on the rural landscape of Kerala, but the region still supports a wealth of distinct flora and fauna. Walking on less frequented beaches or through the rice fields of the coastal plain, you'll encounter dozens of exotic birds, while the hill country of the interior supports an amazing variety of plants and trees. The majority of the peninsula's larger mammals keep to the dense woodland of the Western Ghat mountains, where a cluster of reserves affords them some protection from the hunters and loggers who have wrought such havoc on India's fragile forest regions over the past few decades.

Flora

Something like 3500 species of flowering plants have been identified in Kerala, as well as countless lower orders of grasses, ferns and brackens. In the Western Ghats, it is common to find one hundred or more different types of tree in an area of just one hectare. Many species were introduced from Europe, South America, Southeast Asia and Australia, but there are also many indigenous varieties that thrive in the moist climate.

Along the coast, rice paddy and **coconut** plantations predominate, forming a near-continuous band of lush foliage. Spiky **spinifex** helps bind the shifting sand dunes behind the miles of sandy beaches lining the coast, while **casuarina** trees stand as windbreaks where coconut palms have been felled.

In towns and villages, you'll encounter dozens of beautiful **flowering trees**. The Indian **laburnum**, or cassia, throws out masses of yellow flowers and long seed pods in late February before the monsoons. This is also the period when mango and Indian **coral trees** are in full bloom; both produce bundles of stunning red flowers.

One of the region's most distinctive trees, found in both coastal and hill areas, is the stately **banyan**, which propagates by sending out roots from its lower branches. The largest specimens spread out over an area of two hundred metres. The banyan is revered by Hindus, and you'll often find small shrines at the foot of mature trees. The same is true of the **peepal**, which has distinctive spatula-shaped leaves. Temple courtyards often enclose large peepals, which usually have strips of auspicious red cloth hanging from their lower branches.

The Western Ghats harbour a wealth of flora, from flowering trees and plants to ferns and fungi. **Shola** forests, lush patches of moist evergreen woodland which carpet the deeper mountain valleys, exhibit some of the greatest biodiversity. Sheltered by a leafy canopy, which may rise to a height of twenty metres or more, buttressed roots and giant trunks tower above a luxuriant undergrowth of brambles, creepers and bracken, interspersed with brakes of bamboo. Common tree species include the kadam, sisso or martel, kharanj and teak, while rarer sandalwood thrives on the higher, drier plateaux in the mountains above Munnar. There are dozens of representatives of the fig family, too, as well as innumerable (and ecologically destructive) eucalyptus and rubber trees, planted as cash crops by the Forest Department.

Mammals

Although peninsular India boasts more than fifty species of wild mammals, visitors who stick to populated coastal areas are unlikely to spot anything more inspiring than a monkey or the occasional mongoose. Most of the larger animals have been hunted to the point of extinction; the few that remain roam the dense woodland lining the Western Ghats, in the sparsely populated forest zones of the **Nilgiri Biosphere Reserve**.

The largest Indian land mammal is, of course, the Asian **elephant**, stockier and with much smaller ears than its African cousin, though no less venerable. Travelling around Kerala, you'll regularly see elephants in temples and festivals, but for a glimpse of one in the wild, you'll have to venture into the mountains where, in spite of the huge reduction of their natural habitat, around six and a half thousand still survive. Among the best places for sightings are Periyar (see p.159) and the twin reserves comprising the Wayanad Wildlife Sanctuary (see p.236). Today, wild elephants, which are included under the Endangered Species Protection Act, are under increasing threat from villagers: each adult animal eats

---

"Elephant madness"

There exists in Malayalam a term for a kind of mania that Keralans succumb to en masse during the winter festival season: *anapraanth*, or "elephant madness". Various manifestations of this uniquely South Indian mentality occur, but the most pervasive is the tradition of parading elephants around temple precincts during festivities, accompanied by ear-splitting drum and brass *panchavadyam* orchestras and firework displays. Tens of thousands turn up to adore the assembled tuskers, which are always caparisoned with gold headdresses, while teams of boys wearing white *mundus* stand on their backs performing choreographed routines with sequined silk parasols, yak-tail fly whisks and giant peacock-feather fans. It's an amazing spectacle, especially when the temple is large enough to afford a long line (up to seventy elephants can be employed in the biggest events).

A total of around seven hundred live in captivity in Kerala, ninety percent of them in the care of temples – though many mosques and churches also use elephants in their celebrations. The largest and best loved enjoy film-star status. One – a massive 3.2-metre-tall tusker called Guruvayur Keshavan who, before his death at the age of 72 in the 1970s, was adored for his exceptional intelligence and devotion to Krishna – has even had his skeleton, tusks, and a life-size effigy of him placed at the entrance to the famous Guruvayur temple, for pilgrims to venerate.

In the form of Shiva's son, Ganesh ("Vingeshwara" in Malayalam), elephants are worshipped all over India as symbols of good fortune and as removers of obstacles. But the increasing popularity, and scale, of festivals in Kerala – where temples vie with each other to lay on the longest lines, with the biggest stars – has placed the pachyderm population under considerable strain. Not only do processional elephants have to stand for hours enduring the cacophony of drumming and fireworks, they also have to walk for up to twelve hours between venues. Moreover, to suppress must (an annual phase of sexual heat in which male elephants grow restless, oozing liquid from glands between their eyes and ears), their *mahouts* sometimes deprive them of water for two or three days at a stretch. In recent years, a couple of randy tuskers have cracked under the strain and gone on the rampage: thirteen people were killed in what the local press dubs as "elephant mishaps" over a six-week period in 2007 – worth bearing in mind if the *anapraanth* takes you and you're drawn too close.

roughly two hundred kilos of vegetation and drinks one hundred litres of water a day, and their search for sustenance inevitably brings them into conflict with rural communities.

Across the state, especially in the hill districts, local villagers displaced by wildlife reserves have often been responsible for the poaching that has reduced **tiger** populations to such fragile levels (see box, p.303). These days, sightings in Kerala are very rare indeed, though several kinds of big cat survive. Among the most beautiful is the **leopard**, or panther (*Panthera panthus*). Prowling the thick forests of the Ghats, these elusive cats prey on monkeys and deer, and occasionally take domestic cattle and dogs from the fringes of villages. Their distinctive black spots make them notoriously difficult to see amongst the tropical foliage, although their mating call (reminiscent of a saw on wood) regularly pierces the night air in remote areas. The **leopard cat** (*Felis bengalensis*) is a miniature version of its namesake, and more common. Sporting a bushy tail and round spots on soft buff or grey fur, it is about the same size as a domestic cat and lives around villages, picking off chickens, birds and small mammals. Another cat with a penchant for poultry, and one which villagers occasionally keep as a pet if they can capture one, is the docile Indian **civet** (*Viverricual indica*), recognizeable by its lithe body, striped tail, short legs and long pointed muzzle.

Wild cats share their territory with a range of other mammals unique to the Subcontinent. One you've a reasonable chance of seeing is the **gaur**, or Indian bison (*Bos gaurus*). These primeval-looking beasts, with their distinctive sleek black skin and knee-length white "socks", forage around bamboo thickets and shady woods. The bulls are particularly impressive, growing to an awesome height of two metres, with heavy curved horns and prominent humps.

With its long fur and white V-shaped "bib", the scruffy **sloth bear** (*Melursus ursinus*) – whose Tamil name (*bhalu*) inspired that of Rudyard Kipling's character Baloo in *The Jungle Book* – ranks among the weirder-looking inhabitants of the region's forests. Sadly, it's also very rare, thanks to its predilection for raiding sugar-cane plantations, which has brought it, like the elephant, into direct conflict with man. Sloth bears can occasionally be seen shuffling along woodland trails, but you're more likely to come across evidence of their foraging activities: trashed termite mounds and chewed-up ants' nests. The same is true of both the portly Indian **porcupine** (*Hystrix indica*), or *sal*, which you see a lot less often than the mounds of earth it digs up to get at insects and cashew or teak seedlings; and the **pangolin** (*Manis crassicaudata*), or *tiryo*, a kind of armour-plated anteater whose hard, grey overlapping scales protect it from predators.

Full-moon nights and the twilight hours of dusk and dawn are the times to look out for nocturnal animals such as the **slender loris** (*Loris tardigradus*). This shy creature, a distant cousin of the lemur, with bulging round eyes, furry body and pencil-thin limbs, grows to around twenty centimetres in length and moves as if in slow motion, except when an insect flits to within striking distance. The **mongoose** (*Herpestes edwardsi*) is another animal sometimes kept as a pet to keep dwellings free of scorpions, mice, rats and other vermin. It will also readily take on snakes – you might see one writhing in a cloud of dust with king cobras during performances by snake charmers.

Late evening is also the best time for spotting **bats**. Kerala has four species, including the fulvous fruit bat (*Rousettus leshenaulti*), or *vagul* – so called because it gives off a scent resembling fermenting fruit juice; Dormer's bat (*Pipistrellus dormeri*); the very rare rufous horseshoe bat (*Rhinolophus rouxi*); and the Malay fox vampire bat (*Magaderma spasma*), which feeds off the blood of live cattle.

△ Macaques in Wayanad

Flying foxes (*Pteropus gigantus*), the largest of India's bats, are also present in healthy numbers. With a wingspan of more than one metre, they fly in cacophonous groups to feed in fruit orchards, sometimes falling foul of electricity cables on the way: frazzled flying foxes dangling from live cables are a common sight in the interior.

Other species to look out for in forest areas are the Indian **giant squirrel** (*Ratufa indica*), or *shenkaro*, which has a coat of black fur and red-orange lower parts. Two-and-a-half times larger than its European cousins, it lives in the canopy, leaping up to twenty metres between branches. The much smaller **three-striped squirrel** (*Funambulus palmarum*), or *khadi khar*, recognizeable by the three black markings down its back, is also found in woodland. The five-striped **palm squirrel** (*Funambulus pennanti*) is a common sight all over the state, especially in municipal parks and villages.

Forest clearings and areas of open grassland are grazed by four species of deer. Widely regarded as the most beautiful is the **cheetal** (*Axis axis*), or spotted axis deer, which congregates in large groups around water holes and salt licks, occasionally wandering into villages to seek shelter from its predators. The plainer, buff-coloured **sambar** (*Cervus unicolor*) is also common, despite being affected by diseases spread by domestic cattle during the 1970s and 1980s. Two types of deer you're less likely to come across, but which also inhabit the border forests, are the **barking deer** (*Muntiacus muntjak*), whose call closely resembles that of a domestic dog, and the timid **mouse deer** (*Tragulus meminna*), a speckled-grey member of the *Tragulidae* family that is India's smallest deer, growing to a mere thirty centimetres in height. Both of these are highly secretive and nocturnal; they are also the preferred snack of Kerala's smaller predators: the **striped hyena** (*Hyaena hyaena*), or *colo*, and **wild dog** (*Cuon alpinus*), which hunt in packs, and the more solitary **jackal** (*Canis aureus*).

The Indian tiger: survival or extinction?

Few animals command such universal fascination as the **tiger**. Small populations exist in several areas, including eastern Russia and Malaysia, but it's only in India that you have a real chance of glimpsing this magnificent beast in the wild, stalking through the teak forests and terai grass to which it is uniquely adapted. A solitary predator at the apex of the food chain, it has no natural enemies save man.

At the start of the twentieth century, up to 100,000 tigers still roamed the Subcontinent, even though **shikar** (tiger hunting) had long been the "sport of kings". An ancient dictum held it auspicious for a ruler to notch up a tally of 109 dead tigers, and *nawabs*, maharajas and Mughal emperors all indulged their prerogative to devastating effect. But it was under the trigger-happy British that tiger hunting reached its most gratuitous peak. Photographs of pith-helmeted, bare-kneed *burrasahibs* and their maharaja buddies posing behind mountains of striped carcasses became a hackneyed image of the Raj. Even Prince Philip (now president of the Worldwide Fund for Nature) couldn't resist bagging one during a royal visit.

In the years following Independence, **demographic pressures** nudged the Indian tiger perilously close to extinction. As the human population increased in rural districts, more and more forest was cleared for farming – thereby depriving large carnivores of their main source of game and of the cover they needed to hunt. Forced to turn on farm cattle as an alternative, tigers were drawn into direct conflict with humans; some animals, out of sheer desperation, even turned man-eater.

Poaching has taken an even greater toll. The black market has always paid high prices for live animals – a whole tiger can fetch up to $100,000 – and for the various body parts believed to hold magical or medicinal properties. The meat is used to ward off snakes, the brain to cure acne, the nose to promote the birth of a son and the fat of the kidney – applied liberally to the afflicted organ – as an antidote to male impotence.

By the time an all-India moratorium on tiger shooting was declared in the 1972 Wildlife Protection Act, numbers had plummeted to below two thousand. A dramatic response geared to fire public imagination came the following year, with the inauguration of **Project Tiger**. At the personal behest of then prime minister Indira Gandhi, nine areas of pristine forest were set aside for the last remaining tigers. Displaced farming communities were resettled and compensated, and armed rangers employed to discourage poachers. Demand for tiger parts did not end with Project Tiger, however, and the poachers remained in business, aided by organized smuggling rings. Undercover investigators repeatedly come across huge hauls of tiger bones and skins, and over the past few years the discovery of tiger carcasses rotting in several reserves indicates that poachers have been resorting to new, more random killing methods. In 2005, eight officials at Sariska National Park in Rajasthan were suspended after it emerged that virtually all of the park's 26 listed tigers had been poached. And in 2006, video footage came to light of a major festival in Chinese-occupied Tibet at which officials and even tourists were shown wearing tiger skins; its highlight was a tent made up of 108 individual pelts.

Today, even though there are 23 Project Tiger sites, numbers continue to fall. Official figures claim a **population** of up to 3750, but independent evidence puts the figure at around half of that. The population rise indicated by counts based on pug marks – thought to be like human fingerprints, unique to each individual – that gave such encouragement in the early 1990s has been declared inaccurate. Poorly equipped park wardens are still fighting a losing battle: in 1998 it was estimated that one tiger was being poached every day, and a decade later the situation is at least as bad. The most pessimistic experts even claim that India's most exotic animal could face extinction within two decades.

Your chances of sighting a wild tiger in Kerala are thus slim, to say the least; but don't rule out the possibility altogether. Visitors to the Periyar Wildlife Sanctuary sometimes spot one, especially in the dry season between March and the monsoons, when drought forces them out to prowl the lake shores, from where they're easily sighted.

A species of mountain goat endemic to the Western Ghats, whose last stronghold is the grassy uplands surrounding the tea-plantation town of Munnar in central Kerala (see p.217), is the delightful **Nilgiri tahr**. The tahr's famously inquisitive nature made it an easy target for hunters in colonial times: sportsmen could shoot them for supper without leaving their fireside chairs in camp. Numbers had plummeted by the 1940s, but are on the rise again thanks to the strict protection they're accorded in the Eravikulam National Park, just outside Munnar, where herds of tahr congregate a stone's throw from the main car park.

Long-beaked **dolphins** are regular visitors to the shallow waters of Kerala's more secluded bays and beaches. They are traditionally regarded as a pest by local villagers, who believe they eat scarce stocks of fish. However, this long-standing antipathy is gradually being eroded as local people realize the tourist-pulling potential of the dolphins.

Finally, no rundown of Keralan mammals would be complete without some mention of **monkeys**. The most common species is the mangy pink-bottomed **macaque** (*Macaca mulatta*), or *makad*, which hangs out anywhere scraps may be scavenged or snatched from unwary humans: temples and picnic spots are good places to watch them in action. The black-faced Hanuman **langur**, by contrast, is less audacious, retreating to the trees if threatened. It is much larger than the macaque, with pale grey fur and long limbs and tail. In forest areas, the langur's distinctive call is an effective early-warning system against big cats and other predators, which is why you often come across herds of cheetal grazing under trees inhabited by large colonies of langurs. The Silent Valley National Park in Palakkad district (see p.220) is one of the world's last strongholds of the extremely rare **lion-tailed macaque**. Only a few hundred of these distinctive primates survive in their native habitat of southwestern India, and the population in Kerala's parks is the most robust. Distinguished by their corona-style mane of blonde fur and amber-coloured eyes, lion-tailed macaques, sometimes called "wanderoos", have traditionally been hunted for their meat and fur by the indigenous tribes of the Western Ghats.

Reptiles

Reptiles are well represented in the region, with more than forty species of snakes, lizards, turtles and crocodiles recorded. The best places to spot them are open, cultivated areas: paddy fields and village ponds provide abundant fresh water, nesting sites and prey (frogs, insects and small birds).

Your hotel room, however, is where you are most likely to come across tropical India's most common reptile, the **gecko** (*Hemidactylus*), which clings to walls and ceilings with its widely splayed toes. Deceptively static most of the time, these small yellow-brown lizards will dash at lightning speed if you try to catch one, or if an unwary mosquito or fly scuttles within striking distance. The much rarer **chameleon** (*Chamaeleonidae*) is more elusive, mainly because its constantly changing camouflage makes it virtually impossible to spot. They'll have no problem seeing you, though: independently moving eyes allow them to pinpoint approaching predators, while prey is slurped up with their fast-moving 40cm-long tongues. The other main lizard to look out for is the **Bengal monitor** (*Varanus bengalensis*). This giant brown-speckled reptile looks like it has escaped from *Jurassic Park*, growing to well over a metre in length. It used to be a common sight in coastal areas, basking on roads and rocks.

However, monitors are often killed and eaten by villagers, and have become increasingly rare.

The monsoon period is when you're most likely to encounter **turtles**. Two varieties paddle around village ponds and wells while water is plentiful: the flap-shell (*Lissemys punctata*) and black-pond (*Melanochelys trijuga*) turtles, neither of which are endangered. Numbers of Olive Ridley marine turtles (*Lepidochely olivacea*), by contrast, have plummeted over the past few decades as a result of villagers raiding their nests when they crawl onto the beach to lay their eggs. This amazing natural spectacle occurs each year at a number of beaches in the region, notably Kolavippalam, near Kanhangad in the far north of the state.

An equally rare sight nowadays is the **crocodile** (*Crocodylidae*). Populations have dropped almost to the point of extinction, although the backwaters support vestigial colonies of saltwater crocs, which bask on mud flats and river rocks. Dubbed "salties", they occasionally take calves and goats, and will snap at the odd human if given half a chance. The more ominously named mugger crocodile, however, is harmless, inhabiting unfrequented freshwater streams and riversides.

Snakes

Twenty-three species of snake are found in Kerala, ranging from the gigantic **Indian python** (*Python molurus*, or *har* in Konkani), a forest-dwelling constrictor that grows up to six metres in length, to the innocuous worm snake (*Typhlops braminus*), or *sulva*, which is tiny, completely blind and often mistaken for an earthworm.

The eight **poisonous snakes** in the region include India's four most deadly species: the cobra, the krait, Russel's viper and the saw-scaled viper. Though these are relatively common in coastal and cultivated areas, even the most aggressive snake will slither off at the first sign of an approaching human. Nevertheless, ten thousand Indians die from snake bites each year, and if you regularly cut across paddy fields or plan to do any hiking, it makes sense to familiarize yourself with the following four or five species, just in case; their bites nearly always prove fatal if not treated immediately with anti-venom serum – available at most clinics and hospitals.

Present in most parts of the state and an important character in Hindu mythology, the **Indian cobra** (*Naja naja*), or *naga*, is the most common of the venomous species. Wheat-brown or grey in colour, it is famed for the "hood" it unfurls when confronted and whose rear side usually bears the snake's charac-teristic spectacle markings. Its big brother, the **king cobra** (*Naja hannah*), or *Naga raja*, is much less often encountered. Inhabiting the remote forest regions along the Kerala–Karnataka border, this beautiful brown, yellow and black snake, which grows to a length of four metres or more, is very rare, although the itinerant snake charmers who perform in markets occasionally keep one. Defanged, they rear up and "dance" when provoked by the handler, or are set against mongooses in ferocious (and often fatal) fights. The king cobra is also the only snake in the world known to make its own nest.

Distinguished by their steel-blue colour and faint white cross markings, **kraits** (*Bungarus coerulus*) are twice as deadly as the Indian cobra: even the bite of a newly hatched youngster is lethal. **Russel's viper** (*Viperi russeli*) is another one to watch out for. Identifiable by the three bands of elliptical markings that extend down its brown body, the Russel hisses at its victims before darting at them and burying its centimetre-long fangs into their flesh. The other common poisonous snake in Kerala is the **saw-scaled viper** (*Echis carinatus*). Grey with an arrow-shaped mark on its triangular head, it hangs around in the cracks between stone walls, feeding on scorpions, lizards, frogs, rodents and smaller snakes. They also hiss when threatened, producing the sound by rubbing together serrated scales located on the side of their head. Finally, **sea snakes** (*Enhdrina schistosa*) are common in coastal areas and potentially deadly (with a bite said to be twenty times more venomous than a cobra's), although rarely encountered by swimmers, as they lurk only in deep water off the shore.

Harmless snakes are far more numerous than their killer cousins and frequently more attractive. The beautiful **golden tree snake** (*Chrysopelea ormata*), for example, sports an intricate geometric pattern of red, yellow and black markings, while the **green whip snake** (*Dryhopis nasutus*), or *sarpatol*, is a stunning parakeet-green. The ubiquitous **Indian rat snake**, often mistaken for a cobra, also has beautiful markings, although it leaves behind a foul stench of decomposing flesh. Other common non-poisonous snakes include the wolf snake (*Lycodon aulicus*), or *kaidya*; the Russel sand boa (*Eryx conicus*), or *malun*; the kukri snake (*Oligodon taeniolatus*), or *pasko*; and the cat snake (*Boiga trigonata*), or *manjra*.

Birds

You don't have to be an aficionado to enjoy Kerala's abundant **birdlife**. Breathtakingly beautiful birds regularly flash between the branches of trees or appear on overhead wires at the roadside.

Three common species of **kingfisher** frequently crop up in the paddy fields and wetlands of the coastal plains, where they feed on small fish and tadpoles. With its enormous bill and pale green-blue wing feathers, the stork-billed kingfisher (*Perargopis capensis*) is the largest and most distinctive member of the family, although the white-throated kingfisher (*Halcyon smyrnensis*) – which has iridescent turquoise plumage and a coral-red bill – and the common kingfisher (*Alcedo althis*), identical to the one frequently spotted in northern Europe, are more alluring.

Other common and brightly coloured species include the green, blue and yellow **bee-eaters** (*Merops*), the stunning **golden oriole** (*Oriolus oriolus*), and the **Indian roller** (*Coracias bengalensis*), famous for its brilliant blue flight feathers and exuberant aerobatic mating displays. **Hoopoes** (*Upupa epops*), recognizeable by their elegant black-and-white tipped crests, fawn plumage and distinctive "hoo...po...po" call, also flit around fields and villages, as do **purple sunbirds** (*Nectarina asiatica*) and several kinds of **bulbuls**, **babblers** and **drongos** (*Dicrurus*), including the fork-tailed **black drongo** (*Dicrurus macrocercus*) – which can often be seen perched on telegraph wires. If you're lucky, you may also catch a glimpse of the **Asian paradise flycatcher** (*Tersiphone paradisi*), which is widespread and among the region's most exquisite birds: males of more than four years of age sport a thick black crest and long silver white streamers, while the more often-seen females and young males are reddish-brown.

Paddy fields, ponds and saline mudflats usually teem with water birds. The most ubiquitous is the snowy white **cattle egret** (*Bubulcus ibis*), which can usually be seen wherever there are cows and buffalo, feeding off the grubs, insects and other parasites that live on them. The **great egret** (*Casmerodius albus*) is also pure white, although lankier and with a long yellow bill, while the **little egret** (*Egretta garzetta*), sports a short black bill. Look out too for the mudbrown Indian pond heron, or "**paddy bird**", India's most common heron.

Distinguished by its pale green legs, speckled breast and hunched posture, it stands motionless for hours in water, waiting for fish or frogs.

The hunting technique of the beautiful **white-bellied sea eagle** (*Haliaetus leucogaster*), by contrast, is truly spectacular. Cruising twenty to thirty metres above the surface of the water, this black and white osprey stoops at high speed to snatch its prey – usually sea snakes and mackerel – from the waves with its fierce yellow talons. More common birds of prey such as the **brahminy kite** (*Haliastur indus*), recognizeable by its white breast and chestnut head markings, and the **black kite** (*Milvus migrans*), a dark-brown bird with a fork tail, are widespread around towns and fishing villages, where they vie with raucous gangs of house **crows** (*Corvus splendens*) for scraps.

Other birds of prey to keep an eye open for, especially around open farmland, are the **white-eyed buzzard** (*Butastur teesa*), the **oriental honey buzzard** (*Pernis ptilorhyncus*), the **black-shouldered kite** (*Elanus caeruleus*) – famous for its blood-red eyes – and the **shikra** (*Accipiter badius*), which closely resembles the European sparrowhawk.

Forest birds

The region's forests may have lost many of their larger animals, but they still offer exciting possibilities for bird-watchers. One species every enthusiast hopes to glimpse while in the woods is the magnificent **hornbill**. The Malabar grey hornbill (*Ocyceros griseus*), with its blue-brown plumage and long curved beak, is the most common, although the Indian pied hornbill (*Anthracoceros malabaricus*), distinguished by its white wing and tail tips and the pale patch on its face, often flies into villages in search of fruit and lizards. The magnificent great hornbill (*Buceros bicornis*), however, is more elusive, limited to the most dense forest areas, where it may occasionally be spotted flitting through the canopy. Growing to 130cm in length, it has a black-and-white striped body and wings, and a huge yellow beak with a long curved casque on top.

Several species of **woodpecker** also inhabit the interior forests, among them three types of flameback woodpecker: the common black-rumped flameback (*Dinopium bengalense*) has a wide range and also ventures into gardens and hotel grounds. A bird whose call is a regular feature of the Western Ghat forests, though you'll be lucky to catch a glimpse of one, is the wild ancestor of the domestic chicken – the **jungle fowl**. The grey or Sommerat's jungle fowl (*Gallus sonneratii*), has dark plumage scattered with yellow spots and streaks.

Wildlife viewing

Although you can expect to come across many of the species listed above on the edge of towns and villages, a spell in one of Kerala's nature reserves (see box, p.308) offers the best chance of viewing wild animals and birds. These reserves are a far cry from the well-organized and well-maintained national parks you may be used to at home, although at the larger and more easily accessible wildlife reserves – such as Periyar and Eravikulam – a solid infrastructure exists to transport visitors around, whether by Jeep or, in the case of the former, boat and bamboo rafts. Don't, however, expect to see much if you stick to these standard excursion vehicles laid on by the park authorities. Most of the rarer animals keep well away from noisy groups of trippers. Wherever possible,

Kerala holds fourteen separate reserves set aside for the protection of wildlife, covering a little under five percent of the state's total surface area. Most are up in the Western Ghat range, which preserves the highest concentrations of biodiversity anywhere in peninsular India. Given in alphabetical order, the following list rounds up the best of the region's reserves and parks; all receive full coverage in the Guide section of the book (follow the page references for more details).

Chinnar Wildlife Sanctuary. Located 58km from Munnar in the depths of the mountains, this reserve is much drier than neighbouring Eravikulam, but is a birding hot-spot, with 225 species listed. It also hosts an enigmatic white bison. Best time to visit: Oct–March. See p.217.

Eravikulam National Park. Located 17km northeast of Munnar, amid South India's highest peaks. Famous for its thriving population of Nilgiri tahr, a rare antelope that lives only here, on rolling grassy uplands. Your best sightings will be on longer treks. Best time to visit: Nov–April, though note that it's closed for several weeks in Jan–Feb during the rutting season. See p.217.

Kumarakom Bird Sanctuary. On the eastern shores of Vembanad Lake, between Kottayam and Alappuzha, in the heart of the backwaters district of southern Kerala. Tourism has badly disrupted the peace and quiet of this famous reserve, but it's still a good site for spotting migrant birds during the winter. Best time to visit: Nov–March. See p.155.

Peppara Wildlife Sanctuary. Amid the hills inland from Thiruvananthapuram, and the least rewarding of the state's nature reserves, though it does still hold breeding populations of lion-tailed macaques, as well as wild elephants. Best time to visit: Jan–April. See p.122.

Periyar Wildlife Sanctuary. A former maharaja's hunting reserve, centred on an artificial lake high in the Cardamom Hills. Occasional tiger sightings, but you're much more likely to spot an elephant. Well placed for trips into the mountains and tea plantations, with good accommodation, including remote jungle lodges which you have to trek to. Best time to visit: Oct–March. See p.159.

Silent Valley National Park. The most remote, and thus far least visited, of all Kerala's forested mountain valleys – recently saved from the dam builders. Its pride and joy is a thriving troupe of lion-tailed macaques; this is where you're most likely to sight them, but infrastructure is minimal. Best time to visit: Nov–March. See p.220.

Thattekkad Bird Sanctuary. Kerala's number one bird reserve, easily reachable between Munnar and Kochi. Spread along the banks of the Periyar River, its 25 square kilometres host 275 species, the majority of them endemics. Best time to visit: Nov–March. See p.175.

Wayanad Wildlife Sanctuary. Split into two separate reserves – Muthanga and Tholpetty – Wayanad encompasses some of the finest scenery in southern India, as well as Kerala's most imaginatively constructed eco-resorts. Most of the large fauna of the Western Ghats, and an amazing wealth of plant life, can be seen here – though tiger sightings are extremely rare. Best time to visit: Nov–March. See p.236.

try to organize **walking safaris** with a reliable, approved guide in the forest. In Periyar, guides are recruited from the area's indigenous minorities – formerly responsible for most of the region's poaching – and possess a wealth of local knowledge.

Books

For a region with such a long history of literacy and colonial rule, surprisingly few books have been written about Kerala in English. This neglect may well be reversed as the state's tourist boom gathers momentum, but in the meantime, most titles are either lavish coffee table tomes with little substance or dry academic studies on economics, politics and the anthropology of sacred arts.

The titles listed below aim to appeal to a broader readership, and will serve as ideal primers before your trip, or deepen your understanding of Kerala if you've been inspired to find out more by reading our "Contexts" essays. While some are stocked by high-street bookshops in Western countries, those published in India tend only to be available in Kerala itself, or via online retailers. If you can wait until you get to Kochi, the wonderful **Idiom Bookshop** in Fort Cochin (see p.191) holds the best selection of literature on Kerala assembled in any one place – and at much lower prices than you'll pay for the same books back home.

The publishers, and – where books are not published in the UK or US – the country of publication are listed in parentheses. Titles marked ⅄ are particularly recommended.

History and travel

Eric Axelson *Vasco da Gama: the Diary of his Travels through African Waters 1497–1499* (Stephan Philips). An anonymous first-hand account of Da Gama's voyage to Calicut, written by one of his crew, which was rediscovered in the nineteenth century after lying forgotten in the library of a Portuguese convent. It's framed by a detailed introduction by Axelson outlining the efforts of other explorers and mariners to reach India.

Alexander Frater *Chasing the Monsoon* (Penguin). Frater's wet-season jaunt down the Malabar Coast and across the Ganges plains took him through an India of muddy puddles and grey skies: an evocative account of the country as few visitors see it, and now something of a classic of the genre.

⅄ **John Keay** *India: a History* (HarperCollins). In this, the most recent of his five consistently excellent books on India, John Keay manages to coax a clear, impartial and highly

readable narrative from five thousand years of fragmented events. The best single-volume history of India currently in print, though it focuses more on the North than the South.

John Keay *The Honourable East India Company* (HarperCollins). In characteristically fluent style, Keay strikes the right balance between commentators who regard the East India Company as a rapacious institution with malevolent intentions, and those who present its acquisition of the Indian empire as an unintended, almost accidental process.

William Logan *Malabar Manual Vols I&II* (Asian Educational Services, India). Logan was the last British Collector of the Malabar, and his rambling account of the region under his charge, originally published in 1887, still serves as its major reference book. It's packed full of history, ethnography and background on religion and tradition that's still relevant today. Widely available in bookshops locally, but expensive abroad as it comes in two hardback volumes.

A. Sreedhara Menon *A Survey of Keralan History* (S.Viswanathan, India). A comprehensive survey of the region's past – from Prehistoric times to the present day – by Kerala's best-known historian. While much of it comprises dry, bare-bone lists of dynastic rulers and their various achievements, Sreedhara Menon also draws on cultural, economic and social history to fill out the picture. Not the easiest of reads, but the best general introduction currently available.

Stark World *Kerala* (Stark World, India). Not a pebble in the state is left unturned in this unbelievably thorough, 820-page guide. It's the size of a New York telephone directory and weighs far too much to be of practical use on holiday, but serves as an excellent reference guide, and is generously illustrated with top-quality colour photos.

Sanjay Subrahmanyam *The Career and Legend of Vasco da Gama* (Cambridge University Press). An erudite biography of the great fifteenth-century Portuguese discoverer, based on a mass of published and unpublished sources in Portuguese and other languages, which gets behind the self-made myth of Da Gama. As well as putting his achievements in context, it provides a compelling account of the voyages themselves, including the violent episodes on the Malabar.

Photography

Raghubir Singh *Kerala* (Thames & Hudson). This wide-ranging selection of 87 colour images by India's most acclaimed photographer gives a rounded and memorably vivid portrait of the state in the mid-1980s. Singh's genius lay in his ability to spot the telling detail amid swirls of Indian life, and there are plenty of quirky offbeat moments fixed here, as well as sumptuous set-pieces from his famous National Geographic commission, when he turned his eye on Thrissur Puram and snake boat races to dramatic effect.

Jonathan Watts & Laurent Aubert *Kerala: Of Gods and Men* (Five Continents, Italy). A superb study of the state's sacred arts, assembled over five years of ethnographic trips to temples, village shrines and festivals across Kerala. Watts' colour images capture with particular vividness the intensity of *theyyattam*, from make-up to midnight firebrand swinging.

Literature

Anita Nair (ed) *Where the Rain is Born* (Penguin, India). An eclectic anthology of essays, short stories, poems and extracts from published works (both in English and Malayalam) about Kerala. Arundhati Roy, Salman Rushdie, William Dalrymple and Alexander Frater number among the foreign contributors, and a string of local authors recall childhood memories and reflect on the changing face of the modern state. The perfect introduction to Kerala and its many complexities.

Arundhati Roy *The God of Small Things* (Flamingo/Harper-Collins). Haunting Booker Prize-winning novel about a well-to-do Syrian-Christian family caught between the snobberies of high-caste tradition, a colonial past and the diverse personal histories of its members. Seen through the eyes of two children, the assortment of scenes from backwater life are as memorable as the characters themselves, while the comical and finally tragic turn of events says as much about Indian history as the refrain that became the novel's catch-phrase: "things can change in a day."

Salman Rushdie *The Moor's Last Sigh* (Jonathan Cape/Pantheon). A typically spleen-ridden portrait of India's paradoxes, told through the life story of Moraes Zogoiby, aka "Moor" – the only son of a wealthy, aristocratic family who leads a life of depravity in Bombay before becoming embroiled in a financial scandal in London. Its early chapters are set in Cochin, and give a delight-fully lurid evocation of the ancient port city, with its mixed Jewish and Portuguese legacies. The novel won the Whitbread Prize for Rushdie.

Society

Achamma Chandersekaran (ed) *Daughters of Kerala* (Hats Off Books, US). An anthology of 25 short stories by Keralan women authors, written in direct, accessible prose that brims with insights into what it's like to be female in contemporary Kerala.

Nathan Katz and Ellen S. Goldberg *Kashrut, Caste and Kabbalah: the Religious Life of the Jews of Cochin* (Monohar, India). A candid portrait of Cochin's vestigal Jewish population, written by two anthropologists who lived, ate and worshipped with the community. It stresses the extent to which "Indianess" and "Jewishness" intermingle in this fast-disappearing culture.

Edward Luce *In Spite of the Gods* (Abacus, London). "An unsentimental evaluation of contem-porary India" is how this book bills itself, and there's no more authorita-tive, penetrating account of the current state of the nation in print. Written by a former South Asia correspondent of the FT, it's packed full of sobering statistics and myth-busting facts that challenge common misconceptions about India, yet somehow manages to remain eminently readable throughout.

Susan Visvanathan *The Christians of Kerala: History, Belief and Ritual among the Yakoba* (OUP, India). A great contextualizer for anyone with more than a passing interest in Syrian-Orthodox Christianity, written by an insider of the community who nevertheless retains an objective eye.

The arts and religion

Stuart H. Blackburn *Inside the Drama House: Rama Stories and Shadow Puppetry in South India* (University of California Press). The disappearing traditions of Palakkad district's Tamil shadow puppeteers, whose epic, month-long performances require almost as much skill and stamina as Rama needed to kill the demon Ravana – the subject of their shows.

Albrecht Frenz & Krishna Kumar Marar *Wall Paintings in North Kerala: 1000 Years of Temple Art* (Arnoldsche, Germany). Popular, readable and richly illustrated introduction to Kerala's forgotten Hindu murals – the benchmark book on the subject, though it only covers the north of the state.

Kannur Tourism *Theyyam Guide* (DTPC, India). Illustrated booklet, available through information counters around Kannur district, which provides one of the most practical rundowns of *theyyam* currently in print, listing locations, dates and descriptions of the four hundred or so rituals still in existence.

Ramu Katakam & Joginder Singh *Glimpses of Architecture in Kerala* (Rupa & Co., India). Beautifully photographed introduction to the architecture of Kerala, including many images of temple interiors, palaces and aristocratic residences normally off-limits to visitors.

Mohan Khokar *Traditions of Indian Classical Dance* (Clarion Books, India). Detailing the religious and social roots of Indian dance, this lavishly illustrated book, with sections on regional traditions, is an excellent introduction to the subject.

Parsram Mangharam *Raja Ravi Varma: the Painter Prince* (Bangalore,

India). Reproductions of 76 of the Keralan artist's most famous works, drawn from museums and private collections all over the country, with a biography which describes Varma's travels around India in engaging detail.

George Michell *The Hindu Temple* (University of Chicago Press). The definitive primer, introducing the significance and architectural development of Hindu temples.

Amina Okada & Martine Chemans *Sacred Walls of Kerala* (India Research Press). The latest and most scholarly work on Kerala's unique temple murals.

Phillip B Zarrilli *When the Body Becomes All Eyes* (Oxford University Press, India). This paperback's catchy strap line is "Paradigms, Discourses and Practices of Power in Kalarippayattu, a South Indian Martial Art", which perfectly conveys its rather turgid academic style, but there's no better overview of *kalari*, in all its arcane, bewildering complexity.

Wildlife and the environment

P. V. Bole & Yogini Vaghini *Field Guide to the Common Trees of India* (OUP, UK/US). A handy-sized, indispensable tome for serious tree spotters.

Grimmet & Inskipp *Birds of Southern India* (Helm, UK). The birders' bible, a beautifully organized, written and illustrated 240-page field guide listing every species known in South India. It's a tailored, region-specific version of the heftier *Pocket Guide to the Birds of the Indian Subcontinent* by the same authors (Helm), which lists all 1300 species spotted in South Asia.

Kamierczak & Van Perlo *A Field Guide to the Birds of the Indian*

Subcontinent (Pica/Helm, UK). Less popular than Grimmet and Inskipp's competing guide, but just as thorough, expertly drawn and well laid out, with every species named.

Insight Guides *Indian Wildlife* (APA Publications, UK). An excellent all-round introduction to India's wildlife, with scores of superb colour photographs, features on different animals and habitats and a thorough bibliography.

S. Prater *The Book of Indian Animals* (OUP, Bombay Natural History Society). The most comprehensive single-volume reference book on the subject, although only available in India.

Romulus Whitaker *Common Indian Snakes* (Macmillan). A detailed and illustrated guide to the Subcontinent's snakes, with all the Keralan species included.

Yoga

B.K.S. Iyengar *Yoga: the Path to Holistic Health* (Dorling Kindersley). The definitive guide to yoga by the world's leading teacher, and the only book of its kind recommended by practitioners from across the yoga spectrum. Some 1900 colour photos illustrate step-by-step instructions on how to achieve the postures, and there's a copious introduction giving the philosophical background and history. Too heavy to cart around India with you, but indispensable as a reference tool. A lighter (and much less expensive) version – fully endorsed by the great man, though modelled and written by three of his senior pupils – is *Yoga: the Iyengar Way*, by Silva, Mira and Shyan Mehta (also Dorling Kindersley).

Language

Language

Language

Malayalam, the official state language of Kerala, is spoken by an estimated 37 million people worldwide. It is closely related to Tamil, from which it diverged around the fifth century AD, but boasts its own script, recently boiled down from a bewildering 900 characters to a more keyboard-friendly 51 – including 16 separate vowels. Reflecting the region's complex cultural history, lots of Romance, Hebrew, Arabic, Portuguese, Dutch and English words have their place in the Malayali lexicon, although only four English words – teak, catamaran, coir and copra – have travelled in the opposite direction. The first Malayalam—English dictionary was written in 1872, by the German missionary Herman Gundert (grandfather of the novelist Herman Hesse). As any India trivia lover will tell you, Malayalam is also one of the longest single-word palindromes in English.

India's official national language, **Hindi**, has a place in Kerala, too, largely thanks to the increasing number of settlers from the north of the country and the popularity of "Bollywood" movies. However, the language of higher education, law and the quality press is English, which is so prevalent in the resorts that you can easily get by without a word of Malayalam. Even fluent English speakers, though, will be flattered if you attempt a few words of their native tongue.

Malayalam words and phrases

The lists of words and phrases below are intended as an aid to meeting people and travelling independently around more off-the-beaten-track areas of the state, where English is less commonly spoken.

Meeting and greeting

Namaskaram	Hello		Ennodu kshamikkoo	I am sorry (formal apology)
Aa	Yes		Veendum kaanaam	Goodbye
Illa	No		Suprabhaatham	Good morning
Nanni	Thank you		Shubha raathri	Good night
Uppakaarm	Thank you		Engane?	How are you?
Kshemikkoo	I'm sorry (quick courtesy)		Sukhamayiriknu	Fine (formal)

"ZH"

In English transliterations of Malayalam, the letters "zh" refer to a reflex consonant that sounds somewhere between a "d" and an "r", only pronounced in a distinctively South Asian way, beginning with a flick of your tongue from the roof of your mouth (rather than your teeth). Ask a Malayali to say the word 'Alappuzha' and you'll get the idea soon enough.

Kozhappam illa	Fine (informal)
Ente peru David	My name is (David)
Entha ningalude peru perenthaa?	What is your name? (formal)
Entha ningalude perenthaa?	What is your name? (informal)
Njaan England'il/ USA'il/Australia'il ninnu	I'm from England/ the USA/Australia/ etc

Mansillayilla	I don't understand
Ningal Inglishu samsarikkumo?	Do you speak English?
Enikku malayalam samsaarikkan ariyilla	I don't speak Malayalam
Swagatham	Welcome
Irikku	Sit down

Getting around

Nilkkoo	Stop
Adutha stop	Next stop
Namukku pkaam	Let's go
Eniku ivide eranganam	I want to get out/ down here
Etra duramanu . . .?	How far is . . .?
Ei vellam kudikkan kollamo?	Is this water ok to drink?
Kochikku ticket ethra rupayanu?	How much is a ticket to Kochi?
Kochikku oru ticket venam?	One ticket to Kochi, please

Tren	Train
Bus	Bus
Engottanu ee tren/bus pokunnathu?	Where does this train/ bus go to?
Evide annu kochikkulla tren/ bus?	Where is the train/ bus to Kochi?
Ee tren/bus Kochi nirutthumo?	Does this train/bus stop in Kochi?
Ivide niruthan paadilla	No parking
Vega paridhi	Speed limit

Directions

Idathekku	Left
Valathekku	Right
Nere	Straight ahead
Theruvu	Street
Idatthekku thiriyuka	Turn left
Valatthekku thiriyuka	Turn right
Nere povuka	Straight ahead
Kazhinhu	Past
Munpu	Before

Koodicherunna sthalathu	Intersection
Vadakku	North
Thekku	South
Kizhakku	East
Padinjaru	West
Kayattathil	Uphill
Irakkathil	Downhill
Bus standilekku vazhiyethu?	Which way to the bus stand?

Accommodation

Ivide oru muri ozhivundo?	Do you have any rooms available?
Onno/rendo perkkulla murikku vaadeka ethra aanu?	How much is a room for one person/ two people?
Aadyam muri kandote?	May I see the room first?
Virippe	Bedsheets
Kulimuri	Bathroom

Valiyathu	Bigger
Vrithiyullathu	Cleaner
Vila koranjathu	Cheaper
Njan edukam	OK, I'll take it
Njan onu/ randu raatri thamassikkum	I will stay for one/ two night(s)
Muri onnu vrithiyakkanam	Please clean my room

Shopping

Ithu ethra vilayanu?	How much is this?
Athu villa koothuthalanu	That's expensive
Kurachu	Less
Kooduthal	More
Enikyu athu venda	I don't want it
Ningal enne chadikyukayannalle	You're cheating me
Sari, njan itheduthollam	OK, I'll take it

Time

Ippol	Now
Pinne	Later
Samayam enthayi?	What is the time?
Ravile	Morning
Uchha	Afternoon
Vaikunneram	Evening
Paathi rathri	Midnight
Rathri	Night
Innale	Yesterday
Innu	Today
Naale	Tomorrow
Azhcha	Week
Maasam	Month
Varsham	Year
Iyazhcha	This week
Kazhinhayazhcha	Last week
Adutha azhcha	Next week
Mankoor	Hour
Divasam	Day

Days of the week

Thingalazhcha	Monday
Chovvazhcha	Tuesday
Budhanazhcha	Wednesday
Vyazhazhcha	Thursday
Velliyazhcha	Friday
Shaniyazhcha	Saturday
Nhayarazcha	Sunday

Numbers

Paadi	half	Irupathuh	20
Onnu	1	Irupathonnuh	21
Randu	2	Irupathirunduh	22
Moonnu	3	Irupathimoonuh	23
Naalu	4	Muppathuh	30
Anju	5	Nalpathuh	40
Aaru	6	Anpathuh	50
Eezhu	7	Arupathuh	60
Ettu	8	Ezhupathuh	70
Onpath	9	Enpathuh	80
Pathh	10	Thonnooru	90
Pathinonuh	11	Nooru	100
Pantharunduh	12	Irunooru	200
Pathimoonuh	13	Munnooru	300
Pathinaaluh	14	Aayiram	1000
Pathinanjuh	15	Randayiram	2000
Pathinaaruh	16	Pathu-laksham	One million
Pathinezhuh	17	Nooru kodi	One thousand million (one crore)
Pathinettuh	18		
Pathombathuh	19		

Each of Kerala's many religious and caste communities have their own dishes and food terms, and a full glossary would be almost impossible to compile. The following list, however, covers most of what you regularly encounter on menu cards.

aadu nirachathu	lamb with a rich stuffing of chicken and egg
achar	a type of sour pickle
appam	steamed pancake made from semi-fermented rice-flour, with speckled holes
avial	steamed root vegetables, coated in roughly ground coconut and yoghurt – generally without oil
avioli	a kind of flatfish
bagheri	small aubergine
biriyani	rice baked in clay pots with saffron or turmeric, whole spices and meat, and often hard-boiled egg; a Muslim speciality of northern Kerala
chakka	jackfruit
chapati	unleavened bread made of wholewheat flour and baked on a round griddle-pan
chatni	a tangy paste; in Kerala traditionally made from ground coconut and finely chopped fresh green chillis
chena	elephant yam
chikoo	a fruit that resembles a kiwi but tastes like a pear
chop	minced meat or vegetable surrounded by breaded mashed potato
chota peg	small measure used for spirits (whiskey, rum, etc)
cutlet	minced meat or vegetable fried in the form of a flat cake
dhal	spicy stew made with a base of lentils
dosa	rice pancake – should be crispy; when served with a filling it is called a masala dosa and when plain, a *sada* dosa
elakka	cardamom
erachi olathu	pieces of lamb simmered in ground fennel seeds and other spices until dry
eshtew	meat stew enriched with coconut, cinnamon, ginger, pepper and chillis, traditionally eaten in Kerala's Christian community
ghee	clarified butter sometimes used for festive cooking, and often drizzled over food before eating
gram dhal	a variety of lentil
halwa	sticky Keralan sweet made from rice flour, coconut, *jaggery* (sugar cane) and ghee, often brightly coloured
iddiappam	a kind of vermicelli made from finely ground rice
iddli	steamed rice cake, usually served with *sambar*
iddli-vada-sambar	light meal comprising one *vada* (lentil-flour doughnut), *iddli* and servings of *sambar* and chutney (*chatni*).
inji thayyir	pungent ginger-based condiments
ishtew	see "*eshtew*"
jaggery	unrefined sugar made from sugar cane
jeera rice	rice cooked with cumin seeds
jeerakam	cumin
kada	quail
kadala	a spicy mixture of chickpeas and onions
kakairachi	oysters
kallmakaya	mussels
kallu	toddy (alcohol made from fermented pure coconut sap)

kambalanga	bottle gourd (a vegetable similar to a cucumber)
kappad	tapioca, usually steamed or sautéed
kariyappila	leaves of the curry (a type of laurel) plant, a prime ingredient of savoury Keralan dishes (*karhipatta* in Hindi).
kariampu	cloves
karimeen	a river fish
karimeen pollichathu	river fish marinated in spices and steam-baked in a banana leaf
keema	minced meat (usually lamb or goat)
khichari	rice cooked with lentils in various ways, from plain to aromatic and spicy
kodampuli (also known as kokum)	a kind of tamarind, used as a souring agent in Keralan cooking
kofta	balls of minced vegetables or meat in a curried sauce
kootu	maize flour and lentils cooked with plantain, elephant yam and snake gourd
kozhi curry	country chicken curry, traditionally eaten in Kerala's Christian community
kurumulakku	pepper
malli	coriander seeds
malli illa	coriander leaf
manjal	turmeric
masala	any mixture of spices
meen moillee	fish curry simmered in coconut juice, green chillis, ginger and curry leaves
meen vattichathu	fish (usually mackerel or sardines) cooked in red curry sauce and soured with tamarind
methi	fenugreek
mulligatawny	curried vegetable soup, a classic Anglo-Indian dish
naan	white, leavened bread kneaded with yoghurt and baked in a tandoor
nakkam	mango and lime pickles
olan	a type of stew, often made of lentils and cucumber
ozhikan	dhal and *sambar* served in little terracotta pots for pouring over rice
paan	a digestive and mild stimulant
pachadi	vegetables coated with curry leaves and mustard seeds
pachari	white rice
pachhakai	plantain
pachha mulaku	green chilli
padavalanga	snake gourd (a long, dark green vegetable)
palak	spinach
papad/papadam	crisp, thin cracker
paratha	North Indian wholewheat bread made with butter, rolled thin and griddle-fried; a little bit like a chewy pancake, sometimes stuffed with meat or vegetables
parotta	South Indian bread, made by griddle frying a wheat-flour dough that's been partly fermented and wound into a coil
pathiri	rice-flour bread, a speciality of the Moppila communities of northern Kerala
patta	cinnamon

payasam	sweet rice and mung bean pudding, typically flavoured with cardamom. *Paal payasam* is made with rice and sugar; *parippu payasam* with mung beans and molasses; *pazham payasam* with pineapple and banana
pilau	see pulau
pollitchathu	steamed in a gravy of coconut milk, turmeric, chillis, ginger, garlic and shallots
pomfret	a flatfish, often stuffed with spicy paste or tandoori baked – tasty but with many bones
pootu	cylinders of roughly pounded rice and coconut steamed together
pulau	also known as *pilaf* or *pullao*, rice, gently spiced and pre-fried
puri	crispy, puffed-up, deep-fried wholewheat bread
puzhukkalari	red-streaked variety of Keralan rice with plump, separate grains
rasam	spicy, pepper water often drunk to accompany "meals"
roti	loosely used term; often just another name for chapati, though it should be thicker, chewier and may be baked in a tandoor
sadya	a traditional feast served at Onam (Hindu harvest festival)
sambar	soupy lentil and vegetable curry with asafoetida and tamarind; used as an accompaniment to *dosas*, *iddlis* and *vadas*
sharkaravaratti	fried plantain chips smothered in *jaggery*
tahorava kootu	duck curry, traditionally eaten in Kerala's Christian community
tarka	hot oil infused with mustard seeds and curry leaves
thaaravu	duck
thali	combination of dishes, chutneys, pickles and rice and bread served, especially in South India, as a single meal on a banana leaf or stainless steel thali dish
thoran	vegetables coated in a paste made from fresh coconut and shallots
toddy	(*kallu* in Malayalam) : Keralan "beer" – made from fermented coconut sap
udipi	brand of strict vegetarian fast-food cooking named after the pilgrimage town in coastal Karnataka where it originated. The ubiquitous masala dosa is *udipi* cuisine's hallmark snack
unakka mulaku chuvanna	red chilli
upperi	fried plantain chips
uppma	popular breakfast cereal made from semolina, spices and nuts, and served with *sambar*
uttapam	thick rice pancake often cooked with onions
vada	also known as *vadai*, a doughnut-shaped deep-fried lentil cake, which usually has a hole in its centre
vattichathu	spicy casserole flavoured with chillis, turmeric, garlic, fenugreek, black pepper and shallots, and traditionally cooked in a clay skillet
vazhuthanaga	small aubergine
vellarika	cucumber
vindaloo	hot and spicy sauce of Portuguese-Goan origin, whose sour taste comes from a combination of garlic and vinegar.

Emergencies and hassle

Rakshikkoo!	Help!
Enne thaniye vidoo	Leave me alone
Enne thodaruthu!	Don't touch me!
Njaan policine vilikkum	I'll call the police
Nilkoo! kallan!	Stop! Thief!
Enikku ningalude sahaayam venam	I need your help
Ithu athhyaa vashyamaanu	It's an emergency
Njaan vazhithetti	I'm lost
Ente bag nashtappettu	I've lost my bag
Ente purse nashtappettu	I've lost my wallet
Enikku oru kananam vakkeeline	I want to talk to a lawyer
Njan ippol oru fine adachotte?	Can I just pay a fine now?
Enikku sukhamilla	I'm sick
Enikku doctorude sahaayam venam	I need a doctor
Njaan ningalude phone upayogichootte?	Can I use your phone?
Toilet evideyaanu?	Where is the toilet?

Eating out

Prathal	Breakfast
Oonu	Lunch
Athazham	Supper
Hallo/chetta	Excuse me, waiter?
Njan mathiyakkuvaa	I've finished
Gambeeram	Delicious
Chutulla/thanuppulla	Hot/cold
Erivulla	Spicy
Menu card kanikku	The menu please
Billu taru	The bill please
Njan sasyabhojiyaa	I'm a vegetarian
Randu beer tharoo	Two beers, please
Eppozha adakkunnathu?	When is closing time?

Glossary

Acharya Religious teacher.

Adivasi Official term for tribal person.

Agarbati Incense.

Ahimsa Non-violence.

Arak Liquor distilled from rice or coconut.

Arati Evening temple puja of lights.

Asana Yogic seating posture; small mat used in prayer and meditation.

Ashram Centre for spiritual learning and religious practice.

Ashtanga Brand of yoga, founded by Shri Krishnamarcharya and his student, Shri Pattabhi Jois of Mysore, and popularized in the West by stars such as Madonna and Sting.

Atman Soul.

Avatar Reincarnation of Vishnu on earth, in human or animal form.

Ayurveda Ancient system of medicine employing herbs, minerals and massage.

Azulejos Portuguese-style blue-and-white ceramic tiles.

Baksheesh Tip, donation, alms, occasionally meaning a corrupt backhander.

Bandh General strike.

Banyan Vast fig tree, used traditionally as a meeting place, or shade for teaching and meditating.

Banyain Cotton vest.

Batta Tip.

Bazaar Commercial centre of town; market.

Beedi Tobacco rolled in a leaf; the "poor man's puff".

Betel Leaf chewed in *paan*, with the nut of the areca tree; loosely applies to the nut.

Bhajan Devotional song.

Bhakti Religious devotion expressed in a personalized or emotional relationship with the deity.

Bharatanatyam Classical Indian dance form that originated in the south of India.

Bhawan (also *bhavan*) Palace or residence.

Brahmin A member of the highest caste group, traditionally priests.

Bundh (also *bandh*) Literally "closed", which is why it also denotes a general strike.

Burra-sahib Colonial official, boss or a man of great importance.

Calico Printed cotton cloth, derived from the name of the city Kozhikode (Calicut).

Cantonment Area of town occupied by military quarters.

Caparison Decorative covering, or armour, worn by animal; see "nettippattom".

Caste Social status acquired at birth.

Chappal Sandals or flip-flops (thongs).

Charas Hashish.

Chauri Fly whisk, used in elephant processions.

Chayakada Tea shop.

Chenda melam Keralan drum orchestra.

Chillum Cylindrical clay or wood pipe for smoking *charas* or ganja.

Chital Spotted deer.

Choli Short, tight-fitting blouse worn with a sari.

Chowkidar Watchman, caretaker.

Coir Woven fibre from coconut husk.

Cot Bed.

Crore Ten million.

Cupola Small delicate dome.

Dalit "Oppressed", "out-caste"; the term, introduced by Dr Ambedkar, is preferred by so-called "untouchables" as a description of their social position.

Dargah Muslim shrine.

Darshan Ritual viewing of a deity or saint.

Devadasi Temple dancer.

Devi Goddess.

Dhaba Roadside food stall selling local dishes, mainly to truck drivers.

Dham Important religious site, or a theological college.

Dharamshala Rest house for pilgrims.

Dharma Sense of religious and social duty (Hindu).

Dhobi Laundry-man.

Dhurrie Woollen rug.

Dewan Chief minister.

Dowry Payment or gift offered in marriage.

Dravidian Ancient culture of southern India.

Eve-teasing Sexual harassment of women, either physical or verbal.

Ezhavas One of the lower castes, now among the more upwardly mobile; 29 percent of Hindus in Kerala are *ezhavas*.

Filmi Bollywood soundtrack music – can also be applied to Bollywood influenced clothing, etc.

Finial Capping motif on temple pinnacle.

Ganja Marijuana leaf (grass).

Gaur Indian bison.

Geiser Hot-water boiler.

Ghat Mountain, landing platform, or steps leading to water.

Ghazal Melancholy Urdu songs.

Ghee Clarified butter.

Godown Warehouse.

Gopi Young cattle-tending maidens who feature as Krishna's playmates and lovers in popular mythology.

Gopura Towered temple gateway, common in South India.

Guru Teacher of religion, music, dance, astrology, etc.

Gurukkal Master of *kalarippayattu* martial art.

Haj Muslim pilgrimage to Mecca.

Harijan Title – "Children of God" – given to "untouchables" by Gandhi.

Hartal Strike.

High ranges Name for the area of the Western Ghat mountains around Periyar and Munnar.

Illam Ancestral home of Namboodiri-Brahmin (upper, priestly-class family).

IMFL Indian-made foreign liquor.

Janmis Hindu landlord, usually member of Brahmin caste.

Jati caste, determined by family and occupation.

-ji suffix added to names as a term of respect.

Kalam painting; sometimes used as a shorter form of *kalam ezhuttu*.

Kalam ezhuttu elaborate floor painting.

Kalari see "kalarippayattu", also a traditional Keralan gym.

Kalarippayattu Keralan martial art.

Khalasi Muslim caste of labourers employed in shipyards.

Kannadi Keralan metal mirrors.

Kathakali Traditional Keralan dance-drama.

Kettu vallam Traditional Keralan rice boats, many of which are now used in the tourist trade.

Kettumaran Catamaran; log-raft.

Khadi Home-spun cotton; Gandhi's symbol of Indian self-sufficiency.

Kirtan Hymn.

Kshatriya The martial caste.

Kodai Short for "Kodai Kanal" – a hill station in neighbouring Tamil Nadu.

Kumkum Powder, used to draw a red mark on the forehead.

Kuttambalam Traditional Keralam temple theatre, where *kathakali* and other ritual dance drama was performed.

Kudiyattam Ancient Keralan form of ritual theatre – the forerunner of *kathakali*.

Lakh One hundred thousand.

Lathi Sturdy bamboo cane used by police for crowd control.

Lingam Phallic symbol in places of worship, representing the god Shiva.

Lunghi Male garment; long wrap-around cloth – North Indian term for a *mundu*.

Lusitanian Portuguese.

Maha- Common prefix meaning great or large.

Mahadeva Literally "Great God", a common epithet for Shiva.

Mahadevi Literally "Great Goddess", a common epithet for Shiva's wife, Parvati.

Maharaja (*maharana*, *maharao*) King.

Maharani Queen.

Mahatma Great soul.

Mahout Elephant driver or keeper.

Maidan Large open space or field.

Malabar/Malabar Coast The northern coastal part of Kerala, although in times past used to designate the entire region.

Malayalam Official language of Kerala.

Malayali Keralan (speaker of Malayalam).

Mandala Religious diagram.

Mandir Temple.

Mantra Sacred verse or word.

Marg Road.

Masjid Mosque.

Math/Matha Hindu or Jain monastery.

Memsahib Respectful address to European woman.

Minaret High slender tower, characteristic of mosques.

Mohiniyattam Keralan classical dance form performed by women.

Montane Highland areas below the treeline.

Moppila Keralan Muslim.

Mridamgan Drum used in Carnatic classical music.

Mundu Length of cotton worn as a sarong by men or women; in Kerala, it's traditionally off-white with a gold border.

Mutt Hindu or Jain monastery.

Namboodiris Highest caste of Brahmins, traditionally employed a priests in temples.

Nadumattam Middle of Hindu household's central courtyard – a ritually auspicious point.

Naga Mythical serpent; cobra.

Nairs Kerala's martial caste (Nayars).

Nangiarkoothu An ancient theatre form of female mono-acting, associated with kudiyattam.

Natak Drama.

Natya Dance.

Nettippattom Golden headdress worn during festival parades by elephants.

Nilavilakku Bell-metal oil lamp.

Nilgai Blue bull.

Nilgiris "The Blue Hills" – Tamil name for the Western Ghats.

Niwas Building or house.

Om (Aka AUM) symbol denoting the origin of all things, and ultimate divine essence, used in meditation by Hindus and Buddhists.

Onam Keralan harvest festival (Hindu).

Ottamthullal Costumed mono-acting; an irreverent, satirical kind of ritual theatre, performed by a green-faced jester figure wearing a gold headdress.

Paan A basic *paan* consists of areca nut, lime, calcium and aniseed wrapped in a betel leaf and is chewed as a digestive; it is mildly addictive.

Paikappal Traditional ocean-going ship, in common use over the last millennium, now built in small numbers for the wealthy Gulf Arabs.

Palanquin Enclosed sedan chair, shouldered by four men.

Pali Original language of early Buddhist texts.

Pali Old mosque or church in Kerala.

Panchakarma Ayurvedic internal cleansing of the body.

Panchaloha An alloy of five metals – often called "bell metal" – used since ancient times in India to cast ritual and ayurvedic utensils.

Panchavadyam Traditional Keralan orchestra, comprising five ("panch") different instruments, deployed for Hindu festivals.

Panchayat Village council.

Pradakshina patha Processional path circling a monument or sanctuary.

Prakara Enclosure or courtyard in a temple.

Pranayama Breath control, used in meditation.

Prasad Food blessed in temple sanctuaries and shared among devotees.

Pugri Literally "turban" – often tied with an ice-cream-wafer-shaped fan at the top by *Indian Coffee House* waiters in Kerala.

Puja Worship.

Pujari Priest.

Pukka Correct and acceptable, in the very English sense of "proper".

Purana A genre of ancient Hindu texts, generally in Sanskrit.

Puruthalum Raised veranda at the front of a Hindu *tharavadu* (ancestral house).

Raga/Raag Series of notes forming the basis of a melody.

Raj Rule; monarchy; in particular the period of British imperial rule 1857–1947.

Raja King.

Ramayana Much-loved Hindu epic recounting the story of Lord Rama, Prince of Ayodhya.

Rangoli Geometrical pattern of rice powder laid before houses and temples.

Rath Processional temple chariot.

Sadhu Hindu holy man with no caste or family ties.

Sagar Lake.

Samadhi Final enlightenment; a site of death or burial of a saint.

Samsara Cyclic process of death and rebirth.

Sangam Sacred confluence of two or more rivers; an academy.

Sangeet Music.

Sannyasi Homeless, possessionless ascetic (Hindu).

Sari Usual dress for Indian women: a length of cloth wound around the waist and draped over one shoulder.

Satyagraha Literally "grasping truth": movement that included Gandhi's campaign of non-violent protest.

Scheduled castes Official name for "untouchables".

Shaivite Hindu recognizing Shiva as the supreme god.

Shala Practice hall, usually in the form of an open-sided shelter, for yoga and meditation.

Shastra Treatise.

Shloka Verse from a Sanskrit text.

Shola High-altitude, stunted, evergreen forest, prevalent in the Western Ghats.

Shri Respectful prefix; another name for Lakshmi.

Sudra The lowest of the four castes or *varnas*; servant.

Sutra (*sutta*) Literally "thread": verse in Sanskrit and Pali texts.

Swami Title for a holy man; lord or master.

Swaraj "Self-rule"; synonym for independence, coined by Gandhi.

Tagore Rabindranth Tagore (1861–1941): famous Bengali mystic-philosopher, artist, composer, novelist and cultural icon.

Taluka District.

Tandoor Clay oven.

Tantra Body of esoteric religious practices rooted in Dravidian forms of worship of the Mother Goddess, in which the power of the deity is invoked and internalized.

Thali Plate containing a combination of spiced broths, gravies, sauces, chutneys and rice (a dish traditionally served on a fresh plantain leaf).

Travancore Former kingdom of southern Kerala whose capital was Thiruvananthapuram (Trivandrum).

Tharavad/Tharavadu Ancestral Keralan aristocratic home – often made of teak, with gabled tiled roofs, and incorporating rice granaries.

Thattukada Literally "hot food" -- street stalls selling freshly cooked Keralan cooking.

Theyyam/Theyyattam A kind of spirit-possession ritual, involving elaborate masked costumes, performed in northern Kerala.

Thiruvathirakali Folk dance performed by women at Onam.

Topi Pith helmet – now refers to any hat or cap.

Union territory Administrative division of India, ruled directly from New Delhi – unlike states, which are semi-autonomous. A status accorded former Portuguese and French colonies, including Goa and Pondicherry.

Untouchables Members of the lowest strata of society, formerly considered polluting to all higher castes.

Utsavam Hindu temple festival.

Vahana The "vehicle" of a deity; the bull Nandi is Shiva's *vahana*.

Vallam Boat.

Valia vilakku Giant oil lamp at the entrance to the main shrine of a Hindu temple.

Vijayanagar The last great Hindu empire to rule southern India (1336–1565), from its capital in the Deccan.

Vedas Sacred texts of early Hinduism.

Wallah Suffix implying occupation, eg *paan*-wallah, rickshaw-wallah.

Yogi *Sadhu* or priestly figure possessing occult powers gained through the practice of yoga (female: *yogini*).

Zamorin Title given to the former rulers of Calicut.

Zenana Enclosed portion of a Muslim house where the women would have lived in seclusion (*purdah*).

Travel store

D: Rough Guide
DIRECTIONS for
short breaks

Available from all good bookstores

ROUGH GUIDES

Complete Listing

ROUGH GUIDES

Visit us online

www.roughguides.com

Information on over 25,000 destinations around the world

- **Read** Rough Guides' trusted travel info
- **Access** exclusive articles from Rough Guides authors
- **Update** yourself on new books, maps, CDs and other products
- **Enter** our competitions and win travel prizes
- **Share** ideas, journals, photos & travel advice with other users
- **Earn** points every time you contribute to the Rough Guide community and get rewards

BROADEN YOUR HORIZONS

NOTES

NOTES

NOTES

NOTES

NOTES

NOTES

Small print and

Index

A Rough Guide to Rough Guides

Published in 1982, the first Rough Guide – to Greece – was a student scheme that became a publishing phenomenon. Mark Ellingham, a recent graduate in English from Bristol University, had been travelling in Greece the previous summer and couldn't find the right guidebook. With a small group of friends he wrote his own guide, combining a highly contemporary, journalistic style with a thoroughly practical approach to travellers' needs.

The immediate success of the book spawned a series that rapidly covered dozens of destinations. And, in addition to impecunious backpackers, Rough Guides soon acquired a much broader and older readership that relished the guides' wit and inquisitiveness as much as their enthusiastic, critical approach and value-for-money ethos.

SMALL PRINT

These days, Rough Guides include recommendations from shoestring to luxury and cover more than 200 destinations around the globe, including almost every country in the Americas and Europe, more than half of Africa and most of Asia and Australasia. Our ever-growing team of authors and photographers is spread all over the world, particularly in Europe, the USA and Australia.

In the early 1990s, Rough Guides branched out of travel, with the publication of Rough Guides to World Music, Classical Music and the Internet. All three have become benchmark titles in their fields, spearheading the publication of a wide range of books under the Rough Guide name.

Including the travel series, Rough Guides now number more than 350 titles, covering: phrasebooks, waterproof maps, music guides from Opera to Heavy Metal, reference works as diverse as Conspiracy Theories and Shakespeare, and popular culture books from iPods to Poker. Rough Guides also produce a series of more than 120 World Music CDs in partnership with World Music Network.

Visit www.roughguides.com to see our latest publications.

Rough Guide travel images are available for commercial licensing at www.roughguidespictures.com

Rough Guide credits

Text editor: James Smart
Layout: Nikhil Agarwal, Pradeep Thapliyal
Cartography: Katie Lloyd-Jones
Picture editor: Mark Thomas
Production: Rebecca Short
Proofreader: Martin Moore
Cover design: Chloë Roberts
Photographer: Tim Draper
Editorial: London Kate Berens, Claire Saunders, Ruth Blackmore, Alison Murchie, Karoline Densley, Andy Turner, Keith Drew, Edward Aves, Nikki Birrell, Alice Park, Sarah Eno, Lucy White, Jo Kirby, Natasha Foges, Róisín Cameron, Emma Traynor, Emma Gibbs, James Rice, Joe Staines, Duncan Clark, Peter Buckley, Matthew Milton, Tracy Hopkins, Ruth Tidball; **New York** Andrew Rosenberg, Steven Horak, AnneLise Sorensen, Amy Hegarty, April Isaacs, Ella Steim, Anna Owens, Joseph Petta, Sean Mahoney; **Delhi** Madhavi Singh, Karen D'Souza
Design & Pictures: London Scott Stickland, Dan May, Diana Jarvis, Jj Luck, Nicole Newman, Sarah Cummins; **Delhi** Umesh Aggarwal, Ajay Verma, Jessica Subramanian, Ankur Guha, Sachin Tanwar, Anita Singh

Production: Vicky Baldwin
Cartography: London Maxine Repath, Ed Wright; **Delhi** Jai Prakash Mishra, Rajesh Chhibber, Ashutosh Bharti, Rajesh Mishra, Animesh Pathak, Jasbir Sandhu, Karobi Gogoi, Amod Singh, Alakananda Bhattacharya, Swati Handoo
Online: New York Kristin Mingrone; **Delhi** Manik Chauhan, Narender Kumar, Rakesh Kumar, Amit Verma, Rahul Kumar, Ganesh Sharma, Debojit Borah
Marketing & Publicity: London Liz Statham, Niki Hanmer, Louise Maher, Jess Carter, Vanessa Godden, Vivienne Watton, Anna Paynton, Rachel Sprackett; **New York** Geoff Colquitt, Megan Kennedy, Katy Ball; **Delhi** Reem Khokhar
Manager India: Punita Singh
Series Editor: Mark Ellingham
Reference Director: Andrew Lockett
Publishing Coordinator: Helen Phillips
Publishing Director: Martin Dunford
Commercial Manager: Gino Magnotta
Managing Director: John Duhigg

Publishing information

This first edition published October 2007 by
Rough Guides Ltd,
80 Strand, London WC2R 0RL
345 Hudson St, 4th Floor,
New York, NY 10014, USA
14 Local Shopping Centre, Panchsheel Park,
New Delhi 110017, India
Distributed by the Penguin Group
Penguin Books Ltd,
80 Strand, London WC2R 0RL
Penguin Group (USA)
375 Hudson Street, NY 10014, USA
Penguin Group (Australia)
250 Camberwell Road, Camberwell,
Victoria 3124, Australia
Penguin Books Canada Ltd,
10 Alcorn Avenue, Toronto, Ontario,
Canada M4V 1E4
Penguin Group (NZ)
67 Apollo Drive, Mairangi Bay, Auckland 1310,
New Zealand

Cover concept by Peter Dyer.
Typeset in Bembo and Helvetica to an original design by Henry Iles.
Printed in Italy by Legoprint S.p.A.
© David Abram 2007
No part of this book may be reproduced in any form without permission from the publisher except for the quotation of brief passages in reviews.
352pp includes index
A catalogue record for this book is available from the British Library
ISBN: 978-1-84353-853-0
The publishers and authors have done their best to ensure the accuracy and currency of all the information in **The Rough Guide to Kerala**, however, they can accept no responsibility for any loss, injury, or inconvenience sustained by any traveler as a result of information or advice contained in the guide.

1 3 5 7 9 8 6 4 2

Help us update

We've gone to a lot of effort to ensure that the first edition of **The Rough Guide to Kerala** is accurate and up to date. However, things change – places get "discovered", opening hours are notoriously fickle, restaurants and rooms raise prices or lower standards. If you feel we've got it wrong or left something out, we'd like to know, and if you can remember the address, the price, the time, the phone number, so much the better.

We'll credit all contributions, and send a copy of the next edition (or any other Rough Guide if you prefer) for the best letters. Everyone who writes to us and isn't already a subscriber will receive a copy of our full-colour thrice-yearly newsletter. Please mark letters: "**Rough Guide Kerala Update**" and send to: Rough Guides, 80 Strand, London WC2R 0RL, or Rough Guides, 345 Hudson St, 4th Floor, New York, NY 10014. Or send an email to **mail@roughguides.com**

Have your questions answered and tell others about your trip at
www.roughguides.atinfopop.com

SMALL PRINT

Acknowledgements

First and foremost, thank you to editor James Smart, for maintaining his composure through three months of missed deadlines and random grumpiness. Cartographers Katie and Maxine did a fine job, putting in extra hours to produce the most accurate set of maps of Keralan towns and resorts ever published. Thanks also to Martin Moore for proofreading this first edition, Pradeep Thapliyal for typesetting it, Tim Draper for photography, Mark Thomas for picture editing; and to Kate Berens and Martin Dunford for wanting to publish a guide to Kerala in the first place.

In Kerala, thanks to José Navarro, Sarah Cohen, Joseph Iype and Mr Varghese of the Tourist Desk in Ernakulam.

At home, Baby Morgan, alias Gloworm Maggs, was minus two-and-a-half months when this book was researched. Thank you to him for not showing up until South India was finished, and to his mum for enduring a year of long absences and late homecomings.

The editor would like to thank James Rice, Alison Murchie, Lucy White, Ed Aves, Joanna Kirby and Jessica Subramanian for all their help.

Photo credits

All photography by Tim Draper © Rough Guides except the following:

Introduction
Lighthouse Beach © Joe Beynon/Axiom
Nishangandi Festival © David Abram
Ayurveda © Ayush Image
Snake boat races © Hornbil Images/Alamy
Scuba diving, Lakshadweep © Hornbil Images/
  Alamy

Colour section: Kuttanad backwaters
Snake boat © Hornbil Images/Alamy

Selected images from our guidebooks are available for licensing from:

ROUGHGUIDESPICTURES.COM

Index

Map entries are in colour.

INDEX

347

INDEX

Map symbols

maps are listed in the full index using coloured text

▬▬ ▪▪	State boundary		👹	Mosque
▬▬ ▪▪	District boundary		🛕	Temple
▬ ▬ ▬	Chapter boundary		⛪	Church (regional)
═══	Main road		🏛	Monastery
────	Minor road		ⓘ	Tourist office
▨▨▨▨	Steps		⊠	Post office
▬▬▬	Railway		@	Internet access
─ ─ ─	Path		★	Bus stand
────	Coastline/river		Ⓗ	Helipad
─ ─	Ferry		🅿	Parking
────	Wall		⊞	Hospital
▲	Peak		▪	Building
⌂	Cave		⊞	Church
🇽	Waterfall		⬯	Stadium
✈	International airport		▨	Park
♦	Point of interest		▨	Beach
🗼	Lighthouse		▨	Marshland
⊠—⊠	Gate		▨	Forest